Continued on back end-papers

Novels
and
Novelists

NOVELS
and
NOVELISTS

A GUIDE TO THE WORLD OF FICTION

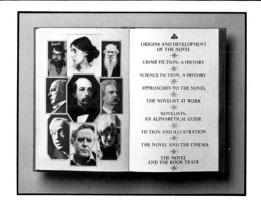

Editor
Martin Seymour-Smith

St. Martin's Press
New York

First published in the United States 1980
by St. Martin's Press Inc.,
New York, New York 10010

ISBN 0-312-57966-7
Library of Congress Catalog Card Number 79-5173

Devised, edited and designed
by Shuckburgh Reynolds Ltd,
8 Northumberland Place, London W2 5BS

Typesetting by SX Composing Ltd, Rayleigh, Essex, England
Printed and bound in Hong Kong
by South China Printing Co.

Designer: Roger Pring

Assistant Designer: Mark Newcombe

Illustrations by: Paul Ailey, Rene Eyre, Carole Johnson,
David Mallott, Sheilagh Noble, Roger Pring and Bill Sanderson

Picture Research: Linda Proud

Jacket pictures (top left to bottom right)
front John Fowles, Virginia Woolf, Leo Tolstoy, Henry James, Charles Dickens,
Mark Twain, Saul Bellow, John Le Carré, Alison Lurie.
back Colette, Kingsley Amis, Mary McCarthy, Émile Zola, Ernest Hemingway,
Humphrey Bogart in *The Big Sleep*, James Lackington's bookshop (*c.* 1800),
E. M. Forster, Huckleberry Finn by E. W. Kemble.

Picture sources
Numerals refer to page numbers (abbreviations: l, left; r, right; c, centre; t, top; b, bottom).

Allen and Unwin Ltd 227; American Academy 45; Godfrey Argent 198, 200 tr, 201; Ashmolean Museum 12; Associated Press 70, 135 l, 266; BBC copyright photographs 10; Sophie Baker 50; Jerry Bauer back jacket tcr, 80 r, 158, 159, 178 l; The Bodley Head Ltd 234 b; Book of the Month Club 274; The Boots Co Ltd 273 r; Hal Boucher 83 b; John Calder (Publishers) Ltd 186b, 212 b; Erskine Caldwell 109; Camera Press Ltd 66 t, 66 b (photo Cecil Beaton), 67, 77 t&b (photos Snowdon), 182 l; Jonathan Cape Ltd 138 t (photo Horst Jayppe), 174 r, 177 l, 179 (photo Lon Van Keulen); Barbara Cartland 81; Chatto and Windus Ltd 190, 251 r; Constable and Co Ltd 129 r (photo Beck and MacGregor), 210 l, 235; Cooper-Bridgeman Library Ltd 13; Corgi Ltd 63; Crystal Palace F.C. (Richard Coomber) 240 l; Len Deighton 84 b, 85 b; André Deutsch Ltd 181 l, 191 (photo Michael George), 210, 230 (photo Jerry Bauer); Dial Press 104 l (photo Francis Hamit); Foster Studio 145; Giulio Einaudi S.p.a. 197 r; Esquire 250 b; Eyre Methuen Ltd 107, 149 r, 163 r, 181 r (photo Janna Malamud), 220 t, 234 l; Joel Finler 254 b, 257 t, 259 r, 261 r, 262 l, 264 tl&tr; Fontana Ltd 84 l; Garden City Publishers 41 c&r; Mark Gerson back jacket tcl, 90 b, 173, 222 br; Maeve Gilmore (photos Roger Pring) 75 tl, tr&b, 243 b; Fay Godwin front jacket tl, 140 t, 202 l; Victor Gollancz Ltd 92, 116 (photo Billye Cutchen), 125, 162 r (photo Shyla Irving), 203 r, 281; Granada Ltd 82, 104 r, 177 b; Gyldendalske Boghandel Nordisk Forlag 102 l; Robert Hale Ltd 208 l (photo Floyd B. Hall); Philippe Halsman (photo) 128; Hamish Hamilton Ltd 216, 226 c; Harcourt Brace and World 100 (photo James Barker Hall); Harper and Row, Publishers 239 t, 273 l;

Heinemann Group of Publishers Ltd front jacket br, 177 tr, 184, 231, 239 b; Andreas Hermann (photo) front jacket bc, 172 r; Hodder and Stoughton Ltd 114; Hutchinson Publishing Group Ltd 139 r, 169 r; Jean Photographs 86; Michael Joseph Ltd 97 l; J. Lamotte (photo) 114; Allen Lane Ltd 206; Lord Leicester 14 r (photo E. P. Microform Ltd); Macmillan & Co Ltd 127 (photo Jill Krementz), 147 l (photo Alex Gotfryd), 187 r (photo Leonid Skvirsky), 218 b (photo Joel Fried), 220 l (photo Jerry Bauer), 247 tl&tr; Mansell Collection front jacket cl, back jacket tl, tr, bl, br, 7, 9 l&r, 17, 18 t, 21, 26 l, 38, 40, 52, 71 tl, tr&b, 72 l, 79 l, 95, 112, 118, 119, 122, 136 r, 138 b, 146, 148, 154 r, 161, 164, 185 l&c, 199, 204, 211 (photo Nadar), 222 tl, 229 l, 240 r, 241, 244 l, 245 l, 246 t&b, 268, 271; Michael Mason 244 tr&br, 245 r, Gladys Mitchell 51 c&b; Julian Nangle Collection (photos Jon Wyand) 65 (Panther 1969), 251 t (Jonathan Cape 1970), 252 t (Heinemann 1933), 252 c (Macmillan & Co 1960), 252 b (Macmillan & Co 1968), 275 (Penguin 1935); British National Film Archive back jacket cr (Warner Bros), 253 (MGM), 255 l (MGM), 255 r (United Artists), 256, 257 b (MGM), 263 t (Paramount), 263 bc (Warner Bros), 263 cl (MGM), 263 cr (United Artists), 263 bl (RKO), 263 br (Avco Embassy); National Portrait Gallery, London front jacket tc, c, 24, 26 t, 90 t, 99, 106 (by Branwell Brontë), 108 l&r, 112 (by Lewis Carroll), 117 r, 124, 126, 129 l, 132, 135 r, 136 l, 153, 162 l, 175 (self-portrait), 185 r, 188, 200 b, 213 (by Sir Edwin Landseer), 215 r, 218 c, 222 c (by Sir Joshua Reynolds), 222 r, 226 l, 232 l&c, 234 r, 238; New Directions 202 b; Newsday 155 (photo Thomas R. Koeniges); Novosti Press Agency front jacket tr, 30, 72 r, 73 tr&b, 196 r; Harold Ober Associates 120; Pan Books Ltd 140 b, 152 l, 174 l, 193 r, 215 l, 221 r, 226 r; Peter Owen Ltd 123, 192; Paramount Inc 254 t, 264 b, 265; Penguin Books Ltd 102 r, 103, 111, 166 r, 197 l, 223; Judy Piatkus

224; Popperfoto Ltd 76, 78 b, 80 l, 84 tr, 144, 156; Roger Pring 83 t; Radio Times Hulton Picture Library back jacket cl, 37, 39, 44, 72, l, 73 tl, 78 t, 79 r, 110, 117 l, 137, 160, 163 l, 267, 270 t; Random House Inc 194 (photo Anne Zane Shanks); Saturday Evening Post 247 b; Secker and Warburg Ltd front jacket bl (photo Jill Krementz), 96, 98 r (photo Jill Krementz), 141 (photo Jerry Bauer), 149 l (photo RAMA, Berlin), 182 r, 186 l, 187 l, 189 l (photo Jerry Bauer), 195, 200 l, 205 (photo Fay Godwin); Danielle Smith 218 t; Snark International 14 l, 15, 16, 18 b, 20, 28, 33, 170; Stanza della Segnatura, Rome (Scala) 11; Tate Gallery, London 23 l, c&r; Taylor Stroehr 147 r (photo Regula Davis); University of Virginia 74 l, r&b; Victoria and Albert Museum, Crown Copyright 243 t; Viking Press Inc 196 l; Western Americana Picture Library front jacket cr, 229 r; Young Artists 53 l&r.

Illustrations
Paul Ailey 55; Rene Eyre 58, 61, 114, 128, 131, 139, 150, 207, 208, 212, 217, 236, 237; Carole Johnson 51, 88, 97, 157, 172, 180, 193, 219; David Mallott 57, 63, 64, 65; Sheilagh Noble 58, 93, 94, 98, 117, 142, 143, 152, 166, 168, 176, 189, 202; Bill Sanderson chapter headings.

Shuckburgh Reynolds Ltd would also like to thank the following: Mike Jarvis and Bob Aldridge of SX Composing; APT Photoset for additional typesetting; the information department of the National Book League, London; Kate Caute; Sarah Dale; Elly King; Jimmie Caffrey and Brian Corbett.

EDITOR

Martin Seymour-Smith has been a full-time writer on literary matters since 1960. He has written, compiled or edited more than 25 books including *Who's Who in Twentieth-Century Literature* and the four-volume *Guide to Modern World Literature* (in U.S., *Funk and Wagnall's Guide to Modern World Literature*). His biography of Robert Graves is shortly to be published. He is fiction and poetry reviewer for the *Financial Times*. In 1971–72 he was visiting Professor of English at Wisconsin University.

CONTRIBUTORS

Brian W. Aldiss is a prolific writer of science fiction, in both novel and short story form. He is a critic, the author of a history of science fiction, *Billion Year Spree* (1973), and the editor of *Science Fiction Art* (1975).

H. R. F. Keating is a novelist known primarily for his crime stories. He has been crime fiction reviewer for *The Times* since 1967. He edited *Agatha Christie: First Lady of Crime* (1977) and *Crime Writers* (1978), and wrote *Sherlock Holmes: the Man and his Work* (1979).

Michael Mason is Lecturer in English at University College, London. He is the author of *James Joyce: Ulysses* (1972). He reviews fiction for the *New Statesman*, *The Times Literary Supplement* and the *London Review of Books*.

David Pirie is film critic, and former film editor, for *Time Out* magazine. He is a regular reviewer for BBC Radio 4's *Kaleidoscope*, and presenter of the BBC World Service's *Soundtrack*. He is the author of *A Heritage of Horror* (1972) and *The Vampire Cinema* (1977).

Gamini Salgado is Professor of English Literature at the University of Exeter. He has reviewed for many periodicals, including *British Book News*, *The Listener*, the *New Statesman* and *Encounter*. He has published *D. H. Lawrence's Sons and Lovers* (1966), *Eyewitnesses of Shakespeare* (1975), *The Elizabethan Underworld* (1977) and several other books. In 1965–66 he was visiting Professor at Earlham College, Indiana. He is shortly to take up a Huntingdon Library Fellowship in California.

J. A. Sutherland is Reader in English at University College, London. He has reviewed fiction for the *New Statesman* and *The Times Literary Supplement*, and has written on the book trade for *The New Review* and *New Society*. He has edited novels by Trollope and Thackeray for the Penguin English Library, and is the author of *Thackeray at Work* (1974), *Victorian Novelists and Publishers* (1976) and *Fiction and the Fiction Industry* (1978).

CONSULTANTS TO *NOVELISTS: AN ALPHABETICAL GUIDE*

Brian W. Aldiss, H. R. F. Keating, Martin Seymour-Smith

David Holloway Literary Editor of *The Daily Telegraph*, and author of several works of non-fiction including *A Short Life of Galsworthy* (1968).

Carol H. Smith Professor of English, Douglass College, Rutgers University; author of *T. S. Eliot's Dramatic Theory and Practice* (1963) and contributor to many periodicals including *The Nation*, *Contemporary Literature*, *Women's Studies*, and *Women in Literature*.

CONTRIBUTORS TO *NOVELISTS: AN ALPHABETICAL GUIDE*

David Holloway, H. R. F. Keating, David Pirie, Martin Seymour-Smith, J. A. Sutherland

Melvyn Barnes Borough Librarian and Arts Officer, Royal Borough of Kensington & Chelsea; author of *Best Detective Fiction* (1975) and editor of the "Deerstalker" series of classic detective fiction.

Hugh Bredin described by Jilly Cooper in *The Sunday Times* simply as a wit, but also a short-story writer, book reviewer and freelance publisher's consultant.

Kathleen Hancock College Librarian at Willesden College of Technology.

W. B. Hart Lecturer in Philosophy at University College, London; formerly Assistant Professor at the University of Michigan.

Marianne Korn Principal Lecturer in English at Middlesex Polytechnic; the author of several books for children.

Anthony Lejeune author of several books including six mystery novels; reviewer of crime fiction for *The Tablet*.

Jessica Mann author of several works of crime fiction; reviewer for *British Book News* and *The Times Literary Supplement*.

Jerry Palmer Senior Lecturer in General Studies at the City of London Polytechnic; formerly Books Editor of *Time Out*; author of *Thrillers. Genesis and Structure of a Popular Genre* (1978).

C. B. Preston freelance writer and researcher.

Kenneth Richardson Principal Lecturer at Kingston Polytechnic teaching contemporary English and American literature; editor of *Twentieth Century Writing* (1969).

Brian Stableford prolific science fiction novelist and reviewer for the SF journal *Foundation*; Lecturer in Social Sciences at Reading University and holder of a Doctorate in the Sociology of Literature.

Nigel Thomas journalist and book reviewer.

CONTRIBUTORS TO *THE NOVELIST AT WORK*

H. R. F. Keating, Gamini Salgado, Martin Seymour-Smith

Rosalind Franey journalist and reviewer whose work has appeared in many places including *The Sunday Times*, *The Guardian*, *New Society* and *Time Out*.

Linda Proud freelance writer and researcher.

John Smallwood editor for a New York publisher.

INTRODUCTION

A Town Critic Hunting down Authors.

London, Pub.by Thomas Tegg, III, Cheapside, July 1-1810.

The novel could not have had such a long and persistent history had it not been for public demand. There now exist, side by side, a still voracious public appetite for the novel, and an enormous critical apparatus for analyzing it. The public is largely, though not wholly, unaware of the critical apparatus, but those responsible for the building of this apparatus – mostly teachers in universities – tend to disregard the power and influence of the public, and the importance of the story element in novels. There is an ever-widening gap between the "general reader" and the "Professor of Literature". *Novels and Novelists* has been compiled in the hope that this gap, opened largely as a result of misunderstandings and mistrust, might be closed – or at least narrowed – for at least some readers.

We have shown how fiction began, and

why it has so powerful an appeal. We have given a brief history of its fortunes and its development. We have given quite detailed accounts of how (and why) certain important and popular writers work, and of their attitude to their work. We have examined the relationship of the novel to other visual media, and traced the influence exerted on the novel by the economics of the book trade. Chiefly, we have provided a critical guide to the lives and work of some 1300 writers of fiction. We have not ignored either the very exclusive "highbrow" writer, nor the very popular one. No reader will accuse of a bias towards the "literary" and the exclusive: we have been at too much pain throughout to show that all fiction has its basis in the experience of the common man. But one of our chief hopes for this book is that it will demonstrate to many readers that the fiction they have hitherto thought of as being too "difficult" is in fact perfectly accessible. To assert that the very popular novel is automatically the very bad novel would be absurd, and we do not fall into this error. But we have attempted to show why some very successful fiction, dealing in cheap fantasy rather than reality, is inferior to some other fiction that is not so successful in sales.

This book is above all intended to encourage people to increase their enjoyment of fiction: by indicating writers that may be new to them; by placing books in their historical context; by pointing out certain critical approaches while stressing that the reader's own critical response is the most important to him or her. Despite years of criticism of the novel, there is still no single theory of the form. However, some critical specialists help to deepen our responses, and are well worth reading. It is our hope that this book will help bridge the gap between critic and reader.

M. S-S.

ORIGINS AND DEVELOPMENT OF THE NOVEL

The novel as we know it, which can be simply defined as the telling of a fictional story in 40,000 words or more of prose, originates with the Spaniard Miguel de Cervantes' *Don Quixote*, which was published in two parts in 1605 and 1615. However, neither Cervantes nor the modern novel can be fully understood except in terms of their origins. The word "fiction" derives from the Latin *fingere*, which originally meant to fashion in clay. The verb then came to mean to invent, to imagine, and even to pretend. Our word "feign" derives from the same root. Novel readers may feel that lying is too strong and emotive a word to use in connection with the innocent art of fiction. But it is not – any more than the art of fiction is truly innocent.

The Greek philosophers Plato and Aristotle, the two most important early thinkers and perhaps still the most influential of all, exemplify two opposing views of this phenomenon of fiction. Plato (*c* 427–347 BC), although he himself wrote a few poems, banned the works of Homer

Below left *Cervantes near the end of his life, writing with his daughter's assistance.*

Below right *The title page of the first edition of* Don Quixote: *Part I.*

and all poetry from the famous and influential utopia which he described in his *Republic* (380 BC). Homer's *Iliad* and *Odyssey* are among the very earliest completed examples of fiction, and Plato banned Homer for what he called his "lies".

In his *Republic* Plato was sincerely and thoughtfully concerned with the "good society". He was therefore concerned with education, and believed that children must be told good things, and not bad ones: wrong ideas must not be suggested. Of the story of the Battle of the Gods in the *Iliad* he said: "These tales must not be allowed in our State, whether they are meant to have an allegorical meaning or not. Youngsters cannot judge what is allegorical and what is not." For Plato, true knowledge consisted of the timeless *ideas* of things, and not of the things themselves. Material things, and even human thoughts, were for him unimaginably distorted shadows of perfection, which was immaterial. Truth was pure spirit. So he rejected literature (actually it was poetry he specifically rejected, but what he said

EL INGENIOSO
HIDALGO DON QVI-
XOTE DE LA MANCHA,

Compuesto por Miguel de Cervantes Saauedra.

DIRIGIDO AL DVQVE DE BEIAR,
Marques de Gibraleon, Conde de Benalcaçar, y Bañares, Vizconde de la Puebla de Alcozer, Señor de las villas de Capilla, Curiel, y Burguillos.

Año, 1605.

CON PRIVILEGIO,
EN MADRID, Por Iuan de la Cuesta.

Vendese en casa de Francisco de Robles, librero del Rey nro señor.

applied to all literature), on the grounds that it cut people off from the truth, from the ideal non-material forms. Homer was, for Plato, at three removes from perfection, since this existed only as *idea*.

We too may seem to be at least three removes from our subject; but in fact the arguments of Plato and those opposed to him pervade the whole of literature. Everyone can see that Plato's arguments are in one sense naive; and that he himself undermines them by using the "lying" devices of literature to get his *Republic* across to his audience. But Plato should not therefore be rejected out of hand: naive or not, he pointed to a deeply disturbing fact. Literature, which we take for granted as being a good and virtuous thing – just as many of Plato's contemporaries regarded Homer, only with more intensity, as being almost god-like – does consist of lies.

We have to be grateful to Plato for bringing up the question; and also for apparently contradicting himself in other works, in which he praises (unless he was being sarcastic, which some have suggested) the true poet as a deliverer of the word of God, and goes on to say that: ". . . he who, having no touch of the Muses' madness in his soul, comes to the door and thinks he will get into the temple . . . he, I say, and his poetry are not admitted; the sane man is nowhere at all when he enters into rivalry with the madman." Plato is saying that true poetry can only be written when the senses are disordered; this is a remarkable anticipation of not only poetry, but also fiction. Plato also here defends himself, so to say, against himself (the quotation above is probably later than the *Republic*), and we may confidently subsume "novelist" into the Platonic "poet", as will shortly be explained. He argues that lying can be divine and inspired. We are unused to thinking in such terms, and they may seem unsophisticated, but Plato's audience was anything but unsophisticated, and it is against the background of such ultimately religious notions that literature developed.

Plato's chief opponent in this matter, apart from himself, was his younger and more sober contemporary Aristotle (384–322 BC), whose first argument is that literature is superior to history (real facts) because it imitates not what is but what ought to be. In effect Aristotle turned Plato's argument on its head. For him, fiction (he was thinking of the plays of Aeschylus and the other Greek tragedians, but again his arguments apply to the novel) is actually better than history because it is based, not on literal truth, but on probability. It is, Aristotle might have said, more real than real, because it provides the reader with the essence of the truth. Consider which of the following you prefer: Robert Graves' frankly imaginative novels about the Emperor Claudius, or one of the two or three historical studies of Claudius? You might answer that you certainly

prefer Graves' fiction, but that if you wanted to know something about the real Claudius then you suppose you would have to read one of the dry factual books, but you would rather not if you did not have to. If sales figures tell a story then this lack of interest in the historians, worthy as they are, is confirmed. The question is worth pursuing a little further. Not much is known about Claudius, and the non-fiction books about him are as frankly boring (except to a few specialists) as Graves' books are frankly imaginative (as he admitted to his friend Lawrence of Arabia). Now since Graves' books are very well researched indeed – the accuracy of his accounts of the manners, customs, habits and practices of the Romans was not challenged by historians – and since he "brings Claudius to life", may it not be that his fiction, being highly probable, is superior to historians' attempts to construct the "real" facts? It is a view worth considering, because it is a version of the Aristotelian argument – and one which anyone can well appreciate who has either read the novels or seen the fine television adaptation of them.

In order to appreciate the modern novel it is not necessary to agree with either Plato or Aristotle, but it is helpful to appreciate the fundamentals of their thought, because this is the basis upon which many of the world's greatest novels, especially modern ones, have been written. Essentially, Plato believed in *Idea* being the basis of all things, whereas Aristotle believed that *Substance* fulfils this fundamental role. Aristotle, who is on the side of literature, had a materialistic temperament, whereas Plato, who is against literature, had a spiritual temperament. It is the word "temperament" which is crucial here.

All novels are, to adapt a phrase of the French novelist Emile Zola, life seen through a temperament. Certain critics have tried to deny this, but most agree that the novel by the known individual – the writer who seeks to express himself – is and must be the product of a temperament. And that temperament will be Platonic (spiritual, theoretical), Aristotelian (materialistic, empirical) or some kind of mixture of the two. The nearer we get to the present, the more complex a mixture this becomes: the individual becomes freer, less tied by rigid conventions, and the scope of fiction becomes wider. There are temperaments which try to reconcile the two approaches; tempera-

Above Left *Derek Jacobi as Claudius in the BBC production of I, Claudius* by Robert Graves

Above *Robert Graves on the set of the BBC's* I, Claudius *with George Baker who played the Emperor Tiberius.*

ments which reflect an anguished conflict between them; temperaments which express one or the other in more or less pure forms; and so on. The combinations are endless, and reflect two fundamental aspects of man's attitude to the enigma of his existence: this is their fascination.

The first fiction

The origin of lying, in its sense of "feigning" or "pretending" – which as we have seen may often be a strenuous attempt to discover, or to tell, the truth – is in the human cortex, whenever that developed. The word "human" implies "speaking", because it is the speech centre of the human brain that most sharply differentiates it from that of animals. It would be fruitless to theorize here about the origins of religion, or its exact meaning, but it does seem as though fiction, the telling of stories, arose from man's need to ritualize, to explain himself to himself, and to account for himself to an authority or creator, exterior to himself, and possessed of superior powers.

The first fiction then was mythology and folklore. Much of the most recent important (and indeed unimportant) fiction is also, significantly, mythology: we call it mythopoeic, meaning producing myths. Homer's *Iliad* and *Odyssey* are partly mythology, but within their mythological framework are several forms of novel: love stories; adventure stories; ghost stories; a famous story about a dog (animal stories have always been popular); and others. But Homer, it may be objected, is in verse, and is in no way a novel. This is true, but the connection of Homer with the novel is very close. James Joyce's *Ulysses* (1922) is only one of countless novels to refer to, or be based upon, Homer or parts of Homer. Although we do not know who or what Homer was, we do know that the material of which the two epics consists was originally orally transmitted. We do not know when this process began, although there are certain features in the text we possess which date back many centuries earlier than the century in which it was once supposed the work was (orally) "composed" – the seventh century BC. The two written poems are either records of particular performances by bards, or – possibly more likely – they are the work of an inspired man (or a group of inspired men) who put the material into order. To what extent he or they imposed his or their own personality on the myths is unknown.

The two stories are in verse because they were originally told around campfires by professional bards. Verse is much easier to remember than prose; and it is more natural to chant to a musical instrument, which is what bards usually did, in verse than it is in prose. It has been shown, too, that the bards were able to memorize these very long chunks of material by means of certain patterns (called *formulae* by modern scholars), which could be accommodated in verse but not in prose. We will never completely explain Homer; but we do have Homer, and in all his versatility he is one of the fathers of the modern novel. If he should turn out not to be a man at all, but a folk-poem, then it will not matter except to those who like to think of the "blind poet of Smyrna". The earliest surviving written texts date

Raphael's "School of Athens": at the centre Plato points upwards while Aristotle turns his palm to the earth, an indication of their different philosophies.

from the Middle Ages, and are the work of monks; although the surviving work of some Greek authors includes a few fragments from the epics.

But where do we find the first novels themselves? There are other epics, such as the Babylonian *Gilgamesh*, which are earlier than Homer. These often resemble Homer in their mythical nature, but they are more fragmentary: they lack Homer's grand sweep and his general consistency. The first known prose novels come from Egypt, and are dated between about 2200 and 2000 BC. Now that new dating techniques have destroyed the old notion of the Middle East as the "cradle of civilization", it is possible that there were other novels, from other civilizations; but no such novel has been discovered, nor is it likely to be.

The Egyptian novels and short stories are much nearer to Homer to what we regard as fiction. There are comic tales which, rather surprisingly, make fun of the figure of the Pharaoh; there are lewd stories, sentimental stories and love stories.

An ostracon, or limestone flake, dating from the Nineteenth Dynasty in Egypt, showing part of a student's copy of the novel Sinuhe. *The complete novel has been pieced together from flakes of this kind.*

The most serious of the Egyptian novels is *Sinuhe*, about a man who suffered shipwreck (a common theme in fiction long before Daniel Defoe's *Robinson Crusoe*), lived in exile, and finally returned. It provides one of the earliest examples of the political, the philosophical and the adventure novel.

What is most interesting about this body of literature is that it was designed solely to entertain. For the first time, as far as we know, there arose a body of fiction of varying quality – ranging from the silly and unreal love story to the relatively thoughtful *Sinuhe* – which was designed to please (as well as, sometimes, to instruct), and which must have been created by demand. These were books for an audience, a "public", produced in quantity. But the "books" were of course papyrus rolls copied out by scribes. Unhappily, in all this Egyptian literature nothing has survived that is truly outstanding; no one would recommend even *Sinuhe* except as being of historical interest.

There are only five Greek novels surviving, all of which date from the first and second centuries AD, although it is known that novels were written in the time of Alexander, the fourth century BC. The five were also circulated on papyrus, and of them only the *Daphnis and Chlöe* of Longus, which the German writer Goethe admired, is now read really widely, although the others, particularly the *Aethiopica* of Heliodorus, are interesting and have merit. What is significant about these novels is that they were written to entertain (or in Henry James' terms: to interest, by which he meant to interest by exciting the mind constructively) a new class, which is best described as "lower-middle". The form was certainly regarded as disreputable by learned men: they do not refer to the novels in their writings. But the authors were themselves skilled and educated.

The novel, as will be seen, has for most of its history had to struggle against various sorts of hostility from two extremes: the learned and scholarly philosophers, and the genteel ignorant moralists. It got much of its strength and vigour from this struggle, and there was a demand for it. These Greek novels survived: they were translated into several languages in the sixteenth century, and were all read until well into the nineteenth. In our century only *Daphnis and Chlöe* is a truly popular book (a Penguin paperback); but the *Aethiopica* has influenced centuries of writers, and is also still read.

Curiously, it was the Greek novels, rather than the later Latin ones, which survived to influence the development of the novel proper (by which is meant the printed novel). A Greek work, the *Milesiaka*, which was written or arranged by the historian Aristides in about 100 BC, lies behind both the Latin novels that have survived in substantial form. This, and almost all of a translation of it into Latin, are lost; but we know that these *Milesiaka* were tales about the author's native Miletus, and that many of them were erotic and some bawdy. *The Satyricon* of Petronius (d. 65 AD) is the earlier of the Latin novels. It is not complete and what we have shows it to have been rather long; it contains two and maybe more of the *Milesiaka*. Lucius Apuleius (124–?164 AD), in his more profound *The Metamorphoses*, known to us as *The Golden Ass*, made even greater use of Aristides, for his main narrative is interrupted by many tales from the *Milesiaka*. *The Golden Ass* was the first unequivocally great novel and contains a bit of everything: adventure, humour, bawdy, magic, religion and the exquisite love story of Cupid and Psyche. Lucius was a priest who had been initiated into the mysteries of Isis, and parts of *The Golden Ass* are autobiographical; but for his main theme he went back to a Greek narrative, perhaps written by Lucius of Patras. Yet another version of the story may be the work of the Syrian or Greek writer Lucian (?115–180+ AD) who was not a novelist, but is influential as one of the earliest satirists and parodists, a learned man and a wit who exposed the follies of his times. One of his tales begins: "All that follows is a lie: don't believe a word of it." This anticipates a fundamental concern of novelists from Cervantes onwards.

From this time until the invention of printing in the mid-thirteenth century in Europe and the subsequent wide dissemination of the novel, the form diversifies and is lost for the long duration of the Dark Ages.

Some have gone so far as to say that the love story is the real basis of the novel; but this is overstating the case. It is, however, an essential ingredient in all or nearly all novels. *The Tale of Genji*, written by a Japanese noblewoman, Lady Murasaki, in the very first years of the eleventh century, is in essence a story of heartbreak through love; it remains one of the greatest novels ever written, and Arthur Waley's translation (1925–33) is a twentieth-century classic in its own right. The earlier popular novels – those of ancient Egypt and Greece – had happy endings.

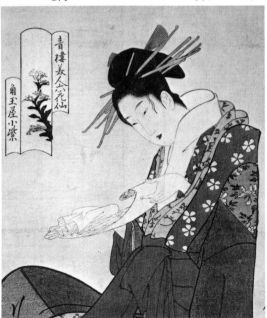

Lady Murasaki, as depicted by Chobunsai Eishi c. 1794.

Precursors of the modern novel

The public has always demanded happy endings, perhaps in part to compensate for the effort they have been required to make in following the course of frustrated or unhappy love. But Lady Murasaki is a sad writer – as well as one of the greatest of all time – and does not give us what could be called a happy ending. She is an analytical writer, timeless, and therefore of course astonishingly "modern".

The Chinese had printing from about the sixth century, and a form of movable type by the eleventh. But although there are early examples of delicate love stories, and tales of the supernatural, they produced nothing of the quality of *The Tale of Genji*.

The modern novel, by which is meant the novel since Cervantes, cannot be defined beyond the vague dictionary short-hand "extended fictional narrative in prose" – and even this does not include some works generally thought of as novels. It is most profitable to think of the modern novel as arising from the demand of a literate public to be entertained. From the beginning, as has been seen, there have been novels whose sights are set deliberately low: the authors desire to hold the reader's attention, and that is all – they therefore manipulate "happy endings" and the behaviour of their characters in the interests of the readers' demands for an entertainment which will allow them to escape from the real world. But man – least of all perhaps a novelist – cannot work all the time, and never play. And so throughout the history of the form there has evolved the novel of sheer entertainment which is improved in one way or another. Sentimentality can be made beautiful by style, crude improbable adventure can be rescued from bathos by ingenuity or fine style. Literary quality is not incompatible with power to entertain, as Charles Dickens most ably demonstrated.

Realism, as we shall see, is only a technical term in literary criticism: the appropriate name given to a strand in the history of novel-writing that culminated in the nineteenth century. However, all forms of the novel attempt to be realistic in the broad sense of the word: they represent true reality as it is seen by the author. Here it is instructive to remember what Plato meant by "reality", and to contrast it with what it means in the Aristotelian tradition. For Plato dreams are more real than anything else; for Aristotle they are dangerous and misleading trash. The novel reader need not choose: he may enjoy the best of all worlds. All he asks is that his interest be held and maintained. But of course at its best the novel has always worked hard to be serious and useful while it performs its primary job of entertaining. One of the measures of the entertainment-value of a novel is, in fact, its seriousness – not the kind of seriousness which is synonymous with earnestness, but a seriousness

nineteenth centuries a distinction was made between romances – fanciful tales of far away and long ago – and novels, "realistic" stories which were "probable". We now, unless we are being very technical, call all these novels. So that what we think of as the novel embraces everything from the trivial news item to the grand impossible amorous adventure.

The psychological novel

The best and most famous examples of the *novella* are to be found in the *Decameron* (1353) by the Italian Boccaccio (?1313–75), whose works include much that is instructive to students of the development of the novel. He wrote a long prose romance, *Filocolo* (c 1336), which is a rather improbable love-narrative, interrupted by other tales, but early in his career he began to introduce a note that would eventually lead to the modern novel. His *Elegy for Madonna Fiammetta* (1345) is one of the first true psychological novels. The psychological novel is, of course, primarily a

which embraces humour. Leo Tolstoy's *War and Peace* is of a higher quality than Harold Robbins' *The Carpetbaggers* because it is more serious – and no one denies this.

Roman and novella

The development of the modern novel has taken place in a vast arena: it stretches from heroic romance at one end to mere ordinary anecdote at the other. This is reflected in the words used to denote it. Our own word "novel" derives from the Italian *novella*, which suggests something anecdotal, "newsy", topical, true. But the word *roman*, used in almost all European languages to designate the novel, indicates its roots in medieval romances: such works as the Arthurian cycle, the stories of Charlemagne, and so on (the origins of these are lost in obscurity, but they crystallized in the Middle Ages). Romance is deliberately not realistic or topical or "newsy": romances are tales of gallant loves, chastity rewarded, magic adventures, unusual events. In the eighteenth and

A page from a fourteenth-century French illuminated edition of Robert de Borron's chivalric romance, Histoire de Saint Graal.

Above right *A detail from the Holkham* Decameron, *an Italian manuscript dating from approximately 1460, showing Fiammetta, one of the ten storytellers in Boccaccio's great work.*

study of the motives and mental make-up of its characters. It describes not only actions, but the reasons for actions. Boccaccio also wrote allegory and tried his hand (unsuccessfully) at pastoral.

Allegory

Allegory is very important, as it is often used today – if not in a pure form. Allegory proper is a sustained metaphor in which everything in a narrative – the people, their actions, all objects – stands for something else (moral, religious, social, political), that something else being outside the narrative. Fables and parables are forms of allegory. John Bunyan's *Pilgrim's Progress* (1678) is very near to allegory. The difficulty about the form, especially as it is practised nowadays, is that the narrative itself tends to sway the reader's interest towards itself – and so he misses the "message". Critics have claimed that Franz Kafka is an allegorist, but such a position is difficult to maintain; however, his novels are influenced by allegory. An allegory is not the same as a symbolic novel, though the line between the two is in practice difficult to draw: in the latter the narrative is intended to be as important as the symbolic matter.

Pastoral

Pastoral is rather less important nowadays, but has historical significance. The term has numerous meanings, but it is the pastoral romance in prose which relates to the modern novel. This is a long and usually complicated narrative, with a strong element of plot, in which the characters bear the names of shepherds and shepherdesses (pleasantly familiar, humble, "simple" people who live close to nature) and in

Geoffrey Chaucer, from an illuminated manuscript dated 1402. Chaucer's Canterbury Tales, *written in verse, are outstanding examples of the early English moral tale.*

MAJOR WORKS OF FICTION: 2200 BC–1599 AD

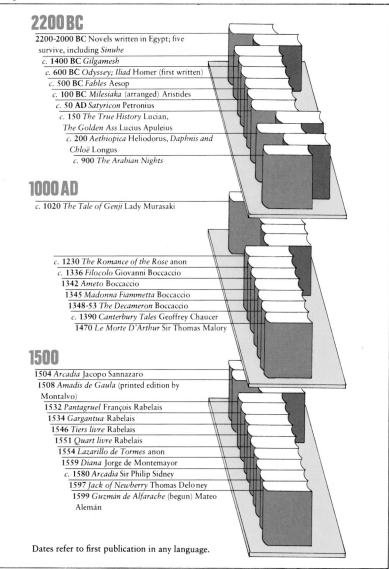

2200 BC

2200-2000 BC Novels written in Egypt; five survive, including *Sinuhe*
c. 1400 BC *Gilgamesh*
c. 600 BC *Odyssey; Iliad* Homer (first written)
c. 500 BC *Fables* Aesop
c. 100 BC *Milesiaka* (arranged) Aristides
c. 50 AD *Satyricon* Petronius
c. 150 *The True History* Lucian, *The Golden Ass* Lucius Apuleius
c. 200 *Aethiopica* Heliodorus, *Daphnis and Chloë* Longus
c. 900 *The Arabian Nights*

1000 AD

c. 1020 *The Tale of Genji* Lady Murasaki

c. 1230 *The Romance of the Rose* anon
c. 1336 *Filocolo* Giovanni Boccaccio
1342 *Ameto* Boccaccio
1345 *Madonna Fiammetta* Boccaccio
1348-53 *The Decameron* Boccaccio
c. 1390 *Canterbury Tales* Geoffrey Chaucer
1470 *Le Morte D'Arthur* Sir Thomas Malory

1500

1504 *Arcadia* Jacopo Sannazaro
1508 *Amadis de Gaula* (printed edition by Montalvo)
1532 *Pantagruel* François Rabelais
1534 *Gargantua* Rabelais
1546 *Tiers livre* Rabelais
1551 *Quart livre* Rabelais
1554 *Lazarillo de Tormes* anon
1559 *Diana* Jorge de Montemayor
c. 1580 *Arcadia* Sir Philip Sidney
1597 *Jack of Newberry* Thomas Deloney
1599 *Guzmán de Alfarache* (begun) Mateo Alemán

Dates refer to first publication in any language.

which pastoral conventions (based on rural ways: singing contests, courtship customs and so forth) dominate – usually in a very artificial way. This began in Greek poetry, and the *Daphnis and Chlöe* of Longus is essentially pastoral. Boccaccio's *Ameto* (1341–42), a mixture of prose and verse, is a very early revival of pastoral. The real importance of pastoral lies in the stress it places on the notion of plot in the novel. Aristotle made the first important remarks about plot: "the first principle . . . and soul of a tragedy." It is, he said, an "arrangement of incidents" and an "imitation of action". A story does not need a plot: it can be the description of a series of incidents in chronological order. However, a plot very often makes a story more meaningful, even though it may introduce an element of artificiality. The plot introduces the factor of causality. At its best, when it is not neat for the sake of neatness, it represents an intelligent view of the events depicted, which has some kind of emotional colouring. The pastoral also made some contri-

bution to the development of characterization, though characters tend to be undifferentiated, to resemble one another too closely.

And so in Boccaccio, even without the *Decameron*, there are many of the germs of the modern novel. The hundred tales in his major work, however, cover a vast range: there is social realism, comedy, tragedy, and, above all, a very "modern" insistence on the earthy, anti-abstract quality of human nature (in this sense Boccaccio was very much opposed to Plato's view of the world). He is now thought of as "bawdy"; but he did not seem so to his readers: puritanism as we know it had not then been invented.

The pastoral novel was actually established in Italy, by Jacopo Sannazaro (*c* 1456–1530) in his *Arcadia* (1504). Jorge de Montemayor (*c* 1520–61), a Portuguese who came to Spain and wrote in Spanish, produced perhaps the most influential pastoral novel in his *Diana* (1559). Miguel de Cervantes' first novel, *La Galetea* (1585), is an exercise in pastoral.

Chivalric romance

While the pastoral novel was flourishing in Spain, so was the novel of chivalry. This form, although dying out when Cervantes (1547–1616) started his great work, was responsible for *Don Quixote* (1605 and 1615). The chivalric romances derived directly from the French romances based on the Arthurian cycle, which were being translated into Spanish throughout the fourteenth and fifteenth centuries. The most widely read chivalric romance during the fifteenth century was the fourteenth-century, native Spanish (or, probably, originally Portuguese), essentially Arthurian *Amadis de Gaula*. The author is unknown; the work was published in a text of 1508 by Montalvo, who probably added a fourth book of his own and who made insertions and alterations in the text of the first three books; but the work itself certainly existed by the middle of the thirteenth century. Amadis is a great and valiant knight, who falls in love with the daughter of the King of "little Britain". The book as we have it can only loosely be called a novel, but has considerable merit.

There were many more Spanish chivalric romances after *Amadis*, which were influenced by it. Literate people were crying out for entertainment, and for some seventy-five years they obtained it in greatest measure from this type of fiction. But a time came when the chivalric ideal had to die. It had been sustained by the personality of Charles V, who actually abdicated and retired to a monastery (a very unusual event in a royal life), in exact accordance with the chivalric ideal. It suffered from the personality of the only half-sane melancholic Philip II, and finally died in 1588, when the Armada was destroyed and with it all the more grandiose dreams of Spain.

The picaresque

The new spirit, necessary to Spain, had effectively been born on the Peninsula in 1554, when the very short picaresque novel *Lazarillo de Tormes*, was published. The author is unknown. His book is deliberately episodic: the incidents are strung together like beads on a string. It is also, in marked contrast to the romances of chivalry and the pastorals (and the mixtures of the two modes), realistic. It gives the reader, through the eyes of a sharp-witted, fairly unscrupulous but sympathetic character, a truthful sociological picture of the real Spain of the time: vicious tricksters, fraudulent and hypocritical priests, pretended gentlemen, a society whose chief feature is the harsh struggle for existence.

Lazarillo, though it drew on earlier material, was the first picaresque novel. The origins of the word "picaresque" are not absolutely clear. But what we now call a picaresque novel may be defined as a novel which has many, perhaps most, but not necessarily all, of the following elements: it is an episodic chronicle, relating the progress

François Rabelais: painted in the sixteenth century by an unknown artist.

through life of a rascally but not seriously criminal person of the lower classes; there is some degree of satire on the social structure; it is often told in the first person; it contains vivid detail. Later on in England Thomas Nashe and then, more importantly, Daniel Defoe, took up the picaresque manner, as did Lesage in France and most significantly Cervantes in Spain. The older picaresque novels are now much more popular than the old romances. It is often said that picaresque novels lack plot, and this is true in a strictly technical sense. But the best of them adequately compensate for it by consistency: in the matter of the psychology of the *picaro* (rogue), the central figure, and in the nature and pointedness of the satire, *Lazarillo* is a profound and, oddly enough, gentle work; clearly the author was a master.

The author of *Lazarillo* did not call his central character a *picaro*, but Mateo Alemán's *Guzmán de Alfarache* (1599) is explicitly one. It is with this that the form becomes established.

The development of the picaresque signifies a great and necessary lurch towards real life; the original masters of the form, such as Francisco Quevedo (1580–1645), were usually ironists who wished to draw attention to false outward as distinct from true inward moral concepts (particularly that of "honour"), and they had very different ways of doing this. When literature gets away from the life of the people it becomes thin, attenuated, and eventually absurd. The picaresque was also a response to the needs of an audience that was on the increase and that wanted common sense as well as romance; it also represented the voice of ordinary people. The printing press made all this possible.

Rabelais

Cervantes was preceded by another major figure, the most important precursor of the modern novel, the Frenchman François Rabelais (?1494–1553). Although Rabelais' four (or five, for those who believe *Cinquième Livre* to be his) separately published books (1532–52) are not, as will be seen, real novels, they have probably had almost as much influence on the twentieth-century novel as has Cervantes. But Rabelais is in a sense very much of a modern discovery. The English knew him through Urquhart's Elizabethan translation, and those who enjoyed him did so for the most part as a lewd and funny buffoon of great intelligence. But Urquhart's translation (it was completed badly by Motteux) is more of an English adaptation, a work in its own right, than it is true Rabelais. For modern translations the English had to wait until the nineteenth century – and still not one of them is satisfactory, though Putnam (in intelligently abridged form in paperback) comes as near as anyone is likely to come.

Rabelais, a radical Catholic and a typical

Gustave Doré's frontispiece for a nineteenth-century edition of Rabelais' Gargantua.

Renaissance man (the scope of his knowledge was enormous), began the *Adventures of Gargantua and Pantagruel* (1532 and 1534) as a fantastic tale of giants, but ended it as a philosophical and psychological critique of existence, masked as riddling comedy. The book is not a unified work. It contains acute sociological comment, criticisms of education, fairy tales, popular almanac material, and an underlying theme of the utmost seriousness and wisdom whose exact philosophical nature has always presented a puzzle to critics: Rabelais is deliberately recondite. But it is certain that the finer points of Rabelais – his questioning of the difference between the real and the illusory, his essentially sceptical and cryptic temperament – have not long been rediscovered. The great French essayist Michel Montaigne (1533–92), another central figure in the history of liberal thought, had to pretend that he was not interested in him and called him "simply amusing": even fifty years after his death it was dangerous for a man of position, as Montaigne was, to admit that there was deep meaning to be found in him. Like the novel itself at its greatest, Rabelais' great proto-novel was religious and political dynamite.

Rabelais' true heirs are Jonathan Swift (1667–1745) and then a host of twentieth-century modern novelists, who have eschewed conventional form in favour of sly humour and a deliberately obscure intention. It is singularly

unfortunate that the adjective "Rabelaisian" should have come to mean "coarse, especially in respect of the eliminatory functions", because this is dangerously misleading. Rabelais' "coarseness" (not apparent to his contemporaries) is hardly relevant to the main tenor of his versatile work, which deals with the nature of true wisdom and the meaning of humour.

The first modern novels

The history of the novel in the main European countries can now be traced. The first place to look for the modern novel is Spain because it produced the first true example, and then, after the time of Cervantes, France, where the novel developed most vigorously in the earlier part of its history. Then attention can move to England, where the novel did not come to full fruition until 1740. Italy and Germany were made up of small principalities until the nineteenth century, and development in these was slower and more sporadic. Russia has always been a special case. America, for obvious reasons, comes in last but by no means least.

Don Quixote

When Miguel de Cervantes began *Don Quixote*, he was certainly simply burlesquing the serious reader of the old chivalric romances. But even at this point he knew that while the genre was on the wane, the "chivalric" attitude persisted in his fellow countrymen. He had an even broader view. He wished to probe imaginatively at the practice of blind idealism. What begins as high comedy – a crazy squire setting off on crazy adventures in the mistaken belief that he is a knight-errant and that the rules of knight-errantry still apply – ends as high and heart-rending tragedy. Don Quixote the madman and Sancho Panza the down-to-earth, simple, cowardly and apparently materialistic peasant, grew and developed as he wrote. The book was published in two parts, in 1605 and 1615, but it has a unity and consistency not found in Rabelais. It is a true novel, because Cervantes was writing at a time when the story-telling convention was better established.

So Cervantes, pressed for money, started out with a plan to make his readers laugh by parodying a worn-out literary vogue, and ended by engaging the attention of all types of readers for ever after. A great work always transcends the intentions of its writer, however profound these are. Pressure to solve problems comes from the unknown depths of the mind, the imagination is rooted in the irrational (the dream, the daydream, the reverie, the involuntary feelings), and authors (and all of us) assimilate the problems confronting their times. The reasons why *Don Quixote* engages the attention of all readers are manifold; the main ones are too instructive to ignore.

First, Don Quixote becomes interesting to us as a character and not a type. He is a madman

with lucid intervals. Sometimes he says things of great wisdom, and when he does so he is undoubtedly a spokesman for his creator. The study of Don Quixote is a study in a certain kind of madness. Remember what Plato (in a mood apparently different from the one in which he wrote the *Republic*) wrote about poetry (literature) and sanity and madness; we may take this to refer to the connection between madness and inspiration. To create great works of the imagination a person is often called upon to make great sacrifices: he has to submerge his intelligence into the depths of the mind, perhaps as savage and terrible as the *id* postulated by Freud. How

can we know about ourselves (a practice recommended as essential by Plato) unless we take the risk of looking into ourselves? Cervantes had a most eventful life: we may guess at the extent of his soul-searchings and his sufferings as he pursued his adventures, and fought to find a way out of his predicaments, which were dire.

Secondly, is there not something of the figure of the holy fool about Don Quixote? After all, mad as he is, and even damaging in his madness, and wrong as his means are, does he not seek with all his heart to redress wrong, to bring justice, beauty and truth to the world? Is he not a battler against evil? And who can deny the beauty of his last understanding of himself, as he dies? "In last year's nests there are no birds this year. I was mad, and now I am sane; I was Don Quixote de la Mancha, and now I am . . . Alonso Quijano [his real name] the good." These words, in their context, have enormous and moving significance for humanity.

Thirdly, there is Sancho Panza, and no novel as great as this could fail to have the voice of the "ordinary man" in it. In contrast to Don Quixote, who is learned (if only in dangerous books) and a gentleman, Sancho is unlettered, and thinks of life in terms of saws and proverbs. He says he is out for gain, yet he turns out to be less materialistic than he seems, even to himself. As Quixote becomes more sane and sobered by his harsh experiences, so Sancho becomes more embroiled in fantasy. He has his "island" just as Quixote has his "giants" (which are windmills). But Sancho really is deluded. Don Quixote is mad, but his madness is wilful: he knows very well that his illusions are illusions.

Don Quixote and Sancho Panza (leading the donkey): a nineteenth-century illustration by Gustave Doré.

Madame Geoffrin's salon: the bust is of Voltaire; Diderot stands in the centre of a group of three behind the seated man in green; Rousseau is in profile, standing sixth from the left; Pierre Marivaux is standing second from the left. The painting is by Lemonnier.

Fourthly, why is it that the modern novel takes its point of departure from Cervantes? An important subsidiary reason has been mentioned: it is psychologically consistent. But the main reason is this: its real subject is the *nature of reality*; it seeks to answer the question, "What is true and what is false, and how do we tell the difference between the two?" This answer is here given: we can't, but we must go on trying. We have a novelist repudiating – fiction! He is doing this by questioning its validity, by carefully drawing our attention to the fact that it is lies. This is literary realism, to which the novel always swings back. Yet it is poetic, meaning supra-realistic, fiction too. And it is about a man writing a novel: the reader discovers this very early on, when he learns that Cervantes has had to get hold of the true history of this extraordinary man Quixote from a manuscript by an "Arabic historian". It also contains inset stories, to the extent that it may fairly be called a variation on the *rahmenerzahlung* (German term for "narrative frame in which are contained other narratives"; *The Arabian Nights*, the *Decameron* of Boccaccio and Chaucer's *Canterbury Tales* are all of this type).

Don Quixote also represents the most radical adjustment ever made of literary form to the circumstances of life. Yet it is a long way from being just drab realism. It is poetic, puzzling, funny, tragic – and the experience of reading it shakes all sensitive people to the core of their beings. Although the great literary realists are pragmatists (many of them have started by parodying works of predecessors: for example Henry Fielding and Jane Austen), they are not necessarily against poetry or the mysterious or the wonderful. Cervantes himself was a good

Catholic, though an audacious and liberal one. But invariably the impulse of such writers is to point out attitudes that are stupid. That is not a bad thing.

Seventeenth-century France

Spanish literature continued vigorously for a time after the death of Cervantes, but in the realm of poetry. Quevedo extended the scope of the picaresque novel, but the form fell into decay on the peninsula until the hugely important Benito Pérez Galdós began writing in the nineteenth century. (He has been scandalously and almost totally neglected in the English-speaking world.) The novel proper developed in France before the end of the seventeenth century: in the *salons*, the houses where the people with excellent minds – and high social position – used to meet and discuss affairs of the past and present, as well as gossip.

At the beginning of the seventeenth century France emerged from a long period of barbarism: the religious wars. Decent people were looking for civilized reading, which is of course closely connected with civilized living. Honoré d'Urfé's long, mythological pastoral *l'Astrée* (1607–27), which no one reads now and of which there is no modern translation (an abridgement might please many readers), scored an enormous success. It is fair to say that this was the first French novel. D'Urfé (1567–1625) found the inspiration for his immensely long book both in pastoral, particularly in Montemayor, and in translations by Jacques Amyot (1513–93) of the early Greek novels of Longus and Heliodorus. There is also a veiled autobiographical element. The novel has a single theme, but there are scores of inset stories. The setting is supposedly the fifth century, the religion "Druidic", which enabled the author to

avoid dangerous theological controversy. The real subject is love, the rules of which are drawn up. The ideal is "Honest Love", and the novels of the next half-century tend to be dominated by the search for this.

L'Astrée led the salon hostess Mlle de Scudéry (1607–1701) to write her own novels, such as *Clélie* (1654–60). Another more sensitive and gifted woman (her letters are among the finest ever written) was Madame de Sévigné (1626–96). Her letters deal in facts, but they come close to good fiction because she saw, as she was fond of remarking, that everything was "many-sided". Her imagination, intelligence and sensibility pervade these letters which she wrote to her daughter, who lived outside Paris but wanted to know what was going on there. Two of her close friends were the aphorist François La Rochefoucauld (1613–80) and Madame de Lafayette (1634–93). The latter married, had children, but then amicably left her husband to his estates while she came to Paris to live in the Rue Vaugirard, and to see much of Madame de Sévigné and La Rochefoucauld. Here she established a salon of her own. It should be noted that the focus has suddenly switched to women – and it should be emphasized that without women the novel could never have developed. Women have written fewer novels than men, but in a certain very important sense they have – from Lady Murasaki onwards – controlled the novel's development. They know more about love than men; and they know more about men. These are inestimable advantages.

Madame de Lafayette tried her hand at two quite ordinary novels before she published *The Princess of Clèves* (1678). She could not avow authorship, for although women of her class had considerable freedom at that time it was not done to admit officially to doing things like writing novels: some of the readership would feel it wrong. She undoubtedly had some help from La Rochefoucauld and others, but nonetheless the book is her own – it is quintessentially a novel by a woman.

The literary influences on *The Princess of Clèves*, besides the love-theme in d'Urfé, include the *Works* of Pierre Brantôme (1540–1614), a military man who was crippled by a fall from a horse and took to subtle, cool and accurate description of the court life of the sixteenth century, and the novels of Mlle de Scudéry and Gauthier de Costes, Sieur de La Calprenède (1614–63). But the true influences were her intelligent milieu and, above all, her own experience – which, however, she transforms perfectly into a story. This is essentially what T. S. Eliot meant by an "objective correlative": an author has a personal experience, and he imaginatively constructs a fiction that exactly covers the case, but more universally: he thus transcends the personal elements, and can communicate its essence to others.

Set ostensibly in the court of Henry II, but really alluding to Madame de Lafayette's contemporaries, *The Princess of Clèves* is an apparently simple tale. A married woman suddenly conceives a passion for another man. She does not act upon it, but instead dutifully informs her husband. The other man overhears her confession. He does not keep the secret. So the husband dies miserable – of jealousy – and the honest woman is forced to refuse the offer of the man she loves when she is widowed. This has been described as a book about the destructive effects of passion; and Nancy Mitford said that the author was coldhearted. The first judgement is extremely limited and the second is grotesque. It is a story told with great self-control, about what a tangled web we can weave when we practice to undeceive, about corruption, about the amoral and involuntary nature of passion, about the sadness of life. What is affirmatory in it is the beautiful and meaningful sense of order that is imposed on this almost horrifying story: that sense of order represents the classical novel at its best, and displays the power of woman's sensibility in adverse circumstances. All those who

Madame de Sevigné, painted in about 1665 by Claude le Febvre.

love the classical novel love *The Princess of Clèves*, and most other readers do as well. There is no substitute for reading it; and most women, whatever their reading habits, immediately know what it is about.

Several contemporaries of d'Urfé and of Madame de Lafayette had been continuing the pastoral and picaresque traditions, although some of them were actually reacting against these forms. In 1627, the year in which the last volume of *l'Astrée* appeared, Charles Sorel (1602–74) published *Le Berger extravagant*, which is much influenced by Cervantes. Sorel had previously written a picaresque novel, and now he set out to mock d'Urfé: in one of its editions the subtitle is actually "anti-novel". A young urban man goes off to the country and tries out "pastoral" life: the jokes are based on how real life intrudes on his dream. It is weak Cervantes. A more original and effective anti-novel was by Antoine Furetière (1619–88), whose *Roman Bourgeois* (1666), although episodic and scrappy, is "modern" enough to make such jokes as that its author did not know what happened upon such-and-such an occasion because he wasn't there . . .

Behind all this realism there lies the example of Cervantes, of course. Cervantes had clearly assimilated the picaresque approach: it is present in Don Quixote – and he wrote one short novel, *The Colloquy of Dogs* (in *Exemplary Novels*) which is pure picaresque. The tradition was carried on in France by Alain-René Lesage (1668–1747) in *Gil Blas* (1715, 1724, 1735), which is in many ways highly original. Lesage remains episodic, relying on speed of narration; but his characterization has been underrated. There is enough blending of narrative and portraiture to make him into a genuine novelist in our modern sense, although he has not enough genius to impress us deeply.

After *The Princess of Clèves* the next French masterpiece is the Abbé Prévost's *Manon Lescaut* (1731). This is a subtle work, the outstanding volume in a long quasi-picaresque series, in which Prévost (1697–1763) pretends to be using the novel to instruct in conventional morality (he may have thought he was doing so). This would remain a tactic of good novelists for the whole of the eighteenth century, for the novel still had powerful enemies. It may be said, as a broad generalization, that the ruling classes do not like the pursuit of truth: it is not in their interests. There are countless individual exceptions that test this, but it is and has always been the case with the mass of civil servants, of churchmen when the church wielded power, and of politicians. When Pierre-Ambroise-François Laclos wrote *Liaisons dangereuses* (1782), *the* French masterpiece of the eighteenth century, he shocked everyone. But Marie Antoinette had it on her shelves – in plain binding.

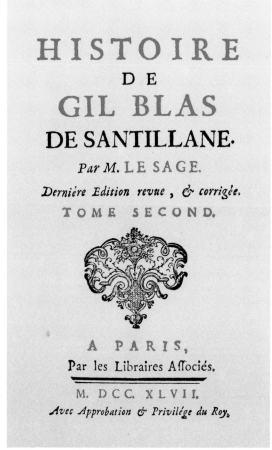

The title page of an early, 1747, edition of Alain-René Lesage's Gil Blas.

Seventeenth and eighteenth-century England

In seventeenth-century England there had been early picaresque, in such works as those of Thomas Nashe (1567–?1601); there had been romance (Spenser's *Fairy Queen*, though in verse, is an example); and there had been pastoral, well exemplified in Sir Philip Sidney's *Arcadia* (c. 1590). But none of these works came near to being real novels. In that empirical country the chief influences on the novel proper, apart from the continental writers, were historical chronicles such as Clarendon's *History of the Rebellion and Civil Wars in England* (1702–4), works about exploration, and "realistic" (in the modern, ordinary sense) theological and philosophical doctrine. It is foolish to try to state categorically which was the first true English novel, because this would involve a large amount of obscure abstract argument. John Bunyan's allegorical *Pilgrim's Progress* (1678 and 1684) is clearly not a novel proper. But its homeliness and paradoxical dependence on actuality profoundly influenced the novelists of the eighteenth century. His book was in almost every literate household; few who could read could avoid reading it.

Daniel Defoe certainly launched the idea of the

MAJOR WORKS OF FICTION: 1600–1799

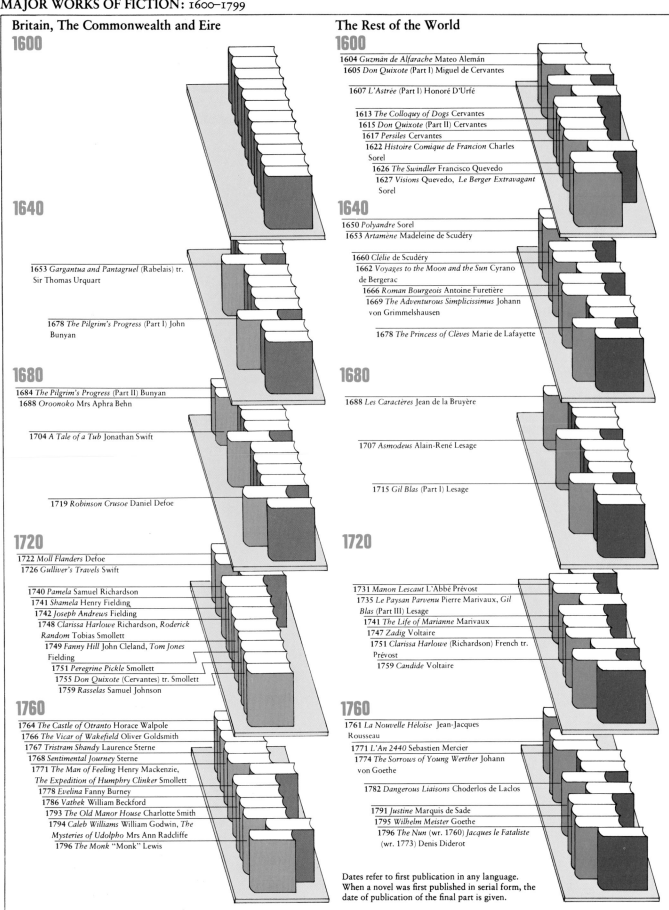

Britain, The Commonwealth and Eire

1600

1640

1653 *Gargantua and Pantagruel* (Rabelais) tr. Sir Thomas Urquart

1678 *The Pilgrim's Progress* (Part I) John Bunyan

1680

1684 *The Pilgrim's Progress* (Part II) Bunyan
1688 *Oroonoko* Mrs Aphra Behn

1704 *A Tale of a Tub* Jonathan Swift

1719 *Robinson Crusoe* Daniel Defoe

1720

1722 *Moll Flanders* Defoe
1726 *Gulliver's Travels* Swift

1740 *Pamela* Samuel Richardson
1741 *Shamela* Henry Fielding
1742 *Joseph Andrews* Fielding
1748 *Clarissa Harlowe* Richardson, *Roderick Random* Tobias Smollett
1749 *Fanny Hill* John Cleland, *Tom Jones* Fielding
1751 *Peregrine Pickle* Smollett
1755 *Don Quixote* (Cervantes) tr. Smollett
1759 *Rasselas* Samuel Johnson

1760

1764 *The Castle of Otranto* Horace Walpole
1766 *The Vicar of Wakefield* Oliver Goldsmith
1767 *Tristram Shandy* Laurence Sterne
1768 *Sentimental Journey* Sterne
1771 *The Man of Feeling* Henry Mackenzie, *The Expedition of Humphry Clinker* Smollett
1778 *Evelina* Fanny Burney
1786 *Vathek* William Beckford
1793 *The Old Manor House* Charlotte Smith
1794 *Caleb Williams* William Godwin, *The Mysteries of Udolpho* Mrs Ann Radcliffe
1796 *The Monk* "Monk" Lewis

The Rest of the World

1600

1604 *Guzmán de Alfarache* Mateo Alemán
1605 *Don Quixote* (Part I) Miguel de Cervantes

1607 *L'Astrée* (Part I) Honoré D'Urfé

1613 *The Colloquy of Dogs* Cervantes
1615 *Don Quixote* (Part II) Cervantes
1617 *Persiles* Cervantes
1622 *Histoire Comique de Francion* Charles Sorel
1626 *The Swindler* Francisco Quevedo
1627 *Visions* Quevedo, *Le Berger Extravagant* Sorel

1640

1650 *Polyandre* Sorel
1653 *Artamène* Madeleine de Scudéry

1660 *Clélie* de Scudéry
1662 *Voyages to the Moon and the Sun* Cyrano de Bergerac
1666 *Roman Bourgeois* Antoine Furetière
1669 *The Adventurous Simplicissimus* Johann von Grimmelshausen

1678 *The Princess of Clèves* Marie de Lafayette

1680

1688 *Les Caractères* Jean de la Bruyère

1707 *Asmodeus* Alain-René Lesage

1715 *Gil Blas* (Part I) Lesage

1720

1731 *Manon Lescaut* L'Abbé Prévost
1735 *Le Paysan Parvenu* Pierre Marivaux, *Gil Blas* (Part III) Lesage
1741 *The Life of Marianne* Marivaux
1747 *Zadig* Voltaire
1751 *Clarissa Harlowe* (Richardson) French tr. Prévost
1759 *Candide* Voltaire

1760

1761 *La Nouvelle Héloïse* Jean-Jacques Rousseau
1771 *L'An 2440* Sebastien Mercier
1774 *The Sorrows of Young Werther* Johann von Goethe
1782 *Dangerous Liaisons* Choderlos de Laclos
1791 *Justine* Marquis de Sade
1795 *Wilhelm Meister* Goethe
1796 *The Nun* (wr. 1760) *Jacques le Fataliste* (wr. 1773) Denis Diderot

Dates refer to first publication in any language. When a novel was first published in serial form, the date of publication of the final part is given.

novel in England; but Samuel Richardson's *Pamela* (1740) is usually considered to be the first true novel. Defoe's fiction, which is in a class above that of Richardson, hardly consists of novels simply because he has no real plots; Richardson does. It is significant that both Defoe and Richardson were tradesmen rather than gentlemen; the English novel proper originated not in the universities, but in the world of commerce.

After a career in trade Daniel Defoe (?1660–1731) began writing with an *Essay on Projects* (1697) which proposed radical and practical reforms in a clear, businesslike prose. Yet he was a very complex man. Some of his financial dealings in business may have been shady, and he went bankrupt and then rescued himself – both spectacularly. A serious dissenter, he was also a spy, who worked for both the Whigs and the Tories. His *The Shortest Way with the Dissenters* (1702) puts forward the case against his position with real conviction, though it is also undoubtedly an essay in irony. In short, he is a mystery man. He was fifty-nine before he came to fiction, and he did so by accident. The story of Alexander Selkirk, who had lived alone on a remote island for four years, was well known. Defoe's political reputation was sinking because

Three of the series of twelve paintings depicting scenes from Samuel Richardson's Pamela *completed by the English portrait painter Joseph Highmore in 1745.*

of his known duplicity, and his health was failing. He decided to write about a castaway, but the experiences of Selkirk (whom he may have talked to) were too well known. He started to invent: to, in his own words, "lie like truth". His intention was to produce a piece of fictitious journalism, and the result was inspired fiction on the theme of survival in a hostile environment: *Robinson Crusoe* (1719).

Defoe went on to write several more novels, of which the best is *Moll Flanders*. All of these were swindles, and were called such: fictions skilfully posing as truths, to capture the market. Defoe span out his tales, wrote at great speed, packed his material with factual detail (most of it at second hand) and was strongly influenced by the picaresque (he spoke six languages and read seven). However, he developed the novel because he brought the authentic realistic note into fiction, and above all he persuaded the reader to identify with the main character. Knowing that large numbers of people were opposed to fiction because it told lies and encouraged immoral behaviour, Defoe pretended to be acting in the interests of morality, and also pretended that his fictions were real stories.

Samuel Richardson (1689–1761), a well-to-do printer and a much less ambiguous moralist than Defoe, also led his readers into identifying with the main characters. He told his stories in the form of letters written by his main characters (Laclos, too, had used this epistolary form), so that the reader sees each character at the moment of his or her crisis. In his *Pamela* the heroine is a servant girl who rejects her master's attempts upon her virtue and eventually gets him to marry her; the book instantly seized the attention of the public. It presented the point of view of a mere servant, and for the first time took it with the utmost seriousness. The social implications are obvious. The sub-title is "Virtue Rewarded".

However *Clarissa Harlowe* (1747–8) rather than *Pamela* is Richardson's best novel. It is of immense length, but held its contemporary readers' attention throughout. It is about the relentless pursuit of a woman by a dissolute man; eventually he rapes her while she is drugged, in a brothel. She wastes away and dies; he is killed in

MAJOR WORKS OF FICTION: 1790–1799

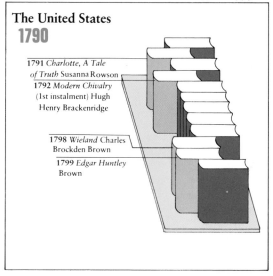

The United States

1790

1791 *Charlotte, A Tale of Truth* Susanna Rowson

1792 *Modern Chivalry* (1st instalment) Hugh Henry Brackenridge

1798 *Wieland* Charles Brockden Brown

1799 *Edgar Huntley* Brown

a duel; and vice is seen to be unrewarded. Although ostensibly and consciously obsessed with virtue, Richardson gains his power by erotic manipulation. The reader is kept in suspense as the climax, the rape, is delayed. However, more important is the fact that Richardson fulfilled his intention of gripping the reader. He intelligently defended his technique by pointing out that in the epistolary novel "the letters are written while the hearts of the writers must be supposed to be wholly engaged in their subjects (the events at the time dubious), so that they abound not only with critical situations, but with what may be called instantaneous descriptions and reflections". Obviously he had stumbled upon something of prime significance. Other writers would drop the letter-form but retain the technique, which eventually developed into "stream-of-consciousness". Richardson also cashed in on the extreme emotionalism of the period: as the book came out, volume by volume, readers wrote to him begging him to "save" Clarissa, to "reform" the villain, and so forth. It is significant that an ostensibly virtuous man had helped convert a public hostile to the novel – to lying – to such an extent that they now thought of lies as if they were true, just as some today believe in the real existence, or convince themselves that they do, of characters in television soap operas. The poet Samuel T. Coleridge was forced to exclaim that although he much admired Richardson his "mind is so very vile a mind, so oozy, so hypocritical, praise-mad, canting, envious, concupiscent!" This remains true for most readers; although some sociologically-oriented critics find him superior in all departments. It is certainly true that John Cleland's (1709–89) *Fanny Hill* (1749), which does not use a single "offensive" word, springs directly from Richardson, and is in one sense more decent – in that it is candidly sexual. But Cleland had not Richardson's very powerful psychological insight into, not the human heart, but the strategies of sexual desire. That Richardson presents them in a way "vile" to many readers cannot detract from his achievement. He had a huge influence on the European continent, especially on Prévost, but very often the adaptations and translations of his works cut out the moralizing and shortened them considerably.

Henry Fielding (1707–54) was of higher social class than Defoe or Richardson, and was more conscious of what he was about: he was educated at Eton and at a Dutch university, and became an excellent reforming magistrate – even though earlier in his life his plays had caused the authorities to extend their powers to ban "subversive" performances. Fielding is more literary and calculating than Richardson, and his first novel *Shamela* (1741) parodies Richardson's *Pamela* on the sophisticated grounds that Richardson's conception of virtue was wrong-headed. Later, when Fielding had found his way in fiction, he

Samuel Richardson, painted in 1750 by Joseph Highmore.

saw Richardson's virtues.

Fielding's first full-scale novel *Joseph Andrews* (1742) was, as its sub-title announced, written "in the manner of Cervantes". Fielding, like Cervantes, was a master of the comic, which of course, as *Don Quixote* makes clear, embraces the tragic. His first great character Parson Adams, in *Joseph Andrews*, is "quixotic" in that he is absurdly innocent and yet absurdly, or at least abnormally, good: he believes that virtue ought to be practised. Fielding, as much as Defoe and certainly more than Richardson, was appalled by the social conditions of his time. A direct satirist, he mocked at the idea of success as it is usually interpreted: externally. His semi-fictional *Mr Jonathan Wild* (1743) tells the story of a famous real criminal as if he were not only a good but a supremely great man. As Thomas Hardy was later to say of all good art, at the bottom of it some kind of protest is being registered. Fielding had thought a great deal about *Don Quixote*, and it may be that the majority of his critics have not seen all that he saw in it – and how this crept into his masterpiece *Tom Jones* (1749).

In the development of the English novel *Tom Jones* perfects the element of plot. It shows plot as a technique to have point, for the ultimate effect of the book is only seen when, after reading, the plot is contemplated. *Tom Jones* creates a world of its own, exposes tyranny (in Squire Western), and gives us an exact evaluation of the extent of sexual sins as distinct from others. There is an oblique criticism of Richardson here. The latter shows that major fiction can spring from nastiness and average intelligence; Fielding shows that it can derive from humane enlightenment and high intelligence. *Tom Jones* is the first great realist novel in English. Fielding, as the critic Walter Allen says, is "the great original in English fiction".

Tobias Smollett (1721–71) is less important,

but still a major figure. Like Defoe, he is more the journalist than the literary man. His novels are wholly picaresque in technique. He is emotional, angry, jeering, spiteful. He does not control his emotions as did Defoe or Fielding; nor has he Richardson's solid confidence in his own virtue. He is rough, but he sparkles with energy, and is highly intelligent; he is also very funny in a robust and very Scottish manner. Significantly, he translated Lesage's *Gil Blas*, as well as Cervantes' *Don Quixote* (his was the standard version for a hundred years, and it is still read). He had been to sea as a ship's surgeon, and his novels deal with life at sea and in foreign parts as well as with London. Dickens could not have existed without Smollett, who was the first to master the art of pure caricature.

Now that the novel has reached fruition it is useful to bring in the famous and useful distinction between "flat" and "round" characters, made by E. M. Forster in his *Aspects of the Novel*. The flat characters "vibrate". They are constructed around a single quality or characteristic, and they give the illusion of being alive. They are never surprising. They please us by acting true to type, like the absurder schoolteachers of our youth. Round characters have the "incalculability of life", they can surprise without straining our credibility, they are complexly constructed. But a note of caution should be added: the pure types of "flatness" and "roundness" are seldom found – except that in very popular fiction they are all, naturally enough, flat and even flimsy. A popular writer's skill in handling flat characters, in stiffening them so that they can vibrate convincingly, is a measure of not only his skill but his worth.

Smollett's characters tend to be flat, though his energy compensates for this in his best novels, *Roderick Random* (1748) and *Peregrine Pickle* (1751). He is careless and his novels are always flawed, but he gives a marvellous bird's-eye picture of his times, and his inventiveness seldom flags. He is savage – all men becoming in his eyes grotesque caricatures – and untrusting, but vital. As the twentieth-century novelists lose control of the form, they tend to read him and to try to imitate him. And if they have his gusto, they can do it. Walter Allen suggests Joyce Cary as one such, and the comparison is just. Many others have been similarly influenced.

Jonathan Swift's *Gulliver's Travels* (1726) has not been mentioned because this is pure satire. It is worth noting that in this cruel dissection of the human race Swift used, initially, the methods of Defoe, whom he affected to despise (he thought there was "no enduring him"). He gets the reader to identify with the sailor, to get interested in him – and then traps him. The reader is thus led to see himself and his kind in a mirror that is by no means merely a distorting one.

Laurence Sterne's *Tristram Shandy* (1760–67), though it turns the eighteenth-century novel on its head, cannot be dealt with so shortly in even a condensed guide to the main developments of the novel. It anticipates modern practice, and by its rejection of the techniques established by Defoe, Richardson and Fielding, highlights them, tests them, and paves the way for their development in changed times.

Sterne (1713–68) is best described as a pragmatist; he offers his fiction for the use of readers. It is interesting that although his profound work should have delighted both his contemporaries and subsequent generations for quite unprofound reasons (in other words, he is readable), he infuriated the narrow, though gifted, twentieth-century critic F. R. Leavis, who thought *Tristram Shandy* was "irresponsible" and "nasty". No dogmatist can really like this open-ended novel, and it is a pity if readers are put off by Leavis. Nor should they be influenced by the fact that Sterne was a clergyman: this was a refuge for the poor but learned man in those times, and he was not happy in the role. He undeniably created a world of his own; yet it is very obviously not a "real" world, and he does not pretend that it is. Sterne's intention is to show that feeling is meaningless without thought, but that thought is also meaningless without feeling: an impossible thing to demonstrate, a fact which he paradoxically enjoys. *Tristram Shandy* offends the novelist's traditional code – just established – by denying its utility. What is the use, he seems to ask, of planning fiction? So his Shandy (Sterne himself) writes as he feels. Thus he too anticipates "stream-of-consciousness", though in a different way from Richardson. He offers the reader a perfectly conventional novel, but so broken up and rearranged as to look plain crazy.

Sterne has been a major influence on the twentieth-century novel; but what he did may be seen as quite unsurprising in the context of his own times. He combined the cult of sentimentality which swept over England (and elsewhere) in the eighteenth century, with the philosophical views of John Locke – who did not regard the workings of the mind as rational (modern psychology on the whole bears him out).

It must be remembered that in the eighteenth century the word "sentimentality" had different connotations: feeling had to assert itself as sentiment if it was to assert itself at all. Nowadays much of this sentiment, especially that of the French writer Jean Jacques Rousseau (1712–78), seems idealistic and excessive. But seen in its context it was an inevitable reaction. An important element in it, after all, was "sensibility", which really means "susceptibility to tender feelings". In Sterne there is sensibility at its best; and in the popular and very fluently written novel by Henry Mackenzie, *The Man of Feeling* (1771), it appears at its worst, its most sickly, sentimental and unsophisticated.

Much later, after the cult of sensibility had been

assaulted by Jane Austen and others, the word acquired an entirely new, and yet not altogether unrelated, meaning. It came to mean the faculty of "being vividly interested in things", awareness of flux. It is found in James Joyce, Virginia Woolf, Marcel Proust, and it is a feature of modernism. We also find this form of sensibility, though, in Sterne.

The two meanings of sensibility are useful in discussion of the novel. The earlier meaning connotes a necessary escape from rationalism. The exponent of this idealistic form of sensibility cared about feelings but he was also interested in wildness, ruggedness and madness. In the end this was overdone, and there had to be a reaction to it. Dr Johnson (1709–84), who said of Sterne that "his nonsense suited his reader's nonsense", was against it in its own time because he suffered from an intermittent mental disorder and believed that the consequences of sensibility could lead to total derangement. *Rasselas* (1759), his one novel, is about this problem, and it is not as opposed to moderate sensibility as some critics think. But Johnson tended to be fixed in his opinions: that was his dramatic style. In his art he was more open-minded, despite himself.

We cannot leave the English novel in its first great phase without mentioning two further important elements: the fact that in the seventeenth century (from Mrs Aphra Behn onwards), women were always writing; and the rise and demise of the Gothic novel. Critics used to despise all the female novelists of this period, many of whom were imitators of Richardson (Fielding's sister, Sarah, was one of them). Some were certainly rather thin, but then the works of many men, whose names are now lost in obscurity, were also. Some of the much maligned Mrs Manley's work is still readable, though regrettably it is not in print. She was not as good as Charlotte Smith, whose best novel *The Old Manor House* (1793)

Samuel Johnson, a contemporary painting by James Barry.

The effects of reading "Monk" Lewis' Gothic novel, The Monk, *as portrayed by Gillray in 1802.*

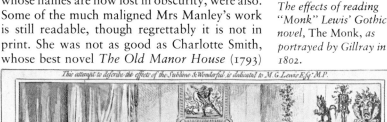

has been reprinted. The succession of women who wrote through the eighteenth century are an important factor in the rise of the form, and they have so far been unduly neglected.

Horace Walpole's *The Castle of Otranto* (1765) marks the beginning of the development of the Gothic novel, though there is a hint of it in Smollett's *Count Ferdinand Fathom* (1753). The form was both a reversion to the past because characterization was neglected, and a pointer to the future, for it was a precursor of romanticism, the development that must be considered next. The Gothic novel arose as a rediscovery of the mysterious past within the general framework of sensibility. Walpole's novel is fairly bad, in the sense that it is very contrived and melodramatic, but it is typical. The setting is medieval; there are supernatural events; the atmosphere is fraught with tension (suddenly slamming doors and the whole paraphernalia now familiar to every late-night television viewer of "tales of horror"). Sometimes an oriental note was added, as in William Beckford's *Vathek* (1786).

The most successful practitioners were "Monk" Lewis (1775–1818) and Mrs Radcliffe (1764–1823); but the best of all novels in the genre (though it is not wholly Gothic) is Mary Shelley's *Frankenstein* (1818). Though well known, this is underrated, its excellences having been submerged by continuous exploitation of its ingenuities and terrors. The fine achievement of the television adaptation by Christopher Isherwood helped greatly to draw attention to the author herself, and what she meant. The Gothic novel eventually collapsed under the weight of ridicule (*Northanger Abbey* (1818), a parody of the genre, gave Jane Austen her start), but many elements of it survived. Thus there is a touch of it in the ghost stories of Henry James, though there it is refined almost out of existence.

Eighteenth-century France

It is often asserted that French novels are the best of all novels. This is true in at least a structural sense: France is the home of the classical novel, pure in form. It is certainly the most appropriate country to employ as the crucible in which the modern novel grew. This is probably because the French are keener on movements, modes, styles, than are the English or the Americans. They are more eager to express their views than the English-speaking peoples, but not too much so.

The inconsistent but enormously influential Rousseau was certainly one of the chief progenitors of *sensibilité*. In him were concentrated most of the "irrational" and paradoxical feelings of his age: the notion of the "noble savage"; the idea that social and all other kinds of progress pervert goodness; the idea that men are born free but are everywhere in chains; the cultivation of candour (in his *Confessions*). He was the playwright who attacked the theatre; the author who had to fly from political persecution and who died in a state of acute paranoia; the immoralist (he abandoned his children) who proclaimed the sanctity of the moral law. His real message, though he was inconsistent in expressing it, is consistent: it is that the natural man is superior to the civilized man. This is an involuntary attitude of mind. It is seen today in those who cannot help, even though they are aware of their impracticality, mourning the rise of godless technocracies in favour of the old rural ways. So, without here trying to discover the key to Rousseau himself, we can appreciate the enormous influence of his point of view, which caused novelists – directly or indirectly – to depict the countryside with a feeling accuracy, to set their characters within their environments and to show the relationships between them, and to concentrate upon the power of instinctive behaviour. Rousseau's epistolary novel *La Nouvelle Héloïse* (1761) was as successful in France as *Clarissa Harlowe* had been in England. It showed the triumph of the family, the natural unit, over the forces of society. The novel itself now bores us, since it is a vehicle for ideas rather than a human document (at one point a character writes a letter to the girl who is about to give herself to him: she is downstairs). But the ideas have influenced all the generations that followed, negatively or positively.

Neither Voltaire (1694–1778) nor Denis Diderot (1713–84) wrote true novels; but both are supremely important in the development of the form – the latter the more so, but less obtrusively. Voltaire, in *Candide* (1759) and other *contes* (a *conte* is a French tale; later it acquired the meaning of long-short-story), adopts the point of view of the reasonable man who satirizes the absurdity of the world but withdraws from it in civilized horror; his satire is malicious and severe, but as funny as it is savage. Diderot, a much more complex character who pretended he was an atheist, anticipated almost every modern ten-dency, and showed in his *contes* a grasp of mind-in-action and characterization that was quite beyond Voltaire. But Voltaire's passion for justice has always been influential, too.

Romanticism

Apart from Benjamin Constant's *Adolphe* (1816), there were no really important French novels between Laclos' *Liaisons dangereuses* (1782) and Stendhal's *The Red and the Black* (1830); but in that period romanticism became established. This is a vague and yet indispensable term. It is best studied in cosmopolitan terms, rather than in those of any single country, and for this reason we will shortly catch up with developments in Germany and Italy – and in Russia. But France, because of its passion for classification, provides the appropriate starting point, even if to many people the English romantic poets provide the most obvious first examples of what we call romanticism.

The word romanticism comes from romance, and "roman" in the sense already described: the romance novel. In the seventeenth century the word came to be used in a derogatory sense: over-fanciful. But then, throughout the eighteenth century, it gradually acquired a more favourable connotation: a romantic place was a pleasant nostalgic wild one. This is a Rousseauist notion, and demonstrates the huge influence of Rousseau. But it was – in so far as it was anyone in particular – a great woman, Madame de Staël (1766–1817), who first made the famous distinction between classicism and romanticism. As a lover and friend of Constant, she knew Germany and the Germans well, and it was in her book about Germany (*De l'Allemagne*, 1810) that she clearly distinguished between classical and romantic poetry. Two Germans, the Schlegel brothers, began the habit of discussing the classical-romantic polarity; but Madame de Staël, who knew them, contributed more usefully to this discussion, because she was less abstract.

It is generally agreed that Mme de Staël was the first person to conceive of literary history "in the modern sense". She contrasted the northern tendency towards sadness, romantic fantasy, agonized complexity, with the southern tendency towards contentment, fixed form, simplicity, happy pagan warmth. This was really a rediscovery of the virtues of such as Cervantes and Shakespeare, both of whom had been condemned by the neoclassical eighteenth century for their faults, although their virtues had been recognized. For the first time there arose a consciousness that while classical art could be perfect and "correct", imperfect romantic art could be much deeper, could mirror human nature (seen as imperfect) more profoundly. In England the philosopher Shaftesbury (1671–1713) had anticipated Rousseau by recommending a "natural" religion towards which men would naturally turn: look into nature, he suggested, for nature is good. Mme de Staël herself had written a study of Rousseau – and her attitude in it is romantic because she does not try to assess him, but rather records the effect he has on her sensibility. A classical mind is impelled to evaluate, and very often, unhappily, is impervious to the fact that literature is not a science: that judgement is finally a relative matter. The romantic puts imagination above formal rules.

However, the romantic-classical opposition is far more easily seen in poetry than in fiction. In the neo-classical period poetry became exceedingly constrained – and as early as 1730, when James Thomson's *The Seasons* appeared, poets were trying to escape from the constraints. Now the picaresque is by no means romantic; but it is energetic and it lacks discipline. It was easier for novelists to escape the constraints put upon them by rules. The only way we can trace the emergence of true romanticism in the novel is to watch how sensibility flowered into the full and confident expression of individuality. The best novelists seem to make nonsense of sharp distinctions: we certainly don't get a full sense of how and why they are rewarding if we try to categorize them. Yet the distinction is necessary, because in the nineteenth century very different novelists do show similar characteristics: love of freedom, expression of emotion, spontaneity, individualism, willingness at least to accept the existence of non-conformity. All these characteristics had manifested themselves separately, but as a cluster they only appear with romanticism. It is in Mme de Staël's own two novels, the best of which is *Corinne* (1807), that we first meet the modern woman. That this is so is certainly a consequence of romanticism.

An illustration from the 1782 edition of Jean-Jacques Rousseau's Émile, or Man's Education Begins at his Birth; a bust of Rousseau stands in an appropriately pastoral setting.

Germany

We should expect romanticism to express itself early in Germany, and so it does. But Germany was very late in producing a modern novel, and had to rely on translations of Cervantes and other authors for some time. Only Johann von Grimmelhausen's highly original, and basically picaresque, *Simplicissimus* (1669) is truly great; there is nothing to equal it in the realm of the novel until Johann von Goethe almost a century later. Goethe's *Werther* (1774), technically a product of the self-explanatory *Sturm und Drang* (Storm and Stress) movement of which he was the leading figure, is certainly a bridge between sensibility and romanticism, with the balance strongly in favour of the latter. It is, as is universally agreed, an absurd book, and Goethe himself mocked it. Yet it took Europe by storm, and was regarded with terrible seriousness by its readers. One can still discern its power, and it is still read.

However, Goethe went on to produce *Wilhelm Meister* (1795), the first *Entwicklungsroman* (novel dealing with the development of a personality; the *Bildungsroman* deals with the education of a personality, so that there is often a confusion between the two terms), and *Elective Affinities* (1809), in truth his best novel, and certainly the most readable today. In producing these novels, his drama, poetry and essays – and, indeed, his *Novelle* (short novels or stories) – Goethe unfortunately put a stranglehold on the German novel, and indeed on German literature, from which it had reluctantly to release itself. He had this effect simply because of his powerful personality and his huge gifts. Thus the substantial realistic novel does not begin in Germany until much later than elsewhere.

Italy

In Italy events were similar, except that there was no Goethe. Alessandro Manzoni's *The Betrothed* (1840–42), one of the world's masterpieces, is entirely exceptional: there is nothing at all like it elsewhere in fiction. Sir Walter Scott, to whom we shall come, had some influence on the form Manzoni chose; but nowhere else can we find such translucent, gentle optimism enclosed within a boldly yet placidly outlined circle of terror and despair. Manzoni, poet and philologist, for whose soul Verdi wrote his majestic Requiem, was the chief founder of the Italian language. We have to wait until the last quarter of the nineteenth century when Antonio Fogazzaro (1842–1911), the magnificent Giovanni Verga (1840–1922), and to a much smaller extent Luigi Capuana (1839–1915) were writing, before the true Italian novel begins.

Russia

Russia, as has been stated, is a special case. It is not only a European but an Asiatic country. It has always been ruled tyrannically and intolerantly, by networks of secret police and spies; so that literature has flourished (literature being a kind of protest), but at great cost to its practitioners.

The novel in Russia begins with a story in verse: Aleksandr Pushkin's *Eugene Onegin* (1823–31). This, and the English romantic poet Byron (the contemporary cult of whom on the continent can hardly be exaggerated), and other purely Russian influences, lie behind the short prose masterpiece *A Hero of our Time* (1840) by the poet Mikhail Lermontov. Lermontov here arranges five *contes* in the form of a novel. The plot is highly complicated, but is certainly present – though in no obvious way. The central figure is seen through other eyes, and through his own. As readable as anything by any popular author, *A Hero of Our Time* is a deliberate puzzle, and an enigma. It quite transcends the "Byronism" which is part of its background. Byronism elsewhere in Europe had a Gothic, strained, sensationalist quality: heroes were attractive but sinister, almost as in modern Gothic novels. Lermontov exquisitely modified this melodramatic tendency.

But Russian realism (each of the "realisms", as we shall see, is different in the different countries) did not dominate the literature before the 1840s. A dramatist turned critic, Vissarion Belinsky ("Furious Vissarion", 1811–48), initiated the movement: the so-called *Natural School* (1846–47). Belinsky, whose efforts inspired Turgenev, Goncharov, Dostoyevsky, Tolstoy and others – even though most of these made different political solutions to his own, which was revolutionary – rejected the literature of mere entertainment: his message was that literature must improve life, by exploring it and by exposing its abuses. Compared to the novelists whom he influenced, Belinsky was crude and political; but in the especially foul circumstances of Russia his Natural School was indeed "natural", and he was radiantly sincere, and no fool either.

Belinsky interpreted the *Dead Souls* (1842) of Nikolay Gogol (1809–52) as just the sort of literature Russia needed. He forgot that one of the half-mad genius Gogol's characters (from another book) had exclaimed "Gentlemen, this world of ours is a bore!" That, too, was a part of Gogol's message. Belinsky was wrong: *Dead Souls* is not a social work. It is, as the increasingly deranged Gogol saw, a series of projections of himself. Yet Belinsky was justified: a work of art of that magnitude does transcend its author's intentions, and so *Dead Souls* does, though incidentally, expose the social madness and injustice of Gogol's times. The lesson to be learned from *Dead Souls* seems to be that from the writer's point of view literature has its own autonomy, and that it functions in the best interests of society when it is allowed to possess this autonomy. The argument as to whether literature should set out to further social progress, or remain autonomous, was to persist in Russia until the promulgation of socialist realism in 1932.

In Russia there was also an argument about whether Russia was unique, and had nothing to learn from the West, or whether she depended on the West for spiritual and all other kinds of sustenance. The cosmopolitan Ivan Turgenev (1818–83) represents the "reasonable", Western point of view: he loved his country, loved justice, hated oppression, and was always civilized and sane in his approach. In his great novels romanticism exists as melancholy, feeling for landscape, regret for wasted energy (as of that of the "nihilist" Bazarov in *Fathers and Sons*, 1862); realism exists as good sense and sad comedy. Turgenev believed in no religion, but rather in people's playing the cards life has given them to their best advantage – within a code of decency. Yet he was obsessed by terrorists, and kept their pictures on his desk. He was much loved by the French novelists, especially Flaubert, and Zola, whom he came to know; and Henry James went out of his way to praise his exquisite spirit.

At the other end of the spectrum is Fyodor Dostoyevsky (1821–81), who believed in "Holy Russia", saviour of the world – and whose final ideas as laid out in his journalism are half-mad (if one takes them at face value). His reactionary position is understandable, since for no good reason he had as a young man been persecuted and imprisoned for being associated with a radical group. Yet the moralist was a compulsive gambler, who even had to borrow money from Turgenev, the man he loathed so much that he tried to depict him as a sick traitor to truth in *The Possessed* (1871–2). The portrait is unfair and wrong; but the novel is gigantic. For Dostoyevsky, though undeniably reactionary (not conservative), does point to a certain unavoidable deadness at the heart of all revolutionary thinking and feeling. There is much of the picaresque in his feverish novels. To realism he brought a recognition of the horrors of the city – its distortion of the selves of its inhabitants – and the first full-scale investigation of the reasons for escapism, and of its moral results. Most important of all, Dostoyevsky was realistic about the consequences of the ways in which the religious impulse (whatever this is: no one has been able to explain it) works itself out in man. He explores these through his characters, as variegated a crew as inhabits the pages of any novelist; he is concerned – morbidly fascinated – with the moral state of affairs that would prevail if men rejected altogether the notion of God, and is thus an important precursor of the existentialists. His wholly "good" characters fail, his villains and "mixed" ones bristle with an energy sometimes radiant, sometimes diabolical. The arena of his concerns is to be found in its most succinct form in Ivan's story of the Grand Inquisitor in *The Brothers Karamazov* (1879–80). It is a large arena.

Ivan Goncharov (1812–91) showed in *Oblomov* (1859) that illusion could lead only to disaster, though he showed it with great regret: he is intellectually realistic, but emotionally idealistic.

Aleksey Pisemsky (1820–81) is the most sharply realistic of all the mid-century Russian novelists: his portrait of Russian society in his best novel, *A Thousand Souls* (1858), portrays it as a useless entity: he is a destructive writer, but not destructive in a bad cause. Leo Tolstoy (1828–1910), a divided character who ended by rejecting art and simultaneously practising it (here he resembles Plato), combined almost all modes in his fiction. *War and Peace* (1865–9) is unsatisfactory as an expression of a philosophy of history but triumphant as a panoramic view of the Russian past. He called it a "book" rather than a "novel". But it does have a plot, provided not only by history but also by the author's genius in putting contrasting characters together. Tolstoy is a realist in his presentation of his differing characters, but he makes no effort to withhold his own approval or disapproval.

In *Anna Karenina* (1875–7) there is more conflict: a dogmatic work (Tolstoy was a dogmatist always), it reads as a much less opinionated one. There are small superb details which add to verisimilitude, and distract the reader's attention from Tolstoy's hobby-horses, which are not running as strongly as in *War and Peace*. In the portrayal of character, especially those of Anna, Vronsky and Levin, a near perfect realism is achieved.

From 1932 the doctrine of socialist realism was adopted in Russia. The ailing Maxim Gorky (1868–1936) allowed himself to be associated with this, although he did not practise it. In itself it is a creed designed to keep writers in line, to perpetuate the rule of philistine thugs. It is a crude perversion of Belinsky's arguable position that literature ought to further progress and justice. It is on a par with Nazi book-burning; and as absurd

Leo Tolstoy and Maxim Gorky in 1900.

MAJOR WORKS OF FICTION: 1800–1869

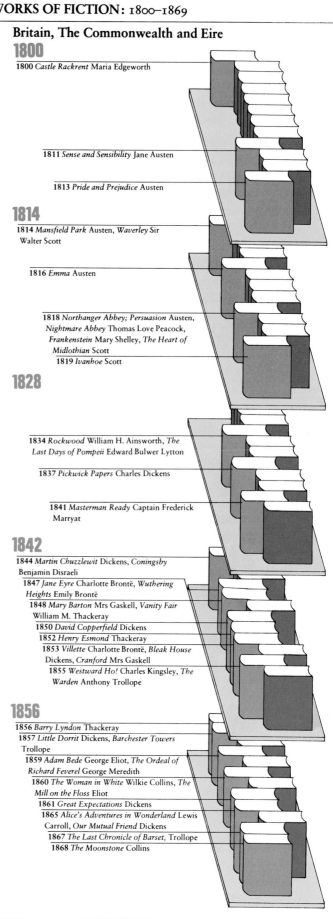

Britain, The Commonwealth and Eire

1800
1800 *Castle Rackrent* Maria Edgeworth

1811 *Sense and Sensibility* Jane Austen

1813 *Pride and Prejudice* Austen

1814
1814 *Mansfield Park* Austen, *Waverley* Sir Walter Scott

1816 *Emma* Austen

1818 *Northanger Abbey; Persuasion* Austen, *Nightmare Abbey* Thomas Love Peacock, *Frankenstein* Mary Shelley, *The Heart of Midlothian* Scott
1819 *Ivanhoe* Scott

1828

1834 *Rockwood* William H. Ainsworth, *The Last Days of Pompeii* Edward Bulwer Lytton

1837 *Pickwick Papers* Charles Dickens

1841 *Masterman Ready* Captain Frederick Marryat

1842
1844 *Martin Chuzzlewit* Dickens, *Coningsby* Benjamin Disraeli
1847 *Jane Eyre* Charlotte Brontë, *Wuthering Heights* Emily Brontë
1848 *Mary Barton* Mrs Gaskell, *Vanity Fair* William M. Thackeray
1850 *David Copperfield* Dickens
1852 *Henry Esmond* Thackeray
1853 *Villette* Charlotte Brontë, *Bleak House* Dickens, *Cranford* Mrs Gaskell
1855 *Westward Ho!* Charles Kingsley, *The Warden* Anthony Trollope

1856
1856 *Barry Lyndon* Thackeray
1857 *Little Dorrit* Dickens, *Barchester Towers* Trollope
1859 *Adam Bede* George Eliot, *The Ordeal of Richard Feverel* George Meredith
1860 *The Woman in White* Wilkie Collins, *The Mill on the Floss* Eliot
1861 *Great Expectations* Dickens
1865 *Alice's Adventures in Wonderland* Lewis Carroll, *Our Mutual Friend* Dickens
1867 *The Last Chronicle of Barset*, Trollope
1868 *The Moonstone* Collins

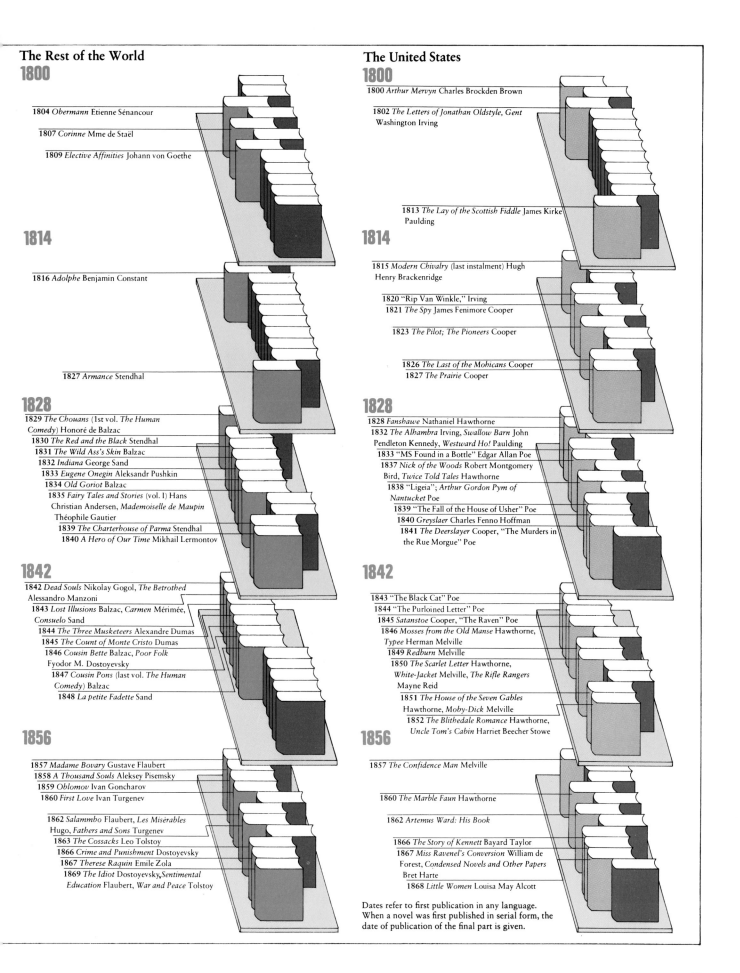

The Rest of the World

1800

1804 *Obermann* Etienne Sénancour

1807 *Corinne* Mme de Staël

1809 *Elective Affinities* Johann von Goethe

1814

1816 *Adolphe* Benjamin Constant

1827 *Armance* Stendhal

1828

1829 *The Chouans* (1st vol. *The Human
Comedy*) Honoré de Balzac
1830 *The Red and the Black* Stendhal
1831 *The Wild Ass's Skin* Balzac
1832 *Indiana* George Sand
1833 *Eugene Onegin* Aleksandr Pushkin
1834 *Old Goriot* Balzac
1835 *Fairy Tales and Stories* (vol. I) Hans
Christian Andersen, *Mademoiselle de Maupin*
Théophile Gautier
1839 *The Charterhouse of Parma* Stendhal
1840 *A Hero of Our Time* Mikhail Lermontov

1842

1842 *Dead Souls* Nikolay Gogol, *The Betrothed*
Alessandro Manzoni
1843 *Lost Illusions* Balzac, *Carmen* Mérimée,
Consuelo Sand
1844 *The Three Musketeers* Alexandre Dumas
1845 *The Count of Monte Cristo* Dumas
1846 *Cousin Bette* Balzac, *Poor Folk*
Fyodor M. Dostoyevsky
1847 *Cousin Pons* (last vol. *The Human
Comedy*) Balzac
1848 *La petite Fadette* Sand

1856

1857 *Madame Bovary* Gustave Flaubert
1858 *A Thousand Souls* Aleksey Pisemsky
1859 *Oblomov* Ivan Goncharov
1860 *First Love* Ivan Turgenev

1862 *Salammbo* Flaubert, *Les Misérables*
Hugo, *Fathers and Sons* Turgenev
1863 *The Cossacks* Leo Tolstoy
1866 *Crime and Punishment* Dostoyevsky
1867 *Therese Raquin* Emile Zola
1869 *The Idiot* Dostoyevsky, *Sentimental
Education* Flaubert, *War and Peace* Tolstoy

The United States

1800

1800 *Arthur Mervyn* Charles Brockden Brown

1802 *The Letters of Jonathan Oldstyle, Gent*
Washington Irving

1813 *The Lay of the Scottish Fiddle* James Kirke
Paulding

1814

1815 *Modern Chivalry* (last instalment) Hugh
Henry Brackenridge

1820 "Rip Van Winkle," Irving
1821 *The Spy* James Fenimore Cooper

1823 *The Pilot; The Pioneers* Cooper

1826 *The Last of the Mohicans* Cooper
1827 *The Prairie* Cooper

1828

1828 *Fanshawe* Nathaniel Hawthorne
1832 *The Alhambra* Irving, *Swallow Barn* John
Pendleton Kennedy, *Westward Ho!* Paulding
1833 "MS Found in a Bottle" Edgar Allan Poe
1837 *Nick of the Woods* Robert Montgomery
Bird, *Twice Told Tales* Hawthorne
1838 "Ligeia"; *Arthur Gordon Pym of
Nantucket* Poe
1839 "The Fall of the House of Usher" Poe
1840 *Greyslaer* Charles Fenno Hoffman
1841 *The Deerslayer* Cooper, "The Murders in
the Rue Morgue" Poe

1842

1843 "The Black Cat" Poe
1844 "The Purloined Letter" Poe
1845 *Satanstoe* Cooper, "The Raven" Poe
1846 *Mosses from the Old Manse* Hawthorne,
Typee Herman Melville
1849 *Redburn* Melville
1850 *The Scarlet Letter* Hawthorne,
White-Jacket Melville, *The Rifle Rangers*
Mayne Reid
1851 *The House of the Seven Gables*
Hawthorne, *Moby-Dick* Melville
1852 *The Blithedale Romance* Hawthorne,
Uncle Tom's Cabin Harriet Beecher Stowe

1856

1857 *The Confidence Man* Melville

1860 *The Marble Faun* Hawthorne

1862 *Artemus Ward: His Book*

1866 *The Story of Kennett* Bayard Taylor
1867 *Miss Ravenel's Conversion* William de
Forest, *Condensed Novels and Other Papers*
Bret Harte
1868 *Little Women* Louisa May Alcott

Dates refer to first publication in any language.
When a novel was first published in serial form, the
date of publication of the final part is given.

as the 1973 Chilean junta's destruction of (among others) the works of Dame Agatha Christie as dangerous communist propaganda. But the tensions produced by struggle between the tendency towards the social view and the view of literature as autonomous during the 1920s produced several powerful works, most of them written in the 1920s by members or associates of the Serapion Brothers, a group who wanted to help direct the progress of the revolution but who wanted to concentrate their energies into literature rather than into political activity. Trotsky, the only Russian communist leader with literary taste and discrimination, encouraged the group as *fellow-travellers*. Yergeniy Zamyatin's *We* (1920) is one of the main works to emerge from this period: drawing on the satirical tradition of Swift, the science-fiction exercises of H. G. Wells (of whom he was an admirer), and the psychological realism that had originated in Sterne and others, he produced one of the first of the great twentieth-century dystopias, anti-utopias expressing disgust with society, seen as more than Gogol's "bore": seen as a threat to individuality.

French realism

Now all "realism" means, in general terms, is "verisimilitude to reality". But in terms of literary criticism it indubitably implies emphasis on the real, in the sense of "truths which are not acceptable to the political elite"; on the seamy side of life; on the unsentimental; on motives (which may not be at all nice); on the truth – however difficult or unpleasant this may seem to be. This literary "realism" everywhere is really no more than an assertion of individuality. Writers were prepared to risk unpopularity in order to express themselves.

Stendhal (the pseudonym of Henri Beyle, 1783–1842) and Honoré de Balzac (1799–1850) in France wrote with the advantage, so to speak, of the rediscoveries of romanticism; but both were proto- (or early) realists, although in very different ways. Stendhal, unappreciated as a novelist in his own time (except by Balzac himself and a very few others), was a prophetic novelist who put his own romantic aspirations, in the guise of his characters, under a realist microscope; but the microscope was of a highly advanced nature. He anticipates modern psychological techniques even while remaining a master teller of tales. He foretold the time when he would be widely read, and wrote his fiction for that time and indeed we read him now as a modern novelist, though we try to allow for his historical context. Being an extremely complex man, he needed a simple precept to guide him in his fiction. So he used the old one of the mirror: the writer holds up a mirror to nature (shows nature as it really is, not as it ought to be), and he adds, characteristically, can he help it if some of the people who walk past it are ugly? Discussion of the quality of Stendhal's mirror take us far beyond mere categorization.

Both Stendhal and Balzac – half-baked mystic and observer of minute sociological detail rolled up into a bewildering one – were early inspired by Sir Walter Scott (1771–1832), the cult of whom in Europe equalled that of Byron.

Scott was a Tory, but he appealed to liberals (Stendhal was a liberal; Balzac ostensibly of the right) because in his novels he was forced to be a democrat, taking his "low" characters with as much seriousness as his royal ones. Robin-Hood figures, rogues, were not treated in a picaresque manner by Scott: he took them more seriously because he had to in order to produce exciting tales of the past. He needed money: therefore he needed popularity. He was honest, and although his insight into character was limited (his imagination is of the narrative sort), he saw as far as he did see very clearly. We are reminded that literature functions best when it is allowed to remain autonomous – even though it may be argued that it cannot achieve this. Imagine Scott writing as a polemical Tory; his genius would have been crippled, just as it would had he been an anarchist. He provided huge and intelligent enjoyment, and he still does now – though on a far smaller scale than in his own century. He may seem to us to have been overvalued, but his historical importance is undeniable. He stimulated Stendhal and helped to inspire Balzac.

Balzac was less intelligent than Stendhal, but more fertile. Most of his best effects are carried out in spite of his conscious intentions. His "philosophy" was a mish-mash of rubbish mixed with mysticism and perfectly sensible ideas. But the fact that it would never have attracted the least attention had it not prompted him to write fiction is quite unimportant. What is important is this: what does it mean as a whole? And the answer, of course, is to be found in the fiction as a whole. Balzac was the first novelist, with the enormous and ambitious collection of novels *The Human Comedy* (about ninety novels and stories, 1829–47), to try to depict the history of the manners and the morals of a whole society in a single scheme. Characters recur in novel after novel, and the whole is an account of the corruption of society on the grandest scale ever attempted. (Marxists prize his analysis of capitalist society.)

Balzac was certainly an early sociologist: his observation of detail that has now disappeared was meticulous and is of inestimable value to social scientists. His characters are definitely "flat" (Stendhal's are "round"), but the method by which he sets them into "vibration" gives them a special kind of depth. His idea of character is a man's face, gestures, clothes – and possessions. His way of showing character thus is possibly his greatest contribution to technique in fiction; and no novelist can have had better descriptive powers over such a vast range. Nor can any novelist have written more convincingly of finance – which in his work consists of one vast swindle. Doubtless

Balzac learned about this subject from his own experiences: he was always in debt, and often obliged to seek humiliating refuge from debt-collectors.

French realism proper begins with Gustave Flaubert (1821–80), even if he claimed that he wrote *Madame Bovary* (1856–57) because he hated reality; and denied that he was a realist. This seems difficult; but it is instructively explicable.

The French realist movement, whose beliefs are enshrined in the first issue of a magazine called *Rèalisme* (1856), was a crude affair – though the way it manifested itself is interesting. The two chief progenitors, Champfleury (Jules Husson, 1821–89) and Duranty (1833–80), were not important as critics or as novelists. Duranty was led to promulgate realism by the example of Champfleury, who, measured against Flaubert, was only semi-literate. He was a hack storyteller who published provincial novels in which he tried to please a low-brow public by describing the events and people in them with what exactitude he could muster. Duranty's manifesto was simple-minded: the novel should be a documentary; imagination and art were distractions, and were bad; topicality was the desideratum; the unusual was to be eschewed; and so forth. The products of this were drab, badly written, squalid tales.

Flaubert wrote *Madame Bovary* in anguish. He loathed it. He wrote it, in fact, for the opposite of all the reasons advanced by Duranty and his friends (Duranty's own review of it was uncomprehending and hostile). For Flaubert imagination was the means of salvation, and he is everywhere regarded as one of the supreme geniuses of the novel; but praise has almost always been grudging. For he really did hate reality, and in particular he hated the mechanistic and predictable habits of the middle classes. He might easily have become an "art-for-art's-sake" elitist, or a bad, precious poet. But he knew at heart that he was not a poet: that is, he knew that he could not express all that he felt and thought in verse. He had a vivid sense of beauty, but was oppressed by the corruption of the social order and by bourgeois behaviour. He was at heart a liberal; but, as he displays in *The Sentimental Education* (1869), he had no faith whatever in the machinations of the left, and felt that the liberals were politically feeble and ineffective. In part he was disgusted with himself. Almost the only successful expression of the positive side of Flaubert is the *conte A Simple Heart* (1877); this is one of the loveliest tales in world literature, and shows us the soul of the man.

Flaubert was a true artist: very tough on himself. He would eschew, he felt, all idealism. He would take the most sordid and ordinary story he could find – one of provincial adultery, an absolutely commonplace affair – and he would force himself to write truthfully about it. "What a bloody stupid notion I had to pick on this subject!" he once exclaimed in fury, during the years it took him to get it on to paper. Most critics and some readers seem to find more misanthropy than beauty in *Madame Bovary*. Certainly it puts its finger unerringly on the irrational imbecility of the human species: on Emma Bovary's serious assimilation of cheap romantic novels (we may be reminded here of Cervantes) and its catastrophic consequences; and on the hypocrisy of churchmen and free-thinkers alike. Only an idiot and a tax collector are decent – and they play tiny parts in the plot. But a few critics and most readers find true pathos in the book, because they feel that Emma Bovary, despite her faults, gets more than she deserves – and that this is tragic. They find in her a certain nobility, and in the novel a great depth of feeling. Whether Flaubert succeeds in his attempt at true realism, or whether the novel is marred by his judging his characters too harshly is finally a question for the reader. This epoch-making novel can be fruitfully approached with the question: does Flaubert justify his facing of the truth by doing so without demeaning anyone beyond the degree to which they have demeaned themselves? Does he diminish any of his characters (as bad satirists do)?

Gustave Flaubert, painted by Giraud.

Spanish realism

The first great Spanish realist was Benito Pérez Galdós (1843–1920), who wrote a substantial and extremely competent cycle of novels about Spanish history (*National Episodes*, 46 vols) and many more important novels on Spanish themes. The way for realism had been prepared in Spain not only by the example of the French, but also by a seemingly trivial type of fiction called *costumbrismo*. This is a Spanish form of "regionalism", a form best exemplified by the works of Maria Edgeworth, to whom we shall come when we consider the development of the nineteenth-century English novel. But *costumbrismo*, though quintessentially Spanish, was originally an import: it began with imitations of foreign sketches of local customs and types. There was only one substantial *costumbrista* novel, Fernan Cabal-lero's *The Seagull* (1849); this is hardly readable now, but is important because it unites a series of sketches of all aspects of Andalusian life by presenting them (not very credibly) as the sum of perfection.

Pérez Galdós made use of the little exactitudes of *costumbrismo* in order to give verisimilitude; but his achievement was to give a picture of his people, and to provide a uniquely warm and subtle view of human psychology. He is probably a better and more consistent novelist than Balzac, yet he has been astonishingly neglected, and a quarter-of-a-century ago could even be studied as having been a simple-minded liberal. His two early influences were Charles Dickens and Balzac, but he had greater psychological insight than either. His *Fortunata and Jacinta* (1886–7), one of the greatest novels of the nineteenth century, anticipates the discoveries of Freud, and combines accurate portraiture of most aspects of Madrid life with wit and a piercingly penetrating insight into the male mind. Over his long career he wrote historical chronicles, realistic novels, naturalistic novels (shortly to be discussed), and modern anti-novels. He found his natural understanding of Cervantes useful for all these purposes: it is in the Spanish character to question idealism meaningfully, because idealism is a specially Spanish disease (for example, when it functions as "honour").

Pérez Galdós died in 1920, by which time the status of the novel was being questioned. He had himself questioned it as fruitfully as any twentieth-century novelist. His historical significance is that in his encyclopedic work may be found all the kinds of novel written in the nineteenth and twentieth centuries. Once his numerous works have been made available in English, which they almost certainly will be in the 1980s, he will become one of the major sources of pleasure and wisdom of the next decade.

After a long lean period in fiction Spain produced a crop of good novelists, some of whom have been translated. Vicente Blasco Ibáñez (1867–1928) was not the best, but was the most internationally popular. A few Spanish novelists of this century, true to the tradition of Cervantes, wrote in a style given the name *esperpento*, which means "funhouse distorting mirror". They deliberately presented reality as through a distorting mirror. The best known of these novelists, one who did not always write in this way, was Ramon del Valle-Inclán (1866–1936), but his work has not yet become internationally known.

The Civil War had a bad effect on literature, but eventually produced the so-called *tremendista* novel, much disliked by the totalitarian regime but not actually suppressed. *Tremendista* is not a very elegant literary term; it meant simply that something absolutely tremendously awful would happen in the novel. The tendency had been

MAJOR WORKS OF FICTION: 1870–1919

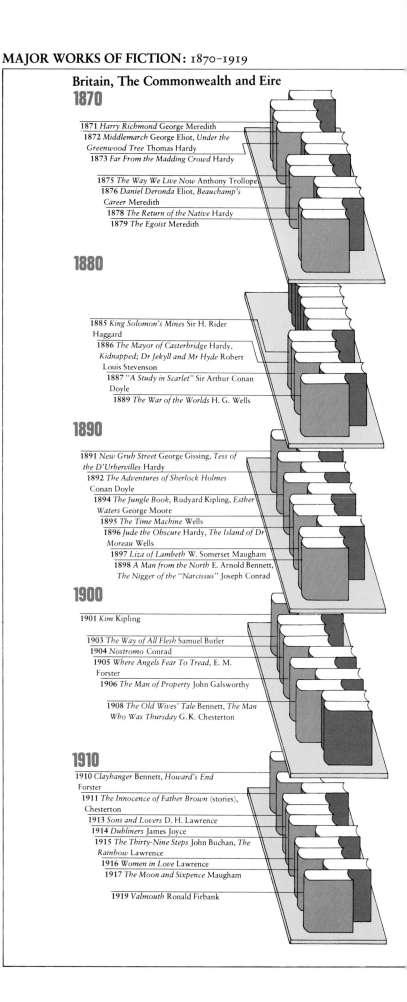

Britain, The Commonwealth and Eire

1870

1871 *Harry Richmond* George Meredith
1872 *Middlemarch* George Eliot, *Under the Greenwood Tree* Thomas Hardy
1873 *Far From the Madding Crowd* Hardy

1875 *The Way We Live Now* Anthony Trollope
1876 *Daniel Deronda* Eliot, *Beauchamp's Career* Meredith
1878 *The Return of the Native* Hardy
1879 *The Egoist* Meredith

1880

1885 *King Solomon's Mines* Sir H. Rider Haggard
1886 *The Mayor of Casterbridge* Hardy, *Kidnapped; Dr Jekyll and Mr Hyde* Robert Louis Stevenson
1887 *"A Study in Scarlet"* Sir Arthur Conan Doyle
1889 *The War of the Worlds* H. G. Wells

1890

1891 *New Grub Street* George Gissing, *Tess of the D'Urbervilles* Hardy
1892 *The Adventures of Sherlock Holmes* Conan Doyle
1894 *The Jungle Book*, Rudyard Kipling, *Esther Waters* George Moore
1895 *The Time Machine* Wells
1896 *Jude the Obscure* Hardy, *The Island of Dr Moreau* Wells
1897 *Liza of Lambeth* W. Somerset Maugham
1898 *A Man from the North* E. Arnold Bennett, *The Nigger of the "Narcissus"* Joseph Conrad

1900

1901 *Kim* Kipling

1903 *The Way of All Flesh* Samuel Butler
1904 *Nostromo* Conrad
1905 *Where Angels Fear To Tread*, E. M. Forster
1906 *The Man of Property* John Galsworthy

1908 *The Old Wives' Tale* Bennett, *The Man Who Was Thursday* G. K. Chesterton

1910

1910 *Clayhanger* Bennett, *Howard's End* Forster
1911 *The Innocence of Father Brown* (stories), Chesterton
1913 *Sons and Lovers* D. H. Lawrence
1914 *Dubliners* James Joyce
1915 *The Thirty-Nine Steps* John Buchan, *The Rainbow* Lawrence
1916 *Women in Love* Lawrence
1917 *The Moon and Sixpence* Maugham

1919 *Valmouth* Ronald Firbank

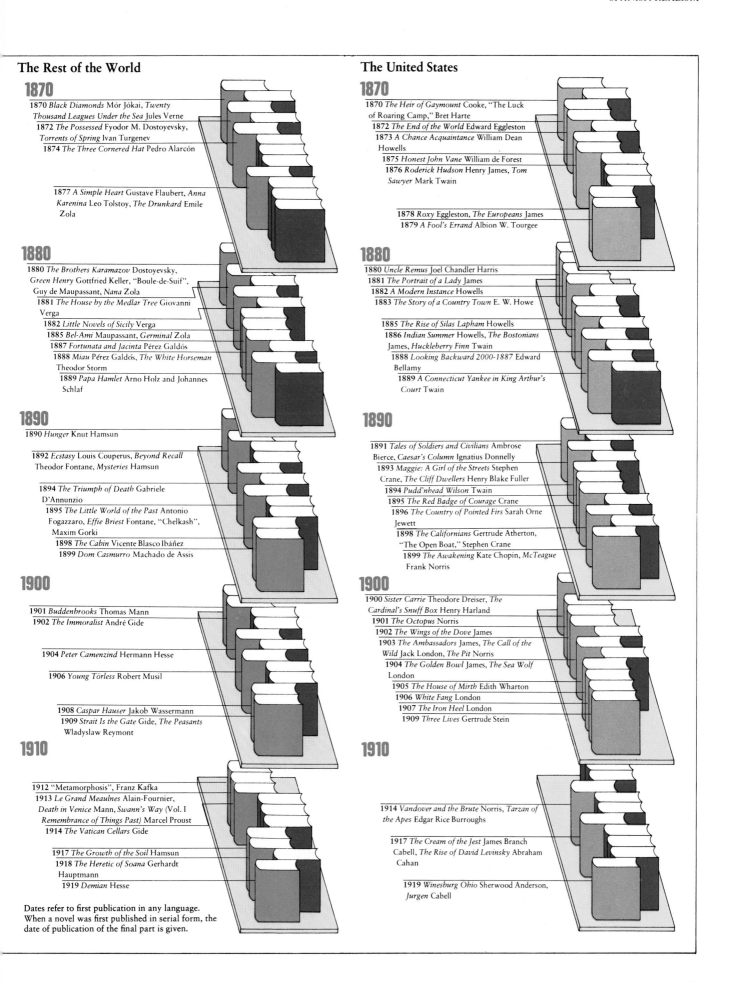

The Rest of the World

1870

1870 *Black Diamonds* Mór Jókai, *Twenty Thousand Leagues Under the Sea* Jules Verne
1872 *The Possessed* Fyodor M. Dostoyevsky, *Torrents of Spring* Ivan Turgenev
1874 *The Three Cornered Hat* Pedro Alarcón

1877 *A Simple Heart* Gustave Flaubert, *Anna Karenina* Leo Tolstoy, *The Drunkard* Emile Zola

1880

1880 *The Brothers Karamazov* Dostoyevsky, *Green Henry* Gottfried Keller, "Boule-de-Suif", Guy de Maupassant, *Nana* Zola
1881 *The House by the Medlar Tree* Giovanni Verga
1882 *Little Novels of Sicily* Verga
1885 *Bel-Ami* Maupassant, *Germinal* Zola
1887 *Fortunata and Jacinta* Pérez Galdós
1888 *Miau* Pérez Galdós, *The White Horseman* Theodor Storm
1889 *Papa Hamlet* Arno Holz and Johannes Schlaf

1890

1890 *Hunger* Knut Hamsun

1892 *Ecstasy* Louis Couperus, *Beyond Recall* Theodor Fontane, *Mysteries* Hamsun

1894 *The Triumph of Death* Gabriele D'Annunzio
1895 *The Little World of the Past* Antonio Fogazzaro, *Effie Briest* Fontane, "Chelkash", Maxim Gorki
1898 *The Cabin* Vicente Blasco Ibáñez
1899 *Dom Casmurro* Machado de Assis

1900

1901 *Buddenbrooks* Thomas Mann
1902 *The Immoralist* André Gide

1904 *Peter Camenzind* Hermann Hesse

1906 *Young Törless* Robert Musil

1908 *Caspar Hauser* Jakob Wassermann
1909 *Strait Is the Gate* Gide, *The Peasants* Wladyslaw Reymont

1910

1912 "Metamorphosis", Franz Kafka
1913 *Le Grand Meaulnes* Alain-Fournier, *Death in Venice* Mann, *Swann's Way* (Vol. I *Remembrance of Things Past*) Marcel Proust
1914 *The Vatican Cellars* Gide

1917 *The Growth of the Soil* Hamsun
1918 *The Heretic of Soana* Gerhardt Hauptmann
1919 *Demian* Hesse

Dates refer to first publication in any language. When a novel was first published in serial form, the date of publication of the final part is given.

The United States

1870

1870 *The Heir of Gaymount* Cooke, "The Luck of Roaring Camp," Bret Harte
1872 *The End of the World* Edward Eggleston
1873 *A Chance Acquaintance* William Dean Howells
1875 *Honest John Vane* William de Forest
1876 *Roderick Hudson* Henry James, *Tom Sawyer* Mark Twain

1878 *Roxy* Eggleston, *The Europeans* James
1879 *A Fool's Errand* Albion W. Tourgee

1880

1880 *Uncle Remus* Joel Chandler Harris
1881 *The Portrait of a Lady* James
1882 *A Modern Instance* Howells
1883 *The Story of a Country Town* E. W. Howe

1885 *The Rise of Silas Lapham* Howells
1886 *Indian Summer* Howells, *The Bostonians* James, *Huckleberry Finn* Twain
1888 *Looking Backward 2000-1887* Edward Bellamy
1889 *A Connecticut Yankee in King Arthur's Court* Twain

1890

1891 *Tales of Soldiers and Civilians* Ambrose Bierce, *Caesar's Column* Ignatius Donnelly
1893 *Maggie: A Girl of the Streets* Stephen Crane, *The Cliff Dwellers* Henry Blake Fuller
1894 *Pudd'nhead Wilson* Twain
1895 *The Red Badge of Courage* Crane
1896 *The Country of Pointed Firs* Sarah Orne Jewett
1898 *The Californians* Gertrude Atherton, "The Open Boat," Stephen Crane
1899 *The Awakening* Kate Chopin, *McTeague* Frank Norris

1900

1900 *Sister Carrie* Theodore Dreiser, *The Cardinal's Snuff Box* Henry Harland
1901 *The Octopus* Norris
1902 *The Wings of the Dove* James
1903 *The Ambassadors* James, *The Call of the Wild* Jack London, *The Pit* Norris
1904 *The Golden Bowl* James, *The Sea Wolf* London
1905 *The House of Mirth* Edith Wharton
1906 *White Fang* London
1907 *The Iron Heel* London
1909 *Three Lives* Gertrude Stein

1910

1914 *Vandover and the Brute* Norris, *Tarzan of the Apes* Edgar Rice Burroughs

1917 *The Cream of the Jest* James Branch Cabell, *The Rise of David Levinsky* Abraham Cahan

1919 *Winesburg Ohio* Sherwood Anderson, *Jurgen* Cabell

present in Spanish literature earlier in the century, but *tremendista* did not arrive until Camilo José Cela's *The Family of Pascal Duarte* (1942). Some might argue that since then it has petered out; but many protest novels – which could not be overt – did contain *tremendista* elements.

Naturalism

Realism was bound to turn, at least for a time, into naturalism. This term has different meanings in different contexts. In literature, however, it implies a narrowing down of realism, and it is associated with the theories of the important French novelist Emile Zola (1840–1902). However, it is the American novelists, such as Frank Norris, Theodore Dreiser and J. G. Farrell, who have proved more receptive to the theory than those of any other nationality. Zola's theory, which he himself did not believe in, maintained that the novel was really scientific: the novelist would select truthful instances in his work, and put them to test, as in a laboratory. Society, he claimed, could then be improved. However, the work of Zola and his disciples seemed to advocate what has been well described as a "pessimistic materialistic determinism". He concentrated on the seamy side of life, on the animal, the brutal. He saw life as a matter of blind animal instinct destroying all impulses towards reason, civilization or beauty.

Zola's fiction is actually more complicated than this. As he himself admitted, all that is seen by a novelist is seen through a temperament. He wrote a vast cycle of novels, dealing with the various branches of a family which he caused to be tainted by alcoholism and other destructive tendencies. Heredity and its determining effects are an important arrow in the quiver of the (rare) pure naturalist novelist. But it has to be pointed out that Zola's great cycle of novels undermine their own theoretical intention, as every critic has

Theodor Fontane, from the painting by E. Beiber completed shortly before Fontane died in 1898.

realized. They pulsate with energy and comedy which derive from Rabelais and the fantastic Dutch painter Hieronymus Bosch, and they have a strong element of romanticism in them. Zola was really less preoccupied with defeat than with human energy, especially sexual energy. Sometimes he is sensationalist to the point of surrealism, the deliberately crazy, pro-subconscious, anti-rationalist, anti-social, subversive, post World War I movement which produced few novels, but which influenced the novel profoundly. There are many incidents in Zola which are totally unrealistic. A man frightens off an official by farting at him, so that he thinks the farts a series of gunshots. Two people consummate their love after they have eaten their clothes, in a flooded mine, when the girl is at the point of death – a corpse has floated near them for some time, that of a man killed by the lover. This is Rabelaisian and surreal.

Naturalism gave novelists the opportunity to deal in impolite material, or to express their pessimism, or to demonstrate how huge concerns dominate and ruin individual lives. The much misunderstood Thomas Hardy has misleadingly been called a naturalist because he refused to please his readers with optimistic views. George Gissing, Frank Norris and Theodore Dreiser were enabled to portray life in the raw, as they wished to portray it. The extremism of the theory arose simply as a social protest against the concealment of the fact that poverty and exploitation existed in the world – as well as gentility.

In Germany realism began most effectively in the form of *novelle*, a form of the *novella* or *conte* or long-short-story which the Germans made peculiarly their own through the work of Theodor Storm (1817–88) and many other writers now forgotten. The great nineteenth-century German novelists were Gottfried Keller (1819–90) in fact a Swiss, and Theodor Fontane (1819–98). Keller's *Green Henry* (1878–80) is a *Bildungsroman* which he wrote in two versions: the first is romantic and subjective, the second, a marked advance, is critical and realistic. The true subject is himself, but in the protagonist he finds a good "objective correlative". Fontane, a really great writer, did not start writing novels until he was fifty-nine years old. He began with historical novels, but then proceeded to write analytical, moving, quietly perceptive fiction about contemporary life. *Effie Briest* (1895), a novel of adultery, is prophetic of Nazism (though very unobtrusively), and is certainly a key novel in international terms. It is revealing to compare *Anna Karenina* (woman's adultery Russian style) with *Madame Bovary* (provincial French style) and *Effie Briest* (provincial German style). In the last the final solution is decided in Berlin in a style simultaneously gentlemanly, Prussian, brutal and senseless.

Though naturalism is in theory narrow, it is nevertheless from naturalism as well as from attempts to advance realism, that modernism sprang. What could be more truly realistic than the attempt to record the exact thoughts of a character as they pass through his mind? This "sekundstil" technique was employed by a German, Arno Holz (1863–1929), in collaboration with another writer. It was of course a dismal failure; it can't be done. We do not understand the nature of thought as it passes through people's minds; psychologists have been working on the problem for decades. Holz was a naturalist, who wanted to fulfil the naturalist programme. Yet his misguided efforts are only a form of the "stream-of-consciousness" method which dominated the early twentieth-century novel, and it can be argued that in changed form it dominates even the contemporary novel. As will be seen when the modernist novel is discussed, authors found that painstaking description of passing thoughts was not viable. The British writer Dorothy Richardson (1873–1957) in *Pilgrimage*, her *roman fleuve* (the term for a long series of novels dealing with the same theme or themes), is often called a pioneer of stream-of-consciousness. She was not; for most of the time she was merely employing the Holz technique, but modifying it by selection. True stream-of-consciousness, as we shall see, employs a quite different method. However, both of these methods have as their aim the achievement of the greatest possible realism.

Maria Edgeworth, a drawing by Joseph Slater.

Nineteenth-century England

The novel during the eighteenth and nineteenth centuries increasingly took on the characteristics of the countries where it was being produced. It became self-consciously nationalistic. The American novel became completely American late, with Mark Twain, and it therefore deserves separate consideration. The British novel, too, differed from the European.

Sir Walter Scott has already been discussed because he was of great service to the European novel. Paradoxically, however, he did great harm to the English novel, because his works are not organic and because he was lacking in perception. He imposed plot on events; it did not arise either from the events themselves or from the characters, and although he was a great storyteller, the subtleties escaped him. A historical novelist such as W. H. Ainsworth (1805–82) might have done much better – had to work much harder – if Scott had never existed. Scott inspired a whole group of historical novelists to write second-rate fiction by demonstrating that novels could be done to a formula. His disciples did not have his gifts, his stolidity.

Maria Edgeworth (1767–1849), whose name is less famous than the most famous of her novels, *Castle Rackrent* (1800), is a great novelist *manquée*. She may have failed to fulfil her promise because she devoted so much of her life to her father, an educationist bent on introducing Rousseau's ideas into Britain. Rousseau left his mark on her, though not in any very obvious way. Her work is important historically, because she bridged the gap between the eighteenth and the nineteenth centuries, and "invented" the British regional novel. She is now underrated and underread. Although inferior to Jane Austen, she has a much wider scope; she influenced Scott himself, who could only admire Jane Austen.

Jane Austen (1775–1817) worked within astonishingly severe limitations. This was her strength. Her chief limitation was her propriety, in which she believed totally. The sincerity of this belief, combined with her involuntary psychological percipience and her high intelligence, enabled her to revolutionize the English novel. Her thesis was that individual behaviour must at all costs be regulated by the conventions of society, and everything she wrote firmly reflects this view. But, fortunately for us, she wrote under a misapprehension. The conventions she believed in were not those of society at all; they were her own. She was a marvellously exact observer of the society in which she moved – but of society at large she fortunately knew nothing at all. Thus she is a forerunner of Henry James and other moral analysts. Sometimes the innocence or primness of this spinster may irritate; but her observations of social custom, of the misuse of power in small circles (family and social), of the qualities of men, disarm such feelings. She has complete integrity, complete confidence. Her theme is always the same; her superbly designed canvases ask a single question, and then answer it: who should a young woman marry? She is anti-romantic, utterly impervious to sensibility, strict to just short of a fault. Her portrait of the society she knew – upper-class naval and church men and their wives and children – is so accurate and honest that it has delighted Marxists. Jane Austen set an example by her meticulousness, and she made her successors conscious of form and what form could do.

The generation that followed Jane Austen's included Thackeray, Dickens, Trollope, George Eliot, Mrs Gaskell and Mrs Oliphant. The reputation of William Thackeray (1811–63) has declined very sharply; only *Vanity Fair* (1847–8)

remains highly rated. Charles Dickens (1812–70) has more than held his own. Anthony Trollope 1815–82) has increased his reputation enormously. George Eliot (Marian Evans, 1819–80), in some ways the most serious of all the novelists of her generation, has come to seem more and more valuable.

Thackeray had genius, but somehow lacked depth. *Vanity Fair* is perhaps as brilliant as any novel ever written; but there is a shallowness about it. It is a tour de force, and it succeeds in exposing the absurdities of the Regency society it depicts. But Thackeray's main weakness is his inability to portray his good characters with anything like as much power and energy as his unscrupulous ones. He lacks a centre of moral gravity, and therefore his brilliance is disproportionate to his seriousness. He was not really an important influence, for he represents an extension of the picaresque and of the methods of Fielding, upon which he was too content to rely.

Dickens is believed by some, perhaps most, to have been the greatest of all novelists. He owed much to Smollett, but much more to the fact that his novels were serialized. He did not write them and chop them up; he kept ahead of his public by only a few chapters, and used public reaction to modify the events in the novels – sometimes well, sometimes badly. He reflects his audience's needs with uncanny precision. These needs were to be

entertained in an instructive manner: in the ways of Christian humanitarianism, individualism, jovial humour, proper means of social reform. He was an actor who gave hugely successful readings from his own work (the energy he put into these helped kill him at fifty-eight), and his style is more oral than any other novelist until the Frenchman Louis-Ferdinand Céline (1894–1961). He was melodramatic and histrionic: the Dickens world, which certainly exists, is very much of a theatrical show. Those who did not share his political views enjoyed his humour and his extreme sentimentality. He is anti-analytical; everything and everybody in his world is magnified, put on show on the Dickens stage. His excited imagination ran riot, producing surrealist characters and passages of symbolic force. None of his successors has been like him, but many (Gissing is an example) tried to imitate his energy.

Dickens provides an embarrassment to critics because he lacks the "high seriousness" they demand: thus the once influential F. R. Leavis dismissed him from the "great tradition" of the English novel. He lacked analytical control; neither knowing nor caring what he was doing in a "literary" way. Yet no one can deny that he combines greatness and success. His one attempt to look at himself in depth, *David Copperfield* (1849–50), is fine in parts but, as is generally conceded, fails as a whole. Yet he was a part of his age.

Above left *Becky and Jos in William Thackeray's* Vanity Fair: *from a painting by Lewis Baumer.*

Above *The title page of Chapman and Hall's edition of Charles Dickens'* Dombey and Son, *with an illustration by Phiz.*

Evil seemed much more real to him than good, and, like Thackeray, he was weak at depicting virtue, which soon turns into sentimentality. He preferred to make us laugh, or to teach us to forgive (as in the case of Mr Micawber). His true influence has been immense: he anticipated the twentieth-century abandonment of the realist method as best exemplified in the archetypal realist George Eliot. His world is internal, subjective. Thus such novelists as Franz Kafka instinctively understood him.

If Thackeray was not as good as he ought to have been, then Trollope is better than, at first sight, he ought to have been. In his immense output, including clusters of novels about the same people and communities (the Barchester series is the most famous) he rivals Balzac. It has been said that to put him beside Balzac is ridiculous; but, lacking the extreme eccentricity of Balzac's pseudophilosophy, he is in his way as satisfying a novelist. He had, said Henry James, "a complete appreciation of the usual". As the solid, common-sense realist he has had immense influence. He covered the whole spectrum of society with equal skill, and what he called his "pathos" is often exquisitely felt portrait-in-depth. Dickens' characters "vibrate" violently; Trollope's are round. He does not use types, though very often the reader will at first imagine that he is encountering a mere type. Like Dickens he wrote for serial publication, but he took less note of the feedback.

Trollope, who (appropriately) designed the English postbox and led a life of strict but in no way puritanical routine, is the great calming influence on the English novel. He is the last unartistic realist. His plots are improvisations that do very well, but he entirely lacks the pure art, the sense of order, of Jane Austen or George Eliot. His bitterness about society is extreme, but extremely unobtrusive. In his day politicians were held in high repute, but he put his finger, unerringly, on some of the main reasons for their present ill-repute: he demonstrated just how it is that politics, which most certainly should not be a game, becomes one. In this respect he is prophetic. Critics tend to underrate him because his style is humdrum and because he wrote for money. But readers get out of him much more than they think. He is the novelist of average and unalarmed decency, and that has been his real if subterranean influence. The notion that he wrote "fairy tales", which has been put forward with seriousness, should be resisted – and is resisted by his continuing popularity with intelligent readers.

Realism proper came to England with George Eliot (1819–80), and it did not come via Europe and Flaubert's *Madame Bovary* but from the indigenous arising of a notion that novelists ought to have a moral seriousness. Of course Fielding had had moral seriousness, and so for that matter had Bunyan before him. But George Eliot felt that moral seriousness must be fortified by making the novel artistic, as perfect as possible, "literary". This isn't a matter of "progress". Many people, quite reasonably, prefer Fielding. But to write like Fielding at the time Eliot published her first novel would not have been effective: the novel would have suffered. And writers want to have an effect – either through sales or by changing men's hearts and minds. The former helps the latter, of course. Flaubert and Dostoyevsky were struggling in their novels with problems fundamental to man. If asked whether they were entertainers, then they would have said they were not. Trollope would of course have said that he was, and that does not of itself make Trollope inferior. Cervantes would have said that he was an entertainer, and would have added – if given the opportunity of viewing the history of the novel from *Don Quixote* to today – that he damned well had to be. He might even have told certain modern novelists of today not to try to be so literary and serious, but he would have agreed that George Eliot and Flaubert and the others had no alternative in their time but to "improve" and "elevate" the novel in a literary way.

George Eliot was an honest woman who had to acknowledge that the Victorian observation of Christianity would not do. She became a reluctant rationalist, an agnostic. She inevitably felt guilty about this – she had been brought up as an Anglican and had then gone through a fiercely Methodist period – and she compensated by becoming a rigid moralist. But that did not prevent her from living with a married man, a shocking thing to do in Victorian times. She was influenced by the rationalist thought of her day, and she believed as fervently as any naturalist in hereditary determinism. Though possessed of a grimly severe humour (she is never "funny") she regarded herself, a trifle primly, as a teacher with high responsibilities. That is why the novel in her hands became so strictly "realistic". She deliberately rejected anything improbable, even though life is full of improbabilities. She considerably curbed her gifted imagination, but the results were good because the frustrations that arose from this drove her into a rage for order – and the order she imposes has the authority of a massive, humane and above all female intelligence.

In *Middlemarch* (1871–2), sociologically meticulous, broad in its canvas, she traces the emergence of the female sensibility and demonstrates how easily the male sensibility is defeated and debased. This is the blueprint of the utterly rational but tenderly felt social novel. But she does not avoid sentimentality at the end, since the marriage of her heroine is unconvincing, and so is her husband. In *Daniel Deronda* (1876), her last novel, she seems to have been feeling out towards something even more profound. Despite her failures, "intelligence" and "artistry" are the keywords to Eliot and to her influence. Modern novelists have tried to write like her, but have

Anthony Trollope, a contemporary cartoon which appeared with the caption: "To parsons gave up what was meant for mankind", a reference to the large number of clerics in Trollope's novels.

failed to understand that modern society is too turbulent and volatile to stand up to such treatment. That is one of the reasons for the inevitable rise of modernism, which is largely a reversion to old modes against a background of godless technocracy operated by people (they once had character) who are for most of the time, to employ a phrase of Wyndham Lewis', "hallucinated automata". Such people (ourselves, doubtless, in whole or part) are alienated from their true beings. We (or they) can be depicted only as abnormal. What could Trollope write about today? He would produce popular outdated yarns of little merit. And Eliot? She would be a preacher or an educational writer or both.

George Meredith (1828–1909) is a complex case. He is regarded as a great novelist, is still read, but is simultaneously thought of as "neglected" or "scarcely readable". If Trollope has no style, then Meredith, usually, has far too much. He was a considerable poet as well as a novelist; his prose is extravagant and convoluted, increasingly highly wrought. But he must be classed as proto-modernist and will assuredly be revalued. In his first novel, *The Ordeal of Richard Feverel* (1859), he gives an account of an act of masturbation. Naturally, he does it circumspectly, and it was not noted publicly for seventy years, but this demonstrates just how far ahead he was of his times. George Eliot would not have dreamed of trying such a thing. Meredith is a "comic" novelist in the sense that he regarded comedy as a means of regulating passion. But his theory of comedy, set forth in *An Essay on Comedy* (1897), is basically concerned with the difference between illusion and reality.

Significantly, Meredith despised the public, subsidized himself by writing journalism, and refused to compromise in order to gain sales. At the end of his life he suddenly became famous; but after his death his reputation soon faded. He is a proto-modernist because all the time he is trying to put across subconscious actions and thinking. His powerful social satire is incidental to this. He was at heart a poet; his prose is sometimes tediously abstruse because, naturally, he wanted to annoy his uncomprehending reader. But he is not rhetorical, and he is the first modern writer to attempt, consciously, to describe states of mind. When he is looked at again by the academics, it is likely that he will be seen as a pioneer: an odd one, but nevertheless a pioneer.

Thomas Hardy (1840–1928) is the most poetic novelist in the English language, and is a unique case. He cannot be read profitably as a realist, as the earlier contrasting of him with George Eliot demonstrates. He wrote his novels in serial form, but, unlike Dickens, violently resented this, believing that it crippled his intentions. His direct influence has been slight – a few minor regionalists have thought they were writing in his manner – but what he represents, the poetic

novelist, is a vital element in the history of the novel. Herman Melville (1819–91) too is poetic, but in a grander and more specifically American way. There may be said to be a trace of naturalism in Hardy; but the only English novelist who, mostly by accident, is at times truly naturalistic is George Gissing (1857–1903): this is to be put down to his gloominess of temperament more than anything else. There were also a few minor novelists, such as Arthur Morrison (1863–1945), who may be called naturalistic inasmuch as they explored the seamy side of life with meticulousness and power.

An illustration from the first serialization of Thomas Hardy's The Mayor of Casterbridge.

The American novel

James Fenimore Cooper (1789–1851) was called the "American Walter Scott", which label he resented. In retrospect he is more truly American than he seemed to be to his more American-minded contemporaries, whom he embarrassed. During the nineteenth century in America a powerful Anglo-American tradition developed. It culminated in Henry James (1843–1916), who eventually made his home in England and in the last year of his life became an English citizen. The American part of this tradition, the major part, was welcome; but some felt that it was not truly native. They therefore welcomed Mark Twain (Samuel Langhorne Clemens, 1835–1910), whose *Huckleberry Finn* (1886) marks the beginning of a truly indigenous American literature. He wrote nothing else as good, but this is one of the world's greatest books.

Melville and Nathaniel Hawthorne (1804–64) revived the old English Puritan dilemma in their novels – in very different ways both are concerned with sin and expiation – but with the advantage that they were aware of the developing European novel. Strictly speaking, Melville was inspired in his greatest work, *Moby-Dick* (1851) –

"Tom Sawyer's Band of Robbers", one of E. W. Kemble's illustrations for the first edition of Mark Twain's Huckleberry Finn.

Captain Ahab above right, and Queequeg above, from an edition of Herman Melville's Moby-Dick *published in 1937 with illustrations by Rockwell Kent.*

which went unrecognized until the early 1930s – by Hawthorne's more cosmopolitan fiction. Hawthorne began with a gothic novel, *Fanshawe* (1828), but even in this he was well aware that he was trying new methods. He was an original, working within a good knowledge of the contemporary European tradition but experimenting outside it by reverting to earlier models. He dealt with realist issues – attempts to establish utopias, female emancipation and others – but is in essence a symbolic (a term shortly to be discussed) and partly allegorical writer. He used the theme of the American in Europe, and this profoundly influenced Henry James.

Melville is wilder: so wild that he failed to gain the attention of the public with his major fiction, and, like Stendhal, had to wait fifty years. Indeed some contemporary readers thought him mad. His pessimistic, hell-raising *Moby-Dick* has had imitators, but is too big to have exercised a direct influence. Rather it provided a gigantic example of an American poetic novel. If it can be classed at all, then it is a symbolic allegory. Just as Melville was successfully inspired by Shakespeare (as well as by Hawthorne and by his own sea experiences), so countless American novelists have been inspired by him. He was a considerable poet as well as a prose writer. So far his achievement has not been equalled in modern times on such a scale.

Hawthorne's dark, Calvinistic vision is utterly obvious throughout his writing; so is Melville's. It is hard to wring consolation from either of these writers except at a profound level of awareness – perhaps they are best understood by their readers in periods of grief, perplexity, extreme mental suffering. Twain began as humourist and journalist; but he too had a dark vision. He is not a simple writer, but perhaps the over-simplification that is nearest to the truth about him is that he fused his high spirits with his dark vision by means of discovering a totally American vernacular. *Huckleberry Finn* is a perfectly realized book, containing within it both the American Dream

(of Eden) and its taking-away. It is a popular book in the sense that none of Hawthorne's nor Melville's could ever be. This is perhaps significant, for there is no telling whether the simple and "uninstructed" reader's enjoyment of it is not as profound as the most informed critic's. It exists vitally at every level.

Naturalism really took on in America. Twain apart, the indigenous American novel has its origins not in Melville or Hawthorne but in regionalist novels such as, in particular, E. W. Howe's *Story of a Country Town* (1883). Frank Norris (1870–1902), initially a fervent romantic, went to Paris and learned at first hand about naturalism. He wrote of animal instincts in *McTeague* (1899) and *Vandover and the Brute* (1914), and of the effects of great business enterprises in *The Octopus* (1901) and *The Pit* (1903). Like all the great naturalists, he is as symbolic as he is realistic.

Theodore Dreiser (1871–1945) was attracted to naturalism by his deterministic temperament and early upbringing. But he had a poetic side (though his verse is execrable), and is one of the very few novelists to have been substantially influenced by

Hardy. His masterpieces, *Sister Carrie* (1900) and *An American Tragedy* (1925), both transcend their sketchy naturalist programme: they embody deep feeling and compassion, and are – as much as any novels of the twentieth century – steeped in the thick of life; the reader feels the atmosphere rubbing against him. Dreiser's "bad style" – clumsy, circumlocutory, awkward, inelegant – actually contributes to this power, which is itself often clumsy but springs from a caring heart. His essays and polemics are undistinguished and scarcely articulate: he is a fine example of a writer who can express himself imaginatively or not at all.

Henry James (1843–1916) demonstrates the power and prestige of which the American novel had become capable, but he did this by becoming international. He is one of the giants, and his legacy is inestimable. His feminine sensibility has made him important to many female novelists, such as Elizabeth Bowen. He could not face the subject of sex directly, but in this lies his strength. He is not as constrained as Jane Austen, but constrained enough to avoid – strategically – direct reference to such matters as lust. He is therefore enormously suggestive. He realized that his fear of sexuality was neurotic, but turned this into an artistic strength: the reader has little work to do to grasp the sexual implications in his novels. His love affairs are not polite or sentimental matters. He analyzes the relationships, often exposing hidden corruptions; and the sexual element is implicit. Since sex really is dangerous, his own involuntary connection of it with evil was not at all far from the mark. But for all that he is not a novelist of love, but, in general, of the corruption of love.

In his first period (culminating in *The Portrait of a Lady*, 1881) he deals with the relationship between America and Europe; in the second (*The Bostonians*, 1886, is perhaps the masterpiece of this period) with political matters; in the third (culminating in the three novels *The Wings of the Dove*, 1902, *The Ambassadors*, 1903 and *The Golden Bowl*, 1904) with more personal relationships, and with technique. His technique is important and has been influential, though more through his criticism than through his novels. He aims to give a representation of life, regards "schools" as ultimately limiting, and depends for his effects on the single point of view and on metaphor, which he uses in a highly individual way. He would have resisted "expressionism" (which will be discussed later as a facet of modernism) and, indeed, all deliberate lack of coherence. But in him lie the seeds of the modernistic. He died just in time: he saw the established order smashed with the advent of war, but died in the middle of it, before the results began to become evident. They would have broken him, for he was highly vulnerable – and, as things were, his vulnerability was one of his great strengths.

MAJOR WORKS OF FICTION: 1920–1945

Britain, The Commonwealth and Eire

1920

1920 *The Mysterious Affair at Styles* Agatha Christie, *Bliss and Other Stories* Katherine Mansfield

1921 *Chrome Yellow* Aldous Huxley

1922 *Ulysses* James Joyce

1923 *Whose Body?* Dorothy L. Sayers, *Leave It To Psmith* P. G. Wodehouse

1924 *A Passage to India* E. M. Forster
1925 *Mrs Dalloway* Virginia Woolf

1925

1926 *The Murder of Roger Ackroyd* Christie, *Debits and Credits* (stories) Kipling, *The Plumed Serpent* D. H. Lawrence
1927 *To the Lighthouse* Woolf
1928 *Point Counter Point* Huxley, *Lady Chatterley's Lover* Lawrence, *Decline and Fall* Evelyn Waugh

1929 *A High Wind in Jamaica* Richard Hughes, *The Good Companions* J.B. Priestley

1930

1930 *Cakes and Ale* W. Somerset Maugham
1931 *The Waves*, Woolf

1932 *Cold Comfort Farm* Stella Gibbons, *Brave New World* Huxley, *A Glastonbury Romance* John Cowper Powys

1934 *I Claudius* Robert Graves, *Goodbye Mr. Chips* James Hilton

1935

1935 *The House in Paris* Elizabeth Bowen, *Mr Norris Changes Trains* Christopher Isherwood

1936 *A Gun for Sale* Graham Greene

1937 *The Hobbit* J. R. R. Tolkien

1938 *Murphy* Samuel Beckett, *Brighton Rock* Greene, *Pilgrimage* Dorothy Richardson

1939 *Finnegans Wake* Joyce

1940

1940 *The Power and the Glory* Greene, *Darkness at Noon* Arthur Koestler, *Strangers and Brothers* C.P. Snow

1944 *Fair Stood the Wind for France* H. E. Bates, *The Razor's Edge* Maugham

1945 *Animal Farm* Orwell, *Brideshead Revisited* Waugh

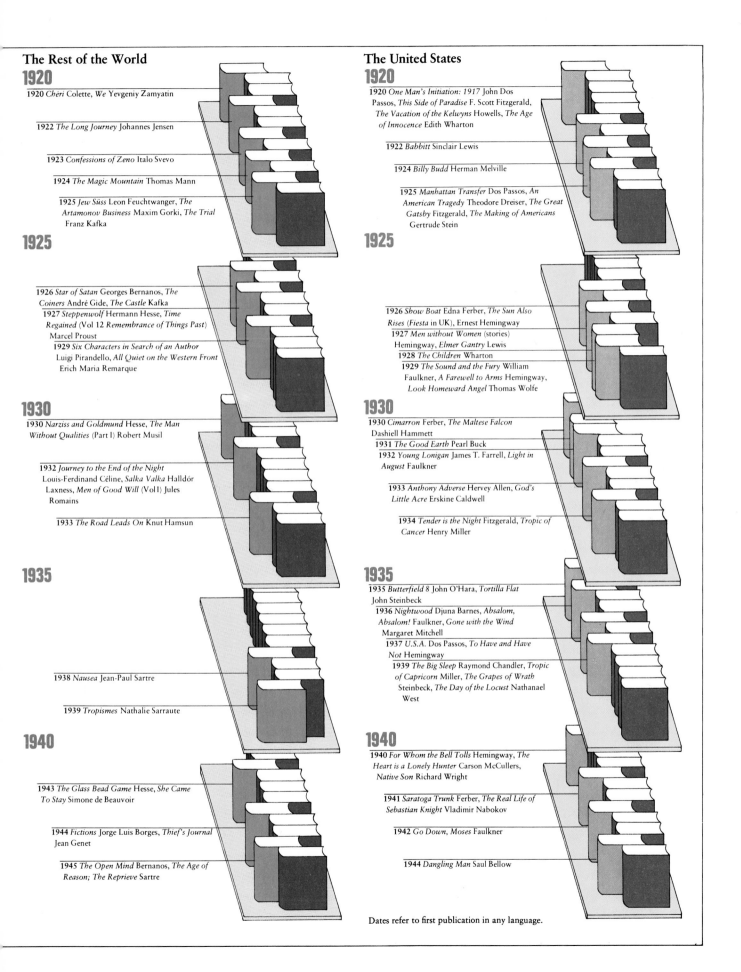

The Rest of the World
1920

1920 *Chéri* Colette, *We* Yevgeniy Zamyatin

1922 *The Long Journey* Johannes Jensen

1923 *Confessions of Zeno* Italo Svevo

1924 *The Magic Mountain* Thomas Mann

1925 *Jew Süss* Leon Feuchtwanger, *The Artamonov Business* Maxim Gorki, *The Trial* Franz Kafka

1925

1926 *Star of Satan* Georges Bernanos, *The Coiners* André Gide, *The Castle* Kafka
1927 *Steppenwolf* Hermann Hesse, *Time Regained* (Vol 12 *Remembrance of Things Past*) Marcel Proust
1929 *Six Characters in Search of an Author* Luigi Pirandello, *All Quiet on the Western Front* Erich Maria Remarque

1930

1930 *Narziss and Goldmund* Hesse, *The Man Without Qualities* (Part I) Robert Musil

1932 *Journey to the End of the Night* Louis-Ferdinand Céline, *Salka Valka* Halldór Laxness, *Men of Good Will* (Vol I) Jules Romains

1933 *The Road Leads On* Knut Hamsun

1935

1938 *Nausea* Jean-Paul Sartre

1939 *Tropismes* Nathalie Sarraute

1940

1943 *The Glass Bead Game* Hesse, *She Came To Stay* Simone de Beauvoir

1944 *Fictions* Jorge Luis Borges, *Thief's Journal* Jean Genet

1945 *The Open Mind* Bernanos, *The Age of Reason; The Reprieve* Sartre

The United States
1920

1920 *One Man's Initiation: 1917* John Dos Passos, *This Side of Paradise* F. Scott Fitzgerald, *The Vacation of the Kelwyns* Howells, *The Age of Innocence* Edith Wharton

1922 *Babbitt* Sinclair Lewis

1924 *Billy Budd* Herman Melville

1925 *Manhattan Transfer* Dos Passos, *An American Tragedy* Theodore Dreiser, *The Great Gatsby* Fitzgerald, *The Making of Americans* Gertrude Stein

1925

1926 *Show Boat* Edna Ferber, *The Sun Also Rises* (*Fiesta* in UK), Ernest Hemingway
1927 *Men without Women* (stories) Hemingway, *Elmer Gantry* Lewis
1928 *The Children* Wharton
1929 *The Sound and the Fury* William Faulkner, *A Farewell to Arms* Hemingway, *Look Homeward Angel* Thomas Wolfe

1930

1930 *Cimarron* Ferber, *The Maltese Falcon* Dashiell Hammett
1931 *The Good Earth* Pearl Buck
1932 *Young Lonigan* James T. Farrell, *Light in August* Faulkner

1933 *Anthony Adverse* Hervey Allen, *God's Little Acre* Erskine Caldwell

1934 *Tender is the Night* Fitzgerald, *Tropic of Cancer* Henry Miller

1935

1935 *Butterfield 8* John O'Hara, *Tortilla Flat* John Steinbeck
1936 *Nightwood* Djuna Barnes, *Absalom, Absalom!* Faulkner, *Gone with the Wind* Margaret Mitchell
1937 *U.S.A.* Dos Passos, *To Have and Have Not* Hemingway
1939 *The Big Sleep* Raymond Chandler, *Tropic of Capricorn* Miller, *The Grapes of Wrath* Steinbeck, *The Day of the Locust* Nathanael West

1940

1940 *For Whom the Bell Tolls* Hemingway, *The Heart is a Lonely Hunter* Carson McCullers, *Native Son* Richard Wright

1941 *Saratoga Trunk* Ferber, *The Real Life of Sebastian Knight* Vladimir Nabokov

1942 *Go Down, Moses* Faulkner

1944 *Dangling Man* Saul Bellow

Dates refer to first publication in any language.

Modernism

Modernism, yet another term which cannot be exactly defined, is the result of certain, specifically twentieth-century, developments: the rise of technocracy and therefore of (often involuntarily) "heartless bureaucrats" (men and women, who "at home" are not at all heartless); the paradoxically malign effects of the advance of knowledge, which cannot but damage established orders and thus cause men and women to feel lost – "strangers and afraid/In a world they never made"; and the nature of new knowledge itself, whose chief feature, again paradoxically, is to show that what we thought we knew we do not know at all. Wisdom flourishes in ordered societies, even if those societies are unjust. It is hard to be wise when only experience teaches. But Hardy (a liberal who advocated reform) wrote, cruelly, that "experience *un*teaches . . ." Men ought to be happier, but they are not.

There are a myriad reactions to all this. Some write to show how the political order may be perfected. They are mainly Marxists: popular Soviet writers; but C. P. Snow in his "Strangers and Brothers" sequence of novels hints at a possible utopia of properly functioning committees. Some write to show the opposite: that order cannot be attained (Patrick White, William Faulkner, Graham Greene, almost all of the leading novelists). Some write to show that God still has meaning (Greene). Others write to show that God is dead (or that, even if he was ever alive, he is now dead): this is Samuel Beckett's bleak message. Some Catholic writers such as Georges Bernanos write to demonstrate that the world is literally a battlefield between the forces of good and evil. Other Catholic writers – of whom Graham Greene is the foremost – write of the world as a squalid place, but one capable of being illuminated by sudden shafts of light, of grace.

The many-faced nature of modernism has been determined by what new, often philosophical, investigations have seemed to reveal. William James (1842–1910), the psychologist and philosopher brother of Henry James, saw the mind as in a state of disorganized flux. Henri Bergson (1859–1941), the French philosopher who was awarded the Nobel Prize for Literature, came to similar independent conclusions at about the same time. These thinkers and others like them had a strong influence on novelists. It was seen, for example, that clock-time was not the same, in human experience, as personal time. Everyone knows this if they think about it. Sometimes events seem to pass quickly, at other times they seem to pass slowly. The new psychologically based philosophy gives this kind of personal experience a factual status, which it does have. Thus a dream, a fantasy, a wrong impression – all these, too, are in one sense real and true. Further, they have an effect on behaviour.

The work of Freud gave the dream an entirely new status, and this profoundly influenced the novel. This is not to say that novels were written about dreamers, but they did deal with the way in which overt behaviour is the result of subconscious motivations. Freud thought the surrealists were mad, but their leader André Breton got his inspiration from Freud.

Plato had said that the ideal forms, the perfect non-material timeless things, were inherent in their names. For this and for other reasons connected with age-old folk-belief, writers began to look at the power of words-in-themselves. Gertrude Stein (1874–1946), William James' pupil, experimented ceaselessly with "nonsense": to discover if what failed to make logical sense nonetheless made emotional sense. She played every possible game with words. Writers despaired of the old clichés, sought for new ways of saying old things, or old ways of saying new things.

Thus modernism is confused, but it is inevitable. Some novelists continue in the old tradition, but those who are notably successful base themselves on such proto-modernists as James or even Meredith. The more popular novelists adapt the old formulas successfully to modern life. All that remains constant is that people love being told stories. Even modernists who seem incoherent are telling stories.

Modernism is in one sense an examination of the novel to see if it is of any use. Thus there are many novels about novelists writing novels: André Gide's *The Counterfeiters,* Flann O'Brien's *At Swim-Two-Birds,* Proust, even Anthony Powell's *A Dance to the Music of Time* by implication, and many others. Thomas Mann (1875–1955) used the picaresque mode to portray the artist as confidence man in *The Confessions of Felix Krull* (1954); all Mann's novels are about tricksters and fraud and illness; in *Doctor Faustus* (1947) he sees art as having its source in sickness and even in the devil.

Stream-of-consciousness and surrealism

James Joyce (1882–1941) began by using traditional means, but in *Ulysses* (1922), the story of one man's day in Dublin, he was forced, felt himself forced, to have recourse to "stream-of-consciousness" and "interior monologue". At the same time, he goes right back (as his title shows): to myth. Stream-of-consciousness, as we have seen, can be attempted by conventionally realistic means, as can interior monologue. But the true forms of these innovations are not conventional. Since thought cannot be translated into words – the indefinable flux cannot be presented as if a person were talking to another person – the author invents symbols, metaphors and other devices to give his impression of the stream of consciousness. Virginia Woolf (1882–1941) presents a hybrid form, in which there is much intrusion of "she/he thought". In the pure form the consciousness is nakedly presented, as in parts of Joyce: at first the writing seems crazy, until we understand that what Joyce is trying to do is to render, realistically (in its widest sense), the ordinary thoughts of ordinary people. Molly Bloom, whose great interior monologue ends *Ulysses*, is as ordinary as any of Trollope's characters – in fact she is more ordinary. But to Joyce's first readers she seemed extraordinary because he did not represent her thinking in a conventional manner. Nowadays however, Joyce is understood by a far wider readership.

Surrealism, an extreme movement which abandoned rationality and gave supreme status to the dream, to irrationality, to all that was the opposite of the "ordinary", produced no full-scale novel, only some three or four short novels. But its influence was immense. Franz Kafka (1883–1924) was most certainly not a surrealist, but his strange novels were more easily understood by those who were aware of surrealism and the reason for it: this was, in short, the failure of reason to control irrational forces (war being the supreme example of the irrational, when grown men kill each other without understanding why). Kafka is unique; his increasingly convincing fiction grew out of a combination of personal circumstances and qualities which included: illness; the alienated plight of the intelligent Jew; prophetic wisdom; a feeling for folklore; the necessity of scepticism in an uncertain world. He now seems more and more a realist, as anyone who has applied for any kind of state document or allowance will be fully aware. Sometimes we do not know who we are, we do not know where we are going, we feel guilty but we don't know altogether why. We resemble the character K of *The Trial* and *The Castle*.

American modernism

In America Edith Wharton (1862–1937) carried on in the Jamesian tradition, though she added much of her own. William Faulkner (1897–1962) used stream-of-consciousness to extraordinary effect: his great tapestry of a part of the South, reflecting the defeated and yet surviving "old Americans", has a tinge of naturalism (he was a deeply pessimistic man), but is wholly modernist. Ernest Hemingway (1898–1961) combined his journalistic skill, and the styles of Stein and Sherwood Anderson, into a technique that for a time expressed the feelings of people who were lost but who were determined to create a code of decency in spite of there being no basis for one. F. Scott Fitzgerald (1896–1940) exposed the crudity and yet purity of the American Dream of Innocence (the New World, Paradise on Earth) in *The Great Gatsby* (1925). His technique is realistic, but his symbols arise naturally from his descriptions, his selections of events.

Later Saul Bellow (1915), Bernard Malamud (1914) and Norman Mailer (1923) stuck to coherence of presentation, but made new use of the old forms to give a powerful Jews'-eye view of America. In their work the American Dream persists, even though it is rudely probed and savaged and even spat upon. More recently in America a series of less coherently presented, more immediately difficult novels have appeared, which mix extreme erudition (or very erudite-looking allusions) with all past forms. John Barth (1930) is an archetypal example of such an intellectual writer. Thomas Pynchon (1937) is another, though he is more adventurous and inventive. Richard Wright (1908–60) and James Baldwin (1924) have dramatized the predicament of the Negro, as has Ralph Ellison (1914), in his single novel *The Invisible Man* (1952). This last, reckoned to be the most successful (and moderate) of Negro novels, is far more modernist in procedure than anything by Wright or Baldwin: it draws on Kafka, and uses stream-of-consciousness, surrealism and symbolism. Here most of the modern methods are seen to be fused together into a coherent whole – so that each method remains unobtrusive.

The modern Italian novel

Towards the end of the nineteenth century Italy began to make up for lost time. Giovanni Verga (1840–1922) developed *verismo* (the best definition of this is Sicilian naturalism), which utilized the Italian vernacular, much as Twain had utilized the American. Luigi Pirandello (1867–1936), most famous as a playwright but as distinguished as a writer of fiction, concerned himself with the question of human identity and with the difference between illusion and reality. (He is

Sherwood Anderson in the late 1930s.

invariably compared by critics to Cervantes.) He did this in a compassionate way, though he had a streak of despairing scornful opportunism in his nature which caused him publicly to support fascism while privately denouncing it. That element in him does not get into his work. Very few twentieth-century writers worth the name have been fascists, and not one of them unambiguous ones. And all the communist writers have become disillusioned or, as in the case of Mikhail Sholokhov (1905), their work has fallen off or they have ceased to write. Totalitarianism is not a good atmosphere for invention – unless the writer criticises it from exile, or uses allegory or other means to trick the politicians. (Alberto Moravia (1907) tried this in Italy, but Mussolini – an ex-"novelist" himself, like Goebbels – saw through the trick.)

Italo Svevo (1861–1928) in *Confessions of Zeno* is a case apart in Italian literature: he wrote poor Italian because he was a native of Trieste, and he went unrecognized until Joyce and others urged a foreign public to read him in translation. He is too unique to be influential, but he offers a prime example of early modernism. Like Kafka, he is prophetic: he prophesied the atomic bomb. And he bases his comic novel on his investigations of Freud (at whom he simultaneously has a good laugh) and of philosophical thought (hence his title, referring to the founder of Stoic philosophy). He is above all concerned with time and its nature and, like the great comic novelist he is, he connects this with cigarette-smoking: time is measured by cigarettes, and his hero is always giving up smoking – because he thus enjoys each "last cigarette" so much the more. The book is not difficult to read, but it contains the essence of modernism.

In the mainstream of Italian literature Ignazio Silone (1900) wrote political novels and in his development is seen the oft-repeated process of communism continually modified. Alberto Moravia, whose presentation, like Silone's is usually coherent, began as a political, anti-fascist, novelist, but after playing fruitfully with allegory and surrealism, concentrated on the inadequacies of a central way in which people relate or try to relate to one another: sex. He could be warmly lyrical on this subject; but his clear "message" is that mankind's attitude to sex is tragically mistaken and has tragic consequences. Pier Paolo Pasolini (1922–1976) concerned himself with violent expressions of rebellion against all accepted political solutions (including, eventually, communism), basing his impulses on an extremely sensitive humanitarianism and on his homosexuality (which last tragically cost him his life). Elio Vittorini (1908–1966) also regarded the novel as a form of political engagement.

For obvious reasons – the long fascist rule and the existence of a huge gap between rich and poor – politics has tended to dominate the recent

MAJOR WORKS OF FICTION: 1946–1970

Britain, The Commonwealth and Eire

1946

1947 *Eustace and Hilda* L. P. Hartley, *Under the Volcano* Malcolm Lowry

1948 *Cry, the Beloved Country* Alan Paton

1949 *1984* George Orwell

1950 *Morning at the Office* Edgar Mittelholzer

1951

1951 *Molloy; Malone Dies* Samuel Beckett, *A Question of Upbringing* Anthony Powell, *The Masters* C. P. Snow
1952 *Martha Quest* Doris Lessing, *Hemlock and After* Angus Wilson

1953 *Casino Royale* Ian Fleming

1954 *Lucky Jim* Kingsley Amis, *Lord of the Flies* William Golding, *Under the Net* Iris Murdoch, *Lord of the Rings* J. R. R. Tolkien

1956

1956 *Time for a Tiger* Anthony Burgess, *The Towers of Trebizond* Rose Macaulay

1957 *Room at the Top* John Braine, *Justine* Lawrence Durrell, *Saturday Night and Sunday Morning* Alan Sillitoe, *The Ordeal of Gilbert Pinfold* Evelyn Waugh, *Voss* Patrick White

1958 *Things Fall Apart* Chinua Achebe, *I Like It Here* Amis, *Billy Liar* Keith Waterhouse

1961

1961 *A Burnt Out Case* Graham Greene, *A House for Mr Biswas* V. S. Naipaul, *Riders in the Chariot* White

1962 *A Clockwork Orange* Burgess

1963 *Occasion for Loving* Nadine Gordimer

1964 *How It Is* Beckett

1965 *The Red and the Green* Murdoch

1966

1966 *Wide Sargasso Sea* Jean Rhys, *The Solid Mandala* White

1967 *No Laughing Matter* Wilson

1968 *I Am Mary Dunne* Brian Moore

1969 *The Green Man* Amis, *The French Lieutenant's Woman* John Fowles

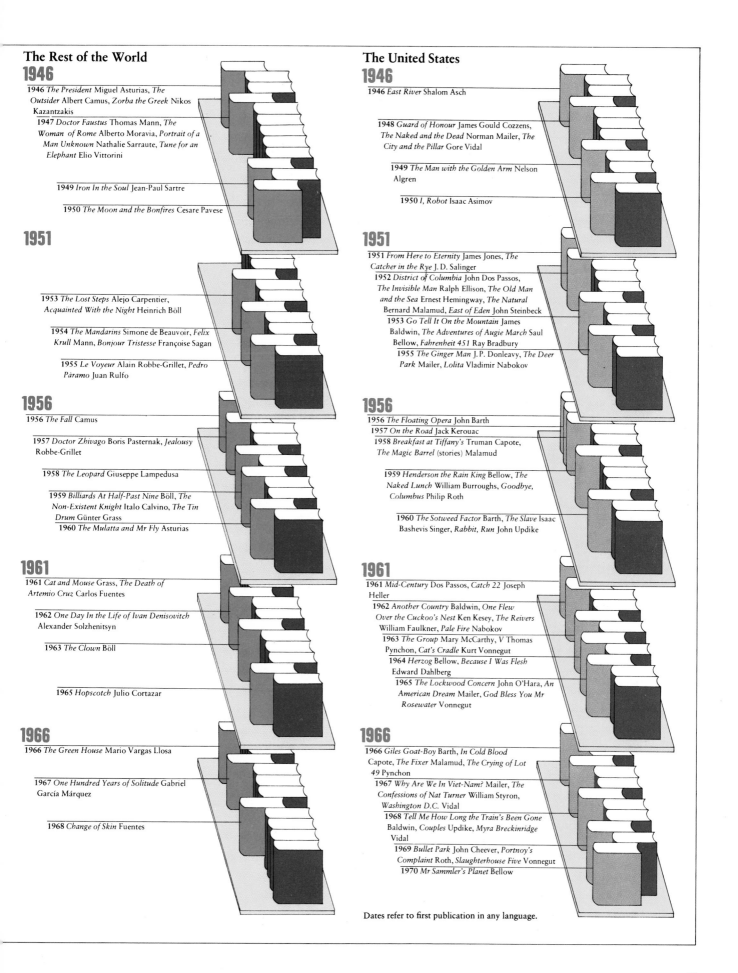

The Rest of the World
1946

1946 *The President* Miguel Asturias, *The Outsider* Albert Camus, *Zorba the Greek* Nikos Kazantzakis

1947 *Doctor Faustus* Thomas Mann, *The Woman of Rome* Alberto Moravia, *Portrait of a Man Unknown* Nathalie Sarraute, *Tune for an Elephant* Elio Vittorini

1949 *Iron In the Soul* Jean-Paul Sartre

1950 *The Moon and the Bonfires* Cesare Pavese

1951

1953 *The Lost Steps* Alejo Carpentier, *Acquainted With the Night* Heinrich Böll

1954 *The Mandarins* Simone de Beauvoir, *Felix Krull* Mann, *Bonjour Tristesse* Françoise Sagan

1955 *Le Voyeur* Alain Robbe-Grillet, *Pedro Páramo* Juan Rulfo

1956

1956 *The Fall* Camus

1957 *Doctor Zhivago* Boris Pasternak, *Jealousy* Robbe-Grillet

1958 *The Leopard* Giuseppe Lampedusa

1959 *Billiards At Half-Past Nine* Böll, *The Non-Existent Knight* Italo Calvino, *The Tin Drum* Günter Grass

1960 *The Mulatta and Mr Fly* Asturias

1961

1961 *Cat and Mouse* Grass, *The Death of Artemio Cruz* Carlos Fuentes

1962 *One Day In the Life of Ivan Denisovitch* Alexander Solzhenitsyn

1963 *The Clown* Böll

1965 *Hopscotch* Julio Cortazar

1966

1966 *The Green House* Mario Vargas Llosa

1967 *One Hundred Years of Solitude* Gabriel García Márquez

1968 *Change of Skin* Fuentes

The United States
1946

1946 *East River* Shalom Asch

1948 *Guard of Honour* James Gould Cozzens, *The Naked and the Dead* Norman Mailer, *The City and the Pillar* Gore Vidal

1949 *The Man with the Golden Arm* Nelson Algren

1950 *I, Robot* Isaac Asimov

1951

1951 *From Here to Eternity* James Jones, *The Catcher in the Rye* J. D. Salinger

1952 *District of Columbia* John Dos Passos, *The Invisible Man* Ralph Ellison, *The Old Man and the Sea* Ernest Hemingway, *The Natural* Bernard Malamud, *East of Eden* John Steinbeck

1953 *Go Tell It On the Mountain* James Baldwin, *The Adventures of Augie March* Saul Bellow, *Fahrenheit 451* Ray Bradbury

1955 *The Ginger Man* J.P. Donleavy, *The Deer Park* Mailer, *Lolita* Vladimir Nabokov

1956

1956 *The Floating Opera* John Barth

1957 *On the Road* Jack Kerouac

1958 *Breakfast at Tiffany's* Truman Capote, *The Magic Barrel* (stories) Malamud

1959 *Henderson the Rain King* Bellow, *The Naked Lunch* William Burroughs, *Goodbye, Columbus* Philip Roth

1960 *The Sotweed Factor* Barth, *The Slave* Isaac Bashevis Singer, *Rabbit, Run* John Updike

1961

1961 *Mid-Century* Dos Passos, *Catch 22* Joseph Heller

1962 *Another Country* Baldwin, *One Flew Over the Cuckoo's Nest* Ken Kesey, *The Reivers* William Faulkner, *Pale Fire* Nabokov

1963 *The Group* Mary McCarthy, *V* Thomas Pynchon, *Cat's Cradle* Kurt Vonnegut

1964 *Herzog* Bellow, *Because I Was Flesh* Edward Dahlberg

1965 *The Lockwood Concern* John O'Hara, *An American Dream* Mailer, *God Bless You Mr Rosewater* Vonnegut

1966

1966 *Giles Goat-Boy* Barth, *In Cold Blood* Capote, *The Fixer* Malamud, *The Crying of Lot 49* Pynchon

1967 *Why Are We In Viet-Nam?* Mailer, *The Confessions of Nat Turner* William Styron, *Washington D.C.* Vidal

1968 *Tell Me How Long the Train's Been Gone* Baldwin, *Couples* Updike, *Myra Breckinridge* Vidal

1969 *Bullet Park* John Cheever, *Portnoy's Complaint* Roth, *Slaughterhouse Five* Vonnegut

1970 *Mr Sammler's Planet* Bellow

Dates refer to first publication in any language.

Italian novel. But Aldo Palazzeschi (1885–1974) was able to write from the position of "autonomous writer" and Massimo Bontempelli (1878–1960) is one of those credited with a method called "magic realism" (his works are not translated). This is used to describe novels which have been written in a conventional manner, but whose subject matter is frankly impossible. It could be applied to Mann's *Doctor Faustus*, and certainly it describes the work of Ernst Jünger (1895). It is not of course new; but it is new in this century.

The post-war Italian novel reached its heights with Cesare Pavese (1908–50), whose suicide shocked and hurt the nation. Pavese is decidedly the autonomous writer; but he was concerned both with politics, with which he was disillusioned, and with sex (his failure to find sexual happiness was one of the reasons for his suicide, but it seemed and seems symbolic). However, Pavese was modernist and his importance in the understanding of modernism is that he wrote the kind of novel which has a very definite future. This would be conceded by most critics including those who believe that other sorts of novels also have a future, as some probably have. Pavese preserves coherence. He is accessible to the common reader. He is wholly adequate to the demands of his times, and in killing himself, left hope. For him, reality consists of the recapturing of the true meaning of myth. He makes personal myths, as in *The Moon and the Bonfires* (1950), and he thus returns to the past. Yet his novels are totally integrated; and they take into account every important manifestation of modern life.

The modern novel in Germany

The German novel has of course been similarly concerned with the totalitarian past (and with prophecy of it). Not a single important German novelist wholly endorsed the Nazis, which is surely highly significant, and thus arose the terms, applied to those who stayed, "inner exile" and "inner emigrant". Thus, while Thomas Mann can explore, disturbingly, the connections between art and evil, he also condemns the Nazis unequivocally, from a liberal standpoint. Some have questioned his formulations and the sincerity of his liberalism; but he could not and would not support Hitler: he totally rejected him.

Mann, like his more left-wing brother Heinrich (1871–1950), preserved coherence. So did the liberal Catholic Heinrich Böll (1917), though he built into all his earlier novels an awareness of modernist methods. In *Billiards at Half-Past Nine* (1959) and in many of his stories he makes full use of interior monologue and timeshifts, and uses the ancient technique of flashback in a new way. Many people find *Billiards at Half-Past Nine* hard to read; in its successor *The Clown* (1963) the central character, who protests at the Nazi past of the Germans, is modernist but the style is not. Böll embraces a non-dogmatic form of Christianity under the influence of the Danish Christian existentialist thinker Kierkegaard, who defined faith as an irrational, but necessary, leap into the dark.

Expressionism

Günter Grass (1927), who is now probably more widely read than Böll, combines magic realism, the surrealistically grotesque, the picaresque, and expressionism to write his more violent novels of protest at that element in the Germans which permitted the Nazis. Expressionism was a specifically German movement which began before World War I and ended a few years after it. It is seen mainly in the theatre and poetry, rather than in the novel; but there is a sense in which expressionism stands for modernism.

Expressionism is technically anti-realistic, though of course in the interests of achieving a greater overall realism. It is best described by way of example. Suppose a novelist wants to express a man's sudden horror and grief. To take a highly dramatic example: his wife burns his beloved dog, whom she has previously seemed to love, and he discovers her doing this. The author may choose to try to describe his emotions realistically. He will do better than "he felt horrified", but he is limited in his resources; for the cruelty of man to man in this century (hence the violent example), while it may not have grown in fact, has obtruded itself terribly because it is continually being practised on a mass scale. Therefore even personal emotion has taken on a sombre hue. The expressionist, feeling that "ordinary" words are not adequate to express horror and other violent emotions, invents a metaphor – or it presents itself to his imagination. He will write that the earth broke, the man fell through. Or that the man exploded. Something "impossible", but nonetheless more "expressive" – he believes – than mere "realist" description.

Once one understands what modernist authors are trying to do when they seem to be being absurd, it is easier to follow them. Every kind of apparent incoherence in the modern novel may be explained as a kind of expressionism. This includes the open-ended novel, where the reader may choose the ending for himself. The British novelist John Fowles (1926) uses this technique in *The French Lieutenant's Woman* (1969). The reader is allowed to choose his interpretation because it is recognized that this is what in any case he has been doing with all books. One generation sees Quixote as a funny buffoon, another as a tragic figure – and so forth. The apparent irrationality of the process (how can a story end in a number of different ways?) is answered by the extension of a fact: that when we read there are, ultimately, even after the text has been fully examined, several interpretations open, several ambiguities. We are subjective. We cannot help being so.

The influence of modern physics

Novels are not mathematics. But is not the mathematics of the higher physics "surrealist"? The eminent novelist Arthur Koestler (1905) has used just that word of them. How can a wave be a particle at the same time as it is a wave? How can two particles do two different things at the same time, being two different things as they do it? The neutrino is described as "stable" and without electrical charge. It has a measure: its "spin". Yet it has no mass! True, in this case the problem is resolved (or is it?) by saying that it has no "rest mass". This is surely a postulate as strange as a mad dream.

So is there such a gap as C. P. Snow proposes between art and science? Are not twentieth-century novelists, too, concerned with the question of entropy, the apparent truth that energy in the universe is finite? Modernists are certainly dealing with the problem of entropy, or what used to be called "the heat death of the universe". What can be the point of anything that will die? But does entropy really operate?

Some of the more difficult modern novels can be thought of as black holes. Most astronomers believe that these exist, but they cannot explain much about them yet. They are matter which has collapsed into so dense a condition that not even the light they "eat" can escape from them. What is on the "other side" of them? White holes, generating energy? The comparison is not made for fun. Black holes are mysterious, and make the idea of the universe we inhabit seem strange. Even if our existence is a dream, of our own or someone else, who is the dreamer, or who made the dreamer? Novelists have touched on this, too. So even if black holes exist in a dream, what are they? Certainly they are utterly different from the old easily assimilated and explicable physics of even so advanced a thinker as Newton. They seem to suggest that what we think we experience is not really what we experience at all . . .

The most notable novelist to be influenced by physics was Robert Musil (1880–1942), the Austrian author of *The Man Without Qualities*. Musil had been a pupil of the physicist-philosopher Ernst Mach, and was himself a scientist. Mach's Principle, as it is called, is, put briefly: that everything that happens in the universe affects the rest of the universe. All objects possess inertia, he postulated, because the universe itself wants to maintain a status quo. Mach was not a literary man, but his implications are enormous. Among them are the fact that our emotions (electro-chemical impulses) are affecting the universe now – and that our inertia (in any matter) is caused by a force over and above us. Of course a leap is needed to see Mach's ideas in an artistic way, to transform them to psychology. Yet if his Principle is true then it must have psychological consequences.

Musil in his great novel gives a comic view of the Austro-Hungarian Empire on the verge of collapse, but itself and its subjects believe that it is stable. His hero knows that the whole edifice is tottering, but has inertia, lacks "qualities". Now Musil was influenced by others as well as Mach, and he was not only influenced by Mach's Principle. It is noteworthy that Mach, to whom Einstein acknowledged a debt, was an empiricist, a pragmatist (inasmuch as he conceived of theories in terms of their utility rather than their truth, which he regarded as inaccessible) and an enemy of metaphysics. Musil's complex novel also draws on myth (in particular that of Isis and Osiris), and one of his central themes is incest, the taboo upon which has not been explained fully by any anthropologist. We take the taboo for granted. But why? The novel and science use different languages, but are they not seeking the same kinds of answers – in this instance the reason for inertia?

Every kind of novel has been written in America; it is the place from which most of the profounder and more lucid studies of modernism emanate. A study of some of the more notable American novelists immediately reveals that they experiment with almost every kind of modernism. There is also a kind of modernism that is practised because it is fashionable: the author may not understand the reasons for it. Sometimes he is successful because he has written from instinct, but he is often pretentious. It is, of course, for the reader to decide who is pretentious and who is not. It is hard not to be pretentious. The Australian Patrick White (1912), a profound novelist, has sometimes had to play about with modernist ideas that he cannot make convincing. Yet how otherwise could he have produced his truly powerful works?

The modern novel in Britain

Britain produced great early pioneers of modernism: Joyce, Woolf, Ford Madox Ford (1873–1939), and it may fairly claim Joseph Conrad (1857–1924), who was Polish by birth, since he chose England to live in and English to write in. Now Britain is somewhat behindhand: the best authors seem to be the older ones: Graham Greene (1904), and Anthony Powell (1905), who pays open homage in his *roman fleuve* "The Music of Time" to Proust and is certainly modernist, though coherent and conservative in outlook. But such novelists as Kingsley Amis (1922), Anthony Burgess (1917), and others have used modernist techniques to effect, and there are signs that a younger generation is profiting from these. Angus Wilson (1913) is the most gifted and interesting of those novelists who tried to recapture the old style; he did not use modernist techniques to any great extent until later in his career. Meanwhile the intelligent popular novel flourishes and so does science fiction, the best of which – H. G. Wells, Olaf Stapledon, Brian W. Aldiss,

J. G. Ballard and others – relies heavily on modernist techniques.

The modern novel in France

France has remained a seedbed of new ideas. Jules Romains (1885–1972), with the 27-volume *Men of Good Will* (1932–46), developed the *roman fleuve* as far as, perhaps, it can be developed. Jean-Paul Sartre (1905), the philosopher, has been the centre of reference since the end of World War II – even if only as a figure against whom to revolt. In his first novel *Nausea* (1938) he described his disgust with existence. He is an atheist who believes everything to be accidental unless a suitable effort of human will is made to defeat the sense of emptiness that assails modern man. As a philosopher he has tried to suggest a version of Marxism as a solution; but, never a member of the communist party, he is not satisfied with his modifications of Marx. In his great unfinished *roman fleuve* – *The Age of Reason* (1945), *The Reprieve* (1945) and *Iron in the Soul* (1949) – he employs the methods of the American John Dos Passos (1896–1970): use of the continuous present, interpolation of documentary into the narrative, the bringing in of public figures. The technique is sometimes called *simultaneousism*. What Sartre and the many influenced by him give the reader is a phenomenological description of existence. "Phenomenology" is the name given to the philosophy of Edmund Husserl, who investigated the philosophical possibilities of *inner* experience. He influenced Sartre profoundly. But he was not interested in novels. Sartre is an existentialist: he believes that particular individual existences are more important than (Platonic) essences, that all that happens – including dreams, day-dreams, and every kind of inner experience – is significant, and that human beings, to escape their deadly boredom, must be "committed". He is magnificent at describing the processes undergone by people who are trying to become committed, and he makes us see vividly how much we want to be committed to whatever it is that we ourselves truly are; but he does not know exactly what it is to which we should commit ourselves. Like Robert Musil, he could not conclude his novel.

Sartre's influence contributed to the *nouveau roman*, or "new novel", and the school of the new novelists took for granted much of what he said. The pioneer was Alain Robbe-Grillet (1922). His theory (though not everyone agrees that his novels embody his theories) is that the world is indifferent to us, that we are too anthropomorphic (human-orientated) in our attitudes. The novel is like life, and life is a game. In one of his novels a detective is put to work on a crime which he himself committed (perhaps); we are deliberately reminded of Oedipus, who did not know that he had married his mother. But Robbe-Grillet in employing symbols and mythological allusions

Gabriel García Márquez.

seems to be parodying them. He was originally an agronomist by profession and is influenced by behaviourism, the psychological theory that states that investigation of all introspection and inner experience is useless: the only things that are significant are those that can be measured scientifically. Robbe-Grillet's own novels have been popular; but the new-novel style, which took hold of France in the 1960s, has given way to more psychological types of novel: the former tended to be arid and to bore the reader.

Latin America

Modernism has flourished most recently in Latin-America. This is because it is a place of great political oppression, which generates protest provided it is not too open (dictators do not understand modernism), and because its exotic and largely unexplored landscape provides a natural metaphor for the unknown, the mysterious – which is the real subject of modern literature. Then there are the Indians. Nearly all the great novelists of Latin-America draw on the wisdom and poetic mythologies of the supposedly "primitive" Indians, who have been treated badly by the colonists. The political flavour of all Latin-American fiction is broadly left. Miguel Asturias (1899), the Guatemalan who won the Nobel Prize, is typical: he published one powerful and terrifying novel about the horrors of dictatorship, *The President* (1946), but then went on to try to translate the wisdom of the Indians into an acceptable Spanish. It looks complex, and is complex, but if the reader takes a little trouble, by reading about the Indians, their ways and folklore, he begins to understand Asturias' language.

The Argentinian Julio Cortázar (1914) plays games as Robbe-Grillet does, and has experimented with different arrangements and endings. Gabriel García Márquez (1928), the Colombian, is more universal: his presentation is more immediately coherent, although he is quite as modernist. He is a popular writer and a great one.

The question that is asked, and should be asked, nowadays is: must a novel be modernist to have true literary merit? The answer is yes, but this must be clarified by pointing out that what is modernist by no means needs to look modernist. Anthony Powell looks old-fashioned, but is not: a few critics might call Cesare Pavese old-fashioned because his novels make immediate sense, but they are in a small minority. The novel of pure entertainment need not be modernist; it is frankly escapist, and why not? It simply has less literary merit than the serious novel. We do not always read for literary merit. But it helps if we know what we are doing. And in the end all good serious fiction becomes popular, at least to a degree.

Crime Fiction: A History

Ever since man has told stories to man there has been crime fiction. A crime story *The History of Bel* is to be found in the Apocrypha of the Bible; there is another among the tales of the Greek demi-god Herakles or Hercules. As soon as there were societies of any sort there had to be rules, but rules restrict and so inevitably are resented. Crime writing is the literature of that resentment and the subsequent acknowledgement that, despite it, the rules must be upheld.

So there have always been books and stories appealing to that fascination with crime that lurks in all of us. A convenient label for this sort of writing is "Sensational Literature", a category which came to life with the advent of cheap printing. In Britain there were the *Annals of Newgate* from 1776 onwards and the broadsheets of James Catnach (*The Red Barn Murder* is said to have sold a million in 1828); in America there was among much else the legend of Jesse James. But crime writing is not only sensational storytelling: it is also an art. And that art can confidently be said to have begun with one man, Edgar Allan Poe (1809–49).

In just three short stories, published in the early 1840s, Poe laid down most of the canons – the role of the Great Detective, the importance of

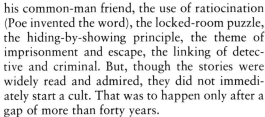

G. K. Chesterton, author of the Father Brown stories.

A banquet held by the Detection Club in 1932. Members wear a white flower to distinguish them from their guests. G. K. Chesterton sits at the centre of the top table. Other prominent members are singled out below (left to right): E. C. Bentley; Freeman Wills Crofts; Dorothy L. Sayers; Anthony Berkeley; Gladys Mitchell.

his common-man friend, the use of ratiocination (Poe invented the word), the locked-room puzzle, the hiding-by-showing principle, the theme of imprisonment and escape, the linking of detective and criminal. But, though the stories were widely read and admired, they did not immediately start a cult. That was to happen only after a gap of more than forty years.

It was then that a struggling young doctor, Arthur Conan Doyle (1859–1930), created the greatest Great Detective of them all, Sherlock Holmes. Though his first appearance in the novel *A Study in Scarlet* (1887) was by no means an instant success, with the publication of the short stories in the *Strand Magazine* from 1891 on the puzzling crime story seized the public imagination on both sides of the Atlantic. The time was just ripe for mystery stories with an atmosphere of scientific method.

Holmes was so popular that scores of imitators and anti-imitators sprang up. Arthur Morrison (1863–1945), the low-life novelist, produced his Martin Hewitt, Holmesean in method, un-Holmesean of face and figure. G. K. Chesterton (1874–1936) created Father Brown, dumpy and prosaic yet all-conquering thanks to spiritual, unscientific methods. In America later there was

The death of Sherlock Holmes at the Reichenbach Falls as depicted by Sidney Paget in 1893. Holmes' popularity was such that Conan Doyle was almost forced to resurrect him and write several further series of stories.

John Dickson Carr regularly foxed their large publics, while in Britain Agatha Christie established perhaps a yet greater supremacy. Her name was coupled with that of Dorothy L. Sayers, but this latter began to add new ingredients to the genre. She set her books against interesting backgrounds and, more important, she made her characters increasingly like the figures-in-depth to be found in the pure novel, a development soon well taken up.

However, in America reaction against the restrictions of the Detection Club school was altogether more explosive. Taking strength from the line of Sensational Literature (which, of course, had never died and had even produced from writers like Mary Roberts Rinehart books of lasting merit) a group of writers associated with the pulp magazine *Black Mask* brought murder back, in the words of one of them, Raymond Chandler, to the people it belonged to, the people of the mean streets.

In both countries in the years after the so-called Golden Age of detective fiction, crime-writing increasingly brought real people back to its pages. It rejoined to a great extent the mainstream of literature, if in its more turbid, bloodstained current.

In the course of this movement it swept up a small sub-section of literature that had long existed, though somewhat obscurely: the spy story. Again, this can be found in the earliest times with such works as the fourteenth-century Chinese *San Kuo*. But it needed another wide popular success to cause it to flourish again, and this it got with the James Bond novels of Ian Fleming from 1953 onwards. Rapidly, reactions against this super-smooth hero sprang up with the acerbities of Len Deighton and the sadnesses of John Le Carré and later in America Charles McCarry.

Yet, although crime-writing has now taken on many of the qualities of the novel proper, it still remains a thing apart. Dostoyevsky's *Crime and Punishment* has never been classed with the genre. Why? Because crime-fiction is essentially entertainment: it puts the reader's needs above those of the writer. There are, of course, many borderline cases where it might appear that the writer's desire to tell us something has smothered our demand simply to enjoy (Patricia Highsmith is a case in point), but in principle this test would seem to be the separating factor.

And it is likely so to remain. Crime-writing in the years to come can scarcely go back to the purer artificial form which flourished during the inter-war years. It will be concerned with almost every aspect of human activity (none more so perhaps than the subject it almost cut out at the height of the Golden Age, sex). Whatever is new it will seize upon, and one thing that is old in us, that ineradicable lurch towards the rule-forbidden, will as always be its mainspring.

the heavily scientific sleuth Craig Kennedy created by Arthur B. Reeve (1880–1936) and Uncle Abner the backwoodsman imbued with religious conviction by Melville Davisson Post (1871–1930). The chain continues to this day.

Because of Holmes' extraordinary success, a pattern for the crime tale, or detective story as it became generally called, rapidly formed to harden almost absolutely over the first third of the twentieth century. The process culminated in the founding of the rule-pledged Detection Club in 1932 with its notion of fair play as between author and reader in books, that were more puzzle contests than novels. With the Belgian Simenon the only noteworthy exception, crime fiction was then, and almost remains still, an Anglo-American preserve.

In America S. S. Van Dine, Ellery Queen and

Science Fiction: A History

Science fiction is the branch of literature which most remarkably exhibits the quality for which the novel itself was named: novelty. Its narratives generally feature a divergence of some kind from what we regard as the norm.

The history of science fiction itself represents a kind of divergence. It is no surprise to find that its earliest examples coincide with the marked divergence in society which took place following the Industrial Revolution: in France, with Sebastien Mercier's *L'An 2440* in 1771, in England with Mary Shelley's *Frankenstein* in 1818.

These novels, as well as their successors, owe much to previous writings, respectively to the utopian tradition as represented by Francis Bacon and the eschatological tradition, with its belief in heaven and hell, as represented by Milton and Goethe. They also exhibit divergences in the history of thought. Mercier introduces Enlightenment ideas concerning the progress of society, Mary Shelley shows Man, in creating life by scientific means, taking over the role of God.

Much of the science fiction written last century is forgotten, although Jules Verne (1828–1905) is now receiving renewed critical attention. His divergences from the norm are characteristically expressed through rebellious heroes who, aided by machines, colonize the remote points of the globe; Captain Nemo of *Twenty Thousand Leagues Under the Sea* (1869) is a good example. Later, Verne's vision became darker, and ever since then science fiction can scarcely be described as sunny.

Left An illustration by Bob Layzell for the jacket of The Best SF of J. G. Ballard.
Right Terry Oakes' illustration for the jacket of André Norton's Wraiths of Time.

The other great figure to set beside Verne is H. G. Wells (1866–1946). Wells's sense of the continuity of history is evident in his science fiction. His divergences are remarkable in that they paradoxically demonstrate the underlying continuity; the creatures on *The Island of Dr Moreau* (1896) remain animal despite their man-like form.

With Wells, SF acquired stature and popularity. The popularity was reinforced when magazines appeared devoted to science fiction. Audiences grew with the arrival of the paperback; nowadays, one tenth of all fiction sales lies in the SF market. Most of the vast output is designed as ephemeral entertainment; some achieves philosophical import, often by adhering to the original principal of divergence.

Such divergences cover a wide range of phenomena, from simple climatic changes, such as the onslaught of a new ice age or a drought, to the introduction of new elements into society, such as the invention of androids (human-like robots) or the arrival of aliens (extra-terrestrial beings). One of the finest alien invasion stories remains H. G. Wells's *The War of the Worlds* (1898), which utilized interest in the planet Mars to introduce an adroit mixture of sensationalism, didacticism, adventure, and extrapolative thinking on society. This recipe has often proved effective since.

But the divergences proposed in a science-fictional narrative may be more far-reaching than the introduction of one single element, and result in novels of greater structural complexity.

Good examples are Aldous Huxley's *Brave New World* (1932) or Frederik Pohl's *Jem* (1979), in both of which society itself has changed. Here the force of the narrative is derived in part from the way in which we as readers perceive how the parameters of the future society can be discerned in our own times. In the Pohl novel, for instance, the world is divided into three power blocs, Fuel, Food, and People.

In order to deploy any of these changes convincingly, the tale must be set in the future. This represents a novelty in itself; we can say that almost any tale set in the future is classifiable as science fiction. Tomorrow is the plimsol line between science fiction and the ordinary novel.

A more recent development is the SF novel which manages to sidestep the present entirely. In it, the divergence is introduced in the past of the fiction concerned, so that we read of an alternative present. The best example here is Philip K. Dick's *The Man in the High Castle* (1962), in which the Axis Powers won World War II some years before the novel opens, and America is partitioned between the Japanese and the Nazis. Impressive recent examples are Kingsley Amis' *The Alteration* (1976) and Michael Moorcock's *Gloriana* (1978).

Novels about alternative worlds generally delay the revelation of how and why they departed from our received present; this serves as a suspense element. They tend also to be elaborately, if not well, written; perhaps because of a certain self-indulgence in such imaginings.

The most popular type of science fiction is that which features action in space or on other planets, and which may, in quest of novelty, venture into other universes, although when you've seen one galaxy you've really seen them all. Uninformed people still speak of science fiction as "space fiction". Certainly, the spaceship is everyone's favourite uninvented vehicle, and a minor publishing industry is devoted to books which illustrate the interiors and exteriors of such vessels (often as spin-offs from television shows like *Star Trek* and *Battlestar Galactica*).

In all the examples quoted so far, with the possible exceptions of the alternative world, science or technology is in evidence. For this quality the game was named. (The term "science fiction" was coined in 1851, re-coined and brought into currency by the American editor Hugo Gernsback during the early 1930s.) In the popular mind, science fiction and science are inseparable; however, even a literature of change itself changes. One of the noted critics of science fiction, Darko Suvin, has claimed "SF should not be seen . . . in terms of science, the future, or any other element of its potentially unlimited thematic field"; rather he sees the genre in terms of "cognitive estrangement".

To look at SF from a more functional point of view, we can recall the remarks made by the poet Shelley in "A Defence of Poetry". "Man, having enslaved the elements, remains himself a slave . . . We want the creative faculty to imagine that which we know . . ." However fitfully, SF does supply that creative faculty, often through images of great power and mystery.

It is difficult to determine where SF shades off into other forms of writing (is George Orwell's *1984* science fiction or not?), and in particular where it shades off into "Fantasy" – not least because the term fantasy is open to more than one interpretation. But there is a branch of SF which straddles the fantasy frontier; it is generally known as "Sword-and-Sorcery", and is often set on barbarian worlds where problems are solved with the blade. These worlds lie beyond the cognitive norms of the reader's own world-perception, and so are outside SF proper. From this we can say that SF embraces the possible, however remote. The worlds depicted in Ursula Le Guin's *The Dispossessed* (1974) are immediately accessible to our waking comprehension; we could reach them in a hypothetical spaceship if we knew in which direction to travel. If Ms. Le Guin had, as an additional novelty, given her planetary beings an extra head apiece, then the novel would fall towards Fantasy, and lose much of its power.

From this, it does not necessarily follow that SF is the literature of the rational. Its attractions frequently lie elsewhere. We are willing to accept stories set in the future for the sake of the argument, but those stories are never written in the future tense. The further in the future they are set, the nearer they approach the "Once upon a time" atmosphere of fairy tales. Examples are the present writer's *Hothouse* (1962), set when the sun is dying, or Arthur C. Clarke's *The City and the Stars* (1956), which begins in true fairy tale fashion: "Like a glowing jewel, the city lay upon the breast of the desert. Once it had known change and alteration, but now Time passed it by. Night and day fled across the desert's face, but in the streets of Diaspar it was always afternoon, and darkness never came."

SF has been proliferating all round the world over the last quarter-century. The most successful motion picture ever made is *Star Wars*; it has assisted SF's enormous commercial expansion during the 1970s. Among today's most popular authors, apart from those already named, are Poul Anderson (*Tau Zero*), Isaac Asimov (*Foundation*), J. G. Ballard (*The Drowned World*), Harry Harrison (*Bill, The Galactic Hero*), Robert Heinlein (*Stranger in a Strange Land*), Frank Herbert (*The Dune Trilogy*), Bob Shaw (*Vertigo*), Robert Sheckley (*Dimension of Miracles*), A. E. van Vogt (*The Voyage of the Space Beagle*), and Kurt Vonnegut Jr (*Sirens of Titan*).

APPROACHES TO THE NOVEL

Analysis and criticism of the novel has a long tradition, and over the last three hundred years much has been made of the role of the novel, and indeed of the novelist, in society. Many novelists, as well as literary critics, sociologists and philosophers, have had their say; innumerable books and essays have been written. Yet there is no consensus, either about critical approaches to the novel, or about its role in society. What follows is not a summary of contemporary critical concepts; it is a selection of possible angles of approach to the novel, which may help to make reading more rewarding.

Beginnings, middles and ends

The beginning, middle and end of William Golding's Lord of the Flies *are easily identifiable as phases of exposition, complication and resolution. Golding succeeded brilliantly in his intention of creating an allegory on the state of civilization, but on a simple level his novel is an adventure story with a narrative line as straightforward as those found in boys' comics.*

In the oldest treatise on literary aesthetics that is normally referred to, *The Poetics*, Aristotle asserts that tragic drama is of a certain size, and has a beginning, middle and end. The novel is larger in size than tragedy (indeed it is larger than all literary forms except for the defunct epic), but nonetheless it normally has these three segments, corresponding, in narrative terms, to exposition, complication and resolution. When we begin a novel we require certain information to "get into the story"; once in, we follow certain exciting or complicated events which hold our attention; finally, everything is wrapped up.

Since fiction in the twentieth century has become increasingly sophisticated, the phases are not always clear cut, or are sometimes deliberately flouted. William Golding is fairly traditional in his construction methods (see illustration), and indeed his powerful allegory *Lord of the Flies* can be read as a conventional adventure story. However, some of the exposition is scattered and we are fed new information throughout the novel (Piggy's background, for example, emerges only gradually). And the ending, although climactic in the extreme, is in one sense no resolution – or at least it is not reassuring to the reader like the ending of R. M. Ballantyne's *Coral Island*, the book on which Golding modelled his darker twentieth-century fable:

> In the middle of them with filthy body, matted hair and unwiped nose, Ralph wept for the end of innocence, the darkness of man's heart, and the fall through the air of the true, wise friend called Piggy.
>
> The officer, surrounded by these noises, was moved and a little embarrassed. He turned away to give them time to pull themselves together; and waited, allowing his eyes to rest on the trim cruiser in the distance.

Ralph's bereavement, his new comprehension of the "darkness of man's heart", and the incomprehension of the rescuing officer, all mark a horrible beginning rather than the traditional happy ending with its complete "closure". The reader is left disturbed rather than sedated.

The enigma which lasts till the end

For all that many modern novelists defy them, endings remain an important part of our interest in, and of the satisfaction we derive from, fiction. Fiction is essentially teleological – it moves in a linear way to a conclusion or terminus. Once the terminus is reached and expectation satisfied the novel is, in a sense, exhausted of meaning. This is why many, and perhaps most, novels are

BEGINNING: INTRODUCTION TO THE PLANE-WRECKED CHILDREN AND THEIR DESERT ISLAND. ANTECEDENT DATA: THE WAR, THE END OF GLOBAL CIVILIZATION.

MIDDLE: THE SINISTER NATURE OF THE ISLAND EMERGES, THE POWER-STRUGGLE BETWEEN INEFFECTIVE LIBERAL-DEMOCRAT RALPH AND RUTHLESS TOTALITARIAN JACK. THE RITUAL SLAUGHTER OF SAINTLY SIMON AND THE CALLOUS ASSASSINATION OF THE RATIONALIST PIGGY LEAVES RALPH ALONE, TO BE SMOKED OUT AND HUNTED DOWN BY JACK'S TRIBE.

END: LAST-MINUTE RESCUE. RALPH LIES EXHAUSTED ON THE BEACH BETWEEN THE SAVAGE JACK AND THE "CIVILIZED" NAVAL OFFICER.

read once only. Mystery, or "whodunnit?" novels are a prime example of the kind of fiction which loses all interest once the last page revelation is reached. On the other hand, clues ignored or misunderstood on a first reading often release their full significance only in retrospect or on a second reading.

The French critic Roland Barthes has applied a useful term to this detective aspect of our first readings of fiction (as opposed to the reflective aspect of second and subsequent readings). The text of a novel, he suggests, is composed of five "codes". As we read we decipher these codes, and as we do so the novel's meanings take shape for us. Barthes terms one of the principal codes the hermeneutic, meaning that it concerns the enigma which all novels pose the reader in their early, middle and penultimate stages. (Other codes are the cultural, pertaining to shared social and historical reference; symbolic and thematic codes; and the code – or more properly "chain" – of action).

The hermeneutic code answers that state of mind which may be called interrogative, in which every reader initially addresses himself to a novel – what is happening, who is talking, what is going to happen? Take, for example, the opening sentence of Emily Brontë's *Wuthering Heights*: "I have just returned from a visit to my landlord – the solitary neighbour that I shall be troubled with." The enigma posed here is one which dominates the whole subsequent narrative – who is Heathcliff, why is he solitary, what are his mysterious motives? (There is also significance in Lockwood's apparently casual premonition that he will be "troubled with" Heathcliff.) A second enigma (who and what is Lockwood?) is satisfactorily resolved within a page or two, but we never completely reach the bottom of the Heathcliff enigma, although most of the narrative is devoted to him.

A cunning novelist often wilfully manipulates the hermeneutic process to set up false or difficult trails for the reader. Such artful misdirection is found in Jane Austen's *Emma*. The main enigma is much the same as in all Austen's fiction, namely: who will the heroine eventually marry? But in *Emma* there are *culs de sac* up which the reader is quite deliberately led (see illustration). The first arises from the false message by which we are instructed to think that the heroine (the central figure whose marriage fortunes are at stake) is Harriet, with Emma merely serving as ancillary match-maker. After the debacle in which parson Elton declines to marry the penniless Harriet, directing his proposal instead to the heiress Emma, we recognize her and her marriage destiny as the centre of the narrative interest.

Having reached this apparently secure ground, Jane Austen again misleads us into thinking that Emma is fated to marry the *jeune premier*, Frank Churchill, rather than the paternally wise and older man Knightley. In the last scenes of the novel the reader and Emma – who has always known herself only slenderly – discover that Knightley is her future marriage partner. For most of the novel, of course, the reader blunders along with the same misapprehensions as the heroine.

All Jane Austen's novels progress in this way, through complications to resolutions concerning the satisfactory disposition of the heroine in marriage and the acquisition of money sufficient for the principals to live in the approved social style. Habitually, however, as in *Emma*, Austen's narrative structures involve teasing and reader-deluding irony.

Conventional endings

Why, one may ask, should novels have such pronounced endings? And why, conventionally, are certain events regarded as terminal in fiction when, demonstrably, they are not terminal in life, where, as George Eliot puts it at the end of *Middlemarch*, "every limit is a beginning as well as an ending"? Marriage, for example, is a very common limit to fictional narrative – a "happy ending" – yet, as William Thackeray observed in *Vanity Fair* with reference to Amelia's union with George Osborne, novelists take a too easy way out when they assume that weddings actually end everything:

As his hero and heroine pass the matrimonial barrier, the novelist generally drops the curtain, as if the drama were over then: the doubts and struggles of life ended: as if, once landed in the marriage country, all were green and pleasant there: and wife and husband had nothing but to link each other's arms together, and wander gently downwards towards old age in happy and perfect fruition. But our little Amelia was just on the bank of her new country . . .

In Emma *Jane Austen deliberately misleads her readers by making them believe that Emma's view of events corresponds with reality. In fact this is rarely the case, and Emma fails to see the truth about her relationships with each of the three men in the story. Thus the reader is almost constantly under a misapprehension, and considerably surprised at the three denouements when Emma is made aware of the truth. Here, yellow indicates what Emma thinks, red indicates reality.*

Emma thinks she is promoting Harriet's marriage to Elton

Emma is actually encouraging Elton to propose to her

Dénouement entails humiliation and shame for Emma

Emma thinks she is flirting with Frank

Emma is actually a decoy to divert attention from Jane, Frank's true love

Dénouement entails humiliation and vexation for Emma

Emma thinks her relationship with Knightley is that of child ward to adult guardian

Emma's actual relationship with Knightley is that of future wife

Dénouement involves correction and fulfilment for Emma

Nonetheless, when it comes to ending his novel Thackeray himself submits to convention, with Amelia's second (and happy) marriage to Dobbin.

Events other than marriage have traditionally been regarded as finishing posts, notably birth and death. All the fiction of Dickens, for instance, ends with a coincidence of birth, marriage and death. These, of course, are the sacramental moments of everyone's life: events which, even in a secularized society, are habitually dignified with solemn religious ceremony.

Open endings
There is some truth in the contemporary French novelist Alain Robbe-Grillet's assertion that "form in the novel has to move to stay alive". In its evolution over the last 250 years the novel has moved from simplicity to complexity. One mark of growing complexity has been the defiance or undermining of conventional structures, codes and constraints. Open-ended novels, those which do not end in one of the conventional ways stated above, are common in the twentieth century (in the nineteenth century they occurred only when the novelist died while writing). Thus A. S. Byatt finishes her novel *The Virgin in the Garden* (1978) with the perfunctory air of one who is simply tired of talking:

> He gave her a cup of tea and the two of them sat together in uncommunicative silence, considering the still and passive pair on the sofa. That was not an end, but since it went on for a considerable time, is as good a place to stop as any.

A more spectacular open ending is to be found in John Fowles's bestseller, *The French Lieutenant's Woman* (1969). In this work Fowles has deliberately recreated a familiar kind of Victorian novel, in which a "gentleman" and an "upper servant" (meaning a lady's companion or governess) fall in love, despite the class gulf which separates them. In many ways Fowles imitates the forms and conventions of Victorian fiction with uncanny fidelity. Yet, as he observes in an authorial aside in chapter 13, "I live in the age of Alain Robbe-Grillet and Roland Barthes". The tensions involved in writing a modern-Victorian novel are most clearly demonstrated in the last chapters where Fowles offers the reader two quite contrary endings.

The first ending is conventionally Victorian; the hero Charles returns from America to discover Sarah working in the house of Dante Gabriel Rossetti. He makes up his differences with her and we are to suppose they marry and live happily ever after; the last image we have is of her head nestling on her future husband's breast. The alternative ending has Charles and Sarah arguing and parting – their differences unresolved. We are to believe that she will go on to become what late Victorians called a "new woman"; he on his part will subside into Victorian conformity, compounded of orthodox beliefs, self interest and hypocrisy. "You must not think," Fowles tells the reader, "that this is a less plausible ending to their story." In its technical freedom, and also in its freedom of reference to, for example, sexual relationships, Fowles's novel measures precisely the distances covered in a hundred years of fiction.

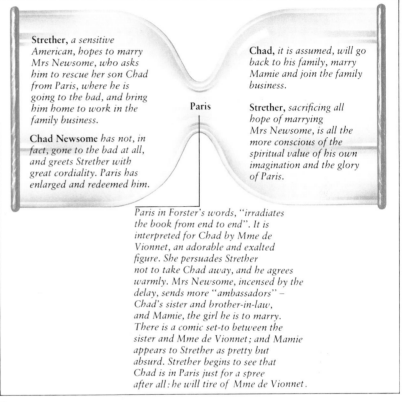

Strether, *a sensitive American, hopes to marry Mrs Newsome, who asks him to rescue her son Chad from Paris, where he is going to the bad, and bring him home to work in the family business.*

Chad Newsome *has not, in fact, gone to the bad at all, and greets Strether with great cordiality. Paris has enlarged and redeemed him.*

Paris

Chad, *it is assumed, will go back to his family, marry Mamie and join the family business.*

Strether, *sacrificing all hope of marrying Mrs Newsome, is all the more conscious of the spiritual value of his own imagination and the glory of Paris.*

Paris *in Forster's words, "irradiates the book from end to end". It is interpreted for Chad by Mme de Vionnet, an adorable and exalted figure. She persuades Strether not to take Chad away, and he agrees warmly. Mrs Newsome, incensed by the delay, sends more "ambassadors" – Chad's sister and brother-in-law, and Mamie, the girl he is to marry. There is a comic set-to between the sister and Mme de Vionnet; and Mamie appears to Strether as pretty but absurd. Strether begins to see that Chad is in Paris just for a spree after all: he will tire of Mme de Vionnet.*

Patterns
It can be seen from some of the novels already cited that a shape, often symmetrical, is frequently apparent, even if it is only a simple inverted "V": exposition, complication, resolution. The element of design has been a major preoccupation for many novelists, who have felt that their work should, like architecture and painting, have a formal structure in addition to its other elements.

In the nineteenth century the "architecture" of the work was often taken to be an essential ingredient, although this was viewed in many different ways. It might encompass plot structure, the balance between plot and characterization, the use of time and indeed many other aspects of the novel.

Henry James felt so strongly about formal structure that he was prepared to make major sacrifices in other ways – including plausibility, and "roundness" of characterization – in order to achieve a balanced and harmonious pattern. The hourglass pattern of *The Ambassadors* (see illustration), noted by E. M. Forster, is certainly achieved with great subtlety and creates a strong sense of satisfaction and harmony. But many

E. M. Forster pointed out that The Ambassadors *by Henry James has a pattern so definite, and so consciously contrived by the author, that it can be summed up in a familiar pictorial image: the hour-glass. Two chief characters, Strether and Chad Newsome, change places both morally and physically, crossing at a central point: Paris.*

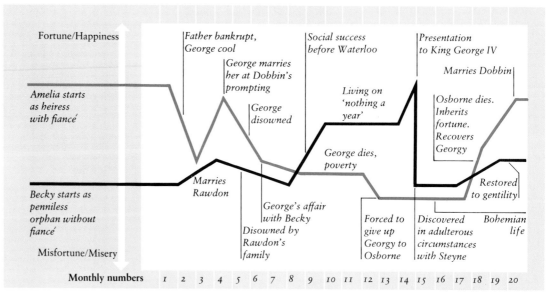

Fortune/Happiness

Amelia starts as heiress with fiancé

Father bankrupt, George cool

George marries her at Dobbin's prompting

George disowned

Social success before Waterloo

Living on 'nothing a year'

Presentation to King George IV

Marries Dobbin

Osborne dies. Inherits fortune. Recovers Georgy

George dies, poverty

Marries Rawdon

Becky starts as penniless orphan without fiancé

George's affair with Becky

Disowned by Rawdon's family

Forced to give up Georgy to Osborne

Discovered in adulterous circumstances with Steyne

Restored to gentility

Bohemian life

Misfortune/Misery

Monthly numbers 1 2 3 4 5 6 7 8 9 10 11 12 13 14 15 16 17 18 19 20

Below W. H. Auden's analysis of the detective story stereotype, as it applies to Ngaio Marsh's Hand in Glove. This, and all conventional detective stories, have five phases, indicated here by the proscenium arches. The phases are of unequal length, the first three being very much longer than the last two. The murder occurs exactly half way through the book, allowing the reader plenty of time to speculate about the motives for a crime which has not yet been committed, but which can be relied on to occur. Until the fourth phase, that of "true guilt and catharsis", suspicious facts, or clues, about each of the characters (introduced below) are gradually revealed. Here, a character appears on the stage whenever a significant fact comes to light. It is interesting to note that the character with the fewest direct clues turns out to be the murderer.

readers today find James' world artificial and his characters thinly-fleshed.

Although many novelists regard shape as an important ingredient, it is rarely carried to the extremes contrived by James, or capable of representation in so clear a solid object as the hour-glass. In Thackeray's *Vanity Fair* a number of different types of shape can be detected, some deriving from the serial publication in which the novel first appeared, and others designed across the book as a whole. The reciprocal "see-saw" pattern in the careers of the heroines Becky and Amelia is particularly marked, because it underlies the general theme of the novel: a satire on notions of "respectability" in society. On a more local level, the novel constantly employs a favourite device of Thackeray's, which has been called "redoubling": we are given a scene; and then the author goes back in time to show us what happened before that scene, gradually

bringing his narrative back to his point of departure. His motive here may have been purely psychological: a fear of the "big scene", and an urge towards a reflective mode of narration.

In some types of fiction the pattern becomes a stereotype: for example, in historical romance or the detective story. W. H. Auden, in an essay entitled "The Guilty Vicarage", provided an analysis of the detective story stereotype, which with a little updating can be applied with extraordinary accuracy to almost any example in the genre. The essential requirements can be classified under five headings:

The milieu This must be a closed and closely related society, like a school, a theatrical company, a group travelling in an overnight train, or the inhabitants of a country village. All the inhabitants can thereby be potential suspects, and the murder itself is violently obtrusive.

The victim He must be good (so that we and the

THE SUSPECTS

Pyke Period

Constance Cartell

Moppett and Leonard

Desirée

Bimbo

Nicola and Andrew

PERIOD OF FALSE INNOCENCE

REVELATION OF THE PRESENCE OF GUILT

Murder of Harold

Upset by Harold's remarks at lunch.

Disliked by all characters except Constance. Andrew has row with Harold about money.

Furious with Harold about his row with Andrew. Harold threatens police over stolen cigarette case.

Something odd about his relations with Harold. Didn't drive away after party.

Left *A see-saw pattern can be discerned in Thackeray's* Vanity Fair. *The two heroines, Amelia and Becky, are opposites, both in character (Amelia has heart and no brain – Becky has brain and no heart) and in the states of their fortune, or happiness, as the novel proceeds. As Becky's fortune rises, Amelia's falls, and vice versa. It is also possible to detect a rhythm in* Vanity Fair *which derives from its having been pulsed out in 20 monthly numbers. Many of Thackeray's best effects are reserved for the ends of numbers. Number 9, in which the action is at Waterloo, ended: "Darkness came down on the field and city: and Amelia was praying for George, who was lying on his face, dead, with a bullet through his heart."*

Digression and elaboration

characters feel remorse and guilt); but he must also be bad (so that everyone may have a plausible motive for wanting him dead). If secondary murders take place, their victims must be more innocent than the first one.

The murderer He is the rebel who claims to be omnipotent, but his rebellion must be concealed. When he is revealed, we must be surprised, but also satisfied that his guilt is compatible with all that we have been told about him.

The suspects They begin as innocents, but their purity must be peeled away, so that all have some degree of guilt: the wish or intention to murder; a desire to conceal their own crimes or vices; or pride causing them to hinder the detectives or confuse the clues.

The detective He is the avenging angel, who exorcizes guilt and restores innocence. If a professional policeman, he represents society's ethics officially; and if an amateur (Sherlock Holmes, Father Brown), he must be obsessively detached from the world of the suspects.

The story is laid out along clearly designed lines (see illustration). It opens with false innocence, the peaceful state before the murder occurs. The murder itself is the revelation of the presence of guilt, when all the characters become suspect through false clues, and secondary murders may take place. Next there is the solution, when real guilt is located, followed by the catharsis of the arrest of the true murderer. Finally, true innocence is restored, in the peaceful state after the arrest.

So far discussion has concentrated on the linearity of narrative, its forward movement. A distinctive characteristic of the novel, however, is its addiction to what Henry James called "solidity of specification". Fiction, that is, always gives the reader a surplus or bonus of concrete

descriptive matter. We are often informed, for example, what a character wears, how a room is furnished, what the weather is doing – although these facts may have no direct, or even indirect, bearing on the action. So, as a novel progresses, it takes time off to digress. Of the three standard components of narrative – scene, dialogue and description – the last is frequently arresting or retarding in effect.

The novelist, as he moves his story onward, is constantly prone to hold things up, for the communication of extraneous detail. Laurence Sterne once calculated that he could never finish his autobiographical novel, *Tristram Shandy*, since it took him a year of his own time to narrate in full detail a day of his hero's life.

Symbolic description

Sterne's dilemma is comically exaggerated. But it does partly explain why the novel is such a physically long form; why it should so often produce what Henry James (who laboured for economy in narrative) called "loose baggy monsters". Contingency and irrelevancy weigh down – may even bog down – narrative movement. But digression is often motivated or functional in complex ways. Consider the following apparently (though only apparently) digressive description of Ian Fleming's arch-criminal, Ernst Blofeld, from the spy-thriller *Thunderball*:

Blofeld's own eyes were deep black pools surrounded – totally surrounded, as Mussolini's were – by very clear whites. The doll-like effect of this unusual symmetry was enhanced by long silken black eyelashes that should have belonged to a woman. The gaze of these soft doll's eyes was totally relaxed and rarely held any expression stronger than a mild curiosity in the object of their focus.

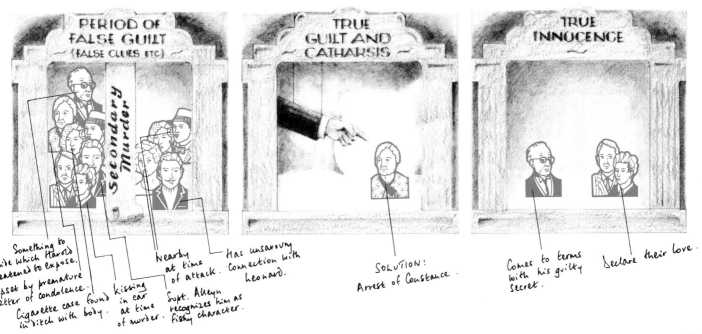

They conveyed a restful certitude in their owner and in their analysis of what they observed. To the innocent, they exuded confidence, a wonderful confidence in which the observed one could rest and relax knowing that he was in comfortable, reliable hands. But they stripped the guilty or the false and made him feel transparent – as transparent as a fishbowl through whose sides Blofeld examined, with only the most casual curiosity, the few solid fish, the grains of truth, suspended in a void of deceit or attempted obscurity. Blofeld's gaze was a microscope, the window on the world of a superbly clear brain, with a focus that had been sharpened by thirty years of danger and of keeping just one step ahead of it, and of an inner self-assurance built up on a lifetime of success in whatever he had attempted.

The skin beneath the eyes that now slowly, mildly, surveyed his colleagues was unpouched. There was no sign of debauchery, illness, or old age on the large, white, bland face under the square, wiry black crew-cut. The jawline, going to the appropriate middle-aged fat of authority, showed decision and independence. Only the mouth, under a heavy, squat nose, marred what might have been the face of a philosopher or a scientist. Proud and thin, like a badly healed wound, the compressed, dark lips, capable only of false, ugly smiles, suggested contempt, tyranny, and cruelty. But to an almost Shakespearian degree, nothing about Blofeld was small.

Blofeld's body weighed about twenty stone. It had once been all muscle – he had been an amateur weightlifter in his youth – but in the past ten years it had softened and he had a vast belly that he concealed behind roomy trousers and well-cut double-breasted suits, tailored, that evening, out of beige doeskin. Blofeld's hands and feet were long and pointed. They were quick-moving when they wanted to be, but normally, as now, they were still and reposed. For the rest, he didn't smoke or drink and he had never been known to sleep with a member of either sex. He didn't even eat very much. So far as vices or physical weaknesses were concerned, Blofeld had always been an enigma to everyone who had known him.

Although Fleming's narrative intentions may strike the reader as fairly low-level here, the functions being performed in the passage are both diverse and intricate. Looking closely, we can see that Fleming is quite artfully setting up a series of oppositions and contradictions in the presentation of Blofeld all of which define him as monstrous – that is to say compounded of unnaturally mixed, or violently incompatible qualities. Consider the following list of cleverly contrived oppositions:

(eyes) "black pools"	"very clear whites"
(eyelashes) "silken . . . doll-like . . . should have belonged to a woman	"An amateur weightlifter in his youth . . . heavy squat nose . . . wiry black crew cut"
most dangerous criminal in the world	"the face of a philosopher or scientist"
"vast belly . . . twenty stone"	"he didn't even eat very much"
(boundless, selfish appetites) "contempt, tyranny, and cruelty"	(asceticism) "he didn't smoke or drink"
(potency) power over others, decision and independence	(impotency) "never been known to sleep with . . . either sex"

The sinister, unnatural and contradictory pairing of qualities which makes up Blofeld's character contrasts with the natural and harmoniously matched set which makes up James Bond (strong, manly, adult, sexually aggressive and "British" in contrast to his opponent's stateless, European origins). In this way the struggle between Bond and Blofeld is turned into an encounter between natural and unnatural.

Superficially neutral description in fiction is often charged with an over-arching symbolism connecting or encapsulating large stretches of narrative. The blasted tree in Charlotte Brontë's *Jane Eyre*, for example, anticipates the mutilation of the hero at the end of the novel. The description of the weather in L. P. Hartley's *The Go-Between* is not just "solidity of specification". The gathering of the heat wave, and the storm with which it breaks, is synchronized with the disclosure and catastrophic consequences of the secret love affair in which the boy Eustace acts as messenger. Dickens is particularly rich in symbolic description – the fog in *Bleak House*, the prison in *Little Dorrit*, the sea in *Dombey and Son*, the river in *Our Mutual Friend*, all have important functions additional to their role as settings.

Character

It was conventional in mid-Victorian fiction to divide novels into two large categories: novels of plot and novels of character. In general the distinction still holds; it may, of course, be elaborated in some such way as "novels primarily concerned with technique, and novels primarily concerned with psychological analysis". Of the two, character is usually taken to be fiction's nuclear element. Thus even a writer as concerned with form and organization as Virginia Woolf admits (in the essay "Mr Bennett and Mrs Brown"): "I believe . . . that all novelists deal with character . . . I believe that all novels begin with an old lady in the corner opposite . . . . We (must be) determined never, never to desert Mrs Brown."

The great nineteenth-century realists (Tolstoy, Balzac, George Eliot) perfected the novel in which characters were autonomous, in which "they came to life" to inhabit a "world" created by the novelist. Trollope, perhaps the most famous Victorian exponent of the novel of character, positively rhapsodizes in his *Autobiography* about the primacy of the living character over the merely mechanical business of plotting:

I have never troubled myself much about the construction of plots, and am not now insisting specially on thoroughness in a branch of work in which I myself have not been very thorough. I am not sure that the construction of a perfected plot has been at any period within my power. But the novelist has other aims than the elucidation of his plot. He desires to make his readers so intimately acquainted with his characters that the creations of his brain should be to them speaking, moving, living, human creatures. This he can never do unless he knows those fictitious personages himself, and he can never know them well unless he can live with them in the full reality of established intimacy. They must be with him as he lies down to sleep, and as he wakes from his dreams. He must learn to hate them and to love them. He must argue with them, quarrel with them, forgive them, and even submit to them. He must know of them whether they be cold-blooded or passionate, whether true or false, and how far true, and how far false. The depth and the breadth, and the narrowness and the shallowness of each should be clear to him. And as, here in our outer world, we know that men and women change – become worse or better as temptation or conscience may guide them – so should these creations of his change, and every change should be noted by him. On the last day of each month recorded, every person in his novel should be a month older than on the first. If the would-be novelist have aptitudes that way, all this will come to him without much struggling – but if it do not come, I think he can only make novels of wood.

It is so that I have lived with my characters, and thence has come whatever success I have attained. There is a gallery of them, and of all in that gallery I may say that I know the tone of the voice, and the colour of the hair, every flame of the eye, and the very clothes they wear.

The creation of fully "rounded characters", as E. M. Forster called them, is no longer fashionable in the advanced reaches of fiction which, in his day, Trollope occupied. In retrospect we can now see that Henry James led a very successful campaign against Trollope's "baggy" kind of fiction, with its "characters" and "worlds",

A flat, a curved and a fully rounded E. M. Forster. Forster's terms "flat" and "round", with reference to fictional characters, have become standard usage for critics and reviewers.

setting up in its place a more "dramatic" ideal. Nevertheless, innumerable twentieth-century novels, and of course soap operas, romances and serials, carry on the tradition of real characters who live in the reader's mind.

In his *Aspects of the Novel*, E. M. Forster distinguished round characters from flat characters.

Flat characters were called "humours" in the seventeenth century, and are sometimes called types, and sometimes caricatures. In their purest form, they are constructed round a single idea or quality: when there is more than one factor in them, we get the beginning of the curve towards the round. The really flat character can be expressed in one sentence such as "I never will desert Mr Micawber". There is Mrs Micawber – she says she won't desert Mr Micawber; she doesn't, and there she is.

Many heroes and heroines in less than good thrillers and romances are completely flat, as are minor characters in the works of many literary writers.

However, novels which contain only flat or moderately curved characters are by no means necessarily bad novels. Many of Henry James's characters are less than round, because they were created to display a point of view. Dickens created very few round characters – some critics would say he failed to create any – yet his novels succeed; they are full of life. This is because a novelist can use his ingenuity and the devices available to him – style and plot – to make, in Forster's terms, a flat character vibrate.

Many successful modern novelists create moderately curved characters who vibrate a great deal. They are not round and do not become someone the reader feels he knows well; he knows a lot about them, but not everything, and he is carried along by their oscillations. Many readers would feel this to be so of Humbert Humbert in Vladimir Nabokov's *Lolita*, Holden Caulfield in J. D. Salinger's *The Catcher in the Rye*, and Herzog in Saul Bellow's novel of that name. If these characters are not completely round, it may be that part of the author's intention is to create an enigma, to puzzle and stimulate the reader.

Plot

Another digressive aspect of narrative which enriches as it retards is the elaboration and underpinning of story which we customarily describe as plot. The distinction between story and plot is neatly expounded by E. M. Forster in *Aspects of the Novel*:

> Let us define a plot. We have defined a story as a narrative of events arranged in their time sequence. A plot is also a narrative of events, the emphasis falling on causality. "The king died, and then the queen died," is a story. "The king died, and then the queen died of grief," is a plot. The time-sequence is preserved, but the sense of causality overshadows it.

It is clear even from Forster's telegraphic example that plots will require more filling in and a slower pace of narration than mere story or historical chronicle. And the more plotted a novel is, the more digression there will be from the simple linearities of narrative.

According to one epigrammatic account, "the history of fiction is simply the decay of plot". The writer is alluding to the increasing "inconsequentiality" of modern and post-modern fiction. In a traditional novel detail tends always to be motivated. If an object, character or descriptive item is introduced, seemingly accidentally, the reader senses that it will be reserved for a later narrative purpose; nothing, in the well made novel, is redundant. Plotting involves the tying up of all loose ends. Thus, for Coleridge, the three best plotted works in literature were *Oedipus Rex*, *The Alchemist* and Henry Fielding's *Tom Jones* – primarily because of the exhaustive way in which everything is finally accounted for – no threads are left hanging. Detective fiction, in the twentieth century, remains the best plotted of genres in this sense.

In the modern "literary" novel the reader often has no secure sense that everything will fall into place. In, for example, Franz Kafka's *The Trial*, details are left hanging, episodes are unmotivated and indeed the whole central business of the trial (what is the offence?) is left unexplained.

Post-modernist novelists like Thomas Pynchon have pushed experimentation with plot in another direction. *Gravity's Rainbow* is thus fantastically profuse in its multiple, spiralling plots. The novel offers us an extraordinary superfluity of links and causal connections. (It has been noted that Pynchon's narrative procedure in this overplotting is akin to the condition of paranoia, where every perceived fact is frantically tied into a "plot" or "conspiracy" against the deranged perceiver – nothing, for the paranoid mind, is accidental or neutral.) Some idea of Pynchon's lavish games with plot can be had from this description of *Gravity's Rainbow* by the American critic Richard Poirier:

> It is impossible to summarize a book of some 400,000 words in which every item enriches every other and in which the persistent paranoia of all the important characters invests any chance detail with the power of an omen, a clue, to which, momentarily, all other details might adhere. The novel clarifies itself only to create further mysteries, as one such pattern modifies or displaces another. This is a cumulative process with no predictable direction so that any summary is pretty much the produce of whatever creative paranoia the book induces in a reader. To complicate matters further, characters are not introduced as they customarily are in fiction, with some brief account of identity and function. Instead, any one of the chapters – which are separated not by numbers but by little squares apparently meant to simulate the sprocket holes in a film – suddenly immerses us in a scene, a mass of persons and furnishings, much as if it were flashed before us on a screen.
>
> In *Gravity's Rainbow* there are some 400 characters all bearing Pynchonesque names (Old Bloody Chiclitz is back, by the way, from *V.* and *The Crying of Lot 49*), along with a fair number of people who, if you bother, can be found in reference books (e.g., such pioneers in organic chemistry as Kekule, von Liebig, and Clerk Maxwell). There are scores of submerged references, including one to "The Kenosha Kid." I guess this is Orson Welles, born in Kenosha, Wisconsin. A most apt allusion, if one thinks of the hero of *Citizen Kane* and of how his last word, "Rosebud," is taken as some clue to the lavish assemblage of his wealth and power, when it is instead the name of a little sled, at the end consigned to junk and fire, that he loved as a boy. Any reference or detail in the book can redeem itself in this way. But no one of them should ever be regarded as a central clue, and the reader need not fret unduly at what he might miss.

The proposition that it is the reader (out of his "creative paranoia") who makes the plot, rather than the author making the plot for the reader to discover, takes the post-modern novel one step further from straightforward "plotless" story telling or the reporting of historical events.

Playing with time

A number of modern novels have accepted Proust's contention that "a work of art is the only means of regaining lost time" and set themselves to capture a full notation of time's passing. In so doing they have slowed down the tempo of narration to the point where a full length novel – traditionally capable of encompassing a whole "life" – may contain nothing more than the events of a single day, as in Virginia Woolf's *Mrs Dalloway* and James Joyce's *Ulysses*. The "stream of consciousness" or "roman fleuve" techniques which such time-conscious novelists typically adopt attempts to create *immediacy* of effect in the face of fiction's conventional historicity. More traditional fiction than Virginia Woolf's simply lives with the contradiction that logically, since the events recorded are past, there can be no legitimate suspense or ignorance. Take this opening from a Mickey Spillane novel:

> The guy was dead as hell. He lay on the floor in his pyjamas with his brains scattered all over the rug and my gun was in his hand. I kept rubbing my face to wipe out the fuzz that clouded my mind, but the cops wouldn't let me. One would pull my hand away and shout a question at me that made my head ache even worse and another would slap me with a wet rag until I felt like I had been split wide open.
>
>   I said, "Goddamn it, stop!"
>
>   Then one of them laughed and shoved me back on the bed.
>
>   I couldn't think, I couldn't remember. I was wound up like a spring and ready to bust. All I could see was the dead guy in the middle of the room and my gun. My gun!

In spite of its historic past tense, this narration has the urgent force of something immediately experienced: we feel that the hero-narrator is living the events, rather than recalling and recording them in tranquil retrospect. Yet that he should be undergoing this adventure while writing about it is clearly nonsensical.

The author and the reader

Above *The author (A), reader (R), work (W) triangle.*
Below *Two explosive pages from Hubert Selby's* Last Exit to Brooklyn.

An early way around this contradiction (first exploited by Samuel Richardson) was the autobiographical narrative, written as a diary or letters, supposedly as the events occurred. This certainly achieved immediacy; but it sacrificed organizing control in what Henry James memorably calls "the terrible fluidity of self revelation". Contemporary novelists, such as Hubert Selby in *Last Exit to Brooklyn*, have made a virtue of "terrible fluidity" of another kind, deliberately flouting the gradations and punctuations of typography and syntax. The effect is to convert a linear narrative into something explosively instantaneous. In another context the novelist Elizabeth Bowen once observed that "the good story is a succession of effective nows". Selby contrives to make a family argument in a Brooklyn tenement into one, continuous, nerve-shattering *now* (see bottom left).

It can be useful to think of the author and reader of a novel as participants in a three-cornered relationship (see illustration), the third member of which is the novel, or work, itself. The triangular relationship can work in several different ways, each of which can be seen as a distinctive style, or mode, of fiction.

The expressive approach

Fiction, like all post-Renaissance literature, originates with the author, A. In some forms of literary utterance the author is indifferent, or substantially indifferent, to the lines A-R and A-W. That is to say, he does not particularly concern himself with his relationship to his audience (or reader), nor is he concerned to create an autonomous "work of art". Where this emphasis predominates the resulting literature can be called "expressive"; at its extreme it may be little more than a *cri de coeur*, a complete subjective outpouring. In fact, because of their length, novels are rarely purely, or even predominantly, expressive; it is hard to sustain a *cri de coeur* over 100,000 words nor would such a work necessarily be interesting reading; as Mark Twain complained, the novel is a confession to everything by a man who has never done anything. Nonetheless the subjective element can be found, if not necessarily on the surface. Following the critic Edmund Wilson's lead new light has been thrown on the intense ambivalences of Dickens's fiction; for example, by quasi-Freudian connections with the novelist's traumatic childhood experiences.

The rhetorical approach

Fiction has traditionally been thought of as a literary form in which strong relationships are set up between author and reader. It is "rhetorical", meaning that the author consciously seeks, by intruding his own personality, to persuade the reader to consider his story seriously and in some

where the smaller ones climbed up the sliding pond, knocking off the even younger kids, stamping on the hands of those who tried to climb the ladder, yanking another one off, kicking another in the face; then they made the rounds of the seesaws, flipping kids off, banging one in the face with the seesaw, the younger kids lying on the ground crying until a few parents, sitting in the sun, looked over and yelled, then the kids ran away to another part of the playground; and some of the bigger kids took a basketball away from the kids on the court and when the owner of the ball started crying for his ball they finally hurled it at him smashing his nose and making it bleed and one of his friends yelled at the fleeing kids calling them black bastards and they came back and told him he was blacker an shit and the other kids said they had black bedbugs and the other kid said his mother fucks for spicks and the kid pulled out a nailfile and slashed the other kid across the cheek and then ran, his friends running with him; and in the far corner of the playground a small group of kids huddled quietly, keeping to themselves, ignoring the fighting and screaming, their arms of comradeship around each others shoulders, laughing and smoking marijuana.

* * * * * *

HURRYUP AND DRESS THE KID. I WANNA TAKE JOEY FOR A HAIRCUT. WHATAYA MEAN HAIRCUT? SHAKING HER HAND IN HIS FACE. WHATS THE MATTA HE GOTTA TAKE A HAIRCUT? SOMETHING WRONG WITH HIS HAIR, EH? WHATZA MATTA YOU WANNA CUT IT OFF? ITS TOO LONG, THATS WHATZA MATTA. LOOK, HES GOT CURLS LIKEA GURL, PULLING JOEY BY HIS HAIR, ALMOST LIFTING HIM OFF HIS FEET, THE KID YELLING AND KICKING AT

278

VINNIE. ITS TOO LONG, THATS WHATZA MATTA. MARY GRABBED A HANDFUL OF HAIR AND SAID WHATZA MATTA WITH THE CURLS? YOU DONT LIKE CURLS SO THE KID GOTTA TAKE A HAIRCUT? NO, I DONT LIKE ALL THOSE CURLS, VIOLENTLY SHAKING THE HAND HOLDING JOEYS HAIR. I DONT WANIM LOOKIN LIKE NO GURL. HES GONNA TAKE A HAIRCUT. YURAZ HES GONNA TAKE A HAIRCUT. I LIKE HIS HAIR LONG AND CURLY AND ITS GONNA STAY LIKE DAT, PULLING SO HARD ON JOEYS HAIR SHE LIFTED HIM FROM THE FLOOR AND HE SCREECHED AND SCRATCHED HER HAND SO HARD SHE OPENED IT AND HE TURNED AND KICKED HIS FATHER AND SCRATCHED HIS HAND AND VINNIE LET GO OF HIS HAIR AND SLAPPED HIM ON THE BACK OF HIS HEAD AND MARY KICKED HIS ASS AND THEY YELLED AT HIM, BUT JOEY DIDNT MIND, HE JUST KEPT RUNNING AND THEY TURNED BACK TO EACH OTHER. VINNIE YELLED AGAIN TA GET THE KID DRESSED SO HE COULD TAKEIM FOR A HAIRCUT AND MARY SAID HE DONT NEED ONE. MEEEEEE, WHAT A FUCKIN JERK. THE KIDS HAIRS DOWN TA HISZASS AND SHE SAYS HE DONT NEED NO HAIRCUT. YEAH. I SAY. I SAY. IT LOOKS NICE. I LIKE IT. HE AINT SUPPOSEDTA LOOK LIKE A GURL. WHO SAYS, EH? WHO SEZ. AND ANYWAY HE DONT LOOK LIKE NO GURL. HE LOOKS CUTE. VINNIE SLAPPED HIS HEAD AND GROANED. MEEEEEE, HE LOOKS CUTE. WHAT KINDDA CUTE WITH ALL DOZE CURLS. WHATSAMATTA WITH CURLS, EH? WHATSAMATTA? DIDNT YA BRODDA AUGIES KID HAVE CURLS AND DIDNT ROSIE

279

instances to believe it as truth. Direct contact between author and reader is particularly prominent – almost a convention – in the Victorian novel. According to Thackeray, the novel was a "sort of confidential talk" between the novelist and his public; Charlotte Brontë could address her reader as she might a close friend – "reader, I married him" the narrator tells us at the end of *Jane Eyre*. George Eliot is somewhat less intimate in her authorial manner, but no less presumes on a sense of community at the end of *Middlemarch*: "the growing good of the world is partly dependent on unhistoric acts; and that things are not so ill with you and me as they might have been, is half owing to the number who lived faithfully a hidden life, and rest in unvisited tombs." Eliot clearly has a strong image of the "you" as she writes, and anticipates agreement with her concluding *sententia*.

In the nineteenth-century novel there is a whole apparatus devoted to cementing the bond between writer and reader: prefaces, envois, asides, footnotes. Novelists were careful to cultivate the sense of fellowship which their public felt – in Dickens's case by public readings and the setting up of journals with a strong communal flavour, such as *Household Words*, which implied that Charles Dickens was a member of the 50,000 or so families that purchased his periodical weekly.

Towards the end of the nineteenth century the bond between author and reading public (except in some quasi-literary forms like journalism) had weakened and even broken altogether. It is often asserted that self-respecting twentieth-century fiction, far from cementing such relationships, must rigidly sever the A-R line. In his famous polemic, *The Dehumanization of Art*, the Spanish critic Ortega y Gasset declares that "modern art . . . will always have the masses against it. It is essentially unpopular; moreover it is antipopular". Although changes in the composition of the reading public make it impossible to re-create a cosy Victorian togetherness, there has been protest against the severely non-rhetorical nature of much modern fiction. In his influential *The Rhetoric of Fiction* (1961), the American critic Wayne C. Booth counter-attacks with the assertion that it is in the nature of the novel as a form to base itself on the act of communication, that it is inherently rhetorical.

The objective approach

Booth writes in the aggrieved tone of a man who knows that his views are unfashionable. The massive influence of Henry James has emphasized the importance of the twentieth-century novelist's responsibility to his work rather than to his reader. For James, writing a novel did not primarily involve setting up a relationship with an individual or generalized reader – and certainly not reaching out to a loyal reading public. What

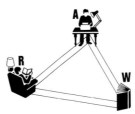

The expressive approach: the author is indifferent to the lines AR and AW.

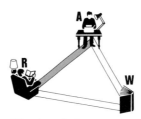

The rhetorical approach: the line AR is most important.

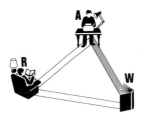

The objective approach: the line AW is most important.

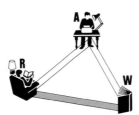

Reader participation: the aim is to make the line WR the most important.

mattered were the decisions the writer made about how actually to write his novel, and the skill with which the project was executed. In James's view the novelist's prime duty – indeed his only duty – is to his work; and it is in the faithful fulfilment of this duty that he achieves his full artistic stature:

> There can be for (the novelist) only one logic for these things; there can be for him only one truth and one direction – the quarter in which his subject most completely expresses itself. The careful ascertainment of how it shall do so, and the art of guiding it with consequent authority – since this sense of "authority" is for the master-builder the treasure of treasures, or at least the joy of joys – renews in the modern alchemist something like the old dream of the secret of life.

Like God, the successful novelist looks on his perfectly executed work and finds it good. And like God, the author is invisible.

The objective approach advocated by James relishes irony, ambiguity and subtlety of narrative design. For the general reader, Booth warns, the result may be "fog" and a specious authority accorded to the "deep readings" of the critics who alone can penetrate the resultingly "difficult" art. A cynic might object, however, that Booth would take us forward into the nineteenth century. And his robust traditionalism has been under pressure from another quarter. The post-war "new novel" (primarily associated with France) has joined forces with the between-the-wars post-Jamesian school to insist on the autonomy of the work and the irrelevance of the reader's demands for the truly creative author. As Alain Robbe-Grillet, main propagandist for the "new novel", declares, "art . . . expresses nothing but itself. It creates its own equilibrium itself, and its own meaning for itself. It stands by itself like the zebra – or else it falls".

Reader participation

These three approaches – expressive, rhetorical and objective – all have one thing in common; they assume the author at the apex of the triangle, originating "meaning". He is active and the reader, if not entirely passive, has only a limited role: interpretation, appreciation, discovery. Some modern critics, however, have demanded an independence for themselves and for the reader they represent; they have sought emancipation from the tyranny of the author's authority. The attitude underlying this liberation is less religious than radically political; it claims autonomy and self-determination for the reader. This is how Roland Barthes conceives the new dominant relationship (W-R on the triangle):

> The goal of literary work (of literature as

THE AUTHOR AND THE READER

work) is to make the reader no longer a consumer, but a producer of the text. Our literature is characterized by the pitiless divorce which the literary institution maintains between the producer of the text and its user, between the owner and its customer, between its author and its reader. The reader is thereby plunged into a kind of idleness . . . instead of functioning himself, instead of gaining access to the magic of the signifier, to the pleasure of writing, he is left with no more than the poor freedom either to accept or reject the text: reading is nothing more than a referendum.

In the famous book-length analysis of a novel from which this declaration comes, *S/Z* – the novel is Balzac's *Sarrasine* – Barthes assumes that he is writing the novel (i.e. creating it) in the act of reading it. And Barthes' practice here is in line with modern experiments (notably by William Burroughs and B. S. Johnson) in cut-up novels which sanction the reader to assemble the unbound, loose-leaf novel as he wants.

Genre and "formula" novels

The preceding triangle is complicated in practice by the fact that very few novelists in any sense "invent" the tools of their trade. Such invention may be an ideal of the supremely artistic writer: for example, Robbe-Grillet asserts that "A book creates its own rules for itself alone". However, the observable fact is that all but a few writers inherit or borrow most of their techniques and methods.

This debt to the accumulated work of others is most evident in genre or "category" fiction – science fiction, detective novels, women's romances, male action and war novels, and so on. These works tend to be formulaic, rule-governed, and often play variations on stock themes (alien invasion, locked-room mysteries, nurse-doctor love affairs to mention three). Frequently the style of genre fiction is hand-me-down and routinized; frequently, too, it adopts a no-nonsense manner which is essentially – anti-style. Thus, for example, Alistair Maclean begins *Ice Station Zebra* with brisk informality: "Commander James D. Swanson of the United States Navy was short, plump and crowding forty." The sense given is of a writer too busy to bother with the niceties of narrative exposition.

B. S. Johnson's The Unfortunates, *a cut up novel: the reader can assemble the book in any order he chooses.*

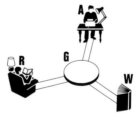

In much genre writing the margin of personal creativity is substantially diminished; the bulk of the story is supplied by an impersonal narrative machinery in which the writer is a kind of joint-stock holder. The novelist makes fewer decisions of his own. With "G" standing for genre, the ARW triangle can be modified. The genre acts as a central switchboard through which author-reader, author-work, and reader-work contact is achieved.

It is to be hoped that the reader has learned from, or at least, been stimulated by, some of the ideas above. However, every reader should be his own critic, should read what he likes and think what he likes about his reading. If the critics and academics have nothing to offer him, then that is a cause for their concern, not his.

THE NOVELIST AT WORK

When Anthony Trollope made the long sea voyage from Marseilles to Perth, the continuously stormy weather he encountered resulted in severe bouts of sea-sickness, but these did not prevent him from sticking to his long-established rule of writing for three hours each day. "I deemed it expedient," he remarked with Victorian severity, "to bind myself to certain self-imposed laws. It was also my practice to allow myself no mercy." On his sea voyage he left his writing desk more than once to be sick, but returned each time and continued grimly until the day's quota was completed.

Trollope is the outstanding example of the writer who succeeds in combining his literary activities with another job (he worked for the Post Office) and harmonizing both with his private life. An extreme example of a writer whose working life is completely and sharply differentiated from his daily existence is Georges Simenon, one of the most prolific producers of fiction ever. Although until recently writing has been Simenon's only occupation for a long time, his routine when engaged on a serious novel involved a complete break with the rhythm of his everyday life. He completed a novel in about eleven days of continuous writing, pausing only for food and sleep, but not leaving the room in which he wrote. He had a medical check-up before and after beginning his work, took no telephone calls and spoke to no one.

The life-styles of novelists, past and present, differ so widely that no generalization can be made. However, from the beginnings of the novel to our own day, surprisingly few novelists have been professionals in the sense of devoting their working life exclusively to the writing of fiction. Fielding was a busy magistrate, Richardson a printer, and Defoe a political and religious pamphleteer. In the nineteenth century Charles Dickens and George Eliot were both editors as well as writers; Trollope, as we have seen, was a Post Office functionary; Edgar Allan Poe was a journalist; and Herman Melville had a variety of jobs, including sailor, farmer and customs officer.

Even today a great many novelists combine some other more steadily lucrative employment, such as academic work, film and television writing, publishing or journalism, with their novel writing. Some novelists, of whom Hemingway is the most celebrated representative, have felt that

Aldous Huxley, who usually wrote only in the mornings.

Mary McCarthy, who often writes throughout the day and refuses lunch dates.

academic activity is dangerously narrowing for a novelist and have preferred a physically more active life; but, as Vladimir Nabokov pointed out, academic work offers the novelist the twin advantages of considerable leisure time and good library facilities, although the latter may be a mixed blessing to the creative writer.

Routine

In their habits of work most novelists resemble Trollope rather than Simenon, in that a steady daily routine rather than a frenzied but sporadic outpouring seems to be the normal pattern. Although few other writers have followed Trollope's self-imposed discipline of writing against the clock, most regard a regular daily output as essential. The early part of the day is the favoured time for work, although there have been notable exceptions, such as Dostoyevsky, who always wrote at night; and on one occasion, according to his own account, Henry Miller planned "the book of my life" in forty pages, which he wrote nonstop from midnight until dawn. Flaubert worked from midday to 4 a.m., during which period he smoked some 15 pipefuls of tobacco; while Anthony Burgess also finds the afternoon a good time for work because "the unconscious mind has a habit of asserting itself in the afternoon".

The most usual pattern is a routine of anything between three and seven hours of writing, starting early in the morning. Hemingway used to find it best to start work as soon after first light each day as possible and continue until noon, and while most novelists do not appear to be such early risers, they have usually tried to arrange matters so that a good part of their writing was completed by noon or early afternoon. Aldous Huxley's is a good example of the most usual routine, completing three or four hours of writing before noon. William Burroughs would rise at 9 in the morning, have breakfast at his hotel (he hated going out for it), and work until 2 or 2.30 in the afternoon. After a 10-minute break for a sandwich and a glass of milk, Burroughs worked on until 6 or 7 in the evening. Henry Miller too used to sit down to his typewriter straight after breakfast – "If I find I'm not able to write, I quit." Other novelists who followed the same pattern of work included: the great Russian novelist Leo Tolstoy; Mary McCarthy (who would refuse most lunch dates when working, because of the interruption to her routine); and the German Nobel Prize-winner Thomas Mann who wrote from 9 until 1 in the afternoon each day.

Getting started

A steady routine obviously depends on the ability to begin work without too much delay each day. Once again Trollope makes the point neatly when he says that the purpose of his rigid self-discipline was to ensure that he did three hours' *writing* each day, instead of sitting nibbling his pen. Not all novelists are as disciplined as Trollope, or as fortunate as Henry Miller who was usually able to start work right away; or Anthony Burgess, who has said that the only writing blocks he has are those he gets from the stationers. Many have devised their own sometimes highly idiosyncratic ways of getting the creative current flowing or, more literally, getting words on paper. As we have seen, reading through the previous day's output is a necessary prelude for a good many writers, but not always a sufficient one. James Jones, the author of several best-sellers including *From Here to Eternity* (1951) and *Some Came Running* (1957), said that although he awoke at 7 or 8 in the morning, he could not get to work until he had spent half an hour or so "fiddling around" smoking several cigarettes and drinking half a dozen cups of coffee. "Finally there's no excuse. I go to my typewriter."

Many writers find that particular physical objects, such as a certain variety of pencil, paper or ink or other articles less closely connected with the physical activity of writing are necessary to get them started, and have what in some cases appears to be an almost superstitious faith in these particular objects. The "daemon" which, according to Rudyard Kipling, guided his pen, abominated blue-black ink and insisted on the blackest possible India inks, as well as favouring specially made writing blocks of blue paper. Hemingway used to begin by writing, standing up, in pencil on onion-skin paper, shifting to the typewriter only when the work was going well and the writing came easily, as dialogue did to him – "Wearing down 7 pencils is a good day's work." Angus Wilson habitually uses school exercise books.

Even the best-regulated writers sometimes find it temporarily impossible to write. The most usual method of getting started again seems to be to read something for a while, as Aldous Huxley used to do. (His aunt, the Victorian novelist Mrs Humphrey Ward, re-read Diderot's *Rameau's Nephew* (1761) before starting work on a new novel, a practice followed by Somerset Maugham who prepared for a new novel by reading Voltaire's *Candide* (1759) which he felt acted as "a touchstone of lucidity, grace and wit at the back of my mind".)

"You don't know what it is," wrote Flaubert to George Sand, "to stay a whole day with your head in your hands trying to squeeze your unfortunate brain so as to find a word. . . . Ah! I certainly know the agonies of style." It was to avoid such agonies that Thornton Wilder took long walks before beginning work and Willa Cather "read a page of the Bible each day". The critic and publisher Malcolm Cowley mentions an agnostic friend who began his writing day by getting on his knees to pray. Among living writers, Truman Capote is perhaps the most ostentatious devotee of the irrational forces that partly govern the art of writing. His homage to such forces includes a refusal to write in a room where there are yellow roses (normally his favourite flower), or to have seven cigarette butts in the same ashtray or to join a flight in which three nuns are passengers. On the other hand there are some writers who follow Maupassant's dictum "Get black on white" literally, considering it their most important task simply to fill paper with words, regardless of quality. Frank O'Connor, best known as a short story writer, has said "I don't give a hoot what the writing's like," and puts down "any sort of rubbish" as long as it has some relation to his general outline. A similar attitude is taken by Nelson Algren, author of *A Walk on the Wild Side* (1956) and *The Man with the Golden Arm* (1949), who finds that "the only way I could finish a book and get a plot going was just to keep making it longer and longer until something happens". Whatever the means adopted to get started and to keep going, the professional writer is by definition one who has found his own particular way to overcome this genuine and formidable obstacle to writing.

Output

Of all the manifold ways in which novelists differ from one another, perhaps none is more immediately striking than the enormous difference in the mere quantity of their productions. This is obviously related to their routine of work and more generally to their life span, but there appear to be other more elusive considerations governing the extent of a novelist's work. Once again the admirable Trollope may serve as a kind of ideal norm. In his view three hours' work a day would produce as much as a man would wish to write; and at his rate of working he produced an average of 40 pages (or 10,000 words) a week.

In a writing career spanning over 40 years, Trollope produced 50 novels of more or less equal length (he always thought of a novel as consisting of so many words, wrote approximately 250 words to a page which he had counted as he went along, and prided himself on delivering as near the exact number of words he had contracted to produce as possible). We may set two twentieth-century novelists alongside the eminent Victorian to mark the extreme limits on either side. A writer who, with a single book written late in life, achieved international prominence was the Italian novelist Guiseppe de Lampedusa. He began work

Somerset Maugham consulting the Oxford English Dictionary. "I could not work without them", he said of the twenty volumes of the O.E.D.

on his only novel, *The Leopard*, when he was in his sixties, and it was published posthumously in 1958. It deals with his ancestral past and is clearly the result of long and patient brooding on his own life and on the history of the family estates in days only just gone by. In that sense *The Leopard*, although its actual writing evidently took only a year or two, is the work of a lifetime. At the other extreme is a writer who has already been cited as a special case. The creator of Maigret, Georges Simenon, has produced over 150 novels under his own name and no less than 350 under various pseudonyms, an output unlikely ever to be exceeded. While he usually took eleven days of feverishly concentrated writing to produce a complete novel, he once finished one in a virtually non-stop bout of twenty-four hours.

A fair way behind the phenomenal pace of Simenon but still prodigiously fast by any ordinary standards comes the creator of Perry Mason, Erle Stanley Gardner, who reputedly took four days to produce a complete novel.

In general, and perhaps predictably, commercially successful fiction in established genres, such as the detective or spy story and melodramatic romance or "disaster" fiction, seems to come more easily to its creators than the kinds of novels whose reading public is more limited. E. M. Forster was a member of this latter group. In a long life (he lived to be 90) Forster produced only six novels, the last of which to be published in his lifetime, *A Passage to India* (1924), came out while he had still over 50 years to live. His posthumous novel *Maurice* (1971), dealing with a homosexual theme, suggests that the barriers to writing (or at least publishing) may have been as much external as internal; but Forster in general represents, if rather exaggeratedly, the relatively limited output of the "serious" novelist, although prolific novelists such as Muriel Spark and Iris Murdoch should warn us against hasty generalization here as elsewhere.

We have already noted that a writer's output, in terms of his daily production, is not necessarily related to the amount of his published work. One reason for this is that a good deal of most novelists' writing consists of revision and re-writing; to say nothing of work abandoned after much time and effort has been spent on it, as happened with at least two projected novels by Norman Mailer and one by Anthony Burgess. We shall look more closely at the business of revision later on in examining novelists' methods, but we may pause briefly to note, through two examples, the place and importance of revision in determining a writer's output. Neither James Thurber nor Roald Dahl are known chiefly as novelists, preferring shorter forms of fiction. But Thurber once spent about two thousand hours whittling down a story of 240,000 words (well over the length of an average novel) to less than a tenth of its original length; while Roald Dahl took six hundred hours over five months licking into shape his celebrated short story "Mrs Bixby and the Colonel's Coat". On the other hand, Elliott Paul, author of *The Last Time I Saw Paris* (in U.K. *A Narrow Street*, 1942), hardly ever revised and could produce three novels in three weeks each (he once had a 60,000 word manuscript stolen and proceeded to rewrite the whole thing in a few weeks).

Most novelists are satisfied if they can produce half a dozen pages each day, and would probably echo in some measure what Dorothy Parker said about her own work: "I can't write five words but that I change seven." Among contemporary novelists who are not large-scale international best sellers, but who have been both "serious" and commercially successful, Vladimir Nabokov, Graham Greene, Anthony Burgess and Iris Murdoch are perhaps the most prolific, with an output of between 18 and 30 novels each. But individual variations are so wide that the idea of an average output, in terms of published work as opposed to daily production, is all but meaningless.

Where novelists work

Does it matter where a novelist sets about the task of writing? The question, like that of output, has two aspects to it, the immediate and the more general environment within which writing takes place. The general environment would include the country where the novelist works and whether he finds a rural or an urban atmosphere more stimulating, while his immediate surroundings would of course be the room or other area in which he sits down (or, like Hemingway and J. P. Donleavy, stands up) to write. Until fairly recent times most novelists have written in the country of their birth, although even here there are numerous exceptions, notably Henry James and Joseph Conrad. For American writers Europe has had a special fascination, especially in the early part of the twentieth century, when novelists such as Hemingway, F. Scott Fitzgerald and Henry Miller produced some of their finest work in Paris and elsewhere on the continent. Notable British exiles have included James Joyce, D. H. Lawrence and Somerset Maugham.

Part of the fascination of an alien atmosphere was perhaps accounted for by Henry Miller when he commented that Europe was a whole new and alien world to him and that his imagination was fired only by the alien, adding that hearing another language can sharpen your own for you. William Burroughs has remarked how, in the earlier stages of his writing career, he found in alien and often exotic places in Europe, South America and North Africa an "extra dimension of character and extremity" which stimulated him as a novelist. But another American writer, Mary McCarthy, has suggested that too long a stay in a place with a language different from that which the novelist uses could present him with difficulties in his writing. She has also said that working in Europe no longer seems to hold much advantage for the American novelist: "I don't feel any more this antithesis of Young America, Old Europe, I think that's really gone. For better or worse, I'm not sure. Maybe for worse." Whatever the reason, the post-war period has seen the return to their native continent of a good many American writers, among them Henry Miller, William Burroughs and Paul Bowles.

When we consider writers' environments in the narrower sense, there is a fairly high degree of uniformity in their preferences. Marcel Proust working away at the contents of his own consciousness in a cork-lined bedroom, and Balzac hiding from creditors in a secret room consuming 50,000 cups of coffee as he produced volume after volume of *The Human Comedy* (1820–1847), stand out as exceptions, as does, once more, Simenon locked away in his self-sufficient room. Most novelists seem, understandably enough, to prefer a quiet, well-lighted place reasonably rather than excessively private. Mary McCarthy speaks for many novelists when she expresses her preference for "a nice peaceful place with some good light", and Burroughs has also remarked that quiet writing conditions in which he can concentrate are more important to him than the exact locale, which in his case was some anonymous hotel room in Europe, America or elsewhere, cluttered with drawers and cupboards full of newspaper clippings.

Both Emile Zola and Rudyard Kipling worked at huge untidy desks covered with a variety of objects including books, papers, letters and momentoes. Marie Corelli, the prolific and best-selling romantic novelist of the late nineteenth and early twentieth century, had a sturdy and substantial gazebo built in the garden of her house in Stratford-on-Avon (it is still there today) to which she would climb each morning to write. Her fondness for looking out at her garden in the intervals of writing is in sharp contrast (appropriately enough) with Norman Mailer who likes a room with a view, preferably a long view, but specifically dislikes looking out on gardens, prefering a prospect of sea or ships, "or anything which has a vista to it".

Most novelists, like other people, prefer working in reasonably comfortable conditions. Some, like Saul Bellow, who are connected with the academic world, have university rooms provided for them. But occasionally we find a writer like Hemingway who seems to find discomfort a stimulus to writing. Henry Miller has expressly said this, and deliberately adopted an uncomfortable position for writing.

A novelist is of course perfectly justified in securing, if he can, whatever physical conditions help him personally to get on with his task. But after we have heard of cork-lined rooms, rooms

without yellow roses, gazebos and the like, it may occur to us that the really professional writer is the one who can work under any conditions. One of the most remarkable science fiction novels ever written, Hinko Gottlieb's *The Key to the Great Gate* (1947), was scrawled secretly in Serbo-Croat on scraps of toilet paper while the author was imprisoned in a German concentration camp, completed in that language in the intervals between his fighting as a Yugoslav partisan, and finally translated by the author into German once he had settled in the new state of Israel. James Jones stated that he found it easy to work anywhere. It is ironical that Jones lost a good deal of the money he made out of *From Here to Eternity* in an unsuccessful attempt to found a writers' colony where ideal writing conditions were to be provided for promising authors. Not one published novel emerged out of this venture.

How novelists work
While most novelists write in roughly the order which will appear in the published novel, this is by no means always the case. The two outstanding examples of novelists whose method of work has no relation to the finished order are Joyce Cary and Vladimir Nabokov. Cary never wrote to a pre-arranged plot, but worked each day on any part of a novel that appealed to his imagination. Similarly, Nabokov wrote his novels on index cards without regard to the narrative order. The cards were often rewritten and continually shuffled. When their final order had been decided, Nabokov would hand the whole stack to his wife who typed them in triplicate.

Some authors' methods vary from one novel to another. Thus, when Norman Mailer began writing *The Naked and the Dead* (1948) he had a file full of notes with a dossier on each of the principal characters, containing many details that never appeared in the finished book. He even had charts to show which principal characters had appeared in scenes with others. He wrote rapidly, working four days a week, two hours in the morning and two in the afternoon ("I usually needed a can of beer to prime me"), producing the first draft in seven months and the second in four. But with his novel *Barbary Shore* (1951) things were very different. The words came slowly, sentence by sentence, and at the end of a day he had no idea where the next day's work would come from. In spite of the regularity of routine of most novelists, these variations from book to book are far from uncommon.

One of the most unusual methods of approach is that adopted by William Burroughs. For his experimental novels, Burroughs used a method which he himself has described as "cut ups" in which scissors and paste are, by his own admission, as important as the typewriter. "Cut ups" consist of newspaper cuttings, quotations from books and other material, interspersed with Burroughs' own writing. He made a habit of keeping a journal in three columns when travelling, one column giving factual details of what happened on the trip, the next recording memories activated by these incidents and the last containing quotations from books read on the journey.

Burroughs' three-column journal curiously recalls a totally different, earlier and greater novelist, Charles Dickens. The conditions of serial publication in magazines largely shaped Dickens' writing, and he was never more than four or five instalments ahead of his readers; indeed, by mid-novel, he was usually only one instalment ahead. Dickens used three sorts of ink on the same page. The middle of the page was devoted to the actual text, while the right-hand margin contained memoranda relating to the story and the left-hand one notes on the general direction of the chapter. Entrances of characters were noted, and characters ticked off when they were disposed of. A dog, which Dickens had introduced into *Dombey and Son* (1848) and inadvertently forgotten, was put back at the proof stage.

William Faulkner working at his home in Oxford, Missouri.

The sources of fiction

Perhaps the most mysterious of all the aspects of the novelist's activity concerns the sources of his art. Where does the novelist get what are loosely called the "ideas" for his novels? Once again, there are almost as many answers as there are novelists, and once again the question itself has a direct and a more remote application. The former is fairly simple and relates to the immediate and conscious origin of a particular work. Thus William Faulkner's celebrated novel *The Sound and the Fury* (1929) began with a visual image of a little girl with muddy pants watching her grandmother's funeral through a window from a tree and giving a running commentary to her brothers on the ground below. By the time all the relationships and explanations surrounding the scene had been dealt with, Faulkner had a full length novel rather than the short story he had envisaged.

But not all novelists begin with a plot or even a scene. The first task for Henry James was to find the atmosphere of the novel, what James himself called "the note absolute". Françoise Sagan and Alberto Moravia are agreed that it is the act of writing which produces the "ideas" rather than the other way about. Many other novelists are also wary of too much planning which might inhibit creativity, and would agree with the attitude underlying E. M. Forster's famous question: "How do I know what I think until I see what I say?" Henry James is the great exception here, meticulously planning each scene of his novels before writing it out.

When we go beyond the question of the *conscious* origin of a given novel to its wider source in the artist's creative depths we are in very dark waters indeed. Writers as different as Kipling, Hawthorne, Bellow and Angus Wilson have borne witness to the importance of unconscious forces, or those of which the novelist is only partly conscious, in initiating and shaping his work. "The devil himself always seems to get into my inkstand," wrote Hawthorne, "and I can only exorcise him by pensful at a time"; while Rudyard Kipling asserted that when a writer's "daemon" was in charge, he should not try to think consciously, but only to "drift, wait and obey". We think of a novelist as sometimes dictating his work, but many novelists have felt that their work was being "dictated" *to* rather than *by* them. As William Faulkner said, "I listen to the voices".

While most novelists take their characters and incidents from real life, this is not invariably the case, and even the novelists who do adopt this practice do not simply give a direct transcription of actual incidents and characters (if only to avoid libel actions!) Mark Twain claimed that every well-drawn character he had encountered in fiction and biography was someone he had already met "on the river" during his years as a steamboat pilot. D. H. Lawrence did not scruple to put incidents and personalities from his personal experience into his novels only thinly disguised, thereby provoking those involved to publish their own versions in innumerable volumes of reminiscence. On the other hand, Norman Mailer finds that real people, if one knows them too well, simply interfere with the reality of the fictional world. "It's not a good idea to try to put your wife into a novel," he has said, "not your latest wife anyway."

Sometimes the "idea" for a novel can come partly as a formal challenge to the novelist's creative powers, as when James Joyce wrote *Ulysses* (1922) as a kind of modern "parallel" to Homer's epic (though this was of course only one of the creative impulses behind the novel); or when Agatha Christie thought of the self-contained episodes in *The Labours of Hercules* (1947) as parallels, centred round Hercule Poirot, to the tasks performed by the legendary Greek hero.

But after we have learned what there is to learn about a novelist's methods, routine and outlook, there is still a core of mystery about the art of fiction which does not yield up its secrets. "I think there is a natural mystique about a novel which is more important than craft," says Mailer; while Angus Wilson has called writing "a kind of magic". Most novelists admit that they do not know just how they produce their work. One of the simplest and most straightforward statements on the subject came from one of the best of living novelists, Saul Bellow. "Well, I don't know exactly how it's done," he said. "I let it alone a good deal".

Emile Zola

L'AURORE
Littéraire, Artistique, Sociale
J'Accuse…!
LETTRE AU PRÉSIDENT DE LA RÉPUBLIQUE
Par ÉMILE ZOLA

Zola's management of his professional life was always very businesslike, and he was highly prolific, publishing 25 novels and some 23 other books during a 31-year writing career. He found the process of writing unusually agonizing, however, and suffered greatly from the strains of creation. He claimed that at times the effort of struggling with a rebellious passage actually caused him to have an erection. Despite marked hypochondria he maintained a remarkably steady output throughout his life, and never started a novel which he did not complete.

ROUTINE Zola regularly spent nine or ten hours a day at his desk, but hours would often pass in which he would sit, chin in hand, staring out of the window trying to recapture scenes or characters and to force them on to the page. In order to overcome these "blocks" he attached great importance to punctiliously regular working methods, accuracy of detail, and rigid discipline. A motto inscribed in his study read: Nulla dies sine linea. While writing he always wore a loose peasant's smock, having a horror of tight-fitting clothes.

OUTPUT Between 1000 and 2500 words per day.
PLACE OF WORK At a huge desk, usually

Zola's novels reflect his intense political and social awareness, but he became actively involved in politics only once, when he interceded in the notorious Dreyfus affair. He was convinced, rightly, that Dreyfus was innocent of the spying charge which led to his exile, and he wrote an open letter to Felix Faure, the President of France, to that effect, beginning "J'accuse". This was published by the French newspapers on January 13, 1898 and made Zola extremely unpopular with the establishment.

Zola worked at a table littered with ornaments, books, paper and writing implements. Here a semblance of his workroom was recreated in a photographer's studio.

cluttered with books, letters, inkstands, mementoes, etc., in his study. From 1878, when he bought a large house at Médan near Paris, he worked there most of the year, and rented an apartment in Paris for the winter season.
METHODS Zola always began to think of a new novel in terms of a general theme, and then of a viable plot in which to develop that theme. His surviving worksheets show that planning the plot was a laborious process, full of false starts and sudden inspirational leaps. It took him four complete attempts before he was satisfied with the plot scheme for La joie de vivre (1884).

The next stage he called "documentation" – a systematic programme of fact-finding, not only elaborate background reading but often prolonged research on the ground. For Nana (1880) he spent several days at the Folies Bergère, and the fact-finding for La faute de l'abbé Mouret (1875) included long conversations with an unfrocked priest as well as Zola's first attendance at mass. He took immense pride in his detailed verification of facts, and insisted (rather illogically) that in his novels he "invented nothing".

The final stage, before beginning to write, involved returning to the plan, modifying it if his research required this, and then drawing up: (a) a synopsis of the plot, chapter by chapter, in considerable detail; and (b) a biographical and descriptive note on each character. This preliminary material often comprised as many as 1000 or 1200 sheets.
SOURCES The characters and settings of Zola's novels derive almost without exception from his own direct experience; either from his upbringing in Aix-en-Provence (the "Plassans" of his novels), or from his own intellectual and social life in Paris, or from the fact-finding research which he undertook for each new novel. The original idea for his novel series Les Rougon-Macquart was based on his admiration for Balzac and his search for an organizing theme comparable to, but sufficiently distinct from, that of La Comédie humaine; and its over-riding social-scientific aims were inspired by the anti-romantic, positivist philosopher H. A. Taine.

Anthony Trollope

Trollope shocked his contemporary readers by confessing in his Autobiography that, apart from the satisfaction of fame and self-esteem, his reason for writing was that it brought him financial reward. He also damaged his reputation by revealing the meticulous matter-of-fact approach which he took towards the writing of novels.

An engraving of Trollope which appeared in the Illustrated London News in December 1882.

ROUTINE *Early in his career as a writer Trollope, who had a full time job at the Post Office, set himself a rigid routine of work. He began the day very early by reading the previous day's output, and from 5.30 a.m. till breakfast time he set himself a target of 250 words every fifteen minutes. He looked at his watch to make sure that he kept to this schedule and kept a diary of his progress. He always delivered his manuscript to the publisher by the agreed date.*

OUTPUT *In a writing career that lasted some 35 years, Trollope produced 47 novels as well as several short stories and travel books and a volume of autobiography. He usually produced 40 written pages (or 10,000 words) a week, but occasionally as much as 112 pages. "This division of time allowed me to produce over 10 pages of an ordinary novel a day, and if kept up through ten months, would have given as its results three novels of three volumes in the year.*

PLACE OF WORK *Trollope's early novels were written in Ireland. After the Barsetshire novels made his name he settled down in Waltham Cross and later in London. But he wrote steadily during his many journeys overseas.*

METHODS *Trollope's writing methods were dictated by the rigid discipline which he imposed on himself as a writer. Inspiration, if and when it came, would be the result of this regular discipline, not its begetter.*

SOURCES *Trollope's most famous series, the six Barsetshire novels, dealing with a quiet cathedral town, was the result of a summer evening's stroll in the grounds of Salisbury Cathedral during his stint as a Post Office Inspector in the West Country. The later political novels may owe something to his experience as an unsuccessful parliamentary candidate. Trollope was an enthusiastic huntsman and clubman and this contact with the Victorian upper classes provided the basis for many of his novels.*

Leo Tolstoy

When Tolstoy was a young boy, his elder brother told him of a little green stick buried at a certain spot on the family estate which had engraved on it a secret formula for ushering in a new golden age. The whole of the great Russian's life and art may be described as a search for this momentous secret. His talent as a writer was always at the service of the general good as he saw it and when he had to choose between art and human welfare, art took second place. Perhaps it is not quite the paradox that appears at first sight that Tolstoy wrote what is often regarded as the world's greatest novel.

ROUTINE *Though he produced much short fiction and discursive writing in a long lifetime, Tolstoy wrote only three novels, the two greatest War and Peace (1863–69) and Anna Karenina (1873–77) belonging to the first two decades of his married life when the restless young sensualist had settled into the quiet domesticity of the family estate at Yasnaya Polyana. Here Tolstoy combined a regular period of writing each day with the active life of a country landowner, gradually sharing more and more the life of the peasants themselves. He worked at his novels for several hours each morning and was convinced that a regular routine was essential. He played patience between bouts of writing, and while at*

A page from the manuscript of War and Peace revealing that Tolstoy doodled as he wrote.

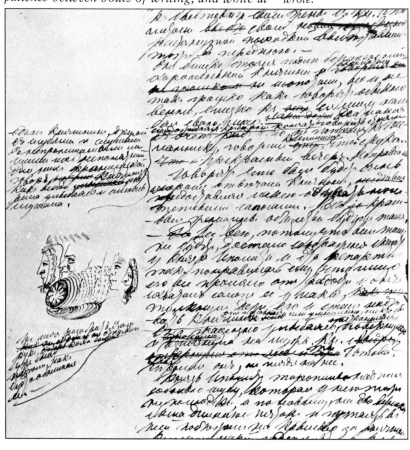

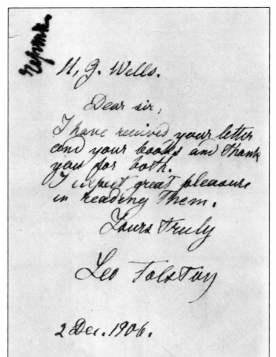

H. G. Wells.

Dear sir,

I have received your letter and your books and thank you for both.
I expect great pleasure in reading them.

Yours truly

Leo Tolstoy

2 Dec. 1906.

work on Resurrection, *he let a game of patience decide whether Katyvisha should marry Nekhlyndov.*

OUTPUT *In addition to his two masterpieces, Tolstoy produced a third novel* Resurrection *(1899) as well as several volumes of short fiction and much non-fiction. He lived to be 82 and his writing career spanned nearly 50 years. His creative works take up 45 volumes in Russian, while a further 45 are devoted to diaries and letters.*

PLACE OF WORK *Tolstoy produced his novels sitting at a large desk in the family mansion at Yasnaya Polyana.*

METHODS *He wrote fluently but also revised extensively.*

SOURCES *Tolstoy is one of the great masters of European realism, though this difficult term should be understood as far more than fidelity to the externals of the world. In addition to a sharp eye for revealing detail, Tolstoy had an intense interest in the workings of the human mind and in the complexities of human relationships. Both*

Above *Tolstoy in 1909, the year before his death.*
Above right *A letter in perfect English from Tolstoy to H. G. Wells. It marked the beginning of a friendly correspondence between the two writers.*
Right *Tolstoy at his desk in 1908.*

his great novels are concerned with family life and come close to his own experience, while War and Peace *draws not only on an immense amount of reading on the Napoleonic wars, but also on Tolstoy's service as an army officer. (While working on the novel he spent three days visiting the battlefield of Borodino, one result of which is the plan of the battlefield that forms the novel's frontispiece). The influence of Rousseau's views on the proper relation between man and nature was decisive in shaping some of his shorter fiction as well as his general philosophical outlook.*

Edgar Allan Poe

Edgar Allan Poe had an immense influence on American and European literature; he was one of the pioneers of science fiction, and in a handful of short stories he invented many of the principles which crime fiction writers have used ever since. After he was thrown out of West Point, Allan, his guardian, refused to help him. He lived in poverty in Baltimore from 1831 to 1835, and this set a precedent: poverty, drink, despair. He added to his distress by marrying the thirteen-year-old Virginia Clemm in 1837; she died ten years later, after a life mostly spent in suffering and sickness. She always gave Poe an acute sense of guilt, and made him feel doomed. By the time of her death his own health was ruined – at least partly as a result of excessive drinking.

ROUTINE *His way of working was not systematic (his health would not have stood this). He worked in wild fits and starts, with intervening periods of depression. His drinking was sporadic, and he does not seem to have composed when drunk (as few, a very few, writers have done).*

OUTPUT *Poe's collected works, comprising stories, poems and an immense amount of criticism, run to 18 volumes.*

PLACE OF WORK *Some of his writing was done in newspaper offices; early on he was editor of the important* Southern Literary Messenger, *and later owned the* Broadway Chronicle *in New York. He found some contentment in the little cottage at Fordham where his wife died.*

METHODS *Poe was a journalist, who had to work to deadlines. No drafts or worksheets of his exist, nor are they mentioned by any of his many biographers. It may be assumed that his planning was minimal, and that his method was essentially inspirational. He was an excitable man and probably wrote quickly and in a disordered way. It is thought that he was incapable of sustained creative effort, and this is why he produced no fiction of great length.*

SOURCES *Although he was original, he drew in the first instance on conventional rather than "personal" horror. If Poe was mad, a critic has said, then "his whole generation was mad with him". Initially he set out to fulfil a need. But the process thus set off forced him to delve into his own subconscious. This interpretation is supported by the fact that he hated coffins, graveyards and the rest of the paraphernalia he employed in his tales. He drew on every available literary source, and began as a writer by deliberately parodying other writers he admired and who were popular. The ingredient he added was the awareness that sensitivity conferred.*

Above The room where Poe worked at Fordham is preserved to this day. *Above left* Poe at work, as depicted by Carl S. Junge. Viewed from a distance, the border reveals the titles of Poe's major works of fiction. *Below left* Poe, painted in oils by Charles Hine in 1848.

Mervyn Peake

It was during his most productive decade, that of 1945–55, that the artist Mervyn Peake wrote his three novels, Titus Groan, Gormenghast and Titus Alone. A fourth book in the series was planned, and perhaps more would have followed had not Parkinson's Disease struck him, twelve years before his death.

ROUTINE Mervyn Peake wrote daily, but under no discipline of time or place. His "desk" could be his drawing-board balanced on the arms of a comfortable chair, or his knees drawn up in bed, or his lap during a train journey. His materials were whatever came to hand: publisher's dummies, exercise books or the backs of envelopes.

OUTPUT Between writing Gormenghast and Titus Alone, Peake produced Mr Pye. It was his only attempt to earn money by writing, and in this it failed. For income he relied upon his earnings from art school tutorials, from the sale of paintings, and from the illustration of books.

PLACE OF WORK Titus Groan was written while Peake was serving in the army in various British camps during World War II. Thereafter, he and his family were forced by financial difficulties to move home frequently. He worked most happily with his boisterous children around him; he was not one for silent retreat until forced into it during the final years of his working life when, to complete Titus Alone, he had to struggle against the tremors of the oncoming disease.

METHODS His method was to write rapidly as passages came to his mind, and then to go over them immediately for careful revision and correction, consulting his wife each step of the way. His

Above left Peake, painted by his wife Maeve Gilmore.
Above right A page from the manuscript of the Gormenghast trilogy. Here Peake wrote and drew in a publisher's dummy, a book filled with blank pages.
Below right One of the many pictures Peake drew of the island of Sark. After World War II he lived for many years on the tiny Channel Island with his young family. The enclosed environment contributed to his vision of Gormenghast.

manuscripts were typed by various willing friends, or by professional typists when they could be afforded. Even then, Titus Groan was virtually re-written on the publisher's galley proofs, incurring such a high expenditure (the book had practically to be reset at the printers) that Peake was obliged to pay a substantial part of it.

SOURCES The enclosed atmosphere of the world of Gormenghast was inspired by the first ten years of Peake's life, spent with his medical-missionary family in a walled city of Imperial China, and later reinforced by the idyllic years he enjoyed on the tiny Channel Island of Sark. The characters with which Gormenghast is peopled, those with unforgettable names like Steerpike, Fuschia and Swelter, though not specifically based on individuals, were inspired by Peake's fascinated observations and sketches of eccentrics met during the singular life of a bohemian family man. He was essentially an artist, and his most powerful sense was visual; novels were therefore a means for more fully expressing a world he could so vividly picture.

Joyce Cary

Cary trained to be a painter in Paris and Edinburgh, but abandoned this ambition and joined the political service in Nigeria after a brief period of service in the Balkan campaign of 1912–13. He remained in Nigeria until the consequences of a severe war wound forced him to take up residence in Oxford where he began his writing career, which lasted for 37 years until his death in 1957.

ROUTINE *Though severely handicapped by ill health and partial paralysis, Cary maintained a steady routine of work at his Oxford home. He spent several years working on his first novel* Aissa Saved *(1932) because he felt he had to undergo a process of intellectual discipline and training before he could satisfactorily resolve the questions which the novel raised as he worked on it.*

OUTPUT *Cary produced 16 novels as well as several short stories. At his death he was still working on his last novel* The Captive and the Free *(1959).*

PLACE OF WORK *Throughout most of his writing career, which was spent at his Oxford home, Cary suffered from a severe physical disability which made it necessary for him to have his pen strapped to his hand while he wrote on a scroll threaded through a special "writing machine" of his own invention. His desk top had an electric roller operated with a switch.*

METHODS *"I do not write and never have written to an arranged plot", wrote Cary. "The book is composed at once like a picture, and may start anywhere, in the middle or at the end. I may go from the end to the beginning in the same day, and then from the beginning to the middle." He wrote very quickly, cancelling and revising often, producing about three times the amount of material which finally appeared, and leaving many passages uncompleted.*

SOURCES *Cary's experiences as a political administrator in Nigeria gave him the material and background for his two early novels* Aissa Saved *and* Mister Johnson *(1939) in which an imagined African outlook is used to examine European moral and social assumptions. His artistic training is evident in many of his novels, especially in* The Horse's Mouth *(1944) whose Gulley Jimson is an eloquent, scurrilous and fiercely independent painter. On one occasion Cary noticed an American woman with a wrinkled forehead on the Staten Island ferry and woke up three weeks later at three o'clock in the morning with a story in his head about a girl with a wrinkled forehead but in an English setting.*

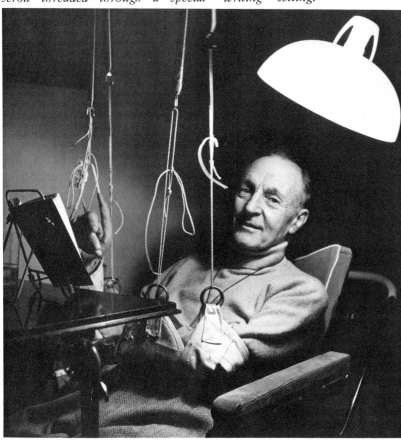

Cary with his arms suspended to enable him to read a book.

Agatha Chris

Above *Agatha Christie at work with notebook and tape recorder at her home in Wallingford, Berkshire.*

Below *Agatha Christie with her husband, the archaeologist Sir Max Mallowan.*

Agatha Christie (née Agatha Miller), who originally wanted to use the pseudonym Mostyn Grey, was, quite simply, the world's biggest selling living author. Yet she wrote almost entirely in a limited genre, the classical detective story, and she confined her settings almost always to a small section of very English society, the upper middle-class. She succeeded by never trying to be other than she was, a very English lady (with a ferocious gift for storytelling and a most cunning touch in mystification).

ROUTINE *Ideas came to Agatha Christie in anything but a routine way, "when I am walking along a street, or examining a hat-shop with particular interest," she says in her autobiography. She agreed with Robert Graves that washing-up was a fine aid to creative thought. She jotted the ideas down in an exercise-book. "So far so good – but what I invariably do is lose the exercise-book." When it came to getting these seeds to grow into a particular book, eating apples in the bath was her preferred way of concentrating her mind. The actual writing was done fast; she aimed to finish a book in six weeks and prided herself on using three, not two, fingers on the typewriter.*

OUTPUT *"A sausage-machine, a perfect sausage-machine," she once called herself, and indeed she produced 83 crime titles in 56 years, plus six romantic novels as Mary Westmacott and a handful of successful plays. She confessed in her autobiography that at least one book, the by no means negligible* Peril at End House *(1932), she could not remember writing at all. In the six years of World War II, beside having a full-time job as a hospital dispenser, she produced twelve books, including some of her best.*

PLACE OF WORK *She never had a room to write in. "All I needed," she said, "was a steady table and a typewriter . . . a marble-topped bedroom washstand table made a good place; the dining-room table between meals was also suitable." She did, however, as her fame increased, acquire two large country houses at the same time, Greenway House on the banks of the Dart in Devon and Winterbrook House near Oxford. Both their gardens were a persistent distraction from the business of providing a Christie for Christmas.*

METHODS *Despite refusing for years to consider herself as "an author", firmly putting "married woman" in her passport, she was very professional. Her typescripts invariably reached her publisher at the promised time, and her proofs were promptly corrected. She was sharp about insensitive editing and had firm views on jackets (putting an absolute, and sensible, ban on representations of Hercule Poirot). The cunning of her plot construction produced a constant tension, which was in no way weakened by her telling her story without the least deviation and mostly in easy-to-read dialogue.*

SOURCES *She was educated at home, and was a voracious reader as a child: Sherlock Holmes was perhaps the prime source for her handling of the classic detective-story, although she did not scruple to seize, and improve upon, ideas from many contemporary whodunnit writers (as witness* Partners in Crime *(1929) in which she imitated a dozen or more, as well as sending up her own Hercule Poirot). Poirot himself owes a little to Belgian refugees she knew of in 1914 but more to anti-Holmesian qualities; and Miss Marple owes a good deal to the author's grandmother. A handful of her books sprang from her second husband's archaeological work, and the rest from sharply observant eyes and ears.*

Ernest Hemingway

When Hemingway committed suicide (as his father had done before him) by shooting himself in Ketchum, Idaho, at the age of 63, he was perhaps grimly acknowledging and responding to the fact that advancing age was making it increasingly impossible for him to continue the active life of physical adventure which he had led since boyhood and which he both celebrated and questioned in so much of his fiction. His life had taken him to bull fighting in Spain, big game hunting in Africa and action and excitement in half a dozen countries spanning half the globe. Three events in this crowded career seem to have shaped Hemingway as both man and writer. The first was a boyhood spent in the still wild country around the Great Lakes which gave him an abiding love for the outdoor life. Next came his years as a provincial journalist, a period during which his distinctive clipped, severely factual prose style was effectively formed. Finally there was the severe head wound he received as a volunteer ambulance orderly during World War I; the experience brought him face to face with the fact of human vulnerability, a theme which runs through all his writing.

ROUTINE A good part of Hemingway's writing life was spent in Cuba where he followed a fairly strict routine of work, getting up at first light and writing standing up, shifting his weight from one foot to the other at intervals. He moved to a chair and a typewriter only when the writing was going well or presented no problems. He kept a chart of his progress on a large piece of cardboard ("so as not to kid myself") and made a point of catching up the following day if he had taken a day off for any reason. He would stop each day, usually around noon, at a point where he was quite certain of what was to follow.

OUTPUT Hemingway's target was between 450 and 575 words a day, but he would write as much as 1250 words to make up for a lost day.

PLACE OF WORK Hemingway had a special work room in a tower in his Havana house, but he preferred to work in his ground floor bedroom. There was a small space for his typewriter on top of a cluttered bookcase. Early in his career Hemingway had developed a capacity to work in almost any conditions.

METHODS Often, though not always, Hemingway's work began with the vague outline of a story. With his novel For Whom the Bell Tolls, for instance, he "knew what was going to happen in principle" but invented each day's events as he wrote. He once said he tried to write on the principle of the iceberg, that is, with the finished work suggesting a whole range of experience which is not present in the novel itself, but whose pressure is felt continuously. The slim novel which, among other things, earned him the Nobel Prize, The Old Man and the Sea could, according to its author, have been a thousand pages long. On the other hand, both To Have and Have Not and Across the River and into the Trees began as short stories.

Hemingway wrote in pencil on onion skin paper, revising when he transferred the work to the typewriter and again at the proof stage.

SOURCES Most of Hemingway's fiction is clearly based on first hand experience. Violent physical action, whether in war or peace, is at the centre, or very close to it, in much of his work. A Farewell to Arms and Across the River and into the Trees are based on his experiences in the First and Second World Wars respectively, while For Whom the Bell Tolls draws on his experiences in the Spanish Civil War. He himself has described The Green Hills of Africa as "an attempt to write an absolutely true book – to see whether the shape of a country and the pattern of a month's action, could, if truly presented, compete with a work of the imagination". Some of his characters were taken from real life, though usually they were invented on the basis of his experience of people, or derived from his own image of himself.

D.H.Lawrence

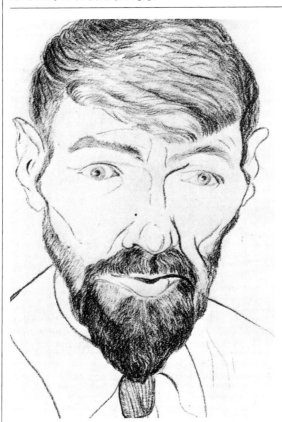

Above *Hemingway at
work in his bedroom at
Finca Vegia, or Look Out
Farm, his house in Cuba.
Left Hemingway
pictured in Europe in
1944, when he came to
observe the war.*

Left *Lawrence: a self-
portrait.*
Above *Lawrence in his
twenties.*

D. H. Lawrence's life was a tempestuous as that of any character depicted in his novels, involving a childhood marked by fierce parental dissension, the final breaking away from an intense emotional attachment to his mother by eloping with a married woman, constant conflicts with authority over the alleged obscenity of his work and other issues, and more or less complete exile from England. He was passionately aware of his working-class origins.

ROUTINE *Lawrence was an amazingly prolific and fluent writer who was capable of working under the most intense pressure, both external and internal. He produced some of his finest work, including* The Rainbow (1915) *and* Women in Love (1920), *during the years of World War I when, in addition to being virtually penniless, he and his German-born wife, Frieda, were subjected to a good deal of harrassment because they were suspected of being German spies. Lawrence had the capacity to immerse himself totally in the act of writing and sometimes wrote for several hours with hardly a break.*
OUTPUT *His death from tuberculosis at the age of 45 ended a writing career that had begun when Lawrence was in his twenties. During this time he wrote ten novels as well as a number of long tales and short stories, in addition to poetry, plays, essays and travel books.*

PLACE OF WORK *Lawrence is the classic example in the twentieth century of the wandering writer. Only four of his ten novels were written in England. The others were produced in places as widely separated as Italy, Australia and New Mexico. His immediate surroundings strongly influenced him and are often directly reproduced in his work.*
METHODS *Lawrence wrote rapidly in longhand and often rewrote whole sections of his work. Two of his greatest novels,* The Rainbow *and* Women in Love, *were originally conceived as one novel, variously called* The Sisters *and* The Wedding Ring. *It was rewritten several times, and at one point Lawrence rewrote it when he had "quite a thousand pages" to discard. He rewrote more often than he revised, but revision was also quite frequent in his practice as a novelist.*
SOURCES *Lawrence's novels are nearly always so closely based on his own experience and acquaintances that the identification of characters and incidents from the novels with their counterparts in real life has become a thriving industry. While Lawrence undoubtedly used autobiographical experience as his chief source, at his best he transformed it to his own imaginative purposes, though the real-life originals of his characters often, understandably, objected to his portrayal of them. Versions of the possessive mother, the "spiritual" woman who will not acknowledge the body's imperatives and the creative fulfilling woman (derived from the three women who shaped his emotional life, his mother, his early love, Jesse Chambers, and his wife, Frieda) recur throughout his work, as do various transformations of the strongly sensuous father-figure he had rejected in boyhood.*

Vladimir Nabokov

Nabokov began his career as a novelist by writing in Russian, but turned to English two years before he emigrated to the USA in 1940. His first English novel was The Real Life of Sebastian Knight, *written in Paris and published in America in 1941.*

ROUTINE *Nabokov combined his writing career with an active and lifelong interest in butterflies. From 1942 to 1948 he was research fellow in entomology at Harvard Museum and from 1945 to 1959 he was professor of Slavic Literature at Cornell University. He once remarked that considerable leisure and good library facilities were two of the advantages enjoyed by a writer with an academic appointment.*

OUTPUT *From 1938 until his death Nabokov produced 15 novels in English and Russian, as well as several short stories.*

PLACE OF WORK *When he first began as an emigré writer in Berlin and Paris, Nabokov often worked in extremely cramped conditions, at one time living with his wife and infant son in a single room which served as bedroom, living room and study. In America he worked in the more congenial conditions of a university campus.*

METHODS *Nabokov produced his fiction by writing on index cards, often shuffling them and commencing the day's work at any point he fancied, regardless of the chronological or final narrative order. When this had been decided the manuscript was typed out by his wife. Nabokov was particular about his materials, insisting on lined Bristol cards and well-sharpened pencils.*

SOURCES *Many of Nabokov's novels are richly allusive and depend for their full enjoyment on a knowledge of other works. But his experiences in Russia and as an emigré provide much of the material for novels such as* Pnin *(1957) and* The Gift *(1963). (The latter novel incorporates a potted history of Russian literature.) In a typically witty comment Nabokov spoke of his characters as "galley slaves" and also said: "The pattern of the thing precedes the thing." He has also affected a scorn of Freudian psychology, referring to Freud himself in such terms as "that well-known Viennese quack".*

Anthony Burgess

"The ideal reader of my novels", Burgess once said, "is a lapsed Catholic, a failed musician, short-sighted, colour-blind, auditorily biased, who has read books that I have read. He should also be about my age." This mildly satirical self-portrait comes from one of the most prolific English writers alive, the author of 18 novels and almost as many works of non-fiction. Anthony Burgess is the best-known pen-name of John Burgess Wilson who has also published work under his own name and as Joseph Kell.

ROUTINE *Burgess began his career as a novelist while a school teacher at Oxford (though his first novel written in 1949 was not published until 1965), and continued it as an education officer in Malaya until he became a full-time writer in 1960. He wrote furiously during one period in which he was given only one year to live by doctors. He has confessed to a dislike of writing and declared that he would give it up if he had enough money. He has said that he finds the afternoon the most productive time for creative work.*

OUTPUT *Burgess has written 18 novels in about 30 years, as well as a large number of other books, ranging from studies of Shakespeare and Joyce (including a shortened version of* Finnegan's Wake) *to books on language and on the Grand Tour.*

PLACE OF WORK *Most of Burgess' working life has been spent away from England, in Gibraltar, Malta, Italy and the United States, and during much of it writing had to be confined to the intervals in a full-time job, which meant that his place of work was determined by considerations other than those of personal choice. Like many experienced writers, he finds conditions of work more important than the place.*

METHODS *"I start at the beginning, go on to the end, then stop", Burgess once said. The implication of a smooth and uninterrupted flow of writing is misleading: he often makes a rough synopsis of a work, including a list of names, but believes overplanning is fatal to creativity and regards his unconscious mind and the act of writing itself as indispensable guides. He does not produce a draft of a whole novel which he then revises, but prefers to get one page finished before he goes on to the next, which involves a good deal of revision and correction. He is fascinated by the possibilities of language, and word-games are an element in much of his fiction.*

SOURCES *Burgess' early novels were based on his military experiences in Gibraltar and his years as a colonial officer in Malaysia. Many of the later ones are sardonic visions of the future where wit and a fertile imagination mingle with a love-hate for what he sees as a declining England.*

Barbara Cartland

In London in the 1920s Miss Barbara Cartland was a member of the social set known as the "bright young people". She was also a contributor to the gossip columns of the Daily Express. *"Lord Beaverbrook taught me to write as a journalist, to get straight to the point and cut out the unnecessary words." Her roots in journalism, her innate professionalism and her apparently limitless facility for storytelling have combined to produce an almost unrivalled success as a best-selling novelist. She was twenty when she began her first romantic novel (though she had written, illustrated and bound a story at the age of five) and was encouraged to finish it by friends who doubted that a young lady who frequently danced all night could actually complete a full-length novel. Her father had been killed in Flanders in 1918, and her family was not rich, so she wrote for money, but "I became hooked on writing; I like it; writing is my life".*

ROUTINE *Barbara Cartland answers letters in the morning, dictates her novels between 1.00 and 3.30 p.m. and conducts interviews in the early evening. She aims to write a chapter per day, and can produce between six and eight thousand words.*

OUTPUT *She takes between two and three weeks to complete a book, and has set the world record for annual output three times: 20 novels in 1975, 21 in 1976 and 24 in 1977. In 1978 she produced "only" 20, because she spent considerable time recording an album of love songs with the Royal Philharmonc Orchestra (at the age of 77). In July 1979 she was working on her 277th novel, and her sales world-wide had topped 100 million.*

PLACE OF WORK *She lives in Camfield Place, Hertfordshire. She dictates from her sofa in her library, a white fur rug over her legs, a hot water bottle at her feet, two dogs beside her and her secretary with a shorthand notebook at the ready behind her.*

METHODS *It was Godfrey Winn who suggested that she should dictate her novels. "Good English, which I require for my serious books, I write in my own hand"; colloquial English, in which her novels are written ("people expect to read the kind of conversation they are now used to hearing from the radio and television") flows more easily through the spoken word. Her books are composed mostly of dialogue; the remaining narrative is deliberately set in short paragraphs so as to resemble dialogue visually.*

Ideas for stories come from her voracious reading of history; she researches the period and, determined to get the facts right, reads twenty to thirty books. The reference books are collected by her chauffeur from the London Library, the
county libraries or from Hatchards in Piccadilly. *She jots notes in a pad and plans in advance the amount of words each chapter will require. When it comes to writing the story, she lives the tale, sees it happening before her and simply allows the words to pour out to be caught and held by the pen of her secretary. Correction and revision are kept to a minimum.*

SOURCES *History is her sole source. A passage in Sir Arthur Bryant's* Years of Victory *on Napoleon's internment of 10,000 Britons in France in 1803 has supplied her with six novels. A visit to Senegal led to what appeared to be a fruitless period of research into the history of Western Africa ("very dull") until she came upon a slim book which told of the importation of white girls as wives for the colonists.*

History, however, provides but the setting for stories which consistently express her belief in perfect love, love which is both physical and spiritual. "It is the highest state man can attain towards God. A young girl should believe in perfect love and not be content with second best. Just because we may end up with second best does not mean we should aim for it. All my heroines are virgins. The sleep-about girl takes the bloom off womanhood, no matter how many pretty words you use."

Barbara Cartland dictating to her secretary Ruth Walles.

Erica Jong

As a student Erica Jong's interest was in modernist literature and in "artifice" and experimentalism; she admired the work of writers like Nabokov and W. H. Auden. Her own prose fiction, however, is concerned essentially with the lives and emotions of modern women; uses direct and conventional means – usually the biographical or confessional, in the first-person singular – and is sharply satirical in intent. Her third novel, not yet published, is a departure from this, being set in the eighteenth century and on a broader canvas; but its central concerns are reported to be similar to her earlier work.

ROUTINE *Erica Jong regularly works six or seven days a week, usually from 10 a.m. to 3.30 p.m. with a break for lunch. She is punctilious and exact about time, as about the other disciplines attendant on the life of a writer – methods of work, output of words per day, dealings with publishers, deadlines, etc. – taking the view that "inspiration grows out of the process" of work, and that a high degree of organization is essential to maintain the level of concentration she needs.*
OUTPUT *Erica Jong has written three novels – the third will be published in 1980 – and a considerable amount of verse. On a good day she completes some 250 to 300 words.*
PLACE OF WORK *Each of Erica Jong's novels so far has been written in a different place; but she now works in a converted loft at the top of her house in Weston, Connecticut. She values a quiet, home-based working environment and continuity of effort.*
METHODS *Erica Jong writes in long-hand on large yellow sheets. She begins merely with an idea (such as the predicament or psychology of a character), prepares a more detailed outline when several thousand words have been written, and alters this outline several times during the course of writing the book (keeping a file of "the roads not taken"). She also revises her work extensively. The eventual novel has thus in each case turned out very differently from the original idea; and this evolutionary process seems to her vital, not only in writing but in reading novels.*

She allows friends to read her work in typescript, but does not place great reliance on the variety of comments they offer. She does, however, believe in listening to the advice of the publisher's editor, and in establishing a strong working relationship with a publisher who shares her own values and concerns.
SOURCES *Although critics and readers have assumed that much of her work is autobiographical, she denies this, describing the process of building the environment of a novel as "taking liberties with" her experience.*

Angus Wells

Angus Wells is the British author of several original paperback series of Westerns, producing one book (50–65,000 words) every month or six weeks. He has never visited the U.S. and is afraid that the reality might be incompatible with the America of his imagination which is based on Western movies. "We are writing about the myth", he insists. "Not the real America."

He is currently writing The Lawman *series for Coronet;* Breed *and* Gunslinger *for Sphere;* Jubal Kaid *and* Gringoes *for Mayflower;* Hawk *for Fontana; and for Corgi a fantasy series called* Raven. *His pen names include J. D. Sandon and William S. Brady.*

ROUTINE *Wells works from 11 a.m. until 7.30 p.m. He is disciplined about fulfilling his daily quota of words, working late into the evening if he has been disturbed during the day. Nonetheless he is often tempted to put off starting in the mornings and there are days when he can produce nothing. When this happens he stops completely.*
OUTPUT *About 3000 words per weekday (ten A4 sheets); a book every four to six weeks.*

Ross Macdonald

A writer of crime fiction who is widely regarded as a major American novelist, Ross Macdonald (the pseudonym eventually chosen by Ken Millar) is the creator of the private-eye, Lew Archer, and a novelist very conscious of what his work implies (he holds an English Literature doctorate with a dissertation on Coleridge). Yet his books are so much in the tradition of popular American crime-writing that they have long been consistent best sellers.

ROUTINE *His first book,* The Dark Tunnel *(1944) (published under his own name), was written by day while he taught creative writing in the evenings. But in 1946 he settled in Santa Barbara, California, and there he works, to quote him, "in the bare muffled room of the professional writer" with his back to the window. He has long since abandoned teaching in favour of full-time devotion to his craft. As one of his former pupils has said, "he kept hammering it into our skulls that writing was Work . . . it had to be hewn, carved, sweated and driven into shape".*
OUTPUT *After an initial spurt of activity when he returned from service in the US Navy and wrote three books in a year, he settled down for a long period to a steady book each twelve*

PLACE OF WORK *At a pine table in a room of his London flat. The room is tidy and museum-like: books (mostly paperback Western, science fiction and fantasy series); magazines and comics; a notice board displaying the specifications of the guns used by his characters; life size full-weight models of the guns themselves; a cowboy hat, cartridge belt and other memorabilia.*

Angus Wells in his study.

METHODS *Wells starts with an idea and allows his characters to take matters into their own hands as the story unfolds. He has made plans in advance, but became bored as he wrote. He has been within 10 pages of the end without knowing how a book will finish, but the plot is always resolved, and the characters manage to extricate themselves from tight corners within the requisite number of pages. His characters are sometimes planned carefully in advance.*

He produces no first draft but writes straight on to an electric typewriter the copy that will go to the publisher after minor corrections the next day. Nor does this entail heavy editing by the publishers, who find his work needs little correction.

SOURCES *Wells sometimes bases entire books on existing characters; the heroes are his friends, or people he likes; the villains may be villains from real life whom he kills off with satisfaction. Events from his own life may also find their way into the plot as it progresses. He draws heavily on the films of John Ford and others, and is influenced by the style of his favourite writers: Chandler, Patricia Highsmith and Ed McBain.*

months. Latterly, however, he has allowed himself longer gaps between volumes. Only since The Galton Case *(1959) has he felt he is wholly himself as a writer, and found, when at last he has hit on his point-of-view for a book, that the "details came unbidden in a benign avalanche".*

PLACE OF WORK *California was where Macdonald was born, although he was taken as a baby to Canada by his sea-captain father (who later deserted his family), and it was of California that his mother never ceased to remind him as they moved from town to town and relative to relative. And to California, where he has lived ever since, he returned to write books almost exclusively set in that state. "The Pacific had lapped like a blue eternity at the far edge of my life," he wrote: "a shining oceanic world" from which he had felt exiled from the age of four when his father had taken him on a short voyage on it.*

METHODS *The tools of Macdonald's trade are spiral notebooks, a red one for the extensive jottings before writing, another for the actual words. But it is delving into the inner depths that turns these tools. His Archer has become "a deliberately narrowed version of the writing self, so narrow that when he turns he almost disappears". Thus he puts himself at one remove*

from subjects he deliberately selects as hard to tackle. He has written of literary detectives, like Poe's Dupin, as being "a kind of welder's mask enabling us to handle dangerously hot material". A mild paranoia, he believes, seems virtually endemic among contemporary writers, himself particularly, and only through a hero like Archer can he act it out, putting him into a plot "as complex as contemporary life, but balanced enough to say true things about it".

SOURCES *His chief source, then, is Ross Macdonald. Asked by a film producer if Archer was based on any actual person, he replied: "Yes. Myself." and received "a semi-pitying Hollywood look". Nevertheless he was happy to find that police detectives he came to know resembled his hero. He admits a debt to Raymond Chandler and Dashiell Hammett before him for their creation of a new type of detective, "the classless, restless man of American democracy". But it is the child who was deserted by his father who fires the books that so frequently feature a father who has to be traced in the past. Oedipus, the exiled, the fated father-killer, appears again and again in the notes for* The Galton Case, *together with discarded titles like "The Castle and the Poorhouse" – reflecting the early poverty – as well as fragments of poetry.*

Michael Moorcock

From a childhood steeped in imaginative fiction, an adolescence making contributions to Tarzan and Sexton Blake magazines, and an adult life producing a stream of science fiction and fantasy novels, Michael Moorcock, now in his 40s, has begun to emerge as an author of substantial achievement. His "Jerry Cornelius Quartet" has been particularly admired.

ROUTINE Moorcock works a strict 5-day week, rarely goes out, and finds writing the least boring of possible activities (including mountain-climbing, which he has tried).

OUTPUT At one stage in his career, while editor of New Worlds magazine, he is reported to have produced as much as 20,000 words per day. This was the period of the "sword and sorcery" novels which established him as a cult figure among the young. In the last decade his output has slowed considerably. The four books comprising the Jerry Cornelius Quartet took 11 years to complete.

PLACE OF WORK Moorcock lives with a clutter of family, friends and fanciful acquisitions in an apartment in London's Notting Hill Gate, an area where the long-haired lifestyle of the late 1960s and early 1970s is perpetuated (if not enshrined). A sign on the front door reads: "Do not knock unless you are expected or making normal service calls. Signed Moorcock-Cornelius." It is frequently ignored by visiting fans.

METHODS The construction of a novel he took from the thriller writer, Lester Dent. He has also applied music theory to writing. His apprenticeship in the pulp magazines he edited for Fleetway Publications taught him the technique of impact. His professional attitude to his work is symbolized by the expensive, self-correcting electric typewriter he uses.

SOURCES He is an avid reader, and authors as diverse as William Burroughs, Dickens, T. H. White, Mervyn Peake and Edgar Rice Burroughs, have combined to influence him. SF inspired him to break SF conventions, just as his taste for High Romance has brought him to satirize the genre in his latest book, Gloriana, a story of a Spenserian Queen with sexual difficulties surrounded by a court of wild characters.

Georges Simenon

Simenon used to write about twenty dense pages each night in pencil. He would correct and type them the following morning.

Best known for the "Maigret series" (begun 1931 and abandoned in favour of more "serious" fiction but revived at the end of the war), Simenon at his peak was evidently a compulsive writer, a fact which has not prevented him from producing several highly distinguished novels both within and outside the "Maigret" framework.

ROUTINE Simenon wrote a "serious" novel in eleven days of continuous writing, having a medical check up before he began and after he finished. He would begin by jotting down the names of his characters (taken from the telephone directory), together with details of their physical appearance, on manila envelopes. He would write a chapter a day, keeping pace with the novel and crossing out each completed day on a calendar. He lived wholly within the world of his characters while writing, seeing them entirely from within and making their anxieties and

Len Deighton

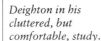

Deighton in his cluttered, but comfortable, study.

Len Deighton revived, with John Le Carré, the espionage novel that presents the realistic, rather than the romantic, face of spying. Yet he is no mere producer of fictionalized documentaries, and indeed went on to write novels not at all concerned with espionage.

ROUTINE With a totally non-literary working class background, he began his first book, The Ipcress File (1962) without any idea even of how long a novel was. (Had he not met a literary agent at a party, he says, it might never have been submitted to a publisher.) Soon, however, he developed an extremely professional way of life

agonies his own, thereby putting himself under immense psychological pressure. The Maigret novels caused him less variation in blood pressure, because the characters are portrayed as seen by Maigret. If he was ill for longer than a day the output produced up to that time had to be abandoned.

OUTPUT *In an interview in the* Paris Review *some years ago, Simenon's output was listed as 150 novels under his own name (or rather under his best-known pseudonym of "Simenon"; his real name is Georges Sim) and 350 under other pseudonyms. Elsewhere he has said that he published about 200 popular novels under 16 pseudonyms between the ages of 20 and 30, and later produced two "Maigret" novels each month for two years.*

PLACE OF WORK *Simenon was a reporter at Liège when, at the age of 17, he published his first novel. At 20, marriage brought a move to Paris and later to Nieul sur Mer where he remained till the German invasion. At 30 he wrote his first "Maigret" novel on board his yacht "Ostrogot". Later he lived in Lakeville, Connecticut and then in Lausanne in Switzerland.*

METHODS *Simenon has said that he always had two or three themes drifting about in his mind, one of which he would consciously take up two days before beginning to write. Next would come a definite atmosphere which would lead to the conception of a little world. He often used a town map to establish exactly where things happened.*

SOURCES *While his early experiences as a reporter and his later wanderings across Europe have obviously provided the raw material for Simenon's work, the distinctive flavour of his novels comes from his absorption in a few recurrent themes – loneliness, the impossibility of full communication between human beings and the individual driven to extremity.*

A piece from an early draft of SS-GB. The manuscript was rewritten several times after this and the contents of this page were not used.

drawing up elaborate preliminary work-sheets for each character, often including a random newspaper picture to indicate general appearance (Deighton trained as an artist and worked in advertizing). He is quick to take advantage of every advance in typewriter technology.

OUTPUT *Largely because of the heavy research programmes he undertakes he now produces only one book every two or three years, although his first volumes came out annually. Melvyn Bragg, interviewing him on BBC television in 1977, described him as "the most hard-working writer I've ever talked to".*

PLACE OF WORK *He lives now in Ireland, with a house in Portugal, and the isolation is very necessary to him, freeing him from distractions;* he achieved this in London by living in the East End and having all his telephone calls either routed via a message agency or sent by teleprinter. In Ireland he lives without television, having calculated that the evenings thus freed give him an extra day a week to work in.

METHODS *A passion for accurate knowledge of technical processes fires the most detailed research before a book is begun. But he is always ready, as a novelist, to sacrifice actuality to invention ("to cheat", as he puts it) so as to produce a vivid impression for his readers. He sees the thriller as a game, and much enjoys playing it. "The stage conjuror", he once said, "is perhaps the only other person permitted to play havoc with the minds of his audience and not be resented." The fragmentation of images that results, adding up only at the end to a logical statement, fascinates him.*

SOURCES *Class differences were perhaps the single greatest source for the Deighton approach, producing in him a sharp amusement rather than bile. In advertising he was the only director of his firm who was not an Old Etonian, and the tension of that situation produced his unnamed spy hero, the jokey rebel against old-school authority. In style, especially of dialogue, he admits his debt to Raymond Chandler, but otherwise, he says, "all writers are made with their own material as part of them". It is on what he has known, both inwardly and outwardly, that he draws. He sees his sort of writer as having a lot in common with the spy. "I like to be able to listen to conversations without people turning round to look at me."*

Beryl Bainbridge

A distinguished and highly skilled writer of painful but comic analyses of frustrated characters and their private agonies in suburban settings, Beryl Bainbridge broadened her canvas somewhat with Private Adolf *(1978) a reconstruction of possible (but improbable) events in the early life of Adolf Hitler, when he visited his waiter brother in Liverpool in 1912.*

ROUTINE *It takes Beryl Bainbridge about four months to write a novel. During this period she begins work at ten each evening and works through until four or five in the morning. After re-reading what she has written she goes to bed, sometimes for as little as three hours, then gets up again and spends the morning correcting and refining the work of the previous night. She neither sees friends nor answers the telephone during this period. Her only contact is with her three children (she is a single parent). Before starting to write in the evening she has to tidy the house: she will wash the dishes, or decide the stairs need cleaning or the hedge needs cutting. She can only work in a perfectly ordered environment.*

PLACE OF WORK *She works at home in Camden Town, London, in a large room with green walls which serves as both study and bedroom. She sits at a small pine table surrounded by books, stuffed birds, Catholic memorabilia (from a long-past conversion), antiques, modern paintings and her children's old toys – all of it in perfect order.*

OUTPUT *Beryl Bainbridge has written nine novels – one a year for the past seven years (1972–79) and two before that. After the four month period of intensive writing she spends the rest of the year writing TV plays and thinking about her next novel. Each one is begun in January and published in September of the same year.*

METHOD *For every nine or so pages written at night there is a rigorous process of honing and rewriting the following morning to produce one page of final draft. Ms Bainbridge approaches her novels with a time-scheme which will allow her to produce one of these "finished" pages a day, but puts off starting until "blind panic" (as she describes it) sets in and she is obliged to produce ten or twelve pages daily to meet the deadline – as much as 100 pages each night. Under this severe pressure her concentration is complete. Once she has a dozen finished pages she will show them to her publisher (who on one occasion made her start again). The first twenty pages are always the most difficult. She will write an opening paragraph in pencil and spend a long time revising it. After that she writes*

Beryl Bainbridge at the small work table in her home in north London.

straight on to a small old-fashioned portable typewriter. At page 50 she becomes elated; her energy is boundless. She is almost too excited to sleep.

Ms Bainbridge places a great emphasis on perfection in the use of language and sentence construction, and on the part played by her editor, whose counsel she considers vital. The creative role of the artist is inseparable from the craft of writing – and this she considers to be a job which the writer cannot do efficiently if he or she is locked in a personal artistic vacuum.

SOURCES *Beryl Bainbridge does not consider herself to be a writer of fiction because every character and place in her books is based on experience. Her heroines are always aspects of herself. The impetus for her writing comes from her past, particularly from her childhood and upbringing. Had it been different she is certain she would not have needed to write at all. The character of Hitler in* Young Adolf *is based on her father. While she manipulates characters and events in her books to serve her purpose, she maintains that ultimately the books manipulate her – because she changes as a result of writing them.*

NOVELISTS:
AN ALPHABETICAL GUIDE

1348 authors and 3284 works of fiction are listed here. The aim has been to include the best fiction writers of every nationality, period and type, the only qualification being that their work should be reasonably easy to obtain in the English language.

The selection of authors has been based on two criteria: popularity with the reading public, and acclaim from critics and reviewers. Hundreds of writers, of course, claim their place on both grounds – what are called "standard authors" of many different kinds. But an attempt has then been made to share out the remaining space equitably between those who have the one and those who have the other. This does not mean that every million-copy seller and every literary award winner is included: there are authors in both categories whose work is now unfashionable or difficult to obtain. At the same time, a number of lesser known, but nonetheless accomplished, authors are included to help the reader find writers that are new to him.

Reading lists and star ratings
The titles of up to three novels or short stories are listed at the end of each entry. These are recommended as the best or most representative introduction to that author, but may not always include his or her most celebrated work, although this will invariably have been mentioned in the entry above. Each title listed has four "star-rating" symbols, each showing up to five stars, for its success according to the four criteria shown below.

Readability This is a broad concept which incorporates style, plot and the pace at which the story moves. Books which score well are considered good entertainment, often because they contain a fast-moving story written in a lively or flowing style. Many of the high scorers are therefore popular thrillers or romances. There are of course several kinds of readability: the romances of Georgette Heyer score highly because they are written in an attractively simple style, and make few intellectual demands. The novels of Dostoyevsky score highly because the content of the work generally makes them compellingly interesting, although the reader may have to work harder.

Characterization Novels with well-observed, memorable or unusual characters score well. Low scores indicate

novels in which the characters are badly drawn and lack credibility, or where there is no character with whom the reader can identify. Many novels which score well on readability get few stars for characterization, reflecting the tendency of many fine story-tellers to neglect the portrayal of character.

Plot Books which rate highly contain a clever, unusual or well-ordered plot. A low rating indicates either a deliberate lack of plot, or a plot which suffers from implausibility or inadequate planning. Good plots are found in books of all kinds.

Literary merit This constitutes an over-all assessment of the novel's artistic achievement, taking into account the originality of the work in its historical context.

The ratings taken together provide a profile of the novel. It has been the contributors' objective to recommend good books, rather than pillory bad ones; and even a score of one star should be taken to indicate some degree of merit. About fifty-four novels score full marks on all four criteria, and represent, in the opinion of the contributors, the finest works of fiction that have been written.

Bibliographical information Abbreviations:
ed.	edition	**sel.**	selection
n.d.	no date	**tr.**	translation
repr.	reprinted	**vol.**	volume
rev.	revised edition		

? preceding a date indicates that the date is conjectural. Empty parentheses indicate that an author's dates of birth or death are unknown or not available.

The year following each novel's title is that of first publication in book form. Where novels have been published under two different titles, both are given. For novels originally published in languages other than English, the dates of first publication and of recommended translations are given.

In general, short stories are only listed as recommended in the case of science fiction writers (in the science fiction field short stores are treated with more respect than elsewhere, and major prizes are awarded for them). The lists do, however, include collections of stories, and in some cases the collected works of a particular writer. The year following the title of a short story is the date of first publication in any form.

A

ABRAHAMS, Peter (1919) South African negro novelist. Much of his early work was done in England; but he now lives in Jamaica. *Tell Freedom* (1954), about his life in a Johannesburg slum, made him famous. His fiction is lucid and dramatic.

A Wreath for Udomo (1956)

This Island Now (1966)

ACHEBE, Chinua (1930) Nigerian novelist and story-writer, generally regarded as the most gifted contemporary African novelist, and certainly the most widely read. *Things Fall Apart* depicts the chaos that resulted from the imposition of European upon African ways; but cosmopolitan, eclectic and moderate-minded, Achebe questions the viability of both ways, and shows that true order can only come from inner standards. *A Man of the People* is a bitter and often very funny satire on African politics.

Things Fall Apart (1958)

No Longer at Ease (1960)

A Man of the People (1966)

ADAMS, Henry (1838–1918) American historian, who influenced many later American writers. He was concerned with the search for unity in what he called the "multiverse": for reconciliation between the Virgin (nature; the thirteenth century) and the Dynamo (science; the twentieth century). Thus he probes at the emotional and intellectual roots of American literature. His novels have important themes: the "unacceptable face of capitalism" and the conflict between religion and science.

Democracy (1880)

Esther (1884)

ADAMS, Richard (1920) Best selling English allegorical, nature-animal novelist. Adams, originally a civil servant, scored a smash hit with *Watership Down,* a tale about rabbits, which delighted children and many adults. *Shardak*, about a bear, was more labouredly allegorical, and was less well received. *The Plague Dogs* which revived the author's reputation, is a grim tale warning of the consequences of animal experimentation. Some critics have alleged that he is politically reactionary and "sexist". His power as a writer lies in his ability to convey to us the way animals experience the world.

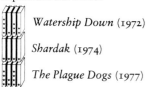

Watership Down (1972)

Shardak (1974)

The Plague Dogs (1977)

AGEE, James (1909–55) American novelist, film-critic and film-writer. The most brilliant film-critic of his age, and a considerable poet, too, Agee did not become famous until after his death, even though he wrote the film script for the Bogart-Hepburn classic *The African Queen*, based on C. S. Forester's novel. *The Morning Watch* finds a perfect objective correlative for the religious-rationalist conflict in its sensitive portrayal of one day in the life of a twelve-year old boy. *A Death in the Family* was also acclaimed and is about the sudden wasted death of the father and husband of a family in Tennessee; it seems like a slice cut through the most nerve-crowded part of life.

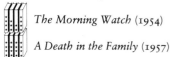

The Morning Watch (1954)

A Death in the Family (1957)

AGNON, S. Y. (1888–1970) Jewish novelist and short story-writer. Agnon was born in Galicia and went to Palestine in 1908. He won the Nobel Prize in 1966, but has never been a best seller except in Jewish communities. He is a writer of genius, although he is less accessible than I. B. Singer. One of his achievements is the creation of an acceptable modern vernacular in Hebrew; he based his style on the Talmud, in which he was learned. *The Bridal Canopy* which is regarded as his greatest novel, has a Don Quixote theme, but is set in nineteenth-century Galicia, and is fascinatingly rich in allusion to its customs. *Only Afterwards* (1947) deals with modern Israel. Agnon has long been regarded by his Jewish readers as the leading Hebrew epic writer, and as a master of the use of symbolism.

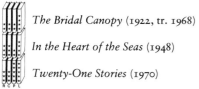

The Bridal Canopy (1922, tr. 1968)

In the Heart of the Seas (1948)

Twenty-One Stories (1970)

AIKEN, Conrad (1889–1973) American poet, novelist, story-writer and critic. Primarily a poet, Aiken was also an esteemed short story-

writer. He used all kinds of modernist techniques, particularly stream of consciousness, and is invariably fascinating; but his novels are not ultimately as satisfying as his best poems, although they cast light on a host of human manifestations. *King Coffin* is his most gripping novel.

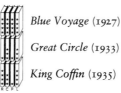

Blue Voyage (1927)

Great Circle (1933)

King Coffin (1935)

Richard Adams

AINSWORTH, William Harrison (1805–82) English journalist and historical novelist. He was a competent, uninspired disciple of Sir Walter Scott. His books are now read mostly by schoolchildren, who profit from them.

Rockwood (1834)

The Tower of London (1840)

ALAIN-FOURNIER (1886–1914) French novelist (real name Henri-Alban Fournier) who was killed in World War I. His one novel, *Le Grand Meaulnes*, translated first as *The Lost*

Domain but published later in English under its French title, is a semi-mythopoeic exploration of adolescent romanticism set in a magical landscape. It was partly autobiographical; but the theme is essentially that of the "Sleeping Beauty". It is unique; but it perfectly exemplifies a Gallic tendency towards the modernistic, sophisticated romance. His greatest achievement was his re-creation of the countryside of the Solagne.

 Le Grand Meaulnes (1913, tr. 1959)

ALARCON, Pedro Antonio de (1833–91) Spanish novelist. His best-known work, because it was made into a famous ballet, is *Three-Cornered Hat* (1874, tr. 1918) – an amusing semi-folktale of the exposing of a wicked official. His best novel is *The Infant with the Globe*, which combines adventure and psychology.

 The Infant with the Globe (1880, tr. 1955)

ALBRAND, Martha (1912) German-born American novelist. She has written under several names, including Christine Lambert, and in Germany as Katrin Holland, whose novel *Carlotta Torrensani* was a best seller in 1938. Since 1942 she has written feminine suspense novels, mostly about espionage in various European capitals, and in 1971 she published a New York police thriller.

 No Surrender (1942)

A Day in Monte Carlo (1959)

ALCOTT, Louisa May (1832–88) American novelist and author of classic children's books. Louisa May Alcott lived all her life in Boston and Concord, and wrote to support herself and her family. Although she wrote on other subjects, she is remembered for *Little Women*. The book is an account of her own impoverished youth, and the closeness of the ties between herself, her beloved sisters, and their parents. *Little Women*, with its charming and sympathetic self-portrait of Jo March, was immediately popular and, with the sequel *Good Wives* which appeared in the following year, made their author's name and fortune. Other sequels followed, full of humour and pathos, describing family life in mid-nineteenth-century Massachussets with a charm which is untarnished even today.

 Little Women (1868)

Little Men (1871)

ALDINGTON, Richard (1892–1962) British poet, novelist, critic and biographer. Primarily a poet and biographer, Aldington achieved temporary fame with *Death of a Hero*, which is simultaneously a bitter satire of pre-war society and a war novel. The bitterness is con-

trolled here, though not in his earlier work.

 Death of a Hero (1929)

All Men are Enemies (1933)

ALDISS, Brian W. (1925) English novelist and anthologist, who has played a leading role in raising science fiction to the level of a serious literary form. His own novels cover a wide spectrum, from remote imagined worlds to stories "merely coloured by the presence of the future"; and are energetically and vividly written. Less well known is his series of semi-autobiographical novels starting with *The Hand-Reared Boy* (1970), which are bawdy reminiscences of life in the British army and elsewhere. His *Billion Year Spree* (1973) is a fine general history of science fiction. His stories are possibly his best work.

 The Primal Urge (1961)

Report on Probability A (1968)

Best SF Stories of Brian Aldiss (rev. 1971)

ALDRIDGE, James (1918) Australian-born novelist and journalist who has lived mostly in England. He has based his fiction on themes of contemporary history and on his love of nature; and several novels – *Signed with Their Honour* (1942) and *I Wish He Would Not Die* (1957) – are based on his experiences as a war correspondent. The main interest of his work is in its sympathetic handling of human concerns in a violent, chaotic modern world.

 The Diplomat (1949)

Goodbye Un-America (1979)

ALEMÁN, Mateo (1547–?1614) Spanish novelist who established the picaresque novel with *Guzmán de Alfarache*. This is vivid, moralizing (but probably only in order to deflect clerical ire) and vitally important in the history of the novel.

 Guzmán de Alfarache (1599–1604, tr. Mabbe 1621, repr. 1928)

ALGREN, Nelson (1909) American novelist, classed as a "Chicago realist". His earlier novels of Chicago's west-side slums had strong naturalist tendencies, and were influenced by Marxist thought. His finest work, *The Man with the Golden Arm*, about a drug addict, has greater psychological depth. Latterly he has written still vivid but more sentimental novels.

 Never Come Morning (1942)

The Man with the Golden Arm (1949)

A Walk on the Wild Side (1956)

ALLBEURY, Ted (1917) English spy novelist. Like many writers in this genre Allbeury's work springs from actual experience (Army Intelligence, 1940–45). He came to fiction late (*A Choice of Enemies,* 1971), used plenty of technical information, and shone chiefly when transcribing personal experiences. Latterly he has tended to use the theme of espionage to illuminate aspects of the human condition, particularly its tragedies, and to expound on such subjects as the Russian mind.

 The Man with the President's Mind (1977)

 The Lantern Network (1978)

The Alpha List (1979)

ALLEN, Hervey (1889–1949) Popular American novelist and biographer. An immensely able journalist, Allen wrote one best selling historical novel *Anthony Adverse*. It deals with the Napoleonic period, and is popularly candid in its treatment of sex, and psychologically credible. Historical accuracy is not one of its merits.

 Anthony Adverse (1933)

Action at Aquila (1938)

ALLEN, H. Warner, see BENTLEY, E. C.

ALLEN, Walter (1911) British novelist and critic. His historical literary criticism has classic status, which unfortunately has led to neglect of his own fiction. His first novels had working-class Midlands settings, and are clumsy – although they have powerful passages. In *Rogue Elephant* (1946) and *Dead Man Over All* he completely changed style, concentrating more on writing from the autonomous position than the political, and on using form to achieve his ends. His masterpiece is *All in a Lifetime*, an old man's view of his past.

 Innocence is Drowned (1938)

 Dead Man Over All (1950) (in U.S. *Square Peg*)

All in a Lifetime (1959) (in U.S. *Threescore and Ten*)

ALLINGHAM, Margery (1904–66) English crime novelist, chiefly known for her detective, Mr Albert Campion. Her first novel *Blacker-chief Dick* (1921) (dictated to her by planchette) was an Essex pirates tale, but thereafter she kept mostly to murder. As might be expected of a novelist who began at 16, she developed rapidly. The ten detective stories up to 1939 show increasing depth, with *Death of a Ghost* (1934) blending man-of-the-world dialogue and interesting characterization, and *Flowers for the Judge* (1936) sharply handling the pub-

Margery Allingham

lishing background and using court scenes which incorporated all the dull bits less skilled writers leave out. She took a leap forward after World War II with *Coroner's Pidgin* (1945) in which Mr Campion became a decidedly intelligent pair of eyes through which his creator could see the complexities of life.

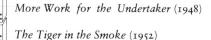

More Work for the Undertaker (1948)

The Tiger in the Smoke (1952)

The Beckoning Lady (1955)

ALTHER, Lisa (1944) American novelist who achieved great success with her first book, *Kinflicks,* partly because it was thought to be part of the current vogue for semi-confessional writing by women. In fact the book has more in common with J. D. Salinger's *Catcher In The Rye* than Erica Jong's *Fear of Flying.*

Kinflicks (1976)

ALUKO, Timothy (1918) Nigerian novelist, an engineer by profession. He relies on documentary, and is psychologically superficial. But his satire is intelligent, funny and sharp: he is best at poking fun, rather than analyzing, the sort of situations with which his compatriot Chinua Achebe deals: the mixture of old and new, Christian and pagan; corrupt civil servants.

One Man, One Wife (1959, repr. 1968)

His Worshipful Majesty (1973)

AMADO, Jorge (1912) Brazilian novelist, most of whose novels are set in his birth region of Bahia. He began as a politically committed left-wing writer, and his novels until *The Violent Land* are powerful, naturalistic but over-simplified accounts of class struggle. *The Violent Land* is still based in Marxist thinking, but its record of the struggle between planters for possession of cocoa groves transcends doctrine by its psychological mastery and its vastly improved technique. Some of its successors are as good, and artistically even better: Amado's interests have shifted from politics to myth, folklore, sly comedy and non-realist techniques.

The Violent Land (1942, tr. 1945)

Gabriela, Clove and Cinnamon (1958, tr. 1962)

Tieta (1978, tr. 1979)

AMBLER, Eric (1909) British writer of spy thrillers, who as early as the 1930s was depicting the seamy realities of the world of espionage convincingly and with an accurate eye for detail. His studiedly unglamorous settings and exquisitely drawn anti-heroes have served as models for the later generation which includes John Le Carré and Len Deighton. His earlier books have somewhat dated. *The Light of Day* (1962, filmed as *Topkapi*) and *Dirty Story* (1967, in U.S. *This Gun for Hire*) feature perhaps his most pleasing protagonist, Arthur Abdul Simpson: stateless, corrupt and cowardly, but always surviving on his wits. *The Levanter* (1972) contains a masterly portrait of the modern terrorist, in this case a Palestinian.

The Mask of Demetrios (1939, in U.S. *A Coffin for Demetrios*)

Passage of Arms (1959)

The Levanter (1972)

AMIS, Kingsley (1922) British novelist and poet. Amis has never done better in terms of sales or popularity than he did with *Lucky Jim,* his first novel. *Lucky Jim,* deriving from *The Card* by Arnold Bennett although set in an academic milieu, was infinitely the best of the so-called "angry young man" novels of its day; and is a splendid debunking of university pretentiousness. After more works in the same genre as *Lucky Jim,* Amis became interested in SF, in Fleming's Bond and in more complex characterization. *The Anti-Death League* is his greatest achievement, since here he displays fine technique and deeper feeling; he allows his imagination to take control, and his prejudices are more evident. Since *The Green Man* (1969) he has experimented with more modernist techniques, and the results have been artistically disappointing since he is essentially a story teller. He conveys what is absurd very

Kingsley Amis

well, but is much less sure in conveying his own warmth.

Lucky Jim (1954)

The Anti-Death League (1966)

Jake's Thing (1978)

AMIS, Martin (1949) English novelist, son of Kingsley Amis, with an acid, clever, gratuitously grubby line on sexual relations. *Dead Babies* (*Dark Secrets*, 1975) has hedonists gathering for a weekend of drugs and debauchery that ends in a Jacobean congress of corpses. Like Amis's other work, this neat but repulsive tract for our times seems a five-finger exercise from an author of huge promise but, so far, only slender achievement.

The Rachel Papers (1973)

Dead Babies (1975)

Success (1978)

ANAND, Mulk Raj (1905) Indian novelist and general writer. He found success when E. M. Forster introduced *Untouchable*. Anand is a humanist who believes that "creating literature is the true medium of humanism as against systematic philosophies", and although influenced by Marxism he believes primarily in "the wisdom of the human heart". In his novels he doesn't hide his furies; but they come off the page like a living voice – sharp, intelligent, comic, indignant.

Untouchable (1935)

The Village (1949)

Morning Face (1968)

ANDERSEN, Hans Christian (1805–75) Danish writer of fairy-tales and novelist. Andersen is best known for his use of the fairy-tale form to express emotions both simple and very highly complex. He is a world-wide children's classic, and is read almost equally widely by adults. His six novels are hardly known, but have merit. *The Improvisatore* is an excellent romance, and *O.T.*, his best novel, is a psychological study.

The Improvisatore (1834, tr. 1863)

O.T. (1836, tr. 1870)

Fairy Tales (1835–72, tr. 1950–60)

ANDERSON, Poul (1926) American science fiction author who is prolific and popular. He uses a clear style to deal in ingenious, if not particularly original, ways with most of the major themes of the genre. His "Trader" series which explores the role of commerce in planetary interaction is clearly based on the experience of the American frontier, and has been influential. His best work extends contemporary characteristics of American society into a technologically different future; although he has written accomplished fantasy.

Guardians of Time (1960)

Trader to the Stars (1962)

The Merman's Children (1979)

ANDERSON, Sherwood (1876–1941) American story-writer, novelist, memoirist and newspaperman, born in Ohio. Anderson was one of the most influential writers of the twentieth century. Faulkner and Hemingway could not have been as good without him, and the former finally acknowledged this. His change-over from businessman to writer, although misrepresented as having been more sudden than it was, became a legend, symbolizing both the rootedness of American literature in "ordinary" life, and the rejection of the commercialism of that life. *Winesburg, Ohio*, connected sketches depicting small-town midwest society and revolt against its conventions, caught the mood of a generation, and combines lyricism with toughness and naturalistic reference to detail. With this he created a public for good fiction. His later work is mixed. The short stories are great and the novels flawed; but some, such as *Poor White* (1920), are profound; and the properly edited *Memoirs* (1969, essentially fictional) are almost as good as *Winesburg, Ohio*. His message, realist yet poetic, is as strong today as it was sixty years ago.

Winesburg, Ohio (1919)

Kit Brandon (1936)

Short Stories (1962)

ANDREWS, Lucilla ( ) English novelist, born in Suez. She joined the British Red Cross in 1940 and later qualified as a nurse at St Thomas's hospital, London. Medicine is the background of all her romantic and humorous novels; indeed the *Guardian* has described her as "the brand leader of hospital fiction".

Hospital Summer (1958)

Edinburgh Excursion (1970)

ANDRÉZEL, Pierre, see BLIXEN, Karen.

ANDRIC, Ivo (1892) Yugoslav (Serbian) novelist and story-writer, who won the Nobel Prize in 1961. He was born in Bosnia, where the Ottoman influence strongly survived, and was an "Austro-Hungarian" until the creation of Yugoslavia. As a Yugoslav nationalist he was imprisoned by the Austrians; but later became a diplomat (ambassador to Berlin until 1940). All this left its mark on his compassionate, epic and rather pessimistic work. *The Bridge on the Drina,* his best known novel, traces the lives of the guardians of the Bridge from the sixteenth to the twentieth century, and the Bridge comes to symbolize man's effort to create meaning out of frightfulness.

The Bridge on the Drina (1945, tr. 1959)

Bosnian Story (1945, tr. 1958)

The Woman from Sarajevo (1945, tr. 1966)

ANDRZEJEWSKI, Jerzy (1909) Polish novelist, much read and translated. Certain Polish critics have a marked distaste for him, regarding him as opportunistic; but he may be genuinely ambivalent. His most sympathetic Polish critic calls him "a writer of seasons" – and certainly he needs to be read by those who wish to understand changes in Poland. His earliest work is right-wing and Catholic (he was launched by a fascist, anti-semitic weekly): self-consciously in the style of François Mauriac. In World War II, however, he gained a reputation and authority for his unequivocally anti-Nazi stand. *Ashes and Diamonds*, later filmed with great success, is his best-known novel – the story of an anti-Russian communist and a pro-Russian one, both of whom are treated with equal sympathy. Since 1957, Andrzejewski has resorted to allegory and to experimentalism.

Ashes and Diamonds (1948, tr. 1962)

The Inquisitors (1957, tr. 1960)

He Cometh Leaping on the Mountain (1963, tr. 1965)

ANTHONY, Evelyn (1928) English romantic and suspense novelist, pen-name of Evelyn Ward Thomas. Beginning with successful historical novels of the better-researched variety, and receiving two U.S. Literary Guild awards, she turned to modern backgrounds of intrigue and international espionage. The latter have shown her to be an accomplished, exciting and ingenious storyteller.

The Tamarind Seed (1971)

The Occupying Power (1973)

ANTHONY, Piers (1934) American science fiction writer born in Britain, pseudonym of Piers A. Jacob. His novels are exuberant exotic adventure stories rich in ideas.

Chthon (1967)

A Spell for Chameleon (1977)

ARCHER, Jeffrey (1940) English thriller writer, formerly international athlete and politician. Archer resigned his seat in Parliament after a financial disgrace, and subsequently made an immense success with his high-powered thrillers.

Shall We Tell the President? (1977)

Kane and Abel (1979)

ARLEN, Michael (1895–1956) English novelist, originally Armenian. His mannered, sensationalist, superficial fantasies of Mayfair highlife were popular between the wars (*The Green Hat* was a best seller), but he has not lasted.

The Green Hat (1924)

Hell! Said the Duchess (1934)

ARMSTRONG, Charlotte (1906–69) American poet, playwright and story-writer who wrote popular suspense novels, often about mysterious threats to children, young girls and old women. She created a strong atmosphere of fear without explicit violence. Most of her novels are set in California where she lived.

The Unsuspected (1946)

Lemon in the Basket (1967)

ASCH, Sholem (1880–1957) Polish-Jewish novelist and story-writer, who became an American in 1920 and is the most acclaimed modern Yiddish writer before I. B. Singer, although not in his class. He was very prolific,

and put plenty of true verve into his intelligent but sentimental stories. *The Nazarene* is a portrait of Christ which sold sensationally but is now hardly read. Altogether more readable is the portrait of New York, *East River*.

Three Cities (1933)

The Nazarene (1939)

East River (1946)

ASHTON-WARNER, Sylvia (1908–78) New Zealand novelist and memoirist. A teacher by profession, she worked to bridge the gap between Maori and white children. *Spinster* is her first and best novel: written in stream of consciousness style without any literary know-how, its naivety becomes moving.

Spinster (1958)

Three (1970)

ASIMOV, Isaac (1920) American scientist and science fiction writer, born in Russia, who continues to have immense influence on the genre despite having written very little fiction

Isaac Asimov

since the 1950s, concentrating instead on works on scientific subjects. "Nightfall", published when he was 21, has been called the greatest short story in the field, and soon afterwards he produced *I Robot* the first of a series, in which, inspired by the influential SF magazine editor John W. Campbell, he worked out the three "Laws of Robotics", an ethical system for artificial intelligences which was quickly accepted by later writers on the subject. His *Foundation* trilogy is an ambitious and readable adventure saga with a theme of social engineering based on the collapse and rebuilding of a Galaxy-sized empire; it was inspired by Gibbon's *Decline and Fall of the Roman Empire*. *The Caves of Steel* is a dystopian view of the consequences of population growth.

I Robot (1951)

Foundation Trilogy (1951–53)

The Caves of Steel (1954)

ASTURIAS, Miguel (1899–1974) Guatemalan novelist, who studied the Mayan civilization and its language in Paris in his youth, under one of the world's leading authorities. He won the Nobel Prize in 1967. His first work was a fine retelling of Guatemalan legends. He was a diplomat under his country's democratic regimes, but lived in exile under the dictatorships. His best known novel is *The President*, begun in 1922 but not published until 1946. It is one of the most powerful of all works about totalitarian rule: the President is seen as pure Evil, and his terrible world becomes, in the vision of Asturias, the incarnation of all modern dictatorships. Later Asturias turned to a different kind of novel: these have been classed as "magic realism"; and while this is sometimes true it fails to do justice to his re-creation of Quiche (the language of millions of Indians) thinking into a viable Spanish. The later novels are more difficult, but worth the effort.

The President (1946, tr. 1963)

The Cyclone (1950, tr. 1967)

The Mulatta and Mr Fly (1960, tr. 1967)

ATHERTON, Gertrude (1857–1948) American novelist, biographer and pseudo-historian. She was a prolific, lively and erratic author, who was very widely read in the 1920s. She owed her success not only to her energy but to the fact that she was called "erotic". *The Black Oxen* is ridiculous and yet readable: it involves a glandular rejuvenation of its heroine.

The Conqueror (1922)

The Black Oxen (1923)

The Californians (1935)

ATWOOD, Margaret (1939) Canadian novelist, story-writer, poet and critic, whose novels are social comedies with elements of fantasy and marked verbal wit. Her themes are the emotional interdependence of men and women and their search for self-discovery and self-reliance.

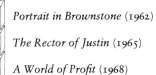

The Edible Woman (1969)

Surfacing (1973)

AUCHINCLOSS, Louis (1917) American novelist, critic and story-writer; a lawyer by profession. Auchincloss's mentors are the novelists of whom he has made lucid, useful and fairly unsubtle studies: Edith Wharton, Ellen Glasgow and other women novelists behind whom stands, usually, the figure of Henry James. Auchincloss is exceedingly accomplished, a master of the well-made novel, and his psychology is sound. Modernism is abhorrent to him. Much of his work deals with New York high society – and particularly with the law – and he conspicuously lacks doubt about the values of the society he depicts.

Portrait in Brownstone (1962)

The Rector of Justin (1965)

A World of Profit (1968)

AUSTEN, Jane (1775–1817) English novelist, daughter of a rector. She was educated at home, and acquired a good knowledge of English literature. Two of her brothers rose high in the Navy, and she learned much about the society in which they moved. She may have once been in love, and have been robbed of fulfilment only by her beloved's death. Nothing she ever did was less than respectable; and it is obvious that as a person, although vivacious, she was something of a calculating puritan, forever dwelling upon what was correct and what was incorrect. Her novels would seem repulsively detached and "snobbish" but for the following qualities: a sense of fun, a superb appreciation of the comic in character, a subtle morality, a meticulously exercised capacity for exact observation, and an ability to dissect real snobbery. Her sense of form was so excellent that she may certainly be said to have invented the conventional English novel. Her plotting is superb – before one climax is reached another is building up – and is perhaps the most lasting example she has left. Her novels are always concerned with whom a girl should marry, and why, and how it happens. If she were not so skilful, we might say that her deficiency is that she leaves us with happy marriages but does not know of what they consist. Her first novel, *Northanger Abbey* (1818) (although she had written apprentice work before that), was a parody of Mrs Radcliffe. Her novels were not published in the order of their composition, which is not

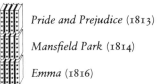

Jane Austen

exactly known. Further posthumous fragments and parts of novels have been published. The important novels, each of which has its champions as her greatest, are *Sense and Sensibility* (1811), *Pride and Prejudice, Mansfield Park, Emma* and *Persuasion* (1818). She is also a great creator of comic characters (Mr Collins, Mr Bates, and many others).

Pride and Prejudice (1813)

Mansfield Park (1814)

Emma (1816)

AVALLONE, Michael, Jr (1924) American novelist of great versatility, who wrote tales of private investigators, spies, science fiction and the supernatural, and used many pseudonyms. His best-known creation, Ed Noon, is personal investigator for the U.S. President. Avallone has an effortless style and specializes in clipped dialogue, fast action and larger-than-life characters.

The Tall Dolores (1956)

The February Doll Murders (1966)

Shoot It Again, Sam (1972)

AYMÉ, Marcel (1902–67) French novelist, story-writer and playwright. Born in the Jura of humble origins, he was self-educated. His essential genius is expressed in his first successful novel *The Green Mare*. He was a savage satirist, drawing mainly on Rabelais for his methods; and is coarse, gross, destructive, but not malicious. He poked gusty fun at everything, and frequently had recourse to fantasy.

He lacks a coherent point of view, but one may discern a sense of values in his doubled-up-with-laughter, mocking attitude. His works were much translated.

The Green Mare (1933, tr. 1935)

The Miraculous Barber (1941, tr. 1949)

The Conscience of Love (1960, tr. 1962)

B

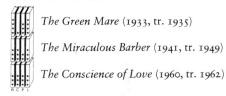

BABEL, Isaak (1894–?1941) Russian-Jewish story-writer and playwright; one of Stalin's victims. He went over to the Bolsheviks in 1917, and fought with the dashing General Budyonny's cavalry on the Polish front. This gave him material for his series of war sketches *Red Cavalry* (1926), his most famous work. Here violence is depicted through the eyes of an intellectual, without political bias; the result is a mixture of luridness, shock, humaneness and apparent cruelty. Other stories present aspects of Jewish life in Odessa, often dealing with the exploits of the Jewish gangster Benya Krik. Babel was an ironist, very much of the "autonomous" school. He is an original writer of great power and dazed intelligence. He told the Soviet authorities that he was working in a "new category": "Silence".

Collected Stories (1957)

BACCHELLI, Riccardo (1891) Italian novelist and journalist. He is a highly gifted novelist who has remained essentially a conventional realist, but has made use of certain modernist procedures such as modified stream of consciousness and romantically heightened description. He is a very fine popular novelist, and the historical *The Mill on the Po*, a trilogy, is a substantial achievement in realist fiction.

 *The Devil at Long Bridge* (1927, tr. 1929)

 *The Mill on the Po* (1938–40, tr. 1952–55)

The Son of Stalin (1953, tr. 1956)

BACH, Richard (1936) American writer and pilot, author of *Jonathan Livingstone Seagull* and four other allegorical books, only superficially concerned with flying. *Jonathan Livingstone Seagull* tells of a bird whose concept of flight for flight's sake introduces him to a world where all limitations are self-induced, and death is "an abrupt change of consciousness". Its message is sincere, and had a wide appeal in the early 1970s. His later books, especially *Illusions*, are merely trite.

Jonathan Livingstone Seagull (1970)

Illusions (1977)

BAGBY, George, see STEIN, Aaron Marc.

BAGLEY, Desmond (1923) British writer of thrillers with the emphasis on action, adventure and exotic settings. Bagley has sacrificed realism to produce masterpieces of sustained excitement. In *High Citadel* (1965) a small group has to fight its way out of a trap high in the Andes. *The Golden Keel* concerns three men sailing from South Africa to Italy, and pays more attention to character.

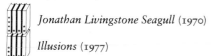 *The Golden Keel* (1963)

Running Blind (1970)

Flyaway (1979)

BAGNOLD, Enid (1889) English playwright and novelist. Her best work has been done in the theatre, but she is an able novelist whose clever and well-informed fantasy *National Velvet* has continued to capture popular imagination.

 *Serena Blandish* (1925)

National Velvet (1935)

BAILEY, H. C. (1878–1961) English detective story-writer, creator of physician-surgeon Reginald Fortune and shyster lawyer Joshua Clunk. His first works were historical novels, but he later specialized in intuitive detective puzzles.

Call Mr Fortune (stories, 1920)

The Red Castle (1932)

Black Land, White Land (1937)

BAINBRIDGE, Beryl (1934) English novelist. She is a black comedian who writes about "outrageous" events in a blandly casual manner. She has acquired a considerable following, as her mastery of the throw-away, comic, and yet tragically oriented, style has increased. *The Bottle Factory Outing* is her most successful exploitation of the half-glimpsed potentialities of the farcical: she elicits from her aware reader the exclamation, "but these are people!", and she means to. In *Young Adolf* (1978) she attempts to blend her broadly Joycean style with intellectual comment on modern history; the result is less assured, although interesting.

Harriet Said (1972)

The Dressmaker (1972, in US *The Secret Glass* 1974)

The Bottle Factory Outing (1974)

BAKER, Dorothy (1907–68) American novelist, married to Howard Baker, the novelist and poet. She began as an imitator of Hemingway but then, as she declared, had to purge herself of her "abject admiration". Her novels are well made, subtle studies written from the "single point of view" of Henry James, but she has none of James' fear of sexual candour. *Young Man with a Horn* is based on Bix Biederbecke, and is her most famous novel. Her uniformly excellent work is now a trifle neglected.

Young Man with a Horn (1938)

Trio (1943)

Cassandra at the Wedding (1962)

BALCHIN, Nigel (1908–70) English novelist. The tense, bomb-defusing drama *The Small Back Room*, which is also a satire on the civil service, was followed by several other competent psychological dramas.

The Small Back Room (1943)

Mine Own Executioner (1945)

In the Absence of Mrs Petersen (1966)

BALDWIN, James (1924) American negro novelist, story-writer, polemicist and playwright. With Richard Wright and Ralph Elison, Baldwin is the most influential modern

James Baldwin

black writer. In the 1970s his energy flagged, and interest in him is dwindling, although his early and best novels remain widely read and discussed. It was felt that *Another Country*, *Giovanni's Room* and *Go Tell It On The Mountain*, contained great passages written by a man who had the potentiality to write a great novel; this was true – but certainly the great novel has failed to come. It is most fruitful to consider Baldwin's literary achievement independently of his polemic, which varies from the beautiful and just to the (understandably) neurotic and over-aggressive. His recent modifications of his violent position may very well lead to a new burst of inspired fiction; but his recent *Just Above My Head* (1979) breaks little new ground. *Go Tell It On The Mountain* dealt with his childhood experiences as a negro and as victim of a fanatic religious sect. *Giovanni's Room* is an exquisite exploration of a homosexual relationship between two white men. Successors are deeply interesting, but have not been received as well.

Go Tell It On The Mountain (1953)

Giovanni's Room (1956)

Another Country (1962)

BALL, John (1911) American writer of detective stories, who created one of the first black detectives, Virgil Tibbs, in *In the Heat of the Night*. He continues to produce books featuring Tibbs, who is just a little too perfect a policeman and family man to be convincing. *Mark One – The Dummy* (1974) was his first book without Tibbs; it is a competent spy thriller.

In the Heat of the Night (1965)

Five Pieces of Jade (1972)

BALLANTYNE, R. M. (1825–94) Scottish writer of boys' adventure yarns of which at least *Coral Island* is still read. He is genteel, but within his limits displayed prodigious energy.

Martin Rattler (1858)

Coral Island (1858)

The Iron Horse (1871)

BALLARD, J. G. (1930) British science fiction author. In his very popular early stories, environmental catastrophe – the end of rainfall in *The Burning World,* the melting of the ice-caps in *The Drowned World* (1962) – triggers a closely examined disintegration; at first social and then personal. Although the ecologist's sense of the fine balance of human existence forms part of these books, they are imbued with a feeling of deeper pessimism about human nature itself. This is made clearer in later novels, like *Crash, Concrete Island* (1974), and *High Rise* (1975), in which the environment, such as motorways and tower block flats, are man-made and already realized but have been heightened and exaggerated. Although he writes in the SF mode, he is in many ways a conventional, if gloomy, chronicler of human fallibility.

The Burning World (1964, in Britain *The Drought* 1965)

The Crystal World (1966)

Crash (1972)

BALZAC, Honoré de (1799–1850) French novelist. His life was a series of disasters; but he drew material from his experiences, and was not as perpetually unhappy as one would expect from an account of his love affairs, debts, defeats, ruinations and unsuccessful enterprises. He was one of the most hardworking of all novelists, and one of the most uneven. Historically he must be judged by his one single work, of ninety or so novels and stories, *The Human Comedy*; but some of the individual novels are very much better than others. The pseudo-philosophical system on which he thought he based his work is, as all concede, a worthless mixture of the occult, and of misunderstandings of the work of natural historians: he was not an intellectual but an instinctive artist, who was really working out his own conflicts. His characters seem flat but are given "roundness" (at their best) by his unique method of description. The verdict of the poet Baudelaire that he was a "visionary" has been generally accepted: he gives a realist picture of French society in his lifetime. He creates his own world, which is vibrant with life; and the quality of his vision is quite as valuable as that of a meticulous historian. His novels are not psychological, they are melo-

Honoré de Balzac

dramatic; but they depict with astonishing success the plight of individuals in their environment.

Old Goriot (1834–35, tr. 1951)

Lost Illusions (1843, tr. 1951)

Cousin Bette (1846, tr. 1948)

BANKS, Lynne Reid (1929) English novelist and playwright who also holds Israeli nationality. Her best known novel is her first, *The L-Shaped Room,* which deals rawly and almost naturalistically with the plight of a woman saddled with a child as a result of a casual, meaningless encounter. Later work is more accomplished but less urgent.

The L-Shaped Room (1960)

The Backward Shadow (1970)

The Adventures of King Midas (1974)

BARAKA, Imamu Amiri, see JONES, LeRoi.

BARBEY D'AUREVILLY, Jules (1808–89) French story-writer, novelist, romantic dandy, Catholic and condemner of realism. His stories are perfervid modified Gothic deriving from

Scott. He was highly original, interestingly self-contradictory – and should be more widely translated.

Bewitched (1854, tr. 1928)

Les Diaboliques (1874, tr. 1925; tr. 1964 as *The She-Devils*)

What Never Dies (1884, tr. 1909)

BARDIN, John Franklin (1916) American suspense writer. Bardin wrote three extraordinary mystery novels, after which he lost touch with his publishers for nearly 30 years; Julian Symons located him, and arranged the republication of the books in paperback. They are haunting, intense and evocative.

The Deadly Percheron (1946)

The Last of Philip Banter (1947)

Devil Take the Blue-Tail Fly (1948)

BARING-GOULD, Sabine (1834–1924) English parson who wrote hymns ("Onward Christian Soldiers"), novels and general works of great usefulness. He was a Devon regionalist; and his work, dramatic and often highly observant, is now undervalued, although John Fowles has introduced a re-issue of *Mehalah*.

Mehalah (1880)

The Gaverocks (1888)

The Broom-Squire (1896)

BARKER, A. L. (1918) English novelist and story-writer who is expert at describing how ordinary people respond to extraordinary events. Her novellas and stories are free from the bleak despair which tends to break into her rambling, episodic novels.

Lost Upon the Roundabouts (stories, 1964)

The Middling (1967)

A Heavy Feather (1979)

BARNES, Djuna (1892) American novelist and playwright whose work has an Anglo-European flavour. She owes her literary reputation to T. S. Eliot's praise of *Nightwood*: he liked its atmosphere of "Jacobean tragedy". Barnes is fascinated by lesbians, diseased personalities, depravity and animals. She is a most original writer whose intelligent sensationalism is beginning to influence many much younger novelists, often militant homosexuals.

A Book of Repulsive Women (1911, repr. 1948)

Ryder (1928, repr. 1979)

Nightwood (1936)

BAROJA, Pio (1872–1956) Spanish novelist who was a doctor and a baker before devoting himself to literature. His numerous formless novels (he defended their "bad style" and lack of shape on the grounds that they thus resembled life) are, at their best, of enormous and affecting power – and have more form than he admitted. He is exceedingly versatile in his subject matter, but most of his characters are underdogs or struggling, and his method clearly derives from the picaresque. His favourite theme was Basque life.

The City of The Discreet (1905, tr. 1917)

Paradox King (1906, tr. 1931)

The Tree of Knowledge (1911, tr. 1928)

BARRIE, J. M. (1860–1937) Playwright (*Peter Pan*), who was at first a novelist. His fiction sentimentally exploited Scottish customs for the amusement of English readers, which much irritated some of his countrymen, who described this kind of patronizing fiction as the "kailyard school".

The Little Minister (1891)

Peter Pan and Wendy (1911)

BARSTOW, Stan (1928) English novelist who scored a great success with his first novel *A Kind of Loving*, a moving before-and-after study of a shotgun marriage. Its sequel, *The Watchers on the Shore* (1966) is more episodic and brashly melodramatic.

A Kind of Loving (1960)

Ask Me Tomorrow (1962)

Joby (1964)

BARTH, John (1930) American novelist, pasticheur and story-writer, born in Maryland. Barth's books are owned by a large proportion of the "highbrow" public. He owes a great deal to Jorge Luis Borges, but genuinely delights fewer readers. Much in his five novels is brilliant. He uses parody of most of the old forms, satire of mythopoeic writing, allegory, fables and games. Whether all this coheres is an open question. *The Floating Opera* (1956) is about a man who decides not to kill himself, and is in part a parody of Dostoyevsky. *The End of the Road* was disliked by many as "nasty", but may well be his most substantial novel, since its central character (who is straight out of Pirandello) is his most psychologically real creation. *The Sotweed Factor* (1960) is a huge, learned, historical fantasy. *Giles Goat-Boy* examines education in just about all the old modes from Plato through Rabelais to Dewey. Barth is unquestionably erudite. But whether he is a critic-playing-novelist, or an original novelist, has not been settled. Critics who can keep up with his allusions call him "great"; but even Terry Southern calls him "overwhelmingly tedious". In short, he is much complained about, and may not be so much read as shelved by the common reader. But a talent is there.

The End of the Road (1961)

Giles Goat-Boy (1966)

Lost in the Funhouse (1968)

BARTHELME, Donald (1933) American story-writer and novelist. Barthelme, a self-confessed existentialist (he was brought up a Catholic), has employed modernist procedures (surrealism, black humour, questioning of the legitimacy of realist procedures) and yet manages to find a wide audience by a clever professionalism. As he has said, he really only believes in fragments, so that his novella *Snow*

John Barth

White is in fragmentary form. He is self-questioning and witty, and he is maturing – as *Sadness* demonstrates. The early Catholic influence now seems to be creeping into his work.

 Come Back, Dr Caligari (1964)

Snow White (1967)

Sadness (1972)

BASSANI, Giorgio (1916) Italian novelist and story writer, who was born in Ferrara of Jewish origin. He writes with subtle sensitivity of the oppressed under fascism, and, latterly, of less starkly clear-cut but equivalent situations. He has perhaps not bettered *The Gold Rimmed Spectacles,* about a decent homosexual doctor destroyed by the fascist state of mind.

 The Gold Rimmed Spectacles (1958, tr. 1960)

 The Garden of the Finzi-Continis (1962, tr. 1965)

 The Heron (1968, tr. 1970)

BASSO, Hamilton (1904–64) American novelist, born in Louisiana. He was a moderate chronicler of Southern habits of life, but *Sun in Capricorn* is venomously exact in its portrayal of a corrupt politician of the Huey Long type.

 Courthouse Square (1936)

Sun in Capricorn (1942)

The View from Pompey's Head (1954)

BATES H. E. (1905–74) English story-writer and novelist. Bates went through several phases. His most artistically successful work was done before 1945, in the realm of the short story. Then he began to write good popular novels, of which *The Purple Plain* (1947) is typical. He found a new audience with his

H. E. Bates

creation of the Larkin family in such novels as *The Darling Buds of May,* which are vulgar, gusty and good-natured farce. He continued to write stories, and it is for these that he will be remembered: the best are soaked in authentic atmosphere, and make of him an English Maupassant.

 Fair Stood the Wind for France (1944)

Selected Stories (1957)

The Darling Buds of May (1958)

BAUM, L. Frank (1856–1919) American playwright, novelist and children's writer. He wrote *The Wonderful Wizard of Oz,* a fantasy of a Kansas schoolgirl, Dorothy, and her adventures in a magic land with the Tin Woodman, the Cowardly Lion and the Scarecrow. The book, immediately popular, was adapted for the stage, and was followed by thirteen more Oz Books. Baum wrote some sixty books, mostly for children.

 The Wonderful Wizard of Oz (1900)

BAUM, Vicki (1888–1960) Viennese-born novelist who became an American. She scored a hit with *Grand Hotel,* in which many personalities are brought together in one setting. She never achieved the same success, but wrote many other entertaining, lively books.

 Grand Hotel (1930)

Ballerina (1958)

BAWDEN, Nina (1925) English novelist and writer for children. Her many admirably constructed novels show a lucid, serio-comic acceptance of the perversities of human behaviour, particularly among the "enlightened" English middle class.

 Tortoise by Candlelight (1963)

Familiar Passions (1979)

BAX, Roger, see GARVE, Andrew.

BEACH, Edward L. (1918) American novelist who made his career in the U.S. Navy and served with distinction throughout World War II. His war novel *Run Silent, Run Deep* has true, authentic excitement.

 Run Silent, Run Deep (1955)

Dust on the Sea (1972)

BEAUVOIR, Simone de (1908) French novelist, essayist and memoirist. Beauvoir has been the companion of J. P. Sartre for over thirty years. *She Came to Stay* illustrates, with rather less ambiguity than Sartre, the possibility of the attainment of the existentialist "authenticity" –

Simone de Beauvoir

which is, briefly, the capacity of a person to act as himself, and to remain uninfluenced by bourgeois or other values. *The Mandarins* is a psychological study of post-war intellectual Paris, still somewhat underrated; it contains portraits of several literary and philosophical figures. Beauvoir does not possess the epic sweep of Sartre as a novelist, but she has as much, or even more, psychological power, especially with female characters.

 She Came to Stay (1943, tr. 1949)

All Men Are Mortal (1946, tr. 1955)

The Mandarins (1954, tr. 1957)

BECKETT, Samuel (1906) Irish novelist, playwright and poet, who has written in both English and French (he has been resident in France for most of his life) – but now only in the latter, which he usually himself translates into English. He was virtually unknown until the performance of his play *Waiting for Godot* in 1953; in 1969 he received the Nobel Prize. Beckett chose to write in French in order to avoid rhetoric and attain discipline and precision. Concentration on a language not his own causes him to express himself in the most disciplined possible manner. He knew Joyce, and was influenced by him; but too much has been made of the influence. He is a more thoroughly philosophical writer. Both his plays and his poems may be described as, essentially, ironic and often humorous investigations into the consequences of meaninglessness. Accepting the existentialist conclusions of Sartre – which he reached, however, by a route of his own – he offers no political or psychological Marxist "humanism" by which life can be given meaning. To appreciate him fully it is necessary to understand something of the thought of a number of philosophers old and new – mostly old. His work has been much explained in these terms in the many books on him. Broken down into categories, his prose is a unique blend of stream of consciousness, naturalist gloom – his chief characters are tramps, bums, derelicts and lunatics – and series of verbal games which undermine, with much pathos, the status of language itself. Of the novels the famous trilogy *Molloy, Malone Dies* and *The Unnameable* (collected as *Three Novels*) is infinitely the most accessible together with *Murphy* and *Watt*. The later prose, especially the novel *How It Is* (1961, tr. 1964), is more recondite, although by no means necessarily inferior.

Murphy (1938)

Watt (1953)

Three Novels (1959)

BECKFORD, William (1760–1844) Eccentric English millionaire writer who wrote his masterpiece, the fantasy *Vathek*, in French. It is a Faust-type story set in the Orient, with Gothic elements: the product of a highly original mind. He was a gifted writer; his two travel books have great style and are still entertaining.

Vathek (1787, tr. 1786; repr. 1970)

BEDFORD, Sybille (1911) English novelist of German parentage. *A Legacy* is set in pre-1914 Germany, a brilliantly evoked picture of the victorious yet enslaved Hohenzollern Reich. After this complex, oddly constructed but triumphant book, Miss Bedford wrote two further novels which, though more accessible and despite a glossy period charm, are disappointing.

A Legacy (1956)

A Favourite of the Gods (1963)

A Compass Error (1968)

BEERBOHM, Max (1876–1956) English novelist, caricaturist, essayist, critic, wit and parodist. Beerbohm concealed a sometimes deadly malice behind a superb elegance. In certain respects he has affinities with Borges, as in his greatest achievement, *Seven Men* (stories). *Zuleika Dobson*, a romance set in Oxford, is an excellent minor fantasy. The parodies in *A Christmas Garland* (of Wells, Bennett, James

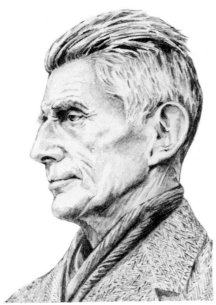

Samuel Beckett

and others) are masterly and unparalleled. Beerbohm was knighted in 1939.

Zuleika Dobson (1911)

A Christmas Garland (1912)

Seven Men (1919)

BEHN, Aphra (?1640–1689) English playwright, poet, novelist and spy, the first woman to keep herself by writing. Her fiction is modelled on continental romance, but introduces elements of realism and anticipates Rousseau (in *Oroonoko*) by presenting a "noble savage". She also anticipated the anti-colonialist and emancipation movements. Many of her novels are well worth reading, and have been undervalued: especially *Oroonoko, The Fair Jilt* and *The Adventure of the Black Lady*.

The Novels of Aphra Behn (1905)

BEHRMAN, S. N. (1893–1973) American journalist and screenwriter, best known as a playwright. Behrman long intended to write a novel, but his single attempt, *The Burning Glass*, did not appear until the end of his life.

The Burning Glass (1968)

BELLAMY, Edward (1850–98) American novelist. His novels are without interest except for *Looking Backward: 2000–1887*, which is historically important as one of the first modern utopias. This was unintentionally prophetic since it seemed to postulate as ideal a society in which economic competition has been eliminated by state capitalism and equal wages.

Looking Backward (1888)

BELLOW, Saul (1915) American novelist born in Canada of Jewish parents. He won the Nobel prize in 1976, and is generally regarded as one of the greatest living novelists. Although he is uneven, his energies have not flagged: his most recent novel *Humboldt's Gift,* a fictionalized portrait of Delmore Schwartz, is unquestionably as good as any of his previous seven – and breaks new ground. Bellow has used almost every variety of fictional mode to explore the condition of man in the twentieth century, but he has remained determinedly coherent. He has drawn greatly on his knowledge of anthropology and psychology, and is only as "modern" as he finds his age demands. As well as being serious in the fullest sense, he is also a magnificent entertainer, knowing that he cannot afford to bore his reader. Even in his less successful novels he is never pretentious. Bellow owes his success in great measure to his conviction that, in what everyone concedes is a difficult and confusing age, the artist must be able to move the human heart. His subject is large; it covers the same ground covered by sociology and religion, but covers it – for many – much more satisfactorily and richly than the majority of sociologists, anthropologists and priests. This subject is the relationship between individual man and his society; and it embraces the more complicated question of the manner in which religious feeling and need survive. His finest novels are *The Victim, Seize the Day* (1956, really a novella), *Herzog*

Saul Bellow

and *Humboldt's Gift*. His first novel *Dangling Man* (1944) is his most conventional; about a man awaiting his draft papers, it is rich in promise. *The Adventures of Augie March* (1953) is sprawling and almost purely picaresque – but the lack of structure did not really suit Bellow's genius. *Herzog* makes innovatory use of epistolary techniques, and arouses emotions of laughter mixed with tears; it is held together by the eponymous hero's persistent efforts to organize his unorganizable past. *Mr Sammler's Planet* (1970) is somewhat too ambitious, attempting too ostensibly to "make sense of life on earth"; but it contains superb passages. *Humboldt's Gift* is a deeply moving study of a good man's descent into paranoia and an absurd death. It epitomizes the plight of the American artist (standing here for the sensitive and intelligent man) who succumbs: fails to fulfil his promise, does not give to the world what he could have given. It is about a non-survivor, and is therefore a tragedy. But the portrayal – the fact that there is a man, subject to the same pressures, who can survive to give us the account – is essentially affirmatory, and gives hope.

The Victim (1947)

Herzog (1964)

Humboldt's Gift (1975)

BEMELMANS, Ludwig (1898–1963) German-Belgian born American novelist and essayist, who came early to America (as a hotel waiter). He wrote whimsical, witty, sentimental, and informative books based mostly on his own experiences.

Hotel Splendide (1941)

The Street Where the Heart Lies (1963)

BENCHLEY, Peter (1940) American writer. A reporter on the *Washington Post,* he also worked for *Newsweek* and wrote speeches for President Johnson. *Jaws* was his first novel and proved to be a blockbuster. This action-packed story about a killer shark was later made into a record-breaking film. *The Island,* which deals with piracy in the Caribbean, has rather less impact than his earlier books.

Jaws (1974)

The Deep (1976)

The Island (1979)

BENEDICTUS, David (1938) English novelist. His first novel, *The Fourth of June,* a satirical study of his Eton schooldays, was a success not equalled by later, better, more serious novels like *World of Windows* (1971) and an ambitious Jewish novel *Twentieth-Century Man.*

The Fourth of June (1962)

Twentieth-Century Man (1978)

BENÉT, Stephen Vincent (1898–1943) American poet, novelist, dramatist and short story-writer. His five novels include *Jean Huguenot* (1923); but better known are his stories,

notably the comic tale "The Devil and Daniel Webster" (in *Thirteen O'Clock*) in which a New Hampshire farmer sells his soul to the devil.

Thirteen O'Clock (1937)

Tales Before Midnight (1939)

BENNETT, E. Arnold (1867–1931) English (Midlands) novelist, journalist and critic. Bennett was the most thorough-going realist of his time. He presented a somewhat vulgar image of himself as a self-made man who was "in literature for cash", but the quality of feeling in his finest novels, his mastery of realist technique, and in particular his *Journals* (1932–3) show him to have been sensitive and compassionate. Moreover, he championed the cause – in his role as fiction critic of the *Evening Standard* – of very many novelists different from himself, including Joyce. His masterpieces are *The Old Wives' Tale, Clayhanger* forming with its two sequels *Hilda Lessways* and *These Twain*, a trilogy which as a whole did not quite live up to its promise – and *Riceyman Steps* (1923). He was a master storyteller, a fine plotter, and his characterization at its best is superb. He had a vivid imagination which he curbed by use of his gift for observation. *The Card* (1911), about a likeable knave who rises to eminence by good sense and clever tricks, anticipated William Cooper, Kingsley Amis and John Wain. *Riceyman Steps* has genuine tragic stature, and is certainly a great novel.

The Old Wives' Tale (1908)

Clayhanger (1910)

Riceyman Steps (1923)

BENSON, E. F. (1867–1940) English novelist and short story writer. Benson's prolific output of novels has not weathered nearly so well as his evocative ghost stories which are frequently anthologized. The very best of these is "The Face" in the collection *Spook Stories*.

Spook Stories (1929)

More Spook Stories (1934)

BENSON, Stella (1892–1933) English novelist who died young of pneumonia. She was a remarkable woman: a devotee of Tolstoy, an inveterate traveller, and possessed of a fine imagination whose qualities have as yet gone largely unrecognized. Only *Tobit Transplanted* did well in terms of sales. She left a diary which she instructed might be published in 1973: this should be made available, as it is likely to prove a classic.

The Little World (1925)

Tobit Transplanted (1931)

Collected Stories (1936)

BENTLEY, E. C. (1875–1956) English detective-story writer and humourist. He created Philip Trent as a conscious reaction against the artificiality of the detective fiction of his day. "It should be possible . . . to write a detective story in which the detective was recognizable as a human being." Bentley's naturalism, humour and characterization placed him among the genre's immortals.

Trent's Last Case (1913)

Trent's Own Case (with H. Warner Allen, 1936)

BERGER, John (1926) English novelist and art critic. His *G* received the Booker Prize but has not appealed to a wide circle of readers, although a few critics admired its highly self-conscious experimentalism.

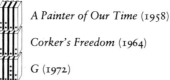

A Painter of Our Time (1958)

Corker's Freedom (1964)

G (1972)

BERGER, Thomas (1924) American novelist born in Ohio. He is a satirical writer of great inventiveness, but is now maturing into a writer of considerable psychological and dramatic power. The Reinhart Novels (*Crazy in Berlin, Reinhart in Love, Vital Parts*, 1958, 1962, 1970 respectively) skilfully chart the progress of an American Schweik (see Hašek). His most ambitious novel is his comic, satirical and yet loving *Little Big Man*, on the legends and realities of the Wild West; and his most serious is *Killing Time*, an absorbing book about a mass killer who regards murder as a favour to the victim.

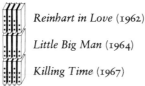

Reinhart in Love (1962)

Little Big Man (1964)

Killing Time (1967)

BERGMAN, Andrew (   ) American detective-story writer who manages with great success to write stories set in the 1940s. The dialogue crackles with an authentic, Chandleresque wit and toughness. Bergman's private eye, Jack Le Vine, tends to happen on people who were famous at the time – Governor Dewey, Humphrey Bogart – and those who would one day be renowned – Richard Nixon.

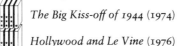

The Big Kiss-off of 1944 (1974)

Hollywood and Le Vine (1976)

Wendell Berry

BERGMAN, Hjalmar (1883–1931) Swedish novelist, story-writer and playwright. His modernism – his awareness of the ambivalence of human nature, and of the problem of personal freedom – stemmed more from his personal need than from the influence of particular writers. Some of his best novels have not been translated: *Clownen Jac* (1930), his final bleak and overly harsh judgement of himself as a prostitutor of his gifts, is one. He is a comedian, a caricaturist and yet a stern moralist; he anticipated black humour and the modern tendency to Gothic but his flavour is uniquely his own.

God's Orchid (1919, tr. 1924)

The Head of the Firm (1924, tr. 1936)

BERKELEY, Anthony, see ILES, Francis.

BERMANT, Chaim (1929) Polish-born British novelist who was brought up and educated in Scotland. As he has written, his "characters are mainly Jewish, hapless but not helpless . . . The treatment is humorous, but the intention is serious." His novels are much enjoyed as comic, but critics tend to prefer his non-fiction. *Diary of an Old Man* is a real tour de force, like all his fiction readable, tender and intelligent.

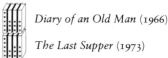

Diary of an Old Man (1966)

The Last Supper (1973)

BERNANOS, Georges (1888–1948) French novelist and essayist. Bernanos belongs to the tradition of Catholic writers who, though fiercely devout, are savage critics of the majority of their co-religionists. He began as a reactionary royalist; but when he saw the atrocities committed by the Church in the Spanish Civil War he denounced them. He is a violent and deliberately intemperate writer; but a fascinating and impassioned one. For him the priest is one who must literally fight Satan (he seriously believed that Gide, whom he savaged in *The Open Mind*, was a representative of the Devil); but he is not without compassion, and his *Diary of a Country Priest* deals poignantly with the problems of a priest who cannot resist evil; it is one of the century's great novels. His work has immense power, and quite transcends its author's plain unfairness and ferocity. His style is chaotic but his religious conviction causes his *Monsieur Ouine* novels to cohere, and even confers an odd, unique structure upon them.

A Crime (1935, tr. 1936)

The Open Mind (1943, tr. 1945, rev. 1955, n.t.)

BERRY, Wendell (1934) American novelist, poet and essayist. His novels deal sensitively with the lives of working men, particularly farmers, and with local Kentucky history.

 Nathan Coulter (1960)

The Hidden Wound (1970)

BESTER, Alfred (1913) American science fiction writer whose small output includes two novels which have become classics of the genre. *The Demolished Man* is a murder story set in a world whose rulers are masters of telepathy. *The Stars My Destination* is a gripping story of interplanetary strife. The best collection of his stories is *The Dark Side of Earth* (1964).

 The Demolished Man (1953)

The Stars My Destination (1956, in Britain *Tiger! Tiger!*)

 The Computer Connection (1974)

BETI, Mongo (1932) Francophone novelist born in Cameroons and educated in France. He treats sympathetically of French malad-ministration in the Cameroons, but his real theme is the plight of the Africans. He is admired for his energetic, Rabelaisian style; his attitude is not aggressive, but satirically comic.

 Poor Christ of Bomba (1956, tr. 1971)

King Lazarus (1958, tr. 1961)

BIERCE, Ambrose (1842–?1914) American story-writer, essayist and aphorist, who van-ished in Mexico during a political upheaval. For years he was dismissed by critics as a minor writer, and was perhaps best known for his cynical *The Devil's Dictionary* (1906), a series of gleefully unpleasant – sometimes forced – aphorisms. Then he began to be taken seriously for his best work, his short stories. He was an elegant, effective ironist, forever contemplating the meaninglessness of existence; he had a superb sense of psychology, especially of that of men under the various stresses of battle – he had fought in the Civil War.

 The Collected Writings (1946)

BIGGERS, Earl Derr (1884–1933) American novelist and dramatist, chiefly remembered for his detective, the imperturbable Charlie Chan, who became the hero of radio dramas, comic strips and films. The mysteries in which he features are unpretentious, conventional and humorous.

 The House without a Key (1925)

Charlie Chan Carries On (1930)

BINGHAM, John (1911) British crime novelist who was among the first to write British crime stories in which the police were not honest and decent. Many of his books convey a strong feeling of the unease of British life in the 1950s, 1960s and 1970s. Intriguing situations, such as a priest, confessor to top people, turning atheist (*God's Defector*) serve him best.

 My Name Is Michael Sibley (1952)

A Fragment of Fear (1965)

God's Defector (1976)

BIRD, Robert Montgomery (1806–54) Ameri-can novelist and dramatist. His novels are lively satirical picaresque, quite liberal in sympathy. *Nick of the Woods* is about early struggles with the Indians.

 Sheppard Lee (1836)

Nick of the Woods (1837)

The Adventures of Robin Day (1839)

BLACKMORE, R. D. (1825–1900) English novelist and poet, famous for one novel, *Lorna Doone*, a historical romance in the manner of Scott. The love affair between John Ridd and Lorna, although stereotyped, has an epic quality, perhaps because of the magnificent description of its West Country setting.

 Lorna Doone (1869)

The Maid of Sker (1872)

Springhaven (1877)

BLACKWOOD, Algernon (1869–1951) English writer of novels and stories of the super-natural. He regarded himself as a serious writer using the medium of the supernatural, but few critics have accepted this claim. Nonetheless, all concede that his best stories have genuine *frisson*, and that he wrote very well.

 The Dance of Death (1927)

Shocks (1935)

Tales of the Uncanny and Supernatural (1949)

BLAKE, Nicholas (1904–72) English crime novelist, pseudonym of the poet, eventually Laureate, Cecil Day Lewis. He wrote in the literary detective tradition but with an icono-clastic left-wing tone. His first books were pure puzzles written frankly for money; he moved on with *The Beast Must Die*, to books that demonstrated what people are. Later his delight in the genre somewhat faded, to blaze up brilliantly in his final, considerably auto-biographical, *The Private Wound*. His cus-tomary detective is Nigel Strangeways, news-paperman.

 The Beast Must Die (1938)

The Private Wound (1968)

BLASCO IBÁÑEZ, Vicente (1867–1928) Spanish novelist, journalist and politician. He set out to be a purely popular novelist, and in many of his novels he is no more than that. But he had important literary qualities. His regional novels of Valencia are based on the naturalism of Zola; his social novels express his republican radicalism; his romantic melo-dramas are more cosmopolitan. He was crude and careless, but had immense verve – and at his best was a master of suspense and signifi-cant detail.

 The Cabin (1898, tr. 1919)

Blood and Sand (1908, tr. 1913)

The Four Horsemen of the Apocalypse (1916, tr. 1918)

BLECHMAN, Burt (1927) American novelist. Blechman calls his work "straight reportage", but it is extremely individual and – in an oblique manner – compassionate. *Stations*, a record of the unhappy world of a Catholic homosexual, is notable. Blechman uses parody and farce, and is often savage; but at heart he is a humanistic writer.

 How Much? (1961)

Stations (1963)

Maybe (1967)

BLISH, James (1921–75) American science fiction writer. His books are intended to make the reader think, and this works both with issues such as a Jesuit's dilemma about divine creation when faced with alien but intelligent life in *A Case of Conscience*, and with almost throw away sentences which challenge the reader's conventional assumptions about a word or an idea. In his *After Such Knowledge* tetralogy, which includes *A Case of Conscience* and *Black Easter of Faust Aleph Null*, he explores the theme of black magic. *Earthman Come Home* begins his *Cities in Flight* series, an intelligent space opera in which whole cities take to space. His greatest gift, which he practised frequently, is his ability to treat magic, religion and philosophy on equal terms with science.

 Earthman Come Home (1955)

A Case of Conscience (1958)

Black Easter of Faust Aleph Null (1968)

Karen Blixen

Heinrich Böll

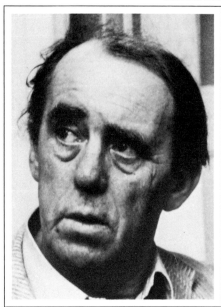

BLIXEN, Karen (1885–1962) Danish story-writer who wrote in English and Danish, many of her books being published in both languages simultaneously. She wrote one novel, *The Angelic Avengers* (1944, tr. 1947) under the name of Pierre Andrezel. She ran a coffee plantation in Kenya from 1914 until 1931. Her best fictional work (she wrote excellent non-fiction about Africa) consists of tales set in nineteenth-century Europe, which she wrote as Isak Dinesen. They have certain affinities with Kleist, with folk tales, with Gothic; but they do not resemble anyone else's work. She carried on the tradition of Andersen but was not a writer for children, and took the fullest account of the times she lived in. Her writing is highly contrived and literary – yet it now appeals to a large audience. Her tales cast a real spell, and are undoubtedly profound.

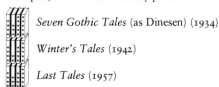

Seven Gothic Tales (as Dinesen) (1934)

Winter's Tales (1942)

Last Tales (1957)

BLOCH, Robert (1917) American writer of suspense stories and science fiction. He wrote the novel on which Alfred Hitchcock's film *Psycho* was based, and his reputation is based on this and similar stories with gruesome final twists.

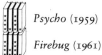

Psycho (1959)

Firebug (1961)

BLOOM, Ursula (?1898) English novelist. Her first book *Tiger* was published privately when she was only seven years old, and she is now one of the most widely read romantic novelists. Her writing has a strong moral undertone. Her pseudonyms include Lozania Prole, Sheila Burnes, and Mary Essex.

Tomorrow for Apricots (1929)

Price above Rubies (1965)

Twisted Road (1975)

BOCCACCIO, Giovanni (?1313–75) Italian story-writer and poet. He wrote a romance, *Filocolo,* and several works in other forms – all important, but none as popular or as enduring as *The Decameron.* The stories vary from social documents to profound allegory; the collection has rightly been called a prose counterpart of Dante's *Divine Comedy. Elegy for the Madonna Fiametta* (1345, tr. 1926) is as good, and as important: it is a love story with genuinely "modern" psychological elements.

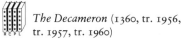

The Decameron (1360, tr. 1956, tr. 1957, tr. 1960)

BODENHEIM, Maxwell (1893–1954) American novelist, poet and dramatist. The "Mississippi Hamlet" – a neurotic, hating, unstable, intelligent, drinking man – he fascinated his contempories. He and his wife were pointlessly murdered, as might have happened in one of his novels, in which he would often attack his best friends. In type the novels are romantic-naturalist: the author, drenched in emotionalism, poses as cynic. But the best have power and conviction.

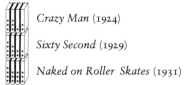

Crazy Man (1924)

Sixty Second (1929)

Naked on Roller Skates (1931)

BOLDREWOOD, Rolf (1826–1915) Australian novelist, born in London but taken to Australia aged three. His real name was T. A. Browne. A prolific novelist in the tradition of Scott, he is most famous for *Robbery Under Arms,* which celebrates the criminal achievements of Captain Starlight while pretending that they are immoral (as a magistrate he probably thought they were). As an adventure novelist he has few equals in his period; his detail is exact and his attitude unsentimental.

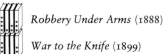

Robbery Under Arms (1888)

War to the Knife (1899)

BÖLL, Heinrich (1917) German novelist and story-writer, who won the 1972 Nobel Prize. He was born in Cologne and served on the Russian front in the war. His first work dealt with the pointlessness of war; and he went on to expose the hollowness of the German "economic miracle", and the moral rot in post-Nazi Germany society, which he sees as uncured (although curable by love). He is a radical Catholic. Wishing to start a fresh German literature he – with Grass and the other members of a group of realistic, anti-Nazi writers who thought like him (Gruppe 47) – started to use terse, economical and simple language. Later Böll became more experimental *(Billiards at Half-Past Nine),* particularly in his use of time-shifts and links between generations. More recently he has moved to a more universal kind of novel *(Group Portrait with Lady),* in which he explores the theme of trampled-upon femininity. Many regard his short stories as his best work: here, it is asserted, his laconic and sardonic humour functions most effectively. He was the writer who met Solzhenitsyn when he was exiled from Russia; he is also the writer who has questioned society's criticism of the Baader-Meinhof group's activities.

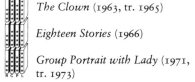

The Clown (1963, tr. 1965)

Eighteen Stories (1966)

Group Portrait with Lady (1971, tr. 1973)

BONTEMPS, Arna (1902) American Negro writer from Louisiana. He is part of the movement known as the "Negro Renaissance"; and wrote in collaboration with Langston Hughes. *Black Thunder* is a vivid historical novel about slave revolts in Virginia in 1800.

God Sends Sunday (1931)

Black Thunder (1935)

BORGES, Jorge Luis (1899) Argentinian poet, essayist, librarian and story-writer. He was educated in Europe, and did not settle in Argentina until 1921. He was for a time involved in a Spanish type of expressionism called Ultraism, but broke with it soon after his return to South America. He made his comparatively late but high reputation when

Jorge Luis Borges

Fictions was translated into English in 1962. He has suffered from progressive blindness for many years. His philosophical position is not unlike Beckett's but he rests on an absolute scepticism and then proceeds to elaborate paradoxically logical fantasies, legends, myths or characters. "A fiction" (*ficcion*) in his special use is an ironic essay-story: Hamlet may be the writer of the play *Hamlet*; the fantasy of a man who is a prisoner in a dark cell in "reality" is treated as more realistic than his condition – and so forth. Borges is a cold writer, but a delightfully ingenious and cunning one; the pleasure to be gained from him is aesthetic rather than emotional – but then his work brings up the status of aesthetics as a valid realm of experience.

Fictions (1944, tr. 1962)

Labyrinths (sel. 1962)

Dreamtigers (1960, tr. 1964)

BORROW, George (1803–81) English writer of fictionalized autobiography. Borrow was not properly educated, but he picked up an amazing amount of knowledge – and twelve languages. His classics *The Bible in Spain*, *Lavengro* and *Romany Rye* belong to the picaresque tradition; he lacked a creative imagination but compensated for it by his exceedingly intriguing manipulations of his adventures.

The Bible in Spain (1843)

Lavengro (1851)

The Romany Rye (1857)

BOSMAN, H. C. (1905–51) South African novelist and story-writer. He started writing early and made a good start; but he accidentally killed his step-brother, was condemned to death, reprieved, and served four years. *Cold Stone Jug* (1949) is a superb autobiography dealing with his prison experiences. His stories of isolated Afrikaans communities are the best in South African literature. Laconic, sardonic, technically assured, he is one of the great as yet unrecognized modern writers.

Jacaranda in the Night (1947)

Unto Dust (1963)

The Best of Bosman (1967)

BOUCHER, Anthony (1911–68) American detective story-writer, translator, anthologist and critic. Best known for his work as a critic, Boucher also produced his own entertaining short detective stories and novels in the classic tradition. His well-plotted puzzles, although not strong on characterization, were presented with literacy and humour. Boucher's series characters include Dr John Ashwin, Professor of Sanskrit, while his stories of wine-soaked Nick Noble are of the "armchair detective" variety. Writing as H. H. Holmes, his novels of Lt Marshall and Sister Ursula are somewhat more ambitious.

 The Case of the Seven of Calvary (1937)

 The Case of the Crumpled Knave (1939)

 Nine Times Nine (as Holmes, 1940)

BOULLE, Pierre (1912) French novelist. Most famous as the author of *The Bridge Over the River Kwai*, he also wrote *The Planet of the Apes* – the novel is more serious than the films. But his best novel is *William Conrad*, about a German spy educated in and partly dedicated to England.

 William Conrad (1950, tr. 1955; in U.S., *Not the Glory*)

 The Bridge Over the River Kwai (1952, tr. 1954)

 Planet of the Apes (1961, tr. 1963)

BOURJAILY, Vance (1922) American novelist. Hemingway thought him the best of America's young writers. His novels are shapeless but accurate and powerful; critics speak of his excellence at "catching characters in action" and of his gift for dialogue. *The Man Who Knew Kennedy* is perhaps his finest achieve-

Vance Bourjaily

ment: in this he examines the American "great man" legend and the corruption at the top.

The Violated (1958)

The Man Who Knew Kennedy (1967)

Brill Among the Ruins (1970)

BOVA, Ben (1932) American science fiction writer and editor. His strong interest in contemporary developments in science enables him to write highly realistic stories of the near future, especially concerned with space travel.

As on a Darkling Plain (1972)

Colony (1978)

BOWEN, Elizabeth (1899–1973) Irish novelist and story-writer. She was distinguished but very uneven, and tended to be overrated by critics during her lifetime. She will be remembered for one novel, *The Death of the Heart*, and for her stories. Her novels are undermined by snobbishness, but all her work is well structured. In her stories her genius is more concentrated, and she can be moving and perceptive.

The Death of the Heart (1938)

Look at All Those Roses (stories, 1941)

The Demon Lover (stories, 1945)

BOWLES, Jane (1918–73) American novelist and story writer, married to Paul Bowles. Her strange work, rightly summed up as showing the "terrible strength of the weak", was hardly known until the reprint in 1964 of her novel *Two Serious Ladies* (1943). This is her chief work: she takes an illogical plot and then works it out with extreme precision. Her technique is to take broadly expressionist material and then work on it with a bland, simple realism.

She exercises great fascination on some readers; others do not understand what her books are about. Her complete naivety and total honesty may offer the clues to her startlingly original achievement.

The Collected Works of Jane Bowles (1967)

BOWLES, Paul (1910) American novelist, story writer, poet, composer, and "translator". Bowles studied music under Aaron Copeland, and has an opera and a quite large opus to his credit. He is a peculiar writer, who has put it on record that his "subconscious . . . knows far better than I what should be written and how it should sound in words". He is competent, lurid, fascinated by all forms of sexual deviation, and decidedly "way out" from any point of view, but always readable. One of his early mentors was Stein and his chief distinction is his musical use of language. His main theme is the conflict between the primitive and the civilized, and there is no doubt that his temperament prefers the primitive. He seems to see morality as illusory and irrelevant in life. His earlier novels were exercises in fairly conventional modern Gothic, and showed his obsession with the Arab world and its values – so different from ours. Later novels are styled "translations", mostly from a young illiterate servant, the Moroccan Mohammed Mrabet. Although these books are essentially his own work, he purports to take down Mrabet's talk on a recorder, and then edit it and render it into English. There are here clear affinities with Genet.

Let It Come Down (1952)

Love with a Few Hairs (from Mrabet, 1965)

Above The World (1966)

BOX, Edgar, see VIDAL, Gore.

BOYD, James (1888–1944) American historical novelist. Meticulous and efficient, Boyd used his experiences of World War I for his reconstructions of the Revolutionary and Civil War periods respectively, in *Drums* and *Marching On*. The action scenes are good, the love interest indifferent.

Drums (1925)

Marching On (1927)

Bitter Creek (1939)

BOYLE, Kay (1903) American poet, novelist, story-writer and essayist, who lived for many years in Europe. Her fiction deals in moral problems presented vividly, subtly and intelligently; her prose presents a clear, immediate rendering of the physical world.

Plagued by the Nightingale (1931)

The White Horses of Vienna (1937)

BRACKENRIDGE, Hugh Henry (1748–1816) American novelist. He was born in Scotland, and taken to America aged five. In *Modern Chivalry* he takes Cervantes' *Don Quixote* as his model to write a wise and witty picaresque tale exploring the French revolution and the complex America of his times. He is the main precursor, in style and attitude, of Mark Twain.

Modern Chivalry (1792–1815)

BRACKETT, Leigh (1915–78) American science fiction and crime novelist and story-writer. Her detective stories are tightly written and realistic, in contrast with her lush and exotic other-worldly romances.

Shadow Over Mars (1944)

An Eye for an Eye (1958)

BRADBURY, Malcolm (1932) English novelist, academic and critic. Under their richly comic surface, Bradbury's three novels reflect the changes in British university life over the last 30 years and the defeat of liberal man. *The History Man* mercilessly dissects the dealings of a radical progressive on the make in a "new" university.

Eating People is Wrong (1959)

Stepping Westward (1965)

The History Man (1975)

BRADBURY, Ray (1920) American author who mixes fantasy and science fiction, and has enjoyed an unusually high reputation for his mastery of conventional literary skills. His vigorous, honest and popular writer.

Ray Bradbury

exploring mood and atmosphere, and his style is an impressive mixture of poetic imagery and psychological observation. He has written one significant conventional science fiction novel, *Fahrenheit 451* (the temperature at which paper burns) – a striking dystopia in which the authorities seek out and burn all books. The novel is notable for its evocation of people living in an unliterate environment; it is this quality of conjuring up unusual facets of human personality in a surreal but convincing way that is characteristic of his best work, most of which is in short story form.

The Illustrated Man (1951)

Fahrenheit 451 (1953)

I Sing the Body Electric (stories, 1969)

BRAGG, Melvyn (1939) British novelist and television arts pundit, born in Cumberland where many of his books are set. Using conventional methods, his main concerns are the narrative patterns of individual lives told in terms of class and regional characteristics. Among the best of these are *Josh Lawton*, a Hardyesque novel about a Cumbrian villager whose tragedy is his goodness, and the two books about the Tallentire father and son: *The Hired Man* (1969) and *A Place in England* which deals with the son growing away from his father. *The Silken Net* is more ambitious; the central character is a woman.

A Place in England (1971)

Josh Lawton (1973)

The Silken Net (1974)

BRAINE, John (1922) English novelist, born in Yorkshire. Braine made a hit with *Room at the Top,* the story of a working class Yorkshireman who ruthlessly pushes his way to the top. It was filmed, and formed the basis of a television series. It is a lively unsubtle, popular novel in poster colour hues. Then followed *The Vodi,* a more interesting and imaginative work – the author's own favourite – which did not achieve the same success. It is about an organization dedicated to the perpetration of injustice. Braine's Roman Catholicism has become more evident in later books, which not a few critics have described in such terms as "dreadful pot-boiling". *The Queen of a Distant Country* restored him to favour with some critics. He is a highly professional, vigorous, honest and popular writer.

Room at the Top (1957)

The Vodi (1959, in U.S. *The Hand of the Hunter*)

The Queen of a Distant Country (1972)

BRAND, Christianna (1907) English detective-story writer. She effectively combines an exuberance of outlook with a skill in devising ingenious, yet not unlikely, plots that equal the very best in the art. Her usual sleuth is Inspector Cockrill.

Green for Danger (1944)

Cat and Mouse (1950)

The Rose in Darkness (1979)

BRAUTIGAN, Richard (1935) American novelist. His novels are off-beat, deliberately zany, completely different. He writes well and can evoke place brilliantly (the Pacific Coast). Most people find *A Confederate General from Big Sur* (1964) extremely funny. *In Watermelon Sugar* (1968) is a utopian fantasy, inspired by the flower children. People either love him or can't read him. The critical consensus might be summed up thus: he has more wit than wisdom.

Trout Fishing in America (1967)

The Abortion (1971)

Willard and his Bowling Trophy (1975)

BREEM, Wallace (1926) English novelist whose historical novels are usually well-plotted, accurate and worthy.

The Legate's Daughter (1974)

The Leopard and the Cliff (1978)

BRINK, André (1935) South African academic and novelist whose *Looking on Darkness* created a sensation when, despite being written in Afrikaans, it was banned in South Africa. *An Instant in the Wind* was nominated for the Booker Prize, but his most impressive achievement is *Rumours of Rain*: a nightmarish weekend in the life of a middle-aged White Afrikaner nationalist. Told from the white man's side, it makes a fitting complement to Alan Paton's *Cry, the Beloved Country.*

Looking on Darkness (1973)

An Instant in the Wind (1976)

Rumours of Rain (1978)

BROCH, Hermann (1886–1941) Austrian novelist who until 1927 worked as a manager in the textile industry. Huge claims have been made for his achievement, especially in *The Death of Virgil*, a long interior monologue of the dying poet's, centring on whether or not to hand his epic to Augustus (he does). Broch is very hard to read, but the experience is rewarding: he has a fine mind, and his questionings of the validity of art are illuminating. He

used most of the modernist technical devices available to him but mainly stream of consciousness.

The Sleepwalkers (1931–2, tr. 1932)

The Unknown Quantity (1932, tr. 1935)

The Death of Virgil (1945, tr. 1946)

BROMFIELD, Louis (1896–1956) American novelist born in Ohio, towards the end of his life a well known right-wing polemicist. He began well as a novelist with the tetralogy *Escape (The Green Bay Tree, Possession, Early Autumn* and *A Good Woman),* which dealt with people's attempts to escape from their American backgrounds. *The Rains Came,* set in India, was a success; but is less serious.

Escape (1924–27)

The Strange Case of Miss Annie Spragge (1928)

The Rains Came (1937)

BRONTË, Anne (1820–49) English novelist. The least accomplished of the three Brontë sisters; but her novels *Agnes Grey* and *The Tenant of Wildfell Hall* have merits which would have caused her to be read today – even if she had not been a Brontë. *The Tenant of Wildfell Hall* is dwarfed by *Wuthering Heights,* but is nonetheless a scarifying and imaginative story of the effects of drinking.

Agnes Grey (1847)

The Tenant of Wildfell Hall (1848)

BRONTË, Charlotte (1816–55) The most successful of the three Brontë sisters with her contemporary public, although Emily's *Wuthering Heights* is the greatest novel produced by the family. Charlotte was more in the mainstream of the English novel; but her work, very strongly masochistic, is an odd hybrid of Jane Austen and the Gothic of Mrs Radcliffe in which the latter predominates. In structure *Jane Eyre* is a sensational melodrama; but the care of the writing, and the implications of the supposedly happy ending, add a whole new dimension. *The Professor* (posthumously published in 1857) is an interesting first novel; and the two later novels are suggestive and fully deserve their continuing popularity. There is a strong element of wish-fulfilment in Charlotte's books, but they are in no way escapist. Mrs Gaskell's *Life* is still the best book on her.

Jane Eyre (1847)

Shirley (1849)

Villette (1852)

Anne, Emily and Charlotte Brontë

BRONTË, Emily (1818–48) English novelist and poet, author of *Wuthering Heights,* one of the greatest novels of all time. An enigma, it seems at first glance to be a piece of gothic melodrama; but in fact it is a most subtle and mysterious narrative, seen from several points of view, and of penetrating psychological force. It is a study in evil, in violence, in distorted recollection, and in passion – and the most successful English poetic novel ever written. Her fame was wholly posthumous.

 *Wuthering Heights* (1847)

BROOKE, Jocelyn (1908–66) English novelist and autobiographer. Brooke's best work, aside from his autobiographies, is in *Private View: Four Portraits* (1954), which comprises fictionalized short biographies of four people he knew. He was a writer of beautifully lucid and penetrating prose. *The Image of a Drawn Sword* is one of the most successful of English Kafkaesque novels.

 The Scapegoat (1948)

The Image of a Drawn Sword (1950)

Four Portraits (1954)

BROPHY, Brigid (1929) Anglo-Irish novelist, critic and polemicist. She and Maureen Duffy ran the Writer's Action Group which, after enormous effort on their part, pressurized the British House of Commons into passing the Authors' Public Lending Right into law. She made her debut with the short novel *Hackenfeller's Ape,* about a laboratory ape who begins to acquire human characteristics. It was acclaimed as a "perfectly executed piece of fantasy", and she herself still believes that it "is probably the best I shall ever write". *Flesh* (1962) is a clever study of how a girl completely changes a man's nature. Since these earlier novels she has become more experimental, and reviewers are finding more to admire in her later work, although for some it still remains "too clever", failing to do her emotions justice.

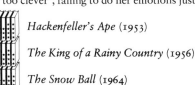 *Hackenfeller's Ape* (1953)

The King of a Rainy Country (1956)

The Snow Ball (1964)

BROSSARD, Chandler (1922) American novelist and dramatist, one of the "beat" generation who is also a conventional novelist of some talent. Critics prefer his earlier work – taking the later to be sensationalist and silly – and most particularly *Who Walk in Darkness,* a study of low-grade New York bohemians. In all his books there are vigorous journalistic passages.

 Who Walk in Darkness (1952)

The Double View (1961)

Did Christ Make Love? (1973)

BROWN, Carter (1923) Australian thriller writer, whose best known series hero is Al Wheeler, a Californian policeman. His investigations invariably bring him into contact with voluptuous young women, whom he is obliged to treat with caution in case they turn out to be on the other side.

 The Lover (1959)

The White Bikini (1963)

BROWN, Charles Brockden (1771–1810) American gothic novelist, whose bizarre, complicated plots draw on both European and indigenous material (religious fanaticism, the American landscape, the Indians). He is an important forerunner of a tradition in American fiction that includes Edgar Allan Poe and aspects of the work of Hawthorne and Faulkner.

 Wieland (1798)

Arthur Mervyn (1799–1800)

Edgar Huntly (1799)

BROWN, Christy (1932) Irish poet, autobiographer and novelist, who has been severely crippled from childhood. His autobiographical novel *Down All the Days* has lyrical force, and was widely praised.

 Down All the Days (1970)

Wild Grow the Lilies (1976)

BROWNE, Gerald A. (   ) American thriller writer who aims for realism and usually succeeds. *Green Ice* concerns the stealing of jewels from an all-powerful crime syndicate.

 Hazard (1973)

Green Ice (1978)

BRUNNER, John (1934) British science fiction author who has written space adventure – *Slavers of Space* (1960) and *Secret Agent of Terra* (1962) – but is best known for his treatment of immediate social and environmental matters such as population in *Stand on Zanzibar,* and urban living in *The Squares of the City.*

 Squares of the City (1965)

Stand on Zanzibar (1968)

BRYHER (1894) English historical novelist. Bryher (pseudonym of Annie Winifred Ellerman) writes of the distant past, setting her tales in times of social dissolution and decay. Her love of history and her strong sense of time and place produce work of haunting intensity.

 The Fourteenth of October (1952)

BUCHAN, John (1875–1940) Scottish statesman and writer of adventure stories. Buchan also wrote highly competent biographies of great military figures such as Cromwell, and other general works. He became Governor-General of Canada, and was made 1st Baron Tweedsmuir. He is most famous for such adventure stories as *The Thirty-Nine Steps* and *Greenmantle*. Everyone agrees that he tells a "good yarn" with a high degree of professionalism; but critics find that the "imperialistic" ideas allegedly underlying his books tend to make them sick at the core. In some recent television adaptations the ideas have even been "sent up". Denigrating his achievement as adventure writer because of his "imperialism" is like denigrating Elgar's music on similar grounds. Buchan was not an artist of the quality of Elgar; but he is infinitely more serious than Ian Fleming whom, it is claimed, he anticipated. He still captures the imagination because his unspoiled settings are so vivid; because his ability to convey the sense of physical danger and exertion is something that many a more literary writer might envy; and because although sentimental he is actually wholesome (in a way in which Yates or Fleming are not). He is well worth reading more carefully than is usually recommended.

 The Thirty-Nine Steps (1915)

Greenmantle (1916)

Mr Standfast (1919)

BUCK, Pearl (1892–1973) American novelist. Pearl Buck was awarded the Nobel Prize in 1938, a controversial decision because the award almost invariably goes to a writer of definite literary merit, and Pearl Buck did not possess this. But she was a truly worthy writer, who did much for Sino-American understanding, and who within her limits wrote fine fiction. *The Good Earth* for which she is most famous is the first part of a trilogy, *The House of Earth* (1931–35). It was popular because it gives a sharply vivid although not profound view of Chinese life – and because it is written in imitation of the Authorized version of the Bible, a style she mastered with great success.

 *The Good Earth* (1931)

Dragon Seed (1942)

The Three Daughters of Madame Liang (1969)

BUCKLEY, William F. (1927) American broadcaster and journalist who has recently produced two spy novels. Both feature Blackford Oakes, a new recruit to the CIA. Buckley's imaginative audacity is in evidence in *Saving the Queen,* when Oakes manages to jeopardize both his cover and his celibacy while staying with the Queen at Windsor. *Stained Glass,* about a potential second Hitler in post-war Germany is more of a pastiche.

 Saving the Queen (1976)

Stained Glass (1978)

BUDRYS, Algis (1931) American science fiction writer born in Germany. He wrote several novels and many good short stories between 1953 and 1960 but his output then declined sharply until he made a recent comeback with *Michaelmas* (1977). The earlier period produced two classic novels in *Who?* and *Rogue Moon,* both of which feature intense studies of the psychology of scientists and those involved with them. His prose is spare and economical and he explores the hypothetical situations in his work with clinical expertise.

 Who? (1958)

Rogue Moon (1960)

BULGAKOV, Mikhail (1891–1940) Russian novelist, story-writer and dramatist whose works are attracting increasing attention in the West as they become available in translation

Pearl Buck

(many have only recently been published in Russian). He avoided murder under Stalin only by a miracle. He is essentially a "magic realist" but he also used symbolism to subtle, extensive and unique effect. Although living under a tyranny, and demonstrating it in his work, he manages to be delightful and humorous.

The Heart of a Dog (1925, tr. 1968)

The Master and Margarita (1966, full tr. 1967)

Black Snow (tr. 1967)

BULWER-LYTTON, Edward (1803–73) English novelist, essayist and politician, who was extremely prolific. He is mainly remembered for *Pelham* and *Eugene Aram,* both based on actual murder cases; Aram himself is a romantic character, attractive despite his guilt, portrayed in a manner reminiscent of Dostoyevsky. Thackeray satirized both books mercilessly in *Vanity Fair* and the "Diary of James de la Pluche." Bulwer-Lytton wrote the best-selling historical novel of the century, *The Last Days of Pompeii,* and an imitation of Sir Walter Scott, *The Last of the Barons.*

Pelham (1828)

Eugene Aram (1832)

The Last Days of Pompeii (1834)

BUNIN, Ivan (1870–1953) Russian novelist, story-writer and poet. He won the Nobel Prize in 1933 while in exile (he left in 1920). He is now seriously underrated, despite his Nobel Prize and the existence of a number of translations. He is a meticulous writer of nostalgic and evocative prose. He began by depicting the terrible lives of the Russian poor in the pre-Revolutionary period, went on to satirize Western degeneracy (especially in the story "The Gentleman from San Francisco") and ended by recalling his lost past in an exquisitely controlled, individual and moving prose.

The Village (1910, tr. 1923)

The Gentleman from San Francisco (stories, 1916, tr. 1923)

The Well of Days (tr. 1933, repr. 1945)

BUNYAN, John (1628–88) English allegorical writer and preacher. Bunyan's literary background was scant and Puritan. He fought for the Parliamentary side in the Civil War, married, and before the Restoration underwent a mystical enlightenment. Under Charles II he spent more than twelve years in prison for preaching as a Baptist without licence. He began to write seriously while in prison. His most famous works are *The Pilgrim's Progress*

John Bunyan

and *The Life and Death of Mr Badman*. These may be read as pure allegories, but their prose is so lucid and their detail so homely that they may also be – and are – read for their realism and for the extreme complexity of their theological and even psychological thinking. Bunyan, most incongruously, is one of the fathers of the modern novel. This is significant: he was in no way self-consciously literary. He managed to touch intimately on ordinary human experience at many points.

 The Pilgrim's Progress (1678–84)

The Life and Death of Mr Badman (1680)

BURFORD, Eleanor, see PLAIDY, Jean.

BURGESS, Anthony (1917) English novelist, critic, scriptwriter, composer and journalist. His real name is John Burgess Wilson. He was a late starter, but has since made up for it: his output of fiction has been immensely prolific, and he has written much for television and film. He has never done better than in his opening trilogy about Malaya, based on his experience there as an education officer: *Time for a Tiger, The Enemy in the Blanket, Beds in the East* (1956–59). Since then he has written an extraordinarily interesting and brilliant series of novels. He has buttressed his disenchantment with modern society by the use of every type of modernist technique, ranging from science fiction through the more or less conventional novel (such as *Nothing Like the Sun*, 1964, a fictionalized biography of Shakespeare) to savage satire *(Honey for the Bears)*. He has used literally every device to achieve his fictional ends, but has not yet quite discovered

what these ends are: he rejects the notion of the meaninglessness of life which seems to be put forward by novelists such as Beckett, and has, indeed, a religious nature; but as he looks about him he sees nothing but nihilism and rot. He is a major writer, always worth reading, who may still produce the great novel everyone expects from him.

 Time for a Tiger (1956)

A Clockwork Orange (1962)

Honey for the Bears (1963)

BURNES, Sheila, see BLOOM, Ursula.

BURNETT, W. R. (1899) American novelist and screenwriter, who fostered the so-called "hard-boiled" school of fiction, best exemplified in the novels of Hammett. Burnett wrote the gangster novel *Little Caesar,* the movie version of which made Edward G. Robinson into a star. He is not the equal of Hammett, but is competent and writes exciting and not too incredible tales of very tough guys.

 Little Caesar (1929)

Underdog (1957)

BURNS, John Horne (1916–53) American novelist. He served in Italy in the war, and on his experiences there based his most famous novel *The Gallery:* a series of impressions, pessimistic and brutal, of American soldiers. *Lucifer with a Book,* on the corrupting effects of education, has everything but urgency and a sense of purpose. Burns died of heatstroke in Italy, written out and disappointed.

 The Gallery (1947)

Lucifer with a Book (1949)

BURNS, Tex, see L'AMOUR, Louis.

BURROUGHS, Edgar Rice (1875–1950) American story writer and novelist. Burroughs began writing because he thought that the fantasies he dreamt up to idle away his unemployment were better than those that appeared in the pulp magazines. In 1914 he published *Tarzan of the Apes.* His stories exploit wellknown fantasy themes: noble savages, jungle wildernesses, fantastic civilizations. These are sometimes mixed together, as in *Tarzan at the Earth's Core.*

 Tarzan at the Earth's Core (1930)

Tarzan and the City of Gold (1933)

BURROUGHS, William (1914) American novelist born in St Louis, Missouri. After conventional beginnings he became a drug addict, shot his wife in an accident, and became for a

time a leading *avant garde* writer, though none of his techniques were new – all were variants of surrealism, SF and gothic. Burroughs' first book *Junkie* (1953), published as by "William Lee", is his most straightforward: it gives an account of the world of the addict. Later novels, which often consist of semi-random rearrangements of his own and other people's prose, are concerned with the symptoms of drug withdrawal, the physiological effects of hanging, police power, homosexuality, and the evil effects of capitalism. He has been put forward as a "major force in 20th century literature", but this is a minority opinion.

 The Naked Lunch (1959)

The Soft Machine (1961)

Nova Express (1964)

BUTLER, Gwendoline (1922) English suspense novelist, also writing as Jennie Melville. She began with a series featuring an odd loner police detective, Inspector Coffin, and moved on to well-researched Victorian stories. As Melville, she has written spy tales and romantic suspense. All her work has a gripping feminine intensity.

 Raven's Forge (as Melville, 1975)

The Brides of Friedburg (1977)

BUTLER, Samuel (1835–1902) English novelist and eccentric thinker. He exercised his greatest influence with *The Way of All Flesh* (1903), which acted as a liberating influence to a generation. It describes the conflict between himself and his extremely unpleasant father; its readers took it as ammunition against the old-fashioned views of their own fathers. Butler's style here, and in his satirical fantasies

Samuel Butler

Erewhon and *Erewhon Revisited*, has given rise to much controversy: he is on the one hand taken to have been complacent and insufficiently serious, but on the other is taken as a subtle ironist who quite transcends his times.

 Erewhon (1872, rev. 1901)

Erewhon Revisited (1901)

The Way of All Flesh (1903)

BUTOR, Michel (1926) French novelist, critic and general writer. Classed as one of the "new novelists", along with Robbe-Grillet, Butor has too much substance to belong merely to a genre – though his earlier techniques did have something in common with the school of the *nouveau roman*. Butor's view of the novel is that it is a vital way of seeing reality: it should provoke the reader into divesting himself of his own sense of reality (false) in order to enter into that of the story, which is truly false (admits that it is so). Thus the reader may realize that he knows nothing, really – and from this realization may arise a real knowledge. Butor has become increasingly difficult to read; but he has feeling, and once the reader understands his purpose the exercise becomes worth while.

 Passing Time (1957, tr. 1961)

Second Thoughts (1957, tr. 1958)

Degrees (1960, tr. 1962)

BYATT, A. S. (1936) English novelist, critic, sister of Margaret Drabble. A. S. Byatt is a thoughtful developer of the well-made novel, less prolific and fashionable than her sister, but more artistically gifted. Like John Fowles she uses modern methods to try to preserve the old strengths of the novel; but she uses apparently recondite moral and psychological analysis. She has puzzled readers, but has much to say.

 Shadow of a Sun (1964)

The Game (1967)

The Virgin in the Garden (1978)

C

CABELL, James Branch (1879–1958) American fantasist who became famous (according to Sherwood Anderson) as a result of a publicity drive and his vogue has not lasted. Nearly all his fiction is set in the medieval country of Poictesme. It is a feeble mix of "naughtiness",

Cervantes, Rabelais, unsatisfactory myth-making and cut-price allegory.

 Jurgen (1919)

The High Place (1923)

The Music from Behind the Moon (1926)

CABLE, George Washington (1844–1925) American fiction writer and historian, who depicts the local colour of Louisiana town life at all levels.

 Dr Sevier (1885)

Bylow Hill (1901)

CAHAN, Abraham (1860–1951) Russian-born American Jewish novelist and editor. *The Rise of David Levinsky* was, until Isaac Singer, certainly the best Yiddish novel America had produced. It tells of an immigrant's rise to power, and is a very well-documented account of life on New York's Lower East Side.

 Yekl (1896)

The Imported Bridegroom (stories, 1898)

 The Rise of David Levinsky (1917)

CAIN, James M. (1892–1977) American crime novelist, described by W. M. Frohock as "surehanded in the manipulation of [his] materials". Although often grouped with Dashiell Hammett and Raymond Chandler as hard-boiled, Cain shows little concern with either private detectives or mobsters. His best works, with great psychological feeling, show lust or greed driving the weak toward criminal acts, and down a path of degradation towards the rough justice of a denouement which makes the reader's sympathy difficult to place. Cain displays extreme economy of words in painting a character or situation, and once stated that he writes as he hears American spoken.

 The Postman Always Rings Twice (1934)

 Double Indemnity (in *Three of a Kind*, 1943)

CALDWELL, Erskine (1903) American novelist, born in Georgia, whose earlier work was both very popular and very good. Later work has been patchy, varying between pulp fiction and sustained flashes of the old brilliance. Essentially Caldwell is a regionalist and a naturalist. He writes of Georgian share croppers, "poor whites", and their coarse and gross ways. He sees that their behaviour appears comic, but he is at the same time profoundly

Erskine Caldwell

concerned at the social climate which produces such personalities. His depiction of them is only slightly sensationalized and his detail is meticulous. The result is comi-tragic. His best work is *The Bastard* (1929), *Poor Fool*, *Tobacco Road* (1932) and *God's Little Acre*. In the 1940s and 1950s he was producing bad, melo-dramatic novels. However, in 1967, he returned to top form with *Miss Mama Aimée*. There is a development in his work, both in the handling of the grotesque element – at first realistic, but later more carefully and sym-bolically considered – and, particularly, in the handling of the short story form, of which he is an acknowledged master. He is somewhat more sensitive than at first appears; his non-fiction has been underrated – and he neither deserves to be, nor will be, forgotten.

Poor Fool (1930)

God's Little Acre (1933)

The Complete Short Stories (1953)

CALDWELL, Taylor (1900) Prolific American romantic novelist, Caldwell is the author of a series of readable best sellers.

This Side of Innocence (1946)

Dear and Glorious Physician (1959)

CALISHER, Hortense (1911) American fiction writer of high literary reputation; she is one of those female writers who owe much to James without being an imitator of him. Her novels and novellas differ greatly from one another, and her achievement requires a full-length study. Her interest is in people, and she has a variety of techniques for looking at them – in some of her stories there is more than one voice. She is an ironist, and an absolute artist – an example of the completely autonomous writer.

Textures of Life (1963)

Standard Dreaming (1972)

Collected Stories (1975)

CALLAGHAN, Morley (1903) Canadian Catholic novelist and story-writer, who has been greatly neglected outside his own conti-nent. He is a major writer, exploring a vast territory with naturalistic precision and low-dogmatic but religious compassion. His style is laconic, his sense of character excellent and his religious faith acts as a strength, not as a didactic weakness. He, more than perhaps any other English-language writer of the century, has a sense of what Christianity means in a post-Christian age. Why so important a novelist should be so neglected is a mystery – as Edmund Wilson and a few other critics have

remarked.

More Joy in Heaven (1937)

A Fine and Private Place (1975)

Stories (two vols. 1963, 1964)

CALVINO, Italo (1923) Italian fiction writer. His first books were realistic; in later fiction he blends SF, fantasy and fairy tale to produce uniquely crazy and delightful books.

The Path to the Nest of Spiders (1947, tr. 1956)

Adam One Afternoon (stories 1949, tr. 1957)

The Non-Existent Knight (1959, tr. 1962)

CAMPBELL, John W., Jr (1910–71) American science fiction writer and long-time editor of *Astounding Science Fiction* (now *Analog*). His early novels were extravagant space operas, and his better and more thoughtful work first appeared under the pseudonym Don A. Stuart.

The Mightiest Machine (1934)

"Who Goes There?" (1938)

The Moon is Hell (1950)

CAMUS, Albert (1913–1960) French writer, novelist, playwright, critic and political philo-sopher. Camus, who won the Nobel Prize in 1957 and who died soon afterwards in a pointless car accident, is one of the key figures of recent times. His adaptations of famous works for the stage were successful, and his essays on seminal matters are essential reading; but it was in the novel that he achieved himself, and came to a point where he was beginning to resolve his conflicts – particularly in *The Fall*, probably one of the greatest novels in all literature. He was born in Algeria of very poor French parents, and began as a communist; he was also a resistance fighter in France during World War II; but he soon quarrelled with communism, and began to criticize it as harshly as he criticized the reactionary right and the fascists. He was essentially a liberal, and his creative life could be described as an agonized and self-critical effort to define a truly viable liberal position. He believed that literature did have and ought to have a social effect; but was greatly pained because it did not have as good an effect as it ought to have. In *The Outsider* his position is semi-nihilistic, and very much in line with the existentialist stance of his friend Sartre, with whom he eventually quarrelled over the role of the Soviet Union. In *The Plague* he comes to a stoical humanism – this is a complex novel, rich in symbolism. *The Fall* is one of the greatest expressions of

Albert Camus

disenchantment with – and yet faith in – literature ever made. It may be read as an account of an individual, with his individual needs tormented by his role in society, a role he knows he needs but which – as society stands – he can find no way of discovering.

 The Outsider (1942, tr. 1946)

The Plague (1947, tr. 1948)

The Fall (1956, tr. 1957)

CANETTI, Elias (1905) Austrian non-fiction writer, dramatist and author of one novel, *Auto da Fé*. This is connected with his lifetime preoccupation with the psychology of fascism, and is a study of moral disintegration in the tradition of Thomas Mann's *Faustus*. Mann, Broch and many others have praised it; but, although easily available, it is more owned than read. It is undoubtedly an important novel.

 Auto da Fé (1935, tr. 1946)

CANNING, Victor (1911) English novelist, who specializes in spy and mystery adventures, usually set in more than one country. He writes fluently, and is adept at both convincing realism and high melodrama, but his plots sometimes seem over-contrived. He is versatile – his romantic sub-plots work well – and immensely professional.

 A Forest of Eyes (1950)

Birdcage (1978)

CANTWELL, Robert (1908) American novelist. Cantwell stopped publishing fiction in 1935. His two novels are starkly naturalistic accounts of the lives of lumber mill workers, but they are not "proletarian" or "political", as is often asserted; they are more concerned with the psychology of the characters.

 Laugh and Lie Down (1931)

The Land of Plenty (1935)

CAPOTE, Truman (1924) American fiction writer born in New Orleans. In Capote there is a disconcerting mixture of degenerate chic, obsession with sexual deviance, genius, powerfully sick Gothic, and slick professionalism. Quite recently he broke down in tears on American television, announcing his totally distraught condition. *The Grass Harp* (1951) is a superb exploration of passive unease against a well realized social background. *Breakfast at Tiffany's* is slick, readable and meretricious. *In Cold Blood* is a brilliant but heartless study of two real-life murderers who were exhaustively interrogated by Capote before they were executed. Capote has for the time being lost his status as a serious author.

The earlier books are the work of a major writer, though their poise must have been hard to achieve.

 Other Voices, Other Rooms (1948)

Breakfast at Tiffany's (1958)

In Cold Blood (1966)

CARGILL, Morris, see HEARNE, John.

CARPENTIER, Alejo (1904) Cuban (of Franco-Russian parentage) novelist and musicologist. Unlike some other writers, he has managed to remain in favour with the government. His novels are inspired by his anthropological and musical studies. His real concern is with the relationship between "primitive" Latin American customs and modernism; *Explosion in a Cathedral* was a commercially successful historical novel.

 The Lost Steps (1953, tr. 1956)

Manhunt, Noon III (1956, tr. 1959)

Explosion in a Cathedral (1962, tr. 1963)

CARR, John Dickson (1906–77) Anglo-American detective story-writer. His first detective stories featured a French police chief. He changed to a very English detective, Dr Gideon Fell, who was frankly modelled on G. K. Chesterton; and, writing under the name Carter Dickson, added a second series about Sir Henry Merrivale ("H.M."), an irascible chief of intelligence at the War Office. The two series were almost indistinguishable, except that H.M. provided more of the knockabout farce with which Carr lightened the atmosphere of menace which he could draw like a curtain across the story. His speciality was the "sealed room" murder. The books of his last period are disappointing, although he experimented at putting his "impossible crimes" into period costume. At his best, he was incomparably ingenious and enthralling.

The Hollow Man (1935)

The Black Spectacles (1939)

The Bride of Newgate (1950)

CARR, Philippa, see PLAIDY, Jean.

CARROLL, Lewis (1832–98) English lecturer in mathematics at Oxford and writer for children. Shy and withdrawn, Carroll (the pseudonym of Charles Lutwidge Dodgson) was only at ease with small girls. *Alice's Adventures in Wonderland* and *Through the Looking Glass* were written to divert Alice Liddell, daughter of the Dean of Christ Church. They unfold a dream-world of inverted logic, satire, parody, word-play and verse that is almost more popular with adults than children. Their characters have passed into folk-lore: amongst them, the White Rabbit, the Mad Hatter, the Cheshire Cat, the White Knight and the Red Queen. This is in part due to the brilliant illustrations by Sir John Tenniel. With Edward Lear's verse, the Alice books launched a tradition of nonsense writing which has influenced countless authors (as varied as "Beachcomber" (J. B. Morton) and J. L. Borges. Carroll was ordained in 1861.

Alice's Adventures in Wonderland (1865)

Through the Looking Glass (1871)

Sylvie and Bruno (1889)

Lewis Carroll

CARTER, Angela (1940) English novelist with a dazzling and highly refined style. Her central theme is sexuality, both as an introspective reality and as a source of much of the tension between people. In the exotic world which she has created and given almost physical presence, the words often convey more of her drift than the meaning of the sentences. The effect of a passage is often contrived to work around the placing of a single word. In the retold fairy tales of *The Bloody Chamber* (1979) this technique has been refined to one of almost terse simplicity in which disturbing shifts of meaning have become the reason for the whole story. Although sharing many concerns and attitudes with the writers of the women's movement, Angela Carter has concentrated on psychology: her books are set in the mind of her characters or readers.

Shadow Dance (1966)

Heroes and Villains (1969)

The Infernal Desire Machines of Dr Hoffman (1972)

CARTLAND, Barbara (1900) English romantic novelist. A larger than life character, she is constantly expounding in public her special interests in health foods, protection of gypsies and charity work. She is very prolific, with an output of more than 230 romantic novels all of which are predictable and conventional in form. Although her beliefs are entirely at variance with contemporary views on the place of women in society, her books are read and enjoyed by millions. She has also written a number of swashbuckling romances under her married name Barbara McCorquodale.

The Coin of Love (1956)

Elusive Earl (1976)

CARUTHERS, William Alexander (?1802–46) American novelist, born in Virginia. Some find him boring, but a majority sees him as having anticipated the Civil War, and as giving a true picture of his age in his gustily humorous novels.

The Kentuckian in New York (1834)

The Knight of the Horseshoe (1845)

CARY, Joyce (1888–1957) Irish novelist who served with the army and the colonial service until bad health forced him to retire. He started writing late, his first book, *Aissa Saved* (1932) being published when he was forty-four. For most of his life he was an invalid. Cary documented his characters with very great care (his files on them were ten times the size of the novels in which they appeared) but he had little sense of form. Invariably the later and better known books appear as exuberant

picaresque. They often look modernist because he is keen on using the present continuous, and because, like his characters, he was eccentric. His point of view was humanist; but he attracts readers not for his intellectual qualities, but for his energy and his power to depict obstinate and courageous people. *Mister Johnson* is probably his best novel: it is a skilful study of the conflict between the West African and the colonial temperaments, and its tolerant message comes across movingly. Later more famous works are full of excellences but do not really cohere – the exception is *The Horse's Mouth*, which is part of a trilogy.

Mister Johnson (1939)

The Horse's Mouth (1944)

Not Honour More (1955)

CASPARY, Vera (1904) American thriller writer, the creator of a small output of stylish, witty thrillers. The best is *Laura*, in which a brilliant plot matches the style.

Laura (1943)

CATHER, Willa (1873–1947) American novelist and story-writer. She was born in Virginia but moved at an early age to Nebraska, an area which figures in much of her best fiction. Her motivations were hatred and resentment of modern ways; an Austenish view of the moral qualities of men; an interest in the function of religion in modern life (she saw religion in the form of Catholicism); a realization of how myth still haunts the "civilized" mind; and a fine understanding of the delicate, virginal sensitivity of women. She wrote a clear and limpid prose, influenced directly by the best of the Latin classics. In *The Song of the Lark* (1915) she comes as near as she dares to an exploration of her sexuality: ostensibly it is the story of an opera singer whose artistic life is threatened by masculine attentions. But her best novels come from the 1920s: *A Lost Lady* (1923), subtly showing the corruption of a woman of fine character; *The Professor's House* – her greatest novel – which contains a mythopoeic section in counterpoint to a realist one; and *My Mortal Enemy* (1926). *Death Comes for the Archbishop* was more popular, but is less well realized.

The Professor's House (1925)

Death Comes for the Archbishop (1927)

Collected Short Fiction (1965)

CAUTE, David (1936) English novelist, historian, dramatist and Marxist, who writes as a "committed" novelist of ideas. One would therefore think that he might be an arid and didactic bore. Sometimes he is; but he has a powerful imagination, and as an artist he understands the tensions between his beliefs and his inclinations. *The Decline of the West*, a study of right-wing fanatics and psychopaths in quest of a French Algeria, should be read not for its thesis, but as a psychological adventure story; as such it is very good indeed, and more than fair to its (mostly) sadistic or psychotic characters. Whatever one may think of Caute's revolutionary activism, he is or can be a very good novelist. But he is a very bad one when, as in *The Occupation*, he curbs his imagination to make political points.

Comrade Jacob (1961)

The Decline of the West (1966)

The Occupation (1971)

CECIL, Henry (1902–76) English county court judge who wrote a series of comic novels about the operation of the law in Britain. *The Brothers in Law* series – a fictionalized collection of the professional experiences of barristers – is both true to its time and extremely amusing.

Brothers in Law (1944)

Sober as a Judge (1958)

CELA, Camilo José (1916) Spanish novelist, essayist and editor. His first novel *The Family of Pascal Duarte*, about a violent peasant murder, pointed towards the injustices of the Franco regime, and was called *tremendista*. Two more novels, *The Hive* and *The Blond* (untranslated) are of comparable stature. Since the 1950s Cela has concentrated more on idiosyncratic essays and stories. Doubtless he is still "the most important Spanish prose writer to emerge since the war" but it seems that his novel-writing days are over.

The Family of Pascal Duarte (1942, tr. 1947, tr. 1964)

The Hive (1951, tr. 1953)

Mrs Caldwell Speaks to Her Son (1953, tr. 1968)

CÉLINE, Louis-Ferdinand (1894–1961) French novelist and doctor. He took up a nihilist stance which led him into crazy anti-semitism and ostensible collaboration (though he stated with his usual wild contempt that Hitler was a Jew). His achievement in his post-war novels, such as *Castle to Castle*, is much greater than has been allowed – since there is considerable ignorance about his real activities and their nature. His *Journey to the End of the Night* and *Death on the Instalment Plan*, both very successful in the 1930s, are unique: they come nearer than any other works of the century to creating the illusion of a living, infuriated, comic, vibrant voice: this voice comes off the

pages of these and his other novels as though it were the pure, real flux of a mind actually working. Really all his fiction is a long interior monologue; as such, it may not easily be surpassed. There is much that was repulsive about the man Céline, but much also that was noble and kindly. As a man he was confused beyond measure throughout his life; but as a writer he reflects the human condition with uncanny exactitude. It should be noted that he found the Vichy Government as absurd as he found democratic France – and that he gave the poor and their children free medical treatment until the end of his life. As he said later, in his anti-semitism he got mixed up in something he knew nothing about.

Journey to the End of the Night (1932, tr. 1934, repr. 1950)

Death on the Instalment Plan (1936, tr. 1938)

Castle to Castle (1957, tr. 1968)

CERVANTES (SAAVEDRA), Miguel de (1547–1616) Spanish novelist, story-writer, dramatist, poet. As the author of *Don Quixote* he can be considered the father of the modern novel: in one way or another he employed all the fictional techniques in existence in the sixteenth and seventeenth centuries – and most of those that have been "invented" since. Son of an unsuccessful doctor, he had an adventurous life. He worked his way up to a position at court but this was insecure, and he was forced to flee because of a duel. He fought as a soldier, lost the use of his left hand, and was captured by pirates and sold into slavery in Algiers. He made several daring attempts to escape, but was eventually ransomed. He became a tax collector, but through no fault of his own was imprisoned because his accounts were said to be out of order. In prison he began his masterpiece. After 1605 and the publication of the first part of *Don Quixote* Cervantes was able to devote himself to writing but he was never rich. His life of adversity and his good humour in face of it (testified to by those who knew him,

Miguel de Cervantes

at all stages of his life) is clearly relevant to his work. *La Galatea,* his first work, is good pastoral romance, and made his name. Apart from *Don Quixote,* the *Exemplary Novels* are his finest work: of these twelve stories, some are picaresque, some cynical, some mythopoeic, and some realistic; one, the "Colloquy of the Dogs", is with Orwell's *Animal Farm* the greatest animal fable in European literature. In this collection Cervantes transformed the Italian novella from a mere form to a high species of art. *Persiles and Sigismunda,* his last work, is a romance modelled on Heliodorus; it has excellences, but shows signs of declining powers. He died as he completed it, and it was published in 1617. His influence is immeasurable.

 La Galatea (1585, tr. 1901-3)

Don Quixote (1605-15, tr. 1905, tr. 1977)

 Exemplary Novels (1613, tr. 1902)

CHAMISSO, Adalbert von (1731-1838) Franco-German story writer and poet, who wrote in German. His *Peter Schlemihl* is one of the greatest of supernatural tales: it is about a man who sells his shadow to the devil for earthly rewards – a variant of the Faust theme. This perfectly symbolizes the psychological conflicts of an age.

 Peter Schlemihl (1814, tr. 1957)

CHANDLER, Raymond (1888-1959) American crime novelist. An ex-journalist and ousted oil executive, Chandler only began writing, for *Black Mask* magazine, at the age of 45. From 1939 on he produced seven novels that have made him, with Dashiell Hammett, the acknowledged exemplar of the hard-boiled school of American mystery writing. With Hammett, Chandler put fictional murder, which for too long had become largely the mechanical spring for pretty puzzles, back where it belongs "in the mean streets", although behind the petty gangsters, the floozies and the cheap homosexuals there is generally a rich man in an opulent California home. All the novels are told in the first person by Philip Marlowe, private eye, depicted by Chandler himself in an essay "The Simple Art of Murder" as "a complete man and a common man" and "a man of honor" who "will take no man's money dishonestly and no man's insolence without a due and dispassionate revenge". In contrast with the sleazy settings, Marlowe cuts an improbably romantic figure with his college education, his chess games and his occasional quotes from T. S. Eliot and Browning. Chandler wrote uncommonly well. Terse vividness was his trademark, as in this comment on old General Sternwood in *The Big Sleep,* "a few locks of dry white hair clung to his scalp, like wild flowers fighting for life on

a bare rock". In dialogue Chandler is scarcely to be faulted, and the talk is salted with that characteristic American product, the wisecrack.

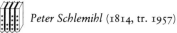

The Big Sleep (1939)

The High Window (1942)

The Little Sister (1949)

CHARTERIS, Hugo (1922-70) English novelist whose early novels were disjointed studies in violence and conflict, often in upper middle-class settings; later his prose became more direct, but some of the power went out of his work.

 A Share of the World (1953)

The Indian Summer of Gabriel Murray (1968)

CHARTERIS, Leslie (1907) American (naturalized 1946) mystery writer, Anglo-Chinese by birth, who created the Saint in *Meet the Tiger* (1928). The Saint is a rugged, good-looking Englishman, descended from Bulldog Drummond, the forerunner of James Bond, yet because of his deliberately unreal, aseptic qualities more enduring than both. There have been over fifteen full-length novels and innumerable short stories. They are fast-moving yarns, in which the Saint invariably excels, physically and mentally, over a clear-cut rascal.

 The Saint in New York (1935)

The Saint Returns (1969)

Leslie Charteris

CHASE, James Hadley (1906) English thriller writer who achieved success in 1939 with the extraordinary *No Orchids for Miss Blandish,*

a bleak book, in which all the characters are unpleasant and meet gruesome ends. His thrillers divide neatly into two groups: a European series, which is very conventional; and an American series distinguished by its chilling amorality.

 No Orchids for Miss Blandish (1939)

Just Another Sucker (1961)

One Bright Summer's Morning (1963)

CHASE, Mary Ellen (1887) American popular novelist of great competence, who was for many years a professor of English at Smith College. *Silas Crockett,* about Maine and its seafarers, is her best known novel.

 Mary Peters (1934)

Silas Crockett (1935)

Lovely Ambition (1960)

CHEEVER, John (1912) American novelist and story-writer. Cheever is a typical writer of the *New Yorker* school: clever, mannered, craftsmanlike, deft. It is interesting to compare him with another *New Yorker* writer, Updike, who has now shown that he is not a mere exponent of the intelligent, well-made tale. Cheever has not progressed to this point. However, his stories are professional, but not so much so that they fail to make their often disturbing point – and his novels deserve their vogue. Cheever is essentially the satirist of the modern technocratic world, comfortless but apparently comfortable, cheerless but apparently cheerful. *The Wapshot Chronicle* expresses this quite straightforwardly; but latterly (in *Bullet Park,* for example) Cheever has turned to black humour, surrealism and a generally modernist (it is often misleadingly called neo-baroque) style with which he seems to be fundamentally out of sympathy. As with almost all *New Yorker* writers, there is some doubt as to his substance: does his appeal reside to a certain extent in his participation in what he satirises? The best of his stories are to be found in the first of his four collections, *The Way Some People Live.* There is no doubt that he can be, as a leading critic called him, "wonderfully funny".

 The Way Some People Live (1943)

The Wapshot Chronicle (1957)

Bullet Park (1969)

CHEKHOV, Anton (1860-1904) Russian story-writer and dramatist. He trained as a doctor, and while doing so began to write sketches for much-needed money. He then married an actress, and wrote some of the world's most famous plays. His life was cut short by tuber-

Anton Chekhov

culosis. His influence on the modern short story has been profound; only Maupassant can challenge him in this. Of the two it is Chekhov who achieves the greatest subtlety and the greatest poignancy: he is unsurpassed. He began as a sheerly comic writer, but soon a melancholy sense of life's transitoriness crept in. His work expresses the paradox of the enormity of suffering in life as set against its absurd shortness – and he is a master at displaying this by the recording of apparently trivial events. He was much influenced by French realism and even naturalism, but retained his own impressionistic method of writing. The influence of his method, of mixing humour and pathos, of concentration on a few very carefully selected details, has been incalculable. The best translations of *The Tales* are by Constance Garnett.

 The Tales (13 vols, 1916–22)

CHESTERTON, G. K. (1874–1936) English novelist, story-writer, poet, essayist, biographer and Catholic apologist (he was converted to Catholicism in 1922). Chesterton as a fiction writer is more complex than is usually asserted: he was not, for example, "optimistic" at all; he was jovial, but at the heart of his work lies a sense of indefinable terror. His Father Brown stories, in which a gentle priest unearths dark mysteries of murder and deceit, are somewhat underrated as literature, although they are of course very widely read. In the figure of Father Brown, Chesterton expresses the best of himself: serene in faith but aghast at the sins going on around him. *The Man Who Was Thursday* is a brilliantly ingenious novel about anarchists and spies. Chesterton was genuinely witty ("If a thing's worth doing, it's worth doing badly").

 The Napoleon of Notting Hill (1904)

The Man Who Was Thursday (1908)

The Father Brown Stories (1929)

CHEVALLIER, Gabriel (1895–1969) French novelist who gave up writing psychological novels such as *La Peur* (1930) for broad comic satire, starting with his masterpiece, *Clochemerle*. This shows how the building of a public lavatory provokes a furore in a Beaujolais village.

 Clochemerle (1934, tr. 1936, tr. 1952)

Clochemerle Babylon (1954, tr. 1955)

CHEYNEY, Peter (1896–1951) English bookmaker and song-writer turned thriller-writer, the first to pander to the public taste for violence with detective heroes who tortured their suspects for pleasure. Feeble plots, poor writing and dreadful mid-Atlantic dialogue notwithstanding, Cheyney's books commanded huge sales at his peak, and the names of his two heroes, Lemmy Caution and Slim Callaghan, were household words on both sides of the Atlantic.

 This Man is Dangerous (1936)

Dark Duet (1942)

CHILDERS, Erskine (1870–1922) Irish political activist and author of one novel, *The Riddle of the Sands,* written to warn Britain of German designs. Set aboard a small yacht in the shallow Baltic waters, it has great charm and enormous suspense. Childers was eventually executed when fighting for the Irish Republicans against the Free State forces.

 The Riddle of the Sands (1903)

CHOPIN, Kate (1851–1904) American novelist whose merits have only recently been discovered. Her first books were of stories about Creole and other local folk; but *The Awakening,* a novel of adultery and mixed marriage, is of major status. Here she anticipated many of the themes still being pursued today; and the psychological quality of the novel is excellent.

 Bayou Folk (1894)

A Night in Acadie (1897)

The Awakening (1899)

CHRISTIE, Dame Agatha (1890–1976) English detective-story writer, the most successful practitioner in the genre; indeed, with world sales estimated as exceeding 300 million, by a quantitative assessment she was the most successful novelist there has ever been. Her triumph was by no means immediate. Her first novel, *The Mysterious Affair at Styles* (1920), although very good of its kind, was rejected by six publishing houses. Thereafter, while she attained a reputation as among the better detective-story merchants, her sales were not large. They rose somewhat when, just after the publication of *The Murder of Roger Ackroyd* (1926), she disappeared for nine days, as a result of strain induced largely by marital difficulties, and was the object of a vast press-inspired manhunt. It was only after her chief British rival, Dorothy L. Sayers, had bowed out that the tidal wave of publicity began to sweep her to phenomenal success. She was possessed of an enormous ingenuity in plotting, playing on her readers' conditioned responses like a maestro, adept at slipping in vital information while apparently doing something else, and swift to take advantage of the tricks the outward world plays on us all with mirrors and similar deceits. But, equally, she was granted the gift of simplicity. She told her admirably straightforward tales largely in easy-to-read dialogue, for which she had a gifted ear. There are duds among her output of some 80 books, including some that feature her dapper, dignified Belgian of "the little grey cells", Hercule Poirot, and her intuitive great-aunt figure, Miss Marple; but the peaks among her books are the best of their kind.

 The Murder of Roger Ackroyd (1926)

Ten Little Niggers (1939, in US *And Then There Were None*)

 Sleeping Murder (1976)

CHRISTOPHER, John (1922) British science fiction writer whose second novel, *The Death of Grass,* remains one of the classic treatments of the human consequences of environmental catastrophe. He has concentrated on the idea of civilization tested to the point of fracture, usually by outside forces.

 The Death of Grass (1956)

A Wrinkle in the Skin (1965)

CHURCH, Richard (1893–1972) English poet, critic, journalist and novelist, who also wrote for children. His fiction is pleasant, conventional, intelligent.

 The Porch (1937)

Prince Albert (1963)

CHURCHILL, Winston (1871–1947) American historical novelist who attained considerable popularity with *Richard Carvel*, a romance of the Revolution. His methods and interpretations were superficial, but he was highly professional.

 Richard Carvel (1899)

The Crossing (1904)

CLARK, Walter van Tilburg (1909–73) American novelist and story-writer, brought up in Nevada. Clark wrote intelligent, well-wrought Westerns. *The Track of the Cat* is too overtly symbolic, but is an exciting tale about the stalking of a panther.

 The Ox-Bow Incident (1940)

The Track of the Cat (1949)

The Watchful Gods (stories, 1950)

CLARKE, Arthur C. (1917) British science fiction writer and tireless propogandist for space travel. His basic form is the space adventure in which the experience of exploration and the alien nature of the environment provide the chief excitement. He is an optimist about the future of humanity, seeing space exploration as a new frontier, the crossing of which provides opportunity for spiritual as well as physical growth. His scientific basis is invariably sound and requires the minimum of unjustified technical assumptions. His greatest achievements have been his short stories. His style is often criticized for its blandness, but his work is attractive for its untarnished sense of

Arthur C. Clarke

wonder, both at what is already known about the universe, and at the immensity of things yet to be uncovered. His non-fiction scientific writings are many, and are as readable as his fiction.

 Childhood's End (1953)

The Nine Billion Names of God (stories, 1967)

 Rendezvous with Rama (1973)

CLARKE, Marcus (1846–81) Australian novelist born in London. His *For the Term of his Natural Life,* though flawed, combines insight into the criminal mentality with a savage indictment of society. Crude and raw, this tale of Tasmanian convicts has all the appeal of naturalism at its best.

 Long Odds (1868)

For the Term of his Natural Life (1872, repr. 1970)

CLAVELL, James (1922) Australian-born film director and novelist. Captured by the Japanese at 18, Clavell was imprisoned at the notorious Changi jail, where his first book, *King Rat,* is set. It is a powerful study of the relationships and characters of the prisoners, British and American, in the face of cruelty and imminent death. He has since written two immensely long and detailed sagas: *Tai Pan,* about the founding of Hong Kong, and *Shogun,* set in seventeenth-century Japan.

 King Rat (1962)

Tai Pan (1966)

Shogun (1975)

CLEARY, Jon (1917) Australian novelist who turned to writing after World War II. His novels combine suspense and intrigue with a sophisticated love interest. One of his most popular characters, featuring in many of his books, is a detective called Scobie Malone who has been likened to an Australian Maigret.

 Forests of the Night (1963)

 The High Commissioner (1966)

A Flight of Chariots (1973)

CLELAND, John (1709–89) English dramatist, journalist, amateur philologist and novelist. After serving as consul in Smyrna and as Bombay agent for the East India Company, Cleland fell on evil times. While in a debtors' prison, he wrote *Fanny Hill, or the Memoirs of a Woman of Pleasure,* for a fee of twenty guineas. A poised, elegant account of a prostitute playing fast and louche with the nobs of

the Town, it was long treasured as a classic of underground erotica and only surfaced, unexpurgated, after much litigation in the mid-1960s.

 Fanny Hill (1749)

Memoirs of a Coxcomb (1751)

CLEMENT, Hal (1922) American science fiction writer, notable for three books which used the device of crash landings on planets to examine in detail the technical implications of radically different environments on human beings. *Mission of Gravity* is set on a world where gravity varies geographically by a factor of several hundred.

 Needle (1950)

Mission of Gravity (1954)

Cycle of Fire (1957)

CLIFFORD, Francis (1917–75) English spy and suspense novelist, in private life Arthur Thompson, a wartime soldier who was decorated after a 1000-mile jungle journey through Burma, and was later an officer of the Special Operations Executive. Clifford came late to writing, finding in it a way of discovering the meaning of his war experiences. But he never forgot the need to ensnare readers and his books are remarkable for their high level of tension, whether set in Franco's oppressed Spain, the Biafran jungle, or a hotel-room in Mayfair under seige.

 The Naked Runner (1966)

Amigo, Amigo (1973)

Drummer in the Dark (1976)

CLOETE, Stuart (1897–1976) South African novelist. Born in Paris, and educated in England, Cloete farmed for twenty years in South Africa before turning to writing, mostly about South African history. His best known novel, *Turning Wheels,* is a saga of the Great Trek.

 Turning Wheels (1937)

CLOUSTON, J. Storer (1870–1944) English writer of comedy thrillers. Amusing and slightly incredible, sometimes farcical, his novels merely sought to entertain, but he was a talented and literate story-teller with an agile mind. His contributions to classical detection, the short stories featuring F. T. Carrington, are now unjustly neglected.

 The Lunatic at Large (1899)

Carrington's Cases (stories, 1920)

COATES, Robert M. (1897) American novelist and art critic, born in Connecticut. Coates was paid scant attention by critics until his first surrealist novel *The Eater of Darkness* was reprinted in 1960. This has great verve, but demonstrates that sustained surrealism has no future in long fictions. He turned to well-made novels, and these have been consistently underrated, especially *Wisteria Cottage,* which is based on an actual murder case.

 The Eater of Darkness (1929, rev. 1960)

 *Wisteria Cottage* (1948)

The Man Just Ahead of You (stories, 1964)

COCTEAU, Jean (1889–1963) French novelist, dramatist, film-maker, man of letters and poet. His best novel, *Children of the Game,* is not

Jean Cocteau

deliberately outrageous – as so much of his work is – and may be his best production. It describes, with a lucid coherence and an unusual seriousness, the consequences of a group's construction of a world of their own in the midst of the real world. This is an outstanding psychological novel. *The Grand Ecart* (1923, tr. 1925) is a French *Bildungsroman* of great sensitivity. *The Imposter* is more modernist, but undoubtedly fascinating and accomplished. It is by his novels (and some of his plays) that he will be remembered.

 Thomas the Imposter (1923, tr. 1925)

Children of the Game (1925, tr. 1955)

Round the World Again in Eighty Days (1936, tr. 1937)

COFFIN, Peter, see LATIMER, Jonathan.

COLETTE, (Sidonie-Gabrielle) (1873–1954) French novelist and memoirist. Colette married the rascal pornographer Willy, who pretended to have helped substantially in the *Claudine* series (1900–07). Better than these are *The Vagabond* (1911) and the earlier *Creatures Great and Small* (1904). *Sido* is a superb and sensitive portrait of her mother. Through her second marriage Colette became a society figure in Paris, but not before she had had to earn her living as a music-hall artist – about which she wrote. The two *Chéri* novels are delightful accounts of a sad affair between a young man and an older woman, but they do not embody the essence of Colette's genius, which was for the understanding of animals and the recollection of the rural past. *Gigi* (1945) fully deserved its mass attention both as novel and (later) film. Of all those who have written of animals in this century, Colette is the

Colette

most realistic – and certainly the greatest. As psychologist she was unsurpassed at tracing instinctive behaviour in people, whom she tended to view as delicate (or sometimes indelicate) animals.

 Chéri and *The End of Chéri* (1920, 1926, tr. 1953)

 Sido (1929, tr. 1953)

A Lesson in Love (1932, tr. 1932)

COLLIER, John (1901) English novelist and story-writer who settled in America in 1942. His early work in some ways anticipates William Golding's; he is a macabre fantasist somewhat in the manner of Roald Dahl.

 His Monkey Wife (1930)

Defy the Foul Fiend (1934, repr. 1958)

The John Collier Reader (1972)

COLLINS, Jackie (1939) English actress turned

novelist. Her best-selling books purport to give the low-down on high-life among showbiz jet-setters, but are each a curiously seedy amalgam of soft porn and stern moralizing.

 The World is Full of Married Men (1968)

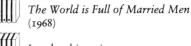 *Lovehead* (1974)

The Bitch (1979)

COLLINS, (William) Wilkie (1824–89) English novelist. Collins was one of the inventors of the modern detective story, in his two classics of the genre *The Moonstone* and *The Woman in White.* These are masterpieces in the sense that the narratives are tailored with a skill hitherto unknown in the realm of popular and sensational fiction. Collins was trained in law, which served him well when he came to plot his melodramatic but meticulous thrillers. But he

Wilkie Collins

wrote other novels of great interest, of which *Armadale* is the most important. This explores, in terms of Victorian Gothic, the pregnant theme of the son who becomes obsessed with the idea that he must re-enact a crime he believes to have been committed by his father. Collins is always immensely readable, and, however melodramatic he may become, his characterization is superb.

 The Woman in White (1860)

Armadale (1866)

The Moonstone (1868)

COMPTON, D. G. (1930) British science fiction novelist, an elegant writer whose main theme is the dehumanization of man by the abuse of technology.

 Farewell Earth's Bliss (1966)

Synthajoy (1968)

COMPTON-BURNETT, Ivy (1892–1969) English novelist. Her strange novels are essentially Gothic melodramas based on the classical precepts of Aristotle but written in a stark, stylized dialogue with some ironically reticent narrative. She posed as an innocent, but saw life as a cesspit of evil. Her themes include incest, blackmail, murder and every other dramatic sin. She said that life had no plot – and so she would supply it with one. Her books are repetitive, but all seventeen (her first is not in the style of the others, and is not counted) are compulsive reading.

 Brothers and Sisters (1929)

CONDON, Richard (1915) American novelist, former Director of Publications for Walt Disney Productions and publicist for Hollywood moguls: Zanuck, DeMille and Howard Hughes. He has written a succession of best sellers, several of which have been filmed. Condon's plots are usually concerned with bizarre political happenings; stories of suspense and adventure.

 The Manchurian Candidate (1959)

Winter Kills (1974)

Death of a Politician (1979)

CONLON, Kathleen (1943) English writer whose novels usually deal with youth, its problems and difficulties. She writes with perception and sympathy.

 A Move in the Game (1979)

CONNELL, E. S. (1924) American novelist, story-writer and poet. Connell's fiction is well made but somewhat more interesting than that of most ultra-professional American writers. He is a little less keen simply to entertain, but is in fact as entertaining as any of his competitors. *Mrs Bridge* and *Mr Bridge* are superb studies of suburban types; Mr Bridge's desire for his daughter, and his bewilderment about it, is a memorable piece of realist writing. *The Diary of a Rapist* is less sure in its account of a frustrated man's disintegration into madness.

 Mrs Bridge (1958)

The Diary of a Rapist (1966)

Mr Bridge (1969)

CONNOLLY, Cyril (1903–74) English writer, critic and novelist. Connolly was an influential critic and reviewer. *The Rock Pool* is interesting but somehow lacks energy.

 The Rock Pool (1935)

CONRAD, Joseph (1857–1924) English novelist (naturalized 1886) born in Poland as Teodor Józef Korzeniowski. He learned French as a child, and spent some years of his youth as sailor, gun-runner, would-be suicide, dueller and adventurer. Then he pulled himself together, joined the British merchant navy, travelled to the Far East, and eventually made the grade as master mariner. He left the service in 1894. He had learned English at the age of 20. He published his first novel *Almayer's Folly* in 1895, but it attracted little attention. He worked at perfecting his peculiar but unquestionably English style of English (this is in itself an extraordinary paradox) for many years, writing good novels in the process, including *Lord Jim* (1900) and *Nostromo*. He became popular with a novel indifferent by his own standards, *Chance* (1913); thereafter his work fell off. Conrad's subjects are the behaviour of men under stress and terror, and the nature of revolution: he appreciated why men and women became revolutionaries, but criticized, with reluctant horror, what became of them when they did. The story "Heart of Darkness" – despite its purple passages – shows him at his most powerful. Here he depicts a man totally alone, and failing – and creates a universal symbol. His style is often blurred and confused; but he is always reaching for a meaning, which makes him continually interesting. At his best he is politically enlightening as well as capable of showing men's inner souls in their external actions. His finest novel by common consent is *Nostromo*.

 Nostromo (1904)

The Secret Agent (1907)

Under Western Eyes (1911)

CONROY, Jack (1899) American proletarian

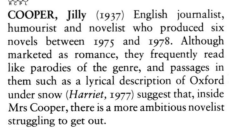

James Fenimore Cooper

novelist, who writes of the fears and uncertainties of working people, from an explicitly Marxist point of view. *The Disinherited,* partially autobiographical, is widely admired as a searing documentary of poetic power. Conroy over-modestly disclaims the appellation "novelist", calling himself simply a "witness to the times".

The Disinherited (1933)

A World to Win (1935)

CONSTANT, Benjamin (1767–1830) French novelist and politician who had a long liaison with Madame de Staël. His short novel *Adolphe* is a detached and yet deeply moving account of a tragic love affair – one of the first great novels of psychological analysis, written in a lucid and candid style. It has exercised enormous influence on the manner in which succeeding novelists wrote of love, and it helped free the novel from excess romanticism.

Adolphe (1816, tr. 1959, tr. 1964)

COOKE, John Esten (1830–86) American novelist born in Virginia, who fought with the Confederates in the Civil War. He was one of the founders of a strong and persistent tradition in American letters: the romanticization of the South. His best novels, set in the pre-Civil War period, are colourful and readable.

The Virginia Comedians (1854)

Henry St John, Gentleman (1859)

COOKSON, Catherine (   ) English novelist. Born on Tyneside, she writes with conviction about the North of England. *Katie Mulholland* (1967) was a best seller, and subsequent novels have added to her reputation; they combine human warmth, pathos, comedy and tragedy. Miss Cookson has a powerful narrative style. Her male characters tend to dominate, although she has created one memorable female character, Mary Ann, the warm-hearted heroine of many of her books. *The Mallen Streak* has recently been produced as a television drama series.

Love and Mary Ann (1961)

Feathers in the Fire (1971)

The Mallen Streak (1973)

COOPER, James Fenimore (1789–1851) American novelist and essayist whose main concern was to analyze the morality of American civilization. His perception that the frontier was the essence of the new civilization seems his most enduring achievement. He wrote excellent adventure stories, to which he added a degree of profundity by drawing on his great knowledge of American history and politics. In *The Last of the Mohicans* he created the formula which was to become the "Western". Natty Bumppo, the Leatherstocking, is the prototype of the "Western" hero, a civilized man, ideally suited to impose order on the wilderness, but personally more drawn to the freedom it provides and to the way of life of the Indian tribes, than to the settled order of the white man's towns.

The Last of the Mohicans (1826)

The Pathfinder (1840)

The Deerslayer (1841)

COOPER, Jilly (1937) English journalist, humourist and novelist who produced six novels between 1975 and 1978. Although marketed as romance, they frequently read like parodies of the genre, and passages in them such as a lyrical description of Oxford under snow (*Harriet,* 1977) suggest that, inside Mrs Cooper, there is a more ambitious novelist struggling to get out.

Emily (1975)

Bella (1976)

Octavia (1977)

COOPER, William (1910) English novelist and civil servant. His picaresque early novel *Scenes from Provincial Life* helped give Amis a model for *Lucky Jim,* although it has little in common with the real master of the genre, Arnold Bennett in *The Card.* By far his finest novel, *Disquiet and Peace,* is the study of a woman of eccentric temperament in Edwardian high society. The early novels, about brash provincials, were very well done; but the later are either feeble, or ill-informed satires (*You Want the Right Frame of Reference*) on modernism. The trouble is not that satire on modernism cannot be funny – it can – but that Cooper does not know what is pretentious and what is not, and shows no notion of why modernist procedures ever arose. His readership has declined, and so has his reputation.

Scenes From Provincial Life (1950)

Disquiet and Peace (1956)

You Want the Right Frame of Reference (1970)

COOVER, Robert (1932) American novelist, born in Iowa. His first novel *The Origin of the Brunists,* about the rise of a fanatic religious sect, showed real promise; since then he has been content to write in more fashionable styles, using neo-allegory, parable, surrealism and other devices. He is linguistically very lively, and has not yet fully and originally exploited this vein in his talent.

The Origin of the Brunists (1966)

The Universal Baseball Association (1968)

Pricksongs and Descants (stories, 1969)

COPPARD, A. E. (1878–1957) English storywriter who might have achieved real greatness in the form had he been able to find roots in a region. As it is, he is one of the finest of twentieth-century short essay-writers. Viewers of the finely televised series *Country Matters*, which filmed stories by him and H. E. Bates, have had the opportunity to make acquaintance with his psychological sensitivity, his mastery of the rural scene, and his poignant lyricism. He adapted the English country folk tale to his own purposes, which owe much to Chekhov and are more sophisticated than they appear.

 Collected Tales (1948)

Lucy in her Pink Jacket (stories, 1954)

CORELLI, Marie (1854–1924) English novelist of immense popularity; her work is devoid of literary merit, but she retains historical interest. Although no longer read in Great Britain or America, she is still popular in certain Commonwealth countries. She pretended that her father was Italian to enhance her image as a writer, but she was in fact the illegitimate daughter of a song-writer called Mackay, who later married her mother. She is interesting as a true popular-professional. The ingredients of her fiction, which made her a fortune and enabled her further to dignify Shakespeare's birthplace by taking up residence there, are: attack on Sin; being "in tune with the infinite"; and the presentation of sentimental themes in a consistent atmosphere of "morality". Now she is herself the subject of investigation, much of it hysterically funny.

 A Romance of Two Worlds (1886)

Thelma (1887)

The Master Christian (1900)

CORTÁZAR, Julio (1914) Argentinian novelist and story-writer who has lived for much of his life in Europe. He began as a critic, and is now an extreme experimentalist whose novels are "open" in the sense that the reader may identify with any character or group of characters he chooses, and may even *(Hopscotch)* read the book in any order he chooses. He offers the reader interesting choices – as between routine-lovers and natural anarchists, or between inner and outer experience. It is a matter of opinion as to how much he has sacrificed readability to experimentalism, or how necessary the radicalism of that experimentalism is. His sense of character is weaker than his interest in ideas – his people are decidedly "flat". But he is rightly regarded as one of the leading experimentalists in fiction of his generation.

 The Winners (1960, tr. 1965)

Hopscotch (1966, tr. 1967)

End of the Game (stories, tr. 1967)

COUPERUS, Louis (1863–1923) Dutch novelist whose works were quite widely read in English translation during his lifetime; some are now being reissued, and more ought to be on the way. He is of major stature. He began in a naturalist vein, but his later, best novels are symbolic: they explore strange states of mind with uncanny accuracy.

 The Hidden Force (1900, tr. 1922)

Small Souls (1914, tr. 1914)

Old People and the Things that Pass (1906, tr. 1918, repr. 1963)

COWPER, Richard (1926) Pseudonym used by the younger John Middleton Murry for his science fiction. His other work appears under the name Colin Murry. Many of his novels are concerned with extra-sensory perception, and some are comedies.

 Breakthrough (1967)

Twilight of Briareus (1974)

COXE, George Harmon (1901) American detective novelist, described by Anthony Boucher as "the professional's professional". Coxe's private eye mysteries, often featuring newspaper photographers Kent Murdock and Jack Casey, are cliché-ridden, predictable, but agreeably fast-moving.

 The Groom Lay Dead (1944)

Deadly Image (1964)

The Ring of Truth (1967)

COZZENS, James Gould (1903–78) American novelist. Cozzens wrote some early novels in the style of Hemingway which were ignored, then *Guard of Honour,* which was critically successful, and then *By Love Possessed,* which was a best seller. He was probably the most able

John Creasey

presenter of the conservative point of view in American fiction; but *By Love Possessed* was written in a portentous pseudo-literary style which angered most critics. His theme is order, and the necessity for it. In his best novel, *Guard of Honour,* he gives a fine picture of the conflicts which arise in air-force leadership in time of war. *By Love Possessed* and *Morning, Noon and Night* are heavy with mystical "style": the author persuades that he is wise because he lacks a moral sense, but blindly and conventionally believes in his own judgement. But he deserved his popularity because he could, in his way, tell a story, and he gave a section of the public the kind of prose it then wanted.

 Guard of Honour (1948)

By Love Possessed (1957)

Morning, Noon and Night (1968)

CRANE, Stephen (1871–1900) American novelist, story-writer, poet and journalist. *Maggie: A Girl of the Streets* (1893) is a good apprentice naturalist novel. But *The Red Badge of Courage* (1895), about the growing up of a young man in the crucible of the Civil War (in a later story Crane killed him off, which is not insignificant), attracted the praise of his major contemporaries, and he suddenly became well known. But his best work is perhaps in his stories, such as "The Open Boat", "The Blue Hotel" and some of the *Whilomville Stories* (1900). Crane's prose is of great originality, it combines impressionism with a use of precise images, and its nervous uncertainty is not a defect but a contributory factor to Crane's psychological perceptions. Crane married a brothel proprietress, became unpopular in his own country, and so came to England. He lived too extravagantly, wore out his health, and died young of consumption in a German sanatorium. Increasing attention is given to his work and its significance.

 The Complete Novels (1952)

The Complete Short Stories (1963)

CRAWFORD, F. Marion (1854–1909) Prolific (fifty-four novels) and once popular American novelist. He was an entertainer, but an intelligent one: his works, scarcely readable now, were mostly historical. *Wandering Ghosts* is a collection of quite good ghost stories.

 Mr Isaacs (1882)

Adam Johnstone's Son (1895)

Wandering Ghosts (stories, 1911)

CRAWFORD, Robert, see RAE, Hugh C.

CREASEY, John (1908–73) English writer of

crime and spy fiction who produced over 600 books and used 26 pseudonyms. The most enduring are the two police procedural series featuring Gideon (written under the pseudonym J. J. Marric) and the "handsome Roger West". In both the reader follows the life of a Scotland Yard detective as he continues the struggle against the London underworld. "The Toff" series – 55 books about a gentleman adventurer – now seems dated. During World War II Creasey wrote topical spy stories under the pseudonyms Norman Deane and Gordon Ashe.

 Withered Man (1940)

Gideon's Wrath (1967)

Murder London-Miami (1969)

CREELEY, Robert (1926) American poet, novelist and story-writer. Creeley is mainly a poet, but his semi-autobiographical novel *The Island* attracted some attention. This reads like the prose of the late James written by one who had not read him. The stories in *The Gold Diggers* lack direction and are hard to read.

 The Island (1963)

The Gold Diggers (stories, 1954, rev. 1965)

CRICHTON, Michael (1942) American novelist, screenwriter and film director who wrote his first best seller *The Andromeda Strain* while completing studies at Harvard medical school. Crichton's scientific background has enabled him to create a unique series of novels, which rely on quantities of thoroughly documented, but wholly imaginary, research: "I never work by amassing information and then distilling the truth from the mass. What I do is tell a story and then invent a fabric of research to underlie it."

 The Andromeda Strain (1969)

The Terminal Man (1972)

CRISPIN, Edmund (1921–78) English detective-story writer, pseudonym of Bruce Montgomery, composer. Crispin wrote eight novels between 1944 and 1951 and a ninth in 1977. He is perhaps the most typical exponent of the detective-story as pure sophisticated pleasure. Fun, frills, fandangles, furbelows, festoons and fal-lals froth and fantasticate in his books, on ground-works of plots as eye-poppingly ingenious as any the art has elsewhere produced. There is much play with the language, marvellously inappropriate metaphors, strict grammatical insistences, and dictionary grubbings; and there are Lewis Carroll-like absurdities which prove at the very last moment to have simple, logical explanations. His detective is Professor Fen.

 The Moving Toyshop (1946)

Love Lies Bleeding (1948)

The Glimpses of the Moon (1977)

CROFTS, Freeman Wills (1879–1957) British detective story-writer, king of the alibi and timetables crime novel. His Inspector French (appearing in most books) works his way ploddingly from initial baffling mystery to ultimate solution, the precursor of all police procedural novels (although the police-work is not particularly accurate). The books have an undeniable fascination, and some sociological interest.

 Inspector French's Greatest Case (1925)

Death of a Train (1964)

CROMPTON, Richmal (1890–1969) Novelist and story-writer remembered for her hugely successful collections of stories about William, a pugnacious and recalcitrant eleven-year-old who first made his appearance in *Just William* in 1922. William's rebellious spirit softened a little over the years, but he remained a breath of bracing air in the anodyne ranks of boy heroes.

 Just William (stories, 1922)

William's Crowded Hours (stories, 1931)

 William the Showman (stories, 1937)

CRONIN, A. J. (1896) Scottish writer, formerly a general practitioner and medical inspector for mines. His first novel *Hatter's Castle* (1931) was an immediate success; a powerful story which contains some of his best writing. Many of his later books are concerned with the conflict between altruism and the pursuit of worldly interests. Latterly he has gained wide popularity as a result of the television series *Dr Finlay's Casebook*, based on his portrayal of a Scottish doctor in some of his early stories.

 The Stars Look Down (1935)

The Citadel (1937)

Keys of the Kingdom (1941)

CROSS, Ian (1925) New Zealand novelist. Influenced to some extent – as are almost all New Zealand novelists – by Sargeson, Cross deals with the problems caused by an excessively genteel society, one of which is that it promotes delinquency and rebellion. *The God Boy* is about a clever schoolboy who believes that he is "chosen" because he is at a convent school; finding that he is not, he decides to take action against God. The two suc-

ceeding novels are not as good; but the first is a tour de force, and is exceptionally well written, in a terse, ironic prose.

 The God Boy (1957)

 After Anzac Day (1961)

CROWLEY, Aleister (1875–1947) Prolific English author, scholar and self-publicist, who wrote a number of works in verse, translations, memoirs, and books on magic and witchcraft. He was notorious for the last, and liked to boast of himself as "the wickedest man in the world". His novel, *The Diary of a Drug Fiend*, was a sensational best seller. Assumed to be autobiographical, it was denounced by some for its descriptions of "the orgies of vice" and praised by others for the morality of its description of the torments of drug-addiction.

 The Diary of a Drug Fiend (1932)

CUNNINGHAM, E. V., see FAST, Howard.

CUSSLER, Clive (1931) American novelist who specializes in sea adventures. His *Raise the Titanic* was an international best seller.

 The Mediterranean Caper (1973, in Britain *Mayday!*, 1977)

Raise the Titanic (1976)

Vixen 03 (1977)

D

DAGERMAN, Stig (1923–54) Swedish novelist, story writer and dramatist. His suicide had almost as much impact on Scandinavian literature as Pavese's had on Italian. He was not in the mainstream of Scandinavian literature, which tends to the complacent. The young felt that he had much to offer them, but he felt that he had dried up. His prose is essentially expressionist, and imbued with the concerns of such thinkers as Kierkegaard; his understanding of insanity was uncanny; and his most powerful books suggest that his vision of the modern world was of a vast lunatic asylum. He was no imitator of Kafka, but is the sort of writer Kafka anticipated. Some of his best work has yet to be translated.

 The Games of Night (stories, 1947, tr. 1960)

 A Burnt Child (1948, tr. 1950)

DAHL, Roald (1916) Norwegian story-writer and writer for children born in Wales. Dahl's most satisfying stories were drawn from his experiences as an RAF pilot during World War II (*Over to You*). He has since concentrated on blackly humorous, usually vengeful anecdotes, each with a neat, usually nasty sting in its tail. For all their wide acclaim, they suffer from a lack of properly developed characters – a fault absent in his excellent books for children.

Over to You (stories, 1946)

Kiss Kiss (stories, 1960)

Switch Bitch (stories, 1974)

DAHLBERG, Edward (1900) American novelist, poet, critic and publicist, whose novels are fictionalized autobiographies. Dahlberg is one of those who alienate the Establishment. He is famous for it. Now that he is old, people would like to forgive him, but in general they have to turn to his early fiction rather than his later, which has fallen off and is less readable. He resembles Céline in his fury, but his prose lacks the Frenchman's precision. However, his long fictionalized autobiography, whether you love him or hate him, has power. The narrative is flawed; he has no sense of form; he is angrily careless; his aphorisms are feeble: yet the whole series, though it falls off as it becomes more obscure and egotistic, has the force of a steamroller.

Bottom Dogs (1930)

From Flushing to Calvary (1932)

Because I Was Flesh (1964)

DALY, Elizabeth (1879–1967) American detective novelist. Her usual cast consists of the East Coast rich; her neat plots are based on inheritance and money, with digressions about cats, books, ghosts and family life.

Evidence of Things Seen (1943)

The House without the Door (1945)

D'ANNUNZIO, Gabriele (1863–1938) Italian poet, dramatist, novelist and hero of fascism. D'Annunzio began as a good minor poet, and his novels were very popular in his lifetime; but they represent that side of him which tried to inflate his small gift into a large one, and their perfervid, decadent sensuality has not stood the test of time. His muse, Eleonora Duse, is vividly portrayed in *The Flame of Life*.

The Triumph of Death (1894, tr. 1898)

The Flame of Life (1900, tr. 1900)

Tales of My Native Town (1902, tr. 1920)

DARCY, Clare ( ) English historical-romantic novelist, one of a band of writers aspiring to don the mantle of the late Georgette Heyer. Her books can best be described as Regency romps.

Georgina (1975)

Victoire (1977)

Eugenia (1978)

DAUDET, Alphonse (1840–97) French novelist and story writer, born in Nîmes. Daudet was an extremely versatile writer, but his real strength lay in his capacity to exploit the anecdote – and in his much admired style. *Little Good-For-Nothing* is a semi-autobiographical novel about the early struggles of a diminutive young man. It was preceded by his most famous work, *Letters From My Mill*, masterly sketches of Provençal life in which Daudet is seen at his best. The *Tartarin of Tarascon* series is less good, but excellent popular fiction; they deal with a boaster who has to make his boasts come true. The first two (translations of these in a single volume are listed below) are easily the best. Zola tried to recruit Daudet to the naturalist school, and some of his novels, such as *The Nabob* (1877, tr. 1902) exhibit a naturalist manner, but Daudet was not a true naturalist: he lacked the power. Although he has a Rabelaisian streak of witty extravagance, his true genius is for the pathetic, the delicate, the intangible.

Little Good-For-Nothing (1868, tr. 1885)

Letters From My Mill (1869, tr. 1966)

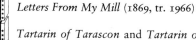

Tartarin of Tarascon and *Tartarin on the Alps* (1872 and 1885, tr. 1896)

DAVIDSON, Lionel (1922) English writer of spy stories, adventure novels and detective stories. *A Long Way to Shiloh* (1966), set in the emergent state of Israel, was based on his own

love of that country; and *Making Good Again* dealt with the meaning of Nazism. Davidson's work shows not only versatility, but great gifts for comic situation and dialogue, and a talent for creating vivid settings and characters.

 The Rose of Tibet (1962)

 Making Good Again (1968)

The Chelsea Murders (1978)

DAVIES, Rhys (1903–78) Welsh novelist and story-writer. Davies' real gift was for the short story, although his novels are more than competent. In the stories and in the novel *Nobody Answered the Bell* he produced unforgettable work.

 Collected Stories (1955)

The Chosen One and Other Stories (1967)

Nobody Answered the Bell (1971)

DAVIES, Robertson (1913) Canadian novelist and dramatist. Davies is by no means typically Canadian, but rather represents a sophisticated continuation of the Anglo-Canadian stream. His novels are mostly quiet but candid satires on Canadian life, and especially on its conventions.

Tempest-Tost (1951)

Leaven of Malice (1955)

The Manticore (1972)

DAVIN, Dan (1913) New Zealand novelist who settled in England and became a leading publisher. His novels deal with New Zealand society and its problems, or with the war *(For the Rest of Our Lives)*, with an urbane and informed intelligence.

 Cliffs of Fall (1945)

For the Rest of Our Lives (1947, repr. 1965)

DAVIS, Dorothy Salisbury (1916) American suspense novelist, remarkable for the feeling she is able to put into books that still remain exciting. Underdogs gain her vivid sympathy and violence gets her unswerving condemnation. Her settings have been varied, including seedy New York, coal-pit Kentucky, college Illinois, and poverty-line Appalachia.

 A Gentle Murderer (1951)

The Pale Betrayer (1965)

A Death in the Life (1977)

DAVIS, Rebecca Harding (1831–1910) American novelist, one of the first realists – although her fiction suffers from sentimentality. She attacked racialism *(Waiting for the Verdict)* and political corruption *(John Andross);* and *Margaret Howth* is a story of slum life.

 Margaret Howth (1862)

Waiting for the Verdict (1868)

John Andross (1874)

DAVIS, Richard Harding (1864–1916) American journalist and fiction writer. Davis was a famous war reporter; his novels were a sideline. They are slick, sensationalist and intelli-

gent – but they gave out a false picture of the young heroic American male which was soon discredited by reality.

 Van Bibber and Others (1892)

Soldiers of Fortune (1897)

The Dictator (1904)

DAY LEWIS, C., see BLAKE, Nicholas.

DAZAI, Osamu (1909–1948) Japanese novelist. He led a legendarily disordered life, although during the war (paradoxically, because he was anti-fascist) he pulled himself together. He made many attempts at suicide before succeeding. But his fiction, which many well-informed critics of Japanese literature find superior to that of Yukio Mishima, does not reflect the disorder of his unhappy life. He is a novelist of international stature. *The Setting Sun,* in effect a study of the reasons for the rise of barbarism and the spiritual collapse of Japan, is an exquisitely touching and profound novel. *No Longer Human,* which traces his own descent into despair, is no less objective and moving.

 The Setting Sun (1947, tr. 1956)

No Longer Human (1948, tr. 1958)

DE CAMP, L. Sprague (1907) American writer of science fiction, fantasy and historical novels. His extensive knowledge of archaeology and ancient technology provides a convincing background for his novels of classical Greece and Rome. Various ancient mythologies provide milieux for his many humourous fantasy novels, some of which were written in collaboration with Fletcher Pratt. *Lest Darkness Fall* is a classic science fiction story in which a time-traveller prevents the fall of the Roman Empire and averts the Dark Ages. De Camp has a strong ironic sense, which adds zest to his work.

 Lest Darkness Fall (1941)

Rogue Queen (1951)

The Bronze God of Rhodes (1960)

DEEPING, Warwick (1877–1950) English popular novelist and doctor of medicine. His large output of romantic novels (many historical) were widely read, but have little literary merit. *Sorrell and Son,* however, does have some force behind its complacency – and is better written than the other sixty-odd books.

 Love Among the Ruins (1904)

Sorrell and Son (1925)

Exiles (1950)

DEFOE, Daniel (?1660–1731) English novelist, tradesman, journalist, economist and dissenter. He had a good, but not an ordered or aristocratic, education. The details of his life are very obscure, and open to varying interpretations. He was held in scorn by his contemporaries, who nonetheless – Swift for example – learned from him. His scope was enormous: he wrote on politics, the supernatural, morals, economics, travel, sociology, crime – and he wrote novels purporting to be biographies, of which he had genuinely written a number. As man and writer he remains an enigma, since his work is full of contradictions: it is hard to discover the exact nature of his imagination, for he always used masks as a device, and it is difficult to be sure if he is being ironic (or using double-irony). The detail with which he described eighteenth-century English life and his early feel for narrative make him a pioneer of the English novel.

Robinson Crusoe (1719)

Moll Flanders (1722)

Roxana (1724)

DeFOREST, John William (1826–1906) American novelist. He was a captain in the Civil War, and drew on his experiences to produce one of America's first truly realistic novels: *Miss Ravenel's Conversion from Secession to Loyalty*. He wrote vividly and accurately of war, and possessed an excellent insight into female psychology.

Miss Ravenel's Conversion from Secession to Loyalty (1867)

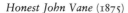

Honest John Vane (1875)

The Bloody Chasm (1881)

De HARTOG, Jan (1914) Dutch novelist and dramatist, who wrote his first novel *Captain Jan* in Dutch – and the rest in English. His novels are well-made adventure stories; his portrayal of character is not deep, but it is accurate. He is at his best when writing of the war and the sea.

Captain Jan (1940, tr. 1952)

The Lost Sea (1951)

The Hospital (1964)

DEIGHTON, Len (1929) English spy fiction writer and novelist. Product of a totally unliterary background, Deighton entered advertising (he is a skilled artist), where he acquired a love-hate feeling towards the Great British Public School Network, and it was this that fired his entry into fiction, coupled with a similar hostility towards the smooth spy world of Ian Fleming. He has a fascination with the technicalities of things (which in the early books resulted in a rash of footnotes). His humour is quietly sharp, and he has a gift for grasping essentials and following through those insights (his insistence on a fresh approach to jacket art-work is responsible for not a little of his initial success). And his unmistakeable personal integrity has stopped him writing "mere bestsellers". From his first book he became a strong influence on the course of espionage fiction in its modern form, helping to steer it away from glossiness into reality. He has at times branched away from espionage fiction – into a novel of the film world, *Close-Up* (1972), into a rationale of the air war of the 1940s, *Bomber* (1970) and into an extraordinary vivid postulation of a Britain conquered in 1940, *SS-GB*.

Billion-dollar Brain (1966)

Spy Story (1974)

SS-GB (1978)

DeLa MARE, Walter (1873–1956) English poet, story-writer, novelist and anthologist. De La Mare is a major poet; but his mastery of the short story of a certain "uneasy" type comes near to the accomplishment of his poetry. He wrote several good, eerie novels, of which the most famous is *Memoirs of a Midget*.

Henry Brocken (1904, rev. 1924)

Memoirs of a Midget (1921)

The Collected Tales (1950)

DELANY, Samuel R. (1942) American science fiction writer, winner of several awards. His early novels, including the trilogy *The Fall of the Towers* (1963–5) and *Babel-17* (1966), have marvellously exotic settings, and the colourful prose is loaded with visual imagery. His works are invariably quest stories of some kind. His recent work is much more intense and has proved very controversial among science fiction readers and critics. Many of his excellent stories were published in *Driftglass* (1971).

Daniel Defoe

Nova (1968)

 Dhalgren (1975)

Tales of Nevèryon (1979)

De La ROCHE, Mazo (1885–1961) Canadian regionalist romantic novelist of great popularity, who dealt with life in rural Ontario. Her series of sixteen novels of the Whiteoak family of Jalna moves back and forth in time and describes the succeeding generations in a close detail which lends realism to her essentially romantic idyll. Her abilities lie in brisk characterization, exciting plot and the solidity of physical setting.

 Jalna (1927)

The Whiteoaks of Jalna (1929)

DELEDDA, Grazia (1871–1936) Italian novelist, born in Sardinia, who won the Nobel Prize in 1926, but has since then been unfairly forgotten. Her first novels were regionalist and have more than a touch of naturalism; her style, bold and simple, is highly original. She developed from a "local colour" writer into one who could achieve great psychological intensity.

 Ashes (1904, tr. 1908)

Nostalgia (1905, tr. 1905)

The Woman and the Priest (1920, tr. 1922, in U.S. *The Mother* 1923)

DELONEY, Thomas (?1543–1600) Elizabethan writer of episodic fiction, and balladeer. He wrote lively historical fiction (*Thomas of Reading*), and used real events as the basis for his stories. He was read widely until the eighteenth century, and is still eminently readable.

 Novels (1961, sel. from *Works*, 1912)

DEL REY, Lester (1915) American science fiction writer. Most of his novels are trivial, except for the prophetic *Nerves*, about an accident at a nuclear power station.

 Nerves (1942, rev. 1956)

The Eleventh Commandment (1962)

DEMBY, William (1922) Black American novelist. He has as yet only a minority audience, although a few critics have admired his modernist technique and his stand against racism.

 Catacombs (1965)

DENNIS, Nigel (1912) English novelist, critic and playwright. Dennis scored a great critical success with *Cards of Identity,* a black satire on modern society much influenced by Swift. Later novels, though worthy, have not been so successful.

 Boys and Girls Come Out to Play (1949)

Cards of Identity (1955)

A House in Order (1966)

De POLNAY, Peter (1906) French-born novelist who lives in Paris and writes in English, he is a prolific author of novels with cosmopolitan settings and characters; crime is sometimes part of the story but not its main feature. His characters are interesting and his view of life wry and worldly.

 The Loser (1973)

DERLETH, August (1909–71) American poet, critic, short story-writer and novelist, founder of Arkham House, the publisher of horror and supernatural fiction. Derleth's popular and prolific writings covered a vast range. He is chiefly remembered for his series of Sherlock Holmes pastiches featuring Solar Pons, and for his mysteries about Judge Ephraim Peck.

 Place of Hawks (stories, 1935)

Evening in Spring (1941)

No Future for Luana (1945)

DÉRY, Tibor (1894–1978) Hungarian novelist and story-writer. His *Niki, the Story of a Dog,* which pretends to deal with the life of a fox terrier, is a savage although humorous indictment of the pre-1956 regime and delighted tens of thousands.

 Niki, the Story of a Dog (1956, tr. 1958)

The Giant (stories, 1965)

The Portuguese Princess (1967)

DESAI, Anita (1937) Indian novelist and teacher, who has been writing since the age of seven ("as instinctively as I breathe"). Her first novels dealt with the effect of modern ways on the entrenched attitudes of upper-class Indians, for whom she shows great sympathy. Later work, almost mystical in its intensity, shows how people paradoxically accept the new ways in terms of the old. Desai's distinction has not yet been fully recognized outside her own country.

 Cry, the Peacock (1963)

Bye-Bye, Blackbird (1971)

Where Shall We Go This Summer? (1975)

DEUTSCH, Babette (1895) American poet, translator, critic and novelist. Babette Deutsch is known primarily for her verse but has also published four novels.

A Brittle Heaven (1926)

In Such a Night (1927)

De VRIES, Peter (1910) American novelist and

Peter de Vries

story writer. He was born in Chicago, and has been a staff member of the *New Yorker* since 1944. He is essentially a writer of connected sketches rather than a novelist, but he makes his books look like novels. His main interest is to let his comic vigour fly to the best effect. Surrealism has influenced him, but he is not surrealist: it is the things his characters say that are surrealist – and they are the kind of things "ordinary" people do say. A careful reading of his large output reveals that he has a more serious theme than may at first seem apparent: he wants to demonstrate that a religious scepticism is a better attitude than a puritan or an atheistic one. He is a superb satirist: on behaviourism; Caldwell; and other institutions.

The Tunnel of Love (1954)

The Tents of Wickedness (1959)

The Glory of the Hummingbird (1975)

DICK, Philip K. (1928) American science fiction writer. Although his work is uneven and inconsistent, his many books contain some of the most fascinating and ingenious ideas and set-pieces in the genre. Distrustful of the future – many of his books are set after some disaster – he is not despairing of human nature. He is able to create convincing dislocations of normal perception, as in *The Three Stigmata of Palmer Eldritch*. His distrust of final and complete answers is mirrored by a strong streak of progressive anti-authoritarianism, but the seriousness of his themes is lightened by a mischievous delight in the humorous aspects of his fantastic creations.

The Man in the High Castle (1962)

The Three Stigmata of Palmer Eldritch (1965)

Do Androids Dream of Electric Sheep? (1968)

DICKENS, Charles (1812–70) English novelist: the most popular, world-wide, of all time. His father, the model for Mr Micawber, went to prison for debt when his son was twelve. Dickens worked in a blacking factory and visited his family in prison on Sundays. He never forgot the experience. He became successful as a journalist (*Sketches by Boz*, 1836), and then decided to work as a writer of serialized fiction. He paid the most scrupulous attention to the way the instalments were received, and modified his plans accordingly. He was successful from his first novel, *The Pickwick Papers,* onwards. Dickens was a brilliant reader of his own fiction – an actor – and this is the key to his artistic as well as his popular success; he pitched his voice as his audience wanted it pitched, but at the same time he was sensitive to needs in his audience of which it was unaware. He was uneven; he could be

nauseatingly sentimental even by the standards of his own day and he could be over-melodramatic. But he cared greatly for justice, and his portraits of cruel and stupid despots – and his satire of bureaucracy (especially in *Bleak House*) – had an effect on society. For he was much loved, and he could move the hearts and minds of those who had previously been indifferent to cruelty and stupidity. He is in no way a realist: he is a magnifier. His art is rooted not in a sensitive intelligence but in a sensitive and largely intuitive response to the (on the whole) noblest needs of his readers. As E. M. Forster said, all his characters are "flat"; but they vibrate more energetically than anyone else's flat characters. There is no denying his power or his significance.

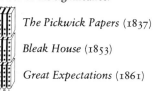

The Pickwick Papers (1837)

Bleak House (1853)

Great Expectations (1861)

DICKENS, Monica (1915) English novelist and great-grand-daughter of Charles Dickens. She had a success with a fictionalized account of how she went out as a household help, *One Pair of Hands* – and a more moderate one with attractively written successors.

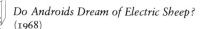

One Pair of Hands (1939)

My Turn to Make the Tea (1951)

Kate and Emma (1964)

DICKEY, James (1923) Well known American poet who has written one novel, *Deliverance,* which was slammed by critics but achieved a moderate sales success, which increased after it was filmed. It is a frankly popular adventure story, with sexual deviation and violence thrown in.

Deliverance (1970)

DICKINSON, Peter (1927) English detective

novelist and children's writer. Dickinson is in the tradition of the great English eccentrics, and brings to his books an imagination of unusual force. His first, *Skin Deep* (in U.S. *The Glass-sided Ants' Nest*, 1968) was set among a New Guinea tribe resident in the attics of a row of London houses. Others have featured a home for children suffering from a sickness (entirely imaginary) that turns them into sleepy, delightful psychic sensitives; and a chimpanzee learning to use grammar who eventually exposes the murderer. Dickinson, by and large, keeps to the form of the classical whodunnit, but he soon began to put behind this facade themes of considerable weight – the relationship of Id, mind and soul (*Walking Dead*), and the danger of not living in the present (*The Lively Dead*, 1975). Besides his rioting imagination, Dickinson possesses a formidable intelligence, a quality that sometimes overloads his work particularly with an extensive, even learned, vocabulary. But he never forgets the need to tell a story, or to maintain tension.

Sleep and His Brother (1971)

The Poison Oracle (1974)

Walking Dead (1977)

DICKSON, Carter, see CARR, John Dickson.

DICKSON, Gordon (1923) American science fiction writer. He is noted for his stories of the "Dorsai", mercenary soldiers of the future.

The Genetic General (1959)

Naked to the Stars (1961)

The Far Call (1978)

DIDEROT, Denis (1713–84) French thinker, dramatist, critic and novelist. Diderot is one of the most interesting of all minds, a prophet and a master of psychology. The scope of his knowledge – as the greatest encyclopedist of all time – was enormous. His fiction anticipates modern techniques, and is psychologically penetrating in a manner not usually found in the creative work of men of ideas. His great novel *Jacques le Fataliste* (1796), has unfortunately not been translated. Diderot's work is not only startlingly relevant to modern preoccupations but also offers devastatingly accurate and subtle character delineation.

The Nun (1760, tr. 1959, tr. 1972)

Rameau's Nephew (?1761, tr. 1972)

DIDION, Joan (1934) American (Californian) novelist. *Run River*, the first of her much-praised novels, deals with the disintegration of the family. *Play It As It Lays* is a brilliantly savage portrait of Hollywood and of the mental collapse of a woman. *A Book of Common Prayer* (1977) is her best stylistic achievement to date. Didion combines a near-naturalist viewpoint with an elegant prose achieving a fine ironic effect.

Run River (1963)

Play It As It Lays (1970)

DINESEN, Isak, see BLIXEN, Karen.

DISRAELI, Benjamin (1804–81) English born of Italian-Jewish parents) Tory prime minister and novelist, who became Earl of Beaconsfield. His achievement as a novelist has been obscured by his huge importance as politician. His earlier novels were sentimental romances; but slashing across this element is an original vein of sardonic, cynical and mordant wit. Byron was the young Disraeli's hero; but he subjected his romantic propensities to microscopic examination, and it is seen in the novels. He has few equals as a political satirist. *Coningsby* and *Sybil* are two of the best political novels in the language: their author knew his subject. *Endymion*, his last complete novel, has been underrated.

Coningsby (1844)

Sybil (1845)

Endymion (1880)

DIXON, Thomas (1864–1946) American racialist novelist and dramatist. He was a Baptist minister, and his novel *The Clansman*, which is not un-readable, is a repulsive vehicle for his hatred of negroes and his love of violence and the KKK. Nonetheless he had some talent for the expression of his crazed beliefs.

The Leopard's Spots (1902)

The Clansman (1905)

The Traitor (1907)

DOCTOROW, E. L. (1931) American novelist whose debut *Bad Man from Bodie* (also known as *Welcome to Hard Times*) established him as a writer of taut prose, with a great sense of period and tearing narrative drive. These assets are stretched almost to breaking-point in his celebrated *Ragtime*: a hectic switchback ride through pre-1914 America. His *The Book of Daniel* examines the fate of the children of parents electrocuted for leaking atom secrets.

Bad Man from Bodie (1961)

The Book of Daniel (1971)

Ragtime (1976)

DODSON, Owen (1914) American poet, novelist, dramatist and teacher, whose novel *Boy at the Window* was much praised.

Boy at the Window (1951)

DONLEAVY, J. P. (1926) Irish-American novelist and playwright. Donleavy was born in Brooklyn and educated at Trinity College, Dublin, the setting for *The Ginger Man*, the adventures of a violent student in flight from continuity and responsibility. In his second novel *A Singular Man* Donleavy emerged from the shadow of James Joyce and Henry Miller to write an inventive and brilliant fantasy about a rich lonely paranoid, George Smith, in a clipped, lyrical telegraphese all his own. The titles of Donleavy's subsequent novels – e.g. *The Beastly Beatitudes of Balthazar B* (1968) – are, sadly, an index to his continuing lapse into inconsequential self-parody.

The Ginger Man (1955)

A Singular Man (1963)

The Destinies of Darcy Dancer, Gentleman (1978)

DONNELLY, Ignatius (1831–1901) American politician and lawyer whose one novel, *Caesar's Column*, is a dystopia about the working classes' violent and brutal revolt against a capitalist slave-state.

Caesar's Column (1891)

DOOLITTLE, Hilda (H. D.) (1886–1961) American poet and novelist. Most famous as a poet, her fiction has been under-rated. *Bid Me to Live* is an outstanding use of stream of consciousness technique, a *roman à clef* about life in literary London towards the end of the

E. L. Doctorow

First World War. Her other novels are historical, and written with precision and understanding.

 Palimpsest (1926)

Hedylus (1928)

Bid Me to Live (1960)

DOS PASSOS, John (1896–1970) American novelist, translator, poet, sociological writer and essayist. Dos Passos was a major technical innovator but his intrinsic achievement does not quite live up to his historical importance. His earlier fiction is excellent in its own way, though some have found it tedious; it is universally agreed that his later fiction is markedly inferior. He began on the extreme left, but over-reacted, and became a too ferocious apostle of the extreme right. His honest hatred of modern technocracy and bureaucracy spilled over into crypto-fascism, although he did not see it as that: he believed that the extreme right wing in America believed in the individual. His technique has three important features: the "camera eye" (seeing lives in parallel, tracing an individual's progress within his general sociological environment); "newsreel" (selections from newspapers, popular songs, etc) and "biographies" (accounts of prominent personalities). The "camera eye" technique includes some use of stream of consciousness. These techniques are seen to best advantage in the trilogy *U.S.A.*, although his finest novel is *Manhattan Transfer*.

 Manhattan Transfer (1925)

U.S.A. (1930–36; 1937)

DOSTOYEVSKY, Fyodor (1821–81) Russian novelist. His father, cruel and despotic (a model for old Karamazov), was murdered by his own serfs. His first novel *Poor Folk* (1846) gave him a good beginning, but his second *The Double* (1846), which is better, was badly received. He was arrested in 1849 on stupid charges, led to execution, and then "spared" – and sentenced to four years hard labour followed by four more years as an army private. This terrible experience left its mark on him: his health was permanently undermined, and he became an epileptic during his martyrdom. His next really significant novel was *Notes From the Underground* (1864), in which he explored his life-long concern with the problem of nihilism. Always Dostoyevsky is asking the question: "If there is no God, no authority, then why should men not behave as they wish?" So he ended up as an apparently paranoiac extremist reactionary. Yet in the great mature novels he accepts, if not ostensibly, the fact that a constructive scepticism is possible. He cannot tolerate it, and so it drives him to certain odd ideological extremes; but the tension between his scepticism and his terrors creates the power

Fyodor Dostoyevsky

of his fiction. He is a great comic novelist, as well as a melodramatic tragedian. All the fiction is constructed around "scenes", which in their sad and crazy absurdity anticipate surrealism. He splits himself up into his various characters, and it is the villains and the divided personalities who are the most vivid. Dostoyevsky is a vibrant and feverish writer; he is at his best when his magnificent imagination gets the better of his ideas. His novels were translated by Constance Garnett in a 12-volume edition, 1912–20, and this is certainly the preferred version. But the translations cited below are also very good.

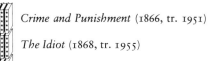 *Crime and Punishment* (1866, tr. 1951)

The Idiot (1868, tr. 1955)

The Brothers Karamazov (1879–80, tr. 1958)

DOUGLAS, Lloyd C. (1877–1951) American Lutheran clergyman who wrote sensationalist "reap the rewards of virtue" novels, and then two inflated Biblical romances which became best-sellers: *The Robe* and *The Big Fisherman*. He could spin a good yarn.

Magnificent Obsession (1929)

The Robe (1942)

The Big Fisherman (1949)

DOUGLAS, Norman (1868–1952) Scottish novelist, travel writer and hedonist. Douglas, who led a "wicked life", made exquisitely exact judgements on his contemporaries. His gift was for living in a pagan manner and disguising his considerable sensitivity. His hedonism and love of Capri is expressed in the novel *South Wind*, but in a deliberately popular manner; its two successors, especially *In the Beginning*, are more serious.

South Wind (1917)

They Went (1920)

In the Beginning (1928)

DOYLE, Sir Arthur Conan (1859–1930) Scottish novelist. Conan Doyle was an immensely versatile novelist: apart from creating Sherlock Holmes, he wrote historical novels and science fiction which are still widely read. But he has virtues that have been neglected by critics, who tend to write him off as a good popular writer. His historical romances, such as *The White Company* (1891), are better than those of Haggard, and his style is vigorous and lucid. But in Holmes (and to a certain extent in Professor Challenger, his SF hero) he was doing something few have noted: he was creating decadent characters under the guise of eccentric types. Holmes is after all a dope fiend who plays the violin (the implications then were devilish and Paganinian); and had Doyle been able to write as his imagination wished, Holmes might have been an ambisexual and a criminal, too. The fascination exercized by Holmes is more literary and serious than is supposed, for his mysteriousness is not at all cosy, as some readers like to think, and as the method of writing suggests. He is decidedly sinister, and is in fact interchangeable with Moriarty and with Mycroft. Doyle became expert in the study of crime, and intervened successfully in certain cases in which people had been wrongly convicted. An imperialist and a spiritualist who believed in fairies, his real interest was in evil. By not knowing he was decadent, Doyle was more successfully so than many self-acknowledged decadents.

The Principal Works in Fiction (1913)

DRABBLE, Margaret (1939) English novelist, critic and radio personality. After a short career as an actress, Drabble took to fiction writing on the model of George Eliot. She produced readable, well-made novels intelligently tailored to the aspirations of literate young women. She was not strident, and in such books as *The Millstone* she reflected the wishes of her readers. She is now less popular, because feminism is now less genteel. Her novels tend to get somewhat bogged down in the over-traditional (without compensating factors), and to present characters who are less humanly convincing than they are impeccably conceived in conventional psychology. Although the daring of her imagination is open to question, all her novels provide a decent and sensible read.

The Garrick Year (1964)

The Millstone (1965)

The Realms of Gold (1975)

DREISER, Theodore (1871–1945) American novelist, story-writer, versifier and essayist. Dreiser, as Saul Bellow acknowledges, was a great novelist, but academic opinion has been against him. He is a writer for writers and readers, not for professional critics, such as Lionel Trilling who viciously attacked him, essentially on the grounds that he wrote about the feelings of disreputable people. Dreiser was

Sir Arthur Conan Doyle

Theodore Dreiser

brought up in conditions of poverty, and his parents were excessively religious. The contrast affected him deeply, although his interest in religion never left him. He became a successful journalist, before writing his first novel – one of his masterpieces – *Sister Carrie*. He got no credit for this at the time despite the support of Frank Norris, because the publisher's wife felt that the heroine, who was "loose" in her morals, did not get her deserts. So the cowardly publisher did not push the book and only after the publication of *Jennie Gerhardt* was the greatness of *Sister Carrie* recognized. The best of Dreiser's later fiction are *Jennie Gerhardt*, the first two volumes of the trilogy about the financier, Cowperwood, *The Financier* (1912, rev. 1927) and *The Titan* (1914) and *An American Tragedy* – a landmark in world literature. The self-study (although the protagonist is a painter) *The "Genius"* (1915) is usually dismissed as thoroughly "lamentable"; in fact it is mixed, consisting of very bad passages interspersed with ones almost as good as Dreiser ever wrote. Dreiser was certainly a naturalist insofar as categories can ever be applied to great writers: he was obsessed with the struggle for survival, he was pessimistic and he seemed to embrace determinism; he certainly concentrated on the seamy side of life. But like Emile Zola he is a symbolist. In *An American Tragedy* the hero decides to murder his girl because she is with child, and likely to ruin his ambitions. She drowns as he has planned. But does he murder her? It is one of the most important moral questions ever posed in fiction. Dreiser often shows characters poised at crises of their lives confronted with temptation, and the decisions they are seen to make demonstrate his mastery of human psychology. Much is made, by academic critics, of his clumsy style. His style is clumsy. But his novels could have been written in no other way. And careful study of the style of *An American Tragedy* shows it to be much more poetic and subtle than it appears. As Sherwood Anderson wrote: "Dreiser, the heavy footed, had tramped through the real wilderness of puritan lies making a pathway for all of us."

Sister Carrie (1900)

Jennie Gerhardt (1911)

An American Tragedy (1925)

DRISCOLL, Peter (1942) South African-born action novelist. Adventure stories underpinned by meticulous and often lengthy research are Driscoll's speciality, though detail is never allowed to interfere with onward-sweeping narrative.

The Wilby Conspiracy (1973)

Pangolin (1978)

DRUMMOND, June (1923) South African writer of murder mysteries. Miss Drummond's elaborate plots are generally based on complex family entanglements. She uses her well-developed style to depict her characters with realism.

The Boon Companions (1974)

The Patriots (1979)

DRUON, Maurice (1918) French novelist. He began by writing novels of contemporary life; then he wrote a somewhat lurid series of historical novels about the kings of France, *The Accursed Kings*. They are vivid and well written, but although Druon had historical help, they are not authentic.

The Curtain Falls (1948–51, tr. 1959)

The Accursed Kings (1955–60, tr. 6 vols 1956–61)

DRURY, Allen (1918) American political novelist. Using his background as a Washington political correspondent, he writes series of over-detailed novels about goings-on in the Senate and White House. His most successful was *Advise and Consent*, which was filmed.

Advise and Consent (1960)

Mark Coffin, U.S.S. (1979)

DUBOIS, William E. B. (1868–1963) Black American novelist, sociologist and historian. DuBois, a learned man, did much for the Black cause in America. His vividly written novels dealt with his "concept of race" with some psychological flair.

The Black Flame (trilogy, *The Ordeal of Mansart, Mansart Builds a School, Worlds of Colour,* 1957–61)

DUFFY, Maureen (1933) English novelist, critic, dramatist and poet. Maureen Duffy is well known in Britain for her part in getting authors a Public Lending Right. Her best novel, *The Microcosm*, deals directly with lesbianism. Other novels, written in a sharply realistic but deliberately off-putting style, are about down-and-outs and freaks. Exposure to her method of prose writing teaches the reader (pleasantly enough) that she is pursuing a new vein in realism in order to match up to her times. She has a good sense of detail, and curbs her tendency to excessive feeling by a laconic, throw-away casualness.

The Single Eye (1964)

The Microcosm (1966)

Capital (1975)

DUHAMEL, Georges (1884–1966) French novelist and essayist, who had a medical training. His first (and some of his later) books were passionately intelligent, humanist condemnations of war and technocracy. He is most famous for *The Pasquier Chronicles*, a superb *roman fleuve* dealing with a man who is desperately anxious to qualify as a doctor, and with his fatuity. This is excellent, but the earlier *Salavin* series represents Duhamel's greatest achievement: it begins with a sudden crazy gesture made by its commonplace hero, and ends with an equally crazy sacrifice by him. This is not as rich in sociological content as the later work; but the psychology of Salavin, a true anti-hero, is as existentialistically viewed as is anyone's character in Sartre or any later existentialist novelist. It is inexplicable that Duhamel's achievement here has not attracted more attention. Certainly the Pasquier series is important, and extremely solid; it contains passages of great insight and pathos. But in the shorter *Salavin* cycle Duhamel summed up the predicament of the "small man"; the work is a metaphor for the spiritual fate of the crushed, of those who want to be good but lack the strength or the intelligence. It is a strange and poetic book, compulsively readable.

Salavin (1920–32, tr. 5 vols 1936)

The Pasquier Chronicles (1933–41, tr. 10 vols 1937–46)

DUMAS, Alexandre (1802–70) French novelist and playwright, now chiefly remembered for his historical novels *The Count of Monte Cristo* and *The Three Musketeers*. His complete works run to 286 volumes. He was one of the first novelists to see history as a source of exotic action and intrigue. His favourite source was the turbulent politics of France's *ancien régime*, and especially the tyrannical practices of absolute monarchs and their ministers. His style is somewhat ornate by modern standards, but his better novels have survived well.

The Count of Monte Cristo (1844, tr. 1906)

The Three Musketeers (1844)

The Queen's Necklace (1850)

DU MAURIER, Daphne (1907) English novelist. Her first novel *The Loving Spirit* appeared in 1931, but her immense and lasting popular success first came with *Rebecca* (1938). This romantic novel, like many of her best stories, is set in Cornwall, and has a brooding Gothic atmosphere, a rich and moody hero and a shy and penniless heroine. Miss Du Maurier is a master of her craft, and her skills can be seen encapsulated in a brilliant short story "The Birds" (1952), about the collaboration of birds to wipe out humanity. It was successfully

Daphne du Maurier

filmed by Hitchcock, as was *Rebecca*. *The House on the Strand* successfully recreates medieval Cornwall in the mind of its protagonist.

 Jamaica Inn (1936)

My Cousin Rachel (1951)

The House on the Strand (1969)

DU MAURIER, George (1834–96) *Punch* cartoonist who turned to fiction when his sight started failing. *Trilby* (a Bohemian romance influenced by Henri Murger), with Svengali mesmerizing the eponymous heroine into becoming a brilliant singer, became one of the smash-hits of all time. Herbert Tree built Her Majesty's Theatre, London, entirely from the profits of the first stage version (1895).

 Peter Ibbetson (1892)

Trilby (1894)

The Martian (1897)

DUNDY, Elaine (1927) American novelist who was married (1951–64) to the critic Kenneth Tynan. Her first novel *The Dud Avocado*, the first-person narrative of a girl living in Paris, was published at a time when neo-picaresque

was fashionable, and was a success. Her later work lacks psychological depth, and her high spirits only partially make up for this.

 The Dud Avocado (1958)

The Old Man and Me (1964)

The Injured Party (1974)

DUNN, Nell (1936) English novelist and journalist. Her books consist of sketches mixed with documentary. *Poor Cow*, the first, was excellent, but its successors, although entertaining and informative, lack cohesion.

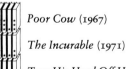 *Poor Cow* (1967)

The Incurable (1971)

Tear His Head Off His Shoulders (1974)

DUNNETT, Dorothy (1923) Scottish conventional portrait painter who has had some success with historical romances.

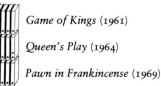 *Game of Kings* (1961)

Queen's Play (1964)

Pawn in Frankincense (1969)

DUNSANY, Lord (1878–1957) Irish dramatist and writer of fiction. Dunsany was most successful as a writer of uncanny fiction. He was popular, but has not had the literary credit he deserves: his world is a strange one, with its own folklore and mythology. Many prefer him to Tolkein; he is certainly more versatile.

 Fifty-One Tales (1915)

 Travel Tales of Mr Joseph Jorkens (1931)

The Curse of the Wise Woman (1933)

DURAS, Marguerite (1914) French novelist, playwright, screenwriter and film director. Marguerite Duras' fiction is influenced by cinematic techniques. An experimental novelist who abandoned conventional modes of narrative, Duras writes increasingly abstract books full of flashing moments of significance in the relationships between two or three characters. She is a sharp painter of people, sensation and emotion; her vision is strange and personal.

 The Sailor from Gibraltar (1952, tr. 1966)

 The Little Horses of Tarquinia (1953, tr. 1960)

 The Square (1955, tr. 1959)

DURRELL, Lawrence (1912) English poet, humorous writer and novelist. For long Durrell, who was born in India (of British parents) and has lived abroad for almost the whole of his life, was thought of primarily as a poet. He became a household word when he published his *Alexandria Quartet: Justine, Balthazar, Mountolive, Clea*. He has since written several more novels, such as *Tunc* (the anagram is rude) in 1968; but while these have received respectful attention, they have not been as widely read as the *Quartet*, on which his reputation as novelist will stand or fall. He had written an earlier novel under a pseudonym, later reprinted under his own name: *Panic Spring* (1937). Before that had appeared *Pied Piper of Lovers* (1935), which although under his own name he seems to prefer to forget. There can be no question of the immediate appeal of the *Quartet*. Young people in particular read it and feel enriched by it. Those who could not take Proust, could take Durrell, who employs every kind of modernist technique in a fluent, readable manner. As instruction-books in the modernist method alone these novels earned their keep. The *Quartet* is startlingly simple in structure. It tells the same story from different points of view, and is based on the theory that nothing can be absolutely true because of Einsteinian relativity. The *Quartet* gives us an evocative sense of life in Alexandria, and a sense of profundity: here are three books which display events spatially, and a final one which displays them temporally. But there are problems. Of Durrell's fluency there can be no doubt. But a certain (growing) body of critics have begun to wonder how "profound" he really is. Is the *Quartet* poor man's Proust or Joyce, or cut-price Einstein? His eventual status provides an intriguing critical enigma. But it is safe to say that for some time yet younger readers will go to the *Quartet* and get real value from it. That it is the "timeless masterpiece" which members of the Durrell cult, now diminishing, once pronounced it seems unlikely; some have repented their enthusiasm. It seems most likely that it was a remarkable tour de force, which is destined to fade beside the greater books from which it partly derives. Durrell has written witty, lightweight, travel sketches – and some claim that *The Black Book*, from the period of his association with Henry Miller, is a major work.

 The Black Book: An Agon (1938, repr. 1973)

 The Alexandrian Quartet (1957–60)

Livia, or Buried Alive (1979)

E

EASTLAKE, William (1917) American novelist. Eastlake is highly versatile, and has puzzled many critics by his virtuosity and apparent changeableness. But, as he has said, "The artist's job is to hold the world together . . . with magic . . ." By far the most successful of his novels, artistically and commercially, is *Castle Keep*. His other work is uneven but exuberant and almost always worth reading.

 Go in Beauty (1956)

Castle Keep (1964)

Dancers in the Scalp House (1975)

EBERHART, Mignon G. (1899) American mystery novelist whose early works often featured a lady in danger, normally Nurse Sarah Keate, with police detective Lance O'Leary hastening to the rescue. She later turned to psychological suspense, blending detection with terror.

 While the Patient Slept (1930)

Another Man's Murder (1958)

 Run Scared (1963)

George Eliot

EDGEWORTH, Maria (1767–1849) Irish novelist, born in England. Through her father, a rich eccentric quasi-Rousseauist, she met many different kinds of people, and was a friend of and influenced Sir Walter Scott. Her first novel was a collaboration with her father, and he kept an eye on all her writings until his death in 1817. She was an intelligent woman whose achievement is not as far from Jane Austen's as her lesser reputation would suggest. The didacticism of her novels is very shrewdly undermined by her sense of comedy, which is often a good deal more subtle than her critics realize. She wrote of Irish life and used local speech to great effect; she wrote of peasants with realism, although she never identified with them. Her scope is much greater than Austen's: she could face and deal with the driving need people have for cash – a theme which was quite beyond Austen's range. But she is less subtle in her character delineation, and she has little interest in plot or structure.

She is an important and rather neglected novelist, and in many ways a pioneer.

 Castle Rackrent (1800)

Belinda (1801)

Patronage (1814)

EDMONDS, Walter D. (1903) American historical novelist, whose novels are lively and often have original and well-researched settings. One of his most popular books, *Chad Hanna*, is a story of the early history of the circus in America.

 Erie Water (1933)

Drums Along the Mohawk (1936)

Chad Hanna (1940)

EDSON, J. T. (1929) British writer of Western novels. Edson was a postman in an English country town, totally fascinated by Western novels and films, who thought he could do better than the authors he read. Within twenty years he has produced around 100 novels with titles like *Trail Boss* and featuring Dusty Fog, Waco and the Ysabel Kid, which are equally popular both sides of the Atlantic.

Waco's Debt (1964)

The Ysabel Kid (1964)

EGGLESTON, Edward (1837–1902) American clergyman, journalist and novelist. The best known of his readable but sprawling novels is *The Hoosier Schoolmaster*, which gives a lively picture of Indiana. He was important as a pioneer of regionalism.

The Hoosier Schoolmaster (1871)

The Circuit Rider (1874)

The Graysons (1888)

ELIOT, George (1819–80) English novelist, born Mary Ann Evans. She was brought up in a religiously orthodox household, but early fell under the spell of her teacher's evangelicism. She later rejected all formal belief, and eventually went to live with a married man, G. H. Lewes – a well known literary critic. Her religious fervour stayed with her, however – and her status as a woman "living in sin" made her exceedingly anxious to maintain a high moral tone in her writings. In her best novels, *The Mill on the Floss, Middlemarch,* and *Daniel Deronda,* she transcends it. At the end of her life she married a younger man called Cross – as though to end up respectably. Eliot is the paradigmatic realist, in the sense that in the greatest and most complex of her novels, *Middlemarch,* she sticks so earnestly to "probability" that she achieves a totally improbable – but as it happens artistically convincing – effect. *The Mill on the Floss,* an objective correlative for her own early efforts to break away from family influence, is more lyrical. *Middlemarch* studies the sensibility of two characters: an idealistic doctor whose altruism is wrecked by his wife's vanity, and an intellectual and independent-minded woman whose sensitivities are wrecked (convincingly) by marriage to a scholar and rescued (unconvincingly) by a second marriage to a radical. The work as a whole gives an incomparable picture of a provincial society at all levels. As a realist George Eliot has no equals. But in *Daniel Deronda* she began to realize the limitations of pure realism. This is a failure, but a very important book – and one which incidentally demonstrates Eliot's intelligence. It is about a man who tries to discover himself, and in the course of doing so discovers that he is a Jew. The analyses of Judaism in the book

are masterly. So is the analysis of the predicament of the heroine, who is trapped in a marriage that denies her fulfilment. But the two themes do not come together, and *Deronda* is two novels in one. Yet each novel, had it been written completely, would probably have outstripped her earlier work. George Eliot's achievement as a novelist must be judged as one of the greatest; yet her potentialities were by no means completely fulfilled. Her truly happy liaison with Lewes perhaps cost us this complete fulfilment.

The Mill on the Floss (1860)

Middlemarch (1871–2)

Daniel Deronda (1876)

ELKIN, Stanley (1930) American novelist, story-writer and Professor of English at Washington University. Elkin displays his greatest talent as a short story-writer; one of his best collections is *Searches and Seizures* (1973) (in Britain, *Eligible Men,* 1974). He has a remarkable gift for original imagery; and although there is a brutality about his descriptions which can be repellent his words are always memorable. His novels tend to be episodic, but they are full of social satire and are often hilariously funny.

Boswell (1964)

The Dick Gibson Show (1971)

The Living End (1979)

ELLIN, Stanley (1916) American writer of thrillers and short stories. Ellin manages to sustain a sometimes breath-taking excitement, while drawing his characters well and making subtle observations of the workings of social groups. In one of his best, *Stronghold,* four ex-convicts plan to extract a large sum of money from a Quaker banking family; the real confrontation is between two very different philosophies of life. In *The Panama Portrait* (1962) a young American is caught between peasant savagery and patrician opulence in South America.

The Eighth Circle (1958)

Stronghold (1974)

The Luxembourg Run (1977)

ELLISON, Harlan (1934) American science fiction writer and anthologist, whose collections of the work of other writers, in *Dangerous Visions* (1967) and other volumes, have been very influential in the science fiction field. Although he has written a few novels, he is primarily a story-writer with a very wide range of subject-matter and a muscular style. A powerful vein of social criticism runs through

his work. *Earthman, Go Home* was originally published as *Ellison Wonderland* (1962).

Earthman, Go Home (stories, 1964)

Over the Edge (stories, 1970)

No doors, No Windows (stories, 1975)

ELLISON, Ralph (1914) Black American novelist, whose one novel (although he has long been at work on a second, and has published sections of it), *Invisible Man,* has long been regarded as the most substantial work by (and about) an American negro. It blends rich and comic realistic detail with a kind of oblique interior monologue. His hero has an identity, and yet he ends up as a nonentity, a nobody. Or does he? No, he rather discovers a new identity – he literally goes underground (into hell), to seek illumination. There is no doubt that *Invisible Man* is one of the most profound and cohesive novels of the century. Ellison has also written a number of (uncollected) stories and a fine volume of essays, *Shadow and Act.*

Invisible Man (1952)

ENRIGHT, D. J. (1920) English poet and critic, who has written four lively and underrated satirical novels. *Academic Year* should be better known: it puts Malcolm Bradbury's *The History Man,* which is celebrated, in the shade.

Academic Year (1955)

Heaven Knows Where (1957)

Figures of Speech (1965)

ERDMAN, Paul E. (1932) American writer of financial crime stories and ex-president of a Swiss bank. Erdman was tried *in absentia* in Switzerland and sentenced to eight years imprisonment after $40 million of depositors' funds were illegally used by some of his employees for speculation in commodity futures. *The Billion Dollar Sure Thing* (1973) is an exciting and convincing account of currency manipulation. His best, *The Crash of '79,* is a frighteningly topical and realistic story about oil and the demise of the West.

The Billion Dollar Sure Thing (1973, in Britain *The Billion Dollar Killing*)

The Crash of '79 (1976)

ESSEX, Mary, see BLOOM, Ursula.

EVANS, Caradoc (1883–1945) Welsh story writer, novelist and dramatist. As a writer of stories about the Welsh peasantry, Evans enraged his countrymen by depicting their narrowness, hypocrisy and greed. But he did not in fact hold back his love for their better qualities. His style is compressed and powerful.

My People (1915)

Capel Sion (1916)

The Earth Gives All and Takes All (1946)

F

FAIR, A. A., see GARDNER, Erle Stanley

FALLADA, Hans (1893–1947) German novelist, whose real name was Rudolf Ditzen. His life reads like a Dostoyevskian crime novel: would-be suicide, killer of a man in a duel, drug and drink addict, certified madman, shooter of his first wife (he did not kill her – his second was an alcoholic), post-war mayor . . . While he was doing all this he was able to become a successful farmer, an accurate and sharply aware journalist and a best selling author. He is a major novelist of great versatility, the excellence of whose output was interrupted only by the Nazis, whose regime obliged him to write hack novels in order to escape the concentration camp. *Little Man What Now?* is his most famous but not his best novel; but it is a very good and sympathetic analysis of the predicament of ordinary poor folk in the immediately pre-Nazi period, and shows why Germany fell for Hitler and his "solutions". Its immediate successor appeared before the Nazis cracked down on literature. An earlier novel about a farmers' revolt is probably his best, but it has not yet been translated. The best of the translated novels, which presents his own predicament, is *The Drinker*.

Little Man What Now? (1932, tr. 1933)

Who Once Eats Out of the Tin Bowl (1934, tr. 1934)

The Drinker (1950, tr. 1952)

FARMER, Philip José (1918) American science fiction writer. His work is noted for its interest in sex, religion and baroque theology, all of which were rare in science fiction when he began writing. He is, however, primarily a writer of exotic adventure stories.

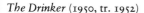

The Lovers (1961)

Night of Light (1966)

To Your Scattered Bodies Go (1971)

FARRELL, J. G. (1935–79) Anglo-Irish novelist, born in England. He made his reputation with *Troubles*, a historical novel about Ireland at the time of the "troubles". His method in this, and its successor about the Indian Mutiny, is to take a historical event and through it to focus his readers' awareness of the present. He was much influenced by Sartre's concept of the novel; but his style is more reminiscent of Samuel Beckett's, although in considerably modified form. A symbolic novelist, he exercises a fairly consistent control over his lilting, Irish rhetoric. He was one of the more interesting serious novelists of his generation.

Troubles (1971)

The Siege of Krishnapur (1973)

The Singapore Grip (1978)

FARRELL, J. T. (1904–79) American novelist, story-writer and critic. Farrell was one of the leaders of the American naturalist school; but, as with all substantial naturalists, his novels are more than mere deterministic slices of seamy life. He never quite equalled his masterpiece, the trilogy *Studs Lonigan*, a moving account of the life and early death of an Irish Catholic Chicagoan. This is an utterly satisfying work, dealing less with ineluctable fate than with weakness of the will. It has something of the savage and massive power of Dreiser's *An American Tragedy*. The other later novels, also forming cycles dealing with particular men, are not quite as good, but nevertheless much better than they have been taken to be. Farrell was a fine, lucid psychologist, and a great storyteller.

Studs Lonigan (trilogy, 1935)

Gas House McGinty (1933, rev. 1950)

New Year's Eve/1929 (1967)

FAST, Howard (1914) American writer of action-filled historical novels expressing his identification with the oppressed. His concern with American history produced *The Last Frontier* (1941), about the flight of the Cheyenne Indians in 1878, and the popular *Freedom Road* (1944), set in the South in the Reconstruction period. Roman and Jewish history inspire others such as *Spartacus* (1951), written after Fast's imprisonment during the McCarthy era. Later titles include *Torquemada* (1966), about the Spanish inquisition, and *The Immigrants* (1977). Fast also writes science fiction, and (as E. V. Cunningham) excellent thrillers and "entertainments" (*The Case of the Poisoned Eclairs*, 1979).

The Last Frontier (1941)

Freedom Road (1944)

Spartacus (1951)

FAULKNER, William (1897–1962) American novelist who grew up in Oxford (Mississippi) and lived there for most of his life. This and its surroundings (Lafayette County) are the basis of the Yoknapatawpha County of most of his fiction. He won the Nobel Prize in 1950. Faulkner is not a conventional realist; but his use of modernist techniques, which was instinctual (he was not an intellectual), is pretty well justified and demonstrates that the modern age demands to be represented in new and apparently irrational ways. Like most great writers, Faulkner was not consistent. His famous locale is never quite the same from novel to novel. He wrote crude melodrama for money (for a description of the experience, suitably magnified, see the section in *The Wild Palms* in which, in Chicago, the unhappy anti-hero turns out rubbish for pulp "true confession" magazines), and later in his life his work became ponderously allegorical, laboured, a shadow of its former grand self. Yet he is a very great writer. Apparently blackly pessimistic, unequalled as a portrayer of the squalid and the cruel and the raw and the unjust and the murderously foul, his heart is full of pity and understanding. At his best his form *is* his content. What a sympathetic imagination it must have taken to employ the stream of consciousness technique by which the idiot Benjy is portrayed in *The Sound and the Fury*! Faulkner's first inspiration, in his truly great work, was Sherwood Anderson, to whom he paid handsome and proper tribute later in his life. But he was a very different kind of writer. He drew on his family's history, local lore and on the violence of the South – which is, in his work, essentially a metaphor for the fearful violence within all men. He was, in himself, a genial and polite man; but he was also subject to fits of black depression which he would try to cure by savage drinking bouts. For a time he worked in Hollywood at scripts (including one based on a book by Raymond Chandler), purely for the money. For he did not earn much from his writings until after his best work was done. There is controversy about which books by Faulkner are the best, but the general consensus is that they comprise: *The Sound and the Fury, As I Lay Dying* (1930), *Light in August* (1932), *Absalom, Absalom!, The Wild Palms, Go Down Moses* (1942) and possibly *Intruder in the Dust* (1948), which won him the Nobel Prize. His subject matter is frequently strange and bizarre – but by his technique he shows that it is no more so than men's minds. He helped familiarize his readers with themselves. Even at his most experimental, he is telling a story. In *The Wild Palms* the reader is constantly waiting to discover what will happen, even though he seems to be confronted by two quite separate tales. It is significant that this writer from the heart (for that is why he was no nihilist, even though he chose to face the grimmest facts of life), apparently so difficult, is now increasingly read: understanding the reasons for his experimentation, we see

William Faulkner

that in every case his aim was to tell a story as truthfully as it could be told.

The Sound and the Fury (1929)

Absalom, Absalom! (1936)

The Wild Palms (1939)

FEARING, Kenneth (1902–61) American poet, novelist and journalist. His novels deal ruthlessly and laconically with what a critic called "the Fearing subject: an urban, mechanical society in which even the forms of belief have been lost". *The Hospital* takes a cross-section of life in a hospital at a particular moment; *The Big Clock* (a famous film) is a fine murder story.

The Hospital (1939)

The Big Clock (1946)

The Crozart Story (1960)

FEINSTEIN, Elaine (1930) English poet, translator and novelist. Feinstein's novels are essentially an extension of her poetry. They treat of male-female relationships intensely but in detached prose.

The Circle (1970)

The Glass Alembic (1973)

The Children of the Rose (1974)

FERBER Edna (1887–1968) American novelist, who won a Pulitzer prize in 1925 for her novel *So Big*. She is best known for *Showboat* (1926) on which the famous Kern and Hammerstein musical was based. Her stories are usually set in colourful surroundings, such as the oil fields of Texas, or Oklahoma during the land rush of the 1880s.

Cimarron (1930)

Giant (1952)

Ice Palace (1958)

FERRARS, Elizabeth X. (1907) British crime novelist, pseudonym (with the X, which stands for nothing, in America only) of Moura Brown. Producing something like a book a year since 1940, she has made a substantial contribution to the crime scene. Her characters have become increasingly life-like and her situations ever more intriguing.

Zero at the Bone (1967)

Foot in the Grave (1973)

In at the Kill (1979)

FERRIER, Susan (1782–1854) Scottish novelist. She is one of the creators, with Scott, of the Scottish regional novel. Her sense of humour is highly original, but her sentimentality spoils her capacity to create characters.

Marriage (1818)

The Inheritance (1824)

Destiny (1831)

FEUCHTWANGER, Lion (1884–1958) German novelist, critic and dramatist, a very successful and prolific historical romancer. *Jew Süss* gained him international popularity, but his best book is *Moscow*. He was intelligent and a good man; but his fluent historical novels have not stood the test of time.

Jew Süss (1925, tr. 1926)

Moscow (1937, tr. 1937)

The Devil in France (1941, tr. 1941)

FIEDLER, Leslie (1917) American critic, poet, novelist and story-writer. Most famous as a critic, Fiedler has been rather neglected as a novelist. His fiction reflects somewhat predictably his critical preoccupations and his desire to outrage. It is very readable, although convoluted and frequently over-provocative. His first novel *The Second Stone* is his most organized, and his best.

Pull Down Vanity and Other Stories (1962)

The Second Stone (1966)

Nude Croquet and Other Stories (1969)

FIELDING, Gabriel (1916) English novelist, the pseudonym of Dr Alan Barnsley who left medical practice to teach English in the United States. His early novels, like *In the Time of Greenbloom* and *The Birthday King*, were much admired for examining large moral themes in terms of personal relationships.

In the Time of Greenbloom (1956)

The Birthday King (1963)

FIELDING, Henry (1707–54) English novelist, journalist, dramatist and reforming magistrate. He began as a burlesque dramatist, having squandered all his money. Then he took up law and novel writing. As Justice of the Peace for Westminster he broke up London gangs and helped develop the Bow Street Runners. He was most influential in establishing a tradition of the novel which steered a course between picaresque literalism and smug virtuousness, such as that of Samuel Richardson. His prose is meticulous and balanced, but transcends the general artificiality of Augustanism by its irony and sly bawdy. He learned directly from Cervantes that the novel was not and could not be "true", which in his time meant distinguishing it from journalism. Thus he is securely in the Aristotelian tradition. *Tom Jones* is magnificently plotted, a masterpiece of storytelling. It is usually held to be his greatest work; but some critics argue for *Amelia*, which is certainly less satirical and more psychologically serious in intention. But the ironic *Jonathan Wild* (in *Miscellanies*, 1743), although less substantial in some ways, may be as good as either. It is now fashionable to accuse Fielding of being "uncertain about his point of view", because he was a pioneer of

Henry Fielding

"authorial intrusion" (essay-like comments inserted into his narrative). The uncertainty arises from Fielding's humility, his desire to free himself from the didacticism of such as Richardson, his intelligence, his awareness that fiction is artificial. It is complained that *Amelia* is a tragedy which is forced into an eventual comedy because of this authorial uncertainty. But the assertion that *Amelia* ought to be tragic may be a piece of academic impertinence; Fielding, an ironist, may have been aware of what he was doing. Certainly his fiction has the kind of authority that transcends the prescriptions of non-creative critics.

Joseph Andrews (1742)

Tom Jones (1749)

Amelia (1751, dated 1752)

FIGES, Eva (1932) German-born English experimental novelist, associated in the public mind with the more intelligent and subtle aspects of the feminist movement; but her novels are much more than polemical expressions of any particular point of view. The basis of her method is a clever use of interior monologue: she traces the significant moments of inner experience, sometimes directly, sometimes by the use of an expressionist narrative of apparently external events.

Winter Journey (1967)

B (1972)

Days (1974)

FIRBANK, Ronald (1886–1926) English decadent-dilletante novelist who had a considerable influence on such major writers as Anthony Powell and Evelyn Waugh. He was an unhappy, chronically ill, neurotic, wealthy homosexual, who combined the decadence and aesthetic exquisiteness of the 1890s with a love

of Roman Catholic ritual; but he was not religious. But as a stylist and a technical innovator he is very important. He presents his slight stories in cinematic style, the narrative consisting of a series of impressions. His lack of robustness is almost a strength, and his love of ritual concealed a true nihilism. Occasionally one catches a near-heartrending glimpse of his shame and loneliness. His best novels are *Caprice* (1917) and *Concerning the Eccentricities of Cardinal Pirelli* (1926), the story of a mad cardinal who dies chasing a choir-boy round the altar.

The Complete Ronald Firbank (1961)

FISH, Robert L. (1912) American detective story-writer. Fish has produced several series heroes including José da Silva, a Brazilian policeman based in Rio de Janeiro, and a New York policeman named Reardon. The most interesting of these is Reardon, an introverted, thoughtful man who features in police procedural stories.

The Fugitive (1962)

Reardon (1970)

A Gross Carriage of Justice (1979)

FISHER, Dorothea Canfield (1879–1958) American novelist, long resident in Vermont. Regionalist and moralist, her novels are concerned with the loves, the family lives, and the spiritual principles of her heroines.

Gunhild (1907)

The Bent Twig (1915)

FISHER, Vardis (1895) American novelist. His prolific fiction is regionalist or historical (on the Mormons), or pseudoanthropological. Of his many works the best is *Suicide or Murder? The Strange Death of Meriwether Lewis*. He tends to run to great length.

Children of God (1939)

Orphans in Gethsemene (1960)

Suicide or Murder? The Strange Death of Meriwether Lewis (1962)

FITZGERALD, F. Scott (1896–1940) American novelist, story-writer and essayist. Fitzgerald became a star of the times he described and criticized: the Jazz Age. A brilliant student at Princeton (although not an academic success), he married a beautiful but unstable wife, Zelda

F. Scott Fitzgerald

Ronald Firbank

– her one work of fiction was recently published: it is of only historical interest – and lived a life of crazy extravagance in the 1920s. He went to Paris and met Gertrude Stein and Ernest Hemingway, and began to drink very heavily. His career opened with a bang: *This Side of Paradise* (1920), a sparkling novel about money, young love, hedonism, religion, and drink. His second novel, *The Beautiful and Damned* (1922), in part an account of his own dissipation, was a failure; but he was in great demand for his stories. In *The Great Gatsby* he found a perfect objective correlative for his own state: of a self-indulgent, self-critical man on the slide. The novel employs symbolic techniques to convey its message about corruption: every metaphor in it enlightens the reader as to the theme, which is essentially a definition of what has happened to the "American dream". Particularly powerful in this book is Fitzgerald's sense of the quality of character, seen at its best in the portrait of Gatsby himself, who seems bad but is not altogether so. *Tender is the Night* is a more complex book, and a more ambitious one. It is inevitably more flawed than *Gatsby*, but perhaps more substantial. It is a criticism and an analysis both of the sickness of modern times and of his own relationship to his wife, who had become mad. Fitzgerald made an enormous effort to pull himself together, and found work in Hollywood. But he did not live to complete *The Last Tycoon*: he died of a heart attack at forty-four. Some feel that this last novel – about a film tycoon – is his masterpiece, others that it is a failure. In terms of subtlety of style it shows an important development in Fitzgerald's work; but as he could not complete it, too large claims are possibly ill-advised. It is clear that despite his illnesses and difficulties, he was one of the most substantial writers of this century.

The Great Gatsby (1925)

Tender is the Night (1934, rev. 1948)

The Last Tycoon (1941)

FITZGIBBON, Constantine (1919) Irish-American novelist. His work has attracted little attention, except for *When the Kissing Had to Stop* (1960) a hysterical but effectively written story about a British Labour government becoming tools of the Russians.

The Arabian Bird (1948)

Cousin Emily (1952)

When the Kissing Had to Stop (1960)

FLAUBERT, Gustave (1821–80) French novelist and story-writer. Flaubert's "realism" is a little too famous, since he had no connections with the French realist movement, which consisted of inferior novelists. One of the greatest and most influential novelists of all time,

Flaubert is also, curiously, one of the most disliked by critics. There are two reasons for this: he is too good, imaginatively, to fit into any set of prescriptions, and he appears to be a misanthropist – his view of life is Swiftian in the sense that he loathes mankind in the mass, but not man individually. The critical conflict over Flaubert is essentially one between the

Gustave Flaubert

autonomous author (the liberal Flaubert soon retreated into his vocation) and the politically (or religiously) committed critic. Flaubert published none of his great mass of early work, although it is now available. It shows him perfecting his art, coming to terms with the element in him that made every experience a disillusion, turning that element into a strength, a constructive scepticism. In *Madame Bovary* (1857) he produced a masterpiece for which he was prosecuted (and acquitted): in a way he has been prosecuted for it ever since, although it remains one of the perennial best sellers. In it every word counts. The novelist admits that he cannot be literally realistic; but each metaphor, every accurate detail, contributes to the whole. Flaubert's next novel, the lush, exotic, historical *Salammbo* (1862), is not as good, but has been unduly ignored. *The Sentimental Education* (1869), is as good – or better – than *Bovary*. It is the sad story of a man's failure to find love, or even to find himself, and there is no doubt that, for optimists on the subject of human nature, the book is extremely hard to take. This novel is incidentally a savage exposée of all the political pretensions of all the factions in the period preceding 1848. It is also a gallery of psychological portraits of great depth. *Three Tales* contains "A Simple Heart", one of the most beautiful stories ever written. The last novel, *Bouvard and Pécuchet*, is a monumental study in bourgeois stupidity – except that Flaubert grew to have a certain affection for his two clerks who set up a farm and plan to "study". He died suddenly before finishing it. Flaubert was without doubt a great novelist. The matter of his loathing of bourgeois conventions (for this he did) will always be counted against him by some of his readers; but others find in this very hatred a source of love for humanity, and can point to "A Simple Heart" as a legitimate key to all the other fiction.

Madame Bovary (1857, tr. 1953)

The Sentimental Education (1869, tr. 1941)

Bouvard and Pécuchet (1881, tr. 1954)

FLEMING, Ian (1908–64) English thriller writer who, although his writing career was short, became much the most famous of his day. Fleming had been a newspaper journalist, and during the war Personal Assistant to the Director of Naval Intelligence, before he wrote *Casino Royale* in 1953. The book introduced the ruthless professional British agent, James Bond, and the various elements – luxurious foreign settings, elaborate and violent set-pieces, fast cars, fast women and a measure of sexual description – which were to be characteristic of all his books. It was well received, but only with his third novel, *Moonraker*, did his popularity and prestige begin to soar. Fleming's books were read by everybody, from President

Kennedy to Cyril Connolly, and were attacked by some critics for dealing in "sex, sadism and snobbery". They were, in fact, sophisticated fairy stories for adults, an updated version of Bulldog Drummond. They seem quite mild today, almost cliché-ridden, because they have been so much imitated; but no-one else in the field has ever quite matched the glossy excitement and sheer inventiveness of Ian Fleming at the height of his success.

Casino Royale (1953)

From Russia, with Love (1957)

Goldfinger (1959)

FLEMING, Joan (1908) British writer of detective and suspense novels, usually in contemporary English settings. She has an original viewpoint and an idiosyncratic style, and the plot of each book is quite unlike the last.

When I Grow Rich (1962)

Young Man I think You're Dying (1970)

To Make an Underworld (1976)

FOGAZZARO, Antonio (1842–1911) Italian novelist: the most important in his country, in his generation, after Verga and Pirandello. He fell foul of both the Church and the liberals: he was open-minded, and wrote as he saw and felt. His most perfect novel, *The Little World of the Past*, is also his most balanced, combining beauty of natural description with painful realism.

The Woman (1881, tr. 1907)

Daniele Cortis (1885, tr. 1890)

The Little World of the Past (1895, tr. 1962)

FOLLETT, Ken (1949) British suspense writer. Follett first produced a number of books with an industrial espionage setting, a fascinating field largely unexplored. He then turned to the more conventional adventure thriller. *Storm Island* is excellent in the genre. Set mostly on an uninhabited islet off England's East Coast during World War II, it gained greatly from its historical perspective.

The Bear Raid (1976)

Storm Island (1978)

FONTANE, Theodor (1819–98) German journalist, poet, memoirist, dramatic critic and novelist who wrote his first novel at the age of fifty-six, and yet became one of the major novelists of the second half of his century. His achievement has not been fully appreciated in English-speaking countries, although the trans-

lation of *Effie Briest* published in 1967 has begun to bring him the readers he deserves. He is a very good example of a realist – in the technical sense – but he is no mere journalist or documenter: his keen and gently ironical observation of the Prussian society which became one of the main components of Nazism is expressed in good-humoured but elegaic mood, with frequent and subtle use of symbolism. *Effie Briest* is the German *Bovary*, and is very nearly as great a novel as Flaubert's.

Trials and Tribulations (1888, tr. 1917)

Beyond Recall (1892, tr. 1964)

Effie Briest (1895, tr. 1967)

FORD, Elbur, see PLAIDY, Jean.

FORD, Ford Madox (1873–1939) English novelist, critic, poet and editor. Although fundamentally a fine and generous man, Ford was on occasions a liar, and his love life was a mess; he attracted considerable spite and hatred, and it is only recently, through the

Ford Madox Ford

efforts of Graham Greene and others, that he has been accorded the recognition he deserves. He was a far less neurotic (and less insufferable) man than, say, D. H. Lawrence whose achievements are not greeted with the same kind of iciness. Ford is in the tradition of Catholic-Tory that is continued, although less consistently, by Anthony Burgess: he is, that is to say, in the Johnsonian rather than the conservative-party tradition. He helped Joseph Conrad to write in English, collaborating with him on two novels, and was at the centre of English letters from 1908 when he founded *The English Review*, which introduced Lawrence and countless others. His greatest novel, *The Good Soldier*, attracted much critical attention; but his tetralogy *Parade's End*, although very nearly as fine, failed to sustain his reputation. It is a richly told story, of the "last Tory", and despite the humour with which it probes pre-war civilization, its underlying pessimism may have had something to do with its failure to get its just deserts. He also wrote some good historical romances; and of the novels after *Parade's End*, probably *When the Wicked Man* is the best.

The Good Soldier (1915)

Parade's End (1924–28)

When the Wicked Man (1932)

FORESTER, C. S. (1899–1966) English novelist. Forester was the very best kind of literary popular novelist. He is most famous for his character of Horatio Hornblower, who is himself quite "flat", a romanticized Nelson figure – but the naval detail is meticulous, and the tales are told at great pace. His best novels, however, are the psychological thrillers *Payment Deferred* and *Plain Murder*.

Payment Deferred (1926)

Plain Murder (1930)

Captain Hornblower, R.N. (1939)

FORSTER, E. M. (1879–1970) English novelist, story-writer, critic, essayist and humanist. Forster stopped writing novels in 1924, when he published his best, *A Passage to India*. The posthumous *Maurice* (1971), about his homosexuality, is very bad – and, although written at the beginning of World War I, shows why his imagination failed him: he was crippled by his sexual condition. His *Aspects of the Novel* is an important critical text, and although it stops well short of a positive critique of all aspects of modernism, it still provides a useful (indeed the most useful) basis upon which to form a coherent view of the novel. His first four novels – and the short stories which preceded them – are well made, well observed essays in humanism; they are romantic, a little soft-headed, but warm in their feeling for the indi-

E. M. Forster

vidual and his rights. In *A Passage to India*, ostensibly a novel about the British raj, and very finely observed (Forster knew India well), he found an objective correlative for his own condition, and produced a masterpiece, although the subject is not homosexuality. Forster's achievement here is to write a fine political analysis of certain sorts of approach to India found in the raj, but at the same time to challenge the sad imperative of *Howards End*, "only connect": by the use of unobtrusive, delicate symbolism and superb characterization he displays the tragic limitations of his own humanism, which was pagan and anti-Christian in character. Here he shows that religious feeling, if ignored, destroys the capacity to see reality. Some interpreters would not agree; but it is hard to see the dark things in this book as anything other than an analysis of religious feeling, despite the pervasive sexuality. The novel is in any event very complex and very successful at all levels.

The Longest Journey (1907)

Howards End (1910)

A Passage to India (1924)

FORSTER, Margaret (1938) English biographer and novelist, who combined the two styles in her pseudo-autobiography of Thackeray (1979). As a novelist she specializes in three kinds of woman: sexy, feckless girls plagued by twinges of guilt; trapped but wayward young wives who exchange adulterous confidences over prams; and dizzy old boots fighting a rearguard action against the encroachments of age. *Georgy Girl*, a "Swinging Sixties" story, was successfully filmed.

Georgy Girl (1965)

The Travels of Maudie Tipstaff (1967)

The Seduction of Mrs Pendlebury (1974)

FORSYTH, Frederick (1938) British writer of best selling spy stories. Forsyth worked for Reuters and then the BBC as a diplomatic correspondent, before going to report the Biafra war as a freelance. He then wrote the hugely successful *The Day of the Jackal* (subsequently filmed) in 35 days. The book describes the attempted assassination of General de Gaulle by a professional killer hired by the OAS. It attained a hitherto unknown level of conviction, because it was written in a realistic documentary style; much of it stemmed from Forsyth's personal knowledge. Most of the characters are real people, some thinly disguised. *The Odessa File* concerns Arab plots against Israel, in which Odessa, an organization of ex-SS men, is involved. It has the same

Frederick Forsyth

realistic virtues as Forsyth's first book, although the story is less sensational. *The Dogs of War* (1974) draws on his time in Biafra; as an adventure story it is slowed by his personal sympathies for the Biafrans.

The Day of the Jackal (1971)

The Odessa File (1972)

The Devil's Alternative (1979)

FOWLES, John (1926) English novelist. Fowles' project, although he is known as (and is) an experimentalist, is to restore solidity to the novel. He has a very high reputation among readers as a modernist; but critical opinion is nervous and divided – is he more a pasticheur and arranger than a genuine novelist? His later work will tell. *The Collector* is about a young man who imprisons a woman he thinks he loves. *The Magus* (later rewritten, although to little point) is about a teacher on an island who gets involved in magic. *The French Lieutenant's Woman*, which consolidated Fowles' reputation with those who like him, is a dazzling pastiche of Thackeray, which is given alternative endings. The theme running through all the novels – and the novellas collected in *The Ebony Tower* (1974) – is the "enigmatic female". Fowles shows how the male punishes the female for her mysteriousness by imprisoning, deserting or betraying her: by manipulating her. His own books are essentially manipulations. There can be no doubt as to Fowles' mastery of pastiche, or his readability. What he has not yet demonstrated is his capacity to sustain a narrative in which he preserves his own viewpoint, or in which he displays his own personality. *Daniel Martin* (1977) is an ambitious novel spanning three decades (and 700 pages), and is more conventional than Fowles' preceding novels. He has described it as "a defence of humanism". Some American reviewers pronounced it "Tolstoyan"; but critics were more wary, and one has called it an example of "boulevard culture". There is no doubt of its high competence, but its exact status cannot yet be decided.

The Collector (1958)

The Magus (1966)

The French Lieutenant's Woman (1969)

FRAME, Janet (1924) New Zealand novelist and story-writer resident in London. Her best novel is *Faces in the Water*, a technically very accomplished study of the world of a woman who has gone mad. Later work consists of elaborations, more or less elegant, of this theme.

Faces in the Water (1962)

Daughter Buffalo (1972)

Living in the Maniototo (1979)

FRANCE, Anatole (1844–1924) French novelist, bibliophile and critic. Although he won the Nobel Prize in 1921, France's work, in the tradition of Voltaire, simply has not lasted. He was witty for his time.

Thaïs (1890, tr. 1909)

The Amethyst Ring (1899, tr. 1910)

Penguin Island (1908, tr. 1909)

FRANCIS, Dick (1920) British thriller writer, once champion jockey. His first book, *Dead Cert* (1962), was an immediate success. With a regular novel a year since, although there have been ups and downs, he has maintained a high standard. His storytelling is direct, but he creates through a remarkable gift for pacing, perhaps derived from race-riding, a heart-stopping tension. Although he is almost always concerned with horses, his human beings are well observed. Francis has no regular hero but

John Fowles

the protagonist of each of his stories is usually a man not afraid of judging, one who sees the people he encounters for what they are, good, bad, a mixture. Often he will carry a burden, too, a wife confined to an iron lung (as Francis's own was), a father's debts, a liability to crippling asthma.

Nerve (1964)

Bonecrack (1971)

Trial Run (1979)

FRANK, Waldo (1889) American novelist, essayist and critic. Frank has had much influence in American letters, but he never fulfilled himself in fiction. He tried his hand at

Dick Francis

both naturalist, more or less Marxist, esoteric and straightforwardly realist novels.

Chalk Face (1924)

Summer Never Ends (1941)

Not Heaven (1953)

FRANKAU, Pamela (1908–67) English novelist, journalist and story-writer, whose genteel mysteries now seem somewhat dated.

The Willow Cabin (1949)

The Bridge (1957)

FRASER, George Macdonald (1925) British popular novelist whose *Flashman* series uses the adult adventures of the school bully in Thomas Hughes' *Tom Brown's Schooldays* to produce comic, but well-researched, accounts of celebrated incidents from nineteenth-century British imperial history. These are bawdy and always readable.

Flashman (1969)

Royal Flash (1970)

Flashman In the Great Game (1975)

FRAYN, Michael (1933) English novelist, dramatist, philosopher, humourist and journalist. Frayn can write conventional or highly experimental novels with equal fluency; his experimental novels (cited below) are his best; but their lack of robustness has led to their neglect.

The Tin Man (1965)

A Very Private Life (1968)

Sweet Dreams (1973)

FREDERIC, Harold (1856–98) American journalist and novelist. He is important for his, for its time, extremely candid account of a Methodist clergyman losing his faith: *The Damnation of Theron Ware*. His other novels are also good.

Seth's Brother's Wife (1887)

The Damnation of Theron Ware (1896, in Britain as *Illumination*)

The Market Place (1899)

FREELING, Nicolas (1927) British detective story-writer, who has lived most of his life in France and Holland. Freeling is a master of the police procedural featuring a detective who works primarily with psychology. His first book, *Love in Amsterdam* (1962), introduced the benevolent, middle-aged Inspector Van der

Valk and his comfortable, still attractive wife; the Inspector's thought processes and the intimate atmosphere of the city were described in an engagingly modern style. Nine more Van der Valk books followed, before Freeling took the bold step of killing his hero off. He has written several other thrillers, the best of which is *Gadget*, a chillingly realistic story about terrorists building atomic bombs. Van der Valk's widow has re-appeared, married to an Englishman, in *The Widow* (1979).

Criminal Conversation (1965)

Gadget (1977)

The Night Lords (1978)

FREEMAN, Mary E. Wilkins (1852–1930) American novelist, story-writer and playwright. She began with Massachusetts regionalist tales of skill and delicacy, and examined the decline of New England into a commercial and mechanistic society drained of vitality. Her portraits of older women are remarkable for their precision. The early tales at least deserve revival.

A Humble Romance (stories, 1887)

The Portion of Labour (1901)

FRENCH, Marilyn (   ) American academic, author of critical work on James Joyce and of *The Women's Room*, the carefully written but overweight account of how Mira French "the wife of the 'fifties" became "the woman of the 'seventies." Ms French is not sufficiently detached from her fiction: it remains far too personal to transcend the confines of the special case – her own. But that case is put with great force and clarity.

The Women's Room (1977)

FRIEDMAN, Bruce Jay (1930) American-Jewish novelist, journalist and playwright. Friedman is an inventive, original and savagely funny chronicler of the misfortunes of failed Jews. His best novel, a modern classic of black absurdist farce, is *The Dick*.

Stern (1962)

The Dick (1970)

About Harry Towns (1975)

FUCHS, Daniel (1909) American novelist, story-writer and scriptwriter. Fuchs' fine opening trilogy failed to attract attention or money, and he went into films – where he made money, wrote indifferent scripts, and spent his time on excellent, clever short stories, only recently collected in *The Apathetic Bookie Joint* (1979). He was "rediscovered" in the 1960s, along with Henry Roth. His much later novel is

excellent, but not as good as the earlier three, of which *Low Company* is the most violent and the most dramatic. Fuchs' technique is derived from the "camera eye" method of John Dos Passos. As a cinematic realist of Jewish ghetto life he is unequalled.

Trilogy: Summer in Williamsburg (1934) *Homage to Blenholt* (1936), *Low Company* (1937)

West of the Rockies (1971)

FUENTES, Carlos (1928) Mexican novelist, story writer, essayist and scriptwriter for Bunuel. The much (but according to most

Carlos Fuentes

Spanish speakers not very well) translated Fuentes is Mexico's leading representative in the world of letters. Much of his work may be read as a savage and meticulous critique of a (one-party) state that pretends to be a socialist democracy but is in fact tyrannical. Like all Latin-American writers he is inspired by the untapped myths of his people, and by the secret beauties of the Latin-American continent. His early technique owes much to John Dos Passos, but latterly he has taken to the more symbolic procedures of his contemporaries such as Gabriel García Márquez. *The Death of Artemio Cruz* is an impressive study of a dying gangster, and conveys a terrible and convincing sense of a country's moral decay.

Aura (1962, tr. 1965)

The Death of Artemio Cruz (1962, tr. 1964)

The Hydra Head (1977, tr. 1979)

FULLER, Henry Blake (1857–1929) American novelist and story-writer. Fuller was a versatile writer, author of romances about Europe, realist novels and satires about America, and hybrids. His stories (e.g. in *Under the Skylight*, 1901) are excellent. Edmund Wilson called him, in the novel of manners, superior to William Dean Howells, which is high praise indeed. *The Cliff-Dwellers*, about Chicago, is an important precursor of the American naturalistic novel.

The Cliff-Dwellers (1893)

The Last Refuge (1900)

Bertram Cope's Year (1919)

FULLER, Roy (1912) English poet and solicitor who has written some moderately successful fiction. His first novel, a crime thriller called *The Second Curtain*, is his best. The style is influenced by Graham Greene and Fuller's friend Julian Symons. Later novels are skilled and competent portraits of the bourgeois – seen from a Marxist angle.

The Second Curtain (1953)

The Ruined Boys (1959)

My Child, My Sister (1965)

G

GADDA, Carlo Emilio (1893–1973) Italian novelist. He lived in exile for much of the time under fascism, but after the war settled in Rome. Gadda is a strange case: he is very difficult; but once the reader gets used to his wild word-spinning and to his habit of apparent digression he understands that he is reading a melancholy-lyrical commentary on a narrative (in principle *any* narrative) on life. Gadda is absolutely non-conformist, and all his work is strictly autobiographical, although never in the style of conventional autobiography. If the effort is made to persevere with this difficult writer, the adventure is deeply rewarding, although painful.

That Awful Mess on Via Merulana (1957, tr. 1965)

Acquainted with Grief (1963, tr. 1969)

GADDIS, William (1922) American novelist who has written one long novel, *The Recognitions*, and a shorter work *JR*. *The Recognitions*, a complex novel about forgery and illusion, was found by most critics to be impenetrable and possibly pretentious.

 The Recognitions (1955)

 JR (1975)

GALE, Zona (1874–1938) American novelist, poet, story-writer and dramatist, whose best novel, *Miss Lulu Bett*, is a clear-eyed portrait of the oppressiveness of mid-western society, set in Wisconsin. It won a Pulitzer Prize, and she rewrote it as a play. August Derleth's biography of her is appropriately entitled *Still, Small Voice*.

 Miss Lulu Bett (1920)

Yellow Gentians and Blue (stories, 1927)

GALLICO, Paul (1897–1976) American best selling novelist. Gallico started as a sports writer and war correspondent, and made his name with *The Snow Goose* which set the pattern for other frankly sentimental stories about animals, like *Scruffy* (1962), and about an English charwoman, Mrs Harris, in a series of novels. Gallico also wrote accomplished thrillers like *The Poseidon Adventure*, about the dramatic sinking of a giant passenger liner.

The Snow Goose (1941)

The Poseidon Adventure (1969)

GALSWORTHY, John (1867–1933) English novelist, playwright, story-writer. He received the Nobel Prize in 1932. Galsworthy is still immensely popular and widely read – in large part because of the successful televising of his long novel-sequence *The Forsyte Saga*. He began well, learning from Turgenev, and from his friend Joseph Conrad. Indignation against social injustice pressured him into writing *The Man of Property*, the first of the *Forsyte* series. This has genuine power and some depth of characterization. But in the rest of the series Galsworthy gradually falls off, a certain smug-

John Galsworthy

ness taking the place of his indignation. Yet the *Saga* has virtues: it is solid, careful in its observation, good-hearted. Galsworthy clung on to his intention of exposing the nature of his age, but lacked the moral force to succeed. The later parts of the *Saga* are therefore static, although they offer serious entertainment.

 The Man of Property (1906)

In Chancery (1920)

To Let (1921)

GALT, John (1779–1839) Scottish novelist famous for the humorous and shrewd, although shapeless, *Annals of the Parish*. He was one of the founders of the truly Scottish novel.

 Annals of the Parish (1821)

The Provost (1822)

The Entail (1823)

GANN, Ernest K. (1910) American novelist, who writes adventure stories with racy dialogue. Many of his best novels are about aviation.

 Blaze at Noon (1947)

The High and the Mighty (1953)

Band of Brothers (1974)

GARCÍA MÁRQUEZ, Gabriel (1928) Colombian novelist and story-writer, the doyen of Latin-American writers of his generation. His *One Hundred Years of Solitude,* set in a town very like the one in which he grew up, is *the* representative Spanish-American novel of its time. It is an ironical chivalric romance; probably the term "magic realism" best describes the technique. It is the story – a story that attains the stature of myth – of how the serpent-gipsy Melquiades brings to the town of Macondo the knowledge of discovery, of how the Buendía family – headed by José Arcadio – rediscovers this knowledge, which brings down war and other sorrows over his descendants. Meanwhile the old ways continue. *No One Writes to the Colonel,* set in the same territory, is a shorter and more personal book, telling of how a colonel awaits a pension that never comes. García Márquez usually chooses to adopt the stance of a comic writer (although *No One Writes to the Colonel* is more elegaic in tone), but his themes are serious and tragic. *The Autumn of the Patriarch* (1977, tr. 1977), about a dictator, is more self-consciously surreal and factitious than *One Hundred Years of Solitude.* Two collections of García Márquez' stories have been translated: *Leaf Storm* (1972) and *Innocent Erendira.* He lives in Spain, and is closely connected with several

extreme left-wing Latin-American movements.

 No One Writes to the Colonel (1961, tr. 1971)

 One Hundred Years of Solitude (1968, tr. 1970)

 Innocent Erendira (stories, 1972, tr. 1979)

GARDNER, Erle Stanley (1889–1970) American detective story-writer. After practising as a trial lawyer he produced two books in 1933: *The Case of the Velvet Claw* and *The Case of the Sulky Girl*; their hero was a California trial lawyer called Perry Mason, assisted by Della Street, his faithful secretary, and a credible private detective, Paul Drake. Through the scores of Perry Mason stories which followed Gardner kept exactly to the original formula. The best of them always had a long courtroom climax, most of them contained a neat legal twist, and none of them wasted time on characterization or description. An illusion of rapid action was created by a narrative consisting largely of curt dialogue. He used a very similar formula for a series featuring District Attorney Douglas Selby; and other, lighter crime stories written under various pseudonyms, including A. A. Fair. Courtroom pyrotechnics have never been more entertainingly presented.

 The Case of the Half-Wakened Wife (1946)

The Case of the Restless Redhead (1954)

GARDNER, John (1933) American novelist, story-writer and scholar of medieval literature. Of the self-conscious American modernists, Gardner is nearest to John Barth in the way he works; but he differs from him in that, for all his apparent modernity, his theme is a simple one: how can mankind regain the art of living gracefully? Much of his material is drawn from medieval allegory, and he is difficult to read – even though his prose is, in itself, very well written. His work rests firmly upon the material from which it is drawn, and this rather restricts Gardner's range of honest readers, although not his range of learned critics. *The Sunlight Dialogues*, although labouredly mythopoeic, is perhaps Gardner's most accessible book: it tells of the conflict between a dazzling but mad magician and an ugly, decent police chief. The stories in *The King's Indian* are poised and less weighted with erudition than his earlier work.

 The Resurrection (1966)

The Sunlight Dialogues (1972)

The King's Indian (1974)

GARFIELD, Brian (1939) American thriller

writer and jazz musician whose most recent works are his best. *Deep Cover* described the Russian take-over of an American missile base and the political consequences. *Line of Succession* and *Hopscotch* both revealed a good knowledge of the inner machinations of American politics, and of the CIA.

Deep Cover (1973)

Line of Succession (1974)

Hopscotch (1974)

GARLAND, Hamlin (1860–1940) American (Wisconsin) novelist. Garland was in the forefront of the realist movement in America, pioneered by William Dean Howells. He even went so far as to try to perfect a form of naturalism he called "veritism", but it proved unsuccessful. He faded out into a conventional novelist – but not before he had contributed much of value to literary life. His best known novel is *Rose of Dutcher's Coolly*; but this has dated more than some of his sketches of regional life in the earlier *Main-Travelled Roads* and *Prairie Folks* (1893).

Main-Travelled Roads (1891)

Rose of Dutcher's Coolly (1895)

GARNER, Alan (1934) English author of children's fantasies set in contemporary Britain but based upon Welsh and early British myth and legend. At his best, his children's novels have a remarkable sense of place.

The Weirdstone of Brisingamen (1960)

The Moon of Gomrath (1963)

The Owl Service (1967)

GARNER, William (1920) English thriller writer, whose *The Andra Fiasco* is a hard, convincing story in the sour espionage school. *The Mobius Trip* has an extremely clever plot.

The Andra Fiasco (1971, in US as *Strip Jack Naked*)

The Mobius Trip (1978)

GARNETT, David (1892) English man of letters and novelist. Garnett made a reputation with his slight fantasies, *Lady into Fox* and *A Man in the Zoo* in the 1920s. He has continued to write competent realistic novels, but more attention has been given to his autobiographies.

Lady into Fox (1922)

A Man in the Zoo (1924)

Plough Over the Bones (1973)

GARVE, Andrew (1908) English crime novelist, who also writes as Roger Bax and Paul Somers. From the classical detective story he turned to thrillers, often concerning a falsely accused central character or one whose dependants are threatened. Sometimes with an international background or outdoor setting, Garve's plots and themes show versatility in the presentation of suspense.

Murder in Moscow (1951)

The Narrow Search (1957)

Frame-Up (1964)

GARY, Romain (1914) French diplomat, soldier and novelist of Russian birth. His first novel, *Education Européene* (translated under two titles, *Nothing Important Ever Dies* and *A European Education*), gained both popular and critical success. In this and subsequent fiction Gary writes about the need for personal integrity and intellectual honesty. His work is well plotted and carefully written; it has been widely translated and in several cases filmed.

The Roots of Heaven (1956, tr. 1956)

Lady L (1959, tr. 1963)

GASKELL, Mrs E. C. (1810–65) English novelist and biographer. Although she did not take up writing until she was thirty-five, Mrs Gaskell became second only to George Eliot in her generation. Her first novel *Mary Barton* (1848), set in Manchester and giving an accurate and sympathetic picture of the textile workers there, attracted much attention. *Cranford* (which is really Knutsford), which followed, is more mature – and has delighted millions with its dry irony and acute observation. But her first major novel is *North and South*, about the relations between working people and their masters. *Wives and Daughters* her greatest novel was not quite finished at her death. Mrs Gaskell's strengths are empathy, subtlety of psychological perception, and the unobtrusiveness of her strongly moral tone. Her forgiving attitude has been sneered at, as has her understanding of the economic issues involved in the situations she depicts; but her warmth is an important function in her work. Some of her novels have been successfully televised.

Cranford (1853)

North and South (1855)

Wives and Daughters (1866)

GASKIN, Catherine (1929) Irish-Australian romantic and historical novelist. She made her name with *This Other Eden* (1946), written when she was fifteen. Her best-known novel *Sarah Dane* (1955) memorably evokes the early settlement of Australia.

Sarah Dane (1955)

Fiona (1970)

A Falcon for a Queen (1972)

GASS, William (1924) American novelist, story-writer, philosopher and theorist of fiction. Gass says that he works in "the tradition of the Symbolist poets", and tells readers to expect "little in the way of character or story". He believes in presenting characters through their speech and thoughts, and not through narrative re-creation. He is difficult to read, but certain passages in his fiction are lively and revelatory.

Omensetter's Luck (1966)

In the Heart of the Country (1968)

Willie Masters' Lonesome Wife (1968)

GAUTIER, Théophile (1811–72) French romantic poet, novelist and journalist. Gautier was an early proponent of "art for art's sake", and his three novels, and especially some short stories, are interesting. *Mademoiselle de Maupin* still has power as an expression of Gautier's anti-moralistic and pagan views. Not many of his stories have been translated.

Mademoiselle de Maupin (1835, tr. 1948)

GENET, Jean (1910) French novelist, dramatist and poet. Genet spent his early life as a petty criminal, and was pardoned from a life sentence by the President of the Republic after the intervention of Jean-Paul Sartre and others. His experience is in conventional terms "disgusting": he is a narcissistic homosexual obsessed with farting, masturbation and with "deviant" sexual acts. But his highly literary style is classical, ritual: he celebrates the

Jean Genet

coarsely commonplace, and provides insights into the sexual condition which are universal, since the "coarse" components of anyone's sexuality resemble those of Genet's. Sartre wrote a long book on him, *Saint Genet*, in which he presented him as the paradigmatic existentialist victim. Genet's novels tell much about the criminal underworld, about the thief's "code", about the mores of the homosexual and the ambisexual criminal. It is a world in which everyone follows their own inclination; it is no happier than the bourgeois world of polite pretence. The most informative of the novels is *Querelle of Brest*. Genet lacks humour and warmth, but it cannot be denied that he creates his own "world", or that he illuminates it. He will probably be remembered for his theatre, which puts forth his thesis more powerfully and less monotonously.

Our Lady of the Flowers (1944, tr. 1964)

Querelle of Brest (1947, tr. 1966)

Funeral Rites (1947, tr. 1969)

GERHARDIE, William (1895–1977) English novelist born in Russia. Gerhardie began with Chekhovian novels of great promise; *Resurrection* suggested the emergence of a major novelist. But he became increasingly eccentric, added an "e" to his name because Dante, Blake and others had an "e" at the end of theirs, and spent his time on a huge (as yet

unpublished) trilogy, *This Present Breath*, which is said to be, in the main, unreadable.

Futility (1922)

Resurrection (1934)

Of Mortal Love (1936)

GHOSE, Sudhindra Nath (1899) Indian critic, scholar, story-writer, educationist and novelist, who lives in England. His collection of *Folk Tales and Fairy Stories from India* and its successors are vividly told. *And Gazelles Leaping* is based on his own Indian childhood, and three further novels follow its hero into early manhood.

And Gazelles Leaping (1949)

Folk Tales and Fairy Stories from India (1961)

GIBBON, Lewis Grassic (1901–35) Scottish novelist. Gibbon's trilogy *A Scots Quair* is still regarded as one of the most notable works of Scottish literature in this century. It traces, from a left-wing point of view, the progress of three generations, and presents the Scots in their own idiom.

A Scots Quair (one vol., 1946)

GIBBONS, Stella (1902) English novelist who

successfully, although not profoundly, parodied "something nasty in the woodshed" country fiction – Lawrence, Deledda and many others – in *Cold Comfort Farm*. Her other fiction is competent.

Cold Comfort Farm (1932)

Conference at Cold Comfort Farm (stories, 1949)

The Shadow of the Sorcerer (1955)

GIDE, André (1869–1951) French novelist, story-writer, dramatist, man of letters. Gide won the Nobel Prize in 1947. His works give out two paradoxical "messages": a belief in sensualism and an almost puritanical moralism. However, a reconciliation between these may be found not only in the *Journals* but also in his best fiction, notably *The Coiners*, a frankly experimental novel which has been consistently underrated. Gide wrote a number of works of fiction which he refused to call novels (he only allowed *The Coiners* this description). *The Vatican Cellars* explores the notion of self-liberation through the committing of a "gratuitous act" – in this case a motiveless murder. *The Pastoral Symphony* (in *Two Symphonies* – the other is entitled *Isabelle*) is his most straightforward novel: the story of a Swiss Pastor's destruction of his wife's and child's happiness. *The Coiners* has

André Gide

Ellen Glasgow

a large canvas; at its centre is a novelist who is writing a novel called *The Coiners*. Gide's achievement here is fruitfully to re-examine the whole enterprise of writing fiction, and simultaneously to provide a moving book in its own right. The territory is Dostoyevskian, but such real people as Jean Cocteau and Alfred Jarry are portrayed (Jarry as himself, Cocteau in disguise), and the techniques employed are varied and modernist. Some feel that *The Coiners* is over-artificial; but it is still read simply as a novel, by intelligent people – this may be an instance of the critics being at odds with the readers. Gide remains a seminal novelist, one who gladly acknowledged all aspects of life – humane, a reformer, an innovator, a profound psychologist.

Two Symphonies (1911, 1919, tr. 1931)

The Vatican Cellars (1914, tr. 1954)

The Coiners (1926, tr. 1950)

GILBERT, Michael (1912) English solicitor, crime writer and dramatist. His work is shrewd, lucid and scrupulously plotted, and draws on his personal knowledge of the backgrounds – legal, local governmental and military.

Smallbones Deceased (1950)

Death in Captivity (1952)

Sky High (1955)

GILL, Brendan (1914) American story-writer and occasional novelist. He is chiefly known for his stories of upper-class Irish Catholic families published in the *New Yorker*, to which he has contributed since 1936. *The Day the Money Stopped* is an exact study of a family dispute over a will.

The Day the Money Stopped (1957)

Ways of Loving (1974)

GILLIAT, Penelope (1924) English novelist, story-writer, film critic and scriptwriter. Gilliat's stories, far more effective than her two novels, are well-made snippets of intelligent commentary about modern life and its Kafkaesque vagaries.

One by One (1965)

What's It Like Out? and Other Stories (1968)

Nobody's Business (stories, 1972)

GILLOTT, Jacky (1939) English novelist, broadcaster and critic whose fiction specializes in late-developers who find their innate values at odds with the world around them. In *Salvage*

a middle-class housewife, suffering from domestic claustrophobia, walks out on her husband and aimlessly hitchhikes through the Home Counties. At times, Miss Gillott seems to have almost too much to say, a good fault which sometimes makes for confusing reading: especially in *War Baby* (1971), a no-holds-barred demolition job on middle-class liberals, and in *The Head Case*, among other things a satire on black magic and the occult.

Salvage (1968)

Crying Out Loud (1976)

The Head Case (1979)

GIRAUDOUX, Jean (1882–1944) Whimsical and desultory, but very popular, French dramatist and novelist. His fiction is at best charming, brilliantly impressionistic and transitory.

Suzanne and the Pacific (1921, tr. 1923)

My Friend from Limousin (1922, tr. 1923)

Bella (1926, tr. 1927)

GISSING, George (1857–1903) English novelist. Gissing had an unfortunate life, suffering consistent poverty, the death of one wife and unpleasantness with a second, but he produced a large and uneven output. He came as near as any English novelist to naturalism; but his best novels owe their peculiar power – surprisingly – to his sense of humour, his capacity to describe the shabby genteel, and to a psychological penetrativeness which at times (especially in *Born in Exile*) is reminiscent of Dostoyevsky. He is extremely readable. *New Grub Street* (1891) is an effective and cruel picture of the literary world of his time.

Born in Exile (1892)

The Odd Women (1893)

In the Year of the Jubilee (1894)

GLANVILLE, Brian (1931) English novelist and journalist. Prolific, accomplished and entertaining, Glanville has faithfully recorded the crackle of crossfire across the generation gap in Jewish families (*The Bankrupts*, 1958; and *Diamond*); and, amongst many other books, produced exact, revealing novels of theatrical life (*A Second Home*; and *The Comic*, 1974).

Diamond (1962)

A Second Home (1965)

The Financiers (1972)

GLASGOW, Ellen (1874–1945) American

novelist and story-writer. Glasgow was one of the leading woman novelists of sensibility of her generation. She wrote best about her native Virginia, studying wealthy families in decay, and the onset of the new (which she hated, although she was fair to it). *Barren Ground* is a powerful and convincing account of a woman's struggle for independence; *The Sheltered Life* contains surprisingly acute characterization. Glasgow was at her best a keen ironist who transcended regionalism by examining the South in the terms of its romantic self-image. She was much influenced by George Meredith.

Barren Ground (1925)

The Sheltered Life (1932)

Vein of Iron (1935)

GLASPELL, Susan (1882–1948) American dramatist, story-writer, novelist and autobiographer. She was the wife of George Cram Cook, whose famous Provincetown Players was responsible for the theatrical apprenticeship of Eugene O'Neill and other notable dramatists. Her novels are sensationalist, but readable and intelligent.

The Glory of the Conquered (1909)

Gifted Masks (stories, 1912)

GODDEN, Rumer (1907) English novelist noted for her sensitive and beautiful evocations of British India (*The River*, 1946, filmed by Jean Renoir) and her imaginative handling of children and adolescents (*The Greengage Summer*, 1958).

Black Narcissus (1939)

The River (1946)

The Greengage Summer (1958)

GODEY, John (1912) American crime novelist. Godey's style, featuring the inept actor Jack Albany in an almost farcical mixture of mayhem with political and mass-media satire, changed with *The Taking of Pelham One Two Three*, a taut tale of hijacking on the New York subway.

 Never Put Off Till Tomorrow What You Can Kill Today (1970)

 The Taking of Pelham One Two Three (1973)

GODWIN, William (1756–1836) English political thinker, journalist and novelist. Godwin was one of the fathers of modern anarchistic thought (*An Enquiry Concerning Political Justice*). His novel *Caleb Williams*, which although clumsy and digressive, has a superb and ingenious plot, is highly revealing of the true position of proponents of "reason". It is in the form of a thriller, and concerns the framing of a good man; it draws on Gothic, and is melodramatic, but has great psychological perception and a genuine *frisson*.

 Caleb Williams (1794)

Fleetwood (1805)

Cloudesly (1830)

GOETHE, Johann Wolfgang von (1749–1832) German poet, dramatist, novelist, storywriter, scientist, man of letters and government minister (at Weimar). Of Goethe's three novels the least well known, *Elective Affinities*, is the most important for our times. It is a perfect example of a more or less "realistic" novel which carries, and bears, an immense weight of poetic symbolism. *Wilhelm Meister* is certainly no less readable than the long novels of Barth or Gardner which try to emulate it. Goethe seems to have anticipated every aspect of modernism, and to go beyond many; all readers find his fiction immensely suggestive.

 Werther (1774, tr. 1957)

Wilhelm Meister (1795–1829, tr. 1824–7)

Elective Affinities (1809, tr. 1960)

GOGOL, Nicolai (1809–52) Russian dramatist, critic and novelist. Gogol's genius is quintessentially Russian; yet his masterpiece *Dead Souls* arises as much from his unstable personality (he died mad) as from his specifically Russian experiences. His versatility was early shown in the four stories contained in *Mirgorod* (1835): "Taras Bulba" is a famous and almost "corny" historical romance, whereas the other stories are fantastic and satirical, and foreshadow the later Gogol. *Dead Souls*, written in a style that carries the Russian language to the extreme of fantastic metaphor,

portrays various types of greed, and life. Chichikov of *Dead Souls* is an early anti-hero. He is a man who only thinks he wants wealth and position, and who deals in false human lives – false because the "wealth" he acquires consists, in fact, of dead serfs. Gogol, despite his furious desire to be a didactic writer, was actually a savage satirist who demonstrated that the Russian language itself could be used as a weapon against the negativity of life – against the lack of the lushly romantic manifestations his Quixotic nature desired. One of his most impressive tricks is to describe people as animated *things* (Wyndham Lewis would later follow him in this). Besides influencing Dostoyevsky and then the early Soviet modernists, Gogol provides a marvellous example of the autonomous writer at war with himself.

 Dead Souls (1842, tr. 1928, 1961)

The Overcoat (1842)

GOLD, Herbert (1924) American novelist, story-writer and critic. Gold is a disorganized, tremendously energetic comic writer, of great sophistication, who has not yet done better than the semi-autobiographical *The Fathers*, which was a long-standing best seller.

 Birth of a Hero (1951)

The Fathers (1967)

GOLD, Michael (1894) American novelist and dramatist. Gold is the most famous of American "socialist realist" writers; but he was not as crude as the Soviet novelists who toed the party line, even though he was a Stalinist. His most valuable critical work was published in the magazine *New Masses*; his attack on Thornton Wilder as "genteel" was famous. *Jews Without Money* is a powerful novel about his own childhood. *120 Million* (1929) consists of vivid sketches of workers.

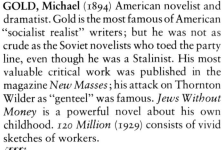 *Jews Without Money* (1930)

GOLDING, William (1911) English novelist, dramatist and poet. Golding has frequently been put forward as the modern English novelist most likely to survive. He was a late starter – he was in his late forties before he published his first novel – and he has not been prolific. *Lord of the Flies* gives a Swiftian picture of how boys would behave if stranded, unsupervised, on a desert island. *The Inheritors* (1955) is a lament for Neanderthal man, and paints another grim picture of *homo sapiens*. *Pincher Martin* (1956) is about the experiences of an apparently drowned sailor; *Free Fall* (1959) investigates most directly what is in fact Golding's main theme, the inevitability of original sin. *The Spire*, his most powerful novel, concerns a medieval dean who

Johann Wolfgang von Goethe

denies all reason by trying to add a spire to his cathedral (with disastrous results). *The Pyramid* was an attempt at realism – or at an ostensible realism – which a few critics liked, but most found disappointing. This may, however, have been because the symbolism was so well concealed. In *Darkness Visible* (1979) Golding has lost none of his power, but for a substantial number of critics he seemed to have increased his mastery of psychology; in many ways this is the most realistic of his books. Golding is enormously ambitious (as, for example, in *The Inheritors*, in which he tries to present in words the non-verbal processes of his postulated humanoids), and there is no consistent line of development in his work: he is "a master of fresh starts". He searches for a pattern that fits over "everything he knows", and he gives readers more to think about than any other English novelist of his generation.

Lord of the Flies (1954)

The Spire (1964)

The Pyramid (1967)

William Goldman

GOLDMAN, William (1931) American novelist, short story writer, dramatist and screenwriter. Goldman's tightly-written, well-constructed novels have a filmic quality, reflecting his prowess as a screenwriter. *Soldier in the Rain* (1960) and *Marathon Man* are his best.

Marathon Man (1974)

GOLDSMITH, Oliver (1730–74) English novelist, dramatist, poet and journalist. Goldsmith, who led an unhappy life, was admired by Dr Johnson. The very widely read *The Vicar of Wakefield* is difficult to classify, since it is probably more ironic than it seems; but in any case it is a unique novel whose appeal rests on the beautifully observed central character.

The Vicar of Wakefield (1766)

GOLON, Sergeanne Pseudonym of Serge Golon (1903) and his wife Anne (1921). These French novelists write a series of "spicy" adventure stories about an improbable French seventeenth-century lady called Angelique, who does everything at every level of society, and has much done to her. The books are skilfully written and have proved popular.

Angelique I (1959)

Angelique II (1959)

Angelique and the Demon (1973)

GOMBROWICZ, Witold (1904–69) Polish novelist, dramatist and story-writer: one of the great experimentalists of the century, who suggested to his puzzled readers that they should "dance with" his books rather than analyze them. This is good advice. *Ferdyduke* is his most interesting novel.

Ferdyduke (1938, tr. 1961)

Pornography (1960, tr. 1966)

GONCHAROV, Ivan (1812–91) Russian novelist. His best novel *Oblomov* is fundamentally a study in inertia, with a universal appeal. It is one of the most moving of nineteenth-century novels. Goncharov's other two works have been underrated.

A Common Story (1847, tr. 1917)

Oblomov (1859, tr. 1954)

The Precipice (1869, tr. 1915)

GOODMAN, Paul (1911–72) American novelist, poet, dramatist, educationalist and anar-

Paul Goodman

chist. Goodman's sprawling, badly written fiction is admired by his followers. In *Making Do* (1963) he examines the problem of his own homosexuality. Study of his novels will come with a study of the man which is overdue.

Parents' Day (1951)

The Empire City (1959)

Adam (stories, 1968)

GORDIMER, Nadine (1923) South African novelist and story-writer. Nadine Gordimer is now the chief representative of civilized South African writing. She is more a psychologically than a politically oriented writer, and (as she has said) had she not been born in South Africa she would not have touched on politics. But as things are, her sensibility has been bound to criticize the racist society in which she lives. Most of her restrained and lucid work is set in Johannesburg, and concerns educated, sensitive people. *A Guest of Honour* is the most accomplished and moving of her novels. She is primarily a psychological novelist trying to convey confused states of mind.

A Guest of Honour (1970)

Selected Stories (1975)

Burger's Daughter (1979)

GORDON, Caroline (1895) American novelist and story-writer. Caroline Gordon is one of the most distinguished exponents of the conservative view of the South. Her well-made novels seek to demonstrate that old-fashioned feudal values can work well. *None Shall Look Back* is about the Civil War. *The Malefactors* is autobiographical, and contains valuable portraits of her husband, Hart Crane and other literary notables.

Penhally (1931)

None Shall Look Back (1937)

The Malefactors (1956)

GORDON, Katharine ( ) Scottish novelist, born in Aberdeen but brought up in India. She travelled the world with her husband and found time to write twenty novels for her own amusement. It was not until 1978 that the first – set in India at the time of the Mutiny – was published.

Emerald Peacock (1978)

Peacock in Flight (1979)

GORDON, Richard (1921) British surgeon and comic writer who has written a series of very English novels about medical life, in which an irreverent view of the medical profession gilds

new translations – of Gorki are overdue.

Mother (1907, tr. 1950)

The Life of a Useless Man (1917, tr. 1972)

The Artamonov Business (1925, tr. 1935)

GOVER, Robert (1929) American novelist. Gover is an intelligent entertainer who uses modernistic techniques – often, as he has said, derived from James Joyce – to try to expose middle-class malaise (mainly sexual). His creation of Kitten, a teenage Negro prostitute, in *One Hundred Dollar Misunderstanding* attracted attention. It was extended to a trilogy by *Here Comes Kitten* (1964) and *J C Jones* (1966). Some critics feel that he positively rejects middle-class values, others that he is "sentimental". He is certainly skilful and observant; but it is difficult to discover a centre of gravity in his work. He has recently been writing under the name O. Govi.

One Hundred Dollar Misunderstanding (1962)

The Maniac Responsible (1963)

Going for Mr Big (1973)

GOVI, O., see GOVER, Robert

GOYEN, William (1915) American novelist, story-writer and dramatist. Goyen is a Texan who writes lyrical, neo-romantic, mythopoeic novels and stories; he combines the Southern grotesque tradition with a careful modernism that is not Southern. *The House of Breath*, his first novel, received full attention; his later work, which is essentially an attempt to recapture the coherence of the nineteenth-century novel, has been misunderstood or ignored.

The House of Breath (1950)

The Faces of Blood Kindred (novella and stories, 1960)

Come, the Restorer (1974)

GRAHAM, R. B. Cunninghame (1852–1936) Scottish adventurer, story-writer and travel writer. An early Scottish Nationalist, he wrote vivid regional stories about Scotland and South America (which he knew well).

The Essential R. B. Cunninghame Grahame (1952)

GRAHAM, Winston (1911) English novelist, many of whose early works are designedly out of print (he is a severe self-critic). Graham first achieved success with his dramatic tales

a well-crafted handling of the traditional devices of farce.

Doctor in the House (1952)

Doctor at Sea (1953)

Summer of Sir Lancelot (1965)

GORES, Joe (1931) American writer of detective stories, formerly a private detective. Gores' private eyes are exceptionally finely drawn and convincing. In *Hammett* Gores pays tribute to Dashiell Hammett, also a former private eye, by making him his protagonist.

A Time for Predators (1969)

Final Notice (1973)

Hammett (1975)

GORKI, Maxim (1868–1936) Russian novelist, story-writer, dramatist and critic. The early Gorki was almost a pure naturalist – which means that he was a perfervid romantic. He helped many writers in the first part of the Soviet period, then left Russia; but he returned and played some part in the establishment of socialist realism, in which he did not believe. Stalin may well have had him murdered. He was over-adulated, but was a more sensitive and interesting writer than is now usually admitted. His early naturalistic work has great power, as *Mother* well demonstrates. His middle period produced works of some ambiguity, and his last long unfinished novel (translated as *The Bystander, The Magnet, Other Fires, The Spectre*, 1930–38), although often dismissed as "weak", has fascinated many readers. *The Confession* (1909, tr. 1916) illustrates his essential independence of Marxist-Leninism. *The Life of a Useless Man* is a gripping and vivid novel about the 1905 revolution. A new assessment – and some more

Robert Graves

of nineteenth-century Cornish families, the Warleggans and the Poldarks. After four novels in the Poldark series he turned to suspense novels in contemporary settings; but he has been drawn back to the Poldarks following a successful TV dramatization, and has produced three more. A fine storyteller, his novels whether modern or historical are highly readable.

Ross Poldark (1945)

The Walking Stick (1967)

The Angry Tide (1977)

GRASS, Günter (1927) German novelist, dramatist, poet and former sculptor. Grass, born in Danzig, is modern Germany's foremost

Günter Grass

writer – despite the fact that the Nobel Prize went to Heinrich Böll. For most of his readers he is the keeper of Germany's conscience in the post-Nazi era. He calls himself a "revisionist", and has worked hard for the socialist party; but essentially he is a gradualist, believing in the slow but sure progress to a humane socialist state. As a writer, however, he is of the autonomous variety: his remarkably energetic imagination remains unfettered by his political convictions. This is so in spite of the fact that his novels seem to be closely related to topical themes (as in the case of *The Flounder*, which seems to be about women's liberation as well as food.) *The Tin Drum*, which brought him international fame, is an expressionist work which traces in minute, surreal detail the fatal split in the German personality which led to Nazism. It is a remarkably unmoralistic book, written in a comic spirit – although it is of course a tragedy. The narration is fake-simplistic, which gives the book its horrifying force, since it reflects

the universal feeling of helplessness towards the Nazi horrors. *Dog Years* is written in a similar spirit, and employs similar techniques. *Local Anaesthetic* (1969, tr. 1970) turns to the German present, and also contains much semi-autobiographical allusion. *The Flounder* is more contorted, but none the less completely controlled: it is an ironic and, as ever, lively and teasing commentary on the unfortunately persistent powers of maleness – and a grim warning to the Germans to eschew the habit of abstraction which has brought them to disaster. Grass continues to develop, and becomes progressively more readable.

The Tin Drum (1959, tr. 1961)

Dog Years (1963, tr. 1969)

The Flounder (1977, tr. 1978)

GRAU, Shirley Ann (1929) American novelist and story-writer. Grau is a tough-minded novelist with an obvious debt to Hemingway. Although she is white, her material is black culture. *The Keepers of the House*, though sensational, is one of the best modern novels about the Ku Klux Klan. She detests racists, yet her portraits of them are unforgettable. Her chief strength is her detachment.

The Keepers of the House (1964)

The Condor Passes (1971)

The Wind Shifting West (stories, 1974)

GRAVES, Richard (1715–1804) English novelist, clergyman and essayist. Graves (an ancestor of Robert Graves) is most famous for *The Spiritual Quixote*, a gentle and perceptive satire on Methodist fanaticism. It has enjoyed success in a scholarly reprint.

The Spiritual Quixote (1773, repr. 1967)

Columella (1771)

Plexippus (1790)

GRAVES, Robert (1895) Anglo-Irish-German-Danish poet, novelist, critic and mythographer. Graves was born in England, the son of a well-known Irish poet and his German-Danish wife. For most of his life he has been best known as the author of *I, Claudius* (1934) and *Claudius the God* (1934). Not a few critics regard this immensely popular work as the best historical novel of the century. Its background detail is impeccable; but the events are in large part imaginary. Graves connoisseurs prefer other novels, notably *The Golden Fleece, Wife to Mr Milton* (1943) and *King Jesus*. Graves has forged a lucid, classical style which influenced E. V. Rieu's famous translation of Homer. His viewpoint is always eccentric, but this adds to the appeal of his

novels, whose narrative exerts persuasive pressure on the reader. The Utopian *Watch the North Wind Rise* (1949, in U.S. *Seven Days in New Crete*) was a radical departure for him, and in a future reassessment may well be seen as yet another major work.

I, Claudius and *Claudius the God* (1934)

The Golden Fleece (1944, in U.S. *Hercules My Shipmates*)

King Jesus (1946)

GREEN, Anna Katherine (1846–1935) American detective story-writer, with a prolific output. Her *Leavenworth Case* (1878) was a best seller, and the first American detective story after Edgar Allan Poe. Her style now appears melodramatic and stilted, but her careful, well-built plots have endured well.

The Leavenworth Case (1878)

The Woman in the Alcove (1906)

GREEN, Henry (1905–73) English novelist. His creative life virtually ended twenty years before his death, with the publication of his last novel *Doting* (1952). He was the most original English novelist of his generation, although he has affinities with Ivy Compton-Burnett – by his extensive use of dialogue – and with James Joyce – by his capacity to see and to convey the poetry in the commonplace. His method was to try to suppress his own attitude; but he was very well aware that no writing is in fact capable of suppressing the writer's point of view. He was thus one of the subtlest of modern writers. Of his major novels, *Party*

Going deals with a group of idle, rich people who are waiting in a railway station for the fog to clear in order to proceed to a pointless party in France; *Loving* is about the servants and masters in an Irish castle during World War II. Green's subjects are happiness (he is at his best a highly lyrical novelist, particularly in *Loving*), which includes the comic, and the nature of detachment and all that this implies. His novels are rich in symbolism, but it does not obtrude.

Living (1929)

Party Going (1939)

Loving (1945)

GREEN, Julien (1900) French dramatist and novelist who was born in France of American parents. Green is a Jansenist Catholic, haunted by a Dostoyevskian terror of a godless universe. His novels have a sensationalist structure; but the melodrama is offset by the extreme spirituality of their atmosphere. His voice is at once lyrical, shrill and powerful. He is highly readable.

The Closed Garden (1927, tr. 1928)

Midnight (1936, tr. 1936)

Moira (1950, tr. 1951)

GREENE, Graham (1904) English novelist, story-writer, dramatist, critic and travel writer. Greene has occupied a pre-eminent position in English letters since the success of his series of novels of the 1930s, a success consolidated by *Brighton Rock*. Since then he has clearly developed, and only after *The Comedians* (1966) has there been any signs of a falling-off, although *The Human Factor* (1978) has been immensely admired. Greene is a converted, "left-wing" Jansenist Catholic all of whose novels have a strong but unconventional theological perspective. He has divided his output into serious novels and what he calls "entertainments" (*Stamboul Train*, 1932; *A Gun for Sale*, 1936; *The Ministry of Fear*, 1943 – and others). He has a lucid prose style strongly influenced by R. L. Stevenson. Most of the novels involve criminal activity. He concentrates above all on two interrelated themes: the squalor of ordinary life, and redemption by grace. His sympathies are always with the sinful, since he clearly regards sin as bringing suffering, and hence a graspable non-abstract redemption. His most conspicuous weakness is his failure to portray women successfully; his great strengths are the lyrical power of his narrative, and the naked honesty with which he conveys his pessimistic, melancholy and yet ultimately yearning attitude. In *Brighton Rock* the vile young hero is heretically presented as capable of grace because he is amoral, because he *feels* good and evil through his experience,

knows their reality, and truly understands the idea of damnation. The drunken priest of *The Power and the Glory*, probably Greene's greatest novel, is presented likewise: close to God just because he knows in his experience what it is to fall short of his duty as priest. More recent work is lighter hearted, although accomplished. Greene has a powerful sense of humour, extraordinary psychological penetration, and a bewitching technique, much influenced by the cinema.

Brighton Rock (1938)

The Power and the Glory (1940)

The Heart of the Matter (1948)

GREENWOOD, Walter (1903–74) English novelist whose one real success was *Love on the Dole*, which was made into a play. It tells movingly of the impact of the Depression on the Lancashire poor.

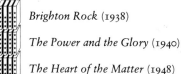

Love on the Dole (1933)

The Secret Kingdom (1938)

Saturday Night at the Crown (1959)

GREY, Zane (1872–1939) American popular novelist. His most famous book, *Riders of the Purple Sage*, sold a million copies in the original edition; and Zane Grey's reputation was assured. His stories of cowboy life are romantic, melodramatic and conventional, with ruthless villains, chivalrous cowboy heroes, and innocent heroines. They are escapist works with

Zane Grey

colourful, authentic settings.

 Riders of the Purple Sage (1912)

GRIFFIN, John Howard (1920) American (Texan) novelist. He is most famous for *Black Like Me* (1961), an account of his experiences disguised as a Negro in the South. *The Devil Rides Outside*, an account of how a young American exorcizes the ugly side of his sexuality through religious (Catholic) experience, is crude but authoritative and original. He has been called "The Texas Balzac".

 The Devil Rides Outside (1952)

Nuni (1956)

GRIMM, Jacob (1785–1863) and **Wilhelm** (1786–1859) German folklorist brothers whose interest in language and culture led them to collect stories from the German oral tradition which they published as *Kinder und Hausmarchen*. The first English translation of these fairy tales was published in 1823. In their most sanitized form they are often thought of as nursery tales, but the archetypal patterns and bare fatalism of such stories as "Rumpelstiltskin", "The Goose Girl", "Jorinda and Joringel", have captured the imagination of writers and anthropologists ever since.

 Fairy Tales (1812–15, tr. 1823)

GRIMMELSHAUSEN, Johann Jakob Christoffel von (?1625–76) German novelist. It was not until the nineteenth century that it was discovered that he wrote *Simplicissimus*, which combines picaresque, symbolic and allegorical elements, and is the finest early German novel.

 Simplicissimus (1669, tr. 1912, tr. 1963, tr. 1965)

GROGAN, Emmett (1942) American crime fiction writer, whose books are tightly written and laced with violence. *Ringolevio* has become a cult classic.

 Ringolevio (1972)

Final Score (1976)

GROSSMAN, Alfred (1927) American novelist. He writes in the picaresque style, taking anti-heroes and following the consequences of their ill-advised adventures in search of their real identities. He is a genuinely comic ironist, but has been accused – not without good reason – of facility and lapses into superficiality. *The Do-Gooders*, however, displayed a more mature talent.

 Acrobat Admits (1959)

Marie Beginning (1964)

The Do-Gooders (1968)

GROSSMITH, George (1847–1912) and **Weedon** (1854–1919) English brothers who wrote the popular and funny series of sketches called *Diary of a Nobody*. This tells of the life of a clerk and describes his opinions, his humour and his family with a photographic realism.

 Diary of a Nobody (1892)

GROVE, Frederick (1871–1948) Canadian realist novelist, whose subject matter was the pioneering of the Canadian West. His pessimism can be oppressive, but he was accomplished and is readable. *The Master of the Mill* is a major novel.

 Fruits of the Earth (1933)

The Master of the Mill (1944)

GUIMARÃES ROSA, João (1908–69) Brazilian novelist, author of one of the great Latin American classics of the century, *The Devil to Pay in the Backlands*. This tells the tale, by means of the interior monologue of the protagonist, of a hunt for revenge preceded by the making of a pact with the devil. The author invented his own complex language in order to convey the psychology of the backlanders (inhabitants of the vast Brazilian backlands). His novel is very difficult, but is at least the equal of Joyce's *Ulysses* in its combination of myth and realistic detail.

 The Devil to Pay in the Backlands (1956, tr. 1963)

 The Third Bank of the River (stories 1962, tr. 1968)

GUTHRIE, A. B., Jr. (1901) American novelist, story-writer and journalist. His romantic

Montana novel *These Thousand Hills* (1956), a successful film, is less good than his others, notably *The Big Sky*, about a nineteenth-century beaver-trapper.

 The Big Sky (1947)

The Big It (stories, 1960)

GUZMÁN, Martin Luís (1887) Mexican novelist who wrote of the Mexican revolution and Pancho Villa in *The Eagle and the Serpent*, one of the best of all accounts of revolutionary activity.

 The Eagle and the Serpent (1928, tr. 1930)

H

HABE, Hans (1911–77) Austrian-American popular novelist born in Hungary. He usually wrote well documented and entertaining semi-thrillers with romantic interest, of which the best, *A Thousand Shall Fall*, was a best seller.

 A Thousand Shall Fall (1941)

The Poisoned Stream (1969)

HAGGARD, Sir H. Rider (1856–1925) English writer of adventure romances; his very successful novels have African backgrounds. His narrative line is superbly judged, and his lush exoticism adds a touch of seamy decadence to his work which he would have deeply deprecated. He is one of the ancestors of the modern adventure novel.

 King Solomon's Mines (1885)

She (1887)

Nada the Lily (1892)

HAGGARD, William (1907) British spy novelist. In a long series of books begun with *Slow Burner* (1958) he has portrayed the highest pinnacles in the hierarchy of British life (and sometimes in that of Russia, seen typically as equally hierarchic). The books have a strong and unique flavour, of unchippable *sang-froid* and an uncompromising scorn for "softy fools" generally of the left.

 The Arena (1961)

The Conspirators (1968)

The Scorpion's Tail (1975)

HAILEY, Arthur (1920) Best-selling American novelist whose rigorously researched novels include in-depth studies of the inner workings of top-level politics (*In High Places,* 1962); a hotel; an airport; high finance (*The Money-changers,* 1975) and electric breakdown in California (*Overload*). Hailey's characters are all cyphers vainly struggling to be stereotypes; but his settings convince.

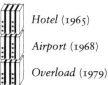

Hotel (1965)

Airport (1968)

Overload (1979)

HALL, Adam (1920) Pseudonym under which Elleston Trevor writes spy stories, the best of which are the Quiller series. Quiller is especially cool and hard-boiled; his detailed self-observation is one of his most intriguing attributes. Under his real name, Elleston Trevor has written some successful war thrillers.

The Berlin Memorandum (in U.S. *The Quiller Memorandum,* 1965)

The Warsaw Document (1971)

HALL, James N., see **NORDHOFF, Charles**

HAMILTON, Donald (1916) American thriller writer who turned early to the combination of crime and espionage that became successful in the 1960s. He uses first-person narrative to good effect, livening conventional plots with sharp dialogue.

The Removers (1961)

The Ambushers (1963)

HAMMETT, Dashiell (1894–1961) American crime-novelist of the "hard-boiled" school – but far above it in achievement. Although Hammett's material is crime and corruption – he had been an experienced detective – he has attracted the admiration of many distinguished writers, including André Gide and Robert Graves. He influenced Raymond Chandler and Ross Macdonald decisively. His style, tough and laconic, has a curious sort of elegance. His novels have gained a wider currency through films: *The Maltese Falcon* and *The Thin Man* and, much later, *The Dain Curse* (TV). His books, the best of which are *Red Harvest* (1929), *The Dain Curse* (1929) and *The Glass Key* (1931), have not only survived but are attracting increasing critical attention.

The Novels of Dashiell Hammett (1966)

The Big Knockover (stories, 1966)

HAMMILL, Pete (1935) American detective story-writer and former columnist on the *New York Post.* Hammill's latest creation, private eye Sam Briscoe, is his best. Briscoe is an ex-journalist, with left-wing views, a devotee of jazz and Jameson's whiskey.

Dirty Laundry (1978)

HAMSUN, Knut (1859–1952) Norwegian novelist, poet and dramatist, who won the Nobel Prize in 1920. Hamsun, of peasant stock, was in his early life a wanderer. His first two novels are by far his most important; and it is what remains of the spirit of these that is valuable in such later work as *The Road Leads On.* Hamsun reacted angrily to the traditional literature of Scandinavia, set himself up as a critic of Ibsen and announced that a literature of the unconscious was required. The first two works, *Hunger* and *Mysteries,* are very early examples of frankly (indeed, aggressively) nihilist fiction. The protagonists are deliberately anti-bourgeois; they set out to defy all convention. They are Dostoyevskian characters "without God", but are puzzled and perplexed rather than evil. There is much rich comedy, much pregnant mystery, and enormous although sly power. Hamsun makes elaborate and brilliant use of interior monologue in *Mysteries,* and he found this technique for himself. Later fiction remains comic, but is coarser because in place of the internal life of tormented protagonists – utterly convincing – he substituted a pseudo-social criticism, based on no more than a distaste for modern life (which is not enough).

Hunger (1890, tr. 1899)

Mysteries (1892, tr. 1927)

The Road Leads On (1933, tr. 1937)

HANDKE, Peter (1942) Austrian novelist,

playwright and film-maker who has lived in Germany and is now resident in Salzburg. Handke is acclaimed by many critics, especially in the U.S. His work is intensely subjective and expressionistic; it is not devoid of humour, and sometimes, as in *The Goalie's Anxiety at the Penalty Kick,* a high level of tension is attained. He sometimes senses the inadequacy of words and uses childlike drawings in their place. *Short Letter, Long Farewell* is a semi-autobiographical account of a young Austrian writer's travels across the U.S.

The Goalie's Anxiety at the Penalty Kick (1970, tr. 1972)

Short Letter, Long Farewell (1972, tr. 1974)

The Left-Handed Woman (1976, tr. 1978)

HANLEY, James (1901) Irish novelist (resident in Wales since 1931) dramatist and story-writer. Hanley has been persistently neglected, despite the admiration of E. M. Forster, C. P. Snow and others. He is a clumsy naturalist, but with the capacity to produce clear passages of passionately lyrical writing describing characters' complex feelings. He was a sailor, and has written much of the sea; his finest work – apart from his plays for TV written in the 1960s – is in his five novels of Dublin life *The Furys* (*The Furys,* 1935; *The Secret Journey,* 1936; *Our Time is Gone,* 1940 – and, with the two preceding, 1949; *Winter Song,* 1950; *An End and a Beginning,* 1958), bleak, relentless but finally affirmatory records of lives blighted from their beginnings by squalor and brutality. *Say Nothing* (1962) is a delicate analysis of one of his favourite themes, the problems of human communication. Hanley's successful breakthrough as a writer of TV plays suggests that his best novels (he has written twenty-four and many books of stories) only await recognition.

The Furys (1935–58)

Collected Stories (1953)

Levine (1956)

HANSEN, Joseph (1923) American detective story writer who created David Brandstetter, a homosexual insurance investigator. Brandstetter is very finely portrayed as a mundane, middle-aged man, who happens to be homosexual and is not at all camp. Some of his cases, but not all, involve homosexuals, and his romantic life is used as a feature of his character in an unremarkable, but realistic, way. The books are set in California.

Fadeout (1970)

Troublemaker (1975)

HANSFORD-JOHNSON, Pamela (1912) English novelist and essayist; the wife of C. P. Snow. She is admired for her earlier work, her later being an eccentric reaction to some aspects of modern life she dislikes for no interestingly stated reason. Probably her best – and last literary – novel is *The Unspeakable Skipton*, the study of a half-mad author.

This Bed Thy Centre (1935)

Too Dear For My Possessing (1940)

The Unspeakable Skipton (1959)

HAN SUYIN (1917) Novelist, born in Peking of a Flemish mother and a Chinese father. She was brought up in China but qualified as a doctor in England. Later she was drawn back to her roots in Asia and her novels reflect her feeling for the country of her birth. Many are frankly autobiographical.

A Many-Splendoured Thing (1952)

And the Rain my Drink (1956)

The Four Faces (1963)

HARDWICK, Elizabeth (1916) American novelist, critic and essayist, a founder editor of the *New York Review of Books*, who was married to the poet Robert Lowell. She is a powerful and intelligent advocate of women's rights.

The Ghostly Lover (1945)

The Simple Truth (1955)

Sleepless Nights (1979)

HARDWICK, Mollie ( ) English writer, whose work ranges from best selling novels to literary studies. She has gained popularity with "novelizations" of popular television series, such as *Upstairs, Downstairs* and *The Duchess of Duke Street*.

Sarah's Story (1973)

Beauty's Daughter (1976)

Lovers Meeting (1979)

HARDY, Thomas (1840–1928) English (Dorset-born) novelist and poet. Hardy was ultimately a poet, although he did not publish his first collection of poems until late in life. He has been called a naturalist because he took a grim view of life, and often concentrated upon unhappiness, frustrated passion and failure; but he is a poetic novelist, not a realist, and as such is unique. His style is not pretty, but it is grand, and is the only one suitable for his purposes. All his major novels are set in Wessex and explore the poetic theme of "character is destiny". They are compelling, improbable on a merely realistic level, often exceedingly shrewd and comic – and tragically exact in their delineations of character. Although Hardy is melodramatic, he does not offer villains or heroes. His only truly "saved" character is Elizabeth Jane in *The Mayor of Casterbridge*. He has been much attacked for his bleakness of outlook; but in his passionate care about consistency of character he shows a great love for humanity; there is scarcely a more moving writer in the language. His imitators (such as Algernon Gissing, brother of George) were merely regionalist. Hardy was successful as a novelist, but the public was never happy about him and he was never happy about it – he wrote for serial publication, and was exactly the opposite of Dickens, in that he

Thomas Hardy

resented the feedback he received, and regarded pleasing his readers as mutilation of his text. Critics write about him with considerable reserve; but his readership has increased steadily, and this is perhaps the best resolution of the problems created by his "difficult" attitude, and by the poetic nature of his fiction.

The Mayor of Casterbridge (1886)

Tess of the D'Urbervilles (1891)

Jude the Obscure (1895)

HARLAND, Henry (1861–1905) American novelist and story-writer. His most successful novel was *The Cardinal's Snuff Box*, a sentimental, but effective, romance.

Mea Culpa (1891)

Grey Roses (1895)

The Cardinal's Snuff Box (1900)

HARNESS, Charles L. (1915) American science fiction writer. His plots are spectacular, usually involving time-paradoxes. *The Paradox Men* is space opera *par excellence*, while *The Rose* is an allegory contrasting the roles of art and science in human affairs.

The Paradox Men (1949)

The Rose (1953)

The Ring of Ritornel (1968)

HARRINGTON, Alan (1919) American novelist whose work reflects fashions with great skill. Some critics find him entertaining, others prolix and feeble.

Life in the Crystal Palace (1959)

The Secret Swinger (1966)

HARRIS, Joel Chandler (1848–1908) American novelist and story-writer. Harris is widely remembered for his careful handling of Negro animal folklore in the *Uncle Remus* stories. He is also inevitably the subject of controversy – which often fails to take into account the Georgian context in which Harris wrote the stories. They are in general very skilful representations of a Negro way of meeting circumstances, and Brer Rabbit, Brer Fox and the others have become a part of all-American tradition. His view is a white Southern one, but is not patronizing.

Uncle Remus (1880)

Nights with Uncle Remus (1883)

Uncle Remus and his Friends (1892)

HARRIS, Wilson (1921) Guyanese novelist, poet and story-writer. Since the *Guiana Quartet*, (*Palace of the Peacock*, 1960; *The Far Journey of Oudin*, 1961; *The Whole Armour*, 1962; *The Secret Ladder*, 1963) – the finest of all the statements of the West Indian predicament, presented in a way that can only be described as anthropological and mythological – he has become increasingly more complex. He is the exact opposite of a James Baldwin in that he does not protest; he wants rather to "resensitize perspectives of community", to awaken the sense of the creative in all men so that they shall reach a greater self-awareness. Inevitably some of the novels and stories fail: they have been swamped by intellectuality. But at his best, as in *Black Marsden*, Harris is as accomplished and impressive a novelist as any in his generation.

The Guiana Quartet (1960–63)

Black Marsden (1972)

Genesis of the Clowns (1975)

HARRISON, Harry (1925) American science fiction writer. He is equally adept at fast-paced adventure stories (*Deathworld*) and humorous fiction (*The Technicolour Time Machine*, 1967). He wrote one of the first overpopulation horror stories in *Make Room! Make Room!* and a classic satire on well-worn science fiction themes in *Bill, the Galactic Hero*.

Deathworld (1960)

Bill, the Galactic Hero (1965)

Make Room! Make Room! (1966)

HARTE, Bret (1836–1902) American story-writer and journalist. Harte worked in the gold mines, and it was his sentimental, highly

Bret Harte

dramatic, deeply felt sketches about miners that brought him fame. A Dickensian energy redeems him from bathos.

Representative Selections (1941)

HARTLEY, L. P. (1895–1972) English novelist and story-writer. Hartley made a distinctive contribution to the English novel in the Jamesian tradition; and he had, like Henry James, a keen insight into the psychology of women. He was always uneven, but his fiction fell off during the 1950s. His chief contributions were the "Eustace and Hilda" trilogy (*The Shrimp and the Anemone*, 1944; *The Sixth Heaven*, 1946; *Eustace and Hilda*, 1947), *The Boat* and *The Go-Between* (made into a memorable film), his finest book. He entirely lacked robustness, but compensated for this, in his best work, by his extreme delicacy of style and ability to portray the weak and vulnerable in a sympathetic light.

Eustace and Hilda (1947)

The Boat (1950)

The Go-Between (1953)

HARWOOD, Ronald (1934) South African actor turned novelist, dramatist and film script-writer. He is a versatile writer whose subjects include a poignant comedy about a lunatic asylum (*The Girl in Melanie Klein*) and the recreation of Paris in the 1870s centred round the revitalising of César Franck as composer and man by a Franco-Irish girl (*César and Augusta*).

The Girl in Melanie Klein (1969)

Articles of Faith (1973)

César and Augusta (1978)

HAŠEK, Jaroslav (1883–1923) Czech novelist and journalist, the creator of the comic soldier Svejk in the unfinished *The Good Soldier Svejk*. But besides giving us the soul of Czech resistence to tyranny, the novel has, since its unexpurgated translation by Sir Cecil Perrott, gained very wide appeal. It is a masterpiece, despite its carelessnesses. Hašek once wrote an obituary for himself headed "A Traitor"; this is the essence of his approach.

The Good Soldier Svejk (1920–23, tr. 1971)

HAUPTMANN, Gerhart (1862–1946) German dramatist, novelist and poet. Hauptmann, who was awarded the Nobel Prize in 1912, is chiefly important for his early plays. But his novels have considerable interest. The best are *The Fool in Christ, The Heretic of Soana, The Island of the Great Mother* (1924, tr. 1925) and the undeservedly neglected *Phantom*, a more

straightforward crime story with Dostoyevskian overtones.

The Fool in Christ (1911, tr. 1912)

The Heretic of Soana (1918, tr. 1923, repr. 1960)

Phantom (1923, tr. 1923)

HAWKES, John (1928) American novelist, story-writer and dramatist. Hawkes is one of the more important modernist writers of America. He makes extensive use of surrealism, but his novels and novellas as wholes are not actually surrealistic. He is violent, neo-Gothic, grotesque. He uses a frequently bizarre language to probe at the more elemental aspects of the mind, and is frequently called "unpleasant" and "uncomfortable". He can be bad, and very mannered, as in his latest *The Passion Artist* (1979); but there is power in the bleakness of his vision and in his lush, rhetorical prose.

The Beetle Leg (1951)

The Lime Twig (1960)

Lunar Landscape (stories, 1969)

HAWTHORNE, Nathaniel (1804–64) American novelist and story-writer. One of the greatest of American writers, although all but one, *The Scarlet Letter*, of his novels are badly flawed. The exception amongst the remainder is *The Blithedale Romance*, a brilliant examination and debunking of Utopian idealism – based on Hawthorne's own experiences at Brook Farm, a Transcendentalist Utopian community – which is deliberately pitched lower than the desperate and tortured complexity of *The Scarlet Letter*, but which is nonetheless major. Like Herman Melville,

Nathaniel Hawthorne

Hawthorne was a man apart. His pessimism has captured the imagination of many disillusioned contemporary Americans, especially at a time when their administration has proved to be corrupt. *The Scarlet Letter*, an inimitable mixture of romance, allegory, myth and psychological realism, is in his own words "hell-fired": it explores his own reluctant tendency towards Calvinism, and at the same time examines nineteenth-century aspirations in the "hell-fired" terms of the seventeenth. It is in one sense a mass of evasions; but somehow the whole text works (except at the very end), since it reflects the confusions of the "American dream", reconstituting them into a near-nightmare of great immediacy. Hawthorne's other romances are readable and interesting, but somewhat laboured. Certain of his short stories such as "Ethan Brand" are as good as anything he ever wrote.

The Scarlet Letter (1850)

The Blithedale Romance (1852)

HAZZARD, Shirley (1931) Australian novelist and story-writer who has lived in America since she was 20. She has published many stories in the *New Yorker*, is technically expert, and specializes in the psychology of women.

Cliffs of Fall (1963)

The Bay of Noon (1970)

HEARN, Lafcadio (1850–1904) American novelist and travel writer. Hearn was of mixed (not American) parentage, but was regarded as an American writer. He travelled in Japan and China, and his books about these countries are now more interesting than his two novels, *Chita*, about the destruction of an American island; and *Youma*, about a slave rebellion.

Chita (1889)

Youma (1890)

HEARNE, John (1926) West Indian novelist, born in Canada. Hearne does not write in the main tradition of post-independence Caribbean fiction. This is not to say that he ignores the plight of the peasants and the urban poor – he doesn't – but rather to point out that he explores the predicament of middle-class intellectuals. He has written two fine thrillers, with Morris Cargill, under the name John Morris: *Fever Grass* (1969) and *The Candywine Development* (1971).

Voices Under the Window (1955)

The Faces of Love (1957)

HECHT, Ben (1892–1964) American novelist,

journalist and showman. Even the best of his fiction is more journalistic than imaginative, although he had considerable fluency and intelligence. *A Jew in Love* is a cruel portrait of Maxwell Bodenheim.

Eric Dorn (1921)

A Jew in Love (1930)

Collected Stories (1945)

HEDGES, Joseph (1936) British thriller writer. His hero, the "Revenger", wages single-handed war against an international crime corporation. Brutal action, explicit sexuality and thin ghoulish humour predominate.

Funeral Rites (1973)

Arms for Oblivion (1973)

The Chinese Coffin (1974)

HEGGEN, Thomas (1919–49) American novelist and dramatist, who made an enormous success with *Mister Roberts*, an uninhibited and bawdy account of boredom on an American cargo carrier in World War II (it was equally successfully dramatized and filmed).

Mister Roberts (1946)

HEINLEIN, Robert (1907) American science fiction novelist and story-writer. Heinlein's imaginative gifts, and his compulsive powers of story-telling, have ensured that he has dominated the field of science fiction for some thirty years. Influenced by Rudyard Kipling and H. G. Wells, anti-materialist and optimistic, he has been more responsible than any other writer for establishing the methods and traditions of modern science fiction.

The Green Hills of Earth (stories, 1951)

Methuselah's Children (1958)

Stranger in a Strange Land (1961)

HELLER, Joseph (1923) American novelist. He was in the air force, and from his experiences there wrote *Catch-22*, a black-comedy anti-war novel that evoked comparisons with Jonathan Swift and Evelyn Waugh. The phrase Catch-22 – the system that traps all the participants, and especially the Assyrian hero Yossarian, into complicity in the crazy enterprise – entered the language. Heller's attitude is one of total scorn – he somewhat alarmingly provides no alternative set of values and is thus nihilistic – and doubts as to his quality seemed to be confirmed by the failure of the ingredients, in the novel's two successors, to mix. But *Catch-22* is more than merely fashionable – even at worst it is a bleak

statement of an intellectual's total rejection of the non-values of a modern world geared to war.

Catch-22 (1961)

Something Happened (1974)

Good as Gold (1979)

HEMINGWAY, Ernest (1898–1961) American novelist and story-writer. Hemingway combined an "outdoor" (boxing, fishing, big-game hunting, bullfighting) life with that of a writer. He shot himself in a fit of depression and the man is now as much a legend as his work. The formative influences on him were Sherwood Anderson, Gertrude Stein, the Mark Twain of *Huckleberry Finn* and his apprenticeship as a journalist. He fought in the war in Italy (as an ambulance driver) and was seriously wounded. Anderson and Stein helped him to develop his laconic, concrete style, which at its best captures reality in an astonishingly precise although never profound fashion. The general consensus is that Hemingway's best writing is to be found in the novel *The Sun Also Rises* (*Fiesta*) and in the earlier stories. Here he presents people facing the ungracious and impossible present with a stoical pride and an insistence on the famous Hemingway "code", a rather more tenuous affair than many critics suggest – but which may best be defined as an insistence upon keeping up the appearances of stoicial acceptance. Jake Barnes, in *The Sun Also Rises*, is emasculated – as Hemingway felt himself to be by his softness and sentimentality. This has genuinely tragic overtones. *A Farewell to Arms* contains a classic war description (the retreat from Caporetto) and much fine writing, but the character of the girl in it is unconvincing. The stories of *Men Without Women* (1927) are among his finest work, and, as the title implies, enable Hemingway to express himself in an unhampered way.

Ernest Hemingway

boys' tales which extol the virtues of the race in lucid and vigorous prose. These are good, patriotic unsubtle yarns, which do not do too much violence to historical fact.

Out on the Pampas (1868)

The Young Franc-Tireurs (1871)

The Lion of St Mark (1889)

HEPPENSTALL, Rayner (1911) English novelist, essayist and critic. Heppenstall has always been an experimental novelist: he has been much influenced by French modernist fiction and, latterly, by astrological symbolism. He is not generally easy to read (although *Blaze of Noon* is an exception), but has much of interest to say.

Blaze of Noon (1939)

The Woodshed (1962)

Two Moons (1977)

HERBERT, Frank (1920) American science fiction writer whose many competent and entertaining works (*The Dragon In the Sea*; *The Eyes of Heisenberg*, 1966) are overshadowed by an undoubted masterpiece. *Dune* is the first of a trilogy of novels set on a desert planet in a galactic civilization which has renounced the technology of machine intelligence and pursued the development of the powers of the human mind. The underlying theme of ecological balance is expressed through a complex relationship between feudal ordering, religious superstitions and mental extremes, all set in the framework of an enthralling adventure of political intrigue and ambition. One of science fiction's most thoroughly realized achievements, it is both stimulating and highly readable, although *Children of Dune* (1976) is a somewhat weak conclusion to the sequence.

The Dragon in the Sea (1956)

Dune (1965)

Dune Messiah (1969)

HERBST, Josephine (1897) American novelist, an important proletarian writer. Her novels are effective, but have been criticized for sacrificing human to socially documentary interest.

Nothing is Sacred (1928)

The Watcher with the Horn (1955)

HERGESHEIMER, Joseph (1880–1954) American novelist. Until *Linda Condon* (1919) Hergesheimer was a serious romantic novelist; after this he sought popularity and sacrificed his integrity to the production of over-erotic

Here he shows men of action blocked from acting by various circumstances, and probes the heart of his own problem: a man of action himself, and a brave one, he was not in fact (despite legend) particularly good at the things he wanted to do – he was always better at drinking. The rest of his life is a saga of powers failing, although he managed to keep up appearances. *For Whom the Bell Tolls* is immensely ambitious, but ruined by sentimentality – and by the fact that the girl heroine, once again, is unconvincing. *Across the River and into the Trees* (1950) is comic self-parody; *The Old Man and the Sea* (1952) although it clinched his claim to the Nobel Prize, which he received in 1954, is not now seen as satisfactory – but rather as "sentimentally perfect", a laboured allegory. But Hemingway, despite his decline, remains one of the major American writers of the century: his version of one way of accepting defeat in the face of intolerable circumstances is – in the earlier work, and in

flashes in the later – absolutely authentic. It is above all a triumph of style, an excellence that was truly worked for.

The Sun Also Rises (in U.K. *Fiesta*, 1926)

A Farewell to Arms (1929)

For Whom the Bell Tolls (1940)

HENRY, O. (1862–1910) American story writer and journalist. He served a long prison sentence for embezzlement and began to write stories after this. His great strength is in his plotting: he produced brilliantly readable, fatalistic, stories; but he has been much criticized for his slick, sentimental and unrealistic neatness.

Best Short Stories (1945)

HENTY, G. A. (1832–1902) English writer of

sensationalist novels which have now lost their interest for the reader. *The Three Black Pennys* is an impressive study of the decline of a Pennsylvanian family over several generations; the iron industry background is accurately and forcefully sketched in.

The Three Black Pennys (1917)

Gold and Iron (1918)

Java Head (1919)

HERLIHY, James Leo (1927) American novelist and story-writer. Herlihy's first two novels *All Fall Down* and *Midnight Cowboy* were memorably filmed. The novels as novels are not quite as good as the films as films. They are written in a misogynous tradition – one more subtly and less shrilly exploited in the plays of Edward Albee and in the novels of Truman Capote and James Purdy – to which they add little. The third novel, *The Season of the Witch* (1971) tries and fails to make the unhappiness of the misfit and the homosexual a glamorous one. His stories are more pointed, although they err somewhat on the side of the grotesque.

All Fall Down (1961)

Midnight Cowboy (1965)

A Story That Ends with a Scream and Eight Others (1967)

HERRICK, Robert (1868–1938) American novelist, teacher and critic. Herrick's best fiction deals with Chicago and its corruption in the era of development, *The Memoirs of an American Citizen* being the outstanding work.

The Real World (1901)

The Memoirs of an American Citizen (1905, repr. 1963)

The Master of the Inn (1908)

HERSEY, John (1914) American novelist and journalist. He has carried on the tradition of Sinclair Lewis, whom he knew well, but has dealt in particular with war. *Hiroshima* (1946) is his most famous piece of work, and is reportage. His novels have become increasingly literary in intent – possibly to their detriment.

A Bell for Adano (1944)

A Single Pebble (1956)

My Petition for More Space (1974)

HESSE, Hermann (1877–1962) German (later naturalized Swiss) novelist, story-writer and poet. Hesse won the Nobel Prize in 1946. He

Hermann Hesse

had three almost separate careers as a writer, although his theme is nearly always the spiritual education of the self. *Peter Camenzind* (1904, tr. 1961) has for its central character a romantic artist who, not very convincingly, discovers self-understanding. The charm of this novel lies in its inventions and its style. Hesse collapsed under the strain of war (he went to Switzerland and renounced German citizenship) and a bad marriage. He then issued *Demian*, not under his own name, and scored a popular success. *Steppenwolf* is a "crisis novel", considered by many to be his best. By this time he had absorbed much from the study of Jung and of Chinese philosophy, and this is reflected in *Narziss and Goldmund* (1930, tr. 1959), a romance which entranced some and irritated others. His last large-scale work which won him the Nobel Prize was *The Glass Bead Game*, a paradoxical novel about a future Utopia in which a game – perhaps Hesse meant something like astrology, although he never gives the "rules" – resolves all paradoxes. Many critics who admire Hesse do so in spite of their belief that his ideas are second-rate, obscure or non-existent: they are entranced by the poetry of his style. It is difficult, however much *The Glass Bead Game* irritates, to deny its serene qualities. Hesse wrote many excellent short stories.

Demian (1919, tr. 1958)

Steppenwolf (1927, tr. 1965)

The Glass Bead Game (1943, tr. 1950 as *Magister Ludi*, tr. 1970)

HEYER, Georgette (1902–74) British writer of historical romances and detective novels who created the genre of the Regency Romance and set standards in it which have not been equalled. Her plots almost invariably turn on a tension between heroine and hero, often compounded by misunderstandings, which is at first mis-

taken for dislike but is finally recognized as love. The inevitable consequence is marriage. Miss Heyer was a leading authority on the social history of her period and the accuracy of detail, linguistic and circumstantial, together with the pointed wit of her dialogue and the confident precision of her craftsmanship, lift her books above the form.

These Old Shades (1926)

The Masqueraders (1928)

The Toll Gate (1954)

HEYWARD, DuBose (1885–1940) American novelist who is most famous for his lively and accurate account of Charleston Negro life, *Porgy* (1925), which he made into a play and Gershwin then made into an opera.

Porgy (1925)

Mamba's Daughters (1929)

Star-spangled Virgin (1939)

HIDAYAT, Sadiq (1902–51) Persian novelist, who killed himself in Paris. His novel *The Blind Owl*, a blistering study in paranoia, is one of the greatest of its decade in world fiction.

The Blind Owl (1936, tr. 1957)

HIGGINS, George V. (1939) American crime fiction writer who was once a District Attorney in Boston. His early books – *The Friends of Eddie Coyle*, *The Digger's Game* (1973), *Cogan's Trade* – are brilliantly realistic portrayals of Boston's underworld, laced with authentic criminal jargon. Unfortunately, Higgins' dialogue was praised so highly that some of the later books, like *A City on a Hill* (1975) are all dialogue of an unreadable naturalism; and his tendency to desert crime for "larger issues" weakens his credibility.

The Friends of Eddie Coyle (1972)

Cogan's Trade (1974)

The Judgment of Deke Hunter (1976)

HIGHSMITH, Patricia (1921) American novelist and story-writer, resident in France. Highsmith is regarded as a crime writer, and is read as one. But she is not a novelist who writes "entertainments", even though she is – in her feline way – very entertaining. There is seldom an element of mystery in her novels, although the reader always wants to know what happens. She made a brilliant start with *Strangers on a Train*; since *Deep Water* (1957) she has been uneven. Her creation of the murderer Ripley, of whom she is clearly very fond, is a tour de force; he runs successfully though

Patricia Highsmith

nervously through many books, beginning with *The Talented Mr Ripley*. Highsmith writes in a deliberately flat style, thus gaining the effect of horror she seeks. She is peculiarly adept at putting people into horrible situations; she then studies them as though they were under a microscope, and with as much skill as a scientist. In her stories, collected as *The Snail-Watcher and Other Stories* (1970), she is usually more determinedly whimsical, but here too she is often horrific, although more professionally so. She is a highly professional writer, who has written some of the finest psychological thrillers of our time. Many of her books have been filmed, most notably *Strangers on a Train* by Alfred Hitchcock.

Strangers on a Train (1950)

The Talented Mr Ripley (1955)

Ripley's Game (1974)

HILL, Christopher (   ) British thriller writer, who has written two gripping, chilling and violent books, *Scorpion* and *Jackdaw*.

Scorpion (1974)

Jackdaw (1976)

HILL, Reginald (1936) English crime novelist. Using broadly the classic detective-story formula, with two sleuths, fat and senior Superintendent Dalziel and trendy sociology graduate Sergeant (later Inspector) Pascoe, Hill has succeeded in combining mystery and social commentary in books showing both intelligence and high spirits. His themes and settings are wholly contemporary.

A Clubbable Woman (1970)

A Fairly Dangerous Thing (1972)

A Pinch of Snuff (1978)

HILL, Susan (1942) English novelist and critic who published her first novel (*The Enclosure*, 1958) when a Yorkshire schoolgirl of 16. She is at her best in *Gentlemen and Ladies* and *A Change for the Better* (1969), and in several short stories; quaintly formal accounts of elderly people in slightly rundown resort-towns. Miss Hill announced her retirement from writing fiction after the appearance of *In the Springtime of the Year*, an over-sentimental but moving story of a 21-year-old girl's adjustment to her husband's sudden death.

Gentlemen and Ladies (1968)

I'm the King of the Castle (1970)

In the Springtime of the Year (1974)

HILTON, James (1900–54) English novelist whose *Lost Horizon* (1933) gave to the English language the word "Shangri-la" – the novel's name for an imaginary Himalayan pass, the site of an earthly paradise. He is most commonly remembered, however, for the immensely popular *Goodbye, Mr Chips*, the sentimental story of the last years of a master at an ancient public school. *Random Harvest* (1941) is about a man suffering from amnesia.

Lost Horizon (1933)

Goodbye, Mr Chips (1934)

Random Harvest (1941)

HIMES, Chester (1909) Black American crime novelist. At odds with his native land (he served a term for jewel theft, and emigrated to Europe in 1953), Himes appears to be less appreciated there than he should be. After early novels, the first written in gaol, Himes established himself with crime in Harlem and two splendid black detectives, Coffin Ed Johnson and Grave Digger Jones, tough, cynical, witty and unimpressed by anything. And in Himes's Harlem there's a lot to impress, lesbians, pederasts, drugs, violent deaths, hustlers, pimps, corruption and religious hysteria. The style is racy and laconic, sometimes obscure and usually exhilarating.

Cotton Comes to Harlem (1965)

Come Back Charleston Blue (*The Heat's On,* 1966)

Blind Man with a Pistol (1969)

HINDE, Thomas (1926) English novelist. He has never bettered his first semi-autobiographical novel *Mr Nicholas*, a study in madness and tyranny. Outstanding among his many others is *The Day the Call Came* (1964), another – more sensationalist – study of madness.

Mr Nicholas (1952)

The Day the Call Came (1964)

The Village (1966)

HINES, Barry (1939) British writer who is adept at capturing the flavour of real speech and at conveying, without exposition, the frustration of young people denied their full humanity and potential by social forces. *Kes*, his best work (first published as *A Kestrel For A Knave*), tells the moving story of a young urchin, neglected at home and school, who catches and trains a hawk, only to have this assertion of his personality cruelly squashed.

The Blinder (1966)

A Kestrel for a Knave (1968)

The Gamekeeper (1975)

HOBAN, Russell (1925) American-born novelist and writer of children's books living in England. The limpid clarity of the text of his picture books for children contrasts sharply with his experimental adult novels, juggling with language and narration, like *The Lion of Boaz-Jachin and Jachin-Boaz* (1972) and *Turtle Diary*.

Turtle Diary (1976)

HODGE, Jane Aiken (1917) English historical novelist, daughter of Conrad Aiken, who has also written a number of suspense stories. Most of her popular historical novels span a period of about fifty years, a time of social and political change at the beginning of the nineteenth century.

Rebel Heiress (1975)

Red Sky at Night (1978)

HODGSON, William Hope (1875–1918) English fantasy writer, killed at Ypres in 1918. His writing career spanned just fourteen years, and achieved only modest fame. He belongs in the company of Poe, Blackwood and Machen, but his curiously congested style and haunting images are very much his own.

The Boats of the Glen Carrig (1907)

The House on the Borderland (1908)

HOFFMAN, Charles Fenno (1806–84) American novelist, lawyer, editor, poet and auto-biographer. His efficient novel *Greyslaer*, based on a real Kentucky murder case, made him famous.

 Vanderlyn (unfinished, 1837)

Greyslaer (1840)

HOGG, James (1770–1835) English poet and novelist, author of the major novel of the supernatural and Calvinist damnation, *The Private Memoirs and Confessions of a Justified Sinner*. This is the ironic tale of a young man who decides that he is "justified" in murdering his brother; it has recently had a strong influence on psychological fiction.

 The Private Memoirs and Confessions of a Justified Sinner (1824)

HOLDING, Elizabeth Sanxay (1899–1955) American novelist, who married a British civil servant. She wrote romantic fiction before turning to mysteries, and was a pioneer in the field of psychological suspense novels. Most of her books are about families fighting inexplicable terrors, and each other.

 The Obstinate Murderer (1938)

The Innocent Mrs Duff (1946)

The Virgin Huntress (1951)

HOLMES, H. H., see BOUCHER, Anthony

HOLMES, John Clellon (1926) American novelist and poet. Holmes made his name with *Go*, which dealt sympathetically with the Beat Generation.

 Go (1952)

The Horn (1958)

Get Home Free (1964)

HOLMES, Oliver Wendell (1809–94) American man of letters, novelist, story-writer, biographer, poet, anti-Calvinist and Professor of Anatomy at Harvard (1847–82). He wrote three novels, which are at base early psychiatric case studies. The best is *Elsie Venner*, which analyzes a schizophrenic girl.

 Elsie Venner (1861)

The Guardian Angel (1867)

A Mortal Antipathy (1885)

HOLT, Victoria, see PLAIDY, Jean

HONE, Joseph (1937) Irish spy story-writer. Hone's first book, *The Private Sector*, is a plausible account of how an innocent English

teacher in Cairo becomes a British secret agent. The sequel, *The Sixth Directorate*, is intriguing, rather than exciting; it uses a complex plot to warn of the consequences of what Hone sees as the weakmindedness of those who believe in the perfectibility of the Marxist ideal.

 The Private Sector (1971)

The Sixth Directorate (1975)

HOOPER, J. J. (1815–62) American (North Carolina) humorous novelist. His character Simon Suggs is a typical late picaro: a Southern frontier rogue who glories in his "shiftiness".

 Some Adventures of Simon Suggs (1846)

HOPE, Anthony (1863–1933) English romantic adventure novelist. Hope created a genre: the Balkan romance. His characters and their actions are not in the least credible, but he was a superb fantasist. *The Dolly Dialogues*, an amusing satire on London society, is more serious than *The Prisoner of Zenda* but less readable.

 The Prisoner of Zenda (1894)

The Dolly Dialogues (1894)

Rupert of Hentzau (1898)

HOPLEY, George, see WOOLRICH, Cornell

HORGAN, Paul (1903) American regionalist novelist, who has written some twenty novels set in the American South West, varying from historical Westerns like *A Distant Trumpet*, to a series of autobiographical fictions about a sensitive young Catholic.

 A Distant Trumpet (1960)

Whitewater (1970)

HORNUNG, E. W. (1866–1921) English crime story-writer, creator of A. J. Raffles, the gentleman burglar. There have been other crook-heroes but Raffles remains the supremely successful example. This is partly because of Hornung's craftsmanship as a writer. But his creation, as George Orwell pointed out, is no crude stuffed aristocrat but simply a gentleman, pure essence of that curious but real ethos: and yet he is, like Sherlock Holmes, no mere formula either but a real person, as is his "Watson", the innocent and loyal Bunny.

 The Amateur Cracksman (1899)

The Black Mask (in U.S. *Raffles: Further Adventures*, 1901)

 A Thief in the Night (1905)

HOUSEHOLD, Geoffrey (1900) English novel-

ist and story-writer, who deals in suspense and adventure of exceptionally high quality. His first book, *Rogue Male*, about an assassination attempt on an unnamed head-of-state and the ensuing animal-like hunt for the would-be assassin, can be read as a clever and timely symbolic account of civilization's slide towards chaos and darkness. Subsequently Household has pursued a single-minded but eclectic literary course. The solitary cat-like heroes of his books look out at society from their hiding-places with a mixture of affection and anger. However, the most notable feature of Household's work is his commitment to landscape and its influence on humans. Whether the setting is Dorset (*Rogue Male*), the Cotswolds (*Watcher in the Shadows*), Somerset (*The Courtesy of Death*) or numerous locations outside England, his spare elegant prose expresses a sense of pantheistic communion with the land.

 Rogue Male (1939)

Watcher in the Shadows (1960)

Dance of the Dwarfs (1968)

Geoffrey Household

HOUSTON, R. B., see RAE, Hugh C.

HOWARD, Elizabeth Jane (1923) English novelist; wife of Kingsley Amis. Howard is a sensible, intelligent novelist in what she calls the "straight tradition". Her novels are skilfully written, and are invariably better when dealing with the problems of older people. But as a "straight", old-fashioned novelist, she could hardly – within her limitations – be bettered.

 The Beautiful Visit (1950)

After Julius (1965)

Odd Girl Out (1972)

HOWATCH, Susan (1940) English novelist who first won recognition in America when her epic saga *Penmarric* (1964) appeared there. She has now settled in New Jersey, and claims that New York stimulates her imagination, although most of her novels are set in typical English or Irish countryside. When *Penmarric* was published Susan Howatch had already written six novels of less monumental proportions; but she is clearly at her happiest with a sweeping canvas spanning several centuries of family history.

 Shrouded Walls (1972)

Cashelmara (1974)

The Rich are Different (1977)

HOWE, E. W. (1853–1937) American novelist, journalist and editor known as "the sage of Potato Hill". His most important work is the novel *The Story of a Country Town*, a cynical and melodramatic portrait of a midwest community. Though crude, it was, as a critic at the time said, "a petard set off under American respectbility"; and it provided Sherwood Anderson with one of the models for *Winesburg, Ohio*.

 The Story of a Country Town (1883)

HOWELLS, William Dean (1837–1920) American novelist, critic, dramatist, and memoirist. Howells played an important part in the development of American realism and naturalism (although he was not himself a naturalist), and his own novels are still much read. He kept his creative vitality to the end, even though his failure entirely to cast off gentility may rob his fiction of greatness. His earlier fiction reflects his European experience; later, as in *A Hazard of New Fortunes*, he pessimistically examines the situation between labour and capital in America. His gifts of characterization are not brilliant, but are marked by high intelligence, sound knowledge, and accuracy. He was universally regarded as "the Dean of American Letters", and attacks on him fell flat.

 A Modern Instance (1882)

The Rise of Silas Lapham (1885)

A Hazard of New Fortunes (1890)

HOYLE, Fred (1915) British astronomer and science fiction writer, who has often written in collaboration with his son Geoffrey. *The Black Cloud* is a classic story of an encounter with an alien intelligence; and *A for Andromeda* (1962) is a fine thriller about mankind threatened by computers.

 The Black Cloud (1957)

October the First is Too Late (1966)

HOYLE, Geoffrey, see HOYLE, Fred

HUBBARD, P. M. (1910) English novelist whose work blends mystery and romance, and evokes the haunting atmosphere of landscape; suspense is built up by hints of menace and unexplained evil.

 A Rooted Sorrow (1973)

A Thirsty Evil (1974)

The Graveyard (1975)

HUDSON, W. E. (1841–1922) English novelist and nature writer. He wrote many books about nature and fictional romances, before *Green Mansions*, the story of a bird-woman, made him famous. The theme is an old one;

William Dean Howells

but his lush treatment is original.

A Crystal Age (1887)

Green Mansions (1904)

Dead Man's Pluck (1920)

HUGHES, Langston (1902–67) American Negro poet, dramatist and novelist, born in Missouri. Hughes was mainly a poet and playwright, but his creation of the Negro Jesse B. Simple made him the most influential Negro writer before the advent of Ralph Ellison and James Baldwin.

Not Without Laughter (1930)

Mortgage of a Dream Deferred (1951)

The Best of Simple (1961)

HUGHES, Richard (1900–77) English novelist, poet and pioneer radio playwright. Hughes was not a prolific writer – only four novels and some short stories – but each of his books received wide attention. *A High Wind in Jamaica* is an interesting variant on the "wicked children" theme. *In Hazard* is a sea tale reminiscent of Joseph Conrad, and is prophetic of the loss of the Empire. He did not live to complete his *roman fleuve The Human Predicament*, but its first two parts (*The Fox in the Attic*, 1961 and *The Wooden Shepherdess*, 1973) are remarkable, a "history of my own times", in which such characters as Hitler appear convincingly. Hughes was a novelist of originality and depth.

A High Wind in Jamaica (1929)

In Hazard (1938)

The Human Predicament (1961–73)

HUGHES, Thomas (1822–96) English novelist immortalized by his novel of Thomas Arnold's Rugby, *Tom Brown's Schooldays*. This advocates "muscular Christianity", but is nonetheless a skilfully told school story.

Tom Brown's Schooldays (1857)

The Scouring of the White Horse (1859)

Tom Brown at Oxford (1861)

HUGO, Victor (1802–85) French romantic poet, novelist and dramatist. He spent the years 1855–70 in exile in Jersey, as an opponent to Louis Napoleon. Hugo is more important as a poet who anticipated his successors (who recognized this) than as the hero-figure who was buried with full state honours. But his novels are important and powerful. The tone of most of his later fiction is set by *Notre Dame de Paris* (1831, tr. 1910) which presents the

Victor Hugo

Cathedral as a symbol of the great Fate, or Ananke, with which man has to contend. *Les Misérables* is more socially aware; the struggle between the criminal Jean Valjean and the policeman Javert has become part of almost everyone's background. *By Order of the King* (*L'Homme qui rit*) is Hugo's strangest work, ostensibly a fantasy about late seventeenth-century England; but it might easily be seen as a quasi-surrealist romance.

Les Misérables (1862, tr. 1906)

By Order of the King (1869, tr. 1901)

Ninety-Three (1874, tr. 1900)

HUMPHREY, William (1924) American novelist. Humphrey writes of Texas somewhat in the tradition of William Faulkner. *Home from the Hill* was a best seller. His novels suffer from flat passages and long-windedness; but he has considerable psychological scope.

Home from the Hill (1958)

The Ordways (1965)

Proud Flesh (1973)

HUNEKER, James Gibbons (1860–1921) American art critic, novelist and story-writer. *Painted Veils*, on the New York art world, was regarded as daring in its day – but Huneker's two volumes of aesthetic short stories contain his best work.

Melomaniacs (stories, 1902)

Visionaries (stories, 1905)

Painted Veils (1902)

HUNTER, Alan (1922) English poet and detective story writer, who has written a long series featuring Superintendent Gently. Most of these are isolated country house murder mysteries, and they display the smooth charm of the best of that form.

Gently Does It (1955)

Gently Floating (1963)

HUNTER, Evan, see McBAIN, Ed

HURSTON, Zora Neale (1901–60) American novelist, storyteller, folklorist, anthropologist and teacher. She retold, with great skill, the tales of the Negroes; her novels treated of their lives with authority and understanding if not with imaginative genius.

Tell My Horse (1938)

Their Eyes Were Watching God (1937)

A Zora Neale Hurston Reader (stories etc, 1979)

HUTCHINSON, R. C. (1907–75) English novelist, who gained his first success with *Testament* (1938). Hutchinson was an excellent craftsman although he deprecatingly described himself as a "standard English bourgeois who has written a few books".

Shining Scabbard (1936)

Elephant & Castle (1949)

A Child Possessed (1964)

HUTH, Angela (1938) English novelist whose books articulate agonized shrieks for help beneath the unruffled comedy of upper-middle-class manners. Her themes and prose-style – crisply economic yet always exacerbatingly brusque – are better suited to short stories, as she demonstrates superbly in the collection cited below.

Nowhere Girl (1970)

Virginia Fly is Drowning (1972)

Monday Lunch in Fairyland (stories, 1978)

HUXLEY, Aldous (1894–1963) English novelist, poet, and miscellaneous writer. Huxley, grandson of the famous biologist T. H. Huxley, would have been a scientist, but eye disease caused him to switch to English while at Oxford. Huxley was a lively and influential writer, but it is generally felt that he failed to produce a great novel. In his early and successful society novels, such as *Chrome Yellow* (1921) ideas and the brittle and cynical tone, rather than characters, are important. He

Aldous Huxley

then moved to more serious fiction with *Point Counter Point*, in which Rampion is a portrait of D. H. Lawrence. Two more serious novels followed: *Brave New World*, a satire on the future which (although it owes a little too much to Zamyatin, whom Huxley refused to acknowledge) is his greatest fictional achievement; and *Eyeless in Gaza*. These are the representative "novels of ideas" of the period; they are successful, but in a Dickensian and satirical sense that Huxley wanted to avoid – he would have liked to build up a solid character, but was hardly able to do so. He was a gifted satirist, and his acceptance of Eastern ideas is an interesting one; but he lacked the capacity to convey emotion in fiction, although he was always energetic and his novels – even the later ones – are good reading.

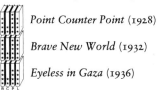

Point Counter Point (1928)

Brave New World (1932)

Eyeless in Gaza (1936)

I

IBUSE, Masuji (1898) Japanese novelist. Ibuse has written both historical and contemporary novels. Most effective of all is *No Consultation Today*, which gives a portrait of a whole town. He is something of a magic realist: his background is meticulously realistic, but his characters are presented in a fantastic or ironic light. The savage and ironic story "Black Rain" is very famous, the black rain of the title being atomic fallout. He is extremely popular in Japan and deserves greater atten-

tion in the west.

John Manjiro (1938, tr. 1940)

No Consultation Today (1949, tr. 1964)

Black Rain (stories, 1969)

ILES, Francis (1893–1970) English crime novelist and, under the name Anthony Berkeley, detective-story writer; he wrote no fiction after 1939. The Berkeley tales are light but extremely ingenious in the classical manner and feature an outrageous journalist sleuth, Roger Sheringham. But two of the three Iles novels are the author's best work. *Malice Aforethought* was the first significant book to turn the detective-story upside down, by starting with a bald announcement of who the murderer is and then tracing the course of the crime and its subsequent ironic detection. *Before the Fact* was a study of a murderer as seen by his victim-to-be. Both books are recounted in a tone of sharp, even vicious, social criticism, and the characters are realistic.

The Poisoned Chocolates Case (as Berkeley, 1929)

Malice Aforethought (1931)

Before the Fact (1932)

IMLAY, Gilbert (?1754–?1828) American novelist, adventurer – and father of one of Mary Shelley's mother's children. He was a revolutionary and a feminist whose epistolary novel in the style of Richardson, *The Emigrants,* has interesting passages and is not unskilfully put together. It reflects his perfervidly romantic view of the innocence of the "New World".

The Emigrants (1793)

INNES, Hammond (1913) English author of best selling adventure thrillers. His novels are about a man's fight not only with human enemies, but with hostile climates and landscapes, vividly described. He is a keen sailor and several books are set at sea; more recently, his interest in conservation made something of a work of propaganda out of *The Big Footprints*. He tightens suspense to an urgent pitch in narratives which are plausible and relentlessly frightening.

Campbell's Kingdom (1952)

The Mary Deare (1956)

The Big Footprints (1977)

INNES, Michael (1906) British detective story-writer, pseudonym of J. I. M. Stewart, novelist and English literature teacher at Oxford University. His first two crime stories *Death at the President's Lodging* (1936, in U.S. *Seven Sus-*

pects) and its successor *Hamlet, Revenge!*, were seen as a new departure, the highly literary, urbanely written dons' story, which has delighted many averagely literate readers. Innes' style has since grown more casual, but most volumes, following his hero, Scotland Yard detective John Appleby, into retirement with a knighthood, have their pleasures. From 1954 on (*Mark Lambert's Supper*) he has written mainstream novels under his own name. Especially to be noted are the five linked volumes, describing mid-twentieth century Oxford life, under the general title *A Staircase in Surrey*.

Hamlet, Revenge! (1937)

The New Sonia Wayward (1960)

The Gaudy (as Stewart) (1974)

IRISH, William, see WOOLRICH, Cornell

IRVING, John (1812–1906) American novelist, lawyer, businessman – and brother of Washington Irving. He wrote his novels under the name John Quod. *The Quod Correspondence*, about legal matters, is lively.

The Quod Correspondence (1842)

Indian Sketches (1888)

IRVING, John (1942) American novelist, highly acclaimed for the best selling *The World According to Garp*, a long, extremely readable, sometimes funny, sometimes gripping, tale of an eccentric Massachusetts family in the years since World War II. The book is reminiscent of the Spanish *tremendista* novel: something unbelievably awful happens from time to time. Part of its attraction is the unwillingness of the hero to give in to circumstance, and the immense energy he gives to maintaining his

John Irving

individuality in the face of contemporary middle-class American society, itself brilliantly depicted. Irving's three earlier novels display the same vitality, but are smaller in compass. *The 158 Pound Marriage* is a closely observed story of wife-and-husband swapping.

Setting Free the Bears (1969)

The 158 Pound Marriage (1974)

The World According to Garp (1978)

IRVING, Washington (1783–1859) American story-writer. Irving was a friend of, and was influenced by, Walter Scott. He was the first American to establish himself as a respected man of letters. His most famous tales, such as "Rip Van Winkle", are adaptations of German legends – he Americanized them well.

The Sketch Book (1820)

ISHERWOOD, Christopher (1904) English novelist, film scriptwriter and memoirist who has lived in America since 1939. As a novelist he has had three phases: two early novels rather in the manner of his friend E. M. Forster, then the episodic *Mr Norris Changes Trains* (1935) and *Goodbye to Berlin* (1939);

and finally, a series of more conventional novels in which he tries to come to terms with homosexuality. He is an extremely lucid and attractive prose writer, always readable even if – latterly – somewhat muddled and lacking in purpose. His two earliest novels are his best, but *Mr Norris* and *Goodbye to Berlin* are highly entertaining.

All the Conspirators (1928)

The Memorial (1932)

A Single Man (1964)

Christopher Isherwood

Washington Irving

JACKSON, Shirley (1919–65) American novelist. Shirley Jackson delighted in the incongruous, and produced several novels in which she caricatured such "ordinary" things as raising children, or, more sinister, fanatical religious beliefs and their consequences. She parodied Gothic in the manner of Charles Addams; but in *The Haunting of Hill House* produced a genuinely good ghost story.

The Bird's Nest (1954, as *Lizzie*, 1957)

The Sundial (1958)

The Haunting of Hill House (1959)

JACOB, Naomi (1884–1964) English novelist, the child of a German Jew. She became a

Catholic in 1914, but her Jewish roots are ever present in her writing which combines humour with a deep feeling for family. Her most popular stories were those which formed part of the Gollantz Saga.

 The Founder of the House (1935)

Gollantz and Partners (1958)

JACOBS, W. W. (1863–1943) English story-writer. Jacobs wrote tales of the sea, of village life, and of the supernatural ("The Monkey's Paw" being his most famous contribution). He was a quiet professional with a good sense of humour and a genuine understanding of his characters.

 Selected Short Stories (1959)

JACOBSEN, Jens Peter (1847–85) Danish novelist and story-writer. Jacobsen's fiction is morbidly concerned with death, with the lack of God, and with the disturbing supremacy of the self consequent upon atheism. Jacobsen was an exact psychologist, worthy of the writers whom he took as his models – notably Flaubert and Turgenev. His fiction (especially *Niels Lyhne*) only needs to be made available once again in translation for it to be widely read.

 Fru Marie Grubbe (1876, tr. 1914)

Niels Lyhne (1880, tr. 1919)

Mogens and Other Stories (1882, tr. 1921)

JACOBSON, Dan (1929) South African novelist and story-writer resident in England and America. His first novels were realistic in manner, and dealt with South African problems humorously and with compassionate understanding. Latterly he has turned to allegory, with rather less success.

 A Dance in the Sun (1956)

The Evidence of Love (1960)

The Wonder-Worker (1973)

JAFFE, Rona (1932) American novelist who first attracted notice with the *Best of Everything* (1958). Her sophisticated love stories tackle the woman's approach to sex and modern living with refreshing frankness.

 The Cherry in the Martini (1966)

The Fame Game (1969)

Class Reunion (1979)

JAMES, Henry (1843–1916) American novelist, playwright and story-writer who settled in

Henry James

Europe and then, in 1876, in England. He became a naturalized British citizen in 1914 on America's failure to declare war. As a psychological novelist (and an acute critic) whose chief aim is to illustrate and define morality – or immorality – in action, James has had a wide influence. Much of the difficulty of his later work is explained by his homosexuality, which did not become widely apparent until the publication of Leon Edel's massive biography. For James himself Europe was perilous, experienced and wicked, whereas America was innocent but thin. However, although his novels deal with Americans in Europe, they are not as simple as this. His first fully mature novel, *Portrait of a Lady*, is above all a study in character. The evil in the book is of a sexual nature, and by understatement James conveys it with extreme power. In *The Bostonians* (1886), a masterly story set in America itself, feminism is examined with great sympathy, but without sentimentality. The major novels of this period are unequivocally great; but there is controversy about the last novels, *The Wings of the Dove* (1902), *The Ambassadors* (1903) and *The Golden Bowl* (1904). The first is more straightforward than its two successors, which strike some as impenetrable and stylistically recondite ("an elephant picking up a pea", said H. G. Wells). Careful re-reading of these "different" novels seems to confirm that, although James was sometimes over fussy about the "right word", he had something new to say: a very complex moral judgement is at work, which exercises an increasing fascination and which moves towards stream of consciousness. James wrote some of the finest stories (such as "The Figure in the Carpet") in English and American literature.

 Portrait of a Lady (1881)

The Golden Bowl (1904)

Complete Tales (12 vols., 1962–65)

JAMES, M. R. (1862–1936) English story-writer. James is the author of some of the most frightening ghost stories in the language. Despite the blandness of his narrative, he did not seek only to entertain: he was actively interested, and highly successful, in demonstrating the forces of evil.

 Collected Ghost Stories (1931)

JAMES, P. D. (1920) English crime novelist. Beginning somewhat late in life, with *Cover Her Face* (1962) P. D. James has re-established the classic detective-story as a vehicle capable both of providing excellent entertainment and of making statements of great penetration and subtlety. She combines the complicated puzzle plot of the old whodunnit with the "round" characterization of figures based closely on real life. In her later work in particular she handles major themes most skilfully, none more so than death itself in *The Black Tower*.

 Shroud for a Nightingale (1971)

An Unsuitable Job for a Woman (1972)

The Black Tower (1975)

JARRELL, Randall (1914–65) American poet, critic and novelist. Primarily a poet and critic, Jarrell wrote one novel which is highly valued: *Pictures from an Institution*. It is both funny and very satirical of the "liberal" viewpoint.

 Pictures from an Institution (1954)

JEFFERIES, Richard (1848–87) English essayist, novelist and naturalist. He wrote unsuccessful novels of aristocratic life but is remembered for his two books about the boy Bevis in the Wiltshire countryside.

 Wood Magic (1881)

Bevis (1882)

JENSEN, Johannes Vilhelm (1873–1950) Danish poet, essayist and novelist, who won the Nobel Prize in 1944. His large-scale work has dated badly, as has his presentation of the theory that civilization spread from Scandinavia. But *The Long Journey*, although in six volumes, still attracts a small audience which likes to read of the development of baboons into men. *The Waving Rye* is quite different: slighter and much more pithy pieces on objects – a kind of Danish equivalent of Joyce's "epiphanies".

 The Fall of the King (1901, tr. 1933)

The Long Journey (1908–22, tr. 1922)

The Waving Rye (1906–44, sel. tr. 1958)

JEROME, Jerome K. (1859–1927) English novelist and dramatist, remembered for his humorous, largely facetious but none the less comic slang classic *Three Men in a Boat*. His other novels were less successful; but this one captures quite accurately a tiny aspect of an era – late-Victorian clerks having time-off fun.

 Idle Thoughts of an Idle Fellow (sketches, 1889)

 Three Men in a Boat (1889)

Three Men on the Bummel (1900)

JEWETT, Sarah Orne (1849–1909) American novelist and story-writer. The sketches of Maine seaport life in *The Country of the Pointed Firs* are universally admired as the cream of nineteenth-century regionalist fiction: influenced by Flaubert, they evoke the atmosphere and illuminate the characters. *A Country Doctor* concerns a New England girl rejecting marriage for a medical career. Jewett had an important influence on Willa Cather, who edited her collected stories.

 A Country Doctor (1884)

The Tory Lover (1901)

The Country of the Pointed Firs and Other Stories (sel. 1925, repr. 1955)

JHABVALA, Ruth Prawer (1927) English novelist and story-writer, born in Germany of Polish parents, and educated in England as a refugee; she married an Indian in 1951. She has said that her subject is India, and that her position – as a non-Indian living in India – is a "half-way" one. Her Indian backgrounds are always meticulous; but her real strength lies in her ability to portray female psychology – and the less attractive side of masculinity. Her portrait of the India-hating, degenerate Esmond in *Esmond in India* is unforgettable. She is a very accomplished novelist who deserves to be read more widely.

 Esmond in India (1957)

Get Ready for Battle (1962)

Heat and Dust (1975)

JOHNS, Capt. W. E. (1893–1968) English writer of boys' adventure stories. His main character, Biggles, was a World War I fighter pilot: the stories are enlivened by a good personal knowledge of airmanship.

 Biggles, Secret Agent (1940)

Biggles Sweeps the Desert (1942)

Biggles Breaks the Silence (1949)

JOHNSON, B. S. (1933–73) English poet, novelist and story-writer, who slashed his wrists when he felt that his powers had failed. His novels were very self-consciously experimental, although it is now clear that his slight gift was for conventional realism.

 Travelling People (1963)

Trawl (1966)

See the Old Lady Decently (1975)

JOHNSON, Uwe (1934) German novelist. The tensions in his fiction originally arose because he lived in East Germany: he believed in the professed aims of the government, but not at all in the government itself. He challenged "socialist realism" with his first novel, *Speculations About Jacob*, written while he was still in East Germany. He is most concerned with problems of identity, and with relativity of outlook, as his second novel *The Third Book About Achim* – on a West German's attempt to write about an East German racing cyclist – demonstrates. He came to West Germany in 1959.

 Speculations About Jacob (1959, tr. 1963)

 The Third Book About Achim (1961, tr. 1966)

 Two Views (1965, tr. 1967)

JOHNSTON, Jennifer (1930) Irish novelist, born in Dublin. Her first novel was *The Captains and the Kings* (1972) and with each successive novel she has grown in stature. There is a haunting lyrical beauty about her prose which reflects much of the troubled state of Ireland today.

 How Many Miles to Babylon (1974)

The Gates (1973)

Shadows on our Skins (1977)

JÓKAI, Mór (1825–1904) Hungarian novelist whose novels were once very popular in translation. He wrote more than 100 books. He had a vivid, romantic imagination, and his novels – most of them historical – vary from light romance to high melodrama. Jókai had a fine grasp of the situation of his country, and treated all of its problems with great intelligence and insight.

 The Day of Wrath (1850, tr. 1900)

Black Diamonds (1870, tr. 1896)

Dr Dumanany's Wife (1891, tr. 1891)

JONES, Jack (1884–1970) Welsh novelist and playwright. Loss of his job as a miner persuaded Jones to try his luck as a novelist, telling stories of the Welsh valleys. His first book *Rhondda Roundabout* (1934) was a success and was followed by others like *Off to Philadelphia in the Morning*.

 Off to Philadelphia in the Morning (1947)

JONES, James (1921–77) American novelist. Jones, from Illinois, won immediate recognition with *From Here to Eternity*. After that he had a wide readership, but was reviled by the critics. His inspiration was Thomas Wolfe, although he is not as powerful as Wolfe. But he has Wolfe's faults: he runs to inordinate length, has no sense of form, and lacks clarity of intellect. But, like Wolfe, he is swept along by fierce passion and curiosity. *From Here to Eternity* is a moving book. His later novels are fascinating failures.

 From Here to Eternity (1951)

Go to the Widow-Maker (1967)

The Merry Month of May (1971)

JONES, LeRoi (1934) American novelist, story-writer, playwright and editor, best known as a Black activist. In 1965 Jones changed his name to Imamu Amiri Baraka, by which he is seldom known. Jones has written one novel, *The System of Dante's Hell*. The subject of this formless semi-autobiographical work is not Dante, but "death-in-life": God is a white man. Jones is more effective as a furious activist and playwright.

 The System of Dante's Hell (1965)

Tales (1967)

JONG, Erica (1942) American poet and novelist noted for her *Fear of Flying*, "the adventures and misadventures of Isadora, the heroine, on her unceasing quest for the Holy Grail of zipless erotic dalliance" to quote the paperback blurb. It is, despite its raunchy reputation, an unintentionally sobering reminder that many people prefer talking or writing about sex to the act itself. Her numerous descriptions of sexual congress itself are muted, uncertain and perfunctory. Isadora's odyssey continues in *How to Save Your Own Life*, a tired sequel.

 Fear of Flying (1974)

How to Save Your Own Life (1978)

JOYCE, James (1882–1941) Irish novelist, story-writer and poet. Early disillusioned with Ireland, Joyce lived for the greater part of his life abroad: in Austria, Switzerland and finally Paris. He spent his life re-creating the Dublin of his youth in a spirit of love-hate. His earliest influences were Ibsen, naturalism,

James Joyce

on his notion of "epiphanies", by which he meant sudden intuitive revelations, insights, set off by apparently trivial or even ridiculous incidents. He was a pioneer of stream of consciousness methods – the soliloquy of Molly Bloom at the end of *Ulysses* is the most famous in all literature. Joyce began with the stories of *Dubliners* (1914), which vary between an exact and highly selective realism, and complex symbolism (eg "The Dead"). *Portrait of the Artist as a Young Man* (1916), concentrating on a man, Stephen, very like Joyce but not him, eventually turned into the epic *Ulysses*, which is one of the first great mythopoeic novels of the century – the progress of the mundane anti-hero Bloom is made to parallel that of Ulysses' wanderings. Readers at first found *Ulysses* hard going; but it is now realized that Joyce's achievement here is to take the life of a very ordinary kind of man, and give it significance. *Finnegan's Wake*, which followed, requires a lifetime's devotion. It is deliberately incoherent, consists of neologisms, puns and learned allusions; and attempts to provide a universal work, a commentary on everything; but its audience is necessarily too restricted. Joyce is unique, and all imitations of him have failed. Most influential has been his theory of epiphanies – of which, it could be argued, all fiction should consist.

Dubliners (stories, 1914)

Ulysses (1922)

Finnegan's Wake (1939)

JUDD, Cyril, see KORNBLUTH, Cyril M.

JÜNGER, Ernst (1895) German novelist and writer. Jünger propounded an aristocratic type of totalitarianism in the early 1930s, and was much praised by the Nazis. But he criticized them, or seemed to do so, in his allegorical *On the Marble Cliffs*, a strange and compelling – but according to many critics repugnant and still totalitarian – fable. *The Glass Bees* is an even more ambitious allegory.

On the Marble Cliffs (1939, tr. 1947)

The Glass Bees (1957, tr. 1961)

K

KAFKA, Franz (1883–1924) Czech-Jewish novelist, story-writer and diarist, writing in German. Kafka, son of a vulgar and dominating merchant, published a few of his stories in his lifetime – and won a prize – but was not very

Franz Kafka

well known until after his premature death from consumption, when his friend Max Brod published all his surviving works – despite his instructions that they should be burned. Posterity has approved Brod's decision. By the end of World War II he was established as one of the century's greatest writers – probably the greatest. Critics have incessantly argued about what his work means, but all – including his detractors – have felt its power. Kafka has been called surrealist, allegorist, symbolist and a number of other "-ists" – but he is none of these: he is entirely original. His writing, which is strangely lucid and serene, is not pessimistic or nihilist; it is rather heroic, because he tackles the major problem of the twentieth century: what is the meaning of existence? Kafka manages to record the consequences arising from the asking of this question (he cannot answer it) without making himself pretentious. Far from being the most recondite writer of the century he is, at a profound level, the most realistic, for his characters progress – or fail to progress – precisely because they are beset by religious uncertainty. Kafka's world was for long taken not to be at all like the "real" world; but with proliferating bureaucracy, computers, tyranny and the lies of politicians and civil servants, the worlds of *The Trial* and *The Castle* come to seem increasingly real. In his two great novels (*America*, 1927, tr. 1938 is less important), Kafka's heroes, each labelled only by the initial K, find themselves in agonized confrontation with an unpredictable and menacing world; this world is certainly not "good" – but it demonstrates to them (or us) their insufficiency, the grand idiocy of their conventions and assumptions. Kafka appeals to the general and "untrained" reader because his work rings a bell in "ordinary" non-literary experience. This applies to the stories – such as

the realism of such as Flaubert, the Roman Catholic Church (which he loathed, but could never quite repudiate) and the atmosphere and character of Ireland. His whole theory of fiction – even in *Finnegan's Wake* – is based

Metamorphosis – as much as to the novels. Kafka is at heart an anti-materialist, caught up in the paradox that the world is a place of such beauty as to be symbolic of salvation, yet not (apparently) "for" man. As the century advances he becomes increasingly important.

The Trial (1925, tr. 1955, tr. 1977)

The Castle (1926, tr. 1953)

Metamorphosis (stories, tr. 1961)

KANTOR, MacKinlay (1904) American popular novelist of high competence. Most of his work, which is well documented although sentimental, is historical; *Diversey* is a good gangster novel.

Diversey (1928)

The Noise of Their Wings (1938)

Valley Forge (1975)

KATEYEV, Valentin (1897) Russian novelist and dramatist. The work he did before Stalin's crack-down on cultural freedom in the late 1920s is his best: he was able to poke discreet fun at Soviet earnestness. *The Embezzlers* is one of the classic crook comedies.

The Embezzlers (1926, tr. 1929)

Forward, Oh Time (1932, tr. 1933)

The Holy Well (1963, tr. 1967)

KAUFFMANN, Stanley (1916) American novelist, dramatist and dramatic critic. Kauffman wrote some highly competent psychological novels about artists; he made history with *The Philanderer*, when an attempt to ban it failed in the British courts.

The King of Proxy Street (1941)

The Philanderer (1954)

Man of the World (1956)

KAVAN, Anna (1901–1968) English novelist, best known for short stories written about, and under the influence of, amphetamines and cocaine. Kafka's writings helped Miss Kavan articulate her nightmares, notably in the short pieces collected under the titles listed below. Her novels are less satisfactory, but she is a gifted and disturbing writer.

Asylum Piece (1940)

Julia and the Bazooka (1975)

KAVERIN, Venyamin (1902) Russian novelist. He was a member of the Serapion Brothers, from which group most of the best Russian writing of the period came. Kaverin is best when dealing with criminal psychology. All his novels are readable and excellently constructed – and they all contain as much criticism of the Russian environment as is possible for him.

The Larger View (1935, tr. 1938)

Two Captains (1940, tr. 1942)

An Open Book (1945, tr. 1955)

KAWABATA, Yasunari (1899–1972) Japanese novelist and story-writer. He won the Nobel Prize in 1968. His atmospheric novels explore the world of decadent and perverted sexuality, with great sensitivity and psychological insight.

Snow Country (1935–47, tr. 1956)

A Thousand Cranes (1947, tr. 1959)

House of the Sleeping Beauty and Other Stories (1969)

KAYE, M. M. (?1908) English novelist, who has a profound knowledge of India and its colourful history. She is the author of several children's books and romantic thrillers, but is at her best writing about India; *The Far Pavilions* is her first best seller.

Shadow of the Moon (1957, rev. 1979)

Trade Winds (1963)

The Far Pavilions (1978)

KAZAN, Elia (1909) American novelist. Kazan turned to writing in his fifties after a successful career as actor, and stage and film director. He specializes in realistic pictures of the rich Hollywood world, as in *The Arrangement*, which was later made into a successful film. Other novels have looked back to his Turkish roots.

The Arrangement (1974)

KAZANTZAKIS, Nikos (1883–1957) Greek poet, dramatist, politician and novelist. His novels (of which *Zorba the Greek*, a famous film, is the best) are rhetorical, rather picaresque, and of immense energy. As a depictor of passionate men, and of the passions in general, he is quite exceptional.

Zorba the Greek (1946, tr. 1952)

Christ Recrucified (1954, tr. 1954)

God's Pauper – St Francis of Assisi (1956, tr. 1962)

KEATING, H. R. F. (1926) English detective story-writer. His early crime novels – the first, *Death and the Visiting Firemen*, appeared in 1959 – were idiosyncratic, even highbrow, in style. To reach a wider market, he invented Inspector Ghote of the Bombay CID, a nervously insecure but persistent and honest detective. Keating had never been to India at the time, but the character and background rang true. This book, *The Perfect Murder*, was a success, and most of his novels since have featured Inspector Ghote. Keating has written three non-crime novels, all highly praised; the most recent is *A Long Walk to Wimbledon* (1978). He has also been crime fiction reviewer for *The Times* since 1967. He is a literate, intelligent and entertaining performer in this field.

Death and the Visiting Firemen (1959)

The Perfect Murder (1964)

Inspector Ghote Caught in Meshes (1967)

KEE, Robert (1919) British historian, journalist and novelist. After two novels based on his prisoner-of-war experiences, Kee wrote *A Sign of the Times*, an ambitious satirical thriller set ten years ahead which brilliantly forecast many trends that emerged in the 1960s.

The Impossible Shore (1949)

A Sign of the Times (1955)

Broadstrop in Season (1959)

KELLER, Gottfried (1819–90) Swiss novelist and story-writer. Keller wrote some fine stories and two novels. The more important of these is *Green Henry,* a major *Bildungsroman* of great charm and insight, in which the author sets up a fruitful tension between duty and the desire to "be oneself".

Green Henry (1854, rev. 1880, tr. 1960)

Martin Salander (1886, tr. 1965)

Keller: A Selection of his Tales (1891)

KELLOW, Kathleen, see PLAIDY, Jean

KELLY, Mary (1927) English crime novelist. She has published only six books since 1961, but the earlier ones were distinguished by her use of backgrounds depicting various modern industries. Her characters are psychologically credible, and her stories are absorbing.

The Spoilt Kill (1961)

Dead Corse (1966)

The Twenty-fifth Hour (1971)

KEMELMAN, Harry (1908) American writer

of mystery stories, whose detective is a quietly thoughtful Boston rabbi. The stories are infused with Jewish culture and tradition, and the reader gets to know the rabbi's family and congregation.

 Friday the Rabbi Slept Late (1964)

Saturday the Rabbi Went Hungry (1966)

KENEALLY, Thomas (1935) Australian novelist and dramatist, who studied for the Roman Catholic priesthood before coming a writer. He is foremost among Australian novelists who are trying to break away from the immense influence of Patrick White. He is a very deft, professional – and yet fashionable – writer, and has been accused of lacking heart. His most finished novel is *Three Cheers for the Paraclete. A Dutiful Daughter* is his attempt at a mythopoeic epic; it impressed some, but left other critics cold, with its genteel treatment of the horrible.

 Three Cheers for the Paraclete (1968)

A Dutiful Daughter (1971)

Passenger (1979)

KENT, Alexander, see REEMAN, Douglas

KEROUAC, Jack (1922–69) American novelist, dramatist and "Beat" personality who died of drink. His first novel was a conscientiously bad pastiche of Thomas Wolfe (*The Town and the City* by "John" Kerouac, 1950). Then he and other personalities (including William Burroughs) created the legend of the Beat Generation. The facts are very different from the "documentary" fiction which we have so far

Jack Kerouac

been given: to a large extent Kerouac is a product of the shrewd business brain of the kindly Allen Ginsberg, otherwise a blurred visionary poet. Kerouac's sprawling *On the Road* influenced a generation: it preached a "spontaneous" life, indulgence in drugs, drink and whatever else you feel like. It has the sick freshness of a youthful candidate for an early death – and its historical importance is undoubted. From then on Kerouac's energies declined, and he became sentimental and vague; his later books tend to undermine the authentic message of *On the Road.*

 On the Road (1957)

Doctor Sax (1959)

Pic (1971)

KESEY, Ken (1935) American novelist and publisher (of *Spit in the Ocean* magazine). Since 1966 Kesey has been turning life into a comic novel in what an enthusiast has called his "messianic LSD scene"; this has made him unpopular with the authorities, who at one point imprisoned him. Before that he wrote two novels, the first of which, *One Flew Over the Cuckoo's Nest,* was very successfully filmed. Kesey had worked in a lunatic asylum, and he wrote this novel from that experience. It is a sharp satire on the mechanized nature of modern life. Kesey's other novel is, surprisingly, more conventional, but less successful.

 One Flew Over the Cuckoo's Nest (1962)

Sometime a Great Notion (1964)

KEYES, Daniel (1927) American writer, author of the classic *Flowers for Algernon,* expanded from one of the best science fiction stories of the post-war era.

 Flowers for Algernon (1966)

The Touch (1968)

KEYES, Frances Parkinson (1885–1970) American novelist. She was the wife of a Senator, and her novels present a rich kaleidoscope of the contemporary American scene. Her plots are usually intricate and ingenious, and her characters are strongly-drawn and colourful.

 Dinner at Antoine's (1949)

Joy Street (1951)

The Royal Box (1954)

KING, Francis (1923) English novelist and story-writer. King, who has been much influenced by Japanese fiction, is suggestive rather than direct. He explores the worlds of the unconscious deviant or the bi-sexual with

elegance and sensitivity. His most successful novel has been *The Custom House*; and he writes very accomplished stories.

 The Custom House (1961)

The Brighton Belle and Other Stories (1968)

 The Needle (1975)

KING, Stephen (1941) American novelist and writer of ghost stories. Several of his novels have been made into major films, notably *Carrie,* about a young girl with psychokinetic powers. He is skilful and readable, although not of the first rank as a psychologist. *Night Shift* (1978) collects his stories, some feeble but others classic in their genre – notably "Quitters Inc.", about a Mafia organization which forces people to give up smoking.

 Carrie (1973)

'Salem's Lot (1975)

The Dead Zone (1979)

KINGSLEY, Charles (1819–75) English parson who wrote novels, poetry and topical works. Kingsley, who suffered from depression, advocated a false optimism (verging on "muscular Christianity") which flaws all his works; some of these are, however, of great energy. The best are *Alton Locke,* whose tailor-poet hero manages – despite his unconvincing conversion to Christianity – to live, and the strange *The Water Babies,* which does (despite denials) survive as a children's book – as its sales show.

 Alton Locke (1850)

Westward Ho! (1855)

The Water Babies (1863)

KIPLING, Rudyard (1865–1936) English story-writer, novelist, poet and imperialist. Kipling was an enormously popular writer. His reputation at the time he received the Nobel Prize in 1907, was at its height; at his death it was at its lowest. Kipling was consciously an imperialist; but critics since his death have seen that his work is interesting because under the imperialism lies a strong undercurrent of doubt, a series of symbols of uncertainty, an *hysterico passio* fear. He had a near-feline insight into human nature, and his artistic conscience would not allow him to get away with falsity. His poetry is a genuine mixture of genius and trash; but the best of his stories are magnificent, especially the allusive and difficult ones (and difficult in a non-literary way) of his last years. *Kim* (1901), an adventure story, is pure fantasy – but it exactly captures the flavour of the childish imagination. Kipling is one of the few major writers who made a virtue out of being

Rudyard Kipling

Arthur Koestler

child*ish* rather than child*like*. His one novel, *The Light That Failed*, is an ugly failure, and points up his one serious defect – his hatred of women. But both in the "children's tales" of *Puck of Pook's Hill* (1906) and *Rewards and Fairies* (1910) and in the later stories, he makes up for this by showing things as he really saw them.

The Light that Failed (1890)

The Jungle Book (1894)

Limits and Renewals (stories, 1932)

KITCHIN, C. H. B. (1895–1967) English barrister, stockbroker and novelist. Kitchin's early works were wild, witty, avant-garde pyrotechnics, in marked contrast to his later books which are technically more conservative, but beautifully shaped and plotted. His best known is *Death of My Aunt*, one of four detective stories narrated by a stockbroker sleuth.

Death of My Aunt (1929)

The Auction Sale (1949)

The Secret River (1956)

KLEIST, Heinrich von (1777–1811) German dramatist and story-writer. Kleist was a manic-depressive who eventually killed himself, a violent romantic who believed that everything was illusion. His eight stories may well be better than his drama, for in them he retains absolute and somewhat aristocratic control over very "wild" material.

The Marquis of O. and Other Stories (tr. 1963)

KNIGHT, Damon (1922) American science

fiction writer, who wrote some fine short stories. His novels are disappointing by comparison.

Hell's Pavement (1955)

A for Anything (1961)

KNOWLES, John (1926) American novelist and story-writer. His brilliant first novel, *A Separate Peace*, is about two senior boys in a very exclusive private school. This has the status of a modern classic, and is in its fortieth printing (1979). Knowles' main concern is self-discovery through wildness in the midst of at least apparently civilized environments of various kinds; but he is ironic about the pretensions of all institutions. The excellence of his first book has been hard to emulate.

A Separate Peace (1959)

Spreading Fires (1974)

KOESTLER, Arthur (1905) Hungarian novelist, journalist and writer on science and religion, resident in England. Koestler wrote first in German; but *Arrival and Departure* (1943) and his subsequent novels are in English. His theme may be summed up in the form of a question: What is the nature of ethical imperatives? He left the communist party in 1938, and, remarkably, did not "go right"; instead he became the soundest guide to the human consequences of communist theory – for which he retained some sympathy – in Europe. All his fiction is of high quality, but *Darkness at Noon*, an account of the trial and murder of a communist (he was suggested by Bukharin) under Stalin, during the purges, is outstanding. This major novel entirely lives up to its tragic theme, and has true Dostoyevskian power.

Other novels include *The Gladiators*, a vivid and critical look at the revolution of Spartacus. *The Call-Girls* is a satire on symposia and "experts".

The Gladiators (1939)

Darkness at Noon (1940)

The Call-Girls (1972)

KOPS, Bernard (1929) English playwright and novelist most of whose work is characterized by his portrayal of London Jewish family life and its problems of adolescence.

The Dissent of Dominick Shapiro (1966)

By the Waters of Whitechapel (1969)

On Margate Sands (1978)

KORNBLUTH, Cyril M. (1923–58) American science fiction writer. Most of his novels were written in collaboration with Judith Merril (as Cyril Judd) or with Frederik Pohl. His short stories are exceptionally fine, but his solo novels are trivial.

The Space Merchants (with Pohl, 1953)

The Syndic (1953)

KOSINSKY, Jerzy (1933) Novelist and psychologist, who has called his escape from Russia to America in 1957 the greatest creative act of his life. Kosinsky has a precocious style which some critics find unsuited to his moral and political seriousness. His first and best novel, *The Painted Bird*, describes in grotesque detail the backwardness of East European peasant life during World War II. *Blind Date*, a bloodthirsty intellectual thriller, demonstrates his dislike of America.

 The Painted Bird (1966)

 Blind Date (1977)

KRIGE, Uys (1910) South African story-writer, dramatist, poet and editor. Krige is a liberal who writes in English and Afrikaans. He has an extensive knowledge of European culture; and his tense stories deal mainly with South African political realities. But his psychological power and literary skill are far beyond those of a merely political writer. He is among the most cosmopolitan and gifted of living South African writers.

 The Dream and the Desert (1953)

 Orphan of the Desert (1967)

KUTTNER, Henry (1914–58) American science fiction writer whose work was in short story form. He used many pseudonyms, the most famous of which is Lewis Padgett. His range extended over most of the themes covered by the magazine market of the 1950s from fantasy to humour.

 Well of the Worlds (as Lewis Padgett, 1952)

 The Best of Kuttner (stories, 2 vols, 1965–66)

KYLE, Duncan (1930) English writer of adventure stories, a master of sustained suspense. *Flight into Fear*, set in an aeroplane, *In Deep*, an arctic adventure, and *A Raft of Swords*, an underwater counter-espionage story, are all excellent.

 Flight into Fear (1972)

A Raft of Swords (1974, in U.S. as *The Suvarov Adventure*, 1973)

In Deep (1976, in U.S. as *Whiteout!*, 1977)

L

LA BRUYÈRE, Jean de (1645–96) French author of *The Characters*, accurate portraits of various go-getters or fools in classically condensed, fast-moving prose.

 The Characters (1688, tr. 1963)

LACLOS, P.-A.-F. Choderlos de (1741–1803)

Marie, Comtesse de la Fayette

French novelist and general. He is remembered for *Les Liaisons dangereuses*, a satirical novel in epistolary form whose heroine takes vengeance on her own restrictive aristocratic society by seeking the widest sensual experiences for herself and the corruption of others.

 Les Liaisons dangereuses (1782, tr. 1961)

LA FARGE, Oliver (1901–63) American novelist who wrote about Indians. His understanding of Indian culture was not "complete", as one incautious critic put it, but it was formidable; and his novels are competent and readable.

 Laughing Boy (1929)

All the Young Men (1935)

Behind the Mountains (1956)

LA FAYETTE, Marie, Comtesse de (1634–93) French novelist. Madame de la Fayette wrote the first real novel in the French language; *The Princess of Clèves* retains its moral force and its power. It is necessary to read the 1950 translation by Nancy Mitford in its revised form, as she "improved" the work though she did not know enough French to translate it properly. The 1925 version is preferable.

 The Princess of Clèves (1678, tr. 1925, adapted 1950, rev. 1972)

LAFFERTY, R. A. (1914) American science fiction writer, noted for the bizarre surrealism of his novels and short stories. He won a Hugo award in 1973 for "Eurema's Dam". He is a Catholic and has a strong interest in mysticism – St Thomas More is the hero of his novel *Past Master*, resurrected to pass judgment on a failed Utopia and to ponder the problem of man's spiritual progress. He is sometimes a very funny writer, as in his futuristic re-casting of the Odyssey, *Space Chantey* (1968), and even when he is at his most serious his prose sparkles with wit. He is one of the finest practitioners of surrealism currently working in the English language.

 Past Master (1968)

Fourth Mansions (1969)

Apocalypses (1977)

LAGERKVIST, Pär (1891–1974) Swedish novelist, poet and dramatist. Lagerkvist won the Nobel Prize in 1951. A self-styled "religious atheist", he was a writer of some power – which he tended to undermine by his ponderous but not very coherent philosophy. He was best at depicting small-town life.

Guest of Reality (1925, tr. 1936)

The Dwarf (1944, tr. 1953)

Barabbas (1950, tr. 1952)

LAGERLÖF, Selma (1858–1940) Swedish novelist and story-writer who won the Nobel Prize in 1909. She became famous with *Jerusalem*, a fanciful epic novel about peasants who went to Jerusalem to try to live like the early Christians. Her *Adventures of Nils* and its sequel, about a boy who can fly, were worldwide best sellers.

Jerusalem (1901–02, tr. 1915)

The Wonderful Adventures of Nils (1907, tr. 1911)

Further Adventures of Nils (1911, tr. 1911)

LAMMING, George (1927) West Indian novelist from Barbados. His first novel *In the Castle of My Skin* describes the village of his birth; later work is more ambitiously allegorical, but highly effective. Like Wilson Harris, he has tried to employ mythology to express the predicament of the West Indian. *The Emigrants* (1954) is semi-autobiographical and deals with the reasons for migration from the West Indies.

In the Castle of My Skin (1953)

Water With Berries (1971)

Natives of My Person (1972)

L'AMOUR, Louis (1908) American self-educated writer of Westerns. L'Amour has been hugely prolific, and his dozens of books have been translated into numerous languages. Writing as Tex Burns, he produced several novels featuring Hopalong Cassidy.

Hondo (1953)

How the West was Won (1962)

LAMPEDUSA, Guiseppe Tomasi di (1896–1957) Italian (Sicilian) Prince whose important novel *The Leopard* was not published until after his death. Written in the last year of Lampedusa's life, *The Leopard* is a violent but nostalgic saga of Sicily from 1860 until the end of the century. It is a late romantic novel which combines melodrama with subtle characterization – a powerful mixture. It was very success-

fully filmed.

The Leopard (1958, tr. 1960)

Two Stories and a Memory (1961, tr. 1962)

LARDNER, Ring (1885–1933) American story-writer and sports journalist. Lardner won a huge popular audience with his cruel sketches, but has had to wait a long time for recognition by critics. He writes with great sadness but deadly accuracy of human stupidity and greed; some prefer him to Ernest Hemingway. He died young through drink and tuberculosis.

You Know Me, Al (1916)

The Love Nest and Other Stories (1926)

Collected Short Stories (1941)

LARKIN, Philip (1922) English poet and novelist. Larkin is primarily a poet; but he has written two novels which have been praised – and reprinted.

Jill (1946)

A Girl in Winter (1947)

LARNER, Jeremy (1937) American novelist whose *Drive, He Said* became a successful movie (he wrote the screenplay with Jack Nicholson). He deals in a black-humoured manner with such themes as the hideousness of society and LSD. His novels are intelligent but somewhat wildly structured and inchoate.

Drive, He Said (1964)

The Answer (1968)

LATHEN, Emma Pseudonym of an American two-woman team comprising Mary J. Latsis, an attorney, and Martha Hennissart, an economic analyst. Most of the books concern murders with complex financial motives; the mysteries are resolved by John Putnam Thatcher, senior vice-president of the Sloan Guaranty Trust. Carefully drawn characters and technical, but intriguing, accounts of financial dealing have made the books immensely successful. *The Times* wrote of Lathen: "She is a sort of Jane Austen of the detective novel, crisp, detached, mocking, economical."

Banking on Death (1961)

Accounting for Murder (1964)

LATIMER, Jonathan (1906) American mystery novelist and screenwriter. Latimer's pre-war detective stories are strongly influenced by Dashiell Hammett, but contain an individual vein of cynical, sometimes bawdy, humour. He used the pseudonym Peter Coffin

for his best book, *The Search for My Great Uncle's Head*.

The Search for My Great Uncle's Head (as Coffin, 1937)

Sinners and Shrouds (1955)

LAURENCE, Margaret (1926) Canadian-born novelist, who has lived in Somaliland and Ghana. She writes with sympathy and understanding about West Africa.

This Side Jordan (1960)

The Stone Angel (1964)

A Jest of God (1966)

LAUTRÉAMONT, "Comte de" (1846–70) French prose-poet, whose real name was Isidore Ducasse. *Maldoror* consists of proto-surrealist, Byronic, decadent prose poetry which was quite original for its time, but is now markedly dated; Lautréamont was an interesting phenomenon who was taken up by the surrealists.

Maldoror (1868, tr. 1944)

LAWRENCE, D. H. (1885–1930) English novelist, story-writer, poet, dramatist and critic. Lawrence, the son of a Nottinghamshire miner, has had a profound influence on modern fiction in England and America. His doctrines should not be confused with his art, although they are intimately connected. His philosophy in its original essence is simple and wholesome: he loathed industrial society, and he believed that sex between men and women was spoiled by being intellectualized, thought about and analyzed ("sex in the head"). Lawrence was not a good thinker, and to the extent that his elaboration of these doctrines – his increasingly neurotic concern with them – interfere with his art, he is a failure: his ideas became more and more confused, and he lacked self-criticism. Yet his art springs from his celebration of human instinct, and when he is studying human behaviour in the light of his intuition he is an exquisite and beautiful writer. Much of the detail in his novels is finely observed (although his style is not outstanding, being rather self-consciously literary, or simply clumsy), but as he developed in the novel he tended to impose ideological structures that undermine the intentions of his heart – which was always, as should be obvious to any reader, "in the right place". This is less often the case in the short story, in which he excels. His first important novel *Sons and Lovers* is a memorable and, for him, detached record of the strains of youth, and contains one of the most acute analyses of a working-class environment ever made. Later novels are more mixed, although when Lawrence is describing the inner workings of personality he is supreme. In *Lady Chatterley's*

D. H. Lawrence

John Le Carré

Lover (final version 1928, repr. 1960) he is excellent on the working class background but misguided in his attempt to purge certain four-letter words of the obscenity they have acquired. In *The Plumed Serpent* (1926), in which his "head" intruded too much, there is more than a touch of spiritual fascism (though he was by then a sick man). In the short – or sometimes long – story Lawrence's touch was more sure, and stories such as "The Prussian Officer" are nearly faultless. In so far as he retained contact with his instincts, he is a great writer.

Sons and Lovers (1913)

Kangaroo (1923)

Complete Short Stories (1955)

LAXNESS, Halldór (1902) Icelandic novelist and dramatist, who won the Nobel Prize in 1955. Laxness was a Roman Catholic, and then a communist. His novels are constructed on a large scale, and are very thoughgoing and intelligent. His communism is less apparent than his lyricism and his feeling for his heroes, who are simple people struggling against hostile conditions.

Salka Valka (1931-2, tr. 1963)

The Atom Station (1948, tr. 1961)

Paradise Reclaimed (1960, tr. 1962)

LAYE, Camara (1928) Francophone Upper Guinea writer, who now lives and works in Senegal. Laye's first two novels made a strong impression, although he was criticized for his

apolitical attitude. *The Dark Child* is about the Malinke civilization in which he grew up: the second, *The Radiance of the King*, is a Kafkaian allegory, in the picaresque tradition, about a man in search of God. It is impressive but its style is ponderous and self-conscious.

The Dark Child (1953, tr. 1954)

The Radiance of the King (1954, tr. 1956)

Dramouss (1966, tr. 1968)

LEACOCK, Stephen (1869–1944) Canadian humourist still immensely popular for his essays and sketches in the tradition of Mark Twain. His nonsense, puns, epigrams and absurdities of style were often directed to the criticism of sham and pretention, although much of his work is purely comic.

Literary Lapses (1910)

Sunshine Sketches of a Little Town (1912)

LEAR, Peter, see LOVESEY, Peter

LEASOR, James (1923) English writer of spy and historical thrillers. He was a foreign correspondent based in the Far East, the background to some of the action novels which involve "Dr Love". A series of historical adventures are set in nineteenth-century China. His enthusiasm for vintage cars plays a prominent part in his fiction.

Passport to Oblivion (1964)

Follow the Drum (1972)

Mandarin Gold (1973)

LE CARRÉ, John (1931) British novelist, formerly diplomat and schoolmaster David Cornwell. With Len Deighton, Le Carré was responsible for removing the spy story from the glossy world of James Bond. He did this with a single tremendous success, *The Spy Who Came in from the Cold*. With its atmosphere of sad and necessary betrayals, its downbeat tone and its squalor, *The Spy* brought back true feeling to espionage writing. Yet its immediate successors failed to improve upon it, and it was only after he had written a conventional novel, *The Naive and Sentimental Lover*, a romantic fantasy which has its fervid admirers as well as its detractors, that he found his form in espionage fiction with two large and linked books dealing with the whole of the British spy machine after a Philby-like betrayal, *Tinker, Tailor, Soldier, Spy* (1974) and *The Honourable Schoolboy*. This latter has a vision and sweep that have hardly been attempted in the genre before. It sets out the appalling dilemma which all espionage poses:

must evil be fought with evil, is it possible to defend human values without using inhuman methods? And it adds: if truth is a real value, how is it possible to defend it by seeing lies and conspiracy everywhere, a quality vital in the good spy-master? In these books Le Carré succeeded in adding considerable doses of the purely intuitive to the rigorously logical world of espionage, as in the memorable opening section of *Tinker, Tailor*, set in a boys boarding school and seen from the point of view of ten and twelve-year-olds.

The Spy Who Came in from the Cold (1963)

The Naive and Sentimental Lover (1971)

The Honourable Schoolboy (1977)

LEDUC, Violette (1907–72) French novelist. Although praised and aided by such writers as Genet and Sartre, she remained unknown until the sudden and controversial popularity of her autobiographical novel, *The Bastard*, in 1964, which explores the loneliness and oppression of women's experience. She has been much criticized for outspoken sexuality and lesbian themes.

The Bastard (1964, tr. 1965)

LEE, Harper (1926) American novelist from Alabama, whose first novel *To Kill a Mockingbird* won a Pulitzer Prize. A slow writer, she has not yet come up with the promised second novel. *To Kill a Mockingbird* is an account of a small Alabama town through the eyes of an eight-year-old girl; her father is a lawyer who defends a black wrongly accused of rape.

The ending is melodramatic; but the earlier part of the novel is a remarkable achievement. It was made into a successful film, and is one of the best selling novels of all time.

 To Kill a Mockingbird (1960)

LEE, William, see BURROUGHS, William

LE FANU, Sheridan (1814–73) Irish novelist and poet whose *Uncle Silas* links the Gothic horror story to modern detective fiction, and is one of the first novels to include a "sealed-room" murder. *In a Glass Darkly*, a collection of "cases" recounted by a Swedenborgian, Dr Martin Hesselius, includes "Carmilla", probably the first story of lesbian love in English fiction.

 The House by the Churchyard (1863)

Uncle Silas (1864)

In a Glass Darkly (1872)

LE GUIN, Ursula K. (1929) American science fiction author whose novels have an increasing reputation outside the genre. After an early start with space opera (*The League of all Worlds* series), she has explored serious and important themes and managed to add a clear but beautiful style and some depth of characterization to the philosophical and conceptual strengths of the genre. *The Left Hand of Darkness* is a remarkable study of gender and its limiting effects on social forms. *The Dispossessed* is one of the most clear-sighted analyses of anarchism in fiction. The *Wizard of Earthsea* trilogy, written ostensibly for children, is sheer delight and deals with an archipelago in which magic is the prevailing technology.

 A Wizard of Earthsea (1968)

The Left Hand of Darkness (1969)

The Dispossessed (1974)

LEHMANN, Rosamund (1903) English novelist and spiritualist. *Dusty Answer* was her first, very successful novel. Her novels are rooted in the methods of Virginia Woolf and Henry James, and she almost always writes of the inner workings of the minds of young women. Her style is delicate, sometimes too self-consciously so. Her best book is reckoned to be *The Ballad and the Source*, concerning a bullying old woman, but seen through the eyes of a child.

 Dusty Answer (1927)

The Ballad and the Source (1944)

The Echoing Grove (1953)

LEIBER, Fritz (1910) American science fiction and fantasy writer. His stories of Fafhrd and the Gray Mouser are fine examples of "sword and sorcery" fiction, and he is one of the few writers able to place convincing stories of the supernatural in contemporary settings – *Conjure Wife* is his greatest success in this vein. Among the best of his stories are the tales of the "Change War" in which time-travelling armies battle to control history. *The Big Time* is set in a relief station serving the participants in a time war spanning several millennia. *The Wanderer* describes the panic on earth when a stray planet approaches the moon. The range of his work is exceptional, and he has a fine sense of theatricality.

 Conjure Wife (1943)

The Big Time (1961)

The Wanderer (1964)

LEM, Stanislaw (1921) Polish writer, best known in translation for his science fiction. *Solaris* is an account of humans struggling to comprehend an alien intelligence. Much of his work is comic or satirical, and does not read comfortably in translation.

 Solaris (1961, tr. 1971)

The Invincible (1963, tr. 1973)

LEONOV, Leonid (1899) Russian novelist. Leonov began, in the 1920s, as an original writer; in the 1930s he was forced to conform, and his work was weakened. *The Badgers* and *The Thief* demonstrate his independence although in both he takes an apparently pro-Soviet line. His style is always distinguished.

 The Badgers (1924, tr. 1947)

The Thief (1927, tr. 1931)

Road to the Ocean (1935, tr. 1944)

LERMONTOV, Mikhail (1814–41) Russian poet and novelist, who was killed in a duel. His very great novel *A Hero of Our Time* is essentially an examination of the consequences of romantic nihilism, and belongs to the tradition of truly poetic fiction. His hero feels that his selfish personality has doomed him, but he struggles with his destiny – only to succumb mysteriously at a point when he has gained a degree of self-knowledge.

 A Hero of Our Time (1840, tr. 1958, tr. 1966)

LEROUX, Gaston (1868–1927) French thriller writer, dramatist and journalist. He was prolific and highly popular. Among his novels are one of the earliest "sealed room" puzzles, *The Mystery of the Yellow Room*, and one of the most-filmed books, *The Phantom of the Opera*.

 The Mystery of the Yellow Room (1907)

The Phantom of the Opera (1911)

LESAGE, Alain-René (1668–1747) French dramatist and novelist, one of the first non-Spanish picaresque writers. *Gil Blas*, which Tobias Smollett translated, is set in Spain and imitates the Spanish manner; but the hero is more an anti-hero than a *picaro*, and inevitably there are French overtones. The novel was of great importance in the development of fiction.

 Gil Blas (1715–35, tr. 1749)

LESKOV, Nikolai (1831–95) Russian novelist and story-writer. Leskov in his sketches – mostly about criminals – invented *skaz*, an untranslatable word meaning something like "a semi-picaresque yarn in the vernacular" – his lower middle-class characters each speak in their own idioms. His use of *skaz* has influenced modern Russian writers like Remizov and Zamyatin. Gorki called Leskov the "most truly Russian of Russian writers".

 The Tales of Leskov (tr. 1944)

The Enchanted Pilgrim (tr. 1946)

Selected Tales (tr. 1962)

LESSING, Doris (1919) English novelist, story writer and polemicist, born in Persia and brought up in Rhodesia. With her Martha Quest novels Doris Lessing gained a very high reputation, and she was eagerly studied in the 1960s both for what she had to say about politics (she was once a communist) and about

Doris Lessing

women's position. But at sixty she seems temporarily obscured and her work during the 1970s has lacked confidence and scope. It has been suggested that she has sacrificed an acute intelligence for a shabby vision, based on the controversial psychological ideas of R. D. Laing; but that would be taking things too far, and *Briefing for a Descent into Hell* (1971) might easily be taken as criticism of Laing. Certainly, however, her interests have shifted from rationalist politics to such matters as Sufism, SF, and madness. Her early work is in any case a great deal more substantial. Her first novel *The Grass is Singing* is the taut tale of the disintegration of a relationship, and for many it remains her best. The *Martha Quest* series (published as *Children of Violence* 1965–66) is, as all admit, somewhat flawed, and very ambitious – but it is full of interest and fascinating detail about the female predicament.

The Grass is Singing (1950)

Martha Quest (1952)

The Memoirs of a Survivor (1974)

LEVER, Charles (1806–72) Anglo-Irish novelist. Lever wrote many very popular, picaresque regional novels modelled on those of Maria Edgeworth. They are ill-organized, but the best are vivid and accurate portrayals of Irish life.

Charles O'Malley (1840)

Arthur O'Leary (1844)

The Fortunes of Glencore (1857)

LEVIN, Ira (1929) American thriller writer and dramatist who established himself as a master

Ira Levin

of the paranoid style at the age of 22 with *A Kiss Before Dying*. His next novel *Rosemary's Baby* inaugurated a vogue for demonic speculation in fiction and the cinema, partly because it was one of the few completely persuasive metaphoric tales of horror since Henry James's "The Turn of the Screw". His most recent book *The Boys from Brazil* used the biological idea of cloning to create the same kind of impact. Levin's devotion to jigsaws reflects his immense skill at plotting, and in this area he has had a great influence on the development of the genre.

A Kiss Before Dying (1953)

Rosemary's Baby (1967)

This Perfect Day (1970)

LEVIN, Meyer (1905) American novelist and journalist. His most successful novel is the taut *Compulsion*, on the Leopold-Loeb murder case. His other novels are more journalistic.

Yehuda (1931)

The Old Bunch (1937)

Compulsion (1956)

LEWIS, C. S. (1898–1963) English scholar, Christian essayist, science fiction novelist and writer for children. The trilogy that began with *Out of the Silent Planet* is allegorical fantasy rather than true science fiction, primarily concerned with original sin and the spiritual origins of catastrophe. His series for children about the magic kingdom of Narnia is still immensely popular.

Out of the Silent Planet (1938)

Perelandra (1943)

That Hideous Strength (1945)

LEWIS "Monk" (1775–1818) English novelist, dramatist and poet. *The Monk*, a ripe Gothic mixture of horror and the supernatural, is the most lurid English tale of its kind.

The Monk (1796)

LEWIS, Sinclair (1885–1951) American novelist. Lewis was the first American to win the Nobel Prize (1930). He became famous with *Main Street* and *Babbitt*, both of which savage American smugness and philistinism. "Babbittry" became a word of opprobrium; but Lewis, partly through a failure of imagination, demonstrated – in the novel itself – that he really agreed with Babbitt's values, and so undermined his own satire. He wrote more as a newspaper reporter/caricaturist than as a literary novelist; but his masses of accurate, accumulated detail have their power, and are

undoubtedly impressive. He was a bad stylist, but, as is often stated, it is hard to imagine American letters without him. His best novel is *Elmer Gantry*, the scarifying portrait of a hypocritical evangelist. *Arrowsmith* (1925) is also outstanding. Lewis remains compulsively readable – and had he had subtlety and more imagination he might have achieved more than he did. His powers failed after 1930.

Main Street (1920)

Babbitt (1922)

Elmer Gantry (1927)

LEWIS, Ted (1940) English writer of crime thrillers. Lewis' underworld protagonists are exceptionally hard-boiled. Jack Carter, a Soho gangster who features in three books, is frighteningly brutal, but a well-drawn, distinctively English character.

Plender (1971)

Billy Rags (1973)

Jack Carter's Law (1974)

LEWIS, Wyndham (1882–1957) English novelist, story-writer, poet, painter, critic and editor. Lewis is unique in twentieth-century letters – and not only because he is the only writer of the age to be distinguished in another art than literature. He was at once a visionary and a satirist. At first he set himself against

Wyndham Lewis

Gertrude Stein, James Joyce and other modernists; but he offered in place of stream of consciousness not traditionalism but a glittering mineral prose based in his practice as painter. Later he analyzed himself in the terrifying and seriously underrated autobiographical novel *Self-Condemned*; after this, taking up his great prose epic *The Childermass* where he had left it off in 1928, he wrote his satirico-visionary masterpiece (unfinished) *The Human Age*. Apart from this – a work with affinities to, but far greater than T. S. Eliot's *Waste Land* – he produced the massive satire *The Ape of God* (1930), *The Revenge for Love* (1937) and several other important novels and stories.

Tarr (1918)

Self-Condemned (1954)

The Human Age (1955)

LEWISOHN, Ludwig (1883–1955) German-born American critic, translator and novelist. His competent and fluent fiction, which deals mainly with Jewish themes, has dated but is still respected.

The Broken Snare (1908)

In a Summer Season (1955)

LEZAMA LIMA, José (1910–78) Cuban poet who wrote one highly original novel, *Paradiso*, which explores the poet's inner world and the accretion of sensual and physical experiences which make up his vision.

Paradiso (1966, rev. 1968, tr. 1974)

LINDSAY, Norman (1879–1969) Australian artist and novelist. Lindsay modelled himself on *fin de siècle* notions of Nietzsche and Rabelais, but usually only succeeded in being smutty; his work has now dated, but *The Magic Pudding* (1918) for children, and his first novel *A Curate in Bohemia*, retain some Bohemian interest.

A Curate in Bohemia (1913)

Saturdee (1933)

Halfway to Anywhere (1947)

LININGTON, Elizabeth (1921) American author of detective and historical novels. She uses several pseudonyms, including Dell Shannon. Her numerous books are about the daily procedures of large urban police forces, and her major personal interest is in active membership of the John Birch Society.

Detective's Due (1965)

Date with Death (1966)

LINKLATER, Eric (1899–1974) Scottish novelist and highly literate middle-brow entertainer, whose most famous work *Juan in America* is a minor classic in the wide-eyed-innocent-abroad genre. Linklater scored several popular successes post-war, including *Private Angelo* (1946), about an Italian soldier farcically abroad in wartime Italy. His most moving and surprising work is *Roll of Honour*, in which a retired schoolmaster muses over his old pupils, killed in the war, in finely orchestrated free verse.

Poet's Pub (1929)

Juan in America (1931)

Roll of Honour (1961)

LINKS, J. G., seeWHEATLEY, Dennis.

LITTELL, Robert (1939) American novelist, chiefly of espionage, former *Newsweek* editor stationed in Communist Europe. His mind is every bit as complex as the most complex of spy stories and to this quality he adds a touch of the bizarre.

The Defection of A. J. Lewinter (1973)

Sweet Reason (1974)

The Debriefing (1977)

LIVELY, Penelope (1933) English writer, primarily for children. Her books skilfully blend past and present and her characters move easily backwards and forwards in time; the stories are told with great imagination and feeling for history.

The Driftway (1972)

A Stitch in Time (1976)

LLEWELLYN, Richard (1906) Welsh novelist and playwright. Llewellyn became famous with his evocation of the vanishing Welsh spirit, published just before World War II, *How Green was My Valley*; and has never bettered it.

How Green was My Valley (1939)

Green, Green My Valley Now (1975)

A Night of Bright Stars (1979)

LOCKRIDGE, Ross (1914–48) American novelist born in Indiana, who in his short life wrote one novel: *Raintree County*. He had such trouble completing this long novel that he killed himself, probably as a result of depression through overstrain. It takes place on one day, 4 July 1892, in an imaginary county in Indiana; and although flawed it is a masterpiece of observation. It was a huge posthumous success.

Raintree County (1948)

LODGE, David (1935) English novelist and academic. Lodge is a serious and intelligent writer who has just failed to develop a satisfactory personal idiom. His realistic novels are underpinned by academic theories and ingenious but stultifying parodic codes.

The Picturegoers (1960)

The British Museum is Falling Down (1965)

LOFTS, Norah (1904) English novelist, whose passion for old houses has provided the inspiration for many of her historical and romantic novels; *Gad's Hall* (1977) deals with demoniac possession in an old Suffolk house.

The House at Old Vine (1961)

Haunted House (1978)

Day of the Butterfly (1979)

LONDON, Jack (1876–1916) American novelist. London was a sailor, adventurer and gold-prospector before he started writing; he had educated himself with a mish-mash of pseudo-Darwinian and pseudo-Nietzschean

Jack London

ideas, and with Kipling, Smollett, Shaw and others; but he had his own real experiences and his genuine sense of the atavistic in man to draw upon. As thinker, he was a crude naturalist fired by an equally crude Marxism; his animal heroes in such books as *White Fang* (1906) and *The Call of the Wild* are more convincing than his human ones. But *John Barleycorn* is at least a very powerful novel about his alcoholism; and the hopefully prophetic *The Iron Heel* (1907), about the Marxist end of three-hundred years of totalitarianism, is at least instructive. He is consistently readable, although sensationalist. He is overrated as a great writer in the Soviet Union; but, although often sentimental and melodramatic, he is hardly ever without interest.

The Call of the Wild (1903)

John Barleycorn (1913)

The Assassination Bureau (completed by R. L. Fish, 1963)

LONGSTREET, Stephen (1907) American novelist, popular historian and screenwriter. In his youth Longstreet went to Europe, and made himself known to such distinguished artists as Utrillo, Chagall and Matisse, and to the expatriate American circle of Gertrude Stein, Elliot Paul and Hemingway. His novels are based on the lives of real people – such as Utrillo (*Man of Montmartre*, 1958) – or incidents in American history; but his reputation particularly rests on the series of family sagas starting with *The Pedlocks, a Family*, about whom he has produced novels regularly for almost thirty years.

The Pedlocks, a Family (1951)

Pedlock and Sons (1966)

Storm Watch (1979)

LOOS, Anita (1893) American dramatist, scriptwriter, novelist and story-writer. As novelist Loos attracted attention and popularity with *Gentlemen Prefer Blondes*, sketches about a grasping blonde flapper; here she wittily captured the style of the 1920s, in both speech and habit. It was one of Churchill's favourite books. She did not repeat her success at this level. *No Mother to Guide Her* is a satire on Hollywood.

Gentlemen Prefer Blondes (1925)

But Gentlemen Marry Brunettes (1928)

No Mother to Guide Her (1961)

LORRIMER, Claire (   ) English best selling novelist and housewife. Her novels, with tempestuous heroines, are colourful historical

romance packed with excitement, adventure, pathos and sex.

A Voice in the Dark (1967)

Mavreen (1976)

Tamarisk (1978)

LOTI, Pierre (1850–1923) French novelist. He wrote numerous tales of romance and adventure set in exotic places – mainly the South Sea islands and the Far East – which he had visited as a naval officer. His style is simple but evocative.

Iceland Fisherman (1886, tr. 1935)

Disenchanted (1906, tr. 1906)

LOVECRAFT, H. P. (1890–1937) American science fiction and ghost-story writer. Lovecraft's works have enjoyed a great revival since his death; there have been films and TV series. In his life-time he published only two books, but many stories in magazines. His expression of "cosmic dread" is inchoate, and not as powerful or pointed as is that of Edgar Allan Poe, one of his masters. But his writing has something of the nastiness and ingenuity of M. R. James, and in his search for cruelty he invented disturbing situations. He was eccentrically learned, and an invalid.

The Best Supernatural Stories (1945)

Something About Cats (1949)

LOVESEY, Peter (1936) English crime novelist. Lovesey's hobby was the history of athletics, and when a British publisher ran a crime-book contest he entered and won with *Wobble to Death* (1970), set amid the walking-races of Victorian times. He followed this with various other Victorian mysteries, constantly gaining in assurance and depth. As Peter Lear he wrote *Goldengirl* (1977) about the programming of an Olympics hopeful.

Wobble to Death (1970)

Swing, Swing Together (1976)

Waxwork (1978)

LOWRY, Malcolm (1909–57) English novelist and poet. Lowry wrote his masterpiece, *Under the Volcano*, while living in a beach-shack in Canada. His life was wrecked by his alcoholism, and he finally killed himself in a small village in Sussex. But in his work he seems, paradoxically, to discover lucidity. He wrote his first novel *Ultramarine* (1933, repr. 1963) under the influence of Joseph Conrad and the Norwegian writer Nordahl Grieg. *Under the Volcano* is an account of the last days, and murder, of a British Consul in Mexico; both

allegorical and symbolic, it is about drink, the rights and wrongs of political commitment, and the death of love. Its "message" is darkly pessimistic, but its beauty of design and majesty of execution contradict such a message: Lowry was defeated by life but redeemed by art.

Under the Volcano (1947, repr. 1962)

Lunar Caustic (1963)

October Ferry to Gabriola (1970)

LOWRY, Robert (1919) American novelist and story-writer. His novels are straightforwardly realistic and usually semi-autobiographical tales. He is often very funny.

Casualty (1946)

That Kind of Woman (1959)

The Last Party (stories, 1965)

LUARD, Nicholas (1937) British writer of spy thrillers, whose special knowledge and contacts have given his thrillers an authenticity known to have rattled both the CIA and MI5. His books usually feature agents who have been isolated by circumstance and are forced to take their own decisions. *The Robespierre Serial* concerns bluff and double-bluff between the CIA and British intelligence; and *Travelling Horseman* (1977) is an intriguingly realistic story featuring the PLO's Black September organization.

The Robespierre Serial (1975)

The Shadow Spy (1979)

LUDLUM, Robert (1927) American bestselling thriller writer. His lengthy plots generally derive from historical incidents, and are embellished with tough stereotyped heroes, fast-talking dialogue and a sprinkling of run-of-the-mill sex. His best was his first, *The Scarlatti Inheritance*.

The Scarlatti Inheritance (1971)

The Gemini Contenders (1976)

The Matarese Circle (1978)

LUNDWALL, Sam (1941) Swedish science fiction writer. His novels are satirical, the earlier ones making fun of science fiction cliches, while *2018 A.D. or the King Kong Blues* is scathing in its commentary on social trends. His *Science Fiction: What It's All About* (1970) is an entertaining introduction to the genre.

No Time for Heroes (1971)

2018 A.D. or the King Kong Blues (1975)

LURIE, Alison (1926) American novelist and lecturer in English at Cornell University. Lurie is undoubtedly the technically most accomplished of all American novelists since the war – although it is alleged that her brilliance of technique has interfered with her presentation of character. She is a novelist of manners, stripping bare the pretensions of "artistic" people – yet, as has been observed by one of her admirers, she does not quite know what to do with the genuine empathy she feels for her "victims". *Only Children* is less brittle and more compassionate than previous novels.

Love and Friendship (1962)

The War Between the Tates (1974)

Only Children (1979)

LYALL, Gavin (1932) English journalist and thriller writer. Lyall served as a pilot in the RAF for two years and has used this experience for several action-packed, literate thrillers. His best is *Midnight Plus One*, in which a man falsely accused of rape tries to evade the French police by flying to Liechtenstein.

The Most Dangerous Game (1963)

Midnight Plus One (1965)

LYTLE, Andrew (1902) American novelist, born in Tennessee. Of his four novels the underrated finest is *The Velvet Horn*, about the growing up of a young man in the Civil War period.

The Long Night (1936)

The Velvet Horn (1957)

M

McALMON, Robert (1895–1956) American story-writer and novelist. McAlmon was an expatriate who was mainly published in France. He is most important for his autobiography and his printing activities; but his fiction is fresh, modernistic in method and still readable.

A Companion Volume (stories, 1923)

Post-Adolescence (1923)

MACAULAY, Rose (1881–1958) English novelist, critic, travel writer and anthologist. A Christian spinster of very high intelligence she published her best novel late in life: *The Towers of Trebizond*. She uses humour to leaven her serious concerns about religion and love, and is an excellent literary novelist.

Potterism (1920)

Told by an Idiot (1923)

The Towers of Trebizond (1956)

McBAIN, Ed (1926) American writer of police procedural novels, born Salvatore A. Lombino, which name he changed legally to Evan Hunter. As Hunter he wrote the acclaimed *The Blackboard Jungle* (1954) about violence and racial tension in New York secondary schools. In 1956, as Ed McBain, he produced

Mary McCarthy

Cop Hater, the first of the 87th Precinct series, which now runs to over 30 titles. These are archetypal police procedural stories set in what must be New York's Manhattan. The series is grimly authentic, though not devoid of humour, and features realistic policemen, whom the reader comes to know well. Its influence on the "procedural" sub-genre has been immense. McBain says he never plans a book; he just sits down and types. Whole paragraphs recur from book to book, but do not seem out of place.

Give the Boys a Great Big Hand (1960)

The Heckler (1960)

Calypso (1979)

McCARRY, Charles (1929) American writer of spy thrillers, former speech-writer for President Eisenhower and former CIA operative. McCarry has produced two outstanding spy thrillers, both superbly written with an exceptional degree of authenticity. *The Tears of Autumn* attempts to explain the assassination of John F. Kennedy as a Vietnamese plot launched in retaliation for the murder of President Ngo Dinh Diem by the CIA.

The Miernik Dossier (1973)

The Tears of Autumn (1975)

McCARTHY, Mary (1912) American novelist, critic, polemicist and story-writer. McCarthy is a shrewd satirist of the intellectual social milieu in which she has moved; her novels are sharp and malicious. *The Groves of Academe* is a satire on intellectual (and leftist) life on the campus, and *The Group* – her best known novel – traces the careers of a number of girls who graduated from Vassar in 1933, the year she herself graduated. Her characterization is weak; she cares – as Harry T. Moore has said – for ideas more than she cares for people, and she is clever rather than in any way compassionate; but within their limits her books are consistently enjoyable, intelligent and truthful.

The Groves of Academe (1952)

The Group (1963)

Birds of America (1971)

McCLOY, Helen (1904) American mystery and suspense novelist. Her plots are always ingenious and full of bizarre details. Many of her more recent novels concern political intrigue, as in *Minotaur Country* (1975).

Through a Glass Darkly (1949)

The Imposter (1977)

McCLURE, James (1940) South African-born crime novelist, now a British resident. In a series of murder mysteries, exciting and well clued, he has done as much perhaps as any writer to portray the land of apartheid, and in by no means a partial way. He writes with subtlety, intelligence and integrity, and in his adventure novel *Rogue Eagle* (1976) he has gone further and produced a book that, while always suspenseful, contrives to paint a picture of a whole nation and its past.

The Steam Pig (1971)

Rogue Eagle (1976)

The Sunday Hangman (1977)

McCORQUODALE, Barbara, see CART-LAND, Barbara.

McCULLERS, Carson (1917–67) American novelist, story-writer and dramatist. Carson McCullers had an unhappy life: she was plagued by ill-health, and her husband was a near-psychotic who eventually killed himself.
Carson McCullers

She never wrote a better novel than her first, *The Heart is a Lonely Hunter*. Here, although she writes of misfits and grotesque characters – the central figure is a deaf mute – the whole work is suffused with tenderness, psychological understanding, and compassion. With the exception of *The Member of the Wedding*, the rest of her work is too self-consciously Gothic – this applies especially to *Reflections in a Golden Eye* (1941). But *The Ballad of the Sad Café* – a novella published with other stories – demonstrates that she never exploited sensationalism; it was the way she saw the world. Even at her most self-conscious she is compulsively readable.

The Heart is a Lonely Hunter (1940)

The Member of the Wedding (1946)

The Ballad of the Sad Café (1951)

MacDONALD, George (1824–1905) Scottish novelist and writer of classic – and superb – children's books (*At the Back of the North Wind*, 1871; *The Princess and Curdie*, 1883). MacDonald remains a neglected writer. At the present time he is chiefly read for his "visionary novels" *Phantastes* and *Lilith* (reprinted in a single volume). These are astonishingly powerful supernatural works, which influenced C. S. Lewis and J. R. R. Tolkein, neither of whom surpassed Macdonald. He also wrote good novels of Scottish life, of which *Robert Falconer* is perhaps the best.

 Phantastes and *Lilith* (1858, 1895, repr. 1962)

 Robert Falconer (1868)

George MacDonald: An Anthology (1946)

MacDONALD, Gregory (1937) American detective story-writer who has achieved an exceptional degree of realism and created two characters who will endure: Fletch, a shifty private eye; and Flynn, a Boston cop. *Running Scared* is a frightening portrayal of a psychotic crack-up in the manner of Patricia Highsmith.

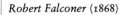 *Running Scared* (1964)

Fletch (1974)

Flynn (1977)

MacDONALD, John D. (1916) American mystery writer best known for the many stories featuring Travis McGhee, a "salvage expert", a man who recovers stolen goods on the condition that he retains a half share. These are some of the best stories in the genre. Although he operates in Florida rather than California, McGhee can be compared with Raymond Chandler's Philip Marlowe and Ross Macdonald's Lew Archer for the unfashionable way in which he confronts moral issues. The only problem with McGhee is that he (and MacDonald) seem to think that sex with McGhee constitutes psychotherapy for unhappy women. MacDonald observes American society with precision and is capable of deep psychological insights. *The Last One Left* includes a keen examination of the psychological problems of refugees from Castro's Cuba. In *Pale Gray for Guilt* (1968) (the McGhee stories always have a colour in the title) MacDonald displays his detailed knowledge of the world of commerce, gained from his early experience as a businessman.

 Nightmare in Pink (1964)

The Last One Left (1967)

The Scarlet Ruse (1973)

MACDONALD, Ross (1915) American crime novelist, famous for his detective Lew Archer (played by Paul Newman in two movies). Macdonald published his first four novels under his own name of Kenneth Millar. He is regarded as the only legitimate heir to Raymond Chandler and Dashiell Hammett, and with good reason. But he is not as "hard boiled"; his plots are superior to Chandler's, but his style is not – and his psychological powers are nowhere equal to those of Hammett. Macdonald has an ability to turn witty and often gruesome epigrams; and he conveys well the sense of corruption that pervades Southern California, where his books are set. He is consistently intelligent; but rather weak in characterization, and his detective Archer, unlike Chandler's Marlowe, seems to be too anonymous and uninvolved.

 The Drowning Pool (1950)

The Doomsters (1958)

Sleeping Beauty (1973)

McEWAN, Ian (1948) British short story-writer and novelist, much acclaimed by critics, whose enthusiasm is tempered only by their bewilderment about his intentions. His narrators, often teenagers, and plausibly unembarrassed by masturbation, nose-picking and the like, innocently exploit the now familiar themes of alienation and sexual perversion to present the reader with haunting images of torture and deterioration. His only novel *The Cement Garden* shares the virtues of his short stories. The setting and events reinforce one another symbolically, a precise prose style reflects the interest in ritual and structured privacy, and by consistently deny-

Ian McEwan

ing us the climax or moral stance his austere vision seems to demand, McEwan shows us that we are watchers of a world in which the four children protagonists of *The Cement Garden* can decide naturally and inevitably to bury their mother in a trunk of cement.

 First Love, Last Rites (stories, 1975)

The Cement Garden (1978)

In Between the Sheets (stories, 1978)

McGIVERN, William P. (1924) American detective story-writer of the hard-boiled school. He is best known for his portrayals of crooked cops (*The Big Heat*, and *Rogue Cop*, 1954), for whom he shows a certain understanding.

 The Big Heat (1952)

Caprifoil (1972)

Soldiers of '44 (1979)

MACHADO DE ASSIS, Joaquim (1839–1908) Brazilian novelist, poet and story-writer. Machado de Assis is the greatest of Brazilian fiction writers. An epileptic, he rose from printer's apprentice to high civil servant. He has been described as the "most disenchanted writer" of the nineteenth century. This is in a sense true; but it is more to the point to say that he was one of the first truly "autonomous" writers: he existed completely only in his novels. The novels he wrote in the last twenty-five years of his life anticipate almost all modernist procedures; but they are more readable than all but a handful of their successors. It is strange that this writer, who conducts a bitter-sweet dialogue with himself, whose characterization is so confident, whose maturity of mind is so evident, should not yet be fully appreciated outside Brazil. The reader can do no better than start with the novel about the mad philosopher, Quincas Borba, and his dog, *Philosopher or Dog?* (1891, tr. 1954). Machado de Assis is as remarkable as Flaubert, and only awaits discovery.

 The Heritage of Quincas Borba (1891, tr. 1954)

 Esau and Jacob (1904, tr. 1966)

The Psychiatrist and Other Stories (tr. 1963)

MACHEN, Arthur (1863–1947) Welsh novelist, translator (of Casanova), story-writer and journalist. Machen was rediscovered in the 1920s, and then again in the 1960s, as an outstanding novelist of the supernatural. *The Hill of Dreams* is an instructive and powerful novel about a man determined to expire in his Celticism. Machen's strange world is well worth a visit.

 The Hill of Dreams (1907, repr. 1968)

 Tales of Horror and the Supernatural (1948, repr. 1964)

 The Novel of the Black Seal and Other Stories (1965)

MacINNES, Colin (1914–76) English novelist and critic. MacInnes became well known for his novel about the world of Black immigrants in Britain, *City of Spades*. This was vivid and full of sympathetic understanding. *All Day Saturday* is his tenderest book; here he drew on his Australian childhood in a manner reminiscent of Chekhov. His last novels were neo-picaresque pastiche of R. L. Stevenson, and though very skilful, show a great falling off in quality.

 Visions of London (1969, in U.S. *The London Novels*; consisting of *City of Spades*, 1957, *Absolute Beginners*, 1959, *Mr Love and Justice*, 1960)

All Day Saturday (1966)

Westward to Laughter (1970)

MacINNES, Helen (1907) American novelist born and educated in Scotland. Her very successful adventure thrillers usually involve innocent Americans who get involved in espionage and intrigue in vividly described European countries. Her books are long, literate, and with undertones of political propaganda. Her villains are usually either neo-Nazis or Communists, reflecting her well-known dislike of totalitarian regimes.

 Assignment in Brittany (1942)

Neither Five nor Three (1951)

The Snare of the Hunted (1974)

McKAY, Claude (1890–1948) Jamaican novelist and poet who established himself in America. His most important novel is *Banana Bottom*, the story of a woman's self emancipation in Jamaica; but *Home to Harlem* sold better because it was set in America. McKay is now often undervalued; but he was the chief pioneer of West Indian fiction.

 Home to Harlem (1928)

Banjo (1929)

Banana Bottom (1933)

MacKENZIE, Compton (1883–1972) Scottish novelist, memoirist, essayist and publicist. MacKenzie began with excellent serious novels

which were praised by Henry James (*Sinister Street* and *Guy and Pauline*). MacKenzie later turned to the novel-as-entertainment, and was one of its best practitioners in this century. Such novels as *Buttercups and Daisies* (in U.S. *For Sale*, 1931) are among the funniest in the language. *Thin Ice* (1956) is a very superior political thriller. MacKenzie was an intelligent entertainer who was careful never to over-manipulate his characters, and who had a much more than superficial insight into the human heart.

 Sinister Street (1913–14)

Guy and Pauline (in U.S. *Plasher's Mead*, 1915)

 The Four Winds of Love (1937–45)

Alistair Maclean

MACLEAN, Alistair (1922) Scottish adventure novelist, former naval officer and teacher. His first novel, a moving and dramatic account of war at sea, *H.M.S. Ulysses* (1955), won public acclaim. He has since written a succession of best sellers, tense, fast-moving adventure stories in most of which a group of characters, a cross section of "types", face danger and death in a hostile environment, and often discover they are harbouring a traitor in their midst, as in *The Guns of Navarone* (1957); Maclean uses this device to build an atmosphere of tension, suspicion and fear. In several of his stories the action takes place amid Arctic desolation or at sea; the thin veneer of civilization is torn away and violence, greed and courage surface among men and women fighting for survival. He writes in an exceptionally terse and economical style – almost an anti-style – and his settings are well researched and impressive. Many of his books have been filmed, none better than *The Guns of Navarone*.

South by Java Head (1958)

Ice Station Zebra (1963)

Where Eagles Dare (1967)

MacLENNAN, Hugh (1907) Canadian novelist. MacLennan is the chief exponent in fiction of the sense of what it is to be Canadian, and many still turn to his sensibility as authoritative. *Return of the Sphinx*, on Quebec separatism, remains highly relevant.

Barometer Rising (1941)

The Watch that Ends the Night (1959)

Return of the Sphinx (1967)

MAILER, Norman (1923) American novelist, essayist, journalist and polemicist. Mailer began with a candid, Dos Passos-like novel about the American army (in which he had served): *The Naked and the Dead*. This was a best seller: but it did not prepare the public for what followed, *Barbary Shore* (1951), which was much more literary and more radical. Mailer makes no secret of his need to "win", and his angry competitiveness has not always served his reputation well; but the deliberately paranoid nature of his much flaunted immaturity, of which he is well aware, makes him a typical American "victim": "mine", he seems to say, "is the only possible fate as an intellectual amongst philistines". Mailer's journalistic work has brought him universal praise, and it is certainly some of the

most outstanding journalism of the century. But none of his fiction, although very widely read indeed, and always interesting, has met with universal critical approval. Yet it has quite properly been observed that unevenness is natural or at least inevitable in what he is trying to do: he is an existential writer, trying to act on his own sense of values, and so his life is as important as his fiction. *An American Dream*, on one level a murder story, is his most choate novel; but *Why Are We in Vietnam?* (1967), being very difficult, was probably undervalued.

The Naked and the Dead (1948)

An American Dream (1965)

Why Are We in Vietnam? (1967)

MAIS, Roger (1905–55) Jamaican novelist and poet. Mais published his important three novels in the last years of his life. They are realistic and humanitarian stories of Jamaican life; about the poor, they are non-political but sharply accurate and sociologically penetrating. In *Face and Other Stories* (1955) he explores the same theme.

The Three Novels of Roger Mais (1966: *The Hills Were Joyful Together*, 1953; *Brother Man*, 1954; *Black Lightning*, 1955)

MALAMUD, Bernard (1914) American novelist and story-writer. Malamud was for long regarded, with Saul Bellow, as the voice of the urban Jew in American society. *The Natural* (1952) combines baseball folklore with Arthurian legend, and also uneasily

combines the two sides of Malamud: the realistic chronicler of the urban Jew, and the would-be experimentalist. *The Assistant*, the finest of the novels, is about an honest Jew and a gentile who first robs him but then helps him, and finally takes his place – he ends by becoming a Jew, and, more important, accepting Jewishness. *The Fixer* was Malamud's bid for the Nobel Prize: it is a historical novel dealing with Russian anti-semitism and the fate of a Russian Jew falsely accused of ritual child murder. It is almost miraculously well stitched together, but ultimately rhetorical rather than truly felt – despite some very fine passages. *Dubin's Lives*, about a middle-aged biographer, marks his return to a more personal mode, and is his finest work to date. His symbolic and allegorical short stories are highly thought of.

The Assistant (1957)

The Fixer (1966)

Dubin's Lives (1979)

MALLEA, Eduardo (1903) Argentinian novelist, essayist and story-writer, whose novels use elements in his own life and experience to explore the essence of his country, and the predicaments of its people.

The Bay of Silence (1930, tr. 1944)

All Green Shall Perish (1941, tr. 1967)

MALRAUX, André (1901–76) French novelist, art critic, adventurer and politician. In retrospect, Malraux's fiction emerges as only one of his "obsessive" romantic gestures as a

Norman Mailer

Bernard Malamud

André Malraux

"man of destiny", seeking to stifle his own nihilistic impulses. After he became a Gaullist, and then De Gaulle's Minister of Culture, he gave up fiction. *Man's Estate* is a Dostoyevskian romantic novel set in the Far East, and really much more influenced by Joseph Conrad than by the author's temporarily leftist affiliations. *Days of Hope* is set in the early part of the Spanish Civil War, and remains the finest and most objective work of fiction about that unhappy event. Malraux's fiction will live as an important example of a convinced Nietzschean trying humanistically to escape the consequences of his beliefs.

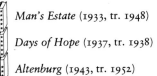

Man's Estate (1933, tr. 1948)

Days of Hope (1937, tr. 1938)

Altenburg (1943, tr. 1952)

MALTZ, Albert (1908) American playwright, screenwriter, novelist and story-writer. Maltz became known during the 1930s as a politically committed writer of the Left. His plays and stories of the period are angry denunciations of poverty and social injustice; "Man on a Road" and "The Happiest Man on Earth", two of his best known short tales, are biting political statements. His novel, *The Journey of Simon McKeever*, is an affirmation of the joy of living, in a journey undertaken through America by a crippled traveller and spiritual optimist.

The Way Things Are (stories, 1938)

The Journey of Simon McKeever (1949)

MALZBERG, Barry (1939) American novelist. He produced science fiction novels in large quantities during the early 1970s. His narratives are intense stream-of-consciousness,

dramatizing (often by means of black comedy and surrealism) existential situations of extreme alienation. His work is disturbing, but frequently very witty.

Screen (1968)

Herovit's World (1973)

Underlay (1974)

MANKOWITZ, Wolf (1924) British dramatist, screenwriter, biographer of Poe, and novelist. He had huge hits with glutinously sentimental novellas about irregularities in the antique trade (*Make Me An Offer*) and a small boy with a "magic" goat in a London East End market (*A Kid for Two Farthings*, 1953). *Raspberry Reich* in which a Marxist cell is discovered in an exclusive Swiss finishing school for girls, an excellent idea, is relentlessly overworked.

Make Me An Offer (1952)

My Old Man's a Dustman (1957)

Raspberry Reich (1979)

MANN, Heinrich (1871–1950) German novelist and story-writer, brother of Thomas. Heinrich is now overshadowed by his younger brother, although he once enjoyed greater fame. Where Thomas was a late and half-reluctant liberal, Heinrich was always well to the left. Although not as clever or versatile as Thomas, his novels are less ambiguous. His chief works are *The Blue Angel* (1905, tr. 1932, tr. 1944 as *Small Town Tyrant*), made into the famous film; *Man of Straw* (1918, tr. 1947); and the historical *King Wren and Henry: King of France* about Henry IV of France. Heinrich might well have achieved the eminence of his brother had he been a less hasty – and a more cunning – writer.

Berlin, the Land of Cockaigne (1901, tr. 1929)

The Little Town (1909, tr. 1930)

King Wren and Henry: King of France (1935, 1937, tr. 1937, 1939)

MANN, Jessica (1937) English crime novelist. The revelation of character within the framework of a more or less classical murder puzzle, set in a British upper-middle class social or academic milieu, is the pattern of this never less than interesting crime writer.

Mrs Knox's Profession (1972)

The Eighth Deadly Sin (1976)

The Sting of Death (1978)

Thomas Mann

MANN, Thomas (1875–1955) German novelist, story-writer, essayist and polemicist. Brother of Heinrich. Mann won the Nobel Prize in 1929, and remained until the end of his life the most respected modern novelist. His fiction developed from the decadent to the eclectic; but at all times he himself played the role of the respectable capitalist. He actively supported the German side in World War I; but took unambiguous objection to Nazism, and after Hitler's ascent to power left Germany for ever (his property was confiscated). He developed a dual viewpoint, and was in consequence an accomplished ironist; thus he loved Wagner, but denounced him as evil. This conflict he tries to resolve in *Doctor Faustus*, whose central character, although a composer, is in part based on Nietzsche (who did in fact compose music) and who pays the price of madness for his gift of art. Some prize him most for the stories "Tonio Kröger" and "Death in Venice" (both in *Stories of a Lifetime*, 1961); these deal more fully and openly with his love of and simultaneous distrust of art than anything else he wrote. His least ambiguous novel is the early *Bildungsroman, Buddenbrooks*, a study in materialistic decline and the growth of spiritual awareness. *The Magic Mountain*, which got Mann the Nobel Prize, is an ironic and pessimistic work which at the time was misread as a novel of affirmation because of its ironic purple passages. The *Joseph* novels (1933–45) are essentially an exploration of the notion that power is best achieved by confidence men. *Lotte in Weimar* (1939, tr. 1940) is a brilliant evocation of the intellectual atmosphere of the court at Weimar in 1816, dominated by the figure of Goethe who is portrayed with reverence. *The Holy Sinner* (1951, tr. 1952) is a beautiful reworking of a chivalric legend. *Felix Krull Confidence Man* (1954, tr. 1958) is a spiritual autobiography in picaresque form and is the novel in which

Mann feels most at home with his reader. Mann is a great writer not because he resolves anything, but because he asks the most interesting questions.

 Buddenbrooks (1901, tr. 1924)

The Magic Mountain (1924, tr. 1927)

Doctor Faustus (1947, tr. 1949)

MANNIN, Ethel (1900–78) English novelist and story-writer. A left-wing writer, Ethel Mannin's early realist work received attention, but in her later years she struggled for recognition. She wrote all her many and competent novels from a consistently Marxist-humanist point of view.

 Sounding Brass (1925)

Selected Stories (1946)

Every Man a Stranger (1949)

MANNING, Olivia (1914) English novelist and story-writer. Manning's chief achievement is *The Balkan Trilogy* (*The Great Fortune*, 1960; *The Spoilt City*, 1962; *Friends and Heroes*, 1965), which is essentially (although it is much else besides) that rare thing, a convincing study of a "good man" – and one who therefore looks a little absurd. The author exploits this paradox to the full. *The Play Room* is an intelligent and dispassionate study of apparent delinquency.

 Doves of Venus (1955)

The Play Room (1969)

The Rain Forest (1974)

MANSFIELD, Katherine (1888–1923) New Zealand story-writer who lived in England, and died young of tuberculosis. Her stories owe a great deal to Chekhov, although they never embody a fully worked out view of life – often they are tinged with a neurotic rancour, arising from the fact that she failed to resolve her discovery that love was not a rosy dream. At her best, when she is writing of children, or evoking atmosphere, or suggesting the quality of people, she is excellent. Her stories recollecting New Zealand, written in England, are her best: she coped beautifully with the remote past, but often failed with the present.

 Collected Stories (1945)

MANZONI, Alessandro (1785–1873) The greatest Italian novelist; also a poet, dramatist and philologist. His only novel, *The Betrothed*, is a triumph of characterization: he portrays good men, and demonstrates the conversion from evil to good, convincingly. At the same time he writes a magnificent ad-

venture novel. His touch is compassionate throughout.

 The Betrothed (1842, tr. 1875, tr. 1924, tr. 1951, tr. 1972)

MARIVAUX, Pierre C. de C. de (1688–1763) French dramatist and novelist. Marivaux was most adept as a playwright, but his two most famous novels – *The Life of Marianne* and *Le Paysan parvenu* – make a contribution to the development of psychological delicacy and exactitude. Both are autobiographical, and in both the moralizing vein is unimportant.

 The Life of Marianne (1731–34, tr. 1889)

Le Paysan parvenu (1734–35, tr. 1735)

MARKSTEIN, George (1928) American writer of spy thrillers, who has a gift for authenticity and for inventing a clever premise which he develops into a rewarding plot.

 The Cooler (1974)

The Man from Yesterday (1976)

MARLOWE, Derek (1940) English screenwriter and novelist, author of an increasingly intricate and horrific series of wittily turned thrillers starting with *Dandy in Aspic*.

 Dandy in Aspic (1966)

Somebody's Sister (1974)

Nightshade (1975)

MARQUAND, John (1893–1960) American novelist. He began his career with romances and detective stories, then turned into a novelist of manners. The first serious novel was *The Late George Apley*. Marquand's world is that of upper-class American business men.

 The Late George Apley (1937)

H. M. Pulham, Esq (1941)

Sincerely Willis Wayde (1955)

MARQUIS, Don (1878–1937) American humorous columnist, playwright and novelist, whose invention of *archy and mehitabel* is his enduring monument. Archy the cockroach and mehitabel the alley cat are comic metaphors around whom Marquis builds a delightful satire on social and intellectual pretensions of many kinds.

 archy and mehitabel (1927)

Sons of the Puritans (1939)

MARRYAT, Frederick (1792–1848) English novelist and naval captain. He was a popular

novelist who wrote, mostly about the sea, in the manner of Tobias Smollett. His work was relegated by later nineteenth-century critics to the status of children's fare; but readers always, and a few critics now, recognize that he has distinct and important virtues. His overt attitude is conventionally moralistic, but his humour, his candour and straightforwardness – as well as his interest in the morbid – show that he has much more to offer than early Victorian moralism.

 Peter Simple (1834)

Mr Midshipman Easy (1836)

The Dog-Fiend (1837)

MARSH, Ngaio (1899) New Zealand detective story-writer who lived for long periods in England and trained as an actress. Her first novel *A Man Lay Dead* (1934) featured a Scotland Yard detective, Superintendent Alleyn. She continues to write detective stories in the classic 1930s mould with Alleyn and his sculptress wife, Troy, as the leading characters. Her settings are often theatrical and her characters actors, musicians and painters. Carefully constructed plots are clothed in extremely literate, although not highly coloured, writing.

 Surfeit of Lampreys (1941)

Opening Night (1951)

False Scent (1960)

MARTIN, Violet, see SOMERVILLE AND ROSS

MARTIN DU GARD, Roger (1881–1958) French novelist and dramatist, who received the Nobel Prize in 1937 for his long and acutely observed *roman fleuve Les Thibault*, the chronicle of a French family before and during World War I. But that is not his best work, worthy as it is: this is to be found in two savage farces about rural life, and a novel about incest. Alas, these remain untranslated.

 Jean Barois (1913, tr. 1949)

Les Thibault (1922–40, tr. 1937–41)

MARTINEAU, Harriet (1802–76) English novelist, political economist and children's writer. Her work included two books for children, collections of tales, and three curious fictionalized accounts of political economy. Her stories are now generally found complacent, sincere and dreary.

 The Playfellow: a Series of Tales (1841)

MARTINSON, Harry (1904–77) Swedish poet and novelist. Martinson shared the Nobel

Prize for 1974. His best known fiction is *Aniara* in verse, about a journey into space. It is interesting in detail, but too long. His other fiction is less pretentious, showing his love for the wandering life and his deep knowledge of nature.

 Cape Farewell (1933, tr. 1934)

The Road (1938, tr. 1945)

Aniara (1956, rev. 1963)

MASEFIELD, John (1878–1967) English poet laureate and novelist. His novels are fresh adventure stories in the manner of R. L. Stevenson, and are still read.

 Jim Davis (1911)

Sard Harker (1924)

Odtaa (1926)

MASON, A. E. W. (1865–1948) English novelist, Liberal Member of Parliament (1906–10) and World War I spy. His detective stories, featuring a French police Inspector, although considered classics at the time, seem dull now; but some of his adventure stories – notably *The Four Feathers* – remain famous and are among the best of their kind ever written.

 Clementina (1901)

The Four Feathers (1902)

At the Villa Rose (1910)

MASTERS, John (1914) English novelist born in India; he was a serving soldier from 1934 until 1948. Masters writes adventure stories about India underpinned by a profound knowledge of the subject matter. *Nightrunners of Bengal*, his first novel, has been called the best English novel on the Indian Mutiny. His psychological powers are less sure.

 Nightrunners of Bengal (1951)

The Lotus and the Wind (1953)

Now, God be Thanked (1979)

MATHESON, Richard (1926) American popular novelist, story-writer and screenwriter. He is best known for the string of chilling fantasies which translated the fears of the cold war period into terrifying visions of cultural and physical mutation.

I Am Legend (1954)

The Shrinking Man (1956)

MATHEW, Harry (1930) American novelist and poet. His novels – although more bril-

liantly ingenious than imaginatively substantial – are exceedingly fascinating but not at all easy reading.

 The Conversions (1962)

Tlooth (1966)

MATURIN, Charles (1782–1824) Irish novelist, priest and dramatist. Influenced by "Monk" Lewis and Mrs Radcliffe, but also by Maria Edgeworth, Maturin wrote one of the most important and accomplished of all Gothic romances: *Melmoth the Wanderer*. It is essentially on the theme of the wandering Jew and is instructively critical of the Roman Catholic religion.

 Fatal Revenge (1807)

The Milesian Chief (1812)

Melmoth the Wanderer (1820)

MAUGHAM, Robin (1916) English popular novelist and thriller writer, nephew of Somerset Maugham. A stream of novels, usually with exotic backgrounds, has appeared since 1945. His best novel, *The Servant*, was filmed.

 The Servant (1948)

MAUGHAM, W. Somerset (1874–1965) English novelist, story-writer, dramatist and critic. Maugham was one of the most accomplished of non-modernist writers of the century. But within his limitations, he experimented a great deal, especially with "mystical" characters by whom he felt fascinated but whom he could not understand (*The Razor's Edge*, 1944). He was highly professional; but, curiously, his finest and most powerful novel, *Of Human Bondage*, is his most carelessly written. He began with an almost straightforward naturalism, with *Liza of Lambeth* (1897); his portrait of the heroine (who came from the slums) is less sentimental than has been assumed by critics, since warmth of heart was a quality very important to him. *Of Human Bondage*, a long and complex book, tries to work out the problem of his bisexuality: the fascinating and faithless waitress Mildred is really a lovely boy. The club foot of the hero is a symbol of his crippled sexuality. He was very prolific, and all his novels are readable and intelligent; but, *Of Human Bondage* apart, he was at his greatest in the short story. The stories are economical, superb in capturing the sense of place (often exotic – he was an inveterate traveller), and always credible. For psychological insight Maugham substitutes a sense of wonder, and this works very well. *A Writer's Notebook* (1949) describes his travels and

W. Somerset Maugham

reveals much about his thinking.

 Of Human Bondage (1915)

Cakes and Ale (1930)

Complete Short Stories (1951)

Guy de Maupassant

MAUPASSANT, Guy de (1850–93) French novelist and story-writer; he was a protégé of Flaubert's, a close friend of his mother's (there was once a rumour that he was his son). He died young, of syphilis. Maupassant was the first master of the "commercial short story"; but he was also much more than this. He had the same regretfully pessimistic view of life as Flaubert; but he also enjoyed life much more. His fiction, which is distinguished by more overtly expressed emotion than Flaubert's, often simply describes his sense of pleasure in life. At other times, as in "Boule de Suif", he expresses a Flaubertian disgust at hypocrisy, and at the same time an affirmation of humanity. He can also be sheerly comic. Some of his less successful stories deal with madness and the supernatural. His best novel is the delightful *Bel-Ami*, which is systematically underrated because it is supposed to be "immoral", on the grounds that the anti-hero prospers through "badness". Other novels are also notable; these include *Pierre and Jean* (1888, tr. 1962) and *A Woman's Life* (1883, tr. 1949).

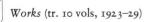 *Works* (tr. 10 vols, 1923–29)

MAURIAC, François (1885–1970) French novelist, dramatist and journalist. Mauriac won the Nobel Prize in 1952. He is one of the outstanding Catholic writers of the century and, like most of these (e.g. Graham Greene, George Bernanos) was severely critical of the religious practice of many of his co-religionists. He opposed Franco, and ended as a critical

Gaullist. His fiction is pessimistic, dealing with men and women helpless in the face of passion and desire; grace is seen as arising from the gestures of love or pity that well up from the depths of their beings. The world of his novels is in many ways an abject one; and he was much concerned with the redemption of criminals, such as his most famous creation, the poisoner Thérèse Desqueyroux. There is little, perhaps no, humour in his work; but it is extremely dramatic and powerful.

 Thérèse Desqueyroux (1927, tr. 1947)

The Dark Angels (1936, tr. 1951)

The Little Misery (1951, tr. 1955)

MAUROIS, André (1885–1967) French biographer, essayist and novelist. Maurois was most notable as a biographer, but his lightweight, intelligent novels achieved some popularity, especially the anglophile *The Silences of Colonel Bramble*.

 The Silences of Colonel Bramble (1918, tr. 1927)

 Bernard Quesnay (1926, tr. 1927)

The Return of Dr O'Grady (1950, tr. 1951)

MAYSON, Marina, see ROGERS, Rosemary

MELVILLE, Herman (1819–91) American novelist and story-writer. Melville went to sea in his youth, deserted, and was for a short time a beachcomber; from these experiences he wrote *Typee* (1846). This is on the familiar American theme of natural (but flawed) paradise and "civilized" hell. He wrote other sea tales, and then *Moby-Dick* (1851), a complex part-allegory of Shakespearean proportions in a prose influenced by the Bible and Sir Thomas Browne. *The Confidence-Man* (1857) is his bitterest and most satirical book; here

Herman Melville

he seems to be attributing devilish powers to God himself, and also to castigate capitalistic society (though there is no trace of Marxism in him). His last prose work is the imposing *Billy Budd*, in which he literally – and successfully – revises the Christian myth: Budd is a truly modern Christ-figure, who dies to satisfy an impressive but futile tyranny posing as "law" and "civilization". He is one of the earliest of truly modern writers. *Moby-Dick* has its longueurs, but is none the less a huge landmark, whose meaning will never be exhausted. His stories, which are highly poetic, explore the same territory.

 White-Jacket (1850)

Moby-Dick (1851)

Billy Budd (1924)

MELVILLE, Jennie, see BUTLER, Gwendoline

George Meredith

MEREDITH, George (1828–1909) English novelist and poet. Meredith is the most "difficult case" of the important novelists of the last century: he still seems hard to read, and yet his name keeps cropping up – no-one can jettison him. Only *Rhoda Fleming* (1865) reads anything like an "ordinary" nineteenth-century novel. His style evokes the unconscious motivations of his characters, which is why it is difficult. Sometimes he is rococo and mannered, the result of his lofty and courageous annoyance with the complacent reader. Among his greatest novels are *The Ordeal of Richard Feverel* (1859), *Rhoda Fleming*, *Beauchamp's Career* (1875) and *The Egoist* (1879). The age in which he has been unfashionable is receding.

 Evan Harrington (1861)

Diana of the Crossways (1885)

The Amazing Marriage (1895)

MÉRIMÉE, Prosper (1803–70) French novelist, story-writer and translator. Mérimée, most famous as the author of the exotic *Carmen*, excelled in the long short story, the *nouvelle*. He is the most trim, sardonic and elegant of the romantics; some of his best tales are of the supernatural. He is almost unsurpassed as a stylish story-teller. His one novel, *Chronicle of the Reign of Charles IX* is also excellent.

 The Abbé Aubin (stories, tr. 1903)

 Chronicle of the Reign of Charles IX (1829, tr. 1889)

Carmen, Colomba and Selected Stories (tr. 1963)

MERRIL, Judith, see KORNBLUTH, Cyril M.

MERRITT, Abraham (1884–1943) American fantasy novelist and crime reporter. He was interested in folk-lore, black magic and the relics of ancient civilizations, and he wove these into a small number of novels and short stories, which were immediately recognized as deserving a place in the first rank of imaginative fiction.

 The Moon Pool (1919)

Dwellers in the Mirage (1932)

Burn Witch Burn (1933)

METALIOUS, Grace (1924–64) American novelist whose fame rests primarily on her novel *Peyton Place*, which became well known to millions when it formed the basis of a television soap opera. It is the story of an American small town, its intrigues and scandals.

 Peyton Place (1956)

Tight White Collar (1960)

No Adam in Eden (1963)

MICHAELIS, Karin (1872–1950) Danish novelist and story-writer. She once enjoyed great international success with her intelligent, rather sensational stories about women and their problems. *The Dangerous Age* was the most popular.

 The Child: Andrea (1901, tr. 1904)

The Dangerous Age (1910, tr. 1912)

Elsie Lindtner (1912, tr. 1912)

MICHENER, James A. (1907) American author of nine novels, many short stories, and a wide range of non-fiction books and articles. Michener based his fiction on his experiences as a Naval officer in the Pacific during World

James A. Michener

War II. Although carefully researched and written, his tales are often criticized for their anecdotal nature, and for their limited characterization; many of his people, especially the women, are flat. Michener's first and most successful work was *Tales of the South Pacific*, a loosely plotted book made into the musical, *South Pacific*.

 Tales of the South Pacific (1947)

The Bridges at Toko-Ri (1953)

Sayonara (1954)

MIDDLETON, Stanley (1919) English novelist. He is a psychologically subtle and compassionate realist, noted for his craftsmanship, integrity and perseverance. He writes of the English Midlands, and explores the bleak yet dogged lives of his usually professional characters with great precision. He has much of the insight of D. H. Lawrence, but is less poetic.

 Harris's Requiem (1960)

Brazen Prison (1971)

Holiday (1974)

MILLAR, Margaret (1915) Canadian novelist, married to Ross Macdonald. She has lived in the U.S. since 1945. Not all her novels are thrillers, but she is best known for her sophisti-

cated psychological mysteries which convey a strong impression of the less conventional aspects of American life; detection is secondary to atmosphere, clues to characterization.

 Beast in View (1955)

A Stranger in My Grave (1960)

How Like an Angel (1962)

MILLER, Henry (1891) American novelist, pornographer and general writer. Miller walked out on a conventional job in New York when he was thirty-three, and went to live in Paris – where he earned a living by writing pornography, and as an editor. His fiction is exclusively autobiographical, and famously candid. Miller educated a smug generation; but what survives in his writing – which is never elegant – is his anti-intellectual frankness, not about sex, but about people (his various wives, in particular). Some of his erotic adventures (as when he steals his fare home from a woman while in bed with her) are uproariously funny; but he displays feeling and perception and pity when he describes the various different people he has met. His influence has been profound, particularly upon Lawrence Durrell. He is a careless writer, and foolish in most of his critical judgements; but his good-heartedness and descriptive exactitude will ensure the survival of his best books.

 Tropic of Cancer (1934)

Tropic of Capricorn (1939)

The Rosy Crucifixion (*Sexus, Plexus* and *Nexus*, 1949–60)

Henry Miller

Margaret Mitchell

MILLER, Walter M. (1922) American science fiction writer, winner of two awards. He wrote relatively little, but was exceptionally accomplished.

 The Darfsteller (1955)

A Canticle for Leibowitz (1960)

MILLER, Warren (1921–66) American novelist, whose three important novels, about Harlem and its gangs, are lucid and knowledgeable.

 The Cool World (1959)

The Siege of Harlem (1965)

MILLIN, Sarah Gertrude (1889–1958) South African novelist, story-writer, dramatist and historian. She was the first true realist in the English language in South African literature. However, she was a racialist, if only of the Smuts variety, and her crude bias robs her fiction of real distinction. Her work declined in later years.

 The Dark River (1919)

Mary Glenn (1925)

The Wizard Bird (1962)

MIRÓ, Gabriel (1879–1930) Spanish novelist. He wrote gentle, naturalistic novels of the countryside and small-town life, in which petty cruelty and religious bigotry contrast with sensuousness and the natural virtues.

 Our Father San Daniel (1921, tr. 1930)

MISHIMA, Yukio (1925–70) Japanese novelist who committed ritual suicide in a neo-fascist demonstration. While he was alive Mishima's many novels attracted much attention; but his ugly and pointless death exposed their essential meretriciousness. His talent cannot, however, be denied. His widely translated books were morbid, sensational and unpleasant; but those which explore his homosexuality are, at the least, psychologically accurate.

 Confessions of a Mask (1949, tr. 1960)

The Sailor Who Fell from Grace with the Sea (1963, tr. 1966)

 Thirst for Love (1950, tr. 1970)

MITCHELL, Adrian (1932) English journalist, playwright, poet and novelist, best known as a committed poet of the Left. He has written several fictional works of note including *If You See Me Comin'*, an imaginative but loosely constructed account of the travels of a Blues singer, and the psychology of his deep despair; and a curious, confused fantasy, *Wartime*, which is a symbolic account of the control of the masses by the ruling class.

 If You See Me Comin' (1962)

Wartime (1973)

MITCHELL, Gladys (1901) English detective story-writer. She dates from the Golden Age of the genre, of which she is an excellent example, but continued writing up to and beyond her fiftieth book, *Late, Late, in the Evening* (1976). Her heroine is the cacklingly reptilian psychiatric adviser to the Home Office, Mrs (later Dame) Beatrice Lestrange Bradley, whose adventures provide ample opportunities for literary and other lore, often of ghost and witch.

 Laurels are Poison (1942)

Tom Brown's Body (1949)

Late, Late in the Evening (1976)

MITCHELL, Julian (1935) English novelist and playwright. A fluent, stylish but curiously uneven writer who produced the best Oxford novel of the 1960s.

 Imaginary Toys (1961)

As Far as You Can Go (1963)

The Undiscovered Country (1966)

MITCHELL, Margaret (1900–49) American novelist, whose only book, *Gone With The Wind*, remains the classic romance of the century. She began writing it in 1926 and

Yukio Mishima

it took ten years to complete. It combines the historical excitements of the American Civil War with the passionate triumphs and tragedies of the heroine, Scarlett O'Hara. Margaret Mitchell was awarded the Pulitzer Prize in 1937.

 Gone with the Wind (1936)

MITCHISON, Naomi (1897) English novelist. Her most popular works have been on historical themes (Greek, Roman and Scandinavian), which she treats with a refreshing and whimsical individuality.

 When the Bough Breaks (1924)

Swan's Road (1954)

Memoirs of a Space Woman (1962)

MITFORD, Mary Russell (1787–1855) English novelist. With *Our Village* she created the genre – the lively sketch about regional life – which Mrs Gaskell perfected.

 Our Village (1824–32)

Belford Regis (1835)

Atherton (1854)

MITFORD, Nancy (1904–73) English novelist and popular biographer. Mitford was successful with her comic novels about upper-class life. She records eccentric speech and behaviour without commenting on it; her secret may be that she did not find it funny herself, but discovered that others do. Such works as *The Pursuit of Love* are revealing in the record they give of how the other one-percent lives.

The Pursuit of Love (1945)

Love in a Cold Climate (1949)

The Blessing (1951)

MITTELHOLZER, Edgar (1909–65) Guyanese novelist. His many (over twenty) novels are uneven, but all except the last few have attracted the interest of critics because of their immense vitality and intensity. Mittelholzer was much concerned with miscegenation and its consequences, especially in his *Kaywana Trilogy* (1952–8). His books are heightened by violence and sadistic imagery.

My Bones and My Flute (1955)

The Weather Family (1958)

Latticed Echoes (1960)

MONSARRAT, Nicholas (1910–79) English best selling novelist best known for his sea stories. Although he started in the 1930s, Monsarrat did not become widely known until the 1940s when he published a series of wartime naval adventures culminating in *The Cruel Sea*, the most successful English novel of World War II, notable for its detailed descriptions of action and its perfunctory characterization. Later novels like *The Tribe that Lost its Head* and *The Kappillan of Malta* showed the same narrative gift marred by a certain crudity in dealing with people.

The Cruel Sea (1951)

The Tribe that Lost its Head (1956)

The Kappillan of Malta (1974)

MONTAGUE, C. E. (1867–1928) English novelist, essayist and journalist. His one important novel is *Rough Justice* (1926), a re-appraisal of pre-First World War values. His stories are satirical, vivid but mannered.

A Hind Let Loose (stories, 1910)

Fiery Particles (stories, 1923)

Rough Justice (1926)

MONTHERLANT, Henri de (1896–1972) French novelist, essayist and dramatist. Montherlant, though not himself a Catholic, except by upbringing, wrote in the Catholic tradition, but modified it by the application of the principles of a "shame" rather than a "guilt" culture. He has been called a Renaissance man, and as a description of his general life-style

this is apt. But in his fiction he is more versatile than is usually allowed – and much more moving (as in the novel about a Spanish anarchist, *Chaos and Night*, 1963, tr. 1964). His aloof and aristocratic attitude put many readers off; but as he grew older he studied the human heart more carefully: his novel *The Bachelors* (1934, tr. 1960) had pointed the way, but the deliberately irritating, though brilliant, *The Girls* tetralogy (1936–9, tr. 1965) seemed to be heartless. In fact Montherlant was exploring the difficult area of his ambiguous sexuality. He has been much misinterpreted and misunderstood; and for this reason it is best to begin by reading his later and more overtly compassionate work.

The Dream (1922, tr. 1965)

The Bullfighters (1926, tr. 1927)

The Boys (1965, tr. 1974)

MOORCOCK, Michael (1939) British science fiction writer and editor who has moved from a massively prolific – and hurried – output of "Sword and Sorcery" fantasy to more considerable work. As the editor of *New Worlds* magazine he was closely involved in what has been called the New Wave of SF, in which writers like Norman Spinrad and J. G. Ballard attempted to revitalize the genre by adding new insights and techniques from psychology, politics, rock music and literary experiment. Moorcock has turned to more serious themes, but has retained the flair for plotting and readability which made his *Elric* and *Dancers at the End of Time* sequences so successful. The *Jerry Cornelius* tetralogy enjoys a growing reputation and a wide audience, despite its complex ideas and plot.

The Final Programme (1969)

A Cure for Cancer (1970)

Gloriana or The Unfulfill'd Queen (1978)

MOORE, Brian (1921) Irish novelist who has lived most of his life in Canada. His first two novels were set in Belfast; later ones are set in Canada, America and elsewhere. His main characters are usually Irish. He is one of the most successful of modern Irish authors: although much concerned with the problem of Catholic dogma, he explores his rich material with compassion, gusto and humour.

The Lonely Passion of Judith Hearne (1955)

The Luck of Ginger Coffey (1960)

The Mangan Inheritance (1979)

MOORE, C. L., see KUTTNER, Henry.

MOORE, George (1852–1933) Irish novelist, story-writer and autobiographer. Moore was a perverse eccentric who said more foolish things than any other major novelist. But his achievement is very great. His point of departure was naturalism, but it is a common error to call his early realistic novels "naturalistic": even though Zola's example gave him a start, he was never concerned to emphasize squalor. The early works are full of robust feeling, and are very well documented – especially *A Mummer's Wife* (1885) and *Esther Waters*. His stories remain sadly neglected: "Albert Nobbs" alone is one of the greatest tragi-comic stories in any language. *The Lake* (1905) is more symbolic, and more like Turgenev. The later books, mostly historical, are entirely original and tell their tale in a "seamless" narrative. *Héloise and Abelard* is a tour de force, and shows a remarkable grasp of the complex philosophical problems set by its subject: Moore gives these real life.

Esther Waters (1894)

The Brook Kerith (1916)

Héloise and Abelard (1921)

MOORE, Ward (1903) American science fiction novelist, a stylish and frequently witty writer. *Bring the Jubilee* is a classic exercise in "alternative history" about a world in which the Confederacy won the Civil War.

Greener Than You Think (1947)

Bring the Jubilee (1953)

MORAVIA, Alberto (1907) Italian novelist, story-writer and journalist. Moravia made something of a sensation with his first novel *The Time of Indifference* (1929, tr. 1953): it was in effect a criticism of fascist society and it drove him into writing in an allegorical style in order to continue saying what he wanted to say. He had to hide out during World War II; but soon after he became famous for his sympathetic portraits of prostitutes and "loose women" (for example *The Woman of Rome*). But this kind of fame was rather misleading, since his real theme is the inability of men to love. Like Jean-Paul Sartre he insists that the true reality of existence is boredom, though he has more faith in the powers of love – if these can be generated. For Moravia sex is the enemy of love. His strength lies in his spare style, his empathy with women (whom he clearly regards as superior to men, although he is unable to say why), and his analyses of the psychological processes which lead men to embrace such repulsive creeds as fascism. He has always been radical, but is not a Marxist; the new Italian terrorists he calls "moralists with guns" – and he does not care for moralists. He has been described as "over-preoccupied with sex"; but he is not more so than most people – and he is more illuminating about it than them. He has been very prolific, and his more overtly modernist novels of recent years have been notably successful. His

Alberto Moravia

best known stories in translation are in *Roman Tales*.

The Woman of Rome (1947, tr. 1949)

The Conformist (1952, tr. 1952)

Roman Tales (1954, tr. 1956)

MORGAN, Charles (1894–1958) English novelist, dramatist and theatre critic. Morgan was once very popular; and the French re-

garded him as a major writer, although English and American critics never did. His novels, of which the most famous is *Sparkenbroke*, are religio-philosophical, allegorical and mystical, and are written in a self-consciously "fine" style. Modern readers find him tiresome and pretentious, but in his heyday he was regarded as "deep". His heart was in the right place; but he had little to say despite his pursuit of what he called "the eternal verities". His early novel *The Gunroom* (1919), straightforward in style and realistic in content, is his best.

The Fountain (1932)

Sparkenbroke (1936)

The Judge's Story (1947)

MORLEY, Christopher (1890–1957) American novelist and essayist, whose popular fiction is carefully made and respects the intelligent reader. His third novel *Kathleen* is set in Oxford, which he attended; and his greatest success was *Kitty Foyle*.

Kathleen (1920)

Kitty Foyle (1939)

MORRELL, David (1943) Canadian writer of adventure stories, who specializes in authentic tales of survival in the wilderness. Morrell has researched his subject-matter first-hand and makes it seem frighteningly real; he sometimes uses an almost surreal style to create a menacing natural world.

First Blood (1972)

Testament (1975)

MORRIS, John, see HEARNE, John.

MORRIS, William (1834–96) English artist, designer, poet, early socialist and writer of epic adventures. Morris was associated with the Pre-Raphaelite Brotherhood, and in their love for the medieval world and Gothic architecture his taste was developed. His prose includes socialist novels like *The Dream of John Ball* (1888); and *News from Nowhere*, an attack on the ugliness of modern industrial society. He also wrote a series of prose romances based on Scandinavian legend, which have some merit despite their archaic style.

News from Nowhere (1891)

The Well at the World's End (1896)

MORRIS, Wright (1910) American novelist. Morris is widely read; he is a very uneven novelist, being at his worst (*Cause for Wonder*, 1963) almost silly, but at his best (*The World in the Attic*, 1949) illuminating and unique.

Wright Morris

His main themes are the helplessness but inevitability of nostalgia for the midwest past, and the consequences of aggressive non-belief. *One Day* (1965) is about the assassination of Kennedy.

My Uncle Dudley (1942)

The Huge Season (1954)

A Life (1973)

MORTIMER, John (1923) English playwright, novelist and lawyer. At 24, Mortimer published an astonishingly poised, stylish satire on the film world, *Charade*. Of his five subsequent novels, *Answer Yes or No* (1950) and *Like Men Betrayed* are the most distinguished; both catch the sour, rancorous mood of many upper-class Londoners in the early 1950s.

Charade (1947)

Like Men Betrayed (1954)

Rumpole of the Bailey (1978)

MORTIMER, Penelope (1918) English novelist. Her novels, which are quite widely read, deal exclusively with the problems of women on the brink of breakdown, held together only by the cement of what they nevertheless cannot come to terms with: their femininity. Terror of abortion, infidelity, loss of attractiveness: these abound in her books. Her portrayal of men is weak, but her insights into female psychology are often compellingly expressed. She is a serious writer, improving all the time, and much appreciated by women who are not attracted to militance.

Daddy's Gone A-Hunting (1958)

The Pumpkin Eater (1962)

Long Distance (1974)

MOSLEY, Nicholas (1923) English novelist and popular historian, the son of the English fascist leader Sir Oswald Mosley. His eight novels show a desire to experiment with the form without much conviction. They were much improved when developed into films as with *Accident* and *Impossible Object*.

 Accident (1964)

Impossible Object (1968)

MOTLEY, Willard (1912–65) Black American novelist. His work is more overtly political than that of James Farrell, whom he admired, but never lacking in power. He never equalled the force of his first novel, *Knock on Any Door*, a story of a young Chicagoan's inevitable development into a criminal.

 Knock on Any Door (1947)

Let Noon be Fair (1966)

MOTTRAM, R. H. (1883–1971) Prolific English (East-Anglian) novelist who became famous for his worthy war trilogy *The Spanish Farm*, and who continued to produce well-made and interesting novels for the rest of his long life.

 The Spanish Farm Trilogy (1927)

The Banquet (stories, 1934)

Maggie Mackenzie (1965)

MOYES, Patricia (1923) Anglo-Irish author of classic-style detective novels set in a variety of countries made attractive by lively description. She uses special knowledge derived from her own leisure interests of skiing, sailing and travelling.

 Down Among the Dead Men (1961)

Falling Star (1964)

The Black Widower (1975)

MPHAHLELE, Ezekiel (1919) South African novelist and story-writer who went into exile, but who (1979) has returned there to teach, although he is unwelcome to the authorities. Mphahlele is a leading representative of the moderate school of Negro thought; but he is none the less committed to freedom and equality. His novel *The Wanderers* (1971) is about the difficulties of exile, and is both accomplished and radiantly intelligent.

 Man Must Live (stories, 1947)

The Living Dead (stories, 1961)

In Corner B (stories, 1967)

MULLALLY, Frederic (1920) English journalist and thriller writer. The adventures of his lubricious heroine *Oh Wicked Wanda* (1968)

are to be followed in cartoon form in *Penthouse* magazine. His other novels are less distinctive.

 Danse Macabre (in U.S. as *Marianne*, 1960)

 Hitler Has Won (1975)

The Deadly Payoff (1978)

MULTATULI, (pseudonym of Edward Douwes Dekker, 1820–87) Dutch novelist. Multatuli was the best Dutch prose writer of the nineteenth century and was much admired by D. H. Lawrence. His experiences of colonialism led him to attack it as unjust and short-sighted; his famous novel *Max Havelaar* expresses his disgust, with profound elegance. It is a very subtle work: its apparent chaos reflects the chaos of the established "order".

 Max Havelaar (1860, tr. 1967)

MUNRO, H. H., see SAKI

MUNRO, Neil (1864–1930) Scottish novelist and writer of sketches now famous for his creation of the humorous Highland character Para Handy, a droll sailor.

 The Vital Spark (1906)

Jaunty Jock (1918)

Para Handy (1931)

MUNTHE, Axel (1857–1949) Swedish author and doctor. His *The Story of San Michele*, a runaway best seller, is autobiography in fictional form. It was written in English.

 The Story of San Michele (1929)

MURASAKI, Lady (?978–?1031) Japanese novelist and diarist. Her long novel *Genji* is still probably the greatest Japanese novel.

 Genji (11th century, tr. 1925–33, tr. 1952)

MURDOCH, Iris (1919) Anglo-Irish philosopher and novelist. Her early books are her best. The first was a refreshingly inconsequential, even existential, piece of Sohopicaresque (*Under the Net*). In *The Flight from the Enchanter* (1956), again set in a twilit ambience of shabby London intellectuals, characters fortuitously impinge on each other as they wrestle with the baleful magnetism of "the enchanter", an international financier. *The Sandcastle* (1957) – about a married headmaster's love for a girl painter – starts realistically but sheers off into contrived parable. Her best book *The Bell* is set in a lay religious community disrupted through the founder's failings, but more by intruders who

dredge the bell from the lake and ring it: death-knell for an experiment in living, "the voice of love but also the cast metal of self-realization" (Anthony Burgess). *The Bell* is an impressive and intensely poetic achievement. *A Severed Head* (1961), an intricately rigged plot of musical beds to the tunes of adultery and incest, marked a decline in Miss Murdoch's work, although not in her popularity. She has since published a book a year, each compromised by faults which only lurked in her earlier fiction: an unreal, febrile, over-charged brilliance; concentration on plot at the expense of developing characters; a *faiblesse* for arch donnish gags; and, above all, symbolism poured thick as treacle over meaning and action. *The Sea, the Sea*, winner of the 1978 Booker Prize, concerned a distinguished actor in his retirement unable to escape disagreeable shadows from his past.

 Under the Net (1954)

The Bell (1958)

The Sea, the Sea (1978)

MURGER, Henri (1822–61) French novelist known for realistic pictures of low life in the Latin Quarter of Paris, who helped to create the legend of artistic Bohemia. His best known work *Scènes de la vie de Bohème* was the basis of Puccini's famous opera, *La Bohème*.

 The Bohemians of the Latin Quarter (1848, tr. 1887, tr. 1949)

MURRY, Colin, see COWPER, Richard

MUSIL, Robert (1880–1942) Austrian novelist, story-writer and playwright. He wrote two great novels: *Young Törless* and the unfinished and unfinishable *The Man Without Qualities*. The stories translated in *Torka* are of similar quality. *Törless* is the most savage and realistic "school story" ever written; and it contains the germ of all Musil's future work. *The Man Without Qualities*, set in the Austrian Empire just before its collapse, is the most intellectually thoroughgoing of all examinations of modern man's predicament: his loss of belief in order, the very collapse of order into meaninglessness, the sense of not-belonging. The main theme of the novel is incest: the incest taboo, although apparently "obvious", is in fact an anthropological mystery, and only the uninitiated feel that it can be "explained". But the book is also a kind of encyclopaedia dealing with the Austro-Hungarian empire, with much satire. It seems at first to be hard to read; but persistence very soon reveals one of the great modern writers.

 Young Törless (1906, tr. 1961)

The Man Without Qualities (1930–43, rev. 1952, tr. 1953–60)

Torka and Other Stories (tr. 1965)

MYERS, L. H. (1881–1944) English novelist best-known for his quartet *The Near and the Far*, set in the India of the Moguls. His other novels include *The Clio*, a "conversation" piece.

The Clio (1925)

Strange Glory (1936)

The Near and the Far (1943)

MYRER, Anton (1922) American novelist. Myrer has written a small group of powerful novels about American life, expressing his despair and disgust with the materialism of modern society. In *The Last Convertible* he tackles a wider canvas: American history from World War II through the Kennedy era.

Evil Under the Sun (1957)

The Violent Shore (1962)

The Last Convertible (1978)

N

NABOKOV, Vladimir (1899–1977) Russian novelist, story-writer, translator and entomologist. Nabokov was born in Russia, but when his family was ruined by the Revolution he became an exile; after a spell in Europe he took up American citizenship, although he spent his last years in Switzerland. His early work, translated from the Russian, is his best; but his later, written in English, was much

more fashionable. The key to his achievement is the agony he endured as an exile. The key to his final artistic ignominy, *Ada or Ardor* (1969), lies in his desire for fame at any cost. This sentimental and contorted novel was admired for a while; few read it now. *Lolita*, his most famous book, is a study in obsession: a man becomes infatuated to the point of madness with a "nymphet". This is a tour de force less substantial than *Pnin* (1957), in which he examines his own predicament as an exiled Russian academic in America. His finest work is in the early short stories and in some of the earlier novels written in Russian: in English, except in *Pnin*, he is usually over-self-conscious, whimsical and desperately insecure. He did know the language well, but felt at heart that he could not (he called his English "second rate"). He is the cleverest of all twentieth-century novelists, and owes a huge debt to Gogol. But his fiction will eventually be seen as a demonstration that you cannot write like Gogol in the English language. He is obsessed with puzzles and games, and far too easily satisfied with smart successes. He is far too passionate to acknowledge feeling. Yet this is true only of the English novels (except, it should be repeated, for *Pnin*). In Russian he can be exquisite and exact, as in *Laughter in the Dark* (*Camera Obscura*, 1932, tr. 1938).

The Luzhin Defense (1929, tr. 1964)

Lolita (1955)

Nabokov's Quartet (tr. 1967)

NAIPAUL, Shiva (1945) Novelist from Trinidad, who lives in England. He is not in the same class as his brother V. S. Naipaul; but he is talented and comic, especially in *Fireflies*, set in Trinidad and dealing with the Hindu community. An indulgence in nastiness for its own sake sometimes mars his work.

 Fireflies (1971)

The Chip-Chip Gatherers (1973)

NAIPAUL, V. S. (1932) Trinidadian novelist of Indian extraction who has lived in England since 1950. Naipaul, one of the six or seven major English-language novelists of his generation, is profoundly admired by Graham Greene, and is without doubt the most accomplished West Indian novelist with the exception of Wilson Harris. His first major novel was *A House for Mr Biswas*, a satire on three generations of Trinidad life centering about a man who was born with an extra finger, symbol of malnutrition and independence of mind. This is comi-tragedy, told with both compassion and wit, about a man who spiritually rejects what he is forced to accept; and its importance and authority are undoubted. In *Mr Stone and the Knights Com-*

panion (1963) Naipaul writes with great sensitivity of an Englishman in England, trying to face the difficulties of old age in poverty. *The Mimic Men* (1967) is more ambitious in that it seeks – with a vanity that is at once tragic and delicious – for the notion of a decent society. Naipaul is sadly humorous, and has great psychological penetration. *In a Free State* (1971) combines three narrative strands, and displays the full range of Naipaul's concerns: the West Indians, the Indians, the Americans, the English, the Africans, exile. . . . It is a vast canvas, painted with concern, wit and understanding.

 The Mystic Masseur (1957)

A House for Mr Biswas (1961)

A Bend in the River (1979)

NARAYAN, R. K. (1907) Indian novelist. One of the most remarkable writers in 20th-century India, Narayan is the author of a long sequence of semi-attached novels about an imaginary South Indian community, Malgudi, combining philosophical discussion of Hinduism with character development. *The English Teacher* and *The Vendor of Sweets* (1967) are particularly notable.

The English Teacher (1945)

NATSUME SOSEKI, see SOSEKI, Natsume

NEAL, John (1793–1876) American melodramatic and sensational novelist and journalist. Neal is less important for his own novels than for his latter-day insistence on an American literature with American roots, written in American. He was well known, eventually, as a writer of crime stories.

 Rachel Dyer (1828)

The Down-Easters (1833)

The Moose Hunter (1864)

NEMEROV, Howard (1920) American novelist, poet and critic. Nemerov is primarily a poet, but in his intelligent novels he works out his persistent *doppelganger* theme with a sardonic sourness and keen wit. *Federigo, or the Power of Love* is his best known novel; it has been taken as a profound investigation of human identity, or a satire on New York manners, or both. It is certainly intelligent and impressive, as is the novel-autobiography *Journal of the Fictive Life*, a novel (unusually) about *not* writing a novel – or, if the reader wants to take it that way, a collection of sketches. Nemerov also writes good stories.

Federigo (1954)

Journal of the Fictive Life (1965)

Stories, Fables and Other Diversions (1971)

NEWBY, P. H. (1918) English novelist. Newby was first known for his complex Lawrentian novels such as *Agents and Witnesses* (1947); then as the comic satirist of Egyptian manners, *The Picnic at Sakhara* (1955) – a tour de force of great wit though little depth. Although Newby is original, especially in the earlier novels, in which he examines with compassion and insight the initiation of young men into love or the professions, he has never entirely detached himself from his sources: D. H. Lawrence, Franz Kafka, E. M. Forster. Yet he is an interesting and gifted writer, who is by now somewhat neglected.

Journey to the Interior (1946)

Mariner Dances (1948)

A Lot to Ask (1975)

NEWMAN, Andrea (1938) English novelist whose modest tale of the penalties of hit-and-run sex amongst students (*A Share of the World*) was meagre preparation for the perverse, clinically disturbing sexual themes obsessively pursued in her later books. In *A Bouquet of Barbed Wire*, for example, a man camouflages his love for his daughter with a nervous walk-out with his secretary (this was the basis for possibly the most explicit treatment of incest on British television). Miss Newman times the twists and turns of her plots with commendable address.

A Share of the World (1964)

A Bouquet of Barbed Wire (1969)

An Evil Streak (1977)

NEXØ, Martin (1869–1954) Danish novelist. Nexø was a well known communist writer in his time. He was born in the slums, and knew what he was writing about. He is a wholesome,

warm and crude writer; his communism is of the honest impracticable and not the totalitarian sort; both the great novel cycles are about proletarian lives; they are accurate, passionate, formless, readable for a few hundred pages, and not psychologically profound.

Pelle the Conqueror (1906–10, tr. 1913–16, tr. 1930)

Ditte (1917–21, tr. 1920–3)

In God's Land (1929, tr. 1933)

NGUGI, James (1938) Kenyan novelist and playwright. *Weep Not, Child* is a moving book about a mission-educated boy whose messianic ambitions are wrecked by the Mau-Mau emergency. *A Grain of Wheat* and *Secret Lives* are among the finest and most accomplished of the novels which take a critical and independent look at the new African leaders. Ngugi has developed into an impressive and mature writer.

Weep Not, Child (1964)

A Grain of Wheat (1967)

Secret Lives (1974)

NIELSEN, Helen (1918) American crime novelist, who has also written screenplays and some non-mystery novels. Her mysteries are about the resolution of threatening situations, rather than straight detection, and are usually concerned with contemporary problems in places where she has lived, including the Midwest and Los Angeles.

Gold Coast Nocturn (1952)

The Crime is Murder (1956)

NIN, Anais (1914–1978) American fiction writer and diarist, of Spanish-Dutch origin, who was associated with Henry Miller in Paris, and whose sometimes interestingly inchoate works are currently enjoying a revival. She employs in her novels all kinds of techniques, but most notably stream-of-consciousness; the results are confused but often impressive mixtures of morbidity, neo-Gothic, sexual squalor and candour. D. H. Lawrence, on whom she wrote a book, has been a potent influence.

Ladders to Fire (1946)

The House of Incest (1949)

Seduction of the Minotaur (1961)

NIVEN, Larry (1938) American science fiction writer who specializes in high-quality, imaginative adventure novels using variations on the

classic alien life theme.

Ringworld (1970)

Protector (1973)

The Mote in God's Eye (with Jerry Pournelle, 1974)

NOBBS, David (1935) English TV-writer and novelist best known for his "Reginald Perrin" novels which were successfully televised. Perrin is a present-day Pooter put upon at home and work who realizes one of his Walter-Mitty daydreams by faking suicide to escape, but force of habit draws him back to his old life. Nobbs is a prodigiously inventive, serio-comic writer who X-rays the mundane to highlight the extraordinary.

A Piece of the Sky is Missing (1969)

The Death of Reginald Perrin (1975)

The Return of Reginald Perrin (1977)

NORDHOFF, Charles (1887–1947) American novelist. Nordhoff wrote a series of novels, beginning in 1919 with *The Fledgling*; but he is primarily known for the exciting sea-stories which he wrote with James N. Hall, especially the trilogy dealing with the mutiny on the *Bounty*.

Mutiny on the Bounty (1932)

Men Against the Sea (1934)

Pitcairn's Island (1934)

NORRIS, Frank (1870–1902) American novelist and critic. Norris was the first and the best of the thoroughgoing American naturalists; and, like all naturalists who amount to

Anais Nin

anything, he was at heart a perfervid romantic. His chief novels, *McTeague* and *Vandover and the Brute*, are both essentially symbolic; both have been misread as naturalistic, which is understandable because this is what the author originally had in mind. More naturalistic is the unfinished cycle about the wheat business, *The Octopus* (1901) and *The Pit* (1903). *The Octopus* is Norris' most socially aware novel; but the heroes McTeague and Vandover have tragic stature.

McTeague (1899)

A Deal in Wheat (stories, 1903)

Vandover and the Brute (1914)

NORTON, André (1912) Pseudonym of Alice Mary Norton, prolific American science fiction and fantasy novelist. Most of her books are aimed at a teenage audience.

Star Man's Son (1952)

Witch World (1963)

NYE, Robert (1939) English novelist, story-writer, playwright, poet and reviewer. *Doubtfire* (called by one critic "rubbish") is a fantasy of adolescence drawing on such sources as Samuel Beckett and the Rabelais of Urquhart (which is not really Rabelais). Scatology is one theme personal to Nye, as was made apparent in *Falstaff*, which won the Hawthornden Prize: this popular book was a free-wheeling fantasy on a rather Victorian notion of Falstaff. Nye is crude but extremely bold, sentimental, and vulgar; and he is a clever and confident *pasticheur*.

Doubtfire (1967)

Falstaff (1976)

Merlin (1978)

O

OATES, Joyce Carol (1938) American novelist and story-writer. Oates' violent novels, influenced by William Faulkner, are very contrived in their "rawness" – recently she has been less read. But in the 1960s and early 1970s she swept many college girls off their feet with grief and rage. She is highly literary, yet there are echoes of Lloyd Douglas in the ultimate confusions of *Wonderland* (1971), a truly scarifying horror book (the horror is not without its unintentionally funny side). Oates has not yet, except in short stories, done full justice

to her undoubted psychological gifts: she is too obsessed with violence. But she remains one of America's most promising writers.

Do with Me what You Will (1973)

The Seduction (stories, 1975)

The Poisoned Kiss (1975)

Edna O'Brien

O'BRIEN, Edna (1932) Irish novelist and story-writer. Edna O'Brien is one of the best of the woman novelists who write candidly of woman's need for sexual attention, and this is what earned her high reputation. But now that popular interest is dying away, it is seen that her sexual candour is by no means her only virtue – her books were until recently banned in her own country, an honour which was accorded to James Joyce and many others. As William Trevor has pointed out, solitude is quite as potent a theme in her work as sex. She sees her country with great accuracy, and she is able to define men as the sex-objects of females. Her novels of Ireland are far more successful than those set elsewhere; and probably her stories of Ireland are the best of all her work. They celebrate life without sentimentalizing it, and do justice to courage in adversity.

Girls in Their Married Bliss (1964)

The Love Object (stories, 1968)

A Scandalous Woman (stories, 1974)

O'BRIEN, Flann (1911–66) Irish novelist, newspaper columnist and essayist. O'Brien's first and best novel *At Swim-Two-Birds* appeared in 1939, but little attention was paid to it (although James Joyce admired him). It was not until the 1960s that he became a famous writer. By that time the "passing of the years", the treadmill of journalism and the civil service, it has been said, "crushed him":

"he was never very lucky". He is an immensely attractive comic writer, whose actual achievement may have been overrated just because he is so delightful, and because some part of him remained undefeated by life. Only O'Brien would have thought of the idea that our water is "too strong", or of depriving Ireland of potatoes and substituting sago. He called his most famous novel a "celestial commode"; it is about a man who is writing a novel about a man who is writing a novel . . . It has been compared to Joyce, but is more like Irish Kafka. Of its successors *The Third Policeman* is the most successful. O'Brien is not a great writer; but he is one of the century's most hilarious ones, a very sad humourist indeed.

At Swim-Two-Birds (1939)

The Dalkey Archive (1965)

The Third Policeman (1967)

Flann O'Brien

O'CONNOR Edwin (1918–68) American novelist and radio producer. He wrote vivid, slightly sentimental but accurate novels about Irish-American types, such as a tough and ruthless city boss with a heart of gold in *The Last Hurrah*. His best novel is his first, *The Oracle*, about a sharp, corrupt, unscrupulous broadcaster.

The Oracle (1951)

The Last Hurrah (1956)

All in the Family (1966)

O'CONNOR, Flannery (1925–64) American novelist and story-writer, from Georgia.

O'Connor, who suffered from a horrible disease and who wrote some horrifying fiction, took her stand as a believing (orthodox) Roman Catholic. She said that only belief could reveal evil – and only evil could remind us of the price of restoration (Christ's sacrifice). But the woman who wrote of a sodomite rape by the devil, and of a man who burns out his eyes with quicklime to attain true sight, felt it improper to read Vladimir Nabokov's *Lolita*. . . . We simply cannot believe that she believed so easily in her Catholicism, or in any Christianity, though she may have done. But this is not to say that her novels, despite their hideousness, are not powerful and disturbing. *Wise Blood* is about a man who preaches a "Church without Christ"; *The Violent Bear it Away,* rather better, is about a man who struggles with the "bleeding stinking mad shadow of Jesus" and apparently goes insane. Her best work is in her stories, such as "The Artificial Nigger": in the shorter form her violence is more concentrated.

Wise Blood (1955)

The Violent Bear it Away (1960)

The Complete Stories (1971)

O'CONNOR, Frank (1903–66) Irish story-writer, novelist and critic. His stories are unpretentious and, at their best, superb examples of unforced art; he could be sentimental, but never when he followed the direction of his own feeling.

The Stories of Frank O'Connor (1953)

Stories Old and New (1964)

Collection Three (1969)

O'DONNELL, Peter (1924) British thriller writer who created the unusual and well-drawn protagonists, Modesty Blaise and Willie Garvin, originally for a strip cartoon. His work is characterized by imaginative plotting and some insight into the psychology of adventure seekers.

A Taste for Death (1969)

The Impossible Virgin (1971)

The Silver Mistress (1973)

O'FAOLÁIN, Seán (1900) Irish novelist, story-writer and biographer. O'Faoláin's high reputation in Ireland is not always realized by his English and American readers. It is in the short story that he excels, but his three novels (all published before he was forty) are good. O'Faolain is an articulate liberal, a pessimist who loves life, a keeper of values; but the "message" of his excellent stories is that what is true to feeling is what is best. O'Faolain

does not clutter his fiction up with ideas, although he has passionately held, and fought against, certain ideas in his time. He is one of the outstanding story-writers of this century.

A Nest of Simple Folk (1933)

The Stories (1957)

Foreign Affairs and Other Stories (1975)

O'FLAHERTY, Liam (1896) Irish novelist and story-writer. Best known for his (filmed) civil war novel *The Informer,* O'Flaherty has published nothing new for almost thirty years. His best work was in the short story: he wrote well of nature, and of primitive emotions.

The Informer (1925)

Insurrection (1950)

The Stories (1956)

O'HARA, John (1905–70) American novelist, story-writer and journalist. O'Hara is something of a latter-day Sinclair Lewis, although he writes more delicately and skilfully: he is an accurate recorder, at the least, of the mores of Pennsylvania in the 1930s; in his later and more diffuse fiction he lost touch. O'Hara is more a good literary journalist than an imaginative writer. He began in stories and in the first novels – for example, *BUtterfield 8* (1935) – as a disenchanted, sharp recorder of the bleakness of country club and similar disgraceful life. He did not hold back his disgust, but is sympathetic in his explanation of his characters' bad behaviour. His vices are stupidity, sentimentality, envy of the "literary", and pretentiousness; while his virtues are honesty,

John O'Hara

a sometimes powerfully nervous and reticent style, and a mastery of external detail. The poverty of his Gibbsville stories is shown up in a literary sense by Sherwood Anderson's *Winesburg* stories; but they are nonetheless impressive, and O'Hara cannot be accused of prejudice or manipulation. *Pal Joey* (1940) was turned by him and others into a very successful musical.

A Rage to Live (1949)

Selected Short Stories (1956)

Ourselves to Know (1960)

OLESHA, Yury (1899–1960) Russian novelist – a victim of Stalin, although "rehabilitated". His *Envy,* which was truly innovatory, is one of the finest of the Russian novels of the 1920s.

Envy (1926, tr. 1936)

The Three Fat Men (1928, tr. 1964)

OLIPHANT, Mrs Margaret (1828–97) English novelist: one of those magnificent nineteenth-century Englishwomen who supported a family by writing, and wrote major fiction, against the odds. Not all her fiction is good, but *Miss Marjoribanks* and *Hester* are superb; and there are other very good novels.

Miss Marjoribanks (1866)

Hester (1883)

The Second Son (1888)

OLSEN, Tillie (1913) American novelist and story-writer. She worked at *Yonnondio,* her extremely precise novel of life in the Depression, for over forty years, and the result is impressive, bleak, psychologically accurate and passionate. She is a modern naturalist using, when she requires them, elementary modernist techniques.

Tell Me a Riddle (stories, 1961)

Yonnondio (1974)

ONETTI, Juan (1909) Uruguyan novelist and story-writer who went to live in the Argentine. He is one of the most important Latin American novelists. His chief concerns are the obstacles to the achievement of inner virtue and the nature of fantasy. He is a great comic writer, who has used modernist techniques with consummate mastery.

The Shipyard (1961, tr. 1968)

ONIONS, Oliver (1873–1961) English novelist and story-writer, highly competent and off-beat, most famous for *In Accordance with the Evidence* (1912), first of a trilogy entitled *Whom*

God hath Sundered completed by *The Debit Account* (1913) and *The Story of Louie* (1913).

 Whom God hath Sundered (1912–13, one vol. 1925)

 The Collected Ghost Stories (1935)

 Widdershins (1939)

ONSTOTT, Kyle (1887–?1978) American writer who began as an expert on dogs; and then wrote *Mandingo*, with which he almost single-handedly invented a new genre: the "slaver" story set in the American South, with a slave hero who has exceptional physical attributes.

 Mandingo (1957)

Drum (1962)

Master of Falconhurst (1964)

ORCZY, Baroness (1865–1947) Hungarian writer of spy novels and historical romances. She wrote in English and is remembered for *The Scarlet Pimpernel*, featuring Sir Percy Blakeney, a master of disguise. Several Pimpernel novels followed; all contained a love story.

 The Scarlet Pimpernel (1905)

A Spy for Napoleon (1934)

ORWELL, George (1903–50) English novelist, satirist, critic and essayist. Orwell was best known in his lifetime for his journalism and for his satirical *Animal Farm* (1945), a fable about the Soviet Union. He seemed to be of

George Orwell

the left within his lifetime, but in retrospect it is evident that his creative work transcends such categories as the merely political. *Burmese Days* came from his experience as a policeman in Burma, a job he abandoned in 1927 for years of near destitution. In 1936 he reported the Spanish civil war *(Homage to Catalonia,* 1938). His early novels such as *Keep the Aspidistra Flying* (1936) and *Coming Up for Air* (1939) have been underrated; and even *1984,* which may well have helped to create such resistance as there is to the conditions it describes, has been patronized. It is now clear that Orwell was chiefly interested in justice and equality, that he was a deeply pessimistic man, and that he had powers of imagination which few of his contemporaries dreamed he had. He was an unlearned essayist, but made up for this by sheer common sense and decency. *1984* is a very literate analysis of trends, and history has proved Orwell right. But his masterpiece is *Animal Farm,* which is in the tradition of the very greatest satires.

 Burmese Days (1935)

A Clergyman's Daughter (1935)

1984 (1949)

OUIDA (1839–1908) English novelist. Marie Louise de la Ramée was born in England of a French father and an English mother. She was a frankly popular novelist, who wrote to please and for money; but her best works have an extra dimension because she was intelligent and genuinely despised her readers' hypocrisy. She was good on dogs.

 Under Two Flags (1867)

Wanda (1883)

An Altruist (1897)

OYONO, Ferdinand (1929) Francophone Cameroons novelist, playwright, actor and diplomat. *Houseboy* is a savage but restrained attack on the colonial presence, and is all too true. Later fiction is more diffuse.

 Houseboy (1956, tr. 1966)

The Old Man and the Medal (1956, tr. 1967)

OZ, Amos (1939) Israeli novelist and story-writer. Oz writes in Hebrew, and has a growing reputation internationally.

 My Michael (1968, tr. 1972)

Unto Death (stories, 1971, tr. 1975)

Touch the Water, Touch the Wind (1973, tr. 1974)

P

PADGETT, Lewis, see KUTTNER, Henry

PAGE, Thomas Nelson (1853–1922) American novelist, one of the many writers devoted to the romanticization of the South. His views are racialist, but his skilfully written books, particularly *Red Rock*, thrilled readers.

 On Newfound River (1891)

Red Rock (1898)

Red Riders (1924)

PALACIO VALDÉS, Armando (1853–1938) Spanish novelist. Palacio Valdés was a sentimental idealist who wrote about the social problems of local and provincial societies in his own day. His portraits of women were particularly admired.

 The Marquis of Peñalta (1883, tr. 1886)

The Joy of Captain Ribot (1899, tr. 1923)

PALAMÀS, Kostìs (1859–1943) Greek patriot and author. Palamàs dedicated himself to the revival of Greek poetry and culture. Although primarily a poet, he wrote some tales dealing with political and cultural revival.

 A Man's Death (stories, 1934)

PALAZZESCHI, Aldo (1885–1974) Italian writer, best known as a romantic poet. Palazzeschi (pseudonym of Aldo Giurlani) was associated with the Futurists in 1908–09. He wrote at least one novel which some considered to be among the major achievements in twentieth-century Italian literature: *Materassi Sisters,* a wry sketch of two old maids.

 Materassi Sisters (1934, tr. 1953)

PALMER, Vance (1885–1959) Australian novelist and dramatist. Palmer was a worthy and competent realist who had a good knowledge of Australian life at all levels. His work is a little monotonous, but informative.

 The Boss of Killara (1922)

Men are Human (1930)

The Big Fellow (1959)

PALUDAN, Jacob (1896) Danish novelist. He is famous for the *roman fleuve, Jörgen Stein,* a savage criticism of his own countrymen and their torpor, set in the second decade of this century.

 Birds Around the Light (1925, tr. 1928)

 Jörgen Stein (1932, tr. 1966)

PARGETER, Edith (1913) English historical novelist and translator from the Czech. Among her best known books are a learned quartet of novels set in medieval Wales. She has also written ingenious thrillers under the pseudonym Ellis Peters.

Scarlet Seed (1963)

Afterglow and Nightfall (1977)

Rainbow's End (as Peters, 1979)

witticisms.

 The Viking Portable (stories etc., 1944)

 The Collected Dorothy Parker (stories etc., 1973)

PARKIN, Molly (1932) British journalist and novelist who has written a series of comedies of sexual manners, in which the joke turns on the explicit expression of desires and feelings that the reader is supposed to be shocked to hear coming from a woman. The device is hard to sustain for a whole book.

 Love All (1974)

Uptight (1975)

Switchback (1978)

Dorothy Parker

PASTERNAK, Boris (1890–1960) Russian poet and novelist. Pasternak was primarily a poet, but became well known when the Soviet authorities refused to allow him to publish his novel *Doctor Zhivago*, which dealt with revolutionary and post-revolutionary times, and subsequently stopped him from going to Stockholm to receive the Nobel Prize (1958). The best part of the novel is the group of poems at the end, supposedly written by the eponymous hero, a doctor. Many critics are agreed that the book as a whole – shot through with beautiful religious imagery – fails to cohere. (It should on no account be confused with the "epic" film made under its title.) The novel does not contradict Soviet policy; it simply takes a different view (which is worse because puzzling to the authorites). In fact Pasternak's prose masterpiece is *Childhood*; but Zhivago is important, if not great. *Childhood* is less often read now that the Western

Boris Pasternak

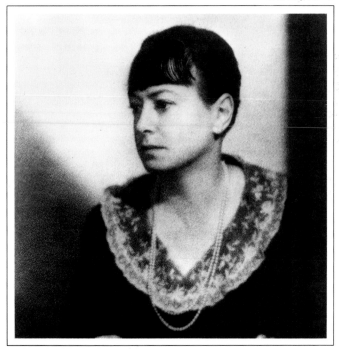

PARKER, Dorothy (1893–1963) American poet, short story-writer and, above all, wit. Her place in literary history remains consistently larger than her work merits. Her short stories have lasted better than her poems, but are mainly read only for their pointed phrasing and their strong "twenties" flavour. They were first collected in *After Such Pleasures* (1933) and *Here Lies* (1939). They are filled with bitter humour, and reflect the writer's despair, her pervading sense of talent wasted, perhaps buried, by her own derisive wit. Dorothy Parker wrote for the *New Yorker* from 1926–55 and helped create the form of that magazine's short story. She was associated with the Algonquin Round Table, the group of minor literary characters who met at New York's Algonquin Hotel to exchange ideas and witticisms.

PASOLINI, Pier Paolo (1922–74) Italian novelist, poet, film director and polemicist. Pasolini, most famous for such films as *Theorem*, was a homosexual who was murdered while he was in nocturnal search of sex. He began as a communist, and always remained politically left. His novels tell with great compassion of the agonies of the poor, the delinquent and the young, and are written precisely in the language of such groups. He was one of the most intelligent and humane of modern Italian writers, and his death was a tragic loss to Italian letters and thought.

 The Ragazzi (1955, tr. 1968)

A Violent Life (1959, tr. 1968)

media have new dissident superstars, but it will be remembered as the monumental failed novel of a major poet.

 Childhood (tr. 1941)

Doctor Zhivago (1957, tr. 1958)

PATCHEN, Kenneth (1911–72) American poet, novelist and graphic artist. His episodic and savagely satirical novel *Memoirs of a Shy Pornographer* is interesting, although other prose work has not worn well.

 Memoirs of a Shy Pornographer (1945)

PATER, Walter (1839–94) English novelist and essayist, associated with the Pre-Raphaelite

Brotherhood. In his Oxford lectures and his many essays he taught that beauty and wholeness of experience are the key to living. The moral implications are explored in *Marius the Epicurean*.

 Marius the Epicurean (1885)

PATON, Alan (1903) South African teacher, novelist, playwright and story-writer, who has also written several works of non-fiction. His subject is the tragedy of apartheid policies in his native land, in which he has continued to live despite strong criticism of his liberal views. Paton's fiction hovers between deep affection for the land itself, and pity at what he perceives to be the tragedy of its people divided by racialism. *Cry, the Beloved Country* is a beautiful and moving study of the destruction of old tribal ways by the ignorance and inflexibility of the whites. *Too Late the*

Alan Paton

Phalarope pictures the lonely humanity of one young Afrikaaner destroyed by ignorance and fear, and the sterility of life in his own community. His experiences as Principal of an African reformatory inspired *Debbie Go Home*.

 Cry, the Beloved Country (1948)

Too Late the Phalarope (1953)

Debbie Go Home (stories, 1961; in U.S. *Tales from a Troubled Land*, 1965)

PAUL, Elliot (1891–1958) American journalist and novelist. Paul wrote a series of autobiographical novels set in Europe and various parts of America, of which the best are listed below. His crime novels, such as *The Mysterious Mickey Finn* (1939) and *The Black Gardenia* (1952) were also successful.

 The Life and Death of a Spanish Town (1937)

 The Last Time I Saw Paris (1942, in Britain, *A Narrow Street*)

PAVESE, Cesare (1908–1950) Italian novelist, poet and translator. Pavese spent some time as a political prisoner in the 1930s – not for activism but for having anti-fascist friends – and, after a very unhappy sexual existence, killed himself. He remains incomparably the greatest of Italian post-war novelists: the doubts he reflects in his novels are still those of decent and intelligent people in civilized societies. Although not a Christian, he saw life as pointless unless lived for others; but he failed to discover a means of achieving such a life. Fortunately, his work hints at one: by the very efforts it records, and by the fact that Pavese is essentially a mythopoeic novelist. His last novel *The Moon and the Bonfires*, examines the whole of Italian life at three levels; it has not been surpassed technically in this century, and is unlikely to be. *The Moon and the Bonfires* amounts to a terrible acceptance of failure; but there is great hope in the mysteries of nature. Pavese was a penetrating psychologist, a much more than merely accomplished technician, and a magnificent stylist. Most of his work has been translated.

 The Harvesters (1941, tr. 1962)

The Political Prisoner (stories, 1955)

The Moon and the Bonfires (1950, tr. 1962)

PEACOCK, Thomas Love (1785–1866) English satirical novelist and poet. In his seven satirical novels, which are unlike anything else in English literature, the learned Peacock uses a romantic historical framework to mock progressive ideas. His main master was Rabelais. The novels are full of interesting talk and farcical action. He was clever, could see both sides of a question, and parades his extensive learning. *Nightmare Abbey* contains revealingly disguised portraits of Shelley, Byron and Coleridge.

 Nightmare Abbey (1818)

Crotchet Castle (1831)

Gryll Grange (1861)

PEAKE, Mervyn (1911–68) English artist, poet, playwright and novelist, best known for the *Gormenghast* trilogy, a major landmark in "other world" writing. The estate of Gormenghast is presented in almost tangible, three-dimensional detail, with its sinister Under-River, its moss-buried battlements, and its eccentric population subjugated by ancient traditions, every member predestined by heredity to his calling. Peake's writing is complex, rhetorical, grandiloquent and sometimes, like his drawings, almost deliberately ugly. But for all its flaws, *Gormenghast* is a triumphantly sustained flight of Gothic fancy; a visionary satire on the grandest of scales, funny and

terrifying by turn.

 *Titus Groan* (1946)

Gormenghast (1950)

Titus Alone (1959)

PENDLETON, Don (1927) American thriller writer whose "Executioner" series now runs to over thirty titles. The Executioner, a Vietnam veteran, wages single-handed war on the Mafia to avenge the deaths of his family.

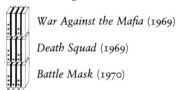 *War Against the Mafia* (1969)

Death Squad (1969)

Battle Mask (1970)

PENTECOST, Hugh, see PHILIPS, Judson

PERCY, Walker (1916) American (North Carolina) novelist, who lives in Louisiana. Percy was originally a doctor, but gave up medicine when he contracted tuberculosis, and published his first novel, *The Moviegoer*, in 1961 at the age of forty-five. He is a Catholic moralist, commenting on the world in the mask of a black humourist. His great strength is his handling of scenes in New Orleans.

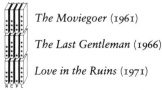 *The Moviegoer* (1961)

The Last Gentleman (1966)

Love in the Ruins (1971)

PERELMAN, S. J. (1904–79) American humorist, renowned for his satirical writing on an infinite variety of topics, notably on advertising and public relations, and on the world of entertainment, much of it published originally in *The New Yorker*. *The Most of S. J. Perelman* (1958) contained many of his most memorable pieces to date.

The Most of S. J. Perelman (1958)

Baby It's Cold Inside (1970)

Eastward Ha! (1978)

PÉREZ GALDÓS, Benito (1843–1920) Spanish novelist. Pérez Galdós has been underrated outside Spain, and is a novelist of at least the stature of Balzac. His series of novels *National Episodes* (1873–1912) examines nineteenth-century Spanish history from Trafalgar. His other and more important works appear at first sight to be "topical", and when he was re-discovered by American critics after World War II, it was fashionable to treat him as a politically radical novelist who was little more than a social commentator. This was very misleading: he played a part in politics, and on the radical side, but even here he was misunderstood. A morally very good man indeed, he remained unmarried but had a number of affairs with girls of the lower class, by one of whom he had children. He thus understood people of all classes, and was able to comment without preconceived notions. His novels in effect slash through hypocrisy and complacency; they also exhibit a profound psychological awareness. *Fortunata and Jacinta* is a vast novel, and one of the best books written in the nineteenth century in any language. In some of his later novels he used anti-realistic procedures, and his progress, through scores of books, was from conventional realist to modernist. He is a great sociological novelist, a great student of psychological abnormality, and a giant in every way. A revival in English is long overdue. Many of the translations from his novels are poor.

Lady Perfecta (1876, tr. 1894)

Fortunata and Jacinta (1887, tr. 1973)

Miau (1888, tr. 1963)

PERRAULT, Charles (1628–1703) French fairy-tale writer and poet. His most famous book he took lightly: his deceptively simple setting down of mostly traditional French fairy tales, including "Cinderella" and "Bluebeard".

Fairy Tales (1697, tr. 1957)

PETERS, Ellis, see PARGETER, Edith

PETERSEN, Nis (1897–1943) Danish poet, novelist, story-writer, alcoholic and tramp. His two novels, the first set in ancient Rome and the other in Ireland in the 1920s, deserve to be better known outside Denmark. He wrote some excellent and very sensitive short stories, which can be found in his *Collected Works* (8

vols., 1962).

The Street of the Sandal-makers (1931, tr. 1932)

Spilt Milk (1934, tr. 1935)

PEYREFITTE, Roger (1907) French diplomat and author. Peyrefitte is well known for his satirical studies of European society. His elegance of style is valued; he has been attacked as a pornographer, a scandal-monger and a "mischief-maker".

Special Friendships (1945, tr. 1958)

Diplomatic Diversions (1952, tr. 1953)

The Keys of St Peter (1955, tr. 1957)

PHILIPS, Judson (1903) American mystery writer, creator of crusading journalist Peter Styles, in books which emphasize action and suspense. Under the pseudonym Hugh Pentecost he writes novels closer to the classic detective mould, featuring hotel manager and linguist Pierre Chambrun. He displays toughness without brutality, and poses an intellectual puzzle.

Sniper (as Pentecost, 1965)

Hot Summer Killing (1969)

PHILLIPS, David Graham (1867–1911) American journalist and novelist, who was murdered by a deranged reader. He wrote more than twenty novels about political corruption and other social issues, of which the best remembered, *Susan Lenox* (which was filmed), charts the downfall of a simple country girl trapped into prostitution.

Susan Lenox (1917)

PIRANDELLO, Luigi (1867–1936) Italian (Sicilian) playwright, story-writer and novelist. Although most famous for his plays, Pirandello was quite as great in the short story and very accomplished in the novel. He received the Nobel Prize in 1934. He is above all the relativist of twentieth-century literature; yet he was all the time intellectually struggling to rid himself of his instinctive belief in the integrity of the human personality. He began as a realist, much influenced by Giovanni Verga; and his sense of reality never slips away into abstraction. His novels are really about human identity, and the crises people have to face when they question who they really are. In *The Late Mattia Pascal* (1904, tr. 1923) he presents a character who tries to "die"; this is the underlying theme of many of his stories (he was very prolific), and yet the best of them never lose touch with their meticulous settings. His art is based in scepticism, concealed tenderness and passion, and

a tragic awareness of the uselessness of integrity. Yet he is affirmative if only in his art.

The Old and the Young (1913, tr. 1928)

One, None and a Hundred Thousand (1926, tr. 1933)

Short Stories (tr. 1965)

PISEMSKY, Aleksey (1820–81) Russian novelist and dramatist. An early realist and satirist of the Russian gentry, Pisemsky's masterpiece is *A Thousand Souls*, about Russia in the earlier part of the nineteenth century.

The Simpleton (1850, tr. 1960)

A Thousand Souls (1858, tr. 1959)

PLAIDY, Jean (1906) English historical novelist. Born Eleanor Hibbert, she writes historical novels as Jean Plaidy, but has also achieved the distinction of best seller status with two other pseudonyms, Victoria Holt and Philippa Carr. Her settings span every period from the middle ages to the Victorian era in England, Spain, Italy and France; and her novels are meticulously researched and bring alive many famous historical characters. As Philippa Carr she writes highly popular light historical romances, and as Victoria Holt she has turned to the Gothic genre, with all the required ingredients of dark brooding houses and menacing terror. Her other pseudonyms include Eleanor Burford, Ellalice Tate, Elbur Ford, and Kathleen Kellow.

Bride of Pendorric (as Holt, 1963)

The Miracle of St. Bruno's (as Carr, 1972)

The Spring of the Tiger (1979)

Jean Plaidy

PLANTE, David (1940) American teacher, novelist and story-writer, who lives in England. His fiction is influenced by the style and psychological concerns of Henry James, as the title of his first novel suggests. His work is a complex working-out of personal relationships.

The Ghost of Henry James (1970)

The Darkness of the Body (1974)

PLATH, Sylvia (1932–63) American poet, novelist and short-story writer. Her single novel *The Bell Jar* describes a successful college girl's decline into mental illness, attempted suicide, and recovery after shock therapy, following the intensification – during a vacation job on a New York magazine – of her feeling that she cannot cope with life. Plath's short stories are also fine.

The Bell Jar (1963)

Johnny Panic and The Bible of Dreams (stories, 1977)

PLOMER, William (1903–73) South African novelist and poet. Plomer found the atmosphere of South Africa stifling, and left it early for England. But some of his best work deals with South Africa, which he has said must be a "black people's country" – or nothing at all. His finest novel *Museum Pieces*, about people who insist on clinging to the past, has not had its due.

Turbott Wolfe (1925)

Sado (1931)

Museum Pieces (1952)

POE, Edgar Allan (1809–49) American story-writer, poet, journalist and critic. Poe was immensely influential not only on American letters but also on Baudelaire and thus on other nineteenth-century Frenchmen. His influence is not yet exhausted: he is one of the founding-fathers both of crime fiction and of the "supernatural tale". Poe was an unstable alcoholic, but his instincts were at times unerring; there is always a stabilizing intelligence or at least sensibility behind the often absurd systematizations. He excelled both in the horror tale and in accounts of abnormal states. He was at his best a psychological realist of the first order, although his very best effects are intermittent. It is probable that his neurasthenic personality has been as influential as his actual work. There are innumerable editions of his *Tales of Mystery and Imagination*.

The Complete Works (17 vols., 1902)

POHL, Frederik (1919) American science fiction author who considers himself as writing "the special kind of SF best described as cautionary literature". He sees inequality, selfishness and trivial ambition as miseries that must be faced in themselves; technological change can only exaggerate, not cure them. Despite the seriousness of this theme he has developed the craft of entertaining narrative to a high degree. His subject matter is usually the alienation of individuals, whether from free choice by advertising (*The Space Merchants*, 1955), by planetary overcrowding (*The Reefs of Space*, 1964), or by computers (*The Age of Pussyfoot*, 1969). He has worked with two important collaborators: C. M. Kornbluth (*The Space Merchants*; *Gladiator-at-Law*; *Wolfbane*, 1959) and Jack Williamson (*Undersea Fleet*, 1956; *The Reefs of Space*, 1964; *Rogue Star*, 1969).

Gladiator-at-Law (1955)

Drunkard's Walk (1960)

Jem (1979)

PONTOPPIDAN, Henrik (1857–1943) Danish novelist and story-writer, who won the Nobel Prize in 1917, but whose work remains largely untranslated. The two translated parts of *Det forjaettede Land* (1891–95) reveal a writer of Tolstoyan stature, and deal with the struggle of a clergyman to realize his ideals.

Emanuel, or Children of the Soil (1891, tr. 1896)

The Promised Land (1893, tr. 1896)

PORTER, Gene Stratton (1886–1924) American novelist and nature writer. She lived with her husband in a cabin on the edge of a swamp in Indiana which provided the setting for many of her books. Her novels are inclined to be sentimental, but they reflect her love of nature. They are still widely read.

Freckles (1904)

Girl of the Limberlost (1909)

Laddie (1913)

PORTER, Joyce (1924) English writer of humorous detective stories, featuring the bumbling Inspector Dover. These are very funny books, but Dover has not developed as the series has lengthened and the joke is beginning to wear thin.

Dover One (1964)

PORTER, Katherine Anne (1890) American novelist and story-writer. She comes from Texas, and is a Southern writer with a difference: while unmistakably of her place and time, she also sees things from the point of view of an expatriate (for many years she lived abroad). She is a strange writer, at her best in short forms; and she has all that Flannery O'Connor has to offer, but is not melodramatic or Gothic. Her originality has hardly been fully recognized. She is seen at her most representative in *Pale Horse, Pale Rider* (1939), which contains the famous "Miranda" novellas. These semi-autobiographical stories about a girl of delicate sensibility are her chief

Edgar Allan Poe

Katherine Anne Porter

Katherine Anne Porter

Anthony Powell

John Cowper Powys

The sequence is extremely subtle, its essence being inspired by Proust, by the painter Poussin, and chiefly by Powell's own elegaic sense of the movement, in time, of things and people and their intimate affairs. Powell is able to examine many facets of twentieth-century experience, including politics (his creation of the go-getter Widmerpool is one of his greatest achievements), the nature of "modern love", and World War II. This is not to mention his comic genius, the greatest since Dickens. His narrator is a novelist like himself, and at first it is hard to understand the direction of his narration, which often seems random. But when the book was finished the mastery of his narrative line became apparent. *Time* is a poetic work, full of psychological insight, and a technical tour de force. Its procedures are unquestionably modernist.

Afternoon Men (1931)

From a View to a Death (1933)

What's Become of Waring? (1939)

POWELL, Dawn (1897–1963) American novelist. She was a witty and satirical realist who wrote of the midwest and then of Greenwich Village, New York.

Whither (1925)

A Time to be Born (1942)

Cage for Lovers (1957)

POWERS, J. F. (1917) American Catholic novelist and story-writer, best known for his stories, who deals with great sophistication with the lives of Roman Catholic clergymen and with Chicago people. He is noted for his technical skill, his ear for dialogue, and his satirical humour. His one novel *Morte D'Urban*, which deals critically with the Church, is perhaps his best work.

Prince of Darkness (stories, 1947)

The Presence of Grace (stories, 1956)

Morte D'Urban (1962)

POWYS, John Cowper (1872–1963) Welsh novelist, brother of T. F. Powys. J. C. Powys has his fervent followers, but he remains widely unread, although from time to time there have been revivals. The earlier books, such as *Rodmoor* (1916), contain profound studies of obscure psychological states. With *Wolf Solent* (1929) and especially the massive *A Glastonbury Romance* (1932) he became recondite, eccentric, interesting but accessible only to the "initiated" (who tend themselves to be eccentric). *Weymouth Sands*, his best novel, is also his most accessible. He was a confessional novelist, and one always of great

triumph; they are bleakly disillusioned, and yet they affirm the inevitability of hope.

Ship of Fools (1962)

The Collected Stories (fullest ed. 1967)

POTOK, Chaim (1929) American Jewish novelist. Potok's well informed, sharply observed and lively novels of Jewish life have been hugely enjoyed.

The Chosen (1967)

The Promise (1969)

POTTS, Jean (1910) American mystery novelist and story-writer, the tension in whose work derives from character more than action. The people and places are firmly planted in everyday experience.

Go Lovely Rose (1954)

The Diehard (1956)

My Brother's Killer (1977)

POURNELLE, Jerry, see NIVEN, Larry

POWELL, Anthony (1905) English novelist, critic and autobiographer. Powell was already an established novelist when he began his famous *roman fleuve A Dance to the Music of Time* (1951–75): he had written some fine comic novels influenced by, but by no means resembling, the work of Evelyn Waugh, Ronald Firbank and Wyndham Lewis. With the publication of the first ten or so of the twelve-volume series he reached the position of one of the very few English novelists who are likely to be regarded as major in the future.

interest – but perhaps finally as a "case" rather than as a fully achieved major writer.

Ducdame (1925)

Weymouth Sands (1936)

Mortal Strife (1941)

POWYS, T. F. (1875–1953) Welsh novelist and story-writer; brother of J. C. Powys. T. F. Powys is hardly better known than his brother; but he has been much more influential – particularly on Dylan Thomas. His works reflect, in a narrow but distinctive compass, the struggle of a sceptical and ribald mind to reconcile itself with Christianity. Ultimately the impression is one of a reluctant Deist – although at times God does intervene, albeit in paradoxical ways, into men's lives. His most famous book is *Mr Weston's Good Wine* (1927), about God "judging" a Dorset village in the guise of a wine-salesman. Or is it? It is a complete and unresolved allegory, flavoured with Powys' characteristically whimsical and black view of humanity. Better are some stories (as in *Feed My Swine, 1926*) and the novel *Mark Only* (1924), in which the cryptic style is less extreme.

Mr Tasker's Gods (1925)

Christ in the Cupboard (1930)

Bottle's Path (1946)

POYER, Joe (1939) American spy thriller writer, often praised for his meticulous research. *The Chinese Agenda* (1972) takes the unusual step of sending a joint American-Soviet expedition into a remote part of China.

The Balkan Assignment (1971)

The Chinese Agenda (1972)

PRATOLINI, Vasco (1913) Italian novelist. Pratolini writes almost naturalist novels about working-class Florence. He is frankly left-wing, and his work suffers from being over-consciously centred on a dialectic *schema*; but his sympathies and understanding are deep, and he draws attention to the development – frustrated though it has been – of a social conscience in the past hundred years in Italy.

A Tale of Santa Croce (1945, tr. 1952)

A Tale of Poor Lovers (1947, tr. 1949)

Bruno Santini (1960, tr. 1965)

PRATT, Fletcher, see DE CAMP, L. Sprague.

PRÉVOST, L'Abbé (1697–1763) French novelist, translator, adventurer and man of letters. He translated and was influenced by Samuel Richardson. His life was a series of "discreditable" episodes (he was nearly hanged for forgery in England) punctuated by meditation. His most famous novel *Manon Lescaut*, is a great work, but has obscured two other important ones: *History of Modern Greek* (1741) and *Memoirs of an Honest Man* (1745); translations of these do not appear to exist. Prévost was one of the anticipators of the modern psychological novel; his portrait of a nice whore is perhaps the best in all literature; and he was a notable examiner of the French manifestations of *sensibilité*. In other words, he wrote "novels of feeling".

Manon Lescaut (1731, tr. 1949)

PRICE, Anthony (1928) English spy novelist. He uses the genre to write about what interests him, military history, archaeology, power ploys, and contemporary social issues (such as women's liberation), but he sees even the most esoteric of his interests always from the human point of view.

The Labyrinth Makers (1970)

Other Paths to Glory (1974)

Tomorrow's Ghost (1979)

PRICE, Reynolds (1933) American novelist and story-writer. Price comes from North Carolina, and has been preoccupied both with life there and with examining the existential consequences of people's thinking and feeling in terms of cliché: the title of *A Long and Happy Life* is just such a cliché, and the book is about a girl who becomes victim to it. Later fiction is more abstract and perhaps less successful, as Price has transferred his "local" vision to an over-lofty concern with the difference between true relationships, which are allegedly "irresistible", and ones only imagined. He is an interesting writer, with a good style, and he has a following.

A Long and Happy Life (1962)

Love and Work (1968)

Permanent Errors (stories, 1970)

PRICHARD, Katharine Susannah (1884–1972) Australian regionalist novelist and journalist, whose work is marked by meticulous personal research and a strong left-wing commitment. Her best novel, *Coonardoo*, charts with restrained savagery the relationship between a cattle-station owner and an aborigine girl in the rough country of Western Australia.

Coonardoo (1929)

Haxby's Circus (1930)

PRIEST, Christopher (1943) British science fiction writer. A careful stylist whose development of ideas is painstaking but occasionally flawed in logic.

Fugue for a Darkening Island (1972)

Inverted World (1974)

A Dream of Wessex (1978)

PRIESTLEY, J. B. (1894) English novelist, dramatist, critic and publicist. Priestley has been an immensely popular novelist, whose very popularity has in recent years contributed to his neglect by critics. He is uneven, but his best is as good as many more "literary" celebrities. *The Good Companions*, his greatest success, is an old-fashioned picaresque novel, sentimental (he has never escaped from this, but his sentimentality is inoffensive) but genuinely wholesome in giving an account of a "merrie England" which is quickly dying out. Priestley is a hugely talented and thoughtful entertainer.

The Good Companions (1929)

Angel Pavement (1930)

Lost Empires (1965)

J. B. Priestley

PRITCHETT, V. S. (1900) English novelist, story-writer, critic and memoirist. Pritchett is best known for his stories, although his novel *Mr Beluncle* (1951) was widely read. His stories are very well made and meticulous in detail; his genius is for spotting and directing the reader's attention to the uniqueness hidden in the commonplace. He is a master of the shabby-genteel, the eccentric and the speech habits of "ordinary" people. He is highly professional, and has not turned out a sloppy page

V. S. Pritchett

in his life.

Dead Man Leading (1937)

Collected Stories (1956)

When My Girl Comes Home (stories, 1961)

PROKOSCH, Frederic (1908) Prolific and elegant American novelist and poet. Prokosch, a lush and very uneven writer, has travelled widely and aims, possibly a little pretentiously, to write "internationally". Yet his novels are original, and show understanding of their themes, which are exile and world crisis – except in the most successful, which are historical. *The Dark Dancer* in particular is a very impressive and fine novel about India.

The Asiatics (1935)

The Dark Dancer (1964)

America, My Wilderness (1972)

PROLE, Lozania, see BLOOM, Ursula

PROUST, Marcel (1871–1922) French novelist and critic. There is undoubtedly a snob cult of Proust, but he is nonetheless a very great writer. The difficulty is that he is praised by intelligent people for different reasons: for his passages about social distinctions; for the "essays" with which he punctuates his long novel; and for his portrayals of character. But he needs to be taken as a whole. Scott Moncrieff's translation, *Remembrance of Things Past*, is elegant but bowdlerised and dated; and it is good news that Terence Kilmartin – the translator of both André Malraux and Henri

de Montherlant, is engaged on a new one in three volumes, which will make Proust much more accessible. Proust, as much as any author, lived for and even through his book. It is a semi-autobiographical work, dealing with the narrator's sexual unhappiness and subsequent dedication to literature (at the end he is setting out to write the novel we have read). It deals with the nature of memory and reverie, with homosexuality (but this is confused because, as André Gide pointed out, Proust makes certain characters female when really he meant them to be male); and with the meaning of art. Its main theme is a religious one: how to recapture through memory the lost innocence of childhood, but without oversimplifying. Literature was Proust's Church. His gallery of characters, especially the Baron Charlus, has hardly been rivalled. There is no defense for the view that Proust is an absurdly over-valued writer, but mystical utterances about him are, it must be admitted, provocative.

Remembrance of Things Past (1913–27, tr. 1922–31)

PRYCE-JONES, David (1936) British novelist, biographer and journalist who began with gentle satires of English middle-class life. He is clever and witty, but has not yet achieved much depth. His new novel, about strange goings-on in a commune in Wales, may show a maturer talent emerging.

Quondam (1965)

The Stranger's View (1967)

Shirley's Guild (1979)

PULMAN, Jack (1928–1979) British suspense novelist and television writer. Much-praised for his TV adaptations (*War and Peace, Crime and Punishment*), Pulman wrote a single but noteworthy novel, *Fixation* (in U.S. as *Collision*). Set in America, it is the story of a clash between titan police chief and titan crook.

Fixation (1978)

PURDY, James (1923) American novelist and story-writer. Purdy had some difficulty in establishing himself, but was taken up by Carl Van Vechten in the United States and by Edith Sitwell in England. His earlier work is very much superior to his later, which is mannered gothic and depends more on publishers' promotion capacities than on its own merits. But the earlier books such as *The Nephew*, about a small-town woman who discovers that her prized nephew killed in the Korean war has been a "bad man", is exquisite, and owes as much to Henry James as it does to the melodramatic and homosexual tradition in which he writes. Later work is sensationalist, though

Marcel Proust

often powerful in patches.

Malcolm (1959)

The Nephew (1960)

I Am Elijah Thrush (1972)

PUZO, Mario (1920) American novelist who is best known for one of the biggest commercial successes ever: *The Godfather* (1969). The story of a Mafia family and its amoral approach to the acquisition of power and wealth, it is written in a detached documentary style, derived from journalistic accounts of the Mafia. This is ideally suited to the many explicit descriptions of violence. Puzo's second book, *Fools Die*, is less competent.

The Godfather (1969)

Fools Die (1978)

PYKE, Robert L., see FISH, Robert L.

James Purdy

PYM, Barbara (1913) English novelist. She writes English novels about enclosed societies (villages in which affairs centre around the Church, etc.) Within her limitations she is acutely observant, and is rightly valued for this. But her view is circumscribed because (as she gladly admits) she does not know much of what goes on in the big world outside, and her moral judgements, while valid, are not quite as astonishing as her admirers suggest.

Excellent Women (1952)

Less Than Angels (1955)

No Fond Return of Love (1961)

PYNCHON, Thomas (1937) American novelist of growing reputation whose books share a common theme. The main character in each is engaged in a search: Herbert Stencil for the truth about his father's death in *V*; Oedipus Maas for the rationale behind the underground mail system of *The Crying of Lot 49*; and Tyrone Slothrop, the disorientated American serviceman of *Gravity's Rainbow,* simply for a way out. These characters are innocents; not really taking part in the world they move through, but driven by their searches on an extended confusing tour of the paranoid subplot to official history that Pynchon has conjured up. The characters who populate this alternative history determinedly pursue their alloted roles in the giant conspiracy which runs the world, accepting coincidence, cruelty and confusion alike with a grim fatalism. His

style, particularly in *Gravity's Rainbow,* reflects this pattern of certainties built on sand. He shifts from technical jargon to journalese to high literature without warning: each passage internally consistent, but its confidence betrayed by the juxtaposition. This is a fascinating – sometimes difficult, sometimes hilarious – technique, but as in the novels themselves the originality is more than skin deep.

V (1963)

The Crying of Lot 49 (1966)

Gravity's Rainbow (1973)

Q

QUEEN, Ellery Pen name used by two American cousins, Frederic Dannay (1905) and Manfred Blennington Lee (1905–71) who collaborated in the writing of thirty-nine detective novels which feature an investigator with the same name, Ellery Queen. They founded and edited *Ellery Queen's Mystery Magazine* and produced many anthologies of detective stories. The novels are lively and written with ease and humour. They are notable for their relentless analysis of events

and clues in the process of deduction.

The Roman Hat Mystery (1929)

Inspector Queen's Own Case (1956)

The Last Woman in His Life (1970)

QUEIROS, José Maria de Eça de (1845–1900) Portuguese novelist. Eça, as he is usually called, spent much of his time abroad as a diplomat. He is the greatest Portuguese novelist, a realist and symbolist who wrote in the tradition of (and partly influenced by) Gustave Flaubert. The subject of his novels is inevitably the decline of Portugal, its inability to adapt itself to the times, the tendency of its people – even the best of them – to fritter away their time in dreaming. He is usually said to have "given up", and to have ended as a "dandy"; but his last books are extremely interesting, although not perhaps on a par with the great novels of his middle period, *The Sin of Father Amaro, Cousin Basilio* and above all *The Maias*. He is notable for his understanding of the Portuguese temperament, his evocation of landscape, his genius for examining bizarre states of mind (for example, incestuous desire in *The Maias*) and his plotting.

The Sin of Father Amaro (1876, tr. 1962)

Cousin Basilio (1878, tr. 1953)

The Maias (1888, tr. 1965)

Ellery Queen: Manfred B. Lee (left) and Frederic Dannay

QUENEAU, Raymond (1903–76) French novelist, poet and editor of encyclopaedias. Queneau was in the tradition of learned buffoons – a sort of French Flann O'Brien. He is both a surrealist and an absurdist; but his chief achievement was to create a slang language of his own. His punning is as extensive as that of James Joyce. He became well known when his zany novel *Zazie in the Metro* (1959, tr. 1960) was made into a film.

 A Hard Winter (1939, tr. 1948)

The Bark Tree (1953, tr. 1968)

Between Blue and Blue (1965, tr. 1967)

QUEVEDO, Francisco Gómez de (1580–1645) Spanish poet, novelist and satirist. As a novelist he is most famous for his important picaresque novel *The Swindler*, which was translated together with *Lazarillo de Tormes* in 1969. In some respects this is the most elegant and subtle of all the picaresque novels: it is the narrative of a villain who has no repentance.

 The Swindler (1626, tr. 1657, tr. 1969)

QUILLER-COUCH, Sir Arthur (1863–1944) English university teacher, critic and novelist. He was an old-fashioned but sound critic. His historical novels, in the tradition of R. L. Stevenson, are well made, literate and still enjoyed.

 Dead Man's Rock (1887)

The Splendid Spur (1889)

The Ship of Stars (1899)

QUOD, John, see IRVING, John.

R

RAABE, Wilhelm (1831–1910) German novelist. He was influenced by Charles Dickens, but made his own distinctive contribution to German letters. His theme is the value of the inner experience over materialistic success, which he despised and described excellently.

 The Hunger-Pastor (1864, tr. 1885)

Abu Telfan (1868, tr. 1881)

RABELAIS, François (?1494–1553) French writer of prose fiction, doctor, geographer, anatomist and man of learning. Rabelais was

François Rabelais

first a monk, then a physician. He satirized theological stuffiness and pedantry. His great work *Gargantua and Pantagruel* grew and changed while he worked at it. Its origins were at first in popular legend; later he took it and himself more seriously, even though the key to the whole is *pantagruelism*, which is essentially "humour" – a whole definition of humour and its educative and imaginative function. His other great subject is education, at all its levels.

 Gargantua and Pantagruel (1532–52, tr. 1937, tr. 1955)

RADCLIFFE, Mrs Ann Ward (1764–1823) English gothic novelist, whose books now seem very dated. Her main plot device has survived well: a terrified girl flees alone through a nightmare landscape, pursued by ghosts and lecherous monks; she is caught and escapes, is caught again and escapes, and so on. Her villain/hero in *The Italian* – evil, passionate, grandiose and lonely – has influenced many writers, including, probably, Lord Byron.

 The Romance of the Forest (1791)

The Mysteries of Udolpho (1794)

The Italian (1797)

RAE, Hugh C. (1935) Scottish crime novelist, who also writes as Robert Crawford, R. B. Houston and Stuart Stern. His stories of violence, enhanced with elements of mystery, explore such concepts as power, corruption and the springs of criminality.

 Skinner (1964)

The Marksman (1971)

The Shooting Gallery (1972)

RAMUZ, Charles-Ferdinand (1878–1947) Francophone Swiss novelist. He began as a sensationalist French realist, but then developed into an effective allegorical writer. Stravinsky collaborated with him on *Histoire du Soldat* for which he wrote the libretto (1918, tr. 1955). *When the Mountain Fell* is his chief work, the story of an avalanche.

 The Triumph of Death (1922, tr. 1946)

When the Mountain Fell (1935, tr. 1949)

RAND, Ayn (1905) Russian-born American novelist whose notoriously ill-written novels preach a "superman" philosophy: to those who have shall be given, and those who have not are nothing. Her cruel message distorts her sense of psychology, but she has a following amongst extreme right-wing circles.

 The Fountainhead (1943)

Atlas Shrugged (1957)

We the Living (1959)

RANSOME, Arthur (1884–1967) English writer best known for his children's novels, the enduringly successful *Swallows and Amazons* series. Mostly set in the Lake District, they capture perfectly the childhood dream of adventure and freedom from adult supervision. All involve sailing and are written with a real feeling for waterscapes.

 Swallows and Amazons (1930)

Secret Water (1939)

Missee Lee (1941)

RAO, Raja (1909) Indian novelist writing in English. Rao is the most gifted literary man to have been influenced by – indeed, to embody – the non-violence advocated by Gandhi. Gandhi did not of course invent non-violence, nor is Rao original; he has taken an old Indian theme and has written about it with wisdom and style. He has also written a number of good stories. E. M. Forster thought Rao's first novel *Kanthapura* to be the best ever written about India in the English language. It is an imaginative but profoundly informative book about life in an Indian village. The two later novels are rather more abstract, but none the less excellent.

 Kanthapura (1938, repr. 1963)

The Serpent and the Rope (1960)

The Cat and Shakespeare (1965)

RAPHAEL, Frederick (1931) Anglo-American novelist and story-writer born in Chicago but educated and resident in England. Raphael has spent much time making reasonably literate adaptations of classics for the large and small screens – and in writing scripts for the same media. His later novels suffer from his main preoccupation. But his earlier ones, after a poor start, suggested that a quite important writer might be in the making. He is intelligent, subtle and aware; he lacks only substance, and conviction.

The Limits of Love (1960)

The Trouble with England (1962)

Lindmann (1963)

RAUCHER, Herman (1928) American screenwriter and novelizer, who has successfully novelized a number of his powerful screenplays.

Watermelon Man (1970)

Summer of '42 (1971)

Ode to Billy Joe (1976)

RAVEN, Simon (1927) English novelist and scriptwriter. Raven's early novels about cads and bad form were exceedingly good and well observed – especially the first *The Feathers of Death*, about homosexuality in the army. He showed a fine sense of what "honour" really is, and how it feels to "break the code" (he himself was, as he says, "compelled to resign my commission because of unpaid gambling debts"). Later novels, all part of a now completed series called *Alms for Oblivion*, are as a whole quite unimportant, though relieved by patches of good writing whenever anyone breaks a code, or is homosexual, or does something in which Raven is interested. The public enjoyed the sequence, and the critics were polite.

The Feathers of Death (1959)

Close of Play (1962)

The Survivors (1975)

RAWLINGS, Marjorie Kinnan (1896–1953) American regionalist novelist who made her home in Florida, which provided the background for much of her writing. Her most successful novel was *The Yearling* (1938) the adventures of a boy with his pet fawn, and reminiscent of *Huckleberry Finn*.

The Yearling (1938)

Cross Creek (1942)

The Sojourners (1953)

RAYNER, Claire (1931) English writer and broadcaster. Her novels show her interest in medicine and the theatre, and include a continuing nineteenth-century family saga *The Performers*.

Gower Street (1973)

Paddington Green (1975)

"READ, Miss" ( ) Pseudonym of English school-mistress and novelist whose hand-knit yarns of enclosed communities in rural England are narrated by a school-mistress of infinite resource and compassion called Miss Read. Her novels comprise cleverly linked stories which lead through neat twists and turns to an invariably happy ending.

Thrush Green (1959)

The Howards of Caxley (1967)

No Holly for Miss Quin (1976)

READ, Piers Paul (1941) English Catholic novelist and journalist. Read began as a very promising and serious novelist, but lately has transferred his attention to big-time journalism, at which he is adept. The best of his novels is the second, *The Junkers*, about the world of the Nazis. This showed a keen understanding of the German character, and Read bade fair to become a major novelist. But *The Upstart* (1973) and *Polonaise* (1976) are by no means in the same class. His excellence seemed to be confined to his journalism, but *A Married Man* (1979) is once again a serious novel of great quality.

The Junkers (1968)

Monk Dawson (1969)

The Professor's Daughter (1971)

Piers Paul Read

READE, Charles (1814–84) British novelist and dramatist, who turned his play *Masks and Faces* into the novel *Peg Woffington* and thereby began a career as a novelist. His stories often have a pointed reforming moral, and are distinguished partly by the research that went into them, but mainly by his considerable ability to tell a compelling story. His best book, *The Cloister and the Hearth*, is a highly readable medieval saga; the central character is torn between the twin paths of worldliness and spirituality and, after a series of journeys and adventures in fifteenth-century Europe, is finally revealed to be the father of Erasmus. It contains an exceptionally fine description of an ascetic mystical experience.

Peg Woffington (1853)

The Autobiography of a Thief (1858)

The Cloister and the Hearth (1861)

RÉAGE, Pauline The pseudonym under which the remarkable *Story of O* was written. Widely praised as the first erotic novel totally lacking in obscenity, it is the story of a young woman's conversion to masochism, told in an entirely non-psychological way, so that the story acquires the character of a fable. The author, known to be a woman, is rumoured to be a close friend of the French essayist Jean Paulhan, who wrote an introduction to the original edition.

The Story of O (1966)

Return to the Château (1971)

RECHY, John (1934) American novelist. Rechy was among the first American writers to explore the world of the homosexual in *The City of Night*. He has no sense of form, but the earlier works were enlightening. His message now seems trite; but he helped create a civilized climate for an ostracized group.

The City of Night (1963)

Numbers (1967)

The Fourth Angel (1972)

REDMON, Anne (1943) American novelist whose *Emily Stone* was a sharp, funny, admirably poised debut about a lonely girl. *Music and Silence* covers less familiar territory: a girl is threatened by mysterious evils in a sinister South-West London household. A baroque, over-convoluted novel, it nonetheless draws a world of multiple tensions together in a vigorous piece of writing.

Emily Stone (1974)

Music and Silence (1979)

REED, Ishmael (1938) Afro-American novelist and poet whose satire criticizes the rationalism, science and technology of American society. Reed's work is based on a return to black cultural origins.

 Yellow Back Radio Broke-down (1969)

REEMAN, Douglas (1924) English novelist, former naval officer, policeman and children's welfare officer. He writes racy sea adventures, mostly set in the present century; and as Alexander Kent he employs the same formula in historical settings.

 Send a Gunboat (1960)

Surface with Daring (1976)

REEVE, Arthur B. (1880–1936) American mystery writer, creator of Craig Kennedy, scientific investigator, unjustifiably called "the American Sherlock Holmes". The books are remarkable for their early use of Freudian psychology.

 The Silent Bullet (1912, in Britain, *The Black Hand*)

 The Clutching Hand (1934)

REID, [T.] Mayne (1818–83) Irish-born American soldier, actor and novelist. He was a very popular romance writer, and drew with skill on the details of his own adventurous life (he fought in the Mexican War). He married a girl of fifteen, which led him to write *The Child Wife* (what she thought about this is not recorded).

 The Scalp Hunters (1851)

The Child Wife (1853)

The Headless Horseman (1866)

REID, V. S. (1913) Caribbean novelist, journalist, critic, playwright and newspaper editor. His first book, *New Day* (1949) is the most popular with his own people, and describes Jamaica's struggle for self-rule through the eyes of a fictional family, the Campbells. It makes interesting use of the rich Jamaican dialect, which derives in part from Welsh, and consequently is full of the cadences and poetry to be found in Welsh writing. A later novel, *The Leopard* (1958), has more general appeal; and recently he has turned with great success to writing for young people, as in *The Young Warriors* and *Sixty-Five* (1960).

 New Day (1949)

The Leopard (1958)

The Young Warriors (1967)

REINER, Max, see CALDWELL, Taylor.

REMARQUE, Erich Maria (1898–1970) German journalist and novelist, who left Nazi Germany to live in America. Remarque fought in the Great War, and, drawing to some extent on a now forgotten book by a dramatist and painter Georg Von Der Vring, wrote a runaway best seller *All Quiet on the Western Front*. It was an honest book, but was psychologically superficial and gained its effects by means of a primitively gothic method of piling horror on horror. Remarque went on to write other best sellers, the best of which is *Three Comrades*. He played quite a large part, and played it well, in the film of his own *A Time to Live and a Time to Die*. He was a competent and good-hearted writer.

 All Quiet on the Western Front (1928, tr. 1929)

 Three Comrades (1937, tr. 1937)

A Time to Live and a Time to Die (1954, tr. 1954)

REMIZOV, Alexey (1877–1957) Russian fiction writer. Remizov is one of the most important modernist Russian writers, following in the footsteps of Gogol and Dostoyevsky. He is the master of twentieth-century *skaz*, and was the genius behind Zamyatin. His prose varies from tales about dreams and folklore to accounts of "ordinary life". But his real subject was the magical power of words: he explored the relationship between language and reality. He went into exile, but did not attack the communists. He died a lonely, half-blind and terrified old man in Paris – writing and exploring his terror until the very end. He is one of the century's greatest modernists.

 The Clock (1908, tr. 1924)

On a Field Azure (stories, 1927, tr. 1946)

The Fifth Pestilence (tr. 1927)

RENAULT, Mary (1905) English novelist. Her work, the best known of which is historical, has been described as being a cross between "nurses' romance" and "woman's fiction"; this is a little unfair. Her narrative skill has gained her a wide audience, especially for her Greek novels, which are flavoured with eroticism. Her sense of history is sound and her research seemingly painstaking, but she can be sentimental.

 The Charioteer (1953)

The King Must Die (1958)

The Persian Boy (1972)

RENDELL, Ruth (1930) English crime and detective novelist. Her books are imbued with a strong feeling of the atmosphere of her home ground, small-town and rural home counties and inner London. The policemen Wexford and Burden are characters who develop in each successive book. Rendell strips the pretences from inadequate personalities with unmerciful perception.

 A New Lease of Death (1967)

A Demon in My View (1976)

A Sleeping Life (1978)

RESTIF DE LA BRETON, Nicholas (1734–1806) French novelist of low life, and printer. He was immensely prolific (over 250 volumes, sometimes composed straight into print). He had little skill, and was a trite moralist, but his *Nights of Paris* is informative on the Revolution.

 Nights of Paris (1790, tr. 1964)

REYMONT, W. S. (1867–1925) Polish novelist who won the Nobel Prize in 1924. Most of his work is very interesting; but his series of novels *The Peasants* is a masterpiece. Reymont explores with remarkable success the life, manners, thinking and above all language of the Polish village people. He treats the peasant community of Lipce in a mythopoeic manner, relating it to the passage of the seasons.

 The Comedienne (1896, tr. 1920)

The Promised Land (1899, tr. 1928)

The Peasants (1902–09, tr. 1925–26)

REYNOLDS, Mack (1917) American science fiction writer. His speculations regarding

Mary Renault

possible socio-economic developments in the near future are interesting.

Black Man's Burden (1961)

The Rival Rigelians (1967)

Looking Backward from the Year 2000 (1973)

RHYS, Jean (1894–1979) British novelist and story-writer. She was utterly neglected after she stopped writing in 1939; but interest in her was revived, and maintained, when she published the novel *Wide Sargasso Sea* in 1966; this is very different from early work, and tells the story of the first Mrs Rochester (of Charlotte Brontë's *Jane Eyre*). Her short stories, in two volumes, are as distinguished as her fine novels; her fiction tells the tales, with great sensitivity and insight and a kind of ravishing gloom, of women badly done by. The novel *After Leaving Mr Mackenzie* (1931) is partly about Ford Madox Brown. She is now regarded as a major writer.

The Left Bank and Other Stories (1927)

Voyage in the Dark (1934)

Tigers Are Better Looking (stories, 1974)

RICE, Craig (1908–57) Pen name of Georgina Ann Randolph, American novelist and author of books about true crime. Of her many detective novels, some are among the few attempts by women writers at the "tough guy" story, and others are comic crime stories.

Trial by Fury (1941)

The Thursday Turkey Murders (1943)

But the Doctor Died (1967)

RICE, Elmer (1892–1967) American playwright whose novels are less well known. *A Voyage to Purilia* (1930) is a Utopian satire on the mythical world of Hollywood; *Imperial City* (1937) is about New York.

A Voyage to Purilia (1930)

Imperial City (1937)

RICHARDS, Frank (1875–1961) British comic children's writer, who used 25 pen names to disguise his authorship of thousands of words each week for school story magazines like *Gem* and *Magnet*. This output was maintained for some 30 years, thanks to a formula of pantomime characterization and mechanical plotting. His most celebrated creation, Billy Bunter, first appeared in 1908.

Billy Bunter of Greyfriars School (1947)

RICHARDSON, Dorothy (1873–1957) English novelist, noted for her twelve-volume *roman fleuve Pilgrimage*, which deals with the life of a woman called Miriam and uses a rather crude approximation to the stream-of-consciousness method. Richardson was hardly the first writer to employ the "interior monologue" method, but she was the first to use it substantially. *Pilgrimage* is rather more than a literary curiosity, even though it is tedious.

Pilgrimage (1915–35, 1938, 1967)

RICHARDSON, Henry Handel (1870–1946) Australian novelist whose real name was Florence Richardson. She lived in England for most of her life; but her masterpiece *The Fortunes of Richard Mahoney* is mostly, though not all, about Australia. It tells of the gradual and terrifying collapse of a doctor, who suffers from "manic depression". Influenced by naturalism, Freud, the nature of Australian life, and her experiences of her own father, it is one of the greatest novels of the century; impeccable in its psychology, quite unequalled in its understanding of the experience of mental illness, and drivingly intelligent and compassionate. It is also thrillingly readable, and a worthy precursor of the works of Patrick White.

Maurice Guest (1908)

The Fortunes of Richard Mahoney (1917–29, 1930)

The End of a Childhood (stories, 1934)

RICHARDSON, Samuel (1689–1761) English novelist and businessman. He wrote his novels with the intention of morally instructing his readers, and managed unwittingly to titillate them instead. Richardson's greatest work is his second, *Clarissa*, in which the heroine symbolizes the titanic lust of the evil Lovelace, who is obsessed with ravishing her. Richardson's epistolary method (the novel is a series of letters) leads to tiresome repetitions and longeurs, but his smug virtuism could not conceal his interest in lust. This epistolary method, very influential in France, also led naturally into the interior monologue – and stream of consciousness – techniques.

Pamela (1742)

Clarissa Harlowe (1747–48)

Sir Charles Grandison (1754)

RICHLER, Mordecai (1931) Canadian novelist and story-writer. He has lived mostly in exile, but is still considered as a quintessentially Canadian (and Jewish) novelist. His is the voice of old Montreal; but the central theme of his books is the conflict between Jew and Gentile. He employs the picaresque method,

and has little sense of structure; but he has plenty of vigour.

The Acrobats (1954)

The Apprenticeship of Duddy Kravitz (1959)

Cocksure (1968)

RICHTER, Conrad (1890–1968) American novelist. Richter was an outstanding historical novelist whose vision of the past was always intelligent and interesting.

The Sea of Grass (1937)

The Light in the Forest (1953)

The Lady (1957)

RINEHART, Mary Roberts (1876–1958) American suspense novelist, chief exponent of the "Had I But Known" story. Her books contain killings a-plenty, and customarily involve an ordinary heroine in a terrifying situation. "This is the story of how a middle-aged spinster lost her mind", is the first line of *The Circular Staircase* but the spinster, Rachel Innes, is a real, credible and humorous person and her adventure has hidden psychological significance.

The Circular Staircase (1908)

Miss Pinkerton (1932, in Britain *The Double Alibi*)

The Yellow Room (1945)

ROBBE-GRILLET, Alain (1922) French novelist, film-maker and critic. Robbe-Grillet is regarded as the inventor of the "new novel", and has taken every opportunity to provoke

Alain Robbe-Grillet

his readers in that role. He concentrates on meticulous description of various objects; and his philosophy is that the world is by no

ROBBINS

means for human beings (although he often seems to ignore the fact that they live in it). He is extremely ingenious, but has not entertained all his readers. His example will remain important; but he is by now a spent force.

The Erasers (1953, tr. 1966)

The Voyeur (1955, tr. 1959)

Last Year at Marienbad (1961, tr. 1962)

ROBBINS, Harold (1912) American novelist, who has written a string of best sellers (most of them filmed) in the wake of his first big success, *The Carpetbaggers*. Set for the most part in high society, his lengthy books are about personal and dynastic empire building and the emotional dramas involved. Brief

Harold Robbins

sexually explicit passages account for some of his success, but he writes with extreme fluency and paces his cleverly contrived plots with precision. The length of his novels is achieved by interweaving the stories of many characters over long periods; complex series of flashbacks lend density to the writing.

The Dream Merchants (1949)

The Carpetbaggers (1961)

The Adventurers (1966)

ROBERTS, Elizabeth Madox (1886–1941) American (Southern) novelist who was encouraged and admired by Ford Madox Ford. Her novels deal with restless Kentucky people, and are notable for their accurate reproduction of the speech habits of the region.

The Time of Man (1926)

My Heart and My Flesh (1927)

Black Is My Truelove's Hair (1938)

ROBERTS, Keith (1935) British science fiction writer. *Pavane*, considered a classic of alternative history, describes what twentieth-century Britain would be like had the Spanish Armada invaded successfully.

The Furies (1966)

Pavane (1968)

The Chalk Giants (1974)

ROBERTS, Kenneth (1885–1957) American historical novelist. His lusty adventure stories are meticulously researched to illustrate lesser-known aspects of the American colonial and revolutionary eras. His writing is vigorous and he is acknowledged as one of the best popular historical novelists of his generation.

Rabble in Arms (1933)

North West Passage (1937)

Lydia Bailey (1947)

ROBINS, Denise (1897) English novelist, who has published more than 170 books since 1924. Her plots and characters tend to be stereotyped, with love invariably conquering all, but she has delighted several generations of readers.

Enchanted Island (1956)

Put Back the Clock (1962)

The Other Side of Love (1973)

ROGERS, Rosemary (1932) American novelist who works for the Solano County Parks Department, California. Her torrid romances reach an immense audience.

Magnificent Animals (as Marina Mayson, 1971)

Sweet Savage Love (1974)

Dark Fires (1975)

ROHMER, Sax (1883–1959) English thriller writer who emigrated to America. Most of his many books feature the diabolically cunning oriental villain Dr Fu Manchu. Despite a somewhat dated style and plotting, the novels continue to be re-issued. After World War II Fu Manchu became strongly anti-Communist.

Dr Fu Manchu (1913)

The Yellow Claw (1915)

The Daughter of Fu Manchu (1931)

ROLFE, Frederick William (1860–1913) English novelist, crook, homosexual and self-

styled head of the Roman Catholic Church. In reality Rolfe's near-surreal life is much more interesting and funny than his work; details of his life can be read in A. J. A. Symons' classic *The Quest for Corvo* (1934). He called himself among other things, Baron Corvo. His most famous work of fiction is *Hadrian the Seventh*, a fantasy about himself as Pope.

Stories Toto Told Me (1898, repr. in *In His Own Image*, 1924)

Hadrian the Seventh (1904)

The Desire and Pursuit of the Whole (1934)

ROLLAND, Romain (1866–1944) French novelist, musicologist and worker for peace. Rolland won the Nobel Prize in 1915. His

Romain Rolland

inspirations were Tolstoy and Nietzsche, and he was friendly with Maxim Gorki. He is most famous for the novel *Jean-Christophe*, which is about a Beethoven-like, German-born composer: modern history is seen in terms of music especially the symphony. It is not a very good – but it is a very worthy – novel.

Jean-Christophe (1905–13, tr. 1910–13)

Clérambault (1920, tr. 1921)

The Soul Enchanted (1922–33, tr. 1925–34)

ROMAINS, Jules (1885–1972) French novelist, dramatist, publicist, general writer, poet and critic. Romains is the chief exponent, although not the originator, of an influential (French) view of life called "unanimism". His early novel *Death of a Nobody* is about a man who takes on a true identity only after his death, through others and by accident. Unanimism is about the relation of the group to the individual and vice versa; it is also about the "relationship" between two people, which is something separate from those people. Romains dealt with two lovers in a series of novels, one of which was translated as *The Body's Rapture*. But his most famous novel is the massive *roman fleuve Men of Good Will*, which lives up to its reputation as being Balzacian. The book is entertaining and funny as well as intelligent and inventive.

 Death of a Nobody (1911, tr. 1914, repr. 1944)

 The Body's Rapture (1929, tr. 1933)

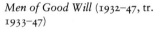 *Men of Good Will* (1932–47, tr. 1933–47)

ROSS, Jonathan, see ROSSITER, John

ROSS, Lillian (1926) American writer long associated with the *New Yorker* magazine. Ross has written biography, witty short stories, and *Picture* (1952), a fascinating account of the making of the film *The Red Badge of Courage*.

 Talk Stories (1966)

ROSSITER, John (1916) British crime novelist, and former Detective Chief Superintendent. He produces skilful police procedural stories as Jonathan Ross, and spy-adventure tales as Rossiter. Direct, sinewy writing and believable characters mark him out.

 The Burning of Billy Toober (as Ross, 1974)

 The Golden Virgin (1975)

A Rattling of Old Bones (as Ross, 1979)

ROSSNER, Judith (1935) American novelist who leans towards feminism, but does not let it cloud her artistic intent. *Nine Months in the Life of an Old Maid* is a hilarious story of the disintegration of a family, all of whose members hate each other. *Looking for Mr Goodbar*, which was filmed in 1977, is a fictional reconstruction of the real murder of a woman in New York; its intention is to examine how a woman's life can lead her into such a situation, and it largely succeeds.

 Nine Months in the Life of an Old Maid (1969)

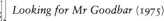 *Looking for Mr Goodbar* (1975)

Attachments (1977)

ROTH, Henry (1907) American novelist who came from Austro-Hungary as a boy, and lived in New York. He has only been able to write one novel: *Call it Sleep*, about the experiences of an immigrant boy like himself. This work has been called a masterpiece, one of the great poetic stories of the century. It is at once visionary and realistic.

 Call it Sleep (1934, repr. 1963)

ROTH, Joseph (1894–1939) Austrian, half-Jewish novelist, the crucial importance of whose work is only just becoming apparent. He led a desperately unhappy life, and recorded his final condition in the painful story *The Drinker* (1939, tr. in *Heart of Europe*, 1943). His two finest novels are *Radetzkymarsch*, a heartrending story, told with extreme tact and restraint, of the old Imperial Austria with its faults and its odd virtues; and *Job* on the theme of the wandering Jew, set in the twentieth century.

 Job (1930, tr. 1933)

Radetzkymarsch (1932, tr. 1935)

ROTH, Philip (1933) Jewish-American novelist, famous for *Portnoy's Complaint*, the confessions of Alexander Portnoy whose vicious, whining mother so sharpens the agonies of adolescence that he is all too literally forced back on himself. Although less literary than Roth's earlier work, it is hilariously funny and sad, a stylistic tour de force. The title novella in *Goodbye, Columbus* (which contains other stories) wittily traces the doomed love affair between two Jewish adolescents from contrasting homes; while *Letting Go* (1962) is an overlong role-reversal story flawed by sentimentality and lack of humour. Roth's other novels include *My Life as a Man* (1976), a witty, no-holds-barred front-line report on the war between the sexes.

 Goodbye, Columbus (1959)

Portnoy's Complaint (1969)

The Ghost Writer (1979)

ROUSSEAU, Jean-Jacques (1712–78) French political and educational theorist and novelist. Rousseau has been influential in many spheres. As a novelist he was essentially a moralist, although a skilful one. He influenced Goethe notably, and countless others. He seems to have believed that man is at heart a noble animal spoiled by progress; indeed, almost any tendency which Rousseau disliked at a given time contributed to man's corruption. He was not a distinguished thinker, but he was a persuasive one, and he had moments of sudden insight into himself which have proved valuable. His message that progress has perverted man, which is paradoxical, is a very important

one and contains much truth. But he himself never approached a solution of the paradox, and his inconsistencies are of a serious and confusing kind. His best work is his fine *Confessions*: but his novel *Julie ou la nouvelle Héloïse*, written in Samuel Richardson's epistolary style, was immensely influential, as was *Émile*.

 Julie ou la nouvelle Héloïse (1761, tr. 1960)

 Émile (1762, tr. 1930)

ROUSSEL, Raymond (1877–1933) French novelist and playwright, an early experimenter in fantasy and surrealism, who much influenced Apollinaire and the French surrealists of the 1920s.

 Impressions of Africa (1910, tr. 1966)

ROWSON, Susanna (1762–1824) English novelist who lived most of her life in Massachusetts. Her romantic and moral tale *Charlotte* was immensely successful, and can still be enjoyed for its picture of the times.

 Charlotte (1791)

ROY, Gabrielle (1909) Canadian Francophone novelist. Roy is a highly efficient, informative and widely read novelist, all of whose work is translated. Her settings vary from Montreal to rural areas, and she is at home in both.

 The Tin Flute (1945, tr. 1947)

The Cashier (1954, tr. 1955)

The Road Past Altamont (1966, tr. 1967)

RUBENS, Bernice (1927) Welsh-born novelist. Her *The Elected Member* (1969, in U.S. *The Chosen People*) is based on the theories of R. D. Laing, and is concerned with Jewish family life. Her view of life is bleak, and sometimes humourless; but she has an individual talent for delineating neurotic characters.

 Sunday Best (1971)

I Sent a Letter to My Love (1975)

Favours (1978)

RULFO, Juan (1918) Mexican novelist and story-writer. His wild mythopoeic novel *Pedro Páramo* is one of the masterpieces of modern Latin-American writing: its characters are dead – in the underworld of a village – and their emotions make the air alive with dread.

 The Burning Plains (1952, tr. 1968)

Pedro Páramo (1955, tr. 1958)

RUMAKER, Michael (1932) American university professor of creative writing, who has published comparatively few short stories and a novel, all critically acclaimed. He writes of misfits, set in a strange cultural wasteland clearly realized; tales like "Gringos" and "Exit 3" contain the best of his skilful writing.

Exit 3 and Other Stories (1958)

The Butterfly (1962)

Gringos and Other Stories (1967)

RUNYON, Damon (1884–1946) American humourist, journalist and dramatist. Runyon is most famous for his superb rendering of the slang of people who hang around sporting arenas and bars: petty gangsters, gamblers, failed boxers and their hangers-on.

Guys and Dolls (1932)

Runyon à la Carte (1944)

Short Takes (1946)

Damon Runyon

RUSSELL, Eric Frank (1905–78) British science fiction writer. His best work is anti-militaristic satire, although he also wrote the classic Fortean melodrama *Sinister Barrier*.

Sinister Barrier (1939)

The Great Explosion (1962)

RUTHERFORD, Mark (1831–1913) English novelist and philosopher, who is now often referred to by his real name, William Hale White. His novels are early and influential exercises in self-analysis. He was excellent on what dissenters were really like, and was much influenced by the philosophy of Spinoza.

Rutherford is interesting because he quarrelled with the Calvinist beliefs with which he was inculcated as a child, at great cost to himself.

The Autobiography of Mark Rutherford (1881)

Mark Rutherford's Deliverance (1885)

The Revolution in Tanner's Lane (1887)

S

SACKVILLE-WEST, V. (1892–1962) Novelist, poet, biographer, gardener and wife of Harold Nicolson. She is best-known for *The Edwardians*, a trenchant indictment of pre-1914 house-party morals. Otherwise, apart from *The Challenge*, recollections of a lesbian love affair uneasily transposed into heterosexual terms, her novels are largely superficial.

The Challenge (1923)

The Edwardians (1930)

No Signposts in the Sea (1961)

SADE, Donatien Alphonse François, Marquis de (1740–1814) French pornographer, who spent much of his life in prison – he was released at the Revolution, but was soon afterwards confined in a lunatic asylum. Although he had notable insights, the case for his being a great thinker has been wildly over-stated. If he anticipated certain modern attitudes towards sex, then he also anticipated Hitler's camps (no small achievement), and many of his tedious works (of which the least monotonous are those about the young woman Justine), describe situations that are not unlike what these became. It is not just now fashionable to denigrate him; but he was not joking. Nonetheless, the life and work (taken together) are worth study.

De Sade Quartet (tr. 1963)

SAGAN, Françoise (1935) Popular and "literary" French novelist whose chief asset is her lucid style. She writes of bored, boring people – usually idlers – and their sexual involvements with a certain insight. She was for a time fashionable, but has not been able to develop.

Bonjour Tristesse (1954, tr. 1957)

Aimez-Vous Brahms? (1959, tr. 1960)

Castle in Sweden (1960, tr. 1962)

SAINT-EXUPÉRY, Antoine de (1900–44) French man of action and writer. Saint-Exupéry, who was killed while flying for his country, is a sort of French T. E. Lawrence. His novels are only an expression of his general philosophy (fulfilment in action, which leads to meditation; celebration of landscape; the quest for nobility by performing useful actions), but they are well told and stylistically excellent. His fairy story *The Little Prince* is delightful, and has the status of a classic.

Southern Mail (1928, tr. 1933)

Night Flight (1931, tr. 1932)

The Little Prince (1945, tr. 1944)

SAKI (1870–1916) British novelist, story-writer and journalist, killed in World War I. H. H. Munro (his real name) is still widely read, but has not yet had the attention he deserves from the best critics. He was a bitter and accurate recorder of human pretensions, and an exposer of human cruelty. His range is wider than his rather whimsical and arch style suggests. He does not show the "beast" in man as triumphant, as is too often supposed, but rather points to its surprising strength. His novel *The Unbearable Bassington* is perhaps his most substantial work.

The Unbearable Bassington (1912)

The Complete Short Stories (1930)

The Bodley Head Saki (1963)

SALINGER, J. D. (1919) American novelist and story-writer who has lapsed into silence for almost twenty years. His novel *The Catcher in the Rye* meant an enormous amount to its first readers, and to a certain extent it is still popular (though life styles have changed since 1951). It tells the story of Holden Caulfield, who has been expelled from school and wanders about testing the world and finding it wanting. The book certainly captures in the

Françoise Sagan

most articulate way the mentality and the unhappy immaturity of an intelligent adolescent, whose predicament is most compassionately rendered. The rest of Salinger's fiction is about the Glass family, and less good: it lends itself to parody too easily and is too chic. Salinger was influenced here by Eastern philosophies, but not it seems in any profound or fruitful manner. He is one of those writers who caught a mood but who has apparently not been able to move on with the times. He is exceptionally fluent and elegant, yet he has shown great integrity in not publishing what he feels does not fulfil his requirements.

 The Catcher in the Rye (1951)

 Nine Stories (in Britain, *For Esmé – With Love and Squalor* 1953)

 Franny and Zooey (1962)

SALKEY, Andrew (1928) West Indian novelist and story-writer, resident in England. He has written many children's books. Salkey's best novel is his first, although he has kept up a consistently high standard. This first is *A Quality of Violence*, a well observed and passionately related tale of a village in Jamaica in 1900. Salkey has continued to depict the West Indian experience, in a variety of fields, in a controlled and psychologically expert way.

 A Quality of Violence (1959)

Anancy's Score (stories, 1973)

Come Home, Malcolm Heartland (1975)

SALTUS, Edgar (1855–1921) American novelist. Saltus was a "decadent" novelist, whose not unreadable – although somewhat jejune – work deals with crime, "Satanism", sexuality and hedonism.

Mr Incoul's Misadventure (1887)

The Truth about Tristram Varick (1888)

The Ghost Girl (1922)

SALTYKOV-SHCHEDRIN, Mikhail (1826–89) Russian fiction writer and satirist. Much of his work is very good satirical journalism, but *The Golovlev Family* is rightly regarded as a masterpiece. This is on a common theme – the decline of a family of gentry – but treats it in a unique and socially aware manner. Some of the characters, especially the famous hypocrite Iudushka, are unforgettable.

The Golovlev Family (1876, tr. 1916, tr. 1916, tr. 1931–34)

Fables (1884–85, tr. 1931)

SAND, George (1804–76) French novelist, famous for her love affairs (particularly with Chopin in Mallorca). She was an early feminist, and despised convention. She was a versatile but not major novelist: her works vary from tales of stormy love through country idylls (the best) to historical and sociological novels. She was over-optimistic in her fiction, but less so in her criticism, which was largely expressed by word of mouth.

Little Fadette (1840, tr. 1849)

Consuelo (1843, tr. 1847)

The Snow Man (1859, tr. 1871)

SANDEL, Cora (1880–1974) Norwegian novelist who from 1921 lived in Sweden. Not until late in her life was she recognized outside Scandinavia. Her tart and brilliant novels are written strictly from a woman's point of view: she is acute at analyzing male shortcomings, but is not malicious. *Krane's Café* is her most famous work, although the masterly Alberte books are now becoming better known.

Alberte and Jakob (1926, tr. 1962)

Alberte and Freedom (1931, tr. 1965)

Krane's Café (1945, tr. 1968)

SANDEMOSE, Axel (1899–1965) Norwegian novelist. He is gloomy, naturalistic and crude; yet at the same time he is subtle, original and interesting – and a master of morbid psychology. His novels – usually about murder and brutality – are all unforgettable.

A Fugitive Crosses His Tracks (1933, tr. 1936, rev. in Norwegian only 1955)

Horns for Our Adornment (1936, tr. 1939)

The Werewolf (1958, tr. 1966)

SANDERS, Lawrence (1920) American novelist and suspense writer. His most successful books rely on a skilful mix of factual detail (gun names, computer technology, sexual positions) and action excitement. The whole is generally told in the barest possible language.

The Anderson Tapes (1970)

The First Deadly Sin (1974)

The Tangent Factor (1978)

SANSOM, William (1912–77) English novelist and story-writer. He made his reputation early with Kafkaesque stories, but his later, odd and atmospheric, novels were rather better – but less widely read. His chief asset, as has often been noted, is the ability to create an unpleasant and menacing atmosphere; but he cannot always go beyond this – and his symbols, although clearly valid for him, are vague to the reader. He excelled in the depiction of the English suburban scene.

The Body (1949)

The Stories of William Sansom (1963)

A Young Wife's Tale (1974)

SANTAYANA, George (1863–1952) Spanish philosopher who was brought up and lived much of his life in America, and wrote in English. He published only one novel, *The Last Puritan*, which became a best seller. A psychologically meticulous and sad study, it is the best novel ever written by a major philosopher.

The Last Puritan (1935)

SAPPER (1888–1937) English writer of thrillers and adventure fiction, pseudonym of Herman Cyril McNeile, creator of Bulldog Drummond. Very popular in his time, Sapper is now regarded as nationalist, right-wing, anti-Semitic and often unnecessarily sadistic. The heroes triumph through a series of cliché

situations; the villains, variously described as "wogs", "dagos" and "unwashed people of that type", invariably meet a sticky end.

Bulldog Drummond (1920)

Temple Tower (1929)

Jim Maitland (1932)

SARGESON, Frank (1903) New Zealand novelist and story-writer. The best of all the New Zealand fiction writers, he was much admired by E. M. Forster. His range is wide: he writes sympathetically of delinquents, of the awful state of mind of most of his countrymen, and of New Zealand suburbia. His method is mainly picaresque; he makes skilful use of apparently wayward interior monologue.

Conversations with My Uncle (sketches, 1936)

Collected Stories (1974)

Joy of the Worm (1969)

SAROYAN, William (1908–78) American novelist, dramatist and story-writer. Saroyan began with great promise, but his reputation declined badly. He is a writer full of zest and energy, mainly picaresque in manner. He was sentimental, but compensated for this by a sense of outrage at injustice and a profound sympathy for the crazy, the afraid, the alienated and the oppressed.

The Human Comedy (1945)

Best Stories (1964)

One Day in the Afternoon of the World (1964)

SARRAUTE, Nathalie (1902) Russian-born French novelist. Sarraute was an important precursor of the new novel in France and was

Nathalie Sarraute

early recognized as such by J.-P. Sartre, who wrote a preface for her second volume *Portrait of a Man Unknown*. However, she has more to offer than Alain Robbe-Grillet: she has a feline and robust humour; and she sees life as governed by involuntary movements (tropisms) which become corrupted by sophistication – and even by "human-ness". She is a subtle and always readable novelist, ironically demonstrating how "proper" behaviour is often a vicious twisting of the initially decent and natural impulse.

Tropisms and The Age of Suspicion (1939 and 1956, tr. 1964)

Portrait of a Man Unknown (1947, repr. 1956, tr. 1959)

The Golden Fruits (1964, tr. 1965)

SARTON, May (1912) American novelist and poet. May Sarton is a versatile novelist who has a small but devoted following. All her novels are more than competent. The finest is based on the life and suicide of the American critic and teacher F. O. Mattheissen: *Faithful Are the Wounds* (1955). She writes in the tradition of Henry James and Edith Wharton, but has her own gentle but searching view of affairs. She is mainly a novelist of relationships, although she can also depict solitude.

The Single Hound (1938)

The Small Room (1961)

The Poet and the Donkey (1968)

SARTRE, Jean-Paul (1905) French philosopher, novelist, dramatist, polemicist, activist and critic. Sartre is one of the most important figures of twentieth-century France. He stopped writing fiction not long after World War II but not before he had produced three distinguished volumes – including his collected short stories, *Intimacy*. His fiction stems from his existentialist philosophy. He is strong in characterization, and skilful in the use of narrative (he learned much, for his long novel – sometimes described as a trilogy – *The Roads to Liberty*, from Dos Passos).

La Nausée (1938, tr. 1969)

Intimacy (stories, 1939, tr. 1956)

The Roads to Liberty (1945–50, tr. 1948–51)

SAYERS, Dorothy L. (1893–1957) English detective novelist, playwright, translator of Dante and amateur theologian. She took to crime in the heyday of the detective-story and at once, with *Whose Body?* (1923), she joined the top flight. To her early books she brought plenty of cleverness and literary allusion as

well as interesting backgrounds. But her principal gift to lovers of the art was Lord Peter Wimsey, a cross between the languid heroes of P. G. Wodehouse and the Scarlet Pimpernel, with a dash of post-1914–18 neurosis thrown in. In a more levelling age he has not worn quite as well as he might have done, but he remains one of the great detectives. Even as early as *The Documents in the Case* (1930), a non-Wimsey, Sayers introduced characters who would not have disgraced most of the conventional novelists of her day, and used subtle symbolism to develop her theme – the contrast between the true and the artificial. She did however, let the words run away with her. She never, to use a phrase of Raymond Chandler's, had "a man come in the door with a gun" until every last drop had been squeezed out of any dialogue. She needed thirty-four close-packed pages to explain all at the end of *Five Red Herrings* (1931). Yet that solution, like almost all of her others, was to a mystery spun with diabolic ingenuity.

The Documents in the Case (1930)

The Nine Tailors (1934)

Gaudy Night (1935)

SAYLES, John (1950) American novelist who deals with working people's lives, and with the failures of left-wing movements in America.

Pride of the Bimbos (1975)

Union Dues (1977)

SCHAEFFER, Jack (1907) American Western novelist whose low-key fictional portraits of typical frontier characters, often seen either through the eyes of a child or from the perspective of old age, are accurate and engaging, if somewhat gruffly sentimental.

Shane (1949)

First Blood (1954)

The Pioneers (1957)

SCHENDEL, Arthur Van (1874–1946) Dutch novelist. Schendel is important for his later novels, not so much for his earlier and very romantic work. His biography of a sailing ship, *The Johanna Maria*, made his name. Later novels are apparently drab; but they grow upon the reader as he begins to realize the mastery with which they tell of men's helplessness, despite their reason and desire to escape from Calvinist "certainty". The later novels – well observed, sparse in dialogue – while depressing, give a picture of Holland that is not to be found elsewhere.

The Johanna Maria (1930, tr. 1935)

The House in Haarlem (1935, tr. 1940)

Grey Birds (1937, tr. 1939)

SCHNITZLER, Arthur (1862–1931) Austrian novelist and dramatist. Schnitzler was a philanderer; but he was also a psychologist who saw through himself, through the sad magnificence of the rotting Empire, and through the bravado of Austrians bereft of that Empire after 1918. He is anti-moralistic; and he has some of the very sad quality of Joseph Roth.

The Road to the Open (1908, tr. 1923)

Rhapsody (1925, tr. 1927)

Thérèse (1928, tr. 1928)

SCHOLEM ALEICHEM (1859–1916) Yiddish story-writer, one of whose many works formed the basis for the successful musical *Fiddler on the Roof*. He was born in the Ukraine but lived most of his life in America. His humour, pathos and liveliness are heart-warming. He did much to demonstrate the special greatness and courage of his people, and their marvellous folk traditions. He is still very widely read.

Stories and Satires (1959)

Collected Stories (1965)

SCHORER, Mark (1908–77) American critic and novelist. His novels, conventional in form, are workmanlike and well-made, and have probably been neglected because of his acknowledged importance as a critic.

A House Too Old (1935)

The Hermit Place (1941)

The Wars of Love (1954)

SCHREINER, Olive (1855–1920) South African novelist. Her best and most famous novel is *The Story of An African Farm*, a neurotic but powerful presentation of life on a remote ostrich farm in the Veld. She was an early, passionate but unintegrated feminist.

The Story of an African Farm (1883)

Dreams (stories, 1891)

Trooper Peter Halket of Mashonaland (1897)

SCHULBERG, Budd (1914) American novelist, dramatist and journalist. Schulberg became famous with his first novel, *What Makes Sammy Run?*, a tough story about the rise of a detestable man from office boy to movie tycoon. His later novels have been less popular, although *The Harder They Fall*, based on the real-life story of the heavyweight Primo Carrera, is a good boxing novel.

What Makes Sammy Run? (1941)

The Harder They Fall (1947)

Sanctuary V (1970)

SCHWARZ, Delmore (1913–66) American fiction writer, poet and critic. The story of his unhappy life and decline into drunkenness is told, in fictional form, in Saul Bellow's *Humboldt's Gift*. He began with great power and intelligence, but gradually became incapacitated – as much, perhaps, by the difficulties of his age as by his own shortcomings as a man. His stories reflect the agonies of lost innocence and the struggle against personal vanity with insight and lyricism.

In Dreams Begin Responsibilities (1938)

The World is a Wedding (1948)

In Love and Other Stories (1961)

SCOTT, Paul (1920–78) British novelist. Army service in India kindled an interest in the country which Scott reflected in a dozen novels, notably *The Jewel in the Crown, The Day of the Scorpion, The Towers of Silence* and *A Division of the Spoils*, which were later published in one volume as *The Raj Quartet*. The quartet deals with the last years of British rule in the Indian subcontinent as it was mirrored, for the most part, by goings on in one Indian princely city. The first two volumes, dealing with the aftermath of an alleged rape of an English girl by a young Indian, seemed slow and heavy but fell into place as they became part of a larger picture completed by the final two volumes. The actual transfer of power and the massacres that followed, described in microcosm, show Scott as a master of his craft. One critic wrote: "When men and women want to know what happened in India in the 1940s . . . they will find a portrait of the real India no formal history can provide."

Scott abandoned his work as a literary agent to write his Quartet, an act of great faith for after the success of his first novel *Jonnie Sahib* (1952) none of his intervening novels had made much money or received high recognition. His final novel, *Staying On* (1976), a short book about the European survivors of the Raj, won that year's Booker Prize, even though it was a much slighter work.

The Chinese Love Pavilion (1960)

The Raj Quartet (1966–75)

SCOTT, Sir Walter (1771–1832) Scottish advocate, publisher, poet, dramatist, antiquarian

Sir Walter Scott

and novelist, who turned to fiction when his reputation as a poet was eclipsed by Byron. He based his famous "Waverley" novels on the troubled history of the Scottish clans, making use of an immense variety of documentary sources, and even first-hand accounts of the last great clan rebellions. Although Scott's literary reputation has never recovered from E. M. Forster's broadside (". . . a trivial mind and a heavy style. He cannot construct . . . has neither artistic detachment nor passion"), his better-known novels are still widely read and enjoyed, for the sweeping picture they give of Scottish history and the Scottish people. His characters are often flat, but a few are genuinely memorable. There is no doubt, too, that he has had a deep influence on English and European fiction, and he is the founding father of historical romance.

 Guy Mannering (1815)

The Heart of Midlothian (1818)

Ivanhoe (1819)

SEAMAN, Donald (1922) British spy thriller writer who spent 24 years at the *Daily Express* as a war and diplomatic correspondent. Under Beaverbrook's direction he spent five years working on the Burgess and MacLean story. His books are tautly written and reveal his hatred of traitors.

 The Defector (1975)

The Duel (1979)

SEGAL, Erich (1937) American novelist whose *Love Story* was one of the biggest best sellers of the 1970s, largely because it was made into a hugely successful movie. It is a perfectly calculated, sad and sentimental romance. The sequel *Oliver's Story* (1977) was less successful.

 Love Story (1970)

SEGHERS, Anna (1900) East German novelist and story-writer. Seghers is one of the better communist novelists of the century: her fiction has seldom suffered seriously from doctrinal manipulation. Her greatest success was *The Seventh Cross* (memorably filmed by Fred Zinnermann). She is psychologically competent, and gains powerful effects from her starkness and laconic style.

 *The Revolt of the Fishermen* (1928, tr. 1929)

 The Seventh Cross (1941, tr. 1943)

 Transit (1947, tr. 1945)

SELBY, Hubert, Jr. (1928) American novelist Selby gained notoriety for his *Last Exit to Brooklyn*, a series of connected sketches which tell of homosexual and transvestite life in Brooklyn in harsh (but rather puritanical) detail. It was foolishly prosecuted in Britain, but the conviction was overturned on appeal. The book gives great insight into the tormented lives of the characters, and is a document of some sociological value. *The Room*, about the sadistic fantasies of a madman who is picked up by police, is more imaginative, and is one of the most searingly truthful and painful accounts of a terrible psychological state ever attempted. Once again, it was accused of being "disgusting": it is disgusting, but it is also truthful – only those who cannot face reality can wish for its suppression. It has much pity. Selby is a very fine and lucid writer; and one of the foremost realists of his time.

 Last Exit to Brooklyn (1964)

The Room (1971)

SELVON, Samuel (1923) West Indian (Trinidadian) novelist and story-writer. He writes of most of the aspects of his native land, and is particularly concerned with the "foreigners" who live there. But his best novel is set in England: *The Lonely Londoners* (1956), in which he handles the scene with great skill and aplomb. Most admired are his stories, where his lightness of touch is most evident. He has considerable comic gifts.

 An Island is a World (1955)

Ways of Sunlight (stories, 1958)

Moses Ascending (1975)

SENDER, Ramon (1902) Spanish novelist. He has had a reputation in the English-speaking world since the publication of *Seven Red Sundays* (1932, tr. 1936). He is a left-wing "committed" writer, who has little sense of structure but great liveliness, sense of justice and intelligence.

 Chronicle of Dawn (1942, tr. 1945)

The Affable Hangman (1952, tr. 1954)

SETON, Anya (1916) English novelist, born in New York. She started writing short stories soon after her marriage to augment the family income. She has written a succession of highly successful historical biographical novels. She chooses colourful and romantic settings – Santa Fé for *Turquoise* (1946), Arizona for *Fox Fire* (1951), the Hudson River for *Dragonwyck* (1945) – and has created a bevy of passionate heroines.

Katherine (1954)

Green Darkness (1972)

SEYMOUR, Gerald (1941) British thriller writer, who produces tense, exciting stories in a realistic manner. He has written breathless pursuit stories: *Harry's Game* and *The Glory Boys* (1976). *Kingfisher* describes the futility of dissent in Eastern Europe.

 Harry's Game (1975)

Kingfisher (1977)

SHADBOLT, Maurice (1932) New Zealand novelist and story writer. Shadbolt is a symbolic novelist much concerned with the presence and function of the artist in society. He has been influenced by Patrick White, and his symbolism is frequently over-obtrusive; but he is an honest and lucid writer, with an effective style.

 The Presence of Music: 3 novellas (1967)

This Summer's Dolphin (1969)

A Touch of Clay (1974)

SHANNON, Dell, see LININGTON, Elizabeth

SHARPE, Tom (1928) British novelist. His raw, farcical brio well suited his accounts of repression, brutality and corruption in South Africa (*Riotous Assembly*, 1971, and *Indecent Exposure*, 1973) but is cruder and more ponderous when switched to British targets such as academic life (*Porterhouse Blue*), publishing (*The Great Pursuit*) and environmental planning (*Blott on the Landscape*, 1975). Their pages are sometimes laced with sexual perversity, especially in *Wilt* (1976); but its successor is very funny.

 Porterhouse Blue (1974)

The Great Pursuit (1977)

The Wilt Alternative (1979)

SHAW, Bob (1931) Irish science fiction writer. He is noted for the originality of his ideas and for the neat and careful way in which he develops them.

 Palace of Eternity (1969)

Vertigo (1978)

SHAW, George Bernard (1856–1950) Irish dramatist, music critic, novelist. Shaw's novels are failures, and attempts to interest readers in them have invariably failed.

 Cashel Byron's Profession (1886, repr. 1979)

 Love Among the Artists (1900, repr. 1979)

Irwin Shaw

SHAW, Irwin (1913) American novelist and dramatist. *The Young Lions* (1948), a best-selling World War II novel, made Shaw's reputation as a topical, sensational (often violent) but challenging writer, whose characters represent various rather stereotyped ideas. *The Troubled Air* (1950), about the broadcasting industry, portrays the betrayal of the liberal by extremists of left and right. The monumental *Rich Man, Poor Man* (1970) traces a family through three generations, questioning many fundamental American beliefs.

The Young Lions (1948)

Rich Man, Poor Man (1970)

The Top of the Hill (1979)

SHECKLEY, Robert (1928) American science fiction writer, primarily noted for his humorous work, which ranges from acidic irony to bizarre slapstick.

Immortality Incorporated (1959)

The Status Civilization (1960)

The Alchemical Marriage of Alistair Crompton (1978)

SHEED, Wilfred (1930) English-born American novelist and story-writer. A Catholic, Sheed uses black humour in the manner of Evelyn Waugh to try to illuminate his convoluted but genuine sense of moral outrage. His style and speed attract readers; but there is considerable critical confusion about what he is actually trying to say.

A Middle Class Education (1960)

Max Jamison (1970, in Britain, *The Critic*)

People will Always be Kind (1973)

SHELDON, Raccoona, see TIPTREE, James, Jr

SHELDON, Sidney (1917) American scriptwriter, playwright and novelist, whose *The Other Side of Midnight* is reported to have

sold over 5 million copies world-wide.

The Other Side of Midnight (1974)

A Stranger in the Mirror (1976)

Bloodline (1978)

SHELLEY, Mary (1797–1851) English novelist, wife of the poet (and daughter of William Godwin and the great early feminist Mary Wollstonecraft). *Frankenstein*, her best known novel, is one of the very best of gothic works.

Frankenstein (1818)

The Last Man (1826)

Tales and Stories (ed. 1891)

Mary Shelley

SHERRIFF, R. C. (1896–1975) English playwright and novelist. His novels have never achieved the popular success of his plays (*Journey's End* etc) but they are eminently readable; they portray the peace and beauty of the English countryside.

The Fortnight in September (1931)

The Wells of St Mary's (1961)

SHIEL, M. P. (1865–1947) British writer of thrillers and futuristic romances. He was fond of stylistic experimentation and bizarre ideas, and he was an extreme Social Darwinist.

The Yellow Danger (1899)

The Purple Cloud (1901)

SHIGA, Naoya (1883–1971) Japanese fiction writer. He was an important influence on other Japanese writers for two reasons: he wrote lucidly and without embellishment, and he

refused to avoid unpleasant subject matter. He was also a very subtle, intriguing and compassionate psychologist. Several of his remarkable stories are translated in various periodicals, including the important "Han's Crime" – a key story on the subject of the nature of guilt – in *Harpers*, November 1956.

Stories (in *Modern Japanese Literature* (1956); *Modern Japanese Stories* (1961); various issues of *Japanese Quarterly*)

SHOLOKHOV, Mikhail (1905) Russian novelist, who won the Nobel Prize in 1965. He has written little in the past thirty years, and there is some evidence that he did not write the whole of his most famous books. But it is clear that, however repugnant Sholokhov's behaviour in going out of his way to attack dissidents and other victims of the Soviet regime, he is possessed of great talent. He is a confident, well-informed and fluent writer: a very good popular novelist who does much more than merely entertain.

And Quiet Flows the Don (1928–33, tr. 1934–40)

Virgin Soil Upturned (1932–33, tr. 1935)

SHORTHOUSE, J. H. (1834–1903) English novelist. He wrote a number of novels, but only one has lasted: *John Inglesant*. The novel is a remarkable, although not fully integrated, account of a seventeenth-century hero who encounters various religious factions, and who also works for Charles I.

John Inglesant (1881)

SHUTE, Nevil (1899–1960) English popular novelist, who had a social conscience and good powers of invention; but he was psychologically limited. He settled in Australia after World War II. The secret of his immense success is his expertise in technical matters (he had been an engineer) and his lucid and superior style. Two of his books, *A Town Like Alice* and the excellent nuclear warfare novel, *On The Beach*, were made into successful films.

The Lonely Road (1932)

A Town Like Alice (1949)

On the Beach (1957)

SIENKIEWICZ, Henryk (1846–1916) Polish novelist of immense popularity; he won the Nobel Prize in 1905. His most famous work is the historical novel *Quo Vadis?* (many times filmed); but *Without Dogma*, more serious and important, is his greatest achievement. Poles say that bad translations make it impossible for non-Poles to assess him, and they defend *Quo Vadis?* He is certainly a successful

and worthy popular novelist, and had great capacity to portray all kinds of characters.

 In Vain (1872, tr. 1899)

Without Dogma (1891, tr. 1899)

 Quo Vadis? (1896, tr. 1898, tr. 1941)

SIGAL, Clancy (1926) American novelist living in England. Sigal has published two documentary novels of great interest: *Going Away*, about a journey through the U.S. in the mid-1950s; and *Weekend in Dinlock* set in a Yorkshire mining village. Sigal is concerned with the dehumanizing nature of technological society.

 Weekend in Dinlock (1960)

 Going Away (1962)

SILLANPÄÄ, Frans Emil (1888–1964) Finnish novelist who won the Nobel Prize in 1939. Sillanpää's basic outlook, a mystical biological vitalism, was rather eccentric. But the comparisons which have been made between him and D. H. Lawrence are not without point. He combines a number of virtues: a love of rural life, a good sense of psychology, a general sympathy with people which is not sentimentalized, and a mellifluous style. His stories are regarded as his greatest achievement.

Meek Heritage (1919, tr. 1938)

Fallen Asleep While Young (1931, tr. 1933)

People in the Summer Night (1934, tr. 1966)

SILLITOE, Alan (1928) English (Midlands) novelist. Sillitoe first achieved fame with *Saturday Night and Sunday Morning*, a realistic and sympathetic story of a young working-class man in Nottingham. This was powerful but badly written; in his stories (including the novella *The Loneliness of the Long Distance Runner*) his writing is much better, and is often distinguished. In the novel he has become bogged down in imitation of D. H. Lawrence, in various ideologies and in hatred of authority (he is not a thinker but a man of instinct, and he writes best when he follows his instinct); but the stories have remained original and fresh – some of the best written by any writer of his generation.

Saturday Night and Sunday Morning (1958)

The Loneliness of the Long Distance Runner (1959)

The Ragman's Daughter (1963)

SILONE, Ignazio (1900–78) Italian novelist. He was at first a communist, but then left the party (1930); however, he remained an opponent of fascism, and most of his novels are on political themes. His later novels are imbued with a new religious feeling, but are not very forceful. He has great sensitivity, but his fiction is somewhat over-dependent on ideas.

 Fontamara (1930, tr. 1934)

Bread and Wine (1937, tr. 1964)

A Handful of Blackberries (1952, tr. 1954)

SILVERBERG, Robert (1934) American science fiction writer, who during the last twenty years has poured out novels, juvenile fiction and short stories, from which he is reported to have made a fortune. His best work shows remarkable imagination and inventiveness, is usually set in the near future, and deals with extensions of contemporary developments, such as a population crisis (*Master of Life and Death*, 1957); the resuscitation of the dead (*Recalled to Life*, 1962); cities of mile-high towers (*The World Inside*, 1971); and the drug culture (*A Time of Changes*).

 Nightwings (1969)

A Time of Changes (1971)

The Stochastic Man (1975)

SIMAK, Clifford D. (1904) American science fiction writer, winner of two Hugo awards. His work contains a strong sense of nostalgia, pastoral settings and an undercurrent of mysticism, which has become more prominent in his recent work, especially *A Choice of Gods* and *A Heritage of Stars* (1977). The story-sequence collected as *City* (1952), in which dogs and robots maintain civilization on an Earth abandoned by men, is one of the classics of 1940s science fiction.

 Time and Again (1951)

Way Station (1963)

A Choice of Gods (1972)

SIMENON, Georges (1903) French novelist and memoirist. Simenon has without doubt raised the crime novel to the realm of literature. André Gide became interested in him, and got to know him; but Simenon felt awkward in such literary company. He is a "natural": his piercing psychological effects, his empathy, his skill in evoking atmosphere, have not been gained from books but from keen observation of life. Not all his books are about crimes, but many of the best are. His

famous Inspector Maigret is simply a shrewd policeman doing his job; but the very best of the many novels do not feature him. The key to all Simenon's work is restraint, lack of moralizing and, above all, a quiet understanding of extreme states of mind. His stature is very high, although few critics can bring themselves to admit this, because he is labelled a "crime writer". Although he does not try to be sophisticated – in fact he distrusts sophistication – he is in reality intensely so. To read Simenon on a family greedy to get their part of a fortune, or on a man determined to kill his wife, or on a man on the run, is to get the fullest possible flavour out of the situation. He has no illusions – and yet a heart of gold.

 *The Simenon Omnibuses* (1–13 to date)

SIMMS, William Gilmore (1806–70) American novelist, poet, critic, editor, legislator and lawyer, born in South Carolina. Simms was an intelligent ancestor of sophisticated Southern writing which culminates in William Faulkner. His first novel, *Martin Faber* (1833), about a crime, was promising; later he turned to border romances, which were exciting and objective.

 The Partisan (1835)

 Beauchampe (1842)

 Eutaw (1856)

SIMON, Claude (1913) French novelist. Simon, one of the most original of modern novelists, was a precursor of the new novel, and was eagerly taken up by this movement when it began in the 1950s. But while his work incorporates some of their discoveries about narrative, it offers much more than theory. His art is based largely on painting, and most particularly on the proto-cubist methods of Paul Cézanne. His works are important for their insight into the inner workings of the mind. He is perhaps the most analytical novelist alive, dwelling upon the manner in which events and people change in memory, and on meticulous description of objects (here influenced not only by painting, about which he knows a great deal, but by Proust). Simon is very hard "to get into"; but the experience is worthwhile, since the persistent reader soon discovers that in reading a Simon novel he is discovering something about how he really thinks and feels and proceeds. Simon is not as "bleak" as he has been made out to be. His earlier novels are more realistic, and the interested reader would do well to begin with *Flanders Road* (1960, tr. 1962).

The Palace (1962, tr. 1964)

Histoire (1967, tr. 1969)

The Battle of Pharsalus (1969, tr. 1971)

SIMON, Roger L. (1943) American detective story-writer whose books are set in southern California in the 1970s. His detective, Moses Wine, has the sour moral depth of Raymond Chandler's Philip Marlowe, but smokes dope instead of swigging rye.

Big Fix (1973)

Wild Turkey (1975)

SINCLAIR, Andrew (1935) Film-maker, dramatist, biographer, historian and novelist. Sinclair began with amiable but hurried novels about national service (*The Breaking of Bumbo*) and lovelorn Cambridge undergraduate life (*My Friend Judas*, 1959). By far his most important novel is *Gog*, about an amnesiac giant washed up on the Scottish coast in 1945, whose comic, sometimes brutally horrific pilgrimage to London turns into an excavation of Britain's past. Sinclair's recent books include an expertly plotted political thriller (*A Patriot for Hire*, 1978).

The Breaking of Bumbo (1959)

Gog (1967)

The Surrey Cat (1976)

SINCLAIR, Jo (1913) American novelist, dramatist and story-writer (her many stories are as yet uncollected). Sinclair's theme is alienation, and she is adept at describing the emotions of weaklings who consult psychiatrists. Her best known novel is her first, *Wasteland*; and although later books are excellent she has not consolidated her success.

Wasteland (1946)

The Changelings (1955)

Anna Teller (1960)

SINCLAIR, Upton (1878–1968) American novelist. Sinclair was a sincere Utopian socialist, whose prolific output of fiction influenced many writers by its realism and its strong passion for justice. His writing had a raw power, but quite lacked art, and was extremely crude. His *The Jungle* (1906), one of

his best novels, led to reforms in the Chicago meat industry (there is a nice detail about a man's finger getting cut off, tinned, and eaten). His main novels (the series is called *World's End*) in the latter part of his long life dealt with a character called Lanny Budd, a kind of poor man's superman who helped tidy up huge international and other messes. Sinclair is to be respected, although not as a contributor to the "art" of the novel.

The Metropolis (1908)

Presidential Mission (1947)

The Return of Lanny Budd (1953)

Isaac Bashevis Singer

SINGER, Isaac Bashevis (1904) Yiddish writer of fiction who was awarded the Nobel Prize in 1977. He was born in Poland, but came early to the United States, where he worked as a Yiddish journalist. His genius as a writer was slow to be recognized. He regards himself, rightly, as a worker for the survival of the Yiddish language, which is threatened with extinction. He has a profound knowledge of the folklore and beliefs of the Jewish people, and no living writer is more capable of making these seem so real and so significant. He moves effortlessly between the Jewish-Polish past and the modern New York scene. Although his novels are impressive (e.g. *The Family Moskat*, 1950), it is in the short story that he excels. He is the most humane and yet unsentimental of writers; Saul Bellow has learned from him (and has translated him) and has some of his qualities of compassion and wonder.

Gimpel the Fool (stories, 1957)

Short Friday (stories, 1964)

The Seance (stories, 1968)

SINGH, Khushwant (1915) Indian novelist and story-writer, born in what is now Pakistan, but living in Bombay. He is best known for *Mano Majra* (in U.S. *Train to Pakistan*), a searing and accurate novel about events on the Indian-Pakistan border just after its creation. Singh is a humanist, but ironic despair often gets the better of his generous impulses. He is one of the most intelligent and robust of Anglophone novelists living in India.

Train to Pakistan (1955, repr. 1956)

I Shall Not Hear the Nightingale (1959)

Black Jasmine (stories, 1971)

SITWELL, Osbert (1892–1969) English man of letters, poet, critic, memoirist and novelist. *Before the Bombardment* is a nearly classic evocation of the doomed Edwardian generation: this was sensitive, and did not possess the wilful waywardness of much of his later work.

Before the Bombardment (1926)

Miracle on Sinai (1933)

Collected Stories (1953)

SJÖWALL, Maj (1935) and **WAHLÖÖ, Per** (1926–75) Swedish husband and wife team, who wrote ten tight, finely observed police procedural novels featuring a Stockholm detective, Martin Beck. Written in a spare documentary style, these have been favourably compared to Simenon; they make the reader care about Beck, his awful marriage, his daughter, his colleagues, his women and his worries about the direction of Swedish society. The Wahlöös were readily able to interchange as authors, sometimes writing consecutive chapters simultaneously.

Roseanna (1967)

The Laughing Policeman (1970)

SLAUGHTER, Frank (1908) American novelist. A doctor, he has written immensely popular novels – the surgery is more accurate than the psychology.

Spencer Brade MD (1942)

Epidemic (1961)

SMITH, Betty (1904) American popular novelist whose *A Tree Grows in Brooklyn* was a bestseller. It was based on her own experiences as a slum child, and became a successful film.

A Tree Grows in Brooklyn (1943)

Tomorrow Will be Better (1948)

SMITH, Mrs Charlotte (1749–1806) English novelist. Charlotte Smith was one of the first, and best, of the women to support herself by writing fiction. *The Old Manor House* is by far the finest of her novels; it is full of shrewd psychology and pertinent observation of the habits of the time.

Celestina (1791)

The Old Manor House (1793)

Marchmont (1796)

SMITH, Cordwainer (1913–66) American science fiction writer, pseudonym of political scientist Paul Linebarger. All his stories are set in a future interstellar culture called "The Instrumentality of Man". His work is romantic and frequently lyrical, and constitutes a futuristic mythology.

The Dead Lady of Clown Town (1964)

Norstrilia (1975)

SMITH, E. E. "Doc" (1890–1965) American science fiction author who gained a Ph.D. in chemistry. His extravagant and crowded adventures, with their monumental plots, gigantic casts of hostile and monstrous aliens, and set-piece battles make him the doyen of "space opera" writers. His two major series, the *Skylark* and *Lensman* books, are amongst the most vigorous and enjoyable examples of SF as escapist entertainment.

The Skylark of Space (1946)

Triplanetary (1948)

Gray Lensman (1951)

SMITH, Wilbur (1933) South African novelist, born in Zambia. He is fully committed to Africa and writes with conviction about the blood and battles of the Boer War and the dangers and drama of mining for gold and diamonds. Smith's novels are virile and uncompromising, and usually contain a lusty love interest: politics play little or no part.

Gold Mine (1970)

The Eye of the Tiger (1975)

A Sparrow Falls (1977)

SMITH, William Gardner (1926) Black American novelist who takes a "moderate" line, and whose fiction is quietly compelling and psychologically precise.

Last of the Conquerors (1948)

The Stone Face (1964)

Wilbur Smith

Tobias Smollett

C. P. Snow

SMOLLETT, Tobias (1721–71) Scottish novelist and translator. Smollett is the most energetic and artless of the picaresque novelists. He knew a great deal about many things – politics, the law, foreign literature, the sea especially – and although he has no sense of structure and is undisciplined, he is very seldom dull. He was extremely inventive, and, in his careless way, anticipated many techniques. He has been most important to twentieth-century writers who want to eschew form; but he also influenced Charles Dickens and other nineteenth-century novelists.

Roderick Random (1748)

Ferdinand, Count Fathom (1753)

Humphry Clinker (1771)

SNOW, C. P. (Lord) (1905) English novelist whose *Strangers and Brothers* sequence has provoked much favourable and adverse comment. The protagonist is Lewis Eliot, a lawyer who is an approximation of Snow himself. The material – power, science, committees, government – something Snow knows well (he was for a short time himself a government minister), is very interesting. The plots of the novels are often melodramatic, and they have seemed to some readers to imply that all is almost well in the *Corridors of Power* (1963), the title of one of the sequence. But this is not Snow's intention. Certainly the books are very sympathetic on the subject of the difficulties of a provincial making his way up in the establishment and as certainly Snow's heart is in the right place; but his style and psychology are not always more than crude. No other novelist has had the information he has or has been prepared to convey it, and there is much valuable documentary material in the novels. There is also a poignant ethical honesty – although this is seldom supported by a really vigorous imagination.

Strangers and Brothers (1940–74, 11 vols)

The Malcontents (1972)

In Their Wisdom (1974)

SÖDERBERG, Hjalmar (1869–1941) Swedish story-writer, novelist and playwright. A poetic but gloomy and disillusioned writer, Söderberg is best known among English-speaking readers for his novel about childhood, *Martin Birck's Youth*; and for *Doctor Glas*, concerning a murder in Stockholm.

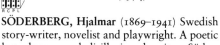

Martin Birck's Youth (1901, tr. 1930)

Doctor Glas (1905, tr. 1963)

SOLOGUB, Fedor (1863–1927) Russian novelist, poet and story-writer. Sologub was

Alexander Solzhenitsyn

hated for his bleak and gloomy outlook, with the result that his genius has been largely overlooked. *The Little Demon* is a masterpiece of malevolence, and the psychology of its chief character cannot be faulted. It is Sologub's inner world of beauty to which one must look if one wishes to obtain full value from his work – and the clue to this is in his poetry.

 The Little Demon (1907, tr. 1962)

The Created Legend (trilogy, 1908–12, tr. 1916)

Little Tales (tr. 1917)

SOLZHENITSYN, Alexander (1918) Russian novelist, publicist, dissident, exile and historian of terror. Solzenhitsyn's best work as a novelist is in his first book, *One Day in the Life of Ivan Denisovich*, and to a lesser extent in *Cancer Ward* and *The First Circle* (the two latter are more flawed than the first, which is a masterpiece of economy and restraint; it is his only novel to appear in Russia, from

which he was suddenly and notoriously expelled in 1974). His *August 1914* (tr. 1973), the first of a projected series, is by common consent a weak novel – but by this time he was more concerned with exposing the horrors of the labour camps in his monumental non-fictional *Gulag* series. *Ivan Denisovich* draws on the author's own experience in a labour camp, and is written with terseness and compassion. Its two successors have exquisite and revealing passages, and are highly informative about life in Soviet Russia; but they are less unified. His first three novels remain important, and he himself remains an increasingly controversial figure. He received the Nobel Prize in 1970. There are rival translations of all his books.

 One Day in the Life of Ivan Denisovich (1961, tr. 1963, tr. 1963, tr. 1971)

Cancer Ward (tr. 1968, tr. 1968)

The First Circle (tr. 1968, tr. 1968)

SOMERS, Paul, see GARVE, Andrew

SOMERVILLE and **ROSS** (Edith Somerville, 1858–1949, and Violet Martin, who used the pseudonym Ross, 1862–1915) Irish novelists, cousins who wrote books individually, but who were successful mainly in collaboration. Their novels of rural Ireland are still enjoyed; they are full of humour and sharp observation. Their rather aristocratic attitude hardly matters, since they reflect it with a witty accuracy.

 The Real Charlotte (1894)

Some Experiences of an Irish R.M. (1899)

In Mr Knox's Country (1915)

SONTAG, Susan (1933) American critic and novelist, who is best known as an acute and original critic. Her semi-surreal works in fiction are generally felt to be failures: they are rather too obviously critical rather than imaginative exercises, and seem pretentious.

 The Benefactor (1963)

Styles of Radical Will (stories, 1969)

SOSEKI, Natsume (1867–1916) Japanese novelist, who with Tanizaki and the inferior Mishima is the most widely translated of the century. From the early whimsicality of *I am a Cat* (1905, tr. 1961) his work developed in two distinct directions, towards naturalism and despair on the one hand, and towards acceptance and Buddhism on the other. He is one of the century's most subtle and enigmatic novelists – in any language. *The Three-Cornered World* (1906, tr. 1965) deals with a man who is torn between the desire for objectivity and the absolute need to express his lovingness.

 Young Master (1906, tr. 1922)

The Heart (1914, tr. 1957)

Star on the Wayside (1916, tr. 1969)

SOUTHERN, Terry (1924) American absurdist novelist and film script-writer. He became famous for *Candy* (with Mason Hoffenberg), an over-extended stretch of girl-can't-help-it soft porn, and *The Magic Christian* (1959). His most impressive achievement is *Flash and Filigree*. Mostly set in cars, it includes a memorable seduction scene in a drive-in movie that is infinitely more erotic than anything in *Blue Movie* (1970), a jaded exercise in sexual surrealism.

 Candy (1956)

Flash and Filigree (1957)

The Magic Christian (1959)

SOYINKA, Wole (1934) Nigerian poet, dramatist and critic. Soyinka, one of the most intelligent of Black writers, fell foul of the authorities during the Biafran civil war and was imprisoned. His drama is his most important work; but in fiction he has written competently and faithfully.

 The Interpreter (1965)

SPARK, Muriel (1918) English novelist. She made her name as a novelist with *The Comforters* (1957). A Roman Catholic, she is very fluent, technically extremely adept, and often funny. *Memento Mori* (1959), black farce about geriatrics, is perhaps her most entertaining book, although to some it seems to take cruel advantage. She lacks charity or depth, and has employed facile and ineffective symbolism. As "clever" novelist she perhaps has no equal in her generation, but as "serious" one she ranks low, although certain critics believe otherwise. She is certainly an entertaining writer – except in her one effort at a major novel, *The Mandelbaum Gate*.

 The Bachelors (1960)

The Prime of Miss Jean Brodie (1961)

The Mandelbaum Gate (1965)

Muriel Spark

Wole Soyinka

SPENCER, Elizabeth (1921) American novelist and story-writer. Her first novels were about her native South; the later are set in the urban North (the very well filmed *The Light in the Piazza*, 1960, has an Italian background). Her best novel is *The Voice at the Back Door*, about a young lawyer who has to sacrifice self-respect to win a place in his corrupt and racially prejudiced environment.

 The Voice at the Back Door (1956)

No Place for an Angel (1967)

The Snare (1972)

SPILLANE, Mickey (1918) American thriller writer who is highly successful. Spillane has no literary pretensions and is proud of it. Notable for the ruthless aggressiveness of his avenging heroes, especially Mike Hammer, he is a master of pace and tension, based on careful use of the first-person narrative.

I, the Jury (1947)

The Deep (1961)

Day of the Guns (1964)

SPINRAD, Norman (1940) American science fiction writer whose *Bug Jack Barron* was seen to combine SF with the iconoclastic attitudes of the so-called alternative culture of the 1960s. A vigorous stylist, he treats some of the genre's standard themes in the light of radical political and psychological attitudes. *The Iron Dream* purports to be a science fiction novel by Adolf Hitler.

The Men in the Jungle (1967)

Bug Jack Barron (1969)

The Iron Dream (1972)

SPRING, Howard (1889–1965) British author whose popular realist novels have their roots in twentieth-century social history. He wrote about exceptional people in a way that allowed him to depict the changing morals and manners of his time, while projecting human nature as subject to unchanging values. *Fame is the Spur* is based on the life of the Labour politician Keir Hardie.

 Shabby Tiger (1934)

My Son, My Son (1938)

Fame is the Spur (1940)

STABLEFORD, Brian M. (1948) British science fiction writer who disguises an ingenious and intelligent imagination behind the form of the other-worldly fantasy. His *Dies Irae* trilogy comes nearest to space opera, but his ability to make a chilling adventure out of difficult scientific and philosophical ideas is most clearly shown in *To Challenge Chaos*.

 Dies Irae (trilogy, 1971)

To Challenge Chaos (1972)

Critical Threshold (1977)

STAFFORD, Jean (1915) American novelist, who writes perceptively about adult isolation and the problems of puberty. She is an accomplished craftsman and a faultless observer of human nature; her leading characters are invariably female.

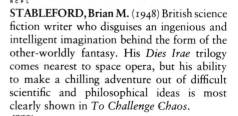 *Boston Adventure* (1944)

The Mountain Lion (1947)

The Catherine Wheel (1952)

STALLINGS, Laurence (1894) American novelist. He is competent and readable, but more or less gave up fiction for drama and film script-writing. *Plumes* was a very popular book, set in World War I.

 Plumes (1924)

STAPLEDON, Olaf (1886–1950) British science fiction author and philosophy lecturer who wrote a handful of books that have had a considerable influence on other authors. *First and Last Men, Star Maker*, and *Sirius* are among the most impressive examples of SF as a literature of ideas. *First and Last Men* tells the story of the remainder of humanity's history – a matter of many million years. Apart from the strength of argument and speculation, there is an humane and cultured ease in the writing that is moving as well as communicative. *Sirius*, the tale of a super intelligence in the body of a dog, is both stimulating and touching in its portrayal of intellect trapped by circumstance. He is said to have written his early books in complete ignorance of any other work in the genre, except that of H. G. Wells.

 First and Last Men (1930)

Star Maker (1937)

Sirius (1944)

STARK, Richard, see WESTLAKE, Donald E.

STEAD, Christina (1902) Australian novelist, who has lived in England, America and New South Wales. Her reputation was not well and truly made until the American reprint of *The Man Who Loved Children*, introduced by Randall Jarrell: since then her gifts have been fully recognized, although she has yet to gain a wider audience for her earlier novels. She is a shrewd, ironic, feline (but never malicious) writer, with a great sense of justice; she has always inclined to the left, but for humanitarian and not doctrinaire reasons. She is a novelist of the very highest quality: restrained, observant, superb at conveying anguish of mind without mawkishness, brilliant at sympathetic portraits of eccentrics. She has called her own novels "scenes from contemporary life", and this is just what they are.

 The Man Who Loved Children (1940)

Dark Places of the Heart (1966, in Britain *Cotters' England*, 1967)

 The Little Hotel (1974)

STEGNER, Wallace (1909) American university professor, editor, novelist and short story-writer. Stegner's subjects are mostly drawn from the history of the American West. He has described the wanderings of a family on the western frontier, recorded in his novel *The Big Rock Candy Mountain* as "a search for a place and a stability", and most of his fiction concerns such a search. His characters typically reveal nobility and bravery in the face of a harsh existence; but their hopes are usually betrayed. His rich and complex stories are written in a clear, realistic prose style.

On a Darkling Plain (1940)

The Big Rock Candy Mountain (1943)

Recapitulation (1979)

STEIN, Aaron Marc (1906) American detective novelist, also writing as George Bagby (the Inspector Schmidt books) and Hampton Stone (the Jeremiah Gibson books). Very prolific, but never slick, often glinting with quiet humour, literate and travelled, Stein is one of the great reliables of crime writing,

and is underrated in Britain.

 Days of Misfortune (1949)

The Murder That Wouldn't Stay Solved (as Stone, 1951)

 Two in a Bush (as Bagby, 1976)

STEIN, Gertrude (1874–1946) American prose writer, experimentalist, popular memoirist and dramatist. Stein studied psychology under Henry James' brother William, and formed an interest in the exact manner in which the mind works, and in the effects that words exercise independently of sense. She experimented along these lines in a series of (usually) short prose works, which considering that they do not make ordinary "sense", are surprisingly readable. Her earliest fiction explores the problems of her lesbianism (*Three Lives*), but she did not go on with this. She was known only to literary critics and to art lovers – she had settled in Paris before World War I – until she published a more straightforward book, *The Autobiography of Alice B. Toklas* (1933); in this she told the story of her own life – as much of it as she wanted – as from the mouth of her tiny but dominating lover, Alice B. Toklas. She then became world famous; and wrote other popular books. In these her prose seems more quaint and amusing than "difficult". But she went on experimenting. She influenced Sherwood Anderson, Ernest Hemingway and a host of others. Her popular books are very skilfully written, but are artistically inferior to her experimental ones. Her first and best prose, in *Three Lives*, was influenced directly by Flaubert, and critics are now finding the more conventional virtues in her prose: sense of place, feeling for country, people, sexual anguish. She has not been underrated; but her more serious prose has.

 Three Lives (1909)

Tender Buttons (1914)

Selected Writings (1946)

STEINBECK, John (1902–68) American novelist, story-writer and screenwriter. Steinbeck received the Nobel Prize in 1962. At the back of most of his fiction lies his lifelong rather uncritical love for the Arthurian cycle. He made his name with *Tortilla Flat*, about a band of outlaws who terrorize Monterey. His work of the 1930s, for which he received his Nobel Prize, is an odd mixture of protest (on behalf of the bad treatment meted out to migrant workers), farce, and an organic view of human "group behaviour". Steinbeck is always, and rightly, criticized for his intellectual inconsistency; on the one hand he showed himself in sympathy with the oppressed (*The Grapes of Wrath*), on the other with the merely irresponsible (*Tortilla Flat*);

and his view of man as a group is never assimilated properly into his fiction. But he wrote movingly, and the ordeal of the Joads in *The Grapes of Wrath* is absolutely convincing. *Of Mice and Men*, too, is a moving tale of two contrasting characters who love each other to the extent that the smaller has to kill the larger to save him from himself. *East of Eden* (1952) is skilful but less powerful, and was made into a successful film. His vision was never clearly expressed, but it was sincere – and its force emerges enough in the work of his middle period for its survival to be assured.

Tortilla Flat (1935)

Of Mice and Men (1937)

The Grapes of Wrath (1939)

John Steinbeck

STENDHAL (1783–1842) French novelist, biographer and memoirist, whose real name was Henri Beyle – hence *Beylisme*, a term used to mean, approximately, that phenomena are studied not for what they mean in themselves, but for what they mean to the person who experiences them. Stendhal's novels – the most famous are *The Red and the Black* and *The Charterhouse of Parma* – are an innovatory mixture of subjectivity, romanticism and cold analysis. He himself realized that his work would not be fully appreciated until fifty years after his death, and, although Balzac admired him, he was right. He was in his lifetime much more successful in the Paris *salons*. His novels demonstrate a very keen revolutionary intelligence coping with a clash between cold reason and high romantic passion; but in this context "revolutionary" has intellectual rather than political implications. Like Flaubert, he was full of *dégoût* against all classes. Stendhal created the "alienated hero", the man at odds with his environment:

Julian in *The Red and the Black* is basically an existentialist hero, since he behaves in order to fulfil himself – rather than to observe the values of society. The same may be said of Fabrice, in the more complex *Charterhouse*. But Stendhal, a perfervid romantic, shows the extreme difficulties of self-fulfilment. He wrote, he said, for a "happy few". His autobiographical writings are of the greatest interest.

 Armance (1827, tr. 1928)

The Red and the Black (1830, tr. 1926)

The Charterhouse of Parma (1839, tr. 1926)

STEPHENS, James (1880–1950) Irish poet and story-teller, remembered above all for his fantasy, *The Crock of Gold*. Stephens lived in Dublin, and during the period of agitation for Home Rule became a student of Gaelic and determined that his task as a writer was to give Ireland a new mythology. His novels, short stories and children's books all make use of Irish material and themes. *The Crock of Gold* is a strange allegorical fable which explores the conflict between abstract reason and the imagination, between head and heart, between the longing for knowledge and the impulse to "gaiety, and music and a dance of joy".

 The Crock of Gold (1912)

STERN, G. B. (1890–1973) English novelist, known chiefly for her popular novels of Jewish life. She also wrote neat short stories, and a series of autobiographies.

 Tents of Israel (1924)

The Young Matriarch (1942)

STERN, Richard (1928) American novelist and story-writer. Stern is a sophisticated writer who has been appropriately described as a "moral realist". His first novel *Golk* is a scarifying satire on the media and their

destructive power. *Stitch* is the only really successful novel to be based on the career (which included a conviction for treason) of the famous American poet Ezra Pound. *Teeth, Dying and Other Matters* (1964) collects rather uneven short stories.

 *Golk* (1960)

In Any Case (1963)

Stitch (1965)

STERN, Stuart, see RAE, Hugh C.

STERNE, Laurence (1713–68) English novelist. His odd, eccentric and innovatory novel *Tristram Shandy* is not in the mainstream of English literature, and yet it has proved very highly influential to twentieth-century novelists such as James Joyce, and it has been very popular. Here Sterne anticipated pretty well every feature of modernism, especially stream-of-consciousness and time displacement. He also inserts "essays" into his narrative. Hs sense of humour is unique, complex and bawdy – it might be said to be the result of hypersensitive and intelligent investigation of the reasons why he felt guilty when he was aroused by pornography. The components of his attitude as it emerges in his novel are not in themselves very interesting or original: sentimentality (the cult of sentiment was then at its height); interest in the psychological ideas of Locke (association of ideas); "dirty-mindedness". But the means by which Sterne combined them, under a Rabelaisian scheme, is original. *Tristram Shandy* is an exploration of the meaning of humour, and while this humour is very different from that of Rabelais (it is much slyer), it is defined in an epoch-making way.

 Tristram Shandy (1760–67)

STEVENSON, Robert Louis (1850–94) Scottish critic, poet and writer of romances, stories, novels and essays. His greatest achievement is the unfinished *Weir of Hermiston*, a

novel much more serious in intention than his previous popular but very efficient romances, most of which have been widely read but somewhat undervalued. His superbly lucid prose, his sense of pace, his skill at telling a story of action: these set a new standard for the adventure story, and influenced many writers, especially John Masefield, perhaps the most effective extender of the Stevensonian tradition. Graham Greene has acknowledged the influence of his style.

 Treasure Island (1883)

The Strange Case of Dr Jekyll and Mr Hyde (1886)

 Weir of Hermiston (1896)

STEWART, J. I. M., see INNES, Michael

STEWART, Mary (1916) English romantic novelist, who scored an immediate success with her first novel *Madame Will You Talk* (1954) and went on to write a number of novels which blend mystery and romance. The plots are always ingenious and plausible but the strength of her writing lies in the colourful and carefully researched settings. Latterly

she has turned to Arthurian legend for her inspiration; the last part of her Merlin trilogy, *The Last Enchantment*, was published in 1979.

 The Ivy Tree (1961)

The Gabriel Hounds (1967)

The Crystal Cave (1970)

STIFTER, Adalbert (1805–68) Austrian novelist and story-writer, who led a difficult life and committed suicide aged 62. Although his importance in German letters is comparable almost to that of Henry James in Anglo-American literature, he has been little read in translation. His tales and fables are complex explorations of the patterns of human intercourse, in which a hostile fate often intervenes.

 Brigitta (1844, tr. 1957)

STOKER, Bram (1847–1912) Irish novelist and journalist, remembered for one book, *Dracula* (1897). Although not the first vampire novel, *Dracula*, written in the diaries-and-letters form used in Wilkie Collins' *The Woman in White* to gain credibility, is the definitive account, forefather of films, plays and TV dramas. It has a good strong narrative line and the atmosphere is evoked with a skill that still chills.

 Dracula (1897)

STONE, Hampton, see STEIN, Aaron Marc

STONE, Irving (1903) American historical novelist who invests the lives of his main characters with large doses of grief, passion and achievement. This exaggerated core of personality is presented against a colourfully realistic background, which throws the main protagonist into clear relief. This technique applied to highly readable and well-researched fictionalizations of historical lives begins to have much in common with myth. Two of Stone's best known books, *Lust for Life* and *The Agony and the Ecstasy* have strongly reinforced the notion of the artist as a tortured romantic, and have shaped the popular, near-legendary pictures of Van Gogh and Michelangelo respectively. *Sailor on Horseback* (1938) is about Jack London.

 Lust for Life (1934)

Love is Eternal (1954)

The Agony and the Ecstasy (1961)

STOREY, David (1933) English novelist and dramatist. Storey, a Yorkshire novelist in the mould of D. H. Lawrence, is an intensely serious writer who wrote, initially, with passion of the things he knew and understood: particularly of rugby football in *This Sporting*

Life (successfully filmed) – and always of working-class life. His later novels suffer from unfulfilled symbolic pretensions, although some critics find him to be an outstanding social realist. He resembles Alan Sillitoe in that he is an instinctive rather than an intellectual novelist; but, apart from *This Sporting Life*, a certain over-solemnity and heaviness gets in the way of his narratives. He has power, but his melodrama and his excursions into various modernist techniques undermine this. Nevertheless he is a readable novelist who never manipulates for the sake of popularity.

 This Sporting Life (1960)

Radcliffe (1963)

A Temporary Life (1973)

STORM, Theodor (1817–88) German poet and writer of *novellen*. His main themes are loneliness and independence of mind; he developed these, and in his final tales gained great tragic power, in a short compass. He was laconic, and is a good example of how the Germans can feel authentic Flaubertian *dégoût*, and yet appear restrained.

 Immensee (1852, tr. 1863)

Beneath the Flood (1876, tr. 1962)

The White Horseman (1888, tr. 1962)

STOUT, Rex (1886–1975) American detective story-writer, hugely popular and revered. He began with psychological novels, but the Wall Street crash (he was a businessman) forced him into more lucrative fiction. His first detective story, *Fer-de-Lance* (1934), introduced the obese, chair-bound Nero Wolfe and his assistant Archie Goodwin; it was a clear

Rex Stout

success. Throughout the long series of novels and three-to-a-volume stories which followed, Wolfe's admirers became familiar with every detail of his old brownstone house in New York, his eccentricities, his love of orchids, beer and good food; and with Archie Goodwin's edged but affectionate style as narrator. The detection itself was always fair and intelligent. He died at a great age having worked with undiminished skill to the last.

 Too Many Cooks (1938)

Plot it Yourself (1959, in Britain, *Murder in Style*)

 The Doorbell Rang (1965)

STOWE, Harriet Beecher (1811–96) American novelist. She is remembered best for *Uncle Tom's Cabin,* a patronizing but worthy semi-anti-slavery novel ("Uncle Tom" is a term of approbation amongst Negroes, and Stowe was not at first even an Abolitionist); better are her later and less well-known novels about New England village folk. She became more liberal as she got older, and *My Wife and I* is a plea for women's rights.

 Uncle Tom's Cabin (1852)

The Minister's Wooing (1859)

My Wife and I (1871)

STRIBLING, T. S. (1881–1965) American novelist whose works made a deep impression on William Faulkner. He writes of Tennessee, his home state, with a humane realism; his characterization is excellent, and his gift for telling a story great. His earlier novels are pessimistic, bitter and sharply satirical in tone. His greatest achievement is his trilogy about Alabama life: *The Forge*, 1931; *The Store*, 1932; and *The Unfinished Cathedral*, 1934.

 Teeftallow (1926)

Bright Metal (1928)

These Bars of Flesh (1938)

STRONG, L. A. G. (1896–1958) Irish novelist, story-writer, poet and general writer. Strong only just failed to become part of the history of the novel: his later books were competent and contained excellent passages, but lacked force. The earlier will be remembered for their romantic passion, craftsmanship and brutal realism.

Dewar Rides (1929)

The Brothers (1932)

The Travellers (1945)

STRUGATSKY, Arkady (1925) and **Boris** (1933) Russian science fiction writers. The elder brother is a linguist, the younger an astronomer. They are the Soviet Union's leading SF writers. Some of their early work – notably *The Second Martian Invasion* (1967, tr. 1970) – was satirical, and the outlook of their other novels, including *Hard to Be a God*, contrasted sharply with the naive optimism of much other Soviet work in the field. After losing favour with the authorities for a time they seem to have reinstated themselves, although some of their work was suppressed in the Soviet Union.

 Hard to Be a God (1964, tr. 1973)

Roadside Picnic (1975, tr. 1977)

STUART, Don A., see CAMPBELL, John W., Jr.

STUBBS, Jean (   ) English novelist who has produced conventional fiction about life's casualties; well-turned but lush romances about Victorian theatricals; and a series of mystery stories set in the same period. They share a genial detective, Inspector Lintoff, are outstandingly well written and have plots of an intricate brilliance.

 The Rose-Grower (1962)

Hanrahan's Colony (1964)

By Our Beginnings (1979)

STURGEON, Theodore (1918) American speculative author whose works hover on the borders of science fiction. He is greatly concerned with character, and especially with the dark lonely sides of human nature which he portrays as mysterious. A strong liberal humanism is present in his writing and he argues consistently for tolerance, compassion and

Jacqueline Susann

co-operation. His *More Than Human* develops this attitude in the tale of a group of strange children, incomplete as individuals, who become more than their sum as "Homo Gestalt", a group individual. Much of Sturgeon's best work is in his short stories.

 More Than Human (1953)

Sturgeon in Orbit (stories, 1964)

The Joyous Invasions (stories, 1965)

STURGIS, Howard Overing (1855–1920) American novelist born in London. He failed to fulfil his potential, and would not be remembered were it not for his pallid – but for its time courageous – novel *Belchamber*, about a young English nobleman who is both a homosexual and a utopian. George Santayana's Mario in *The Last Puritan* is a portrait of Sturgis.

 Tim (1891)

Belchamber (1904)

STYRON, William (1925) American (Virginian) novelist, who draws on Southern history to interpret contemporary personal situations. *Lie Down in Darkness* (1951) recounts a tragedy of family disintegration. In *Set this House on Fire* (1960), set in Italy, an expatriate artist's Southern background provides the perspective for his experience of guilt. The controversial Pulitzer prize winner *The Confessions of Nat Turner* (1967) is an account of the 1831 slave rebellion from the Negro viewpoint.

 Lie Down in Darkness (1951)

The Confessions of Nat Turner (1967)

Sophie's Choice (1979)

SURTEES, R. S. (1805–64) British comic writer who created the character of the rollicking fox-hunter grocer, Mr Jorrocks, born to a station beneath his instincts.

 Jorrocks's Jaunts and Jollities (1838)

Handley Cross (1843)

Hillingdon Hall (1845)

SUSANN, Jacqueline (1925–76) American best selling novelist. *Valley of the Dolls* (1966) established her as purveyor of long, sensational novels about high life and complicated sex. Others, like *The Love Machine* (1969) and *Dolores* (1976), followed the formula.

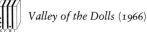 *Valley of the Dolls* (1966)

SUYIN, Han, see HAN SUYIN

SVEVO, Italo (1861–1928) Italian (Triestine) novelist and story-writer. Svevo, whose real name was Schmitz, was a successful businessman (in underwater paint) and a failed writer – until he published his masterpiece *Confessions of Zeno*, which was "pushed" by James Joyce who had known him during World War I. *Confessions of Zeno* succeeds as a comi-tragedy partly because it is written in bad Italian (Svevo's first language was German), an irony typical of this ironist, who prophesied the atomic bomb at the end of his great novel. He makes use of Freudian theory while making fun of it; and it is only towards the end of the novel – told in the first person, but "stolen" from him by his psycho-analyst in revenge for him giving him up – that the reader realizes that he is proceeding to a sombre and indeed terrifying climax. The novel is now reckoned to be on a level with works by James Joyce, Franz Kafka, Robert Musil and Thomas Mann; there is no greater comic novel of the century. Svevo's other work is also excellent, although he achieved no success with it.

 A Life (1892, tr. 1963)

As a Man Grows Older (1898, tr. 1932)

Confessions of Zeno (1923, tr. 1930)

SWADOS, Harvey (1920) American novelist and story-writer. Swados is an efficient left-wing writer who has never fallen victim to the fallacies of "socialist realism".

 Out Went the Candle (1955)

The Will (1963)

A Story for Teddy (stories, 1965)

SWARTHOUT, Glendon (1918) American novelist whose books, set in a variety of times and places, are mainly concerned with the effect on modern America of its Indian and Western past. *The Eagle and the Iron Cross* tells of a German prisoner of war who escapes and falls in with a tribe of Indians. *The Shootist* – about an aging gunfighter dying of cancer – is one of the finest Westerns dealing with the twilight of the frontier age.

 They Came to Cordura (1958)

The Eagle and the Iron Cross (1966)

The Shootist (1975)

SWIFT, Jonathan (1667–1745) English novelist, satirist, poet and pamphleteer, who was born and lived much of his life in Ireland. Swift used prose fiction as a means of satire, and he drew on the practice of Daniel Defoe whom he affected to despise. One of his satires, got out of hand and became an imaginative masterpiece,

Jonathan Swift

which is even abridged for children's consumption: *Gulliver's Travels*. The novel is a satire on mankind, but also a profound and poetic commentary on it (which Swift hardly intended). Its means are not original; but its style and ingenuity are. It used to be thought that Swift, a Dean, had no true Christian faith; it is now realized that he had, and that *Gulliver* is open to the profoundest interpretations. It can hardly be said that the work has been influential, since it has never successfully been imitated; but the Swiftian style of irony has remained immensely influential in British satirical writing. Swift was often upbraided for his harsh views – views that he was expressing ironically, as when he suggested that surplus children be boiled and eaten (*A Modest Proposal*).

A Tale of a Tub (1704)

Travels Into Several Remote Nations of the World by Lemuel Gulliver (1726)

SWINNERTON, Frank (1884) English novelist – friend of H. G. Wells, Arnold Bennett, George Gissing and many others – who has continued to turn out competent novels for the whole of his very long life. *Nocturne* (1917) is everyone's favourite.

Young Felix (1923)

A Tigress in Prothero (1959)

Rosalind Passes (1974)

SYMONS, Julian (1912) English novelist, poet, critic, biographer and social historian. Symons is one of the few writers to have raised the detective story to the level of literature. He has written poor novels, but at his best (in for example *The End of Solomon Grundy*, 1964, in the *Omnibus*) he is a very fine psychological novelist, who can tell a story at a swift and satisfying pace. He is well informed about the art of murder, knows the nature of his reader's interest in it, and exploits this with delight. He is expert on the ways of suburbia.

The Broken Penny (1963)

The Julian Symons Omnibus (1966)

The Plot Against Roger Rider (1973)

T

TAGORE, Rabindranath (1861–1941) Indian poet, playwright, novelist, musician, painter and teacher. He wrote in Bengali, and far too little of his work has been translated. In 1913 he won the Nobel Prize, largely for his poetry. Tagore was a writer of immense stature and influence in his own country.

A Tagore Reader (1961)

TANIZAKI, Junichiro (1886–1965) Japanese novelist and story-writer, probably the greatest of this century. He began as a decadent, a sort of Japanese Oscar Wilde; but he later wrote two different kinds of novel: the long, meticulously realistic one, *The Makioka Sisters*; and the shorter tense psychological study of relationships, of which the much acclaimed *Some Prefer Nettles* is the best example. He was influenced by Western culture and techniques, but remained resolutely Japanese. Although clinical, truthful, morbid and exact, he always had a fine delicacy of touch.

Some Prefer Nettles (1928, tr. 1955)

The Makioka Sisters (1943–48, tr. 1957)

The Key (1956, tr. 1961)

TARKINGTON, Booth (1869–1946) American novelist, best known for his trilogy *Growth* (1918–27). Its central novel, *The Magnificent Ambersons* (1918), which won a Pulitzer prize and was filmed by Orson Welles, concerns the downfall of a genteel Indiana family through their resistance to economic and social change; but the "business heroes" of *The Midlander* (1923), which completes the trilogy, and of *The Plutocrat* (1927), are clearly barbarous.

Alice Adams (1921)

Growth (1927)

The Plutocrat (1927)

TATE, Ellalice, see PLAIDY, Jean

TAYLOR, Elizabeth (1912–75) English novelist and story-writer who infused each of her sixteen novels with a formidable intelligence, wit and compassion, with penetrating psychological insight and a cool, spare, quietly precise style entirely her own. She evoked the joys and sorrows of young love (*In a Summer Season*, 1961), and the problems of retirement (*The Wedding Group*, 1969) with equal skill and clarity, and has a strong claim to be considered as one of the most accomplished and downright enjoyable novelists of her generation.

A View of the Harbour (1947)

A Game of Hide-and-Seek (1951)

Blaming (1976)

TAYLOR, Peter (1919) Novelist and story-writer born in Nashville, Tennessee, whose work springs from the tradition set up by Robert Penn Warren, Andrew Lytle, and the other "Southern agrarians". His achievement is to look back at the awful chaos of Southern history and to make his readers aware of the beauty in it – as well as the terror. There is no clear "message": he is essentially a story-writer.

A Woman of Means (1950)

The Widows of Thornton (stories, 1954)

Collected Stories (1969)

TAYLOR, Phoebe Attwood (1909–76) American writer of a large number of novels in which her detective, a homespun sailor retired to Cape Cod, identified murderers by using his common sense.

The Cape Cod Mystery (1931)

Proof of the Pudding (1945)

Diplomatic Corpse (1951)

TEY, Josephine (1896–1952) Scottish mystery novelist (the pseudonym of Elizabeth MacKintosh) who wrote successful stage plays as Gordon Daviot, and two straight novels. Her interests appear in the details of her novels – theatre, horse racing and breeding and, in particular, history: *The Daughter of Time* (1951), a defence of Richard III in modern mystery style, is regarded by some as a genuine contribution to scholarship. *The Franchise Affair* is a modern re-creation of the eighteenth-century case of Elizabeth Canning. Not all her crime stories are about murder, and each is quite different from the others. All are written with a tart, observant wit, and have original and plausible plots. *Miss Pym Disposes* (1946) draws on her experience as a qualified teacher of physical education.

The Franchise Affair (1948)

Brat Farrar (1949)

To Love and Be Wise (1950)

THACKERAY, William Makepeace (1811–63) English novelist. Thackeray was one of the great nineteenth-century successes. His first successful – and his best – novel *Vanity Fair*, shows his brilliantly penetrating interest in evil, and is a book of the greatest subtlety, although done in a deceptively light-hearted and semi-picaresque mode. Its successors do not quite realize its promise, for Thackeray's vision was a bleak one: he believed that society was fatally misorganized. But in the light of Victorian optimism he did not dare to pursue his insight to its logical conclusion. In a sense his great gifts were wasted – but so brilliantly that few have grumbled.

Vanity Fair (1847–48)

The History of Henry Esmond (1852)

The Virginians (1859)

THÉRIAULT, Yves (1915) Francophone Canadian novelist and story-writer, who also writes in English. He is versatile, uneven and prolific, and specializes in ethnic groups (e.g. Eskimos, Jews). His characterization is excellent and his writing lucid. *Agaguk*, about Eskimos, is his masterpiece.

Agaguk (1959, tr. 1963)

Ashini (1960, tr. 1961)

THEROUX, Paul (1941) American novelist and travel writer, resident in London. Theroux taught in Uganda and Singapore, and used these places as backdrops for his early novels, most successfully in *Jungle Lovers* (1971) and

Saint Jack. He tries to write in the style of V. S. Naipaul, on whom he has written a book, and is also much influenced by Graham Greene. His later novels are more weighty and command respect from some critics, although he tends to be, in the words of one critic, "self-consciously flashy". His best is *Picture Palace*, which tells, with a clever use of flashback, the life story of an elderly, eccentric, female photographer.

Saint Jack (1973)

The Family Arsenal (1976)

Picture Palace (1978)

THOMAS, Craig (1942) British writer of tough adventure stories. His best is *Firefox*, an enthralling espionage story about the theft of an aeroplane from the Russians.

Firefox (1977)

Wolfsbane (1978)

THOMAS, Dylan (1914–53) Welsh poet, fiction writer, radio dramatist and script-writer. Thomas' prose, which simplifies and vulgarizes the methods of T. F. Powys and James Joyce, is very highly amusing, especially when he read it aloud (recordings exist; and the actor Emlyn Williams stood in well for the author). The novels and stories are picaresque-sentimental, and fade on the written page; but as entertainment they are impressive and enjoyable.

The Map of Love (poems and stories, 1939)

Portrait of the Artist as a Young Dog (1940)

Adventures in the Skin Trade (1955)

THOMAS, Leslie (1931) British popular novelist who worked as a journalist before writing

the best selling *The Virgin Soldiers*, an account of young men on National Service in Malaya in the 1950s. His readability, conversational style and, in some cases, choice of bawdy subject matter have obscured the craftmanship of his work. A certain innocence in his central characters – a traditional picaresque device – helps create an attractively light tone which inspires both humour and sympathy.

The Virgin Soldiers (1966)

The Man With Power (1973)

Ormerod's Landing (1979)

THOMAS, Ross (1926) American mystery writer and one-time publicity director for Chief Abafemi Awolowo of Nigeria. His best novels are his early spy stories, especially *The Cold War Swap*, and two novels which came from his African experience: *The Seersucker Whipsaw* (1967) and *The Brass Go-Between* (1960), the latter published under a pseudonym, Oliver Bleeck. His new novel, *The Eighth Dwarf*, marks a return to his old form.

The Cold War Swap (1966)

The Fools in Town Are on Our Side (1971)

The Eighth Dwarf (1979)

THOMPSON, Flora (1877–1947) English writer born in poor rural circumstances, who made her name late in life with *Lark Rise* (1939), a simple, moving autobiographical story of village life. She followed it with two sequels, *Over to Candleford* (1941) and *Candleford Green* (1943), and all three were republished as one volume.

Lark Rise to Candleford (1945)

THURBER, James (1894–1961) American comic writer and cartoonist. Thurber is especially associated with the *New Yorker*

William Makepeace Thackeray

Paul Theroux

Leslie Thomas

J. R. R. Tolkien

where his work appeared regularly for many years. His humour is uniquely black, being focussed on the deepest problems and neuroses of American society, and making use of material which in any other hands would be the stuff of tragedy. Typical of this is his semi-autobiographical sketch, *My Life and Hard Times*, an ironical work describing isolation and alienation in the Ohio of the first decades of the century. One of Thurber's most famous stories, "The Secret Life of Walter Mitty", about a man whose failures and frustrations have forced him to escape into a dream world and abandon the reality of his own identity, was memorably filmed by Danny Kaye. Later Thurber turned to the writing of fables like *The Thirteen Clocks* (1950) or *The White Deer*, in which he explores illusion and reality, hiding a moral vision in the cloak of a fairy tale.

My Life and Hard Times (1933)

My World – and Welcome to It (stories, 1942)

The White Deer (1945)

TIPTREE, James, Jr. (1915) Pseudonym of Alice Sheldon, American science fiction writer who also uses the name Raccoona Sheldon. She is the widely-praised winner of several recent awards, but has a tendency to overwrite.

The Girl Who Was Plugged In (1974)

Up the Walls of the World (1978)

TOLKIEN, J. R. R. (1892–1973) Novelist and professor of philosophy at Oxford, born in South Africa. In his trilogy *The Lord of the Rings* and its satellite works, Tolkein succeeded in creating an original but wholly satisfying fictitious myth cycle. It is the tale of the last great confrontation between the forces of light and darkness in a time when elves, dwarves and goblins still inhabit their enclaves openly, magic still prevails, and the ancient lore has not been abandoned. The winning of this latest round of the Manichaean struggle saps the vitality of the enchanted "Third Age of Middle Earth" and humans, more prosaic, predictable and safe than elves or wizards, inherit the earth. Against this grand pattern, Tolkein creates a fictitious world with all the high seriousness of a Norse saga or a German fairy tale, and it almost achieves the status of these – as a blank archetype of all the moral dilemmas of life. Its solidity is reinforced by the author's philological ingenuity and learning, particularly his invention of the elvish language. The moral patterns are those of a particularly English brand of yeoman Christianity – evil defeated by ale and common sense. *The Hobbit* is a prologue to the trilogy and in-

troduces the characters within the framework of a much simpler tale: *The Silmarillion* purports to be an elvish epic poem predating the events of the "Ringwars" by several thousand years.

The Hobbit (1937)

The Lord of the Rings (1954–55)

The Silmarillion (1977)

TOLSTOY, Count A. N. (1882–1945) Russian novelist, a distant relative of the famous Leo Tolstoy. Tolstoy was at first anti-communist, and fought with the Whites; then he returned to Soviet Russia, and did very well out of it – he was never in serious disgrace. He was a very gifted and versatile minor writer: he wrote Wellsian science fiction and romances, stories about the dying gentry and about Russian emigrés, and (less successfully but readably) on how decent Russians struggled to gain acceptance of Stalinism, and won in the end.

Nikita's Childhood (1921, tr. 1945)

The Death Box (1926, tr. 1934)

The Road to Calvary (1919–41, tr. 1945)

TOLSTOY, Count Leo (1828–1910) Russian novelist, pacifist, thinker, polemicist, story-writer, critic and activist. Tolstoy, as man and as writer, is the supreme example of the clash between the instinctive and the intellectual: he lived the conflict out. He enjoyed life; but needed to moralize – on the strictest principles. He ended by denouncing art; but went on writing. On the whole, the instinctive in him triumphed; yet, had he not moralized, then he would not have been as profound a novelist. *War and Peace*, the great epic centring on Napoleon's useless entry into Moscow, is based on certain arguments about predestination that are not very profound (man has no

free will, but must think he has); but its characters experience these ideas, and exemplify the results of their experiences and come to extraordinary life in so doing. *Anna Karenina*, a novel of adultery, is based on a philosophy, but its characters – again – come to life despite this philosophy. Most readers tend to ignore the moralizing and to enjoy the story. Yet it can be argued that the height of Tolstoy's art is not reached until the story *The Death of Ivan Ilyich* (tr. 1960 in *The Cossacks*), which anticipates Franz Kafka, J.-P. Sartre and Albert Camus. This was not written until 1886, after Tolstoy thought he had rejected art . . . It is often said that Tolstoy the moralist has "little to give" to us today, whereas Tolstoy the writer has. This is true. But it must be remembered that the effect of Tolstoy the moralist and those who thought like him on the conditions of today is enormous.

War and Peace (1865–69, tr. 1957)

Anna Karenina (1875–77, tr. 1954)

Resurrection (1899, tr. 1931)

TOMLINSON. H. M. (1873–1958) English novelist, travel writer and essayist. He wrote of the sea and of exotic places with gusto and verve; and his style is memorably lucid.

Galleons Reach (1927)

All Our Yesterdays (1930)

The Trumpet Shall Sound (1957)

TOYNBEE, Philip (1916) English novelist, critic and journalist. Toynbee began with three conventionally rebellious novels, wrote two experimental "Jungian" novels – which attracted much notice at the time – and then started on a long sequence of novels (the Pantaloon series) written in free verse: these have so far been respectfully ignored, but when the series is complete, it may be found more significant. The two important novels are *Tea with Mrs Goodman* and *The Garden to the Sea*, which suggested that Toynbee was (or would be) the best of the modern English novelists. Yet the appeal of the intense writing has not lasted and is quite different from the superb lucidity achieved by Toynbee the memoirist. The later verse novels are interesting, but it is hard to see where they will lead: they are alternatively rambling and concentrated. Yet Toynbee has always been interesting, and his gift for lucid prose may lead him to write a major novel.

Tea with Mrs Goodman (1947)

The Garden to the Sea (1953)

Views from a Lake (in verse, 1968)

TRANTER, Nigel (1909) Scottish novelist and historian, born in Glasgow. Many of his best and most popular novels are written around the lives of well-known Scots heroes.

Robert the Bruce (1971)

Montrose: the captain general (1973)

Lords of Misrule (1976)

TRAVEN, Ben (1890–1969) German Chicago-born writer, who perhaps lived for much of his life in South America. The mystery of his identity is not fully solved (a 1979 television feature confidently giving the "solution" ignored a quite different and equally convincing solution). "Traven" wrote in German. His novels are vigorous, simple but very intelligent adventure stories, attacking capitalism, but they are not really classically Marxist. The most famous, because of the Bogart film, is *The Treasure of the Sierra Madre* (1935).

The Death Ship (1934)

Government (1935)

The Rebellion of the Hanged (1952)

TRESSELL, Robert (1868–1911) Irish sign-writer and house-painter who was shocked by the plight of his fellow labourers into writing *The Ragged Trousered Philanthropist*: a pioneering, powerful and unexpectedly funny account of the lives and opinions of a group of working men in a small town in the south of England. Hauntingly sub-titled ". . . the story of twelve months in Hell told by one of the damned", it defines poverty and proposes socialism as the solution.

The Ragged Trousered Philanthropist (1914)

"TREVANIAN" Pseudonym of an American Professor of English Literature whose identity has been well concealed. *The Eiger Sanction* is a strange blend of humour, sex, horrific violence, authentic spy jargon and stylishly sparse writing. The characters include: Wormwood, Hemlock, Felicity Arce, Randi Nickers, and Anna Bidet. The opening is ridiculous, but when the action moves to the Swiss mountains, nail-biting tautness and authenticity take over. *The Loo Sanction*, about a British intelligence organization which operates from a former lavatory, is more obviously a spoof.

The Eiger Sanction (1972)

The Loo Sanction (1973)

Shibumi (1979)

TREVELYAN, Robert (1926) English historical novelist who jealously guards his anonymity. His novels feature a swash-buckling Victorian hero, Pendragon; tall, virile ex-cavalry officer of the 11th Hussars who serves as Queen's agent in numerous extravagant exploits.

Pendragon: late of Prince Albert's Own (1975)

Pendragon: the Montenegran Plot (1977)

TREVOR, Elleston, see HALL, Adam

TREVOR, William (1928) Irish novelist, story-writer and TV and radio playwright. Trevor writes novels and stories of high quality in the tradition of William Plomer, Graham Greene and George Moore. He is the master of the seedy southern seaside resort, the haunted country house, the genteel retired old folk, the lonely in the hospital, the ill-treated or victimized anywhere. His range is very wide and his treatment subtle and compassionate.

The Boarding House (1965)

Elizabeth Alone (1973)

Angels at the Ritz (stories, 1975)

TRILLING, Lionel (1905) American champion of liberalism in literary criticism and biographer of Matthew Arnold and E. M. Forster. His one novel *The Middle of the Journey*, is a shrewd and lively portrayal of radical intellectuals in pre-war America. One of its characters, Gifford Maxim, is based on Whitaker Chambers, chief instigator of the case against Alger Hiss (1948).

The Middle of the Journey (1948)

Of this Time, Of that Place, and Other Stories (1979)

TROLLOPE, Anthony (1815–82) English novelist. Trollope, a post office civil servant who travelled widely (and exploited his travels in his fiction), was an uneven but very prolific novelist. He can write very badly; but at his best he writes more densely and more tellingly than it is at present fashionable to admit. At heart he was disgusted with the society in which he lived; but he was also a commercial sentimentalist. *The Way We Live Now*, which is quite savage, shows him at his toughest; the famous Barchester series shows him at his most charming; a number of less well known but still widely read novels show him at his competent worst: sentimental, taking off Dickens, and content to satisfy his wide public. His frank *Autobiography* tells us all about it; it upset some of his readers because it recorded the exact amount he made for each book – and

modern critics seize on this as if to prove that he lacked integrity. He is unequalled in his capacity to show the manners of various sets of people of his time: a good example is the life of commercial travellers, as described in *Orley Farm*. He wrote particularly well of political life.

Orley Farm (1862)

The Way We Live Now (1875)

Phineas Redux (1876)

TRUMBO, Dalton (1905) American scriptwriter and novelist. Trumbo started out as a radical; and his third novel *Johnny Got His Gun*, about a man who loses all his limbs and senses in World War I, shocked liberal sensibilities and may have been suppressed during World War II. Although in the 1950s he was one of the "Hollywood Ten", and was imprisoned for a year, he has not returned to serious fiction.

Johnny Got His Gun (1939)

The Remarkable Andrew (1941)

TRYON, Thomas (1926) American film-actor and best selling novelist. A wordy dabbler in dog-eared grand guignol, he effectively contrasts nasty epidemics of accidents and ritual murders with ravishing pastoral settings (*The Other; Harvest Home*, 1973), but these and other clichés swamp *Lady*, the saga of a kind, beautiful widow who reigns lightly but firmly over a small community for twenty years until cruel fate forces her to disclose a terrible secret long-nursed in agony . . . By contrast, Tryon's *Crowned Heads* is the best "good-bad" Hollywood fiction since *The Disenchanted* by Budd Schulberg.

The Other (1971)

Lady (1974)

Crowned Heads (1976)

TUOHY, Frank (1925) English novelist and story-writer. Tuohy is an efficient realist who has had most success in the short story. He is most adept at demonstrating the bad faith of wealthy idlers.

The Animal Game (1957)

The Admiral and the Nuns (stories, 1962)

The Ice Saints (1964)

TURGENEV, Ivan (1818–83) Russian novelist, story-writer, critic, dramatist and memoirist. Turgenev was the most cosmopolitan of the nineteenth-century Russian writers, disliked

Ivan Turgenev

in his own country but loved elsewhere. *Fathers and Sons* is his greatest novel: it depicts with a perfect balance – as is shown by the fact that it does not satisfy political dogmatists of any colour – the predicament of the would-be reformer in Russia. The character of his "nihilist" Bazarov has been greatly misunderstood: he is rough and aggressive but this hides a gentle heart. Turgenev loved his native Russia, and was fascinated by terrorism; but in the end he opted for art, and was thus able to make comments of lasting value. His theme is the enjoyment, but inevitability of defeat, in love; his mood is mellow and sad; his humour is subtle; and his sense of the ridiculous is precise. A novelist of frustration, he evokes beauty in his style and in his feeling for nature.

A Nest of Gentlefolk (1859, tr. 1959)

Fathers and Sons (1862, tr. 1970)

Smoke (1867, tr. 1949)

TUTE, Warren (1914) English novelist, playwright and popular historian. He began to publish plays and novels when well into his forties. He has subsequently achieved great success with his popular historical works, such as *Hitler: the Last Ten Days* (1973), and with his espionage thrillers.

The Resident (1973)

Honours of War and Peace (1976)

The Cairo Sleeper (1977)

TUTUOLA, Amos (1920) Nigerian novelist. Tutuola is disliked by most Nigerian writers, but it seems that his capacity to capture and convey the meaning and the feeling of African legend is not excelled by any. Each of his narrators is a spiritual hero with supernatural powers; Tutuola seems, perhaps because of his lack of formal education, to have utterly avoided the mistake of trying to be "literary" in his strange and as often chilling as humourous tales. He is a kind of Nigerian Homer, and and although after *The Palm-Wine Drinkard*

and *My Life in the Bush of Ghosts* – his first novels – his manner became familiar to English readers, he has not really lost much of his power. He does no less than tell us, in his own English, the tales of his country, transformed by him. He is a major and a unique writer, who has been neglected in recent years, owing to the emergence of Western-style African literature. But he is possibly the greatest of them all.

The Palm-Wine Drinkard (1952)

My Life in the Bush of Ghosts (1954)

Abaiyi and his Inherited Poverty (1967)

TWAIN, Mark (1835–1910) American novelist, journalist and humourist. His real name was S. L. Clemens, and his pseudonym means "Two fathoms deep!" – the cry of the Mississippi river-sounders: but he took over the name from a writer he was parodying, and it has no especial significance. Twain was an uneven writer, over whom there is some disagreement. All agree, however, that he was the first writer to produce an unequivocally American novel: *Huckleberry Finn*. This is apparently rambling and unstructured, but it has its own mythopoeic pattern – one which Twain himself only half realized as he wrote it. He was a careless writer, and this is his only unflawed novel; but some of his non-fiction, and his short stories such as "The Man That Corrupted Hadleyburg", 1900, achieve a similar perfection. He stands at the head of the tradition of native American letters.

The Adventures of Tom Sawyer (1876)

The Prince and the Pauper (1882)

The Adventures of Huckleberry Finn (1886)

Mark Twain

UHNAK, Dorothy (1933) American police-story-writer who was a policewoman for 14 years. She has written three highly authentic books featuring Christie Opara, a female detective assigned to the Manhattan DA. *Law and Order*, about several generations of a New York police family, is a much more considerable work which deservedly became a best seller.

The Bait (1968)

Law and Order (1973)

UNAMUNO, Miguel de (1864–1936) Spanish poet, novelist and professor of Greek, chiefly remembered for his novel *Mist*, a working-out in fictional form of Unamuno's preoccupation with the problem of free will.

Mist (1914, tr. 1928)

UNDSET, Sigrid (1882–1949) Norwegian novelist who won the Nobel Prize in 1928, for the best seller *Kristin Lavransdatter*, a historical trilogy set in fourteenth-century Norway. This was solid, competent fiction, and unusually accurate. Her later work is religiose and of less interest.

Jenny (1911, tr. 1921)

Kristin Lavransdatter (1920–22, tr. 1930, repr. 1969)

The Faithful Wife (1936, tr. 1937)

UPDIKE, John (1932) American novelist, story-writer, poet and writer of juvenile fiction. Updike began as a perfect *New Yorker* writer, then began to write differently and more adventurously. He combines the erudition of John Barth or John Gardner with a vigour and wit which give his novels and stories a bite of their own: it is not necessary to know the allusions, or to understand every pun. *The Centaur* (1963) is one of his most original and powerful novels: it reads perfectly well at the *New Yorker* level, but is at the same time a parody of Joyce *and* a successful piece of myth-making. Updike has learned to inject his feelings into his prose, and he becomes more versatile with each book. He insists on searching for meaning, and yet ironizes his quest as useless. The closet play *Buchanan Dying* (1974), which could be called a kind of novel, shows him at his best: trying to make sense and truth out of an episode in history which everyone ignores or derides. Updike is a writer of

John Updike

deepening awareness; *The Coup*, set in a newly-independent African country, is a remarkable essay in compassionate satire.

The Poorhouse Fair (1959)

Warm Wine (stories, 1973)

The Coup (1979)

UPFIELD, Arthur W. (1888–1964) English writer of detective stories, who spent most of his life in Australia. He created the half-white, half-aboriginal detective, Napoleon Bonaparte, who solves classic murder mysteries in well realized, remote environments.

The Bachelors of Broken Hill (1951)

Man of Two Tribes (1956)

URIS, Leon (1924) American novelist. His experiences as a marine inspired his first novel *Battle Cry* (1953) which was well received. His third book, *Exodus* (1958), an exhaustively researched account of the making of modern Israel, was a runaway best seller. In his later novels he has explored such varied subjects as the Berlin airlift; a libel case brought by a doctor accused of atrocities against the Jews in Auschwitz; the Jewish uprising in the Warsaw Ghetto; and the contemporary troubles in Northern Ireland. These have all been best sellers.

Topaz (1967)

Q.B. VII (1970)

Trinity (1976)

V

VANCE, Jack (1916) American science fiction writer, noted for his depiction of eccentric semi-barbaric human cultures on other worlds. His work is colourful, but sometimes poorly plotted.

The Dying Earth (1950)

Big Planet (1952)

The Dragon Masters (1963)

VAN DER POST, Laurens (1906) South African novelist, playwright, and travel writer, who has lived in England and farmed in the Orange Free State. Van der Post's novels deal with the problems of South African life, which he presents with descriptive vigour and strong characterization. His first book, *In a Province*, (1934), is typical in its presentation of problems of race relations and in its criticism both of racial injustice and of Communist exploitation of the situation. *Flamingo Feather* recounts an adventurous journey through African jungle; in its vivid wilderness descriptions, it resembles his excellent travel writing.

In a Province (1934)

Flamingo Feather (1955)

The Hunter and the Whale (1967)

VAN DE WETERING, Janwillem (1931) Dutch writer, formerly a policeman and Buddhist monk, who lives in the U.S. and writes police procedural stories set in Amsterdam. The stories are slow, patient descriptions of routine enquiries which eventually lead to the solving of a murder case. Van de Wetering's strength lies in his subtle portrayal of character.

Outsider in Amsterdam (1975)

Tumbleweed (1976)

VAN DINE, S. S. (1888–1939) American detective novelist, pseudonym of art and literary critic Willard Huntington Wright, creator of Philo Vance. He produced *The Benson Murder Case* (1926), asserting that no author "has more than six good detective novel ideas in his system"; of his twelve novels, the earlier were indeed far superior. Vance is a dilettante with a penchant for intellectual one-upmanship and pseudo-English conversation. Equally affected was Van Dine's use of footnotes to amplify literary and artistic allusions. Although ostentatious and humourless, Van Dine combined ingenuity

and literacy with an almost documentary flavour. Ogden Nash felt that "Philo Vance needs a kick in the pance", but he remains a remarkable detective creation.

The Canary Murder Case (1927)

The Greene Murder Case (1928)

The Bishop Murder Case (1929)

VAN DOREN, Mark (1894–1972) American poet and critic, for many years Professor of Literature at Columbia University, New York. His novels about contemporary American manners were never more than respectfully received; it is as poet and critic that he will be remembered.

Windless Cabins (1940)

Tilda (1943)

VAN SLYKE, Helen (1919) American novelist and magazine journalist. Her novels, many of them now best sellers, are bitter romances heavily tinged with tragedy. They are set among the smart set in New York whose despair she paints in rich colours.

The Best People (1973)

Always Is Not Forever (1977)

VAN VECHTEN, Carl (1880–1966) American novelist, literary personality, entrepreneur and critic. His novels are somewhat Firbankian records of life in the 1920s; the best is *Nigger Heaven*.

Peter Whiffle (1922)

The Blind Bow-Boy (1923)

Nigger Heaven (1926)

VAN VOGT, A. E. (1912) American science fiction writer, celebrated for his convoluted and frequently irrational plots. His best known books feature individuals with strange latent powers who move through a series of threatening situations until desperation brings forth their superhumanity. The strong paranoid element in his work gives it a curious intensity, which may distract attention from the arbitrariness of his plot-development.

Slan (1946)

The World of Null-A (1948)

The Weapon Shops of Isher (1951)

VARGAS LLOSA, Mario (1936) Peruvian novelist. He combines keen and hilarious satire on Latin-American backwardness and *machismo*, with more imaginative explorations of the myth and legend of Peru. *The Time of the Heroes* remains his finest book, a savage satire on life at a Peruvian military academy. *The Green House*, also good, is more experimental.

The Time of the Heroes (1962, tr. 1967)

The Green House (1966, tr. 1969)

The Cubs and Other Stories (tr. 1979)

VERGA, Giovanni (1840–1922) Italian novelist and story-writer. Verga was the pioneer of the Italian *verismo*, the Sicilian – and then Italian – form of naturalism. He knew Flaubert and Zola and learned from them. But his greatest feat was to forge a language which truly represented the thinking and feeling of Sicilians. He could not finish his great planned cycle of Sicilian life, *The Vanquished*, for reasons of mental health (he was a depressive). But the two that he did write, *The House by the Medlar Tree* and *Mastro-Don Gesualdo*, are among the classics of Italian literature. His stories, of which "Cavalleria Rusticana" is best known because of the opera, are no less remarkable. Verga's "stories" seem, as has been said, to tell themselves: each and every utterance by any of the characters contributes, with infinite poetry, to the whole. His plots are tragic; but his vision is finally affirmatory: he shows us how we ourselves "go on" despite our disappointments and defeats. It has been suggested that Verga could not finish his cycle because he could not present "the psychology of more sophisticated characters". But Verga in his livelier days had been a very highly accomplished adulterer, and he knew all about the psychology of "sophisticated" people. His earlier society novels are talented but less artistically successful, although his contemporaries preferred them.

The House by the Medlar Tree (1881, tr. 1950)

Cavalleria Rusticana (1883, tr. 1928)

Mastro-Don Gesualdo (1888, tr. 1928)

VERNE, Jules (1828–1905) French writer of adventure stories set either in the future or in places then (and possibly now) thought inaccessible: the deep, the centre of the earth, and so forth. Verne was not as important a pioneer of science fiction as was H. G. Wells but his books are still enjoyed by young readers. He was ingenious and genuinely fascinated by science.

The Jules Verne Omnibus (1951)

VIDAL, Gore (1925) American novelist, story-writer, polemicist, publicist, once a (democratic-liberal) politician, and critic. He is a left-wing activist with aristocratic connections,

and with talent for film scripts (*I Accuse*, about Dreyfus, and many more). His elegant detective stories are published under the name of Edgar Box. He first became famous as author of a novel about homosexuality, *The City and the Pillar* (1948, rev. 1965), which is a compassionate and interesting psychological study. The sex-change novel, *Myra Breckinridge* (1968), shows him as a film-buff and sexjoker: it is an exercise in how to shock, and does not quite come off. But Vidal is very versatile – so much so that he bewilders his readers and himself with the problem of just who and what he is: entertainer or serious author or both? He has written two powerful historical novels, *Julian* (1964), and *Burr* (1973). The political novel *Washington D.C.* is shrewd and gripping, although in the last analysis a trifle facile. Vidal is overflowing with talent, but seems so far to lack just the touch of genius that could make him into a major novelist.

A Thirsty Evil (stories, 1956)

Washington D.C. (1967)

Myron (1974)

Gore Vidal

VITTORINI, Elio (1908–67) Italian novelist. Vittorini's obsession with social justice caused him to go to the left, especially since Italy was fascist when he came to maturity; but this does not make his fiction polemical, since he is most interested in character – feeling that understanding of character is the key to compassion. He experimented ceaselessly with methods of objective narration, and finally lost his capacity to write at all; but his best work *The Red Carnation*, (for eight years suppressed by the fascists) is not inhibited by technical considerations. All his fiction is distinguished, although it offers a perfect target for both right-wing critics and doctrin-

aire Marxists, since it seeks truth and objectivity.

Tune for an Elephant (1947, tr. 1955)

The Red Carnation (1948, tr. 1953)

Women on the Road (novellas, tr. 1961)

VIZINCZEY, Stephen (1933) Hungarian-born critic, essayist and novelist. His best seller *In Praise of Older Women* is a genuinely sensual novel charting the sexual education of a young man who acquires maturity through mature women.

In Praise of Older Women (1966)

VOLTAIRE (1694–1778) The pseudonym of François-Marie Arouet, French novelist, *philosophe*, dramatist, poet and satirist. Voltaire was the master of the *conte*, the short novel. It is for these rather than for his plays and poems – much prized in his lifetime – that he is remembered. Voltaire uses light-hearted fiction, most notably of course *Candide*, to convey a moral message. This message is not profound – it does not amount to much more than "be tolerant; do not fall for high-sounding nonsense" – but it is profoundly humane, and is conveyed in a brilliantly economic and ironic manner. Voltaire's satire is neither deep nor malevolent, but he is elegant and decent, and pinpoints cruelty with an unerring precision.

Zadig (1747, tr. 1959)

Candide (1759, tr. 1959)

VONNEGUT, Kurt, Jr. (1922) Idiosyncratic American novelist who originally worked within the science fiction field, but increasingly developed an individual form of near-fantasy in which ideas, narrative and jokes are combined in an entertaining blend of philosophy and fiction. The result is a body of work which, referring increasingly back into itself, becomes more and more impenetrable to the uninitiated; however the fluency of his writing helps him avoid the backwater of a minority enthusiasm. As a prisoner of war in World War II, he witnessed the bombing of Dresden, and this perhaps explains his deep-rooted gloom about human charity and understanding. *Slaughterhouse Five* tries to capture the meaning of this experience, and as in *The Sirens of Titan* (1959), the futility of human aspiration is expounded in a plot which assumes a fantastic and demeaning alternative explanation for the course of history and the reasons for behaviour. *Cat's Cradle* is his most accessible book, and includes both the creation of a convincing religious philosophy and a global catastrophe of deadening finality: a typical juxtaposition. *Breakfast of Champions* (1963) marks his turn to a more introspective style;

and *Mother Night* (1966) is an attempt to come to terms with the experience of fascism. *Jailbird* (1979) is straightforward post-Watergate political satire, and seems to indicate a refreshing change of direction.

 Cat's Cradle (1963)

Slaughterhouse Five (1969)

Jailbird (1979)

W

WAHLÖÖ, Per, see SJÖWALL, Maj

WAIN, John (1925) English critic, poet and novelist. Wain began with a badly written but lively picaresque novel, *Hurry on Down* (1953). Since then his technique has become more polished, and he has begun to approach the lesser achievements of his master in fiction, J. B. Priestley.

 Strike the Father Dead (1962)

Death of the Hind Legs (stories, 1966)

Winter in the Hills (1971)

WAKEFIELD, H. Russell (1888–1964) English author of mystery and ghost stories. He wrote several novels and reconstructions of classic criminal cases, but remains best known for his short stories of murder and the supernatural. To these he imparted a nice blend of credibility and terror in a very English atmosphere.

 Imagine a Man in a Box (stories, 1931)

The Clock Strikes Twelve (stories, 1939)

WALLACE, Edgar (1875–1932) British crime writer, dramatist and journalist. Wallace wrote a record number of thrillers of near-surreal type; he was energetic and ingenious, but wrote sloppily. He also produced novels about Africa (the first was *Sanders of the River*, 1911). He made a fortune but lost it on horses and high life. His stories are still filmed and televised, and he is still widely read.

 The Four Just Men (1905)

The Crimson Circle (1922)

Green Archer (1923)

WALLACE, Irving (1916) American novelist. He first achieved best selling fame with his long novel *The Prize* (1963), concerning the intrigues surrounding the award of a Nobel Prize. His stories are fast moving and dramatic, and he deals imaginatively with such controversial subjects as a pseudo-sociological sex report, and a black American president.

 The Chapman Report (1962)

The Man (1964)

The Pigeon Project (1979)

WALLACE, Lew (1827–1905) American Civil War general, diplomat and popular novelist. Wallace is remembered for his romance of the Roman Empire, *Ben Hur* (1880), a study of the character and doctrines of Christ. Wallace wrote other historical romances and an *Autobiography* (1906), which contains a personal account of his war experiences in the Union Army.

 Ben Hur: A Tale of Christ (1880)

WALLANT, Edward Lewis (1926–62) American novelist whose early death was a serious loss to American letters. He wrote four tense, passionate, well shaped novels about various tragic aspects of American-Jewish life. They are deceptively simple, very intense – and must have been very difficult to write. Perhaps most memorable is the bitter agony of the husband in *The Human Season* (1960) who has just lost his wife. Wallant remained this simple; and his accounts of how people sometimes come out of pain are unequalled in their pathos.

 The Pawnbroker (1961)

The Tenants of Moonbloom (1963)

The Children at the Gate (1964)

WALPOLE, Sir Hugh (1884–1941) English novelist and story-writer, born in New Zealand. Walpole was a popular and prolific writer best known for two sequences, the Jeremy stories – semi-autobiographical tales of boyhood – and the Herries Chronicle, a sequence of four romantic adventures telling the history of a Lake District family from the eighteenth century to the twentieth. Walpole was a popular author appreciated for skilful narrative, scenic descriptions, and plausible characterization. However, many critics have felt that his early book, *The Dark Forest*, a realistic story of World War I, was the best; and that his later work grew more careless as it became unashamedly romantic and swashbuckling.

 Mr Perrin and Mr Traill (1911)

The Dark Forest (1916)

Jeremy (1919)

WALSCHAP, Gerard (1898) Flemish novelist. Walschap is a realist who has attacked the Roman Catholic Church in Belgium with the authority of one who was once in it. He is a tough and vigorous humanist.

 Marriage: Ordeal (1933–43, tr. 1963)

WAMBAUGH, Joseph (1937) American writer of police procedural novels, who is now more highly regarded than Ed McBain. A former

Edgar Wallace

Sir Hugh Walpole

Los Angeles policeman, Wambaugh shows brutality, corruption, perversion and evil in his cops, as much as courage, dedication and honour.

The Onion Field (1973)

The Choirboys (1975)

WARD, Artemus (1834–67) American printer, journalist, lecturer and writer of comic sketches, whose real name was Charles Farrar Browne. His collection of comic letters, *Artemus Ward: His Book* (1862), was hugely successful. In it Ward presented himself as a crackerbarrel philosopher, sly and irreverent, with comical spelling and problems with verbs. During the Civil War period, he satirized the hypocrisy and corruption of Northern citizens; and he attacked all kinds of still popular butts, including Mormons, women's rights, spiritualism, free love and university students, with a cocky irreverence.

Artemus Ward: His Book (1862)

Artemus Ward: His Travels (1865)

WARD, Mrs Humphrey (1851–1920) English moralistic novelist, who was vehemently opposed to votes for women. Her once popular novels are lurid and dated, although not wholly unintelligent.

Miss Bretherton (1884)

Robert Elsmere (1888)

WARNER, Rex (1905) English novelist, poet and classicist. Warner began with novels in direct imitation of Franz Kafka which received attention at the time (most notably *The Wild Goose Chase*, 1937) but have since been forgotten. His more recent novels are vigorous historical works, written from an orthodox Christian point of view.

The Young Caesar (1958)

The Converts (1967)

WARNER, Sylvia Townsend (1893–1978) English novelist, story-writer, poet, musicologist and biographer. Warner wrote of witches and medieval England (*The Corner that Held Them*, 1948) with uncanny authority. She made her name with *Lolly Willowes* (1926), about a witch. She wrote clever *New Yorker* stories with ease and skill. Many of her best stories are in the collections below.

Mr Fortune's Maggot (1927)

A Garland of Straw (stories, 1943)

The Innocent and the Guilty (stories, 1971)

WARREN, Robert Penn (1905) American poet, critic, novelist and story-writer. Warren's most famous and best novel is based on a career very like that of the populist governor of Louisiana in the 1930s, Huey Long: *All the King's Men* (1946). His other novels, apart from the earlier *Night Rider* (1939) and *The Cave* (1959), have been heavily criticized for being too "Jacobean": too intensely romantic and melodramatic. But few critics deny his power and originality. His stories are exceptionally well made.

World Enough and Time (1950)

Wilderness: A Tale of the Civil War (1961)

Meet Me in the Green Glen (1971)

WASSERMANN, Jakob (1873–1934) German-Jewish novelist. Very widely read in their day, Wassermann's novels explore Dostoyevskian experiences of depravity, eroticism, corrupted innocence, and innocence restored among the beggars.

Caspar Hauser (1908, tr. 1928)

The Maurizius Case (1928, tr. 1930)

WATERHOUSE, Keith (1929) English journalist, dramatist and novelist best-known for *Billy Liar*, a very funny account of a Saturday in the life of an undertaker's clerk, a Walter Mitty (see THURBER, James) who compulsively lies his way into and out of a sequence of appalling contretemps. Its sequel *Billy Liar on the Moon* (1975) is just as diverting, but these books tend to overshadow Waterhouse's wider gifts in his more important novels, including *Jubb*, a painfully funny story of life in a New Town, and *Office Life*, a mordant account of bureaucratic ritual.

Billy Liar (1959)

Jubb (1963)

Office Life (1979)

WATSON, Colin (1920) English crime writer. Watson practises the highly difficult art of farce-crime, in which the former is always in danger of puncturing the suspense of the latter. His books are set in the imaginary Lincolnshire town of Flaxborough and deftly expose provincial hypocrisies of all sorts, but particularly the sexual. He has a gift for the deflations of lavatory humour.

Hopjoy Was Here (1962)

Lonelyheart 4122 (1967)

One Man's Meat (1977)

WATSON, Ian (1943) British science fiction writer. His novels usually develop themes connected with psychology and the possibilities of mental evolution, and are startling in their originality.

The Embedding (1973)

The Martian Inca (1977)

Miracle Visitors (1978)

WAUGH, Alec (1898) English novelist, brother of Evelyn Waugh. He is a competent novelist who has written well-made, well-observed fiction over a long period. His great successes were *The Loom of Youth*, reckoned a daring exposé of public school life when it came out, and *Island in the Sun*, famous as a film starring Harry Belafonte.

The Loom of Youth (1917)

Island in the Sun (1955)

The Fatal Gift (1973)

WAUGH, Auberon (1937) English journalist, critic, satirist and novelist, son of Evelyn Waugh. He used his own experiences to excoriate a Catholic public school (*The Foxglove Saga*), the drab trendiness of Oxford in the late 1950s (*Path of Dalliance*), and the "permissive society" and Fleet Street (*Where are the Violets Now?*, 1965). Although sharply and fluently written, there is a languid, snobbish intolerance about these ill-constructed books happily absent from *Consider the Lilies,* a good-natured, richly comic novel about an idle, agnostic rural rector.

The Foxglove Saga (1960)

Path of Dalliance (1963)

Consider the Lilies (1968)

WAUGH, Evelyn (1903–66) English novelist and satirist. Waugh, a converted Roman Catholic (1930), was the bitterest between-wars satirist: his black comedy in such novels as *Put Out More Flags* (1942) approached the surreal. He had learned from Dickens and Ronald Firbank. He tried to emulate Ford Madox Ford in his larger-scale works such as the trilogy *Sword of Honour* (1965), but this proved just too much for him. He was an alcoholic and a depressive, and in his finest novel of all *The Ordeal of Gilbert Pinfold* (1957), he tried to tell the truth about his unhappiness and sense of madness. *The Loved One* is a frightening satire on the American undertaking industry. At the end, in the trilogy and its recension, he tried to replace his sick humour with tolerance; but it was too late, and the artifice, although sincere, shows through. It is for his comic and satirical

novels that he will be remembered.

Vile Bodies (1930)

Brideshead Revisited (1945)

The Loved One (1948)

WAUGH, Hillary (1920) American detection writer whose recent romantic mysteries are less successful than the earlier police procedural stories. Some are set in Waugh's own New England home, while others, usually more brutal, are about a detective in New York's Homicide Squad.

Last Seen Wearing (1952)

The Late Mrs D (1962)

30 Manhattan East (1968)

WEBB, Mary (1881–1927) English regionalist novelist whose fifth novel, *Precious Bane*, became a best seller when the Prime Minister, Stanley Baldwin, publicized it three years before her death. Her work is original and quirky, uses rural dialect and country traditions and superstitions, and deals with Hardy-like themes – but without his authority and poetic vision.

The House in Dormer Forest (1920)

Precious Bane (1924)

WEIDMAN, Jerome (1913) American novelist and story-writer. Weidman's fiction is about Jewish heels, cheats and rats – and, except from Ernest Hemingway and Robert Graves, has not had its due. His earlier books are much more forceful than the later; they are unique

in their comic, disgusted concentration on sheer greed and nastiness.

I Can Get it For You Wholesale (1937)

What's in It For Me? (1938)

Word of Mouth (1964)

WELCH, Denton (1915–48) English novelist and story-writer, who wrote three sensitive but clear-eyed autobiographical novels mainly about the trivia of his childhood.

Maiden Voyage (1943)

A Last Sheaf (stories, 1951)

WELCOME, John (1914) Irish novelist and anthologist. His interest in gambling and fast cars has been particularly evident in his scenic espionage novels, featuring agent Richard Graham in a series of motorized pursuits.

Run for Cover (1958)

Stop at Nothing (1959)

Hell is Where You Find It (1968)

WELDON, Fay (1933) British novelist and television playwright who writes mainly about the domestic relationships of post-war Englishwomen. A sardonic and epigrammatic style make her writing verbally delightful; but despite the entertaining surface the final impression is of victims conniving in their own oppression.

Down Among the Women (1971)

Female Friends (1975)

Little Sister (1978)

WELLS, H. G. (1866–1946) English novelist, thinker, historian, essayist and story-writer. Wells was one of the most versatile writers of the century. His science fiction has not yet been surpassed for inventiveness, and Henry James much admired his romances of the "little man" (such as *The History of Mr Polly*, 1910). He was astonishingly energetic. First came the great science novels: sinister and ingenious romances such as *The Time Machine* (1895) and *The Invisible Man* (1897). Then the romances, such as *Kipps* (1905), in which, on the very verge of sentimentality – but just, at his best, avoiding it – he humanized the wretched lives of clerks and shop assistants. Later he wrote more experimental novels, including the neglected dystopia *Mr Blettsworthy on Rampole Island* (1932), which is quite close to Orwell's *1984*. His novels of ideas are uneven, but at their best exciting: *The World of William Clissold* (1926), the chief of these, is underrated. He kept up a ceaseless stream of activity, and had more mistresses than any other literary man of his calibre (he treated them well). At heart he was a pessimist and a poet; but he fought against this, as rationalist and official optimist. Finally he gave up and wrote a shattering attack on humanity, *Mind at the End of its Tether* (1945), which is too true for many to have taken more than cursory note of it. His style is not distinguished, and he is uneven; but at his best he is unexpectedly poetic and sombre, and in the science novels – probably his finest work – there are hints of symbols not yet explored. His stories are also extraordinarily rewarding.

Love and Mr Lewisham (1900)

Short Stories (1927)

The Shape of Things to Come (1933)

WELTY, Eudora (1909) American (Southern) novelist and story-writer, who was early encouraged by Ford Madox Ford. Unlike Flannery O'Connor and Carson McCullers, with whom she is often compared, Welty writes of the misfit and the grotesque with much greater control. She has felt as strongly about the South, but she is less sensational, and at first reading less impressive. She is, however, more intellectual and cunning; she is a relativist, who cannily explores the ambiguous nature of reality. She writes of a person not as a single identity, but as a bundle of "I's", each going in a separate direction – except in some magic or significant moment. She is a subtle, difficult but rewarding writer, who is read and appreciated by the discerning.

The Ponder Heart (1954)

Thirteen Stories (1965)

The Optimist's Daughter (1972)

WERFEL, Franz (1890–1945) Austrian poet, novelist and dramatist. Werfel began with poetry and serious novels, but became world-famous with *The Song of Bernadette*, which was nonetheless below the level of his previous artistic achievements. His earlier *Verdi*, in part an attack on Wagner, is a much better novel.

Verdi (1924, tr. 1925)

The Song of Bernadette (1941, tr. 1942)

WESCOTT, Glenway (1901) American novelist, story-writer and poet, whose best works are sensitive, lyrical evocations of his native Wisconsin. He spent his early years in Paris and elsewhere in Europe, and was associated with Hemingway and other expatriate American writers in the 1920s.

The Grandmothers (1927)

Goodbye Wisconsin (stories, 1928)

WEST, Morris (1916) Popular Australian novelist. West has been a publicist, a politican and a Roman Catholic novice monk. His novels are intelligent, sensationalist melodramas about finding God against a background of intrigue, big money, publicity and journalistic scoops. He also writes Biblical romances. He knows his backgrounds, and pleases his readers.

The Big Story (1957)

The Shoes of the Fisherman (1963)

Harlequin (1974)

WEST, Nathanael (1904–40) American novelist who was killed in a car crash. West was one of the great Jewish writers of the 1930s; but he did not gain his large reputation until his rediscovery in the 1950s. Of his four novels the two most important are *Miss Lonelyhearts*, about the male writer of an agony column who decides to involve himself in his readers crazy pain, and dies unjustly for it; and *The Day of the Locust*, a symbolic satire of great depth on Hollywood (and its cult) where West worked. The last work is of Swiftian proportions.

The Complete Works (1957)

WEST, Rebecca (1892) English novelist, critic, essayist, journalist and travel writer. Rebecca West's novels made early use of Freud, and went on to probe at aspects of English life both at home and abroad in a way no one else has done – and yet critics, although respectful, have on the whole failed to study these solid and shrewd books in depth. She writes, as she has said, about what she calls "the majority of people"; she seems to mean that she chooses as her subjects intelligent and unhappy people who do not get written about because they are not sensational or criminal. This perhaps explains the forceful impact of her books, especially the later ones.

The Return of a Soldier (1918)

The Fountain Overflows (1954)

The Birds Fall Down (1966)

WESTLAKE, Donald E. (1933) American crime novelist. He created the inept Dortmunder, Munch and company, who are forever planning lucrative capers that fail to come off. The early books in this series (*The Hot Rock; Bank Shot,* 1972) are brilliantly comic. However, Westlake's success is largely due to his books about Parker, an amoral thief, written under the pseudonym Richard Stark.

The Green Eagle Score (as Stark, 1967)

The Hot Rock (1970)

WHARTON, Edith (1862–1937) American novelist and story-writer (notably of good ghost stories). Wharton wrote in the tradition of her friend Henry James, but had more acidulous things to say of New York society. She is a solid and sharply intelligent novelist, who could leave her accustomed milieu to write a successful book set in rural New England – *Ethan Frome* (1911) – which is very nearly naturalistic. She is satirical about society's values without being political.

The Age of Innocence (1920)

Twilight Sleep (1927)

Collected Short Stories (1968)

WHEATLEY, Dennis (1897–1977) English adventure story-writer. His first novel, *The Forbidden Territory* (1933), was an instant best seller, and his success thereafter was huge and continuous. Some of his most popular novels dealt with Satanism and black magic; a series of large-scale spy stories covered the events of the war; and latterly he concentrated on a series of historical romances, featuring Roger Brook, a secret agent for Mr Pitt, which begins just before the French Revolution and ends after Waterloo. In collaboration with J. G. Links he devised, during the 1930s, a number of fictional "crime dossiers", which included physical clues and photographs (*Murder off Miami*, has recently been republished).

The Devil Rides Out (1935)

The Scarlet Imposter (1940)

The Launching of Roger Brook (1947)

WHITE, Patrick (1912) Australian novelist and story-writer. White won the Nobel Prize for 1973. He began with a book of poems, and then wrote two realistic novels, but his true style emerged in *The Aunt's Story* (1948). He combines satire on Australian suburban life, which he hates with perhaps too Flaubertian a vigour, with visionary writing about grotesques or madmen. The influence of Nietzsche is most apparent in his work. He believes in the vision of the lunatic, and his prose – which is often interior monologue – supports his claim. He is in many ways the most thoroughgoing

Edith Wharton

romantic among modern major writers. Novels such as *Voss* depend entirely on the style, and White here usually succeeds, although he risks being, and sometimes is, pretentious. He is exceedingly powerful, and even those who have doubts about him admit that it is not possible now to tell whether he will last or not. It seems likely that for his best novels, such as *Voss* and *The Tree of Man* (1955), he will. He is a risk-taker, and in much of his dense writing there is an undeniable message.

Voss (1957)

The Solid Mandala (1966)

The Eye of the Storm (1973)

WHITE, T. H. (1906–64) English writer of prose romances and essayist who lived a solitary life on the island of Alderney. White had a huge success with his whimsical version of the Arthurian legend *The Once and Future King*; it was made into the musical *Camelot*. He is a writer who is loved or hated, and his audience remained absolutely faithful. *The Once and Future King* series was designed for children; it is a mixture of cruelty and charm, fantasy and historical fact. White wrote other learned and odd books.

The Once and Future King (1938–58)

WHITE, William Hale, see RUTHERFORD, Mark

WHITNEY, Phyllis A. (1903) American writer of mysteries and children's books. She is most successful with adventure romances in exotic settings, which are usually about ingénue heroines encountering unexpected perils.

Seven Tears for Apollo (1963)

The Winter People (1969)

WILDER, Thornton (1897–1975) American dramatist and novelist. Wilder has often been attacked for being "genteel" and "middle-brow"; but although undeniably pretentious and pseudo-profound he was a very clever craftsman. His very best work of all, free from his usual vices, is the novel *Heaven's My Destination*. *The Bridge of San Luis Rey* (1927), an experiment with coincidence set in eighteenth-century Peru, has meant a great deal to many readers.

Heaven's My Destination (1934)

The Ides of March (1948)

The Eighth Day (1968)

WILLIAMS, Alan (1935) Welsh journalist and writer of spy thrillers. Williams has some experience of intelligence operations and often

uses real people in stories that could have happened. *Gentleman Traitor* featured Kim Philby and postulated that he grew bored with, and quit, Russia, to be given a change of identity and an unpleasant job in Rhodesia by British intelligence.

The Beria Papers (1973)

Gentleman Traitor (1975)

WILLIAMS, Charles (1886–1945) English poet, critic, novelist and dramatist. Williams' novels are spiritual thrillers dealing with esoteric matters, and are very well written. He himself did not like them, but they were his most popular work.

War in Heaven (1930)

The Place of the Lion (1931)

All Hallows' Eve (1945)

WILLIAMS, Gordon M., see YUILL, P. B.

WILLIAMS, Tennessee (1911) American playwright, short story writer and novelist. A Southerner, he writes of sexuality, repression, delusion and loneliness: the stories in *Eight Mortal Ladies Possessed* ranging typically from gentle to grotesque. His published fiction includes *Hard Candy* (1954), *Three Players of a Summer Game* (1960), and the novella with stories, *The Knightly Quest* (1967); but the best is listed below.

The Roman Spring of Mrs Stone (1950)

Eight Mortal Ladies Possessed (stories, 1975)

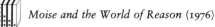
Moise and the World of Reason (1976)

WILLIAMS, William Carlos (1883–1963) American poet, novelist, essayist and memoirist. Williams was born in Rutherford, New Jersey, and lived there for most of his life, practising as a family doctor among the poor and inarticulate who provided him with the subject for much of his most sympathetic writing. Through the poets H.D. and Ezra Pound, Williams became involved in modernist literary movements; and he became one of the leading American poets of the twentieth century. He wrote four novels, concerned with the predicament of being an American, created by American history. The first, *A Voyage to Pagany,* is based on his own travels in Europe and his rediscovery of the old culture. *The White Mule*, a trilogy, pictures immigrants adjusting to American life: *In the Money* (1940) is the story of a middle-class family and *The Build-Up* (1952) continues their story to the time of World War I. Williams' prose is colloquial and sharply precise, and even his most experimental forms are intensely readable. However, the achievement of his fiction lies in the characters and his presentation of the quality of their experience. *The Great American Novel* (1923) and *In the American Grain* (1925) are impressionistic plotless essays on a similar theme to the novels.

A Voyage to Pagany (1928)

The White Mule (1937)

WILLIAMSON, Henry (1895–1977) British novelist whose major work, the 15-book sequence *The Chronicle of Ancient Sunlight*, tells in great detail the life of one Phillip Maddison. However, Williamson's popular fame rests mainly on two quite different works, *Tarka the Otter* and *Salar the Salmon*, which manage to recreate the wonder of the natural life of these animals without mannered condescension or anthropomorphism.

Tarka the Otter (1925)

Salar the Salmon (1935)

The Chronicle of Ancient Sunlight (1951–69)

WILLIAMSON, Jack (1908) American science fiction writer. He made his reputation writing pulp space opera but matured along with the genre. Much of his recent work has been in collaboration with Frederik Pohl.

The Legion of Time (1938)

Darker Than You Think (1940)

The Humanoids (1949)

WILLINGHAM, Calder (1922) American novelist, playwright and scriptwriter, born in Georgia. Willingham is a powerful and original writer, whose talents have largely been devoted to the cinema (his films include *Paths of Glory*, *One-Eyed Jacks*, *The Graduate*, and *Little Big Man*). But as a novelist he has been likened to a twentieth-century Fielding, and his *Eternal Fire* has been called one of the greatest dozen novels in American literature. It is a mock-Southern saga, in which ruthless accounts of villainy and evil are presented with a compassionate sensibility. Willingham believes that "a good story is more than merely entertaining, that characterization, style, philosophical depth, even poetry flow from the story". His short stories are also remarkable: wild, inconsequential, experimental, but

always interesting.

End as a Man (1947)

The Gates of Hell (stories, 1951)

Eternal Fire (1963)

WILLIS, Ted (1918) English television playwright and crime writer. Lord Willis of Chislehurst came late to the novel after much TV work including the creation of the comfortable policeman, Dixon of Dock Green. But a fine storytelling gift and plenty of accurate background has brought him considerable success.

The Left-handed Sleeper (1975)

The Buckingham Palace Connection (1978)

WILSON, Angus (1913) English novelist and story-writer. Wilson began late, but made an immediate success with his wicked and beautifully observed stories about homosexuals and snobs in *The Wrong Set* (1949); the novel *Hemlock and After* (1952) is an unusually sympathetic and shrewd account of a married man who discovers he is a homosexual. Wilson is much praised, but not often enough taken seriously. He believed in the old-fashioned

Angus Wilson

Victorian novel at least enough to try one, and nearly brought it off in *Anglo-Saxon Attitudes* (1956). Thereafter his writing became more experimental. It has continued to be lively and interesting, and he is still one of England's most comic and inventive writers.

The Middle Age of Mrs Eliot (1959)

The Old Men at the Zoo (1961)

As If By Magic (1973)

WILSON, Colin (1931) English critic, novelist and general writer, best known for his famous first work of non-fiction *The Outsider* (1956). He has written a number of novels, including science fiction fantasies, murder mysteries and thrillers, which all in some way relate to his optimistic existentialism, as well as to his preoccupations with criminality, violence and sexuality. They are thus in a sense parodies of their genres, but are plainly written and can be enjoyed at more than one level.

The Killer (in U.S. as *Lingard*, 1970)

The Philosopher's Stone (1971)

The Space Vampires (1976)

WILSON, Edmund (1895–1972) Prolific, wideranging and hugely influential American literary critic. His fiction includes only *I Thought of Daisy*, an entertaining if untidy novel of bohemian life in Prohibition New York; and *Memoirs of Hecate County*, a masterly collection of short stories which include at least two classics, "The Man Who Shot Snapping Turtles", and "The Princess with the Golden Hair" which, on publication, was heavily censored for its sexual frankness.

I Thought of Daisy (1929)

Memoirs of Hecate County (1946)

WILSON, Ethel (1890) Canadian novelist and story-writer. She is a humorous, skilful but superficial writer about contemporary manners and morals and the motives of young women. Her best work is in her short stories.

Love and Salt Water (1956)

Mrs Golightly (stories, 1961)

WILSON, Sloan (1920) American novelist whose first novel, *The Man in the Grey Flannel Suit*, about a corporation man, was an instant – and lasting – success. He has a wry but compassionate eye for the absurdities of social mannerisms, and a spare style.

The Man in the Grey Flannel Suit (1944)

A Summer Place (1958)

Janus Island (1967)

WINSOR, Kathleen (1919) American romantic novelist. Her long and unflaggingly erotic *Forever Amber*, a Restoration novel, was immediately and immensely popular; but later volumes, such as *The Lovers* (1952), *America, with Love* (1957) or *Calais* (1979), have usually missed their targets.

Forever Amber (1944)

WISEMAN, Thomas (1930) English novelist and dramatist born in Vienna. His best-selling titles include *Czar*, about a ruthless Hollywood mogul; and *The Quick and The Dead* an intense, detailed study of Vienna under the Nazis. *A Game of Secrets* is a taut, darkly satirical farce of White House life which, like many of Wiseman's books, collapses into competent but humdrum spy drama after a very promising opening.

Czar (1965)

The Quick and the Dead (1968)

A Game of Secrets (1979)

WISTER, Owen (1860–1938) American novelist, author of the classic Western novel *The Virginian*, and of other stories of the Wyoming cattle country. His protagonists are ideal Western heroes—brave, handsome, athletic and incorruptible.

The Virginian (1902)

WODEHOUSE, P. G. (1881–1973) English novelist, scriptwriter and story-writer. He began with excellent school stories, then graduated to novels about types such as Psmith and Uckridge; he then discovered the world of the "drone" Bertie Wooster and his manservant Jeeves. Wodehouse is the perfect non-serious writer, the learnedly vacuous comedian. He will, says William Trevor, be remembered when many "of the swells with messages" are forgotten. In the Jeeves novels, and certain others, he achieved perfection of style: he wrote just for entertainment, and he meant nothing at all. The stories are indeed perfect entertainment. He has become, with the recent advantage of good television adaptations, an accepted part of life.

My Man Jeeves (1919)

Ring for Jeeves (1953)

Aunts Aren't Gentlemen (1974)

WOLFE, Thomas (1900–38) American novelist, dramatist and story-writer, who died young after a brain operation. He could not organize his material, which had to be cut and arranged for him by his editor (in his first and best novels by the famous editor of Scott Fitzgerald, Maxwell Perkins). He was a supreme egoist and egotist; he wrote the same novel, about himself, four times; and he was bombastic and uncontrolled. Yet for all this his first two novels, *Look Homeward Angel* and *Of Time and the River*, have a great power and appeal. You cannot, a critic has said, withstand the tide when it is coming full at you. He had real wonder and real desire to fulfil himself, and he finally felt unrelated to anyone, and desolately alone – which comes across in

the last novel, *You Can't Go Home Again* (1940).

Look Homeward Angel (1929)

Of Time and the River (1935)

The Web and the Rock (1939)

WOOD, Mrs Henry (1814–87) English novelist. Her one surviving novel, *East Lynne,* was a best seller, and was frequently adapted for the stage. It is the melodramatic but ultimately moral story of an estranged wife who comes back under the guise of governess to her children.

East Lynne (1860–61)

WOOLF, Virginia (1882–1941) English novelist and critic. Her first novel *The Voyage Out* (1915) is traditional. Thereafter she became increasingly experimental. She suffered from an affective disorder, and eventually killed herself—she was depressed by the war, and perhaps by ideas of her own failure to achieve what she wanted to in her fiction. She employed stream of consciousness to much greater effect than Dorothy Richardson, than whom she was considerably more intelligent. But although she achieved some perfection of technique, it is not universally agreed that she created substantial or even meaningful characters. Her novels are strewn with oddly purple passages, and the most experimental ones such as *The Waves* are somewhat directionless. But in *Mrs Dalloway* (1925) she used technique (particularly flashback) so brilliantly that it almost succeeded in creating a robust character. *The Years*, written when she had tried all methods, reverts to a conventional form, and is possibly her finest novel. Yet some believe *Between the Acts* (1941) to be her best; here she uses symbolism in a new way. Opinion about her is divided: some say that she is over-refined to the point of tedium, others that she created an original kind of novel. There is certainly a lack of robustness; but there is also a courageous attempt to define and locate her own often strange states of mind. There can be no doubt of her importance in the history of the novel.

To the Lighthouse (1927)

The Waves (1931)

The Years (1937)

WOOLRICH, Cornell (1903–68) American writer of psychological thrillers, who also wrote as William Irish and George Hopley. Perhaps the finest purveyor of terror against a background of normality, the "enormous impact of the everyday-gone-wrong", Woolrich subordinated everything to the "line of suspense".

The Bride Wore Black (1940)

Phantom Lady (as Irish) (1942)

Night Has a Thousand Eyes (as Hopley) (1945)

WOUK, Herman (1915) American popular novelist, who made his name with the tense and skilfully told *The Caine Mutiny*. He has been unsuccessful with the critics, but hugely successful with the public – although not at the level he would wish. Apart from his "serious" ideas, he has a gift for comic writing.

The Caine Mutiny (1951)

Marjorie Morningstar (1955)

War and Remembrance (1978)

WREN, P. C. (1885–1941) English popular novelist, who was very prolific. His most successful novels were tales of the Foreign Legion – improbable in the extreme, but in an appealingly romantic vein.

Beau Geste (1924)

Beau Sabreur (1926)

Fort in the Jungle (1936)

WRIGHT, Richard (1908–60) American Negro writer. Wright's fiction became richer, then suddenly declined. *Native Son* (1940), influenced by Theodore Dreiser and admired by

him, was a worthy Negro *American Tragedy*. The stories in *Uncle Tom's Children* (1940) are of a similar power, and in their symbolism often anticipate Ralph Ellison, who is only more elegant. Later work has been defended; but the general view is that it lacks the power and conviction of the earlier, which was written before Wright went to France in 1947.

The Outsider (1953)

Eight Men (stories, 1961)

Lawd Today (1963)

Richard Wright

Frank Yerby

WYLIE, Elinor (1885–1928) American poet and novelist, whose four historical novels established her reputation in the 1920s. *Jennifer Lorn* is set among the English ruling class in India in the eighteenth century; and *The Orphan Angel* imagines the poet Shelley in America.

Jennifer Lorn (1923)

The Orphan Angel (1926; in Britain, *Mortal Image*, 1927)

WYNDHAM, John (1903–69) British science fiction author who achieved considerable popularity outside the genre's usual readership, because he paid more attention to character than is customary, and wrote within the conventions of the traditional novel. His method was to take one premise (deadly plant life in a radiation-blinded world – *The Day of the Triffids*; invasion through impregnation of women – *The Midwich Cuckoos*) and to examine its effects on familiar English society and people. *The Outward Urge* is an extremely low-key and convincing account of the likely processes of early space exploration, described in technological terms, but without losing any of the awe of the "Final Frontier".

The Day of the Triffids (1951)

The Midwich Cuckoos (1957)

The Outward Urge (1959)

Y

YERBY, Frank (1916) American novelist, born in Georgia. Most of his stories are set in the South, and are concerned with racial conflict. His heroines are fascinating and tempestuous creatures caught in the turmoil of deep-southern history; and his style in flamboyant and florid.

The Foxes of Harrow (1946)

A Woman Called Fancy (1951)

A Darkness at Ingraham's Crest (1979)

YONGE, Charlotte M. (1823–1901) English author of 120 books whose first novel *The Heir of Redclyffe* was an instant success. Influenced by John Keble, founder of the Oxford Movement, Mrs Yonge propounded High Anglicanism and the virtues of family life through her novels. She also wrote numerous historical romances, notably *The Little Duke* (1854).

The Heir of Redclyffe (1853)

Heartsease (1854)

The Daisy Chain (1856)

YORKE, Margaret (1924) English crime writer, pseudonym of Mrs Margaret Nicholson. First, she produced a series of fairly conventional detective stories featuring Patrick Grant, an Oxford don. She now writes novels of psychological suspense, distinguished for the truth to life of all the characters and often set in an English village or small country town.

Mortal Remains (1974)

No Medals for the Major (1974)

Death on Account (1979)

YUILL, P. B. Pseudonym of British novelist Gordon M. Williams (1934) and Terry Ven-

P. B. Yuill: Gordon M. Williams (left) and Terry Venables

ables (1943), football-club manager. Williams has a good clutch of worthwhile novels under his own name, of which *The Siege of Trencher's Farm* (1969) (filmed as *The Straw Dogs*) is most notable. As a crime-writing combination, Yuill created James Hazell, Londoner private-eye, in a series of books (and TV series) which bring to vivid life the seedy world of Soho and the nerve-jangling metropolis.

The Siege of Trencher's Farm (1969)

Hazell Plays Solomon (1974)

Z

ZAMYATIN, Yevgeny (1884–1937) Russian novelist and story-writer, critic, and dramatist. Zamyatin was one of the most gifted writers of the century but has failed to get his due. His genius comes out most fully in the dystopia *We*, which is, as a work of art, superior not only to Huxley's *Brave New World*, but even to George Orwell's *1984* (both of which it influenced: Huxley denied it and Orwell happily acknowledged it). His stories are expressionist in the profoundest sense.

We (1920, tr. 1960)

The Dragon (stories, tr. 1972)

ZELAZNY, Roger (1937) American science fiction writer, who is particularly noted as a stylist. Zelazny uses this skill to turn character and language into an oblique description of his alternative worlds. It is the language of the monster hunter in the short story, "The Doors of His Face, The Lamps of His Mouth", that makes the piece more than a tale of space adventure. Among his novels *Lord of Light* uses American Indian folklore, and *Damnation Alley* uses the lore of the twentieth-century motorbike gang similarly, in both cases to provide a subtle illumination of the future of mankind.

This Immortal (1965)

Lord of Light (1967)

Damnation Alley (1969)

ZOLA, Émile (1840–1902) French novelist, story-writer and critic. Zola was the leading naturalist, but was in reality a romantic symbolist, at his best when depicting scenes reminiscent of the paintings of Bosch or Breughel. He made his name with the tense murder story *Thérèse Raquin* (1867) and then planned and completed his twenty-novel series *Les Rougons-Macquart*. These are not liked by Marxists because they dwell on the squalid, and have no serious political suggestions to make. Zola was interested in justice, as his behaviour over the Dreyfus case showed (he risked prison in writing his influential *I*

Accuse); but he distrusted revolutionaries, as he demonstrates with the highly convincing character Souverine in *Germinal* – the man who will kill hundreds and then walk away without a thought for them, except that (he claims) he is working for the good of all the exploited. Zola's characters are flat; but they come to life in his crowd scenes, or when they are fighting or eating. He has warm sympathy for the victims of poverty, and is not so bleak as never to show them enjoying themselves. Reading his novels now it is hard to understand how he avoided prosecution: they are cruelly explicit on all sexual and eliminatory matters; this gives an idea of the enormous reputation he created for himself. He was devoted to the truth as he saw it, and admitted that his literary theories were not practical. All his work has been translated.

Germinal (1885, tr. 1954)

The Masterpiece (1886, tr. 1950)

Earth (1887, tr. 1954)

Émile Zola

ZWEIG, Stefan (1881–1942) Austrian novelist and biographer. Zweig was a very fluent and intelligent writer; but he was somewhat over-dramatic. He has paid for his lack of delicacy: since his suicide in Brazil he has been little more than a name. He was a good psychologist, but wasted his efforts in perfervidness.

Amok (1922, tr. 1931)

The Tide of Fortune (1927, tr. 1940)

Kaleidoscope (stories, tr. 1936)

FICTION AND ILLUSTRATION

The literary novel in England and America has hardly ever been illustrated, at least in what is usually thought of as its purest form. That is to say, few first editions of novels by Jane Austen or Thomas Pynchon, Henry Fielding or William Faulkner, have had any kind of accompanying pictorial material (and virtually none has had such material when the "first edition" has also been the first published appearance of the novel or of any part of it). The one exception to this rule is the modern pictorial dust-jacket on a first edition. Many new novels still have purely typographic jackets, but a pictorial constituent is increasingly common, even in the case of serious fiction. Here the old resistance to illustration seems to have broken down for the first time.

This tendency to repel illustration is the more striking because illustration flourishes all round the traditional first edition of the full-length

The Walrus and the Carpenter: one of Sir John Tenniel's illustrations to Lewis Carroll's Alice Through the Looking Glass. *Tenniel's illustrations accompanied the first editions of both of Carroll's "Alice" books.*

literary novel. Remove or qualify the term "literary", for example, and a vigorous history of illustrating activity comes into view. Whenever the literary novel has overlapped with children's fiction, thrillers, light fiction, science fiction or other genres, it has tended to pick up the habit of illustration from these adjoining areas. The novella, too, has had a way of acquiring illustration. Hemingway's *The Old Man and the Sea* (1952), for example, was published with illustrations by the celebrated American artist Noel Sickles chiefly because these illustrations had been commissioned for its first appearance in *Life*.

As a novel moves into subsequent editions it is more likely to be illustrated. A pictorial cover may be devised for the first paperback edition of a modern novel when the original dust jacket was a purely typographic affair. When publishers

Right *Sir Edwin
Landseer's frontispiece
for Sir Walter Scott's*
The Antiquary. *This
edition appeared in 1829
as Volume VI of Cassell's
collected edition of the
Waverley novels.*

have put out new or uniform editions of the
works of successful authors, they have sometimes
been stimulated to commission illustrations.
Above all when a novel is out of copyright a
publisher can afford – and, for competitive
purposes, will need – to enhance the familiar
text with illustrations. The most consciously
artistic novel-illustration ever undertaken in
Britain or America has occurred in projects such
as the "Oxford Trollope", George Macy's
Limited Edition Club editions, Macmillans' 1890s
Cranford Series of reprints, and the publications
of the Folio Society in the 1960s and 1970s. No
copyright restrictions prevented British publishers from reprinting *Uncle Tom's Cabin* in
1852, and in this one year they put out a torrent
of editions. Cruikshank, Leech and Gilbert were
among the artists who contributed to the illustrated versions.

The pre-publication of *The Old Man and the
Sea* in *Life* magazine exemplifies a crucial respect
in which the conventional first edition adjoins an
illustrated form of fiction – in this case, fiction
in periodicals. Major novels since the mid-
nineteenth century have achieved some form of
periodical pre-publication in a variety of ways:
the monthly parts of many Dickens novels,
serialization in monthlies or weeklies of
Thackeray, Trollope, Hardy, James and Howells,
appearances of all or part of novels by Crane,
Conrad, Twain and Nabokov in the American
and British daily press, and excerpts from
important forthcoming novels in periodicals as
diverse as *New Masses, Playboy, The Partisan
Review, Sports Illustrated, Blast,* and *Ramparts.*
In many such cases these novels first came before
the public in illustrated versions.

The eighteenth and nineteenth centuries

The story of novel-illustration only becomes
interesting when serious fiction starts to be
illustrated with the knowledge and approval of
the author. This development can be dated quite
precisely to 1836, the year in which *The Pickwick
Papers* started to appear in monthly parts.

There had been only a few, isolated precedents
during the previous century – in the form of new
editions of already successful novels with illustrative contributions more or less actively arranged by the novelists. Samuel Richardson, for
example, planned to embellish the 1741 second
edition of *Pamela,* Part One, with a series of
illustrations; and he turned first of all to Hogarth.
The two drawings which resulted have vanished,
and were never reproduced by Richardson
because one or both of them had "fallen very
short of the spirit of the Passages they were
intended to represent". The set of illustrations for
Pamela which did finally meet with Richardson's
approval – the thirty-nine by Gravelot and
Hayman attached to the May 1742 edition – are
pretty certain evidence for what he had found
lacking in the "spirit" of Hogarth's work. Both

Gravelot and Hayman made the heroine, in
particular, a figure of almost regal grace and
dignity, in an idiom completely antithetical to
that of Hogarth the engraver. These artists were
both professional illustrators, but the idiom in
question derives from easel painting. Sir Walter
Scott turned to painters proper – Mulready,
Martin, Landseer, Wilkie, Bonington and others
– for frontispieces to the 1829–33 collected
edition of the Waverley novels. He did not think
them a success, and claimed that the project was
undertaken in deference to "the taste of the
town".

Whatever the best way to embellish a reissue of
established novels might be, there could be no
doubt about the norms which would prevail in
the illustrations of a new serialized novel in the
1830s. The Hogarthian mode was at its most
irresistible in cheap serial forms, ranging from
sequences of anecdotal engravings to illustrated
periodicals. When Dickens adopted the technique
of first issuing his novels as parts or in periodicals
he at once had available to him a rich resource of
comic illustrating activity, represented by Leech,
Cattermole, Cruikshank, and above all "Phiz".

Of course the Hogarthian mode was deeply
congenial to Dickens anyway, as many critics
have urged. It suited, and probably nourished,
that part of him which relished the grotesque and
ridiculous in the vividly seen here-and-now, and
which wished to put these elements at the service
of simple, strongly-felt moral lessons. His fiction
has much more in it than this, however. It would
have been poorly served by illustration in a
narrowly comic vein, but Dickens did not allow
this. In his exceptionally careful supervision of
his illustrators, his main purpose seems to have
been to bring their idioms on to the middle
ground – to nudge caricature in the direction of
history painting, and vice versa.

Dickens had a "nervous dread of caricature" in relation to Phiz's representation of Dombey, and requested from him a whole page of sketches for this character, from which he made his selection. But in Phiz Dickens had found an exceptionally responsive and hard-working illustrator, who in many essentially pictorial touches achieved sensitive equivalents for Dickens's text, and who could modify his idiom not just once but continuously to accommodate the author's growing range of content and feeling. The more ambitious and atmospheric social comment in *Bleak House* (1852–53) and *Little Dorrit* (1855–57), for example, was answered in Phiz's "dark plates" – the tonal effects being achieved by an actual advance in engraving technique (involving a preparatory graining of the plate).

The problem of illustrating fiction that is in some sense serio-comic arose with other Victorians. The plates for Thackeray's *The Newcomes* (1853–55), executed by Doyle (another illustrator in the comic tradition), are frankly in one or other of two veins: the grotesque and the sentimental. Thackeray's own work for *Vanity Fair* (1847–48) is technically weak and what strengths it does have in this area are all on the side of caricature. Not only the pure looks of Amelia but even the sensuality and charm of Becky's appearance, so stressed in the text, are outside Thackeray's range. But these illustrations do have the overriding interest of being the author's own. When seen in their entirety and placed exactly in the text as Thackeray intended, they contribute to it in uncountable ways. (There have been more novelist-illustrators than is commonly recognized. The cases of Thackeray and Mervyn Peake are well enough known, but R. M. Ballantyne, Arnold Bennett, John Dos Passos, Evelyn Waugh, D. H. Lawrence, and Joyce Cary all contributed illustrations to their fiction which have generally been lost sight of.)

In the 1860s the problem of harnessing the resources of comic serial illustrations for the novel suddenly changed its character. The tradition extending back from Cruikshank through Rowlandson and Gillray to Hogarth yielded to a quite different manner, best exemplified by George du Maurier's work in *Punch*. The stylistic gap between comic serial illustration and academic painting abruptly narrowed. The illustration of periodical material in general, including fiction, changed similarly. The main cause of anxiety for the novelist attending to his illustrations was now likely to be a blandness or generality in the pictorial handling of his material. Dickens – though there are signs that his vigilance concerning his illustrators had relaxed a little by this date – had to give a prompting to Marcus Stone, working on *Our Mutual Friend* (1864–65), exactly opposite to that required for Phiz in depicting Dombey: Boffin's "oddity", Dickens wrote, must not be "at all blinked". But Boffin's

Above *Phiz's sketches for Mr Dombey: these were produced at Dickens' request, so that the author could choose those which he felt to be appropriate.*
Right *Mervyn Peake's illustration of Steerpike from his* Gormenghast *trilogy.*

Above "Another Wedding", one of Phiz's illustrations for Dombey and Son.

Right Sir John Millais' frontispiece to Trollope's Orley Farm. *The artist copied a photograph supplied by Trollope.*

"oddity" has powerful elements of the Dickensian grotesque ("he was of an overlapping, rhinoceros build") which Stone was quite unable to rise to. Henry James wrote in 1883 that du Maurier's *Punch* work had captured all the foibles of London society; but he surely would not have claimed this for the American scene as it had been blandly depicted by du Maurier three years earlier on the pages of *Washington Square* (1880). Trollope grumbled, in private, that Millais had not made Mr Chaffenbrass in *Orley Farm* distinguishable from other characters; in the text he is decisively enough described – as a "dirty old Jew", "with a hooked nose".

Millais illustrated four of Trollope's novels in the 1860s in serial form. The stylistic rapprochement between academic painting and serial illustration was having the effect of opening the pages of the periodicals to well-known easel painters. Lord Leighton illustrated George Eliot's *Romola* in the *Cornhill* (1862–63). At the same time, and perhaps partly as a result of the decay of illustration as an artistic specialism, the method of illustrative reproduction changed. The wood-engraving process – whereby the artist's illustration is cut by a professional engraver on a wood block – generally came to replace the etched metal plate as the medium of illustrative reproduction in periodicals. The results on the whole were deplorable, and all the more so when complete fidelity to the original was sought. This seemed to be achievable if the artist drew his design (in reverse) directly on the block. In practice, though every mark may have been recorded by the engraver, the quality of the draughtsmanship was always lost. Better results were achieved when the engraver was free to find engraved equivalents for drawing or even painting done off the block. Hence the *Romola* plates look better than Millais' Trollope illustrations, which were drawn straight on the wood. Another case where the reproductive weakness of wood-engraving became its strength was Tenniel's justly famous work for the Alice books. Tenniel

One of Lord Leighton's illustrations for the Cornhill's *serialization of George Eliot's* Romola. *The engraver copied Leighton's drawing which was made on paper.*

submitted rather vague drawings to the engraver, and they were fleshed out with the stiff, dead lines of the wood-block procedure at its most automatic. The resulting images are marvellously apt for the spirit of the books – holding Carroll's thing-persons poised between animate and inanimate, and his dream-monsters, like the Jabberwock, between the poles of terror and comedy.

Illustrators could not be confident that their work would reach the page unimpaired until "photo-mechanical" processes were developed.

Line-block illustrations (made from a plate on which the photographically transferred image had been etched) and half-tone plates (the tones being

E. W. Kemble's drawing of Huckleberry Finn appeared in the first edition of Mark Twain's book in 1884. The illustrations were reproduced photographically as line blocks.

achieved by the varying size of inked dots) steadily replaced the wood-engraving in the periodicals of the 1880s and 1890s. The consequent leap in quality can be seen by comparing the illustrations in *Tom Sawyer* (1876) with those in *Huckleberry Finn* (1884) (admittedly the former are also vitiated by the illustrator's inept conceptions, especially his saccharine version of the hero). Photo-mechanical reproductions were better, and they were cheaper. The result was a vigorous and many-headed revival of illustration. In America, though not in Britain, magazine illustration became a permanent institution within the visual arts, with thousands of practitioners. It has been estimated that even before the turn of the century at least a thousand illustrators would have been required to keep the 30-odd leading American periodicals supplied with material.

The earlier shift to a more academic style of illustration in the 1860s had its effect on the quality of the new photo-mechanically produced work. Academic artists like Millais, du Maurier, Stone and others had pulled illustration towards a new kind of naturalism. Millais, in particular, tried to achieve a Degas-like, impressionist feel of unstructured, instantaneous images of the everyday world. Broadly speaking this has continued to be the spirit of twentieth-century illustration. At the outset the impressionist approach – stressing instantaneousness and naturalism – tended to encourage a rather pedestrian representation of the specific scene, rather than the freer and more symbolic connection of text and illustration which we find, for example, in Phiz's frontispieces and title-pages.

1890 to the present

Almost all the illustrated novels mentioned above were published serially, but in most cases the illustrations survived into the first book edition. With the illustrated magazine boom, however, the illustration of fiction starts to go underground. Novels are furnished with illustrations for their periodical appearance which are never reprinted, or only in part. The main reason was a divergence of periodical and book formats and materials. Magazines became bigger than books, and their illustrations would not fit comfortably on a book page. There was a growing tendency to place illustrations in the big format text, either as small conventionally rectangular plates or as irregular, unframed components. This might entail printing the text on the specially finished paper required for half-tone illustrations. Illustrations were often bunched at the beginning around one short section of the text, the eye-catching page which appeared early in a magazine together with the beginnings of several other items. There had been precedents for the changes in illustrative format in the Victorian period. Phiz occasionally turned the page on its side to get a long horizontal dimension, and his designs were unframed with

plenty of white space around them, so that the focus of interest and the tonal emphasis can shift from plate to plate. But even at this period such features tended not to survive the transition to book form. At this point Thackeray's careful assemblage, in *Vanity Fair*, of text and illustrations in various formats was destroyed, and Millais' chapter-initial vignettes for Trollope's *The Small House at Allingham* were discarded.

The increasingly impersonal character of the illustrated magazines restricted the novelist's possibilities of control over his illustrator, especially in the case of British novelists publishing in American periodicals. Thomas Hardy was still able to give guidance (including sketches of his own) to Arthur Hopkins, his illustrator in the *Belgravia*'s 1878 serialization of *The Return of the Native*, but this possibility does not seem to have been available to him when *The Mayor of Casterbridge* (1886) and *Tess of the D'Urbervilles* (1891) came out in the *Graphic* – one of the pioneers in England of the big, fully illustrated magazine. (*Tess*, incidentally, was illustrated by the well-known painter Herkomer and his pupils; Hardy, who often describes his characters in the language of academic painting and art history, was extensively illustrated in serial form, but the material was not reissued.)

The move from the English, chiefly wood-engraved, magazines to the American half-tone ones is significant. American magazines did not dominate the scene yet, but they offered an alternative serial outlet to the British novelist and a new one for the increasingly vigorous American school of fiction. Hardy's last novel, *Jude the Obscure* (1895), was serialized with excellent

Right *One of Sir Hubert Herkomer's illustrations for Thomas Hardy's* Tess of the D'Urbervilles. *The illustrations appeared when the novel was first published, as a serial in the* Graphic.

illustrations in *Harpers Monthly*. *Harpers Monthly* and its companion *Harpers Weekly* were well-established members of the first generation of American illustrated magazines – relatively expensive periodicals which carried a good deal of new fiction. For example, two novels by William Dean Howells, *A Hazard of New Fortunes* and *The Landlord at the Lions Head*, were run in the *Weekly* in 1886 and 1896 respectively, generally furnished with two plates per episode occupying half the magazine's big page. There was still a tendency, however, for the illustrated periodicals to withhold illustration from their most serious fiction. When Howells' important novel *The Rise of Silas Lapham* (1885) appeared in *The Century* – a monthly broadly similar to *Harpers* – there were no illustrations.

On the other hand an excerpt from *Huckleberry Finn* received five illustrations from a major Twain illustrator, E. W. Kemble – a selection from the 170 or so which eventually adorned the book edition. Twain had appointed Kemble personally and carefully examined all his drawings. Their representation of the grotesque element in the text raised problems that are interestingly reminiscent of Dickens' dealings with his early illustrators. Twain found several of the figures "forbidding and repulsive. . . . An artist shouldn't follow a book too literally, perhaps – if this is the necessary result". Some years later *The Century* serialized another Twain novel, *The Tragedy of Pudd'nhead Wilson* (1894), with large, impressive plates by the French-trained illustrator, Louis Loeb.

The older illustrated monthlies and weeklies were challenged dramatically towards the end of the century by the wave of "10-cent" magazines: *McLures, Munseys, The Cosmopolitan, The Metropolitan*, and others. Most of them aimed to offer as much fiction, as attractively presented, as the more expensive periodicals. These new magazines were attractive to British novelists. *McClures* ran Kipling's *Kim*, for example, in 1900–01 (though not with the full complement of illustrations it received in *Cassells*, where it was serialized simultaneously with work by three different artists, on three different aspects of the subject-matter, and in three different media). Conrad was published in both *The Metropolitan* (*The Shadow Line* ran in 1916, with rather vapid illustrations by the ex-sailor, Anton Otto Fischer) and in *Munseys* (where *Victory* appeared in 1915).

But the "dinosaur" of the cheap American illustrated periodicals in this early period was a weekly, the *Saturday Evening Post*. It carried several serials and short stories in each issue. Important new American fiction was often included, with good illustration. Jack London, a widely serialized novelist, received some of his

An illustration by H. Lanos which introduced the eighth part of H. G. Wells' When the Sleeper Wakes in Harpers Weekly in 1899

The title page of the first issue of The Strand Magazine which appeared in January 1891 costing sixpence. This issue contained Sherlock Holmes stories.

best illustrations in Charles Livingstone Bull's work on *The Call of the Wild* (1903). These stylized, slightly art-nouveau plates by an expert animal illustrator, often dealing with the text in a generalized way, were balanced by plainer, more anecdotal contributions from a specialist in hunting scenes, Philip Goodwin. Sinclair Lewis received early attention from the *Post*, which serialized *Free Air* (1919) with accompanying illustrations by F. R. Gruger in his idiosyncratic pencil and wash technique. The *Post*, like *Harpers Weekly*, was in direct competition with another branch of the illustrated press in America: the Sunday newspapers' magazines. These carried new fiction by both American and British writers. An excerpt from Stephen Crane's *The Red Badge of Courage* (1895), for example, appeared in the *New York Press* magazine with several small line-drawings, and Joseph Conrad's *Chance* (1913) was serialized in the *New York Herald*, with a disappointingly deteriorating series of illustrations by L. A. Shafer.

The British periodical press did, for a time, have fiction-carrying magazines to rival this spate of American publications. The most celebrated of these, the *Strand* and the *Pall Mall*, achieved some striking presentations of new fiction. Probably the best set of illustrations for any Conrad novel, by the painter Grieffenhagen, with plenty of claustrophobic, gloomy atmosphere and well-discriminated characters, accompanied *Typhoon* (1902) in the *Pall Mall*. Then *Strand* furnished H. G. Wells's *The First Men in* the Moon (1901) with brilliant drawings by a highly individual artist, Claude Shepperson. These range in feeling from the comic to the awesome, and in technique from a French lithographic look to anticipations of the modern idiom of science-fiction illustration. Further down the market *Pearson's Weekly* carried another Wells romance, *The War of the Worlds* (1898), with less accomplished but even more gripping illustrations by Warwick Goble, elaborately wound into the text in irregular or broken-framed formats that enhance the menace of the images.

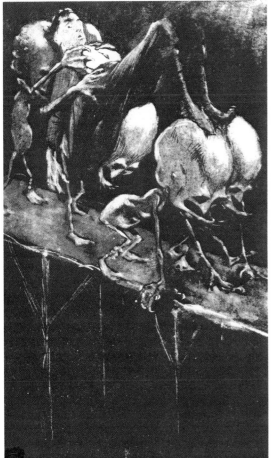

But the illustrated magazine in Britain lost vigour as an institution and, where it survived, seldom published important fiction. Nash's *Pall Mall Magazine* attempted an American look, but its excerpt from Evelyn Waugh's *A Handful of Dust* (1934) (with two quite good illustrations by Marshall Frantz) was well above the usual standard of its fiction. *Lilliput*, also in the mould of American counterparts, carried the tradition of serious fiction-publishing further into the century than almost any other British illustrated magazine – printing, for example, an extract from another Waugh novel, *Put Out More Flags* (1942), with lively though small ink sketches concerning Basil Seal and his evacuees. The daily press has sporadically published excerpts

Below and below left
Two illustrations by Claude Shepperson for H. G. Wells' The First Men in the Moon. *These first appeared in* The Strand Magazine *in 1901.*

In it's long history the Saturday Evening Post *has published fiction of all kinds. In 1961 Erle Stanley Gardner's* The Case of the Bigamous Spouse *was serialized. Della Street, Perry Mason and Hamilton Burger are accurately modelled on the actors who played them in the long-running television series.*

by major novelists with illustration; *The Times* did an episode from Nabokov's *Glory* in 1972 (unfortunately commissioning an artist, William Rankin, who did not seem to know the difference between a punt and a canoe).

For modern British novelists the chief pre-book outlets have been the serious, unillustrated British literary review and the still healthy illustrated American periodical press. For an excerpt from *Brideshead Revisited* in *Town and Country* Waugh received much grander illustration than *Lilliput* had furnished two years earlier, done with obvious relish by the ex-Russian Revolutionary artist Constantin Alajálov. Much more recently, the American technique of very large almost poster-like illustration has been applied quite well to Iris Murdoch's *The Time of the Angels* (1966) in *Cosmopolitan*. Muriel Spark's *The Girls of Slender Means* (1963) was excerpted in the *Saturday Evening Post*. Spark has been one of the most conspicuous of contemporary British novelists in American magazines, though her work has mainly appeared in the *New Yorker*, which does not illustrate its fiction. The modern *Harpers*, which has published Joyce Cary, Evelyn Waugh and Aldous Huxley, follows much the same practice, but the habit of fiction-illustration is widespread in the American periodical press – in literary reviews, for example, whose British counterparts would never deploy illustration (*Sports Illustrated*, for example, printed part of Philip Roth's *The Great American Novel*). The *Kenyon Review* has habitually embellished its fiction-excerpts with a kind of title page, of which the montage of images by H. Danska introducing William Golding's *The Pyramid* (1967) is a good instance.

These mentions of *Cosmopolitan* and *Saturday Evening Post* show that some of the pillars of the

illustrated, fiction-carrying American periodical press had proved extraordinarily durable. But broadly speaking these publications gave a deteriorating service in illustration for the serious novelist, and the magazines which were only thinly or intermittently illustrated often provided more sensitive pictorial contributions. The possibility of a novelist participating in the illustrating plans of a big periodical became even more restricted than in Hardy's day. From at least the 1920s the visual appearance of these magazines was planned as a whole by the house art editor. He gave instructions to the illustrator commissioned for any item, fiction included, which specified shape, treatment, colour and content. And the spirit of the major illustrated magazines separated them and their illustrations increasingly from the serious fiction they printed. The "all-American" character forced on these magazines by the shift from sales to advertising as their main revenue, became at odds with what some of the novelists they published were trying to tell America. *Colliers* kept calling its fiction in the 1940s and 1950s "heart-warming". The epithet may have been appropriate for the O'Hara short novel *The Family Party* (illustrated by one of the most characteristic of American illustrators, Robert Fawcett); but scarcely for J. D. Salinger's *The Catcher in the Rye* – an excerpt of which appeared in 1945 with a heart-warming depiction of Holden Caulfield as an apple-cheeked young rascal.

As recently as 1967 *Cosmopolitan* swathed the opening of an extract from Philip Roth's *When She was Good* with an idyllically clinching couple, a case of the baneful influence on the presentation of fiction of an important twentieth-century newcomer. *Cosmopolitan* by this date was a woman's magazine – no longer the 10-cent family periodical of the 1880s – and one of a large tribe of publications which have contributed a familiar slanting or restriction to the illustration of fiction in magazines. Perhaps the nadir of the woman's magazine style was reached in the 1930s and 1940s. When *Redbook Magazine* announced Sinclair Lewis' *Ann Vickers* as "probably the most important novel he has *ever* written and the *only* one about a woman" the tendency to rugged males and identically elfin females in A. N. Simpkin's plates was predictable. Earlier treatments of *Arrowsmith* and *The Innocents* in the *Designer and Woman's Magazine* and *Woman's Home Companion* respectively were less stereotyped, especially in the case of Worth Behm's illustrations for the latter. The recent woman's magazine specialist Coby Whitmore – in his illustrations to Steinbeck's *The Winter of our Discontent* (1961) in *McCalls*, for example – commands more than a fashion-plate range of imagery.

One new kind of illustrated periodical – exactly antithetical to the woman's magazine –

Von Humboldt Fleisher, the title character in Saul Bellow's Humboldt's Gift, *as depicted by Jean-Paul Goude in the December 1974 edition of* Esquire.

has stemmed the divergence between the modern novel and the spirit of the big magazines. The man's magazine in America has consistently published good new fiction and furnished it with responsive, unstereotyped illustration. Even where the appeal of these magazines is narrowly erotic they have been catholic in their selection and presentation of fiction. *Playboy* has an impressive record of fiction publishing which includes Bellow, Nabokov and Malamud. But the magazine which overshadows all the others is *Esquire*. From the 1950s to the present its editors have been extraordinarily receptive to the major developments in American fiction. Updike, Mailer, Barth, Styron, Bellow, Malamud, Roth and Pynchon make up a diverse group, but they have all been pre-published more or less extensively in *Esquire*. Some of the accompanying illustration has been as good as anything ever provided for the novel.

In addition to this family of magazines there have been several American publications from the 1930s onwards, lying outside the mainstream of the illustrated periodical tradition, which have issued new fiction with thoughtful, sensitive illustration. The literary review, in the form of the *Kenyon*, has been mentioned. *The Paris Review* also quite commonly illustrates its fiction, though the results – such as Albert Eisenlau's drawings for Kerouac's *On the Road* or Robert White's for Styron's *The Confessions of Nat Turner* – are generally more pedestrian. Even the *New York Review of Books* occasionally puts out a piece of fiction with illustration – like the amusing anonymous drawing that accompanied an excerpt from Roth's *Our Gang* in 1971. An entirely peculiar case was the communist magazine *New Masses*. John Dos Passos was a contributing editor, and several extracts from *Nineteen Nineteen* appeared in 1931–32. They were not directly illustrated, but *New Masses* attached great importance to the visual power of the magazine and its pages were filled with angry, forceful work by a number of radical cartoonists. Dos Passos's description of the castration and hanging of Wesley Everest, for example, resonates extraordinarily with this visual context – very far removed from the insipid tone of the woman's magazines of the period. The radical press of more recent times has not carried much fiction, but *Ramparts* published excerpts from two Kurt Vonnegut novels with illustration. *Slaughterhouse Five* had a baffling photographic frontispiece; by contrast Vonnegut's own illustrations for *Breakfast of Champions* (a selection from those in the book) were cunningly literal, as was the bowl of cereal photographed on the title-page.

Although the literary novel's resistance to illustration remains largely unbroken, there have been several interesting exceptions. Thornton Wilder's novel-cum-short story collection, *The*

Bridge of San Luis Rey, came out in 1927 with ten plates and a vignette in imitation woodcut style by Amy Drevenstedt. The following year saw a truly unorthodox piece of novel-illustration – the first edition of *Orlando*, in which photographs of Vita Sackville-West and portraits of her male and female ancestors from Knowle House were brought together by Virginia Woolf as alleged depictions of her hermaphrodite, time-travelling central figure. Almost simultaneously D. H. Lawrence was furnishing the first, French edition of *The Man who Died* (at this stage entitled *The Escaped Cock*) with coloured vignettes and a lurid, amorphous frontispiece in which male and female figures are doing something intense and uncomfortable-looking with a cauldron. Evelyn Waugh executed six illustrations and a wrapper design for his "illustrated novelette" *Decline and Fall*. Surprisingly, all Waugh's plates for this very laconic novel manage to deal with actual episodes within it (except for "Grimes was among the immortals" – a mock-expressionist fantasy of Grimes in convict-dress soaring on a charger over the heads of fellow stone-breakers). But Waugh's idiom – an unmodelled technique in which the even line is interrupted at arbitrary points – matches the reticence of his text. *The Loved One* appeared with illustrations by Stuart Boyle, the subject of a characteristically rude comment in Waugh's diary: "a hardworking, penurious draughtsman of great technical skill and little imagination or taste. Just what I want." Waugh was right about Boyle's technical facility – the plates and vignettes are masterfully composed – but perhaps wrong about his imagination. Boyle's widow denies that he took "dictation" for "every detail", as Waugh claimed. Waugh returned to illustrating his own fiction in 1953 for *Love Among the Ruins*. This short, satirical "Romance of the Near Future" says little about the characters' appearance and an extraordinary flavour is contributed by the neo-classical, sometimes inexplicably sexless, figures in the illustrations (they were assembled by Waugh as "collages" from a book of reproductions of Canova statues etched by the early nineteenth-century English engraver, Henry Moses). Another British novelist with strong pictorial instincts, Joyce Cary, was asked by his publisher to illustrate the 1957 edition of *The Horse's Mouth*. The eight plates have a poignantly thwarted look owing to the impaired action of Cary's hand and wrist. The edition was published posthumously.

The first edition of F. Scott Fitzgerald's *Tender is the Night* (1934) was published with very evocative and clever pen-drawings by Edward Shenton. This was not a true first illustrated edition, since the plates had accompanied the serialization of the novel in *Scribners* (each issue of which Shenton, it seems, was illustrating throughout to the same high standard). But the illustrations were reduced and rearranged for book-publication, and this is a fairly rare instance where a publisher has tried to reconcile the physical differences between the modern periodical and the modern book. In the case of Steinbeck's *The Pearl* the periodical and book versions were simply allowed to diverge, though both were illustrated. Its publication in *Woman's Home Companion* had a single, full page, opening colour plate in typical magazine fashion. For the book version (1947) the Mexican painter Orozco was commissioned to do five ink-drawings, of a completely different character.

Pictorial jackets

Printed or blocked hard covers have rarely been used on novels, and most examples occur around the turn of the nineteenth century, when this kind of work became popular with publishers. Somerville and Ross's *Some Experiences of an Irish R.M.* (1899) had a blocked illustration on its cloth binding. On the binding of Wells' *The Island of Dr Moreau* the island is shown in sinister black with a lowering red sky above; and on *The Invisible Man* appeared a chair, dressing-gown, slippers – and no man.

The technique was in some ways better at not showing things than at showing them. The novel did not have to wait until the advent of the pictorial paper wrapper, however, before it could carry an adequate illustration on its outside. The ancestor of the modern illustrated jacket is the decorated paper binding on Victorian part-published novels – and the presiding genius here, once again, was Dickens. He demanded from his illustrators an unprecedented degree of "shadowing out the drift and bearing" of his novels both in the cover decorations, which were not reprinted in book publication, and in the frontispieces, which were. In his practice and in Thackeray's this concern had a close connection with their innovative efforts to find images or motifs which were representative of the novel as a whole. Hence Dickens sometimes required a frontispiece-like generality for illustrations *within* his text, so lively was his sense of the connections between the illustrated episode and the rest of the narrative. His long list of instructions to Phiz for the meeting of Mr Dombey, Major Bagstock, Edith, and her mother has often been quoted: "a good deal will come of it and I want the Major to express that as much as possible, in his apopleptico-mephistopholean observation of the scene and in his share of it". Thackeray incorporated the imagery of fair, puppet-master, sideshow and so forth, with its teasing implications for his own authorial task, into the cover, frontispiece, and some of the vignettes of *Vanity Fair*. The frontispiece has the melancholy puppet-master, after the show, looking into a mirror. The cross-legged jester in one of the vignettes bears Thackeray's own face. Although the Dickens and Thackeray part-bindings expounded the novels so much more fully than their modern counterparts they also did the modern cover's job of promoting sales. The parts of *Dombey and Son* and *Vanity Fair* were displayed in bookshop windows, where their bindings were meant to catch the eye.

The new vein of naturalistic novel illustration of the 1860s worked against the spirit of the Dickensian and Thackerayean cover and frontispiece. For the frontispiece of *Orley Farm* Millais simply copied a specially commissioned photograph of the real farm Trollope had in mind. But with the advent of pictorial jackets in the early twentieth century new possibilities of generalized novel illustration became available and were exploited. The very fact that the illustrated jacket was a single image relating, at least on first acquaintance, to an unknown narrative content, ensured generalized illustration.

There are signs, however, that the move towards a more general kind of illustration was welcome on other grounds. For in the same period fiction in magazines started to resort to generalized, thematic illustration. In particular it became standard practice in the 1920s to provide a portrait of one of the leading characters at the outset of a serial. If the novelist had inconveniently postponed the character's appearance to a later episode the reader must be kept primed. "This is Alverna, whom you will meet and fall in love with in *Mantrap*," was the caption for one of the opening illustrations to Sinclair Lewis' novel in *Colliers* magazine. Her portrait was again given in the second episode: "Alverna, the dazzling, whose presence you'll begin to feel next week." The illustrations for the *Cosmopolitan*'s serialization of Hemingway's *Across the River and into the Trees* consisted entirely of photographs of prestigious-looking volumes – which were supposed to be the novel in book-form – with captions such as "The novel for which the world has been waiting for ten years". The advantage to the novel-publisher of periodical publication of fiction has been much enhanced by a conspicuous recent development: the eclipse of the serial by the excerpt. Major novels are nowadays hardly ever pre-published in their entirety. When they are, it is done in the minimum of episodes.

The fashion for general, alluring illustrations to excerpts from forthcoming novels has recently produced some brilliant results in the more intelligent of the major illustrated magazines. *The Atlantic Monthly*, with a long history of resistance to illustration, deployed small but telling photographic vignettes for its excerpt from Updike's *Rabbit Redux* – a series of images corresponding to important or recurring motifs in the text: the top of a beer can, a moon-rocket on the television, and so forth. But the most satisfying work in this vein has appeared in the modern man's magazines, especially *Esquire*: the witty sequence of drawings by Jean-Paul

Goude for Bellow's *Humboldt's Gift*, depicting a progressively more jaded and unkempt figure (who might be Humboldt, but doesn't quite correspond to him); or the rivetting full-page plate that introduced part of Thomas Pynchon's *The Crying of Lot 49* (a photograph of a painted triptych of kissing mouths – photography, as in many book covers, enhancing the indirectness of the image). *Cavalier*, a more modest imitator of *Esquire*, did well with its own excerpt from Pynchon's novel a year later, though in the imagery of Oscar Liebman's big design paranoia prevailed too decisively over playfulness.

Book jacket and magazine illustrations overlap in appearance for more than commercial reasons. In America, especially, the strong tradition of periodical illustration was bound to have an influence on the quite minor branch of illustration represented by book covers. In England

Right *Tom Adams's jacket for Patrick White's* The Vivisector.
Below *The spread which introduced* Esquire's *excerpt from Thomas Pynchon's* The Crying of Lot 49 *in December 1965.*
Below right *The jacket for Iris Murdoch's* The Sea, The Sea *(1978) exemplifies the modern tendency to reproduce paintings which are of interest in their own right. The illustration is an eighteenth-century Japanese woodcut: "The hollow of the deep-sea wave off Kanagawa" by Hokusai.*

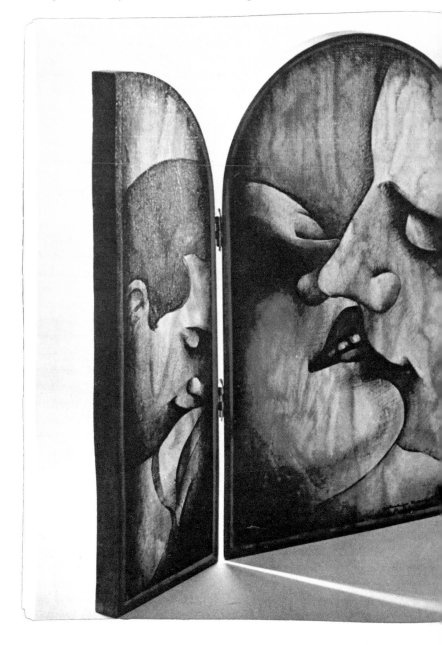

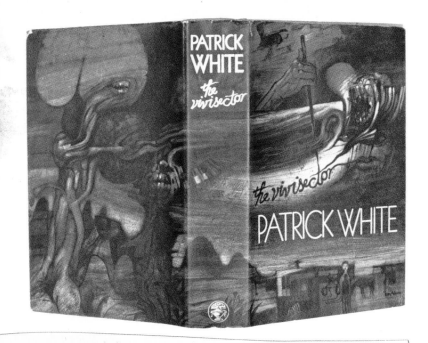

magazine illustrators were never so abundant, and publishers have resorted much more than in America to known easel-painters for cover designs: to Duncan Grant, John Piper, John Minton, Sidney Nolan, and others. A jacket design by an established British magazine illustrator – like Ronald Searle's for Angus Wilson's *Anglo-Saxon Attitudes* – is a rarity.

Jackets are used, in the first instance, to encourage booksellers to stock and display forthcoming books. Hence a form of illustration which necessarily seeks to arouse curiosity has pressed even further in this direction since the 1950s (when one American bookseller characterized recent novel covers as "Guess-What" illustrations). Although no technical obstacles exist to printing illustrations directly on hard covers, several ventures of this kind in recent years have been abandoned – doubtless because of the vital importance of the jacket as a tool of advance promotion.

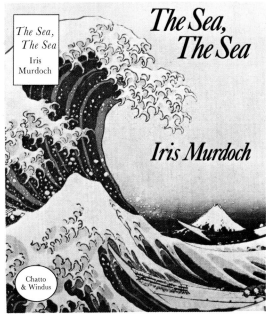

This commercial impulse has also been influenced to some extent by the paperback publishers, whose principal activity has been the reprinting of fiction first published in hardback. Their cover illustrations have been restricted by the need to represent known material, or even known stereotypes of this material – such as the images from the film version of a hardcover success. They have been slower than hardback publishers to introduce photographic covers, and have continued to resort to painted designs in the manner of traditional magazine illustration. And they tend to be ruthlessly commercial in their attitude to the content of novels, often reducing the ingredients to banal stereotypes. On the other hand some paperback houses, Penguin Books for instance, have furnished their reprinted serious fiction with covers which are by no means pedestrian or cynically eye-catching.

Only in hardcovers, however, has there been any survival of the tradition of cooperation between author and artist. Some novelists have even designed their own wrappers – like Dos Passos for *Manhattan Transfer* or Wyndham Lewis for *The Apes of God*. Many more have requested particular artists, such as Patrick White or C. P. Snow, who both nominated Sidney Nolan. It would be pleasing to think that a conjunction as clever as Edward Gorey and *The Sotweed Factor* was due to John Barth's initiative.

Finally, jacket illustration has increasingly drawn more on the broad field of applied art and design than on magazine illustration. The novel covers of any one period will look like the interior decoration, fabric designs, car bodies, and especially the advertising art that surround them. There are distinctively "1920s" jackets with shapes in silhouette, tonally contrasted and drawn with a strong line, learned from French poster technique (though more plainly pictorial covers are also to be found, as they are at all periods, alongside the highly designed variety). In the late 1920s and early 1930s, when an approximation to poster-art in covers was particularly urged by publishers and booksellers, covers still use powerful silhouette, but the shapes and the lettering are highly geometrical. Pearl S. Buck's *The Good Earth* carried a fairly restrained example of this manner. Lettering was often made to stand forward from a broadly treated pictorial ground, as on O'Hara's *Butterfield 8*, and in the late 1930s there was a move against pictorialism. "The calligraphers are in the driver's seat . . . in the last ten to fifteen years," said a commentator in 1948. Lettering on covers (much more cursive now, and often given a hand-executed look) and simple, spidery ornament tended to become dominant. The result was a cover for Fitzgerald's *The Last Tycoon*, for example, very different from that carried by *Tender is the Night* only seven years earlier. Pictorial elements at this period, themselves often calligraphic in treatment, tended to be overlaid with widely separated, rounded patches of colour in bright pastels. In the 1950s "colour break-up" continued with super-imposed panels of colour, often with a wavy contour (though now in the non-primary hues – ochres, turquoises, etc. – so much in fashion). A break-up of the whole cover into areas with distinct pictorial or typographical modes was also common – of the kind achieved by the influential American jacket-designer, George Salter, for Styron's *Lie Down in Darkness*.

Above *The jacket for J. B. Priestley's* Wonder Hero, *published by Heinemann in 1933: an example of the geometrical style of the late 1920s and early 1930s.*
Below *Victor Reinganum's jacket for Muriel Spark's* The Bachelors, *published by Macmillan and Co in 1960.*
Bottom *Muriel Spark's* The Public Image *(1968) was adorned with a simple photo-montage. The technique is still popular, but tends to be used more subtly.*

The two most conspicuous innovations of the last fifteen years are the use of more or less composite photographic images (though these have a longer history in mystery fiction); and the reproduction in widely spread form (often right round the wrapper and bled-off) of a painting actually or supposedly done for it's own sake. The two styles overlap when the painted image is incorporated in a photographic assembly, and indeed they are not so different in principle. Tom Adams' spectacular cover designs for John Fowles's *The Magus* and for Patrick White's *The Vivisector*, for example, are meant to be perceived as reproductions of paintings – paintings of interest in their own right which have only become "about" these texts, as it were, by virtue of the publisher's decision to print them on the jackets. The new idiom has proved extremely powerful, and its success must to some extent be explained by reference, once again, to the illustration of magazines. These developed, in advance of the change in jacket design, a new brilliance in photographic work, which in America has much reduced the role of the traditional illustrator. The new techniques were perhaps most spectacularly deployed in the advertising imagery of the magazines and, indeed, at large in commercial illustration. So the new appearance of the novel jacket must also be seen as a mark of its continuing intimacy with commercial art.

But the new style has worked for the serious modern novel because it offers, in addition, a new tactfulness. The scarcity of illustration in first editions of serious novels is usually explained by economics: it costs too much, it is alleged, to furnish illustrations for books published in such small runs. But in practice publishers nowadays spend sizeable sums on creating illustrations for even the most uncommercial novels – in the form of their pictorial wrappers. The old obstacle to illustrations must in part have been aesthetic. There is almost bound to be something awkward about a literal visual representation of the content of written fiction of any complexity and depth, unless extraordinary, Dickensian efforts are made to get it right. Covers which are overtly the handiwork of one artist can certainly succeed if they are not too literal, but in the struggle against literalness a sense of the specific may get lost. The solution is an image which is specific and yet does not insist that it is truthful: an image – or an image of an image – which uses the photographic medium both as a means of being evocative and as an excuse for being precise.

THE NOVEL AND THE CINEMA

Many twentieth-century novelists have been pessimistic about the novel's chances of survival in the age of cinema and television. The future society of Aldous Huxley's *Brave New World* gives babies selective electric shocks to ensure that they grow up with an instinctive hatred of books but enjoy "feeling pictures". In George Orwell's *1984*, fiction is manufactured "like jam or boot-laces" in the Ministry of Truth, and the tele-screen rules. In Ray Bradbury's *Fahrenheit 451*, an entire civilization is devoted to the mass extermination of literature and reading, while people's homes are dominated by massive wall-to-wall colour screens.

None of these drastic predictions has yet come true, but speculation about the relation between film and literature continues to flourish. There is even a regular journal, the *Literature Film Quarterly* (of Salisbury State College, Maryland) devoted solely to academic discussion of the subject. It has no shortage of material to study, because of the striking degree to which the cinema has leaned on fiction for its plots and ideas.

The history of screen adaptation

Silent films from novels

In its early one-reelers and shorts, the cinema gravitated towards music hall and the stage for its plots and performers. The subjects of the films of the 1890s were substantially the same as those of the peep shows that they succeeded: dancers, prize-fighters, stage cartoonists, slapstick comedians and conjurers. But in the early 1900s the chase became an enormously popular item, represented in full story-form for the first time in Edwin S. Porter's *The Great Train Robbery* (1903). The popularity of the chase is significant because plots involving pursuit are a common feature of the novel, but not of the stage. In cutting back between heroes and villains in *The Great Train Robbery*, Porter was demonstrating an early link between film and novel.

In 1907 a company called Kalem produced a one-reel version of Lew Wallace's novel *Ben Hur*; and was successfully sued by the author's heirs, establishing the important legal precedent that movie producers could not use copyright literary material without the consent of the owner.

Novels became increasingly popular as screen material after World War I. Zola was adapted in France and Dickens in England. Two Hollywood successes included Rudolph Valentino in *The*

Four Horsemen of the Apocalypse from the popular book by Blasco Ibáñez; and Jackie Coogan in *Oliver Twist*; but by today's standards these seem very simplistic and theatrical versions of their originals. The most extraordinary adaptation of the silent era derives from Frank Norris' celebrated naturalist masterpiece *McTeague* (1899). The Austrian director Erich Von Stroheim was attracted by Norris's story, based on the real-life murder of a janitress, and determined to shoot absolutely everything in the novel scene by scene, even amplifying certain background details like McTeague's ancestry. The film was called *Greed,* and accounts of its original length vary between seven and twenty hours. There is no doubt that it remained the most ambitious – certainly the longest – screen adaptation prior to the new TV "mini-series" which will be discussed later; in fact, in its original form *Greed* seems to have run considerably longer than the time it would take to read *McTeague*.

Regrettably hardly anyone has seen the complete version of *Greed* because its backers would not release it. A two and a half hour section, consisting largely of the climax, was eventually shown in 1923 and this flopped at the box office. Von Stroheim's career subsequently foundered and the whole episode demonstrated that the

Rudolph Valentino in The Four Horsemen of the Apocalypse. *The movie was based on the novel by Vicente Blasco Ibáñez.*

Paramount's Tom Sawyer *was one of the first sound adaptations from a novel. The child star Jackie Coogan was considered the movie's main attraction. The name Mark Twain played little part in the promotion.*

"THE KID" Grows Up! Now He TALKS for the First Time!

And the Most Popular Girl on the Screen! Pert and pretty Mitzi Green as Tom Sawyer's unruly "best girl," Becky Thatcher.

Little Jackie Coogan is a big boy now! A fine youngster whom you'll love all over again as the healthy, hearty hero of the most hilarious comedy of boyhood ever written, Mark Twain's

"TOM SAWYER"

WITH

JACKIE COOGAN
MITZI GREEN

A Paramount Picture

economics of cinematic exhibition simply did not allow film-makers to duplicate a novel scene by scene. Some other way had to be found. The Russians, of course, do not have this problem: Bondarchuk's *War and Peace* was made over four years (1963–67), lasted almost nine hours (cut to six in the West), cost £40m ($80m) and was financed by the state.

Early sound adaptations

The first effect of the introduction of sound to the movies was a temporary return to the stage as a source of material; in the wake of Broadway personalities, like Al Jolson, theatre actors with properly trained voices flocked into film production and, for a time, the cinema had to begin all over again. One of the earliest important novel adaptations after the introduction of sound was Universal's 1931 version of Bram Stoker's *Dracula*. Few plots could be more ideally suited to the spatial freedom of cinema: the ride through Transylvania, Harker's escape from the castle, the sea-journey to Whitby, Van Helsing's frantic pursuit of the Count across Europe – most of these elements would be seen again and again in the films of the 1960s and 1970s. But the original Universal producers were so intimidated by the necessity of treating vision and sound (not to mention Dracula's subject-matter) that they were content to borrow most of its action from the Broadway play: almost all of the story, apart from a short prologue, is reduced to a banal series of drawing-room conversations.

A year later the same studio adopted a much more imaginative approach with James Whale's version of Mary Shelley's *Frankenstein*. Whale and his writers were shrewd enough to take the

Right Detail from the publicity poster for MGM's Gone With the Wind.

bare bones of Mary Shelley's idea and build another simpler, but equally disturbing, story around it. Shelley's monster is transformed from an eloquent but ill-used primitive into a beast-like mute. It was a drastic change, but it worked so well that the film's portrayal of Frankenstein effectively replaced the original character in the public imagination, confirming that radical alteration has a greater chance of success than laborious scene by scene reconstruction. This discovery would later cause much heart-ache to living novelists.

By 1934 a Hollywood survey estimated that one third of all film production was based on novels; by the 1950s the figure had probably grown to one half. The sheer quantity of film production in America makes it hard to arrive at reliable figures over the first three decades of sound, but in the smaller British film industry we can be reasonably precise. In 1932, 44 English films were adapted from plays as against only 27 from novels, from a total output of roughly 160 films. By 1938 the figures had levelled out to 28 adaptations from plays and 28 from novels out of a total of 150. But twenty years later in 1958, of the 100 or so films made, 50 were adapted from novels and only 9 from plays. The cinema in Britain had evidently found its preferred source; and in this respect it seems unlikely that the British industry was very different from America or Europe.

The Selznick approach

The conventional "Hollywood" approach to novels is typified by the career of David O. Selznick, whose work came to dominate the first two decades of sound. Selznick grasped more quickly than any other producer the commercial advantages of making glossy, relatively faithful, paraphrases of famous bestselling novels and using Hollywood stars to bolster the portrayal of major fictional characters. Selznick's approach was to choose which stars, or potential stars, best fitted a celebrated novel and then to build the story as conscientiously as possible around them,

DAVID O. SELZNICK'S PRODUCTION OF MARGARET MITCHELL'S "GONE WITH THE WIND"

reconstructing the exterior action of the plot with a few set-pieces. The result was W. C. Fields as Micawber in the star-studded *David Copperfield* (1934), Greta Garbo in a lush but truncated *Anna Karenina* (1935), Ronald Colman and Basil Rathbone in *A Tale of Two Cities* (1935), Freddie Bartholomew as *Little Lord Fauntleroy* (1936), Vivien Leigh and Clark Gable in *Gone With the Wind* (1939) and (his most perfect matching of subject to director) Laurence Olivier and Joan Fontaine in Hitchcock's *Rebecca* (1944).

As his choice of novels shows, Selznick was aware of the cinema's enormous capacity for generating emotional involvement, and he therefore preferred epic love stories, frequently even increasing the high romantic interest of his originals. He was expressly concerned that, like the great popular characters of fiction, his leading characters should be larger than life. In one of the interminable "memos" by which Selznick steered each production, he wrote of a scene in *Gone With the Wind* that "it should by its colours alone dramatize the difference between Scarlett and the rest of the people".

Above *W. C. Fields as Micawber in* David Copperfield.
Above right *Laurence Olivier and Joan Fontaine in* Rebecca.

Another revealing "memo" of Selznick's refers to an unmade biblical picture, and vividly reflects the kind of vulgar energy he was able to inject into his literary adaptations:

You have working for you that greatest of all showmanship combinations – sex and religion. You have father love, brother love; you have lust and sentiment; you have complete blueprints for every conceivable production value. . . . *But* add to these the ultimate in quality and integrity of approach, add to them idealism worthy of a Thomas Mann, and *there* will be a motion picture to be remembered for generations.

As this note suggests, Selznick's treatment of fiction, like his treatment of the bible, was almost triumphantly middle-brow; he would extract the commercial juice from a book while making every attempt to preserve its "integrity" (one of his favourite words). Two other great moguls of the early years, Samuel Goldwyn and Cecil B. de Mille, shared Selznick's craving for respectability, but adapted fewer famous novels: Goldwyn had hacked a conventional love story out of *Wuthering Heights* in 1939, but generally preferred more contemporary material; while with isolated exceptions Cecil B. de Mille tended to work from original scripts based loosely around biblical or epic themes. Selznick's approach was therefore the one that made its mark and it was increasingly imitated by his inferiors; what had been successful in the hands of its originator (with the help of several talented directors) eventually became a recipe for disaster. By the 1950s, solemn and verbose adaptations of turgid blockbuster novels (like *The Rains of Ranchipur* and *Love is a Many Splendoured Thing*) were almost the norm in Hollywood and even Selznick's acumen finally failed him in 1957 when he delivered a ponderous adaptation of Hemingway's *A Farewell to Arms*. It was his last film.

Perhaps it was not surprising that the literary community grew to despise Selznick's popular picture-book readings of the classics. In many ways unfairly, he came to represent Hollywood's parasitic attitude to fiction. In 1957 when he announced that he would pay Ernest Hemingway $5,000 out of the profits of *A Farewell to Arms*, Hemingway replied by telegram that, if by some miracle the film did make a profit, Selznick should have it changed into nickels "and shove them up his ass until they come out of his ears".

The avant-garde approach

The studios' treatment of novels inevitably differed from the approach of more independent film-makers. Following the demise of the studio system in Hollywood and the rise of the independent producer in the early 1960s, there was even more freedom of interpretation available to the individual film-maker. Even so, some of the major directors of the post-war period were disdainful of the idea of adapting fiction. "Film has nothing to do with literature," Ingmar Bergman has said. "We should avoid making films out of books." In a similar vein, Alain Resnais compared the process of filming a novel to reheating a meal. Other directors like Jean-Luc Godard took a more pragmatic view, preferring to utilize the bare bones of their source novels as a kind of springboard for the imagination. In one typical instance, Godard took a thriller called *Obsession* by Lionel White (about an advertising executive who runs off with his babysitter after a murder) and turned it into the extraordinary fragmented odyssey *Pierrot le Fou*, which compares more closely to the great modernist works of twentieth-century fiction than to a crime story. At one point the leading character, played by Jean-Pierre Belmondo (as a medium for many of the director's own ideas), turns to the camera and makes this connection explicit: "I've found an idea for a novel," he announces to the camera. "No longer to write about people's lives, the life of a man, but only life, life itself. What there is between people in space . . . like sound and colours. That would be something worthwhile; Joyce tried, but one must, ought to be able, to do better."

As this implies, Godard's artistic ambitions for the cinema have been as high as any film-maker of the post-war period; yet, at the height of his creative powers during the late 1960s, he consistently preferred to adapt novels with particularly conventional plots. "I do need a story," he said. "A conventional one serves as well. It is with this kind of novel that one can make the best films. . . . The Americans know how to tell stories very well; the French not at all. Flaubert and Proust don't know how to narrate; they do something else."

Godard's attitude echoes the familiar argument that "the worse the book, the better the movie", and it has a sound basis in the difference between the two forms. Films can deal as well as books with external action and narrative, but not with subjective description and commentary; and thus the bulk of Flaubert and Proust may get lost on celluloid whereas a Lionel White thriller can be transcribed very precisely. To White's bare plot a director like Godard can add a substance as meaningful as a "serious" novelist's by using a series of devices that are strictly cinematic (montage, counterpoint between sound and vision, music, voice-over) and cannot therefore be translated directly from any novel. In this respect the most avant-garde and artistically ambitious cinema can hardly be anything more than *analogous* to the most serious fiction, whereas popular cinema can reproduce popular fiction relatively faithfully.

For much the same reason the novelists who have been most consistently preferred by the movie-makers from the 1930s to the 1970s are those who have sometimes chosen to work within clearly defined narrative genres; from the nineteenth century the list includes Conan Doyle, H. Rider Haggard, Bram Stoker, Edgar Allan Poe, Wilkie Collins, Robert Louis Stevenson, H. G. Wells and some but by no means all of Dickens. In the twentieth century there have been: John Buchan, Raymond Chandler, Graham Greene, Somerset Maugham and a host of other popular writers.

Anna Karina and Jean-Pierre Belmondo in Pierrot le Fou. *Jean-Luc Godard based his screenplay on Lionel White's thriller* Obsession.

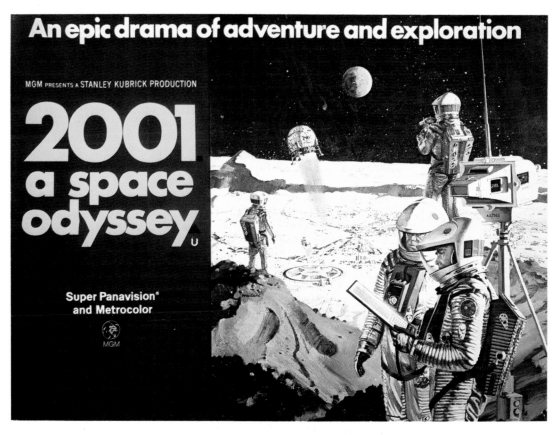

An epic drama of adventure and exploration

MGM PRESENTS A STANLEY KUBRICK PRODUCTION

2001
a space
odyssey

Super Panavision®
and Metrocolor

MGM

Right *MGM publicity for*
2001: A Space Odyssey.

However, the last two decades of cinema have also seen some ambitious attempts by talented film-makers to steer a middle course between the approach of Godard and other members of the avant-garde and simple plot-lifting. Films like *Death in Venice* (1971) and *The Go-Between* (1971), which will be discussed later, are comparatively true to the spirit of their originals.

Developments in the 1970s

As the 1970s end, novels remain a major source of film material; but a close examination of *Variety*'s chart of top-grossing films (tabulated from American box office returns but generally accepted as a fair overall indication of the world market) indicates that original scripts have recently overtaken fiction as the key ingredient of success. The list of the twenty most successful films of the 1950s – according to *Variety* – featured no less than fifteen adaptations of novels, from both classic novels like *Around the World in 80 Days* and *20,000 Leagues Under the Sea* and contemporary bestsellers like *Peyton Place* and *From Here To Eternity*. By the 1960s this figure has dropped as low as nine out of twenty (*Thunderball, Mary Poppins*). And the twenty most popular films of the 1970s so far include only six novel adaptations. But it is worth remembering that even if today's major films like *Star Wars* or *Close Encounters* do not *start* life as a novel, they always end up as paperback novelizations. It is now routine practice for any studio embarking on a big production to com-

Film and novel:
a comparative
analysis

mission a novel from its script as a matter of course.

We are used to regarding narrative sound film as a vivid two-dimensional representation of reality, and therefore as a lazier, more passive experience than reading: the process of absorbing it sometimes seems almost too easy. In spite of devices like flash-backs, the cinema's tense is overwhelmingly present. "By its very nature", writes the novelist Alain Robbe-Grillet, "what we see on

Stanley Kubrick
(left) on the set of 2001
with Arthur C. Clarke
who wrote the novel.

the screen is in the act of happening. We are given the gesture itself, not an account of it."

Confronted by today's mass audience films, which create a high sensory impact by using an extremely elaborate (and expensive) battery of special visual effects, we are inclined to forget that watching a film – even a narrative entertainment film like *Star Wars* – is in certain respects as sophisticated a mental process as reading.

The link between watching film and reading words has been demonstrated most persuasively in a series of anthropological experiments conducted amongst non-literate cultures, including Eskimo and African tribesmen. Professor John Wilson, of the School of Oriental and African Studies at London University, was one of the pioneers in the field; his experimental work in the early 1960s influenced the writings of Marshall McLuhan. When Wilson showed an African audience a simple film about sanitation techniques, he was surprised to find that they were as unable to decipher the film's code of visual images, as they would have been a page of typescript. Instead they picked out the most irrelevant details. Wilson described what happened in an interview in a Canadian journal:

> We showed this film to an audience and asked them what they had seen, and they said they had seen a chicken, a fowl, and we didn't know there was a fowl in it! So we very carefully scanned the frames one by one for this fowl, and . . . for about a second, a fowl went over the corner of the frame. . . . We discovered afterwards that they hadn't seen a whole frame – they had inspected a frame for details. A sophisticated audience focuses a little way in front of the flat screen . . . (to) take in the whole frame. You've got to look at the picture as a whole first and these people did not do that. . . . We found that the film is, as produced in the West, a very highly conventionalized piece of symbolism although it looks very real. . . . We had to begin a process of education in useful conventions.

Audiences, it seems, have to be educated in the disciplines of "reading" film rather as they are taught their letters. Film is *not* simply an easy, direct representation of reality; it involves subliminal processes of mental self-discipline – in particular the ability to see visual shapes as symbols – quite comparable to the deciphering of linear type.

The various similarities that psychologists have found in the way we "read" film and read books may go some way towards explaining why the early film-makers turned with such enthusiasm to the novel as a source of inspiration. Both the cinema and the novel originated as entertainments; together they are unrivalled in their abilities to create private enclosed worlds for the spectator or reader. As McLuhan wrote, in *The Gutenberg Galaxy*, "it would be difficult to exaggerate the bond between print and movie in terms of their power to generate fantasy in the viewer or reader".

The man who is generally credited with the invention of the key techniques of narrative cinema was the American film-maker D. W. Griffith. In a famous and influential essay "Dickens, Griffith and the Film Today", the Russian film-maker Sergei Eisenstein (director of such early silent classics as *Battleship Potemkin* and *Strike*) claimed that the prose of Charles Dickens provided a blue-print for Griffith's discovery of all the major technical cinematic devices, including the dissolve and the close-up. Griffith himself frequently mentioned Dickens as a major inspiration, and is said to have carried copies of his novels on location.

Eisenstein quotes the first line of *The Cricket on the Hearth* ("The kettle began it.") as a key example of a close-up in Dickens's work, and the close-up was a device of fundamental importance to the early cinema in differentiating it from the stage. But it is easy to make too much of the notion of Dickens as the father of modern cinema. Nineteenth-century literature provides us with scores of close-ups, some of them much more compelling than "The kettle began it". For example:

> . . . in one moment, every drop of blood in my body was brought to a stop by the touch of a hand laid lightly and suddenly on my shoulder from behind me.
>
> I turned on the instant, with my fingers tightening round the handle of my stick.
>
> There, in the middle of the broad, bright high-road – there, as if it had that moment sprung out of the earth or dropped from the heaven – stood the figure of a solitary Woman, dressed from head to foot in white garments, her face bent in grave inquiry on mine, her hand pointing to the dark cloud over London, as I faced her.

The dramatic technique of this passage, heralding the first appearance of the title character in Wilkie Collins' *The Woman in White,* has been imitated so many times in suspense cinema that there is no mistaking it: the hand touching the hero's shoulder from off-screen, the cut or rapid camera movement as he turns (precisely mirrored by the short one sentence paragraph) and the full close-up of the figure looming over him. The device is highly theatrical in its impact on the reader, yet it could never be achieved on stage; even the most brilliant lighting effects cannot bring a stage audience so close to the action that it sees only "her face bent in grave inquiry on mine". Clearly Dickens had no exclusive role as the inspiration of cinema. He was simply the most prominent among many nineteenth-century novelists who excelled in dramatic effects of this

and other kinds. D. W. Griffith's enthusiasm for Dickens was merely representative of the cinema's appetite for the carefully managed techniques of the nineteenth-century novel.

Differences between film and novel

The fact that cinema and the novel share so much common ground – an ability to range in space and time, to create a private hermetic world for the viewer or reader and to handle linear narrative – can blind us to their equally essential differences. Film's principal handicaps compared to fiction are that it is awkward in the detailed representation of subjective states of mind, and even worse at communicating concentrated doses of information. A fictional film cannot entirely capture the intense psychological insights of Dostoyevsky, for example, any more than a documentary film can do the work of a psychiatric text book. Cinematic adaptations of writers like Joyce or Dostoyevsky – even when they are attempted boldly and intelligently – almost always seem like very pale shadows of their originals.

An example is Luchino Visconti's ambitious film of Thomas Mann's *Death in Venice*. His recreation of Mann's Venice is elegantly persuasive, making full use of tiny details from the book like strawberries being sold on the beach and the camera left standing on its tripod. But the director is eventually defeated by the story's rich layers of symbolism. On the printed page the beautiful youth Tadzio keeps his distance enough to remain a symbol, embodying the elderly writer (changed to a composer in the film) Aschenbach's unattainable artistic ideal of pure beauty. But in the film he is a potently physical force. This inevitably heightens the sexual undertone, and by the end Aschenbach, with his smeared make-up, seems less like a tragic hero than a pathetic self-

disgusted lecher. The literalness of the cinematic image, its very immediacy, has perverted the intentions of the translator from fiction to film.

Flaubert anticipated this difficulty when he objected to the idea of illustrating his novels with pictures. "A woman drawn resembles one woman, that's all," he wrote. "The idea, from then on, is closed, complete and all the sentences are useless."

The cinema is even less capable of generalizing than an illustration; it cannot say "A woman came into the room". It has to show a specific woman entering a specific room and even the clothes she is wearing, the furniture in the room she enters, the expression on her face. This degree of particularization can be a disconcerting handicap if an artist wishes to make general statements. Unlike the novelist, the film-maker generalizes with difficulty and at considerable risk. His or her task is to particularize and allow the audience to draw the appropriate generalization. But he faces the additional problem that, because visual styles and fashions change, films date far faster than fiction; in general novels of the 1950s seem much more contemporary to us now than films of the period. Graham Greene saw this fact as an advantage to the novelist who sells his work to the cinema: "You take the money, you can go on writing. You have no just ground of complaint. And the smile in the long run will be on your face. For the book has the longer life."

Economic considerations are also important in considering the basic differences between the two forms. Even films made as cheaply as possible for the "art" market – specialist cinemas or television channels catering for middle-class audiences – will today cost a minimum of £80,000 ($160,000) and usually far more, while a commercial feature, like *Jaws* (1975), cost almost £4 million ($7.5 million). Yet the book on which *Jaws* was based could have been written for the price of the paper and its author's time and published in a small way for about £3,000 ($6,000). Clearly there is more

Left *D. W. Griffith, the pioneer of modern cinematic technique, who was enormously influenced by the novels of Charles Dickens.*

Richard Dreyfuss and Robert Shaw in Jaws.

financial pressure on film to be popular, to find an audience at all costs. Graham Greene recognized this basic fact when he wrote that it is "wrong to despise popularity in the cinema – popularity there is a value, as it isn't in a book . . . a film with a severely limited appeal must be – to that extent – a bad film".

Literal adaptation

The "shot" in film parlance is an uninterrupted exposure of numerous frames of film. "Montage" is the process by which various shots are edited together to create meaning (for example, shots of the sun rising, a man sleeping, a hand banging on a door, the man waking up). Enthusiasts of montage, like the great Russian theorist Pudovkin who helped to invent the notion of editing, have often compared it to sentence construction and tried to establish a cinematic equivalent for the word in language. Pudovkin claimed that a single shot "subserves the same purpose as the word of the poet" and, following his example, Sergei Eisenstein tried to transpose passages of Milton's *Paradise Lost* and Pushkin's *Poltava* into shooting script form.

Attempts to achieve this degree of relativity between film and language now seem pointless intellectual games which honour neither medium, particularly when we consider how difficult it is to translate even a short passage of narrative prose literally on to the screen. As an example, here is the first sentence of a famous story that has been filmed three times:

> During the whole of a dull, dark, and soundless day in the autumn of the year, when the clouds hung oppressively low in the heavens, I had been passing alone, on horseback, through a singularly dreary tract of country; and at length found myself, as the shades of the evening drew on, within view of the melancholy House of Usher.

On the face of it the action involved in the opening of Poe's *The Fall of the House of Usher* is straightforward: a man rides towards a gloomy house on horseback; and indeed that is exactly how the film-maker Roger Corman treated it. But a second look confirms just how inadequate, as a direct representation of the prose, this treatment is. Leaving aside Pudovkin's forlorn hope of a direct word-for-word translation on to the screen (how do we film the word "During"?), it seems there are at least three kinds of problem.

The first central difficulty is time or, more precisely, pace: "*During* the *whole* of a dull, dark . . . *day* in the *autumn* of the *year* . . . I *had been* passing and *at length* found myself . . ." The langorous sense of time passing, beautifully underpinned by Poe's alliteration, is not susceptible to filmic translation, nor is the historic tense. There are various clumsy short-hands available to the film-maker (like the rapid movement of clouds in the sky or a series of dissolves) but all of them collapse the day into a few seconds, which is the opposite of the effect required.

Secondly there is the major problem of character and point of view. Poe does not say "A man"; he says "I", nor – at this stage at least – does he particularize the "I". The only cinematic device which even approximates to this use of the first person is the "subjective camera": the camera takes the place of the narrator or leading character and the audience sees only what he sees. The most celebrated continuous use of this device in cinema is Robert Montgomery's adaptation of Raymond Chandler's *Lady in the Lake* (1947) where the director played the private investigator Philip Marlowe from behind the camera throughout, only becoming visible when he looks in the mirror. As a technique this has certain intriguing possibilities, even if it has not proved particularly popular with audiences, but it is doubtful whether even the subjective camera rightly reflects Poe's use of "I" here; the effect of Montgomery's technique is to make the audience become the narrator whereas Poe's "I" is not necessarily meant to be a focus of easy identification, especially since Poe goes on to describe his "utter depression of soul". In this respect, however, it should be added that point-of-view is not always so difficult for the film-maker: where a writer adopts the more conventional stance of the omniscient narrator, the cinema probably finds it easier than any other medium to duplicate the approach.

Thirdly, there is the problem of translating action in such a way as to convey the plot. The plot is generally the most important component of a novel to a film-maker, because in their most basic form, plots are structures independent of any medium. (The simple example of a plot which E. M. Forster gives in his *Aspects of the Novel*: "The king died and then the queen died of grief", could be the basis of a dance, a painting or a song as well as of a novel or a film.) Yet the first sentence of *The Fall of the House of Usher* illustrates the difficulties that are involved in the adaptation of even the most straightforward action, so that it forms part of the plot. To show a man riding towards a gloomy mansion on horseback is only a cursory version of the events Poe describes: his rider is making a long, lonely journey through a very strange kind of landscape – dull, dark and soundless – all negative qualities which a film may find it difficult to convey. The action described in the sentence is its most accessible element, but even this is not easy to duplicate exactly.

Some of these many difficulties might be resolved by using Poe's own text as a voice-over to the film, but this can in turn create its own problems. Off-screen narration undermines the effectiveness of the image; and there is certainly no way of utilizing it continuously without reducing the film to mere illustration.

If Roger Corman's version of *The Fall of the House of Usher* (1960) managed to overcome most of these apparent hurdles, it was precisely because it did not try to be a scrupulously faithful version of Poe's text. Following the example of Whale's *Frankenstein*, Corman merely lifted many of Poe's favourite nightmares and obsessions (the sentience of inanimate objects, premature burial, hyperaesthesia) to build a graphic plot of his own; the result is rough in places but comes nearer to being a "Poe" film, to reproducing the effect of Poe's tale for an audience in the 1960s, than other more literal and literary attempts.

Problems of time and tense

Because it operates essentially in the present tense, film is not nearly as adept as the novel at expressing shifts of time: where a novelist can write simply "Five years later . . ." at the beginning of a chapter, the cinema must resort to all kinds of elaborate and often unsatisfactory devices like a magically changing calendar. By the same token, film is easier with space than the novel, cutting rapidly between detailed locations that may need pages of description in a novel.

James Joyce's *Ulysses* is supposed to observe the unity of time; in other words it covers 18 hours 45 minutes of a Dublin day which is also the approximate duration of an average reading. This is one obvious case where the pace of a book completely defies the cinema, yet in 1967 Joseph

Strick attempted a two-hour version. The fact that Strick was very cautious in his treatment of the text, lifting many passages whole and using a number of cinematic tricks to convey Joyce's style, only served to make the distortion of the original worse. The Homeric metaphor of Joyce's text disappeared completely in the film, and the universal images of Joyce's prose became specific and parochial. Given the film's relative brevity, it was inevitable that Molly Bloom's monologue at the end swamped the rest of the action and remained more or less all that audiences took away from it.

Again and again in the history of fiction adaptation examples like Strick's *Ulysses* suggest that cautious fidelity to an original text can be the easiest way of distorting it on film. This is one reason why "literary" has become one of the most insulting adjectives in film criticism. The film critic Pauline Kael rightly described Strick's *Ulysses* as "an act of homage in the form of readings from the book plus illustrated slides", which was only a kinder way of saying (as her colleague Stanley Kauffmann did) that it was "a facile and ludicrous reduction". A true film version of *Ulysses* would of necessity have to stretch the feature film as radically as Joyce stretched the novel, in which case it would not necessarily follow Joyce at all. Because *Ulysses* is "cinematic" in some of its techniques does *not* mean that it can be transferred directly into cinema.

Below *Robert Montgomery in his own adaptation of Raymond Chandler's* The Lady in the Lake.

Above *Burt Reynolds (left) and Jon Voigt in* Deliverance. *James Dickey successfully adapted his own novel.*

John Schlesinger's *Far From the Madding Crowd* (1967) runs for over three hours, but even so it can do little more than telescope Thomas Hardy's narrative. Although certain scenes, like the sheep-shearing supper, stick closely to the novel, and some of the film's minutest descriptive details (like the leaves dripping on Fanny Robin's coffin) derive from the text, nonetheless the film looks and sounds ponderously theatrical; the settings become far more interesting than the characters.

Above *Robert Redford as Jay Gatsby in Jack Clayton's movie* The Great Gatsby.
Above right *Dominic Guard (left) and Alan Bates in Joseph Losey's adaptation of L. P. Hartley's* The Go-Between.

Another recurrent time problem facing the screenwriter is whether to transpose the original story into a contemporary setting. Joseph Strick's film of Henry Miller's *Tropic of Cancer* (1969) and Tony Richardson's adaptation of Evelyn Waugh's *The Loved One* (1965) were both badly damaged by an awkward updating of their plots. In contrast Jack Clayton's £3¼ million ($6½ million) version of F. Scott Fitzgerald's *The Great Gatsby* (1974) became so involved in the period detail of the Jazz Age that it sometimes seemed to forget that Fitzgerald was more essentially interested in the relationships of his characters than in their period trappings. Nonetheless, in fairness to Clayton's *Gatsby*, at least one of its ingredients – Bruce Dern as Tom Buchanan – was an impressive interpretation of Fitzgerald's text, and perhaps the film was excessively attacked in response to its overblown marketing.

Flash-backs

The cinema's best-known device for expressing a shift in time is the flash-back; this permits the film-maker to interpolate material from a character's past into the present (or, much more rarely, vice-versa) and the audience is usually alerted by some visual device so that it recognizes the transition. But the awkwardness of the flash-back is now so well established that many film-makers refuse to use it.

In adapting Philip Roth's 1969 bestseller *Portnoy's Complaint*, a novel about the sexual problems of Jewish boyhood in New York, Ernest Lehman was compelled to use flash-backs in order to be faithful to the original. Roth's rambling confessional style had allowed him to interpolate amusing anecdotes from his hero's past into the action of his novel with relative ease. But on film the same device served only to break the flow and lose the audience's interest. Richard Brooks had precisely the same problem in making

a film out of Truman Capote's *In Cold Blood*. Capote's book had offered some penetrating insights into the psychology of two psychopathic killers, Dick Hickock and Perry Smith, who murdered the Clutter family. Unable to develop these arguments in the course of his action, Brooks inserted some desultory flash-backs to Perry's childhood and then tried to ram the point home by showing Herb Clutter assume the face of Perry's father just as Perry was about to kill him. In the event, the effect is tritely concrete. Flash-backs are so unnervingly literal in the cinema that they constantly undermine the more subtle time-switches of the printed page.

One of the very few films to get around this problem was *The Go-Between*, scripted by Harold Pinter from L. P. Hartley's novel. Pinter and the director Joseph Losey based their film on a stylistic contrast between the lush sun-drenched flash-backs to Edwardian England and the gray sterile present. Hartley had used a prologue and epilogue in the present to achieve this, but Pinter successfully abandons the prologue, preferring to cut forward in time rapidly and rarely (the reverse of the usual technique). He also eliminated most of the book's commentary (as related by the central character Leo Colston) so that the events of the boy's childhood have an immediate and unfiltered force. The result may not be *The Go-Between* exactly as Hartley wrote it, but it is hard to see how any film could get very much closer.

The mini-series

Ever since Von Stroheim tried to release his lengthy adaptation *Greed*, film-makers have been bedevilled by lack of time in which to develop a novel's plot. However, the "mini-series", which devotes up to 25 hours television time, usually on consecutive nights, to a novel adaptation, provides an opportunity for film-makers to reconstruct novels in as much detail as Von Stroheim attempted. Harold Robbins' novel *The Carpet-baggers* was made into a Paramount film in 1964, lasting just two and a half hours, which is long by movie standards. His novel *79 Park Avenue* as an NBC mini-series in 1977 was very nearly three times that length, and it was short by comparison with other mini-series. James Michener's 1,000-page bestseller *Centennial* lasted 25 hours at a cost of £500,000 ($1 m) an hour.

If the reproduction of plot in its entirety is the real answer to the problems of adapting novels to films, then the mini-series should resolve it. But to date the results have not been encouraging. The dullness of so much of the material suggests that plot convolutions, which are acceptable in a long novel, quickly become exhausting and irrelevant on the screen.

Character

Unless they are aiming for a quasi-documentary approach, like that of Peter Watkins in *Culloden* (1964) and *Privilege* (1966), film-makers rarely comment directly on their characters; consequently they must rely on dialogue, appearance, and external trappings, including props, to develop character. Distinctive articles of clothing, like the hat pulled down over Humphrey Bogart's head in Howard Hawks's version of Raymond Chandler's novel *The Big Sleep*, or props, like the stuffed birds that surround Anthony Perkins in Alfred Hitchcock's adaptation of Robert Bloch's *Psycho*, are made to do some of the work that commentary does in fiction.

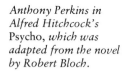

Anthony Perkins in Alfred Hitchcock's Psycho, *which was adapted from the novel by Robert Bloch.*

By creating expectations that can either be cheated or fulfilled, the star system in the film world also adds its own hidden resonance to character. Raymond Chandler once wrote that the best man to portray Philip Marlowe on the screen would be Cary Grant, but most of his readers would surely disagree; Grant's smooth image is so firmly established in the public mind that it would have been asking a lot for them to accept him as Marlowe. Bogart, on the other hand, had built up such a convincing background in tough guy roles that, although he played

Five stars who have played Philip Marlowe, the private detective created by Raymond Chandler: (centre) Humphrey Bogart in The Big Sleep; *(clockwise, beginning top left) Robert Montgomery in* The Lady in the Lake; *Elliott Gould in* The Long Goodbye; *Robert Mitchum in* Farewell My Lovely *(1975); Dick Powell in* Farewell My Lovely *(1945).*

Marlowe only once, he remained Marlowe in the public imagination for ever.

The cinema shuns anonymity in character. In the most recent BBC TV version of Geoffrey Household's classic pursuit novel *Rogue Male* – about a marksman who tries to kill Hitler – Household's anonymous hero became Sir Robert Hunter. When the Len Deighton spy books were adapted to the screen, Deighton's unnamed working class spy was suitably reborn as Harry Palmer. In both cases the "I" of Household and Deighton

had to be pinned down.

In the thriller genre, the reworking of the characterization of the hero (or villain) can occasionally elevate a pedestrian novel into a superior film. Robin Cook's novel *Coma* was a taut but minor thriller about a nurse who uncovers a racket in human transplants. By upgrading the nurse into a crusading woman doctor, and expanding her part into a witty commentary on the problems of professional women, the novelist and film-maker Michael Crichton was

able to make the film *Coma* (1977) into a far more substantial work than its source.

The cinema sometimes demands the hero of a thriller to prove himself through some extra feat of daring that was not in the original book; this can have a negative effect on an adaptation. Don Sharp's version of John Buchan's *The Thirty-nine Steps* (1978), with Robert Powell, based its commercial appeal on the grounds that it was more faithful to Buchan than any previous film. Yet the makers eliminated Buchan's subtle climax in which Hannay strives to penetrate the ultra-English disguise of his opponents, and substituted a ludicrous denouement in which the hero swings from the hands of Big Ben.

Some characters from fiction are so complex, and are drawn with such an accumulation of narrative detail, that they are almost impossible to put on the screen in anything but diminished form. Robert Fuest's version of Emily Brontë's *Wuthering Heights* (1970) portrayed Heathcliff as little more than a shy and moody farmhand; and Omar Sharif as Doctor Zhivago, in David Lean's 1965 film of Boris Pasternak's book, conveyed no sense of intellectual depth. These

failures are perhaps predictable, but it is almost more frustrating when the exigencies of casting undermine an adaptation before a single sequence has been filmed. In William Wyler's production of John Fowles' *The Collector,* the character of the timid, spotty and impotent bank-clerk who kidnaps a girl was allocated to one of the most glamorous leading men of the 1960s, Terence Stamp. Such impossible paradoxes inevitably arise from the collision between accurate reproduction of a novel and marketing considerations.

Paramount's poster for The Blue Dahlia, *which was written by Raymond Chandler from a novel he had abandoned.*

THAT **LADD** IS MIXING IN MURDER!

The Big Three... in a rough, tough shocker by Raymond Chandler, one of the greatest hard-boiled mystery writers that ever lived!

"You ought to know that you can't take chances with a stranger..."

PARAMOUNT presents

ALAN LADD
VERONICA LAKE
WILLIAM BENDIX

in

The **BLUE DAHLIA**

A GEORGE MARSHALL PRODUCTION

with HOWARD DA SILVA · DORIS DOWLING · TOM POWERS · FRANK FAYLEN

Produced by JOHN HOUSEMAN · Directed by GEORGE MARSHALL · Written by RAYMOND CHANDLER

Novelists in Hollywood

"I would rather take a 50-mile hike," Samuel Goldwyn is reputed to have said, "than crawl my way through a book." This was the kind of attitude that earned Hollywood its reputation as a writer's hell and ensured that so many major novelists conceived a deep-seated mistrust of the cinema. From the 1920s Hollywood's salaries for writers were high, but the terms authors were offered for their books were far worse than today. It was not until 1941, when Edna Ferber sold *Saratoga Trunk* to Warner Brothers, that the contract for the sale of a novel called for the rights to revert back to its author after a stated period. In the early days of Hollywood, books were sold outright, sometimes for pitifully small sums, and could be filmed again and again by the studios while their authors received no additional money. The novelists who came to Hollywood to write screenplays were also originally compelled to work in a studio office where they could be more closely supervised. Even as distinguished a novelist as William Faulkner had to cable MGM begging to be allowed to write at home.

One of the most revealing skirmishes in the cold war between Hollywood and the novelists occurred in 1945 while Raymond Chandler was working on a script called *The Blue Dahlia* (from a novel Chandler had decided to abandon) with the producer John Houseman. Chandler tended to hold himself aloof from the vulgarities of studio life but he had consented to work for Houseman on the grounds that they were both "British Public School men" (Chandler had been educated in England at Dulwich during the early 1900s). On this occasion – because the studio's major star Alan Ladd was about to enter the army – the cameras began rolling before Chandler had even finished the script. Slowly the camera began to catch up on the pages Chandler was delivering each day, and an anxious production chief at Paramount, who even at this late date evidently saw a film-writer as a hack rather than an artist, called Chandler in and offered him an additional five thousand dollars if the script was completed on time.

Chandler was deeply offended by the suggestion that his talent could be bought, and his morale was shattered. He informed Houseman he was withdrawing from the film.

In the end an extraordinary secret compromise was reached between Chandler and Houseman: Chandler agreed to finish the script on his own terms, which meant that he would work at home and subsist on alcohol. In the belief that he was ill, the studio provided a relay of secretaries and limousines to type and transport the pages to the studio while a doctor administered the writer with intravenous vitamin injections in place of food. In this way *The Blue Dahlia* was finished on time. Houseman's account of the episode concludes with the observation that Chandler saw himself afterwards in his weakened post-binge state "as a gravely wounded hero who had shown courage far beyond the call of duty".

Today, ironically, Chandler's eccentric working conditions could be demanded by any major screenwriter in Hollywood and a producer or studio would agree at once. Because Hollywood's major studios are no longer factories but agents who assemble packages of talent, the successful screenwriter has assumed considerable power. In a press interview, the producer Robert Evans said "I'd rather have the next five Robert Towne pictures than the next five Robert Redford pictures". Towne is one of the most talented of Hollywood's current crop of writers. Some of this

Raymond Chandler working on The Blue Dahlia, *the script which, in the words of producer John Houseman, he "risked his life for".*

power has been extended to the novelist who wishes to sell his work for film production. John Fowles' best-selling *The French Lieutenant's Woman* has taken years to reach the screen because Fowles insists on personally approving the film's director and has already turned down several famous names.

In spite of the slight shift to original scripts as a source of the biggest and most successful films, popular fiction has never been accorded such enormous status by Hollywood as it is now. Bidding will often begin long before a book is published (in some cases even when it is a first novel by a new author, provided it has a likely subject). And money is not all that is at stake. Michael Crichton's success as a best-selling novelist enabled him to move into film direction with almost no qualifications at all (except the ability to write). The same applies to Nicholas Meyer, author of the best-selling *The Seven Per Cent Solution*. It is striking that a successful novelist will generally find it easier to get a job directing movies than a successful cameraman.

But F. Scott Fitzgerald's distrust of Hollywood was not based simply on the fact that it denied its writers creative control. Like the authors of *Brave New World, 1984* and *Fahrenheit 451*, he had more sweeping fears:

> I saw that the novel . . . was becoming subordinate to a mechanical and communal art which . . . was capable of reflecting only the

tritest thought, the most obvious emotion. As long past as 1930, I had a hunch that the talkies would make even the best-selling novelist as archaic as silent pictures . . . (T)here was a rankling indignity that to me had become almost an obsession in seeing the power of the written word subordinated to another power, a more glittering, a grosser power . . .

Despite Fitzgerald's anxieties, film has not made the best-selling novel archaic. Novels sell in larger quantities today than they have ever done, even in the face of deadlier enemies than the cinema. And the evidence suggests that, far from being fiction's enemy, the cinema actually induces people to read; the sales of every kind of novel – even the most serious kind – tend to increase sharply in the wake of film or television adaptation.

Fitzgerald was most nearly right only in the sense that the cinema has now begun to influence the most commercial spectrum of novel-writing to such an extent that some books almost seem to be written in script form. Thrillers like Frank de Felitta's *Audrey Rose* or Peter Benchley's *Jaws* (sold on a four-page outline to an American publisher for a $7,500 advance, presumably with the film market very much in mind) are more cinematic than literary. On the other hand, popular fiction has always regarded pace and a strong visual atmosphere as a virtue. Film may have made some inroads into the novel but a glance at the high degree of literacy of some recent original Hollywood scripts like *Klute*, *Chinatown* or *The Deer Hunter* suggests that the traffic has not all been one way.

Strangely enough it was Raymond Chandler himself who predicted that the cinema might one day cease to abuse its writers. "I suppose there is hope," he once wrote. "The cold dynasty will not last forever, the dictatorial producer is already a little unsure, the top-heavy director has long since become a joke in his own studio; after a while even technicolour will not save him. There is hope that a decayed and make-shift system will pass, that somehow the flatulent moguls will learn that only writers can write screenplays and only proud and independent writers can write good screenplays and the present methods of dealing with such men are destructive of the very force by which pictures must live."

Not all of Chandler's hopes have been fulfilled. But it seems likely that the spectacular resurgence of the cinema's popularity in recent years has come about partly for the reasons Chandler foresaw: someone finally listened to the writer.

THE NOVEL AND
THE BOOK TRADE

The main structure of the British book trade was laid down early. The eighteenth century saw the innovation of a statutory copyright law, recognizing for the first time that the producer of the written word had an assignable right of ownership over his work. At the same time, the collective use of novels, through the setting up of town circulating libraries, became regularized; and the price of publications became stabilized – at an artificially high level – with concomitantly small editions of new publications. Finally, readers of novels began to form into mass units with a group preference for certain kinds of fiction (e.g. the Gothic vogue in the second half of the century).

In the nineteenth century the interlocking network of competitive "publishing houses" emerged, quite distinct in their role from the bookseller-printer-jobbing publishers of the earlier era. In the 1830s the expensive first-form/cheap reprint sequence was standardized, and it remains with us today as the hardback/paperback system.

The book trade is by nature conservative. Its history consists of long plateaux stabilized by "trade custom" and convention. Change, when it comes, tends to be abrupt and drastic, serving as the prelude to a new long-standing plateau. With the publishing of fiction three such changes stand out as pre-eminently influential: the huge increase in price in the first decades of the nineteenth century, which led to the 31s 6d novel; the almost overnight dropping of the guinea and a half (31s 6d) novel in favour of the 6s standard price of the 1890s; and finally, the post-World War II "paperback revolution". Other factors have had their effects; but these three have more than any others created the environment or "literary climate" in which the novelist has worked.

The American book trade has developed quite differently. American practice has always been less conservative, more competitive and ruled (especially after the 1890s) by a greater degree of *laissez faire*. In the twentieth century America has pioneered the book club, the mass market paperback and the film and television tie-in. The mosaic of independent and relatively small publishing houses still prominent in Britain has largely given way to bigger, industrial-sized combinations in the US. Given the economically dominant nature of the American book trade (in the late 1970s its annual turnover was $4 billion, compared to the British book trade's £500 million) it seems likely that American patterns will increasingly dominate English-language publishing.

Eighteenth-century England

In his classic study *The Rise of the Novel* (1957) Ian Watt indicates the middle-class nucleus around which the literary form grew in eighteenth-century England:

> Novels were in the medium price range. They gradually came to be published in two or more small duodecimo volumes, usually at 3s bound, and 2s 3d in sheets. Thus *Clarissa* appeared in seven and later eight volumes, *Tom Jones* in six. The prices of novels, then, though moderate compared to larger works, were still far beyond the means of any except the comfortably off: *Tom Jones*, for example, cost more than a labourer's average weekly wage. It is certain, therefore, that the novel's audience was not drawn from such a wide cross-section of society as, for example, that of the Elizabethan drama. All but the destitute had been able to afford a penny occasionally to stand in the pit of the Globe; it was no more than the price of a quart of ale. The price of a novel, on the other hand, would feed a family for a week or two. This is important. The novel of the eighteenth century was closer to the economic capacity of the middle-class additions to the reading public than were many of the established and respectable forms of literature and scholarship, but it was not, strictly speaking, a popular form.

Novels were best sellers among the range of books offered the reading public and their sale and dissemination (via libraries, book clubs and family groups) probably catered for the largest combination of secular (as opposed to readers of religious matter) and literary (as opposed to consumers of sub-literary ballads, chapbooks and pamphlets) readers. The population of Britain was between six and seven millions in 1750, of mixed literacy. Catering for the audience which could be reached from this mass (communications outside London were still primitive), Samuel Richardson's *Pamela* went through five editions in a year in 1740. Henry Fielding's

An advertisement for J. Seago, who sold books and prints near St Giles's Circus in London in the eighteenth century.

James Lackington's London bookshop and lending library in about 1800. In this so-called "Temple of the Muses", Lackington, an early and successful exponent of remaindering, boasted, amongst large numbers of novels, 10,000 copies of Isaac Watt's Psalms. The higher the customer climbed in the gallery, the cheaper the books became.

Joseph Andrews, two years later, went through three editions and sold 6500 copies in about the same amount of time. *Clarissa Harlowe*, again by Richardson (1748) seems to have cleared about 3000 copies in two years. In 1751 Fielding's *Amelia* had a legendary sales success, selling 5000 copies in a week or less. Most editions of fiction in this century, however, ran to a moderate 500 or so copies.

The multi-volume eighteenth-century novel was a durable object (they can still be found in use in scholarly libraries), and each purchase may represent up to ten or so readers. J. M. S. Tompkins in *The Popular Novel in England 1770–1800* (1932) estimates that production in the century peaked at about 60 titles a year – which suggests that the avid eighteenth-century reader could, unlike his successors, have read everything that came out in the fiction line. Of course, such a devoted consumer would also have borrowed his reading matter from a circulating library. These emerged in the 1720s, and were a dominant feature of the cultural life of London, large cities, and the spas and watering places by mid-century. As is always the case where readers have a say in what they get, fiction was the main stock held. Subscriptions ran from half a guinea to three guineas annually. An ample supply of servants to collect and return volumes (and doubtless clandestinely read them) solved the "circulation" problem. (Circulation is always a difficulty with "clubs" or "association-based" reading groups – the twentieth-century book club could only really get going on the back of a fully developed and cheap postal delivery system, in collaboration with modern mass advertising methods. One of the things that killed the big commercial London libraries in the twentieth century was that middle-class patrons could no longer afford to send someone to get their books, and the stores themselves could no longer afford to deliver them by van.)

Libraries tend to homogenize the reading public and standardize the product offered them.

They also foster the growth of publishing houses serving them. In the second half of the eighteenth century William Lane brought his Minerva Press to dominance, providing romances for the library trade. He also had his own library, and would supply whole library stocks, from 100 to 10,000, "for sale to grocers, tobacconists, picture-framers, haberdashers and hatters eager for a profitable side line." Although tame enough as we look back at them, the kind of novels purveyed in these "slop shops of literature" raised moral objections, famously guyed in Sir Anthony Absolute's outburst in Sheridan's *The Rivals*: "A circulating library in a town is an evergreen tree of diabolical knowledge! It blossoms through the year! – and depend on it, Mrs Malaprop, that they who are so fond of handling the leaves, will long for the fruit at last."

The booksellers (who were also, in general, the publishers) had shown their corporate force early in the century when they petitioned repeatedly, and in 1709 successfully, for a copyright law. It was their capital which underwrote the expensive business of producing novels (one of their number, Samuel Richardson, was also a novelist). Their function at this time was not, however, consciously enlightened or friendly towards the new literary form. Watt, for example, observes that the booksellers "did little or nothing to promote the rise of the novel directly".

Where the money goes on a hardback novel. The diagrams assume a printing of 5000 copies, all of which are sold. That a British publisher makes a substantially larger percentage profit than his American counterpart on a printing of this size, reflects the considerably smaller size of the British market. A sale of 5000 copies is above average in Britain: in the US it is close to the norm.

On the other hand, they demolished the old author-patron relationship which might have held the form down:

> ...as an indirect result of their role in removing literature from the control of patronage and bringing it under the control of the laws of the market-place, they both assisted the development of one of the characteristic technical innovations of the new form – its copious particularity of description and explanation – and made possible the remarkable independence of Defoe and Richardson from the classical critical tradition which was an indispensable condition of their literary achievement.

The laws of the market place also created that "lottery" aspect to the rewards of fiction which has always since characterized it. Great novelists commanded high, even princely, payment. Fielding received 1000 guineas for *Amelia* (using the previous calculus, this would be enough to feed a labourer and his family for fifty years). At the end of the century Mrs Radcliffe's Gothic romances were sufficiently the rage for her to get sums of over £500 for a string of novels. Meanwhile, at the Grub Street end of the profession, hacks might be offered as little as half-a-guinea per volume for manuscript fiction. According to Tompkins, "usual payment for a library novel

Nineteenth-century England

seems to have been between five and ten guineas," although "the profit could be doubled by a judicious dedication" (the old vestiges of patronage, that is, were not entirely stamped out).

During the Napoleonic Wars two important developments affecting the book trade had a strong influence on the novel. The first was the usual "emergency" intervention by the state in the form of censorship and control (in this war and post-war period, "taxes on knowledge" were imposed which were to encumber the press for over fifty years). As a medium of recreation rather than of information the novel probably gained rather than lost from this government action; a population typically turns to escapist fiction in times of stress. But the production of novels was massively affected by the second of the war's consequences, namely huge price increases. Books, like other commodities, were subjected to unprecedented cost inflation and shortages of materials. The novel, whose price had actually been coming down at the end of the eighteenth century, began to spiral upwards and in 1821 reached the sky-high level of 10s 6d a volume for the three volumes of Sir Walter Scott's *Kenilworth*. Scott left his mark everywhere on the subsequent Victorian novel, but nowhere more so than in its high retail cost and hefty physical format.

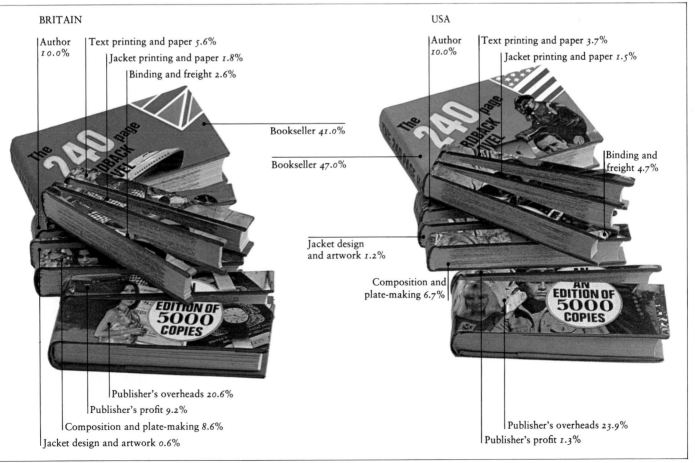

BRITAIN

Author 10.0%
Text printing and paper 5.6%
Jacket printing and paper 1.8%
Binding and freight 2.6%
Bookseller 41.0%
Publisher's overheads 20.6%
Publisher's profit 9.2%
Composition and plate-making 8.6%
Jacket design and artwork 0.6%

USA

Author 10.0%
Text printing and paper 3.7%
Jacket printing and paper 1.5%
Bookseller 47.0%
Binding and freight 4.7%
Jacket design and artwork 1.2%
Composition and plate-making 6.7%
Publisher's overheads 23.9%
Publisher's profit 1.3%

Extraordinarily, the novel remained at the guinea-and-a-half price for the next seventy-three years; and three volumes was the standard (although not invariable) length and format of the new work. Of all the book trade plateaux which the British novel has moved along this is the longest, and the most artificially supported. Everyone agreed that the "three-decker" was overpriced (and usually, in consequence, over-long). But experiments to lower the price were invariably doomed since authors resisted them (their payments in advance would suffer), booksellers resisted them (their pre-sale profit would

be cut into) and the public did not complain since it got fiction from the library, or waited for the cheap reprint. As a Victorian joke had it, there was a man once, somewhere, who bought a three-volume novel for private use, but no-one could remember his name.

The long-lasting standardization of the three-volume novel created stability, and this stability, in its turn, fostered the growth of supportive literary institutions – notably the "leviathan" metropolitan circulating library. The most famous of these libraries was Mudie's, founded in London in the early 1840s. In the next twenty years C. E. Mudie expanded to control a major section of the metropolitan market and, using the newly developed rail, steamship and postal

Charles Edward Mudie, whose circulating library was a dominant force in the British book trade during the 1850s and 1860s.
Left The publisher's expenditure and income on a 1000 copy first printing of Anthony Trollope's The Three Clerks *(1858). From the sale of 852 books the publisher, Richard Bentley, made a profit of £74, or 12½ per cent on his investment. 38 books were used for sales and review purposes. Of the 123 copies left (the printer delivered 13 extra to allow for damage), 97 were sold off at a reduced price the following year, yielding another £33 for the publisher. Figures have been rounded up to the nearest pound.*

ADVERTISING £63

PAYMENT IN FULL TO TROLLOPE £250

BINDING £47 10s

PAPER £91

PRINTING £130

352 SOLD TO THE TRADE some unbound £368

500 SOLD TO MUDIE £288

services, a sizeable portion of the country and overseas market. At his zenith, in the 1860s, he earned up to £40,000 a year in subscriptions – representing a likely readership for his books of 200,000 (assuming four to five readers for every subscriber). His principal selling point was cheapness – especially taken against the face price of 31s 6d for a new novel. For an annual fee of a guinea the customer was entitled to the loan of a volume which could be exchanged as often as he cared. Proportionately more lavish subscriptions were available, and it was calculated that using Mudie's facilities a year's reading for half-a-dozen members of a family could be had for two or three guineas, equivalent to £200 worth of new books bought in the shops. Most of these would certainly be fiction. Of the half million or so volumes Mudie bought between 1853 and 1862, half were novels. All the 150 to 200 three-deckers produced in these bumper years were aimed primarily at Mudie.

Like W.H. Smith, who grew to giant stature at the same period (his first railway station bookshop opened at Euston in 1848), Mudie relied for his success on the new machinery of the Victorian age – its improved roads, newly laid down railways and flat-rate mail service. But Mudie also preserved long past its natural span the archaic and quite pre-industrial three-volume novel. This had invaluable benefits for him: it discouraged people from buying their own fiction; and the three-decker could be simultaneously read by three customers for the price of one copy. Mudie, incidentally, since he enjoyed a near monopoly and by-passed bookshops, could exact huge discounts of 50 per cent and over from the publishers.

Most publishers and most authors were happy enough with the three-decker. It created stability, which is always good for the book trade. Publishers could estimate in advance how many copies of a novel would sell. Small library editions were easy to handle and warehouse. The high price, even after discount, meant that authors could be advanced a reasonable fee for their effort. Everyone might be happy with arrangements such as these. Trollope (see diagram) was well paid – especially since at this period he was turning out two or three books a year; the publisher had a valuable copyright, and a gross profit of 12 per cent on his first edition; Mudie had his copies at less than half price; and the public had an entertaining novel to read. Of course, potential disadvantages are also evident. Mudie's purchasing power was so great that he might, and frequently did, impose his censorship on books which he did not like. Like the equally censorious W.H. Smith – "the North Western missionary" with his railway book stalls – Mudie was a very strait-laced individual. And Trollope was obliged to write at greater length and with more padding for the family readership than he might want. It was partly pressure by English novelists to enjoy the artistic freedoms of their French colleagues, as regards form and content, which led to the abolition of the three-decker at the end of the century.

Around the central, supporting pillar of the three-volume novel alternative forms flourished. The most famous was the novel in monthly parts, inaugurated by Dickens in collaboration with his publishers Chapman and Hall in 1836. This gave the purchaser a full-length illustrated novel in twenty instalments, each costing one shilling. Since the work had to be sold time and again during its year-and-a-half's issue, an unusually close bond was established between author and reading public (the author, that is, soon knew if his work did not please). Techniques had to be developed to keep the purchaser eager to re-purchase ("Make 'em laugh. Make 'em cry. Make 'em wait"). Given the fact that at one pound, even in easy payments, the novel in numbers was not cheap, Dickens's sales were amazingly high. Commonly the early numbers of one of his serials would sell 40,000 or more, averaging around 30,000 overall. But one of the unsolved difficulties with this form of serialization was that no other single novelist was capable of appealing as widely or as consistently as Dickens: Thackeray, for example, who also wrote monthly serials, rarely exceeded 20,000 and often fell below 10,000. Trollope did well if he managed 10,000.

Another form of serialization was kinder to the less than Dickensian writer. This was issue in the fiction-carrying magazine. These established themselves very early in the Victorian period with *Bentley's Miscellany* (originally starring Dickens as editor) which sold as many as 10,000 copies in its first early 1837 numbers. The most spec-tacular success, however, was that of *Cornhill* in 1860 (with Dickens's great rival, Thackeray, as editor). This achieved early sales of 120,000 for its monthly numbers. It did not sustain this circula-tion: a decade later the market it opened had been parcelled out, and *Cornhill*'s share was severely cut down (as low as 12,000 by the mid-1870s). But the magazine had indicated a new dimension to the fiction market. For fiction was the main appeal of *Cornhill*: it regularly carried two serials by "name" novelists, making up about a third of its total length.

The reprinting of fiction in cheap form was regularized in the early 1830s with Bentley and Colburn's "Standard Novels". Costing 6s, these came out a couple of years or more after the the original three-decker. The reprint industry was given a boost in the 1840s with the vast railway expansion. Railway stations were natural places to sell books, given that the travelling public had money and time ahead of it to read on the journey. Of the "railway" publishers, George Routledge was the greatest. In 1851 he

publicly demonstrated his pre-eminence by pay-ing the novelist Bulwer Lytton £20,000 for the lease of his copyrights for his "Railway Library" (by this period the reprint price had fallen to 1s). In the great *Uncle Tom's Cabin* boom of the same period, Routledge was printing up to 10,000 copies of the novel a day (since there was no copyright agreement between Britain and America these were pirated). The scale of the reprinters' operations made them, like the maga-zine and newspaper publishers, progressive in their attitude towards new printing machinery and new modes of distribution.

The jacket of A. H. Wheeler and Co's Indian Railway Library *edition of Rudyard Kipling's* In Black and White. *Publishing editions specifically for sale in railway stations began in England in the 1840s. The idea spread to many parts of the British Commonwealth in the wake of the railways.*

From the novelist's point of view, the Victorian was a golden age – at least for the most successful practitioners. Scott's consistently high payments at the beginning of the century were sustained by a *corps d'élite* of novelists through the century. G. P. R. James, Harrison Ainsworth, Bulwer Lytton had four figure payments in the 1830s. Dickens had monthly payments of from £250 to £600 for his serials; Thackeray from £100 to £250 a month for his. George Eliot made close on £10,000 from *Middlemarch*, first published in 1871–72. Trollope, although he never made as much as the others from any one novel, com-pensated by bringing out 47 works of fiction during his writing career; and in the 1860s at the height of his popularity he could reckon on

£2000 to £3000 for a full length novel. Benjamin Disraeli climbed to the top of this slippery pole, as of all others in his life-time, with £10,000 from Longmans for *Endymion* in 1880.

Throughout the nineteenth century free trade had been the rule of the British book trade. An abortive attempt by the publishers in 1851 to prevent booksellers from underselling (i.e. offering the kind of discount which drove weaker competitors out of business) failed. In the last decades of the century, however, the book trade and literary professions generally organized themselves. The Society of Authors was formed by the energetic novelist Walter Besant in the early 1880s, the Booksellers Association and the Publishers Association in the 1890s. Between them, these organizations set down the ground rules which were to take the British book trade into the twentieth century. Authors successfully campaigned for payment by royalty and the abolition of various forms of publisher's tyranny. Booksellers and publishers between them helped set up the "net book agreement" in the 1890s. This form of retail price maintenance, which still controls the selling of books in Britain, prohibits a bookseller, under threat of trade boycott, from selling a book at less than the publisher's marked price. Its aim is to protect the small outlying supplier against the large metropolitan bookshop, which by virtue of its greater turnover could, in a free market, offer larger discounts to the customer. Another stabilizing innovation of the 1880s and 90s was the arrival on the literary scene of the agent (the two most famous early agents were A. P. Watt and J. B. Pinker). Traditionalists lamented, and still lament, the invasion of the author-publisher relationship by this middleman, but the agent helped ensure rational and fair dealings between parties.

Nineteenth-century America

From the point of view of fiction, another momentous change in the 1890s was the long delayed aboliton of the three-decker in favour of the one-volume 6s novel. This affordable price, together with the Net Book Agreement, revived the British bookselling business.

American publishing benefitted at the cost of American fiction in the nineteenth century. Sharing a language with England, it was only too easy to share its literature as well. And since there was no international copyright agreement until the 1890s Chase Act, the rich harvest of English fiction was open to American piracy. Thus Harper's first catalogue contained 234 titles, of which 90 per cent were English reprints. It was easier to appropriate an English novel than to cultivate and patronize an American novelist, who might, after all one's patronage, produce an inferior article. This logic had a depressing effect on American literature generally; and it tended to drive the great novelists of the second half of the nineteenth century into the magazines. Centred in Boston and New York, these flourished massively with circulations of 200,000 or more. The most famous was *Century Illustrated*, first published in 1881.

The biggest American firms dwarfed their transatlantic equivalents. There was nothing in London to rival Harper and Brothers in 1850, who had seven five-storey buildings and turned out over 2 million volumes a year. Unrestrained by any kind of control other than the "trade courtesy" practised by a comparatively few genteel houses, the American publishing industry boomed. Everything in America was larger, faster, cheaper and earlier than it was in England. In 1823, for example, the firm of Carey and Son produced 1500 copies of Scott's *Quentin Durward*, ready for the shop, in 28 hours. Harper's

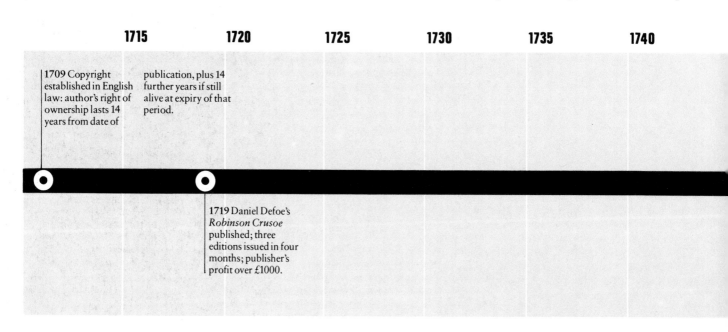

1715	1720	1725	1730	1735	1740

1709 Copyright established in English law: author's right of ownership lasts 14 years from date of publication, plus 14 further years if still alive at expiry of that period.

1719 Daniel Defoe's *Robinson Crusoe* published; three editions issued in four months; publisher's profit over £1000.

reckoned to sell 100,000 copies of Lytton's *The Last of the Barons* in a fortnight. (The English publishers calculated on a first-form sale of about 5000.) In the 1860s the biggest single customer for fiction (mainly English fiction paid for at knock-down rates) in the world, was Harper's *Weekly* which sold at five cents and had a circulation of almost 5 million.

For most of the century the American population was smaller than the British, but literacy was higher. However, the vast sales achieved were the consequence of fierce market competition and extremely low shop prices. (Trollope once found one of his novels, currently selling in Britain at 31s 6d, on offer to the American purchaser at the equivalent price of 7d – more than fifty times cheaper.)

America and Britain 1900–1939

Above, left The beginnings of Harpers' New York empire. By 1853, Harpers' offices and printing works occupied seven buildings in the Cliff Street area. Above, right One of the many branches of Boots circulating library c. 1900.

In Britain the publishing of fiction in this period was relatively sedate. The price of the standard new novel remained stable at 6s, rising to 7s 6d by the outbreak of World War II. The main market for the new novel was the commercial circulating library (the largest were the Boots and W. H. Smith chains with up to 400 branches each in their heyday – though a myriad network of 2d, or cornershop libraries supplied fiction to the whole population). Pandering to its paying subscribers, the commercial library imposed a certain stultifying conformity on the average article and although the business was prosperous the quality of fiction was generally low in the interwar years. (For an indictment, see Q. D. Leavis' *Fiction and the Reading Public* (1932): Claud Cockburn and Colin Watson give more

1750	1755	1760	1765	1770	1775	1780

1748 *Roderick Random* sells 6500 copies in two years.

1774 House of Lords decision abolishes the notion of "perpetual copyright", making possible cheap reprinting of "out of copyright works".

1751 Henry Fielding receives 1000 guineas for the copyright of *Amelia*.

1780 Price of new fiction begins to climb from 2 shillings per volume.

affectionate, but condescending, accounts of the staple fictional commodity in *Bestseller* (1972) and *Snobbery with Violence* (1971) respectively.) Book production in Britain rose to around 10,000 titles annually, of which a quarter were fiction. It is often observed that thanks to the commercial libraries and their multiple orderings of the book of the day, the hardback best seller has never done better than in the 1930s. 80,000 to 100,000 was a relatively commonplace achievement; in the 1970s a British hardback novel which sells less than 20,000 copies can be a best seller.

The American publishing of fiction, and the American book trade generally, had a much rougher ride in this period. The 1890s saw the stabilization of the British scene around price maintenance, the royalty system and the 6s novel. In America the most significant innovation of this decade was the best seller list.

The atmosphere of American publishing throughout the twentieth century was to be much more concerned with hard-selling in an uncontrolled market. It was partly the commercialism of the book trade (combined with Philistine moral censorship and a very favourable post-war dollar-franc rate) which drove the American "lost generation" to expatriate publication in Paris. This adventure was largely curtailed, however, by the Wall Street crash of 1929 and the subsequent slump. The depression had a traumatic effect on the book trade, as on other areas of American business life. It was particularly severe in ripping out the network of bookshops (as holders of slow-moving stock, paid for in advance, they were particularly prone to bankruptcy). In his 1932 survey of the book trade, O. H. Cheney estimated that there were only 500 proper bookshops left in the whole country. To supply the public (who had not, of course, lost their reading habits – although some of their

The Book of the Month Club emblem.

purchasing power was gone) the book club emerged. Originally devised in post-war Germany (which also lost many of its bookshops in the war) the twentieth-century book club aims to substitute mail order for bookshop service; as Harry Scherman of Book of the Month Club put it in the late 1930s: "the book club uses America's 40,000 post offices as book outlets."

The American Book of the Month Club was founded in April 1926, and its great rival the Literary Guild began operations in the same year. Scherman in launching BOMC hit on the brilliant and everywhere imitated idea of a panel of expert judges. These judges were selected to reassure the customer, while at the same time representing the whole range of club membership. The selection board also enabled the supplier to reduce his list to a nucleus of "best books" and thus take full advantage of the economies of scale which have enabled the book club to undersell the orthodox book outlet (in America in the 1970s, 40 per cent is a common reduction on the book club novel, compared with 35 per cent in Britain).

At the end of its first year BOMC had 45,000 members (a period, incidentally, when subscribers were obliged to pay their own postage); 900,000 members in 1946; and 1,250,000 members in 1976. In the year ending June 1975 the club sent out some 12 million books, and spent $12 million on promotion. It was reckoned at this period that some $12 was needed to recruit a new member.

In Britain book clubs have always met chilling resistance from the Publishers and Booksellers Associations, much stronger in their combined power than the equivalent American trade organizations. In the 1930s the American style of club was seen in Britain as a barefaced attempt to rob booksellers of their easy business, "that

1810	1815	1820	1825	1830	1835	1840	1845	1850

1814 First use of steam printing in Britain, Sir Walter Scott's *Waverley* sells 6000 copies in six months.

1821 Scott's *Kenilworth* published in three volumes at 31 shillings and 6 pence.

1830 Bentley and Colburn's "Standard Novel" reprints begin to appear at 6 shillings.

1842 Copyright law further improved in authors' favour, with 42 years of possession after publication, or life of author plus seven years, whichever is the longer.

1848 W.H. Smith's first book- and news-stand at Euston Station, London.
1850 *Harper's New Monthly Magazine* launched.

1852 Legal decision in Britain prohibits price maintenance in books, and licenses "underselling".

1826 Scott ruined by Constable crash.

1836-37 Charles Dicken's *The Pickwick Papers* serialized in twenty monthly parts at 1 shilling. Sales rise from 500 to 40,000 monthly.

1842-45 Price-cutting war in American fiction, sparked off by practice of binding in reprinted (usually pirated) novels as "extras" to newspapers.

1852 Harriet Beecher Stowe's *Uncle Tom's Cabin* runaway best seller. 1½ million pirated copies sold in Britain alone.

section of our turnover," as one book seller put it, "which is compensation for all the non-profit making business we must do". Until 1968 there was a trade agreement that no British book club editions could be issued until a one-year delay had elapsed, with the exception of religious and political items. In 1968 simultaneous publication was finally allowed. Since then the vacuum created by 40 years of trade resistance has created a book club boom in the U.K., led by W.H. Smith (in association with Doubleday) and the German multinational giant, Bertelsmann.

In the 1930s the notion of the mass market paperback originated in America. Allen Lane in England blazed the trail with his Penguin Books in 1935, but from the first, Lane seems to have conceived of his paperbacks as quality books – hardbacks in soft covers. As was said by counsel at the trial in 1960 when Penguin were prosecuted for obscenity in publishing D. H. Lawrence's *Lady Chatterley's Lover*, Lane's intention was "to publish in a form and at a price which the ordinary people could afford to buy, all the great books of our culture". There was initial resistance to Lane's Penguins from the British book trade, but it was dissolved by the war, during which time Penguin established itself as the ideal mixture of austerity and quality. Penguin established bookshops within bookshops (privileged areas which they continued to hold until the mid-1960s). They largely scorned the non-bookshop outlets to which the American paperback accommodated itself. By the 1950s Penguins were an "institution" in Britain – as respectable, indeed more respectable in some cases, than hardback publishers.

The American mass market paperback has a different history. Their innovation is usually credited to Robert de Graff, whose Pocket Books

Andre Maurois' biography of Shelley, entitled Ariel, *was the first Penguin book; it was published in 1935 and carried a list of Penguin's first ten titles on the back.*

Inc. was formed in 1939. From the first, de Graff aimed at the popular, and as he perceived unexploited, end of the market. De Graff was primarily a salesman, and he seems to have been the first to apply market survey techniques to the question of book supply. In 1938 he sent out 25,000 letters and questionnaires to book and magazine readers all over the country, to see what they wanted. 52 titles were provisionally offered from which ten were selected on the basis of advance orders. De Graff spent months experimenting with covers, paper and advertising methods. He decided eventually on eye-catching pictorial covers (in Britain Lane's sober Penguin uniform was not shed until the 1960s, amid much soul-searching). Huge publicity was arranged and a controlled launch of Pocket Books

1860	1865	1870	1875	1880	1885	1890	1895	1900

1860 *Cornhill* magazine launched; early issues sell 120,000 monthly.

1880 Disraeli receives £10,000 for *Endymion*, the highest nineteenth-century payment for a novel.

1891 International copyright between Britain and America agreed.

1894 George Du Maurier's *Trilby* serialized in *Harper's*; in volume form it sells 80,000 in three months.

1896 Publishers Association founded in Britain; it enforces the "Net Book Agreement" by which books may not be sold below the publisher's price.

1870 Universal Education Act in Britain.

1890s First literary agents established in Britain.

1894 "Three-decker" at 31s 6d declines. 6s one-volume novel established as standard in Britain.

1895 *Bookman* starts best seller lists in New York.

set up in New York. From the start de Graff observed that twice as many re-orders came from news-stands and drug stores as from bookshops. These became the main targets for his subsequent sales drive.

Following his early experiments de Graff inaugurated a sales method which was quite different from that of Penguins, who were already on the way to being institutionalized in bookshops. The de Graff technique is described by Malcolm Cowley as: "the saturation method. . . . Instead of being widely advertised the product is simply placed on sale, but in the largest possible number of outlets, and usually in impressive quantities, until it has been displayed to every potential customer and the market is saturated." Over supply worked from the first. Pocket Books sold 4 million books in 1940, and doubled the figure in 1941. The saturation method is still standard in America and means that as many as 50 per cent of paperbacks are returned unsold. *Publishers' Weekly* estimated in 1975 that the average duration of the paperback's shelf life was 15 days (this may be an exaggeration). In Britain the picture is less drastic; it is estimated that less than 15 per cent of paperbacks are returned, and shelf life is considerably longer.

It is evident that the paperback successfully invaded and displaced the territory previously held by magazines on news-stands and in drugstores. The paperback competes with the magazine in terms of immediate illustrative appeal, recurrence and monthly novelty. In the long term, the irresistibly expansionary paperback has probably caused the death of the American middle-market magazine.

Britain, and notably Penguin, resisted the example of the American mass market paperback until the 1960s when Pan (with Ian Fleming as their star author) began regularly selling a

million copies, indicating that American styles of paperback publishing could transplant successfully. (Before the 1960s, and the Bond boom, the million sellers were a motley crew of old favourites, led by Penguin's *Odyssey* and Paul Brickhill's patriotic *The Dam Busters*. By the late 1970s, things had so changed in the British scene, that Pan had a first printing of a million copies for James Herriot's *Vet in a Spin*.) Penguin who can plausibly claim to have started the whole thing in 1935, found themselves, 40 years later, inexorably pushed towards the American style of marketing. In acknowledgement of this, the appointment of Peter Mayer, whose professional achievements have primarily been in the American paperback world, in 1978 as Chief Executive of Penguin, was widely seen as an attempt to "de-institutionalize" the firm.

Genre has been a feature on the literary landscape since the earliest days of the novel. It is, however, a mode of fiction which accommodates particularly well to paperback. Category fiction (as genre is sometimes called) turns over quickly; blockbusters are rare. It sells best if it can be shelved separately in large numbers. The uniform, monthly-issued paperback with a genre identity mark on it is the rational way for these novels to be marketed.

Genre underwent a spectacular boom in the early 1960s (Barbara Cartland, for example, found her annual rate going up from 5 to 20 novels a year in response to market demand). Science fiction expanded vastly to supply a young, largely college-educated readership – by 1976 SF was estimated to account for $40 million annual turnover in the U.S. The new "sweet and savage" romances (more erotic than Cartland's traditional confections) were pioneered as paperback originals by Avon Books; their star per-

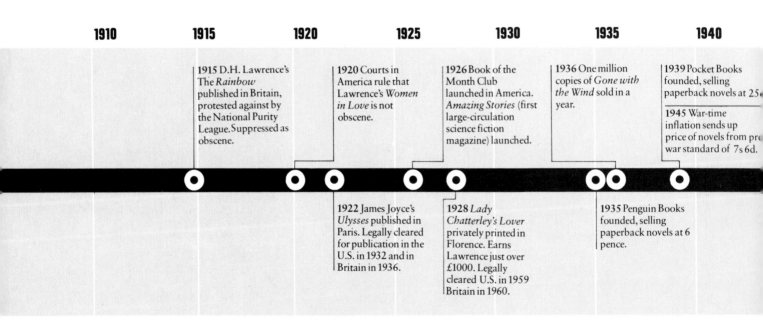

1910   1915   1920   1925   1930   1935   1940

1915 D.H. Lawrence's The *Rainbow* published in Britain, protested against by the National Purity League. Suppressed as obscene.

1920 Courts in America rule that Lawrence's *Women in Love* is not obscene.

1926 Book of the Month Club launched in America. *Amazing Stories* (first large-circulation science fiction magazine) launched.

1936 One million copies of *Gone with the Wind* sold in a year.

1939 Pocket Books founded, selling paperback novels at 25¢

1945 War-time inflation sends up price of novels from pre war standard of 7s 6d.

1922 James Joyce's *Ulysses* published in Paris. Legally cleared for publication in the U.S. in 1932 and in Britain in 1936.

1928 *Lady Chatterley's Lover* privately printed in Florence. Earns Lawrence just over £1000. Legally cleared U.S. in 1959 Britain in 1960.

1935 Penguin Books founded, selling paperback novels at 6 pence.

former, Rosemary Rogers, took over Jacqueline Susann's vacated place in the American best-seller lists.

The post-1960s boom in publishing was largely an American and a paperback phenomenon. It may be regarded as one of the later consequences of the paperback revolution started by Lane and de Graff in the 1930s.

The contemporary period

Post-war austerity in Britain was gradually relaxed (the "wartime regulations" which imposed the economic use of paper had effectively disappeared by the 1950s). Book production increased steadily with the number of titles rising from an annual figure of around 10,000 in the 1940s to over 30,000 in the 1970s. The production of new novels, however, remained constant around 2000 per annum. A major shift of patronage which had important consequences for fiction was the vast growth of the public library system after the war. As the commercial libraries dwindled with the loss of middle class purchasing power, the public system boomed with the "nationalizing" Labour ministry of 1945. By the mid-1970s, the public library service had some 11,000 outlets nationally, and made over 650 million loans a year, 75 per cent of which were fiction. (Boots' and Smith's lending libraries were wound up in the early 1960s; Boots went out of the book business, Smith's stayed but concentrated on the new boom areas of the mass market paperback, the gift book and – in conjunction with the American giant Doubleday – the book club.)

The public library represented a different kind of patronage for fiction than that offered by the pre-war commercial libraries. Public librarians are trained, and take their role as cultural custodians seriously. Since they provide a "free" service (it is paid for, of course, out of taxes)

public librarians are less accountable to their patrons. Public libraries do not buy multiple copies as readily as the old circulating libraries; they go for quality and make their stock last longer. With the public library "safe" sale at 1000 or more for any hardback novel of decent pedigree, publishers could afford to take risks, knowing that their gamble on a new or "difficult" novel was insured against absolute loss-making. According to Tom Maschler of Jonathan Cape, in the late 1960s a first novel in hardback could expect a sale of around 1,200 "of which perhaps as many as 90 per cent are sold to the libraries".

In Britain the "everlasting boom" which the book trade has enjoyed (with a hiccup over the 1973–75 period) has been gradual and self-sustained. In America the trade's expansion has been more violent, and has shaken out old practices and trade formations. The boom in educational books in the 1950s (the GI Bill of Rights and higher education expansion were main factors) led Wall Street to take a new interest in publishing. A series of mergers joined many publishing houses in new industrial-sized combinations. In the 1960s and 1970s the diversification of conglomerates (they are prohibited by trust laws from expanding monopolistically in any single sector) absorbed publishing.

By the late 1970s Random House, Ballantine and Alfred A. Knopf (the most prestigious American literary publisher) belonged to RCA; Simon and Schuster and Pocket Books were part of the Leisure Division (together with Madison Square Garden and Paramount Pictures) of Gulf and Western. Bobbs Merrill belonged to ITT, Putnams to MCA, Holt Rinehart and Winston together with Popular Library and Fawcett to CBS.

Bantam, the largest paperback publisher in the English-speaking world (it has about 14 per

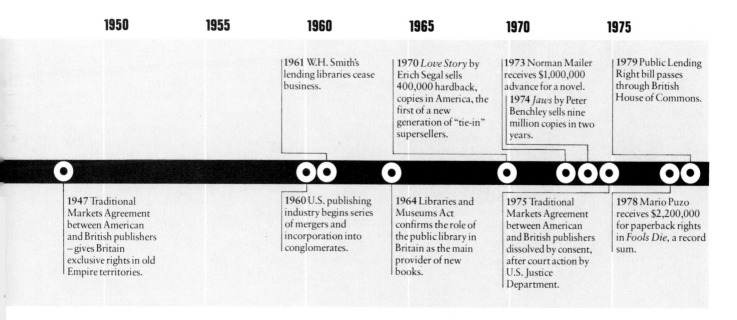

1950   1955   1960   1965   1970   1975

1961 W.H. Smith's lending libraries cease business.

1970 *Love Story* by Erich Segal sells 400,000 hardback, copies in America, the first of a new generation of "tie-in" supersellers.

1973 Norman Mailer receives $1,000,000 advance for a novel.

1974 *Jaws* by Peter Benchley sells nine million copies in two years.

1979 Public Lending Right bill passes through British House of Commons.

1947 Traditional Markets Agreement between American and British publishers – gives Britain exclusive rights in old Empire territories.

1960 U.S. publishing industry begins series of mergers and incorporation into conglomerates.

1964 Libraries and Museums Act confirms the role of the public library in Britain as the main provider of new books.

1975 Traditional Markets Agreement between American and British publishers dissolved by consent, after court action by U.S. Justice Department.

1978 Mario Puzo receives $2,200,000 for paperback rights in *Fools Die*, a record sum.

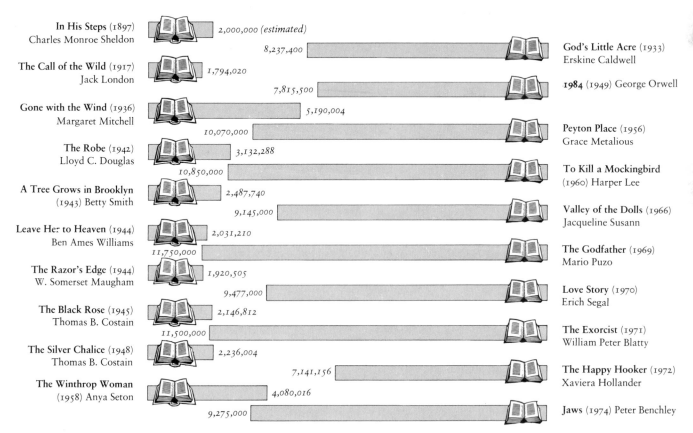

In His Steps (1897)
Charles Monroe Sheldon — 2,000,000 (estimated)

God's Little Acre (1933)
Erskine Caldwell — 8,237,400

The Call of the Wild (1917)
Jack London — 1,794,020

1984 (1949) George Orwell — 7,815,500

Gone with the Wind (1936)
Margaret Mitchell — 5,190,004

Peyton Place (1956)
Grace Metalious — 10,070,000

The Robe (1942)
Lloyd C. Douglas — 3,132,288

To Kill a Mockingbird
(1960) Harper Lee — 10,850,000

A Tree Grows in Brooklyn
(1943) Betty Smith — 2,487,740

Valley of the Dolls (1966)
Jacqueline Susann — 9,145,000

Leave Her to Heaven (1944)
Ben Ames Williams — 2,031,210

The Godfather (1969)
Mario Puzo — 11,750,000

The Razor's Edge (1944)
W. Somerset Maugham — 1,920,505

Love Story (1970)
Erich Segal — 9,477,000

The Black Rose (1945)
Thomas B. Costain — 2,146,812

The Exorcist (1971)
William Peter Blatty — 11,500,000

The Silver Chalice (1948)
Thomas B. Costain — 2,236,004

The Happy Hooker (1972)
Xaviera Hollander — 7,141,156

The Winthrop Woman
(1958) Anya Seton — 4,080,016

Jaws (1974) Peter Benchley — 9,275,000

The best selling novels in the US up to 1975 (figures are taken from A. P. Hackett and J. H. Burke, 80 Years of Bestsellers, 1977). The dates of publication of these best sellers in their different forms indicates the degree to which the "paperback revolution" has accelerated in the 1970s. Taking speed, as well as volume, of sale into consideration, the last published, Jaws, was in one sense the best seller of all time up to 1975.

cent of the U.S. domestic market) is now owned by the multi-national Bertelsmann group (since they have to buy rights in advance, paperback firms need a banker and are more prone than hardback firms to commercial dependence on a financial big brother). The firms which remain are either giants in their own right like Harcourt Brace Jovanovic or Doubleday, or they are consciously eccentric like Farrar, Straus & Giroux, whose chief executive has gone on record in 1976 as saying he did not want to be a department of Kleenex.

This change in structure has brought about consequent changes in style of operation. The old "gentleman publisher" was an early casualty of business rationalisation. As early as 1948 Ken McCormick of Doubleday observed the beginnings of a managerial revolution in the American publishing profession:

> The most important change in an editor's job today is that he has slowly acquired the publisher's responsibility. This is particularly true in the United States. In England, the head of the house, the publisher, still chooses his own list, keeps track of all authors and gives little credit to others. Editors and readers are seen and not heard. In the U.S., editors have come to know a new sort of freedom.

McCormick went on to distinguish between the traditional editor of the Maxwell Perkins kind who had "no interest in anything but the book itself" and the new kind of editor, like himself,

for whom "it is not that simple. . . . Editors must have some business sense, which should be directed to the benefit of the author and the publisher alike."

At any time since World War II one can find American authors complaining about the oppressive materialism of the modern book trade. They are understandably alarmed at such grandiose statements as that of Richard Snyder, President of Simon and Schuster:

> I was the voice that said many many years ago that there was going to be a consolidation in this industry before it even started to consolidate. However it has gone well beyond what I ever thought it could go to. What we are going to see now, if this trend continues, is that like the seven sisters of the oil business we will have seven giant publishing companies.

(Snyder might well have added: "like the five majors who dominate the world record industry." Three of these five, RCA, CBS and Warner Communications also have major interests in publishing.)

Authors have been less sangine than Snyder about this concentration of publishing power, and its links with a nucleus of media corporations. The novelist John Hersey, chairman of the Contract Committee of the Authors' Guild, observed as one of the worst effects of the increasingly corporate nature of American publishing that "publishers are now going for the big book; it is more and more a choice of whether

a book will sell, not whether or not it will contribute to our culture". To this Michael Korda (also of Simon and Schuster) would reply: "There is no such thing as a good book that doesn't sell."

The absorption of publishing into large, diverse combines favours a "synergistic" approach by which one medium is made to serve another. Thus, for example, when the conglomerate CBS, whose most famous property is one of the three TV networks, acquired Fawcett paperbacks in 1977 they advertised their new acquisition thus:

> And now, more than ever, Fawcett/Popular Library gets the CBS sell in, so you'll sell out [the advertisement is directed specifically at booksellers]. There's a lot that's new at Fawcett/Popular Library – new ideas, new books, new and exciting ways to sell them . . . NOW THE WHOLE FAWCETT BOOKS GROUP GETS TURNED ONTO THE CBS TREATMENT . . . television in markets coast to coast reaching over 75,000,000 people.

New "vertical" sequences are possible. Judith Rossner's *Looking for Mr Goodbar* (1975) was published as a hardback by Simon and Schuster, as a paperback by Pocket Books and made into a film by Paramount. All three are divisions of Gulf and Western. Another giant, Warner Communications, owned the *Superman* copyright through DC Comics, one of their many subsidiary holdings. At a cost of $35 million their film division made it into a film, and their publishing division, Warner Paperback Library, brought out nine or more tied-in books, one of which featured Mario Puzo as collaborator. Warner Records produced *Superman* discs. All these combined to create a massive media bandwagon for the *Superman* merchandise.

Given the continuingly open and highly competitive nature of American business – and its phobia about monopoly – verticalization is not universal, nor is it likely to become so. But the new business organizations which dominate the production of American cultural commodities have made the communications industry alive to tie-in possibilities. Paperbacks in the 1970s have sold as never before, and the titles which have sold most (*The Godfather, Jaws, Love Story, The Exorcist*) have all been blockbuster movies as well. In the 1970s the success of TV mini-series such as MCA's *Centennial* (based on James Michener's 1974 novel) indicate a new growth area for novel tie-ins.

A constant apprehension in the British publishing world of the post-war period is that it is becoming "Americanized". Before the war there

Victor Gollancz, one of the pioneers of rights exchange between the U.S. and Britain.

was surprisingly little co-ordination in the trans-atlantic trade. After the war enterprising publishers (notably Victor Gollancz) went to America in search of rights, consolidating the two markets. As the more substantial partner, however, America was felt to dominate – culturally and economically. At one time in the 1960s it was widely feared that America would actually take over British publishing (as she took over a large part, for example, of British auto manufacturing). This did not happen; but insidiously the British book trade was taken over by the American way of doing things – it Americanized itself. Shortly before his death Victor Gollancz, in a letter to one of his authors in the early 1960s, viewed the change of ethos, which he had partly started, with dismay:

> What beastly changes I have seen in my 33 years of publishing. The only thing I am finally concerned about is getting ideas over to the public. The whole economic situation is developing in such a way that it is becoming progressively more difficult, and may soon become impossible, to do this. The British publishing business is rapidly going the way of the American: it is becoming impossible, without the certainty of bankruptcy, to publish really good work by young people or books of social and political importance of the "non popular" kind. Everything is becoming canalised into a few huge sellers.

It is certain that the British book trade is now more international in its outlook, and that it is more best seller conscious (however much the best seller list itself is disdained). Best selling British authors are similarly minded; 80 per cent of Frederick Forsyth's income comes from markets outside Britain, and his novels are careful to have an international appeal (none, for example, is set entirely in any one country). Insofar as one can usefully predict, the future of the British booktrade would seem to promise: 1. a huge increase in the book club business, which was held back for three decades by the protectionist Publishers Association; 2. the absorption of smaller publishing houses by larger, or at least a higher degree of co-operation and "sheltering" relationships; 3. a reduction in the importance of public libraries as patrons, particularly of the novel; 4. continued growth in the paperback section; and 5. a stiff fight to hold on to export markets.

Since the American industry leads the way, it is hard to predict where it may go, unless it is towards more and even bigger-selling paperback tie-ins.

General Index

Novelists referred to in this book are indexed separately on the end-papers. **Bold** numerals indicate the principal reference; *italic* numerals indicate the illustrations. In references to the alphabetical guide to novelists on pp. 87–240, page numbers are followed by the letters a, b or c, indicating the first, second or third columns on the page.

Index of Novelists